ALL
ABOUT
THE
BIBLE

Other Titles in Nelson's A-to-Z™ Series

Where to Find It in the Bible
0-7852-1157-8

Who Was Who in the Bible
0-7852-4240-6

Find It Fast in the Bible
0-7852-4521-9

What Does the Bible Say About . . .
0-7852-4270-8

I Never Knew That Was in the Bible
0-7852-1378-3

ALL ABOUT THE BIBLE

The Ultimate

A TO Z

DICTIONARY

RESOURCE

FULLY ILLUSTRATED

THOMAS NELSON PUBLISHERS

Nashville

Published in Nashville, Tennessee, by Thomas Nelson, Inc.

Most of the material in this book originally was published in another form in *Nelson's New Illustrated Bible Dictionary,* copyright © 1986, 1995 by Thomas Nelson Publishers.

Unless otherwise indicated, Scripture quotations are from the *New King James Version* of the Bible, copyright © 1979, 1980, 1982, 1990 by Thomas Nelson, Inc.

Published in Nashville, Tennessee, by Thomas Nelson, Inc.

All about the Bible

ISBN 0-7852-4600-2

Printed in the United States of America

1 2 3 4 5 6 7 — 06 05 04 03 02 01

A Bible Dictionary
For the Reader in a Hurry

This is a dictionary with an impressive heritage. In 1986 *Nelson's Illustrated Bible Dictionary* was released as an entirely new work, put together under the editorship of Herbert Lockyer, Sr. The 5,500 entries were written by a team of noted scholars and Bible teachers. Almost a decade later, the volume was updated, revised, and expanded by Ronald F. Youngblood, appropriately titled *Nelson's New Illustrated Bible Dictionary*. With more than 7,000 entries, it continues to be a top-selling Bible reference work.

Planning for this paperback edition was guided by one key assumption: People usually turn to a Bible dictionary for basic information, not to identify some obscure person or place. Thus this volume contains the 1,000 most important entries on people, places, things, doctrines, and themes. By leaving out the "extra" details, we have made it easier to get to the essential information you are seeking. In that same spirit, we have trimmed back the longer articles, so that in most cases you will need to read no more than two pages to get the basic facts on a topic.

If you are writing a research paper or boning up for a trivia quiz, you still will want to seek out the exhaustive treatment provided in *Nelson's New Illustrated Bible Dictionary*. But if you are clarifying a point for a Sunday school lesson or just satisfying your personal curiosity, you are holding in your hands all the help you will need.

—The Publisher

AARON [EHR un]

Brother of Moses and first high priest of the Hebrew nation. Very little is known about Aaron's early life, other than his marriage to Elisheba, daughter of Amminadab (Ex. 6:23).

When God called Moses to lead the Hebrew people out of slavery in Egypt, Moses protested that he would not be able to speak convincingly to the pharaoh. So Aaron was designated by God as Moses' official spokesman (Ex. 4:14–16). At Moses' instruction, Aaron also performed miracles as signs for the release of the Hebrews. Aaron's rod turned into a serpent that swallowed the rods of the Egyptian magicians (Ex. 7:8–20). Aaron also caused frogs to cover the land by stretching his rod over the lakes and streams of Egypt (Ex. 8:6).

Aaron held an important place of leadership because of his work with his brother Moses. A central figure in the Exodus from Egypt, he also received instructions from God for observing the first Passover (Ex. 12:1). In the wilderness he assisted Moses in keeping order and rendering judgments over the people (Num. 15:33). Both he and Moses were singled out when the people complained about the harsh conditions of these wilderness years (Num. 14:2).

When the priesthood was instituted in the wilderness, Moses consecrated Aaron as the first high priest of Israel (Ex. 28–29; Lev. 8–9). The priesthood was set within the tribe of Levi, from which Aaron was descended. Aaron's sons (Nadab, Abihu, Eleazar, and Ithamar) inherited the position of high priest from their father (Num. 3:2–3). Aaron was given special robes to wear, signifying his status within the priesthood (Lev. 8:7–9). At his death the robes were transferred to his oldest living son, Eleazar (Num. 20:25–28). The tabernacle, the main sanctuary of worship, was placed under Aaron's supervision (Num. 4). He received instructions from God on the functions of the priesthood and the tabernacle (Num. 18). He alone, serving in the capacity of high priest, went into the Most High Place once a year to represent the people on the Day of Atonement.

In spite of his responsibility for the spiritual leadership of the nation, Aaron committed a serious sin in the wilderness surrounding Mount Sinai. While Moses was on the mountain praying to God and receiving His commandments, the people demanded that Aaron make one or more gods for them to worship. Aaron made no attempt to stop the people and made a golden calf for them (Ex. 32:1–10). Aaron was saved from God's wrath only because Moses interceded on his behalf (Deut. 9:20).

After all their years of leading the people, neither Moses nor Aaron was permitted to enter the Promised Land. Apparently this was because they did not make it clear that God would provide for the Hebrews' needs when they believed they would die for lack of water in the wilderness (Num. 20:12). Aaron died at Mount Hor, and Moses died later in Moab.

Upon arriving at Mount Hor from the wilderness of Kadesh, Aaron was accompanied by Moses and his son Eleazar to the top of the mountain. There he was stripped of his high priestly garments, which were transferred to Eleazar. After Aaron's death, the community mourned for 30 days (Num. 20:22–29).

The Book of Hebrews contrasts the imperfect priesthood of Aaron with the perfect priesthood of Christ (Heb. 5:2–5; 7:11–12). Christ's priesthood is compared to the order of Melchizedek because it is an eternal office with no beginning and no end. Thus, it replaces the priesthood of Aaron.

AARON'S ROD

A rod mentioned on two dramatic occasions in the Old Testament. When Moses and Aaron appeared before Pharaoh, Aaron cast down his rod and it became a serpent. When the magicians of Egypt did the same thing, "Aaron's rod swallowed up their rods" (Ex. 7:12). Later, Aaron struck the waters of Egypt with his rod and they turned to blood (7:15–20).

During the wilderness wandering, Aaron's rod was the only staff that produced buds, blossoms, and almonds, indicating God's choice of Aaron and his descendants as priests (Num. 17:1–10).

ABANAH [AB ah nah]

The chief river of Damascus. The Abanah flowed through the center of the city. With the Pharpar, it supplied an abundance of water, making the country around it a beautiful and fertile spot. When Naaman the leper was asked to bathe in the Jordan River seven times, he complained that he would rather bathe in the Abanah or the Pharpar (2 Kin. 5:12; Abana in KJV, NIV, NRSV). The Abanah River's modern name is Barada.

ABBA [AB ah] *(father)*

An Aramaic word that corresponds to our "Daddy" or "Papa." It is found three times in the New Testament (Mark 14:36; Rom. 8:15; Gal. 4:6). What a privilege it is to be able to call the great Creator, "Our Father"!

ABED-NEGO [uh BED knee goe] *(servant of Nebo)*

The Chaldean name given to Azariah in King Nebuchadnezzar's court when he was chosen as one of the king's servants (Dan. 1:7; 2:49). With Shadrach and Meshach, Abed-Nego was thrown into the fiery furnace for refusing to bow down and worship a golden image. The three men were miraculously protected from the fire (Dan. 3:12–30). Like the three Hebrew men in the fiery furnace, the nation of Israel endured the captivity and were miraculously protected by God.

ABEL [A buhl] *(breath, vapor)*

The second son of Adam and Eve (Gen. 4:2). His brother Cain, who was a farmer, brought an offering of his produce to the Lord. Abel, a shepherd, brought to the Lord an offering "of the firstlings [the best quality] of his flock." Genesis records: "And the Lord respected Abel and his offering, but he did not respect Cain and his offering" (Gen. 4:4–5). Envious of Abel, Cain killed his brother and was cursed by God for the murder.

In the New Testament, Abel is described as a man of faith, who "offered a more excellent sacrifice than Cain" (Heb. 11:4). Cain murdered his brother Abel, writes John, "because his [Cain's] works were evil and his brother's [Abel's] righteous" (1 John 3:12). Jesus spoke of "the blood of righteous Abel" (Matt. 23:35; Luke 11:51) and implied that Abel, the first righteous martyr, anticipated in symbol His own death on Calvary at the hands of evil men. The blood of the New Covenant, however, "speaks better things than that of Abel" (Heb. 12:24). The blood of Abel cried out for vengeance; the blood of Christ speaks of salvation.

ABEL ACACIA GROVE [A bell a KAY shuh grove]

A site northeast of the Dead Sea in the plains of Moab, also called Acacia Grove. It was here that the Israelites camped just before crossing the Jordan and entering the Promised Land (Num. 25:1; Josh. 2:1; 3:1; Mic. 6:5; Shittim, KJV). It was probably the same place as Abel-shittim (Num. 33:49, KJV).

Most scholars identify Acacia Grove with Tell el-Hamman, although some think it was at nearby Tell el-Kefrein. Many notable events occurred while the Israelites were camped here. Here many Israelites took Moabite women for their wives and worshiped Moabite gods. As punishment, God allowed a plague to kill 24,000 Israelites (Num. 25:9).

At this campsite Moses also took a military census of the Israelite tribes, establishing the number of those 20 years old and above who were able to go to war (Num. 26:2). At Acacia Grove God also revealed to Moses that he would not be allowed to cross the Jordan River and that Joshua would be his successor as leader of the people (Num. 27:12–23).

After Moses ascended Mount Nebo and died (Deut. 34), Joshua sent out two spies from Acacia Grove to examine the defense of Jericho (Josh. 2:1). Upon their return, the Israelites broke camp and crossed the Jordan River, finally entering the land that God had promised to Abraham and his descendants hundreds of years earlier (Josh. 3:1).

ABEL BETH MAACHAH [A bell beth MAY uh kah] *(meadow of the house of Maachah)*

A fortified town near the town of Dan in the area of the tribe of Naphtali. It was attacked by Ben-Hadad (1 Kin. 15:20) and Tiglath-Pileser (2 Kin. 15:29), who mentions it in his annals. The name of the town is also given as Abel Maim, meaning "Abel on the waters" (2 Chr. 16:4). It is described as a "mother in Israel"— meaning a place of great importance, having many "daughters," or inhabitants.

ABIATHAR [a BY uh thar] *(father of abundance)*

One of two chief priests in the court of David. Abiathar was the son of Ahimelech of the priestly clan of Eli from Shiloh (1 Sam. 22:20). When the residents of the priestly village of Nob were massacred

by Saul for helping David, Abiathar was the only one to escape (1 Sam. 22:6–23). When David eventually became king, he appointed Abiathar, along with Zadok, as priests in the royal court (2 Sam. 8:17; 1 Chr. 18:16).

When David's son Absalom tried to take his throne by force, David was forced to leave Jerusalem. Zadok and Abiathar carried the ark of the covenant out of the capital city but later returned it at the command of David (2 Sam. 15:29). Both priests remained in Jerusalem to inform David of Absalom's plans (2 Sam. 15:34). After Absalom's death, Abiathar and Zadok carried the message of reconciliation to Amasa and the elders of Judah (2 Sam. 19:11–14).

During the struggle over who would succeed as king, Abiathar supported Adonijah. When Solomon emerged as the new ruler, Zadok was appointed priest of the royal court, while Abiathar escaped execution only because of his earlier loyalty to David. He and his family were banished to Anathoth, and his rights and privileges as a Jerusalem priest were taken away (1 Kin. 1:7–25; 2:22–35).

Some scholars believe Abiathar may have written portions of 1 and 2 Samuel, especially the sections describing the royal court life under David.

ABIB [A bibb] *(sprouting or budding)*

One of the months of the Hebrew calendar (corresponding to our March-April). On the fifteenth of this month, the people of Israel left Egypt. Abib was made the first month of the year in commemoration of the Exodus (Ex. 23:15; Deut. 16:1). The Passover and the Feast of Unleavened Bread were celebrated during the month of Abib. After the captivity, the month was called Nisan (Neh. 2:1; Esth. 3:7).

ABIGAIL [AB ih gale] *(father of joy)*

Wife of Nabal the Carmelite and, after his death, of David (1 Sam. 25:3, 14–42; 2 Sam. 2:2; 1 Chr. 3:1). Abigail's husband, Nabal, was an ill-tempered, drunken man. When David was hiding from the jealous King Saul, he asked Nabal for food for himself and his men. Nabal blatantly refused. Angered, David threatened to plunder Nabal's possessions and kill Nabal himself. Abigail, in her wisdom, gathered enough food for David's men, rode out to meet David, and bowed before him to show her respect. By agreeing with David that Nabal had acted with great disrespect, she stemmed David's anger. To Abigail's credit, she did not leave her godless husband. When Nabal died, apparently from shock at discovering his near brush with death, David married Abigail and she later bore him a son, Chileab.

ABIHU [a BIH hoo] *(he is my father)*

Second son of Aaron and Elisheba (Ex. 6:23). Abihu was destroyed, along with his brother Nadab, in the Wilderness of Sinai for offering "profane fire" (Lev. 10:1) before the Lord. Exactly why the fire was "profane" is not certain; perhaps Abihu and Nadab rebelled against the authority of Moses and Aaron by presuming to bring an unauthorized offering before the Lord. If so, their action implies pride and arrogance, which the Lord despises.

ABIJAM [a BUY jam] *(the sea is my father)*

A king of Judah and son of Rehoboam and Maacah, the daughter of Absalom. When King Rehoboam died, Abijam succeeded to Judah's throne. He had 14 wives, 22 sons, and 16 daughters. When he died, after reigning for 3 years, his son Asa became king (1 Kin. 14:31). He is also called Abijah (2 Chr. 11:20, 22). The

KJV has Abia (Matt. 1:7), listing him as an ancestor of Jesus.

ABILENE [ab uh LEE knee] *(region of Abila)*

A district near the Anti-Lebanon Mountains. It derived its name from Abila, its capital, which was located on the Abanah (modern Barada) River some 18 to 20 miles (29 to 32 kilometers) northwest of Damascus. Originally a part of the Iturean kingdom of Ptolemy Mennaeus (about 85–40 B.C.), Abilene was broken up when King Lysanias I (40–36 B.C.) was put to death by Mark Antony. It became the tetrarchy of a younger Lysanias "in the fifteenth year of the reign of Tiberias Caesar" (Luke 3:1), when John the Baptist began his ministry.

ABIMELECH [uh BIM eh leck] *(my father is king)*

1. The king of Gerar in the time of Abraham (Gen. 20:1–18; 21:22–34). Fearing for his own safety, Abraham introduced Sarah, his wife, as his sister when he entered Abimelech's territory. Abimelech claimed Sarah for his harem, only to be warned in a dream that he had taken the wife of another man. Then Abimelech returned Sarah to Abraham. The two men made a covenant with each other, and Abraham asked God to reward the king by giving him many children. Many scholars believe that the word *Abimelech* is not a proper name but a royal title of the Philistine kings, just as Pharaoh was a title for Egyptian kings.

ABIMELECH [uh BIM eh leck] *(my father is king)*

2. The ruler of the city of Shechem during the period of the judges (Judg. 8:30–10:1; 2 Sam. 11:21). Abimelech was a son of Gideon by a concubine from Shechem. Abimelech tried to become king, and he did reign over Israel for

three years (Judg. 9:22). In order to eliminate all who might challenge his authority, he killed all the other sons of Gideon—his brothers and half brothers—who were potential successors of his father (Judg. 9:5).

Abimelech was killed in a battle at Thebez, a city northeast of Shechem, which he surrounded with his army. When Abimelech ventured too close to the city tower, a woman dropped a millstone on his head, crushing his skull. Abimelech commanded his armorbearer to kill him so it could not be said that he died at the hands of a woman (Judg. 9:50–54; 2 Sam. 11:21).

ABISHAG [AB ih shag]

A young woman from Shunem employed by David's physicians to care for him in his old age (1 Kin. 1:1–4, 15). The treatment implies that through physical contact Abishag's youth could revive a dying David. The treatment failed. After David's death, one of his sons, Adonijah, asked permission to marry Abishag (1 Kin. 2:17). Solomon saw Adonijah's request as an attempt to seize the throne. He had Adonijah killed (1 Kin. 2:13–25).

ABLUTION

The ceremonial washing of one's body, vessels, and clothing for the

ABLUTION

SCRUB BEHIND EARS

purpose of religious purification. This word is not found in the NKJV, but it occurs in Hebrews 6:2 and 9:10 in the RSV. In both places the Greek word is *baptismos* (literally, "dipping"), which can be translated "washings" (Heb. 9:10).

Ablutions have nothing to do with washing one's body for sanitary or hygienic purposes. Rather, these were performed in order to remove ritual defilement. Some of the causes of ritual uncleanness in Bible times were bloodshed (Lev. 17), childbirth (Lev. 12), sexual intercourse (Lev. 18), leprosy (Lev. 12), menstruation (Lev. 15), and contact with dead bodies (Num. 19).

At Mount Sinai, the Israelites were told to wash (literally, "trample") their clothes in preparation for worship (Ex. 19:10, 14). Similarly, the Levites as well as Aaron and his sons were prepared for service by washing their clothes and their bodies (Ex. 12–13).

By New Testament times, ceremonial washings became almost an end in themselves. The Pharisees were preoccupied with ritual purifications (Matt. 15:2; Mark 7:4). Jesus exhorted the scribes and Pharisees to "cleanse the inside of the cup and dish"—that is, cleanse their hearts and spirits—and not just wash the outside by religious rituals. Moral filth cannot be washed away with physical cleansing agents (Jer. 2:22; Is. 1:16). Jesus Christ is to be praised, for He "loved us and washed us from our sins in His own blood" (Rev. 1:5; Rev. 7:14).

ABNER [AB nar] *(the father is a lamp)*

The commander-in-chief of the army of Saul, first king of the nation of Israel (1 Sam. 14:50–51; 17:55).

As Saul's highest military official, Abner occupied a seat of honor in the king's court (1 Sam. 20:25). He was the person who inquired about David after his battle with the giant, Goliath, and who intro-

duced David to King Saul (1 Sam. 17:55–58). Abner also was the commander of the guard that was supposedly protecting Saul when David entered the camp of the king while everyone was asleep (1 Sam. 26:5–7).

After the death of Saul and his three sons in a battle with the Philistines (1 Sam. 31:1–6), Abner established Saul's son Ishbosheth as king. His capital was at Mahanaim on the east side of the Jordan River. Only the tribe of Judah, of the 12 tribes of the nation, followed the leadership of David (2 Sam. 2:8–11). In the warfare that broke out between the forces of David and Ishbosheth, Abner killed a brother of Joab—one of David's military officers—in self-defense (2 Sam. 2:12–3:1).

Still later, a crisis developed between Abner and Ishbosheth when Abner took one of Saul's concubines. Ishbosheth accused Abner of plotting to take over the kingship. The rift between them became so pronounced that Abner eventually shifted his loyalties to David. This move by Abner was significant, because Abner was able to persuade the elders of all the tribes of Israel to follow David's leadership (2 Sam. 3:6–21).

Soon after this turning point in David's political career, Abner was killed by David's commander Joab in an act of vengeance over the death of his brother (2 Sam. 3:22–30). This presented David with a troublesome situation. Abner's death looked like the execution of an opponent who had delivered the tribal loyalties the king needed to establish control over the entire nation. To counter any backlash, David reprimanded Joab publicly and had Abner buried with full honors (2 Sam. 3:27–39).

ABOMINATION

Anything that offends the spiritual, religious, or moral sense and causes extreme disgust. Among the objects described as an "abomination" to God were the carved images of pagan gods (Deut. 7:25–26), the sacrifice to God of inferior, blemished animals (Deut. 17:1), the practice of idolatry (Deut. 17:2–5), and the fashioning of a "carved or molded image" of a false god (Is. 44:19).

ABOMINATION OF DESOLATION

A despicable misuse of the temple of the Lord during a time of great trouble—an event foretold by the prophet Daniel.

The phrase is found in Matthew 24:15 and Mark 13:14 as a quotation from Daniel 11:31 and 12:11. In Daniel, the words mean "the abomination that makes desolate." In other words, Daniel prophesied that the temple would be used for an "abominable" purpose at some time in the future. As a result, God's faithful people would no longer worship there—so great would be their moral revulsion, contempt, and abhorrence at the sacrilege—and the temple would become "desolate."

According to the verses in the Gospels, a similar misuse of the temple would take place in the future. This would show that a time of great trouble was coming on Judea. People should take warning and flee to the mountains (Matt. 24:16; Mark 13:14).

Some believe Daniel's prophecy was initially fulfilled about 165 B.C. when Antiochus IV (Epiphanes), Greek ruler of Syria, polluted the Jewish temple in Jerusalem by sacrificing a pig on the holy altar. This sacrificing of an unclean pig was the worst kind of abomination that could have taken place. A more complete fulfillment, however, occurred when the Romans sacked the Jewish temple about A.D. 70 (Luke 21:5–7, 20–22). But others insist that the final abomination of desolation refers to the idolatrous image or the "man of sin" who will take over God's place in the temple and make people bow down and worship him (2 Thess.

2:3–4). According to this interpretation, this will be the final act of sacrilege that marks the beginning of the end time.

ABRAHAM [AY bruh ham] *(father of a multitude);* originally Abram *(exalted father)*

The first great patriarch of ancient Israel and a primary model of faithfulness for Christianity. Abraham's story begins with his migration with the rest of his family from Ur of the Chaldeans in ancient southern Babylonia (Gen. 11:31). He and his family moved north along the trade routes of the ancient world and settled in the flourishing trade center of Haran, several hundred miles to the northwest.

While living in Haran, at the age of 75 Abraham received a call from God to go to a strange, unknown land that God would show him. The Lord promised Abraham that He would make him and his descendants a great nation (Gen. 12:1–3). The promise must have seemed unbelievable to Abraham because his wife Sarah (called Sarai in the early part of the story) was childless (Gen. 11:30–31; 17:15).

But Abraham obeyed God with no hint of doubt or disbelief. He took his wife and his nephew, Lot, and went to the land that God would show him. Canaan was inhabited by the warlike Canaanites; so Abraham's belief that God would ultimately give this land to him and his descendants was an act of faith.

Because of a severe famine in the land of Canaan, Abraham moved to Egypt for a short time (Gen. 12:10–20). During this trip, Abraham introduced Sarah to the Egyptians as his sister rather than as his wife in order to avoid trouble. Pharaoh, the Egyptian ruler, then took Sarah as his wife. It was only because "the Lord plagued Pharaoh and his house with great plagues because of Sarai, Abram's wife'' (Gen. 12:17), that Sarah was returned to Abraham.

Upon his return from Egypt, Abraham and his nephew, Lot, quarreled over pasturelands and went separate ways (Gen. 13:8–9). Lot settled in the Jordan River valley, while Abraham moved into Canaan. Apparently Abraham headed a strong military force by this time as he is called ''Abram the Hebrew'' (Gen. 14:13). He succeeded in rescuing his nephew Lot from the kings who had captured him while raiding the cities of Sodom and Gomorrah (Gen. 14:14–17).

A common practice of that time among heirless families was to adopt a slave who would inherit the master's goods. Therefore, because Abraham was childless, he proposed to make a slave, Eliezer of Damascus, his heir (Gen. 15:2). But God rejected this action and challenged Abraham's faith: ''Then he [God]

brought him [Abraham] outside and said, 'Look now toward heaven, and count the stars if you are able to number them.' And He said to him, 'So shall your descendants be' '' (Gen. 15:5). Abraham's response is the model of believing faith. ''And he [Abraham] believed in the Lord, and He [God] accounted it to him for righteousness'' (Gen. 15:6).

The rest of chapter 15 consists of a ceremony between Abraham and God that was commonly used in the ancient world to formalize a covenant (Gen. 15:7–21).

According to Genesis 16, Sarah, because she had not borne a child, provided Abraham with a handmaiden. According to this custom, if the wife had not had a child (preferably a male) by a certain time in the marriage, she was obligated to provide a substitute (usually a slavewoman) to bear a child to her hus-

ABRAHAM

band and thereby insure the leadership of the clan. Thus, Hagar, the Egyptian maidservant, had a son by Abraham. The boy was named Ishmael. Although Ishmael was not understood to be the child that would carry on the line promised to Abraham, he was given a favorable blessing (Gen. 16:10–13; 17:20).

The most substantial account of the covenant between Abraham and God is given in Genesis 17—a covenant that extended the promise of the land and descendants to further generations. This covenant required Abraham and the male members of his household to be circumcised as the sign of the agreement (Gen. 17:10–14). In this chapter Abraham and Sarah receive their new names. (Their old names were Abram and Sarai.) The name of the son whom God promises that Sarah will bear is designated as Isaac (Gen. 17:19–21). The practice of circumcision instituted at this time is not unique to the ancient Hebrews, but its emphasis as a religious requirement is a unique feature of God's covenant people. It became a visible symbol of the covenant between Abraham and his descendants and their redeemer God.

After Isaac was born to Sarah (Gen. 21:1–7), Sarah was unhappy with the presence of Hagar and Ishmael. She asked Abraham to cast them out of the family, which he did after the Lord told him they would have His protection. Ishmael does not play an important role in the rest of Abraham's story; he does re-enter the picture in Genesis 25:9, accompanying Isaac at Abraham's death.

God's command for Abraham to sacrifice his beloved son Isaac was the crucial test of his faith. He was willing to give up his son in obedience to God, although at the last moment the Lord intervened to save Isaac (Gen. 22:1–13). The Lord's promise of descendants as numerous as the stars of the heavens was once again reaffirmed as a result of Abraham's unquestioning obedience (Gen. 22:16–18).

The promises originally given to Abraham were passed on to his son Isaac (Gen. 26:3), and to his grandson Jacob (Gen. 28:13; 35:11–12). In later biblical references, the God of Israel is frequently identified as the God of Abraham (Gen. 26:24), and Israel is often called the people "of the God of Abraham" (Ps. 47:9; 105:6). Abraham was such an important figure in the history of God's people that when they were in trouble, Israel appealed to God to remember the covenant made with Abraham (Ex. 32:13; Deut. 9:27; Ps. 105:9).

In the New Testament, Abraham is presented as the supreme model of vital faith and as the prime example of the faith required for the Christian believer (Rom. 4:11; Gal. 3:6–9; 4:28). He is viewed as the spiritual father for all who share a similar faith in Christ (Matt. 3:9; Luke 13:16; Rom. 11:1). If anyone deserves to be called God's "friend," it is Abraham (Is. 41:8).

ABRAHAM'S BOSOM

A figure of speech for the life hereafter. According to the Old Testament, when a person died he went to "be with his fathers" (Gen. 15:15; 47:30; Deut. 31:16; Judg. 2:10). The patriarch Abraham was regarded as the "father" of the Jews (Luke 3:8; John 8:37–40). At death, therefore, the Jew went to his forefathers or, more specifically, to join "father Abraham."

The only use in the Bible of "Abraham's bosom" occurs in Jesus' parable of the rich man and Lazarus (Luke 16:19–31), in which the beggar is described as being "carried by the angels to Abraham's bosom" (v. 22). A great gulf or chasm separated him from the rich man, who was being tormented in the flames of Hades.

ABSALOM [AB suh lum] *(father of peace)*

The arrogant and vain son of David who tried to take the kingship from his father by force.

Absalom was David's third son by Maacah, the daughter of the king of Geshur (2 Sam. 3:3; 1 Chr. 3:2). Of royal descent on both sides, Absalom was a potential heir to the throne. Attractive in appearance and charming in manners, Absalom was also a popular prince with the people and a favorite of his father. He was especially noted for his beautiful long hair, in which he took great pride (2 Sam. 14:25–26).

During the height of Israel's prosperity under David's rule, another of David's sons, Amnon, raped his half sister Tamar—Absalom's sister (2 Sam. 13:1–22). Absalom took it upon himself to avenge this dishonor, eventually succeeding after two years in having Amnon murdered by his servants (2 Sam. 13:23–29). Fearing his father's wrath, Absalom fled into exile. He stayed with his grandfather Talmai in Geshur for three years (2 Sam. 13:37–38).

Since Absalom was one of David's favorite sons, the king longed for his return (2 Sam. 13:39) in spite of his crime. Joab, one of David's advisors, urged that Absalom be allowed to return to Jerusalem on probation but that he not be allowed to appear before David.

Absalom did return to Jerusalem, but this turned out to be an ill-advised move on David's part. Absalom secretly plotted a revolt against the throne. Taking advantage of his natural appeal and his handsome appearance to win the favor of the people, he also aroused discontent by implying that he could rule more justly than his father.

When the plot was ready, Absalom obtained permission to go to Hebron to worship. Meanwhile, he had sent spies throughout the tribes, inviting those favorable to him to meet at Hebron (2 Sam. 15:7–11). After gathering these warriors, he then enlisted Ahithophel, a disloyal official of David, as his aide and advisor (2 Sam. 15:12).

When David learned of these rebellious acts, he fled to Mahanaim, beyond the Jordan River (2 Sam. 17:24). Under Ahithophel's advice, Absalom entered Jerusalem and publicly took possession of the wives in his father's harem who had been left in the city. By this act Absalom demonstrated that he would never be reconciled with his father, and even more of the people rallied to his cause.

Absalom then called a council to determine what action to take against David. Present at this meeting was Hushai, a loyal advisor to David who pretended to follow Absalom in order to spy on the proceedings. Ahithophel advised that Absalom move against the retreating king as quickly as possible, but Hushai countered by pointing out that if the attack failed, his revolt would fail. He advised instead that Absalom gather all his forces for one full-scale attack. Absalom heeded Hushai's counsel, giving David time to assemble an army.

Absalom was formally anointed king after taking Jerusalem (2 Sam. 19:10). He appointed Amasa as captain of his army, then crossed the Jordan River to meet his father's forces. The battle took place in the woods of Ephraim, where Absalom's recruits were no match for David's veterans. Absalom's army was defeated, and 20,000 of his men were killed (2 Sam. 18:6–7).

Absalom tried to flee from the forest on a mule, but his head caught in the thick branches of a terebinth tree. Joab, the captain of David's army, then killed Absalom in spite of David's request that he not be harmed. Upon hearing the news of his death, David moaned, "O my son Absalom—my son, my son Absalom—if only I had died in your place! O Absalom my son, my son!" (2 Sam. 18:33). These are some of the saddest words in the Bible.

Absalom had many talents and abilities. But he was also spoiled, impatient, and overly ambitious. These, along with his vanity and pride, led to his tragic death. His body was cast into a pit, over which a great heap of stones was piled as a sign of contempt (2 Sam. 18:17). A large mausoleum erroneously called Absalom's Monument, located in the Kidron Valley east of Jerusalem, was built centuries after Absalom's death. It can still be seen today.

ABSTINENCE

The voluntary, self-imposed, and deliberate denial of certain pleasures, such as food, drink, and sex. The Israelites were commanded to abstain from eating meat that contained blood (Gen. 9:4). They were to refrain from eating certain animals (Lev. 11). Priests could not drink wine while exercising their holy ministries (Lev. 10:9). Others abstained from drinking wine (Jer. 35:6).

The apostle Paul taught that Christians live by the laws of love and freedom—and that they should voluntarily abstain from food sacrificed to idols, lest it cause a weaker brother or sister in Christ to stumble (Rom. 14:1–23). The Christian is called to live a life of unselfish and sacrificial love.

ABYSS [ah BISS]

The bottomless pit or the chaotic deep. Sumerian in origin, the term referred to a deep mass of waters surrounding the earth. Darkness is said to have been on the face of the deep or abyss (Gen. 1:2).

The term is used in several other ways in the Bible. It describes the prison of disobedient spirits, or the world of the dead (Luke 8:31; Rom. 10:7; Rev. 20:1–3).

Terms like "the pit" and "bottomless pit" represent the abode of all the wicked dead.

ACACIA

A large thorny tree with rough gnarled bark. The orange-brown wood was hard-grained, and it repelled insects. It bore long locust-like pods with seeds inside and produced round, fragrant clusters of yellow blossoms. Many species of acacia grew in the desert of Sinai, in southern Canaan and in Egypt.

Acacia wood was used to build the ark of the covenant and the first tabernacle (Ex. 36:20; 37:1). The acacia is called shittim and shittah in the KJV (Ex. 25:5, 10; Is. 41:19).

ACCAD [ACK add]

One of four cities built by Nimrod in the land of Shinar—which were "the beginning of his kingdom" (Gen. 10:10; Akkad in NIV). The name was extended to the land of Accad, which was the northern division of ancient Babylonia. Accad was the region between the Tigris and Euphrates rivers—where the two rivers are close together and flow in roughly parallel courses.

The dynasty of Accad was founded by Sargon the Great and lasted from the twenty-third to the twenty-first century B.C. The name Accad survives in references to one of the earliest recorded Semitic languages, Accadian or Akkadian, which had two major dialects, Assyrian and Babylonian. It was written in the wedge-shaped characters (Cuneiform) developed by the Sumerians.

The location of Accad is not positively identified, but it is thought by some to be about 9 miles (15 kilometers) from modern Baghdad.

ACCEPT

To receive or treat with favor. In the Bible, a person is accepted by the grace, mercy, or covenant-love of God through faith and repentance. In the primary New Testament passage on acceptance, the apostle Paul explains that God has fully accepted believers through the merits of Christ (Eph. 1:6). God will not reject them; He opens Himself to His own by welcoming them.

ACCO [ACK coe]

A city of Canaan on the Mediterranean coast about 25 miles (40 kilometers) south of Tyre and about 9 miles (15 kilometers) north of Mount Carmel. Situated on the north shore of a broad bay, Acco was at the entrance to the rich, fertile plain of Jezreel. Although Acco was located in the portion of land assigned to the tribe of Asher, the Hebrews were never able to drive out the original Canaanite inhabitants (Judg. 1:31; Accho, KJV).

Acco was mentioned in the Amarna letters of the fourteenth century B.C. In the Hellenistic period the name was changed to Ptolemais. It came under Roman domination in 65 B.C.

Acco is mentioned only once in the New Testament and then as Ptolemais (Acts 21:7), the name coming from Ptolemy, the king of Egypt who rebuilt the city. Sailing from Tyre to Caesarea at the end of his third missionary journey, the apostle Paul docked at Ptolemais and spent the day with his fellow Christians while his ship was anchored in the harbor.

During the Crusades, Ptolemais recaptured some of its former prominence under the name Acre, by which name it is still known today. Its importance has once again waned, being overshadowed by the city of Haifa, which lies directly across the bay.

ACCOUNTABILITY

The biblical principle that we are answerable to our Maker for our thoughts, words, and deeds. The Bible plainly teaches that "the whole world [is] accountable to God" (Rom. 3:19, NASB). We cannot experience God's grace until we first see ourselves as sinners who are without excuse. Christians are accountable to God individually (Rom. 14:12), and corporately as well, "for we are members of one another" (Eph. 4:25).

ACHAIA [ah KAY yah]

In Roman times, the name for the whole of Greece, except Thessaly. The Romans gave the region this name when they captured Corinth and destroyed the Achaian League in 146 B.C. Later it comprised several Greek cities, including Athens.

The apostle Paul passed through Achaia on his way to Jerusalem (Acts 19:21). He also appeared before Gallio, the proconsul of Achaia, when the Jewish leaders tried to convince him to prosecute Paul for worship contrary to Jewish law (Acts 18:13). Gallio refused to accept the case and Paul was set free (Acts 18:12–17).

ACHAN [A kinn]

Son of Carmi of the tribe of Judah who unintentionally brought about the Israelites' defeat at Ai (Josh. 7:1, 18–24). He is called Achar in 1 Chronicles 2:7 and is described as the "troubler of Israel, who transgressed in the accursed thing."

During the Israelites' destruction of Jericho, Achan took a Babylonian garment, 200 shekels of silver, and a wedge of gold and hid them in his tent. Before the battle, the Lord had designated everything in Jericho an "accursed thing" and commanded that everything be destroyed, lest Israel also become cursed because their camp contained Canaanite spoils. The Israelites were defeated near the city of Ai because Achan had brought the "accursed thing" into their camp.

ACHISH [A kish]

A king of the Philistine city of Gath, to whom David fled for refuge when King Saul sought his life (1 Sam. 21:10–14; 27:2–12). David formed an alliance with Achish, who always treated him with great kindness (1 Sam. 28:1–2). Because the Philistine lords resisted the league between Achish and David, Achish was forced to send David away (1 Sam. 29:2–9). Achish is called Abimelech in the title of Psalm 34.

ACHMETHA [AK mee thah]

The capital of the empire of the Medes. Later it became one of the capitals of the Persian and Parthian empires. Achmetha was surrounded by seven concentric walls; since the city was built on a hill, the inner walls thus rose above the outer ones. Each wall was painted a different color.

Achmetha was also a treasure city, known for its luxury and splendor. When Cyrus the Great of Persia captured Achmetha in 550 B.C., he made it his summer residence, seeking escape from the terrible heat of Persia. At the time of Cyrus the imperial records were kept here, according to Ezra 6:2. When Darius I ordered a search of the palace library in Achmetha, a scroll was discovered upon which was written the decree of Cyrus permitting the Jews to return to Jerusalem and authorizing them to rebuild the temple.

In 330 B.C. Alexander the Great conquered Achmetha, destroying its walls and looting its palaces. Hamadan, Iran, occupies the site today, about 175 miles (280 kilometers) southwest of Teheran. Most modern versions (such as NIV, NASB, REB, and NRSV) translate Ecbatana.

ACHOR [A kore] *(trouble)*

A valley near Jericho where Achan was stoned to death during the time of Joshua (Josh. 7:24, 26). The prophets used the phrase "the Valley of Achor" (Is. 65:10) to symbolize the idyllic state of contentment and peace of the messianic age (Hos. 2:15).

ACHSAH [ACK sah]

The only daughter of Caleb (1 Chr. 2:49; Achsa in KJV). Caleb promised Achsah in marriage to anyone who would capture the city of Debir (formerly known as Kirjath Sepher). When Othniel, Caleb's nephew, took the town, Caleb gave his daughter a portion of the Negev (land in the South) as a dowry. Achsah also wanted springs to water her land and thus Caleb gave her "the upper springs and the lower springs" (Josh. 15:16–19; Judg. 1:12–15).

ACHSHAPH [ACK shaf]

A Canaanite city situated in the northern part of the territory conquered by Joshua (Josh. 11:1; 12:7, 20; 19:24–25). It was in the territory allotted to the tribe of Asher. Modern scholarship identifies Achshaph as Tell Kisan, about 6 miles (10 kilometers) southeast of Acre.

ACROPOLIS [uh CROP oh lis] *(topmost city)*

An elevated, fortified part of an ancient Greek city, such as Athens, Philippi, and Corinth. The Acropolis of Athens, the most famous acropolis of all ancient cities, was located on a hill about 500 feet high. It was adorned with stunning architectural works. Among these works was the Parthenon, a magnificent temple with 8 Doric columns in front and rear and 17 along each side.

ACROSTIC

A literary device by which sets of letters (such as the first letter of a line) are taken in order to form a word, phrase, or a regular sequence of letters of the alphabet.

The ancient Hebrews realized the importance of words and various literary devices such as puns, allusions, and acrostics. The best example of an acrostic in the Bible is Psalm 119, based on the Hebrew alphabet of 22 letters, from Aleph to Tau ("A" to "Z"). This Psalm, the longest chapter in the Bible, has 176 verses—eight verses for each of the 22 Hebrew letters.

In the original Hebrew of Psalm 119, verses 1–8 begin with Aleph; verses 9–16 begin with Beth; verses 17–24 begin with Gimel; and so forth. Parts of Psalms 9, 10, 25, 37, 111, 112, and 145 and Lamentations 1–4 are also acrostic—as are the last 22 verses of the Book of Proverbs, which contain a description of a virtuous wife (Prov. 31:10–21).

ADAM [ADD um] *(red, ground)*

The first man, created by God on the sixth day of creation, and placed in the Garden of Eden (Gen. 2:19–23; 3:8–9, 17, 20–21; 4:1, 25; 5:1–5). He and his wife Eve, created by God from one of Adam's ribs (Gen. 2:21–22), became the ancestors of all people now living on the earth. Adam was unique and distinct from the animals in several ways. His creation is described separately from that of the animals and the rest of God's creative acts (Gen. 1:3–25; 1:26–27; 2:7).

God breathed into Adam's body of "dust" the divine "breath of life; and man became a living being" (Gen. 2:7). God also made man in his own image and likeness. The exact words are, "Let Us make man in Our image, according to Our likeness" (Gen. 1:26). The apostle Paul interprets this to mean that God created man with spiritual, rational, emotional, and moral qualities (Eph. 4:24–32; Col. 3:8–10).

God placed Adam in the Garden of Eden, where he was to work the ground (Gen. 2:5, 15) and take care of the animals (Gen. 1:26–28; 2:19–20). God made Eve as a "helper comparable to" Adam (Gen. 2:20), creating her out of one of Adam's ribs so they were "one flesh" (Gen. 2:24).

God told the human pair, "Be fruitful and multiply; fill the earth" (Gen. 1:28). As a consequence, they had a number of children: Cain, Abel, Seth, and a number of other sons and daughters (Gen. 4:1–2; 5:3–4). Created in innocence, they did not know sin (Gen. 2:25).

Genesis 3 tells how Adam failed to keep God's command not to eat of the tree of the knowledge of good and evil. The consequence of this disobedience was death (Gen. 2:17), both physical (Gen. 5:5) and spiritual (Eph. 2:1). Eve disobeyed first, lured by pride and the desire for pleasure (Gen. 3:5–6; 1 Tim. 2:14). Then Adam, with full knowledge of the consequences, joined Eve in rebellion against God (Gen. 3:6).

The consequences of disobedience were: (1) loss of innocence (Gen. 3:7); (2) continued enmity between the seed of the woman [Christ] (Gen. 3:15; Gal. 3:16) and the seed of the serpent [Satan and his followers] (John 8:44); (3) the cursing of the ground and the resultant hard labor for man (Gen. 3:17–19); (4) the hard labor of childbirth (Gen. 3:16); (5) the submission of woman to her husband (Gen. 3:16; Eph. 5:22–23); and (6) separation from God (Gen. 3:23–24; 2 Thess. 1:9). Adam lived 930 years (Gen. 5:5).

The New Testament emphasizes the oneness of Adam and Eve (Matt. 19:3–9), showing that Adam represented man in bringing the human race into sin and death (Rom. 5:12–19; 1 Cor. 15:22). In contrast, Christ, the "last Adam," represented His redeemed people in bringing justification and eternal life to them (Rom. 5:15–21).

ADAMANT

A hard stone of superior strength. The exact identity of this substance is unknown; but it is believed to be corundum, the hardest of all minerals next to the diamond. Pure corundum is colorless; it is the source of such gems as rubies and sapphires.

Because of its hardness, the prophet Ezekiel used adamant as a symbol of the stubborn will of the rebellious Israelites. God strengthened the prophet with a "forehead like adamant stone, harder than flint" to preach to the Israelites (Ezek. 3:9; emery, NASB). Other English translations render the Hebrew word for adamant as diamond (Jer. 17:1, KJV, NASB, NRSV) or flint (Jer. 17:1, NIV).

ADDAN [ADD un]

An unidentified place in Babylonia from which returning captives came with Zerubbabel to Jerusalem (Ezra 2:59; Addon, Neh. 7:61). Some scholars believe Addan was the name of a man who was unable to produce his genealogy to prove he was an Israelite.

ADMAH [AD muh] (red earth)

One of the Cities of the Plain, destroyed with Sodom, Gomorrah, and the other cities (Deut. 29:23). Some scholars identify Admah with the city of Adam (Josh. 3:16).

ADONIJAH [add oh NYE juh] (the Lord is my Lord)

The fourth of the six sons born to David while he was at Hebron (2 Sam. 3:4). Adonijah's mother was Haggith. With the exception of Absalom, David apparently favored Adonijah over his other five sons. When David was old, Adonijah attempted to seize the throne, although he probably knew that his father intended Solomon to succeed him (1 Kin. 1:13).

Adonijah won two important people to his cause—Joab, the captain of the army, and Abiathar, the priest. At an open-air feast at the stone of Zoheleth beside En Rogel, he had himself proclaimed king. But Adonijah had not won over Zadok the priest, Benaiah the commander of the royal bodyguard, or Nathan the prophet. Bathsheba, Solomon's mother, and Nathan told David of Adonijah's activities; David immediately ordered Solomon, who had been divinely chosen as David's successor, to be proclaimed king. When Adonijah sought sanctuary at the altar (1 Kin. 1:5–50), Solomon forgave him.

Adonijah, however, foolishly made another attempt to become king—this time after David's death. He asked that the beautiful Abishag, who had taken care of David during his final days, be given to him in marriage. According to the custom of the day, claiming a king's wife or concubine amounted to the same thing as claiming his throne. This time Solomon ordered that Adonijah be killed (1 Kin. 2:13, 25).

ADONIRAM [ad oh NYE rum] (my Lord is exalted)

The son of Abda and an officer under kings David, Solomon, and Rehoboam. David placed Adoniram "in charge of revenue" (2 Sam. 20:24), and Solomon appointed him "over the labor force" (1 Kin. 4:6; 5:14)—a group sent to work in his enforced labor crews in Lebanon.

When the northern tribes rebelled against Rehoboam, Rehoboam sent Adoniram to force the rebels to obey the king, but "all Israel stoned him . . . and he died" (1 Kin. 12:18; 2 Chr. 10:18). Adoniram also was called Adoram (2 Sam. 20:24; 1 Kin. 12:18) and Hadoram (2 Chr. 10:18).

ADOPTION

The act of taking voluntarily a child of other parents as one's own child; in a theological sense, the act of God's grace by which sinful people are brought into [□]is redeemed family.

In the Old Testament, adoption was never common among the Israelites.

Adoption in the Old Testament was done by foreigners or by Jews influenced by foreign customs. Pharaoh's daughter adopted Moses (Ex. 2:10)

By New Testament times, Roman customs exercised a great deal of influence on Jewish family life. One custom is particularly significant in relation to adoption. Roman law required that the adopter be a male and childless; the one to be adopted had to be an independent adult, able to agree to be adopted. In the eyes of the law, the adopted one became a new creature; he was regarded as being born again into the new family.

The apostle Paul used this legal concept of adoption as an analogy to show the believer's relationship to God. Paul's

ADOPTION

A

emphasis was that our adoption rests with God, who "predestined us to adoption as sons" (Eph. 1:5). Paul also used the term to describe Israel's place of honor in God's plan (Rom. 9:4). However, Gentile believers have also been given the "Spirit of adoption," which allows them to cry, "Abba, Father" (Gal. 4:6).

ADORATION

The act of worship, of paying honor, reverence, and obedience to God. The word *adoration* does not occur in most English versions of the Bible (such as the KJV, NKJV, and NRSV, but the concept of adoration as worship is implied in many places in the Bible.

ADRAMMELECH [a DRAM uh leck]

A pagan god to whom the colonists of Samaria sacrificed their children (2 Kin. 17:31). This deity was worshiped in Mesopotamia under the name Adad-Milki, a form of the Syrian god Hadad.

ADRAMYTTIUM [add rah MITT ee um]

An important seaport of the Roman province of Asia, situated in northwestern Asia Minor, in what is modern Turkey. As a prisoner, Paul boarded "a ship of Adramyttium" (Acts 27:2) on his way to Rome. The site is now called Karatash, but a nearby town, Edremit, preserves the name.

ADRIATIC [a drih AT ick]

A name for the central part of the Mediterranean Sea south of Italy. It is mentioned in Luke's account of Paul's voyage to Rome (Acts 27:27). Paul's courage in the midst of this terrible storm is an inspiration: "Do not be afraid . . . for I believe God" (Acts 27:24–25). The Greek geographer Strabo (63 B.C.?—A.D. 24?) identified the Adriatic as the Gulf of Adria, pointing out that the name comes from the old Etruscan city of Atria. The KJV translates as Adria.

ADULLAM [a DULL um]

A large cave near the city of Adullam (1 Sam. 22:1; 1 Chr. 11:15), where David hid when he was a fugitive from King Saul.

ADULTERY

Willful sexual intercourse with someone other than one's husband or wife. Jesus expanded the meaning of adultery to include the cultivation of lust: "Whoever looks at a woman to lust for her has already committed adultery with her in his heart" (Matt. 5:28).

In the Ten Commandments, God specifically prohibited adultery (Deut. 22:22). Adultery plays havoc with personal, domestic, and national happiness. A case in point is David's affair with Bathsheba. Their adultery led to a cover-up, which was followed by the murder of Bathsheba's husband (2 Sam. 11). Nathan the prophet later came to David, accusing him of his sin and declaring that because of it, violence would become commonplace in David's household (2 Sam. 12:10). One disaster after another struck his family, including rape, murder, and revolt (2 Sam. 13–15).

The apostle Paul catalogued a series of sins that exclude a person from the kingdom of God. The sin of adultery was included in these lists (1 Cor. 6:9).

ADVERSARY

One who opposes or hinders another. In the Bible, this word is often used of Satan, the adversary of God and His plan of righteousness and redemption in the world. Since his fall, Satan has opposed God's plan to establish His kingdom on earth. He tricked Eve (Gen. 3:1–5) in order to use human beings to establish his kingdom rather than God's. Satan later opposed Jesus by questioning His identity as the Messiah and by tempting Him to misuse His powers as God's Son (Matt.

4:1–11). Satan is still the Christian's adversary (1 Pet. 5:8), but we have an advocate, Jesus Christ (1 John 2:1), who enables us to overcome his temptation.

ADVOCATE

One who pleads another's cause before a tribunal or judicial court. The word *advocate* is found only once in the NKJV: "If anyone sins, we have an Advocate with the Father, Jesus Christ the righteous" (1 John 2:1). The Greek word translated as "advocate" here is also found four times in the Gospel of John, all referring to the Holy Spirit (John 14:16, 26; 15:26; 16:7; helper, NKJV).

Christians need an Advocate because of the Adversary, the devil or Satan, who accuses us before God (1 Pet. 5:8; Rev. 12:10). If Satan is the "prosecuting attorney," Christ and the Holy Spirit are the legal advocates, the "defense attorneys," who help, defend, counsel, and comfort us; they plead the Christian's case before God day and night, providing a continuing remedy for sin.

AFFLICTION

Any condition or problem that produces suffering or pain. The Bible speaks of two types of affliction—suffering that represents God's judgment on sin (Is. 53:4; Matt. 24:29; Rom. 2:9), and suffering that brings about the purifying of believers as they identify with Christ (Rom. 5:3–5; 2 Thess. 1:4–7).

God's judgment on the sin of unbelievers is designed to punish them, while the second type of affliction is designed to perfect Christians and prepare them for greater service in God's kingdom.

AGABUS [AG uh bus]

A Christian prophet of Jerusalem who went to Antioch of Syria while Paul and Barnabas were there, and "showed by the Spirit that there was going to be a great famine throughout all the world" (Acts 11:28). Later, when Paul and his companions were at Caesarea, Agabus the prophet gave a symbolic demonstration of Paul's impending arrest. Agabus bound his own hands and feet with Paul's belt. Then he predicted that the owner of the belt would be bound like this by the Jews and delivered into the hands of the Gentiles (Acts 21:10–11).

AGAG [A gag]

A king of the Amalekites whose army was defeated by the forces of Saul. Instead of killing Agag as God told him to do, Saul spared his life. Because of his disobedience, Saul was rebuked by the prophet Samuel and rejected by the Lord. David was then anointed king in Saul's place (1 Sam. 15:33).

AGAPE [ah GAH pay]

A Greek word for love used often in the New Testament (John 13:35; 1 Cor. 13; 1 John 4:7–18). God loves with His will (John 3:16; Rom. 5:8). He can find nothing enjoyable about a sinner on whom His wrath still abides. So He loves by His will; it is His nature to love.

AGORA [ah GOE ruh]

The Greek word for marketplace (Acts 16:19). The agora was a large open space, often found near the gates of cities in New Testament times, where goods were bought and sold. The agora was also the site for public assemblies. While in Athens, the apostle Paul shared his faith with people in the agora (Acts 17:17).

AGRICULTURE

The science, art, and business of cultivating the soil, producing crops, and raising livestock; farming. The Bible indicates that one of the most basic human tasks was to till the soil (Gen. 2:15), so that human beings are seen as having divinely-given abilities to be gardeners or farmers.

Jesus made frequent reference to the land and its products in His teaching, indicating that He and His hearers were quite familiar with such matters. Matthew 13, for example, contains four agricultural parables—the sower (vv. 1–23), the wheat and the tares (vv. 24–30, 36–43), the mustard seed (vv. 31–32), and the treasure hidden in the field (v. 44).

Israelite agriculture included the farming of the land and the rearing of animals. In the days of the patriarchs, livestock farming was the major activity; but as the Israelites settled in the land, the role of animals became less important. Herds and flocks were kept basically for their wealth and for food, although meat was much less important than it is in modern Western society. Most families also owned work animals, the ox being the most valuable and the donkey the most common. Neither horses nor camels were used much in agriculture. Horses were kept mostly for military use and camels for trading purposes.

The growing of crops in ancient Israel was no easy matter. Palestine's location between the Mediterranean Sea and the desert produced unpredictable rainfall. The growth of vegetation in some lowland areas, such as the Jordan River valley and parts of the Plain of Sharon along the coast, were so luxuriant that they contained mostly dense forests. Other areas, mainly in the east, were dry and barren, with stony terrain and only occasional rain. These were impossible to farm and unable to support a settled population. Even the areas that could be cultivated had their continual hazards, such as locusts, hail, desert storms, and invading armies. The Israelite farmer well understood the truth of Genesis 3:19: "In the sweat of your face you shall eat bread."

The Old Testament consistently refers to the three basic Israelite crops: grain, grapes, and olives. Psalm 104:15, for example, speaks of God providing "wine that makes glad the heart of man, oil to make his face shine, and bread which strengthens man's heart" (Deut. 7:13; 2 Kin. 18:32; Neh. 5:11). Of the grain crops, wheat was grown mainly in the central area of the western highlands (Manasseh) and in Gilead and Bashan, east of the Jordan River. Barley was grown in the drier south and east, especially in Philistia. Barley is able to grow in poorer soils than wheat, and it has a shorter ripening period.

Seed was usually broadcast and then plowed or raked into the soil, although occasionally plowing was done before sowing. A single wooden plow with a metal tip was normally used; it was pulled by a pair of oxen or donkeys. The animals were yoked together with either a single yoke or a double yoke with bars over and under the neck. An ox goad, a long staff with a nail or metal tip, was used to control the animals (Judg. 3:31).

Harvest was an important time, and workers were hired especially for the occasion. The standing grain was cut with a scythe or sickle, then brought in bundles to the threshing floor where it was threshed and separated from the chaff. Finally it was stored, either in earthenware jars or in underground silos. The prophet Isaiah referred to the various processes involved in growing grain, observing that it was an occasion for wonder and praise of God (Is. 28:23–29).

Vineyards were concentrated on the terraces of the Judean hills, although they were also found in the Carmel area and in parts of the region east of the Jordan River. Isaiah 5:1–7 gives some idea of the hard labor involved in preparing and cultivating vineyards. Vines were often left to trail on the ground. As the fruit began to ripen from July onward, people built watch-towers, or temporary booths, to keep watch for both human and animal intruders. Harvesting the grapes and making wine were great social occasions. The Old Testament law allowed people to eat grapes while collecting them, but not to put them in their own baskets while in someone else's field (Deut. 23:24). The grapes were mainly used for wine, but some were dried as raisins.

AGRIPPA [a GRIP uh]

1. Roman ruler of Galilee and eventual ruler of the territory previously governed by his grandfather, Herod the Great. Agrippa I persecuted the Christians in Jerusalem (Acts 12:1–23) during his reign in Judea from A.D. 41 until his death in A.D. 44.

AGRIPPA [a GRIP uh]

2. Son of Herod Agrippa I and greatgrandson of Herod the Great. He was appointed by the Roman emperor Claudius as ruler of Abilene, part of Galilee, Iturea, and Trachonitis. Shortly before the apostle Paul was taken prisoner to Rome, he appeared before Herod Agrippa II (Acts 25:13–26:32).

AHAB [A hab] *(father is brother)*

The son of Omri and the seventh king of Israel (1 Kin. 16:30). Under the influence of Jezebel his wife, Ahab gave the pagan god Baal equal place with God. Ahab also built a temple to Baal in which he erected a "wooden image" of the Canaanite goddess Asherah (1 Kin. 16:33). At Jezebel's urging, Ahab opposed the worship of the Lord, destroyed His altars, and killed His prophets. He reigned over Israel for 22 years (873–852 B.C.) (1 Kin. 16:29).

Ahab strengthened the friendly relations with Phoenicia that David had begun when he was king of the united kingdom. He sealed the friendship between the two nations with a political marriage to Jezebel, the notoriously wicked daughter of Ethbaal, king of the

Sidonians (1 Kin. 16:31). Ahab may have been the first king of Israel to establish peaceful relations with Judah.

False religion soon led to immoral civil acts. Because Jezebel had neither religious scruples nor regard for Hebrew civil laws (Lev. 25:23–34), she had Naboth tried unjustly and killed so that Ahab could take over his property (1 Kin. 21:1–16).

Throughout Ahab's reign, the prophet Elijah stood in open opposition to Ahab and the worship of Baal. Ahab also had frequent conflicts with Ben-Hadad, King of Syria, who once besieged Ahab's capital city, Samaria, but was driven off (1 Kin. 20:1–21).

Later, Ahab defeated Ben-Hadad in a battle at Aphek (1 Kin. 20:22–34); but Ahab was lenient with him, perhaps in view of a greater threat, Shalmaneser III of Assyria. In 853 B.C., Ahab and Ben-Hadad joined in a coalition to stop Shalmaneser's army at Qarqar on the Orontes River in Syria. Ahab contributed 2,000 chariots and 10,000 soldiers to this coalition. Still later, Ahab fought Ben-Hadad again. In spite of his precautions, Ahab was killed at Ramoth Gilead (1 Kin. 22:1–38).

Ahab was a capable leader and an avid builder. He completed and adorned the capital city of Samaria, which his father Omri had begun. Archaeological discoveries show that Ahab's "ivory house" (1 Kin. 22:39; Amos 3:15) was faced with white stone, which gave it the appearance of ivory. It was also decorated with ivory inlays. The ivory fragments that have been found show similarities with Phoenician ivories of the period. These findings illustrate the close political and social ties that existed between Israel and Phoenicia. Archaeology has also shown that Ahab refortified the cities of Megiddo and Hazor, probably in defense against growing threats from Syria and Assyria.

Ahab's story is particularly sad because of his great potential. His tragedy was forming an alliance with Jezebel and turning from God to serve idols.

AHASUERUS [ah has you EH rus]
(mighty man)

A king of Persia and the husband of the Jewess Esther. Scholars generally agree that Ahasuerus is the same person as Xerxes I (485–464 B.C.).

The picture of Ahasuerus presented in the Book of Esther—the vastness of his empire (1:1), his riches (1:4), his sensuality and feasting (1:5–12), and his cruelty and lack of foresight (1:13–22)—is consistent with the description of Xerxes provided by the Greek historian Herodotus. Ahasuerus succeeded his father, Darius Hystaspis, in 485 B.C.

The Book of Esther tells the story of how Ahasuerus banished his queen, Vashti, because of her refusal to parade herself before the drunken merrymakers at one of his feasts. Following a two-year search for Vashti's replacement, Ahasuerus chose Esther as his queen. Esther and her people, the Jews, were in Persia as a consequence of the fall of Jerusalem (in 586 B.C.) and the scattering of the Jews into captivity in foreign lands.

Ahasuerus's advisor, Haman, hated the Jews; he prevailed upon Ahasuerus to order them to be wiped out—an order which the king gave with little concern for its consequences. During a sleepless night, Ahasuerus sent for his royal records and read of how the Jew Mordecai, Esther's guardian, had uncovered a plot to kill the king and thus had saved his life. Ahasuerus's discovery led to Mordecai's being raised to a position of honor in the kingdom. Haman's treachery soon led to his own fall, and he and his ten sons were hanged on the gallows he had previously prepared for Mordecai.

In 464 B.C. a courtier murdered Ahasu-erus, and his son, Artaxerxes Longimanus, succeeded him. In Ezra 4:6, the reign of Ahasuerus is mentioned chronologically between Cyrus (v. 5) and Artaxerxes (v. 7).

AHAVA [a HAH vuh]

A town in Babylonia situated near a small river or canal of the same name. Ezra and his companions camped for three days on the banks of this stream as they prepared for the long journey to Jerusalem (Ezra 8:15, 21, 31).

AHAZ [A haz]

A son of Jotham and the eleventh king of Judah (2 Kin. 15:38; 16:1–20; Achaz, KJV). He was an ungodly king who promoted the worship of Molech, with its pagan rites of human sacrifice (2 Chr. 28:1–4).

The reign of Ahaz probably overlapped the reign of his father Jotham and possibly the reign of his own son Hezekiah. His age when he became king was 20 and he reigned for 16 years, beginning about 735 B.C.

Early in his reign Ahaz adopted policies that favored Assyria. When he refused to join the anti-Assyrian alliance of Pekah of Israel and Rezin of Syria, they invaded Judah and besieged Jerusalem, threatening to dethrone Ahaz and replace him with a puppet king (Is. 7:1–6). Pekah and Rezin killed 120,000 people and took 200,000 captives. However, through the intervention of Oded the prophet, the captives were released immediately (2 Chr. 28:5–15).

In view of his precarious circumstances, Ahaz requested help from Tiglath-Pileser III, king of Assyria, offering him silver and gold. At first the plan worked, and Assyria invaded Israel and Syria (2 Kin. 15:29). Ultimately, however, Assyria "distressed" Ahaz, demanding excessive tribute (2 Chr. 28:20–21).

Spiritually, Ahaz stopped following in

the ways of the four relatively good kings who had preceded him (Joash, Amaziah, Azariah, and Jotham). He made images of Baal, offered infant sacrifices in the Valley of Hinnom, and sacrificed on the high places (2 Chr. 28:1–4). He came under further pagan influence at Damascus, where he had gone to meet Tiglath-Pileser III. Seeing a pagan altar there, he commanded Uriah the priest at Jerusalem to build a copy of it. He then installed it next to the bronze altar in the Jerusalem temple.

It was to King Ahaz that Isaiah's announcement of the promised Immanuel was made (Is. 7:10–17). The prophet Isaiah sent a message to the terrified Ahaz, but Ahaz would not turn to God and trust Him for deliverance. Instead, he plunged deeper into idolatry and self-destruction. Ahaz's conduct brought divine judgment to Judah in the form of military defeats. Edom revolted and took captives from Judah. The Philistines invaded Judah, capturing several cities. Rezin of Damascus seized control of Elath, Judah's port on the Gulf of Aqaba (2 Kin. 16:5–6).

At his death, Ahaz was buried without honor in Jerusalem. He was not deemed worthy of a burial in the royal tombs (2 Chr. 28:27).

AHAZIAH [a huh ZIE uh] (the Lord sustains)

The son and successor of Ahab and the ninth king of Israel (1 Kin. 22:40, 49, 51). Ahaziah reigned from 853 to 852 B.C.

The son of Jezebel, Ahaziah followed policies that showed evidence of his mother's pagan influence. After reigning only two years, he "fell through the lattice of his upper room in Samaria" (2 Kin. 1:2) and was seriously injured. Sending his messengers to ask Baal-Zebub, the god of Ekron, about his recovery, Ahaziah was frustrated when the prophet Elijah interrupted their mission

and prophesied Ahaziah's death. Enraged by Elijah's predictions, Ahaziah tried to seize him, but the men sent to capture the prophet were destroyed by fire from heaven and Elijah's prophecy was quickly fulfilled (2 Kin. 1:9–17).

At the time of Ahaziah's ascent to the throne, Mesha, the king of Moab, rebelled because of the tribute imposed on him by Omri, Ahaziah's grandfather (2 Kin. 1:1; 3:4–5). Ahaziah formed an alliance with Jehoshaphat, king of Judah, to build ships and trade with other nations. God judged this effort and it failed (1 Kin. 22:49).

AHIJAH [a HIGH juh] (my brother is the Lord)

The prophet from Shiloh who prophesied Israel's division into two kingdoms because of its idolatries (1 Kin. 11:29–39). While Solomon was king, Jeroboam rebelled against him. Ahijah tore his own garment into 12 pieces and instructed Jeroboam to take 10 of them. This symbolic action indicated that Jeroboam would be king over the 10 tribes which would be known as the northern kingdom of Israel. Ahijah stood up for the people in the face of their oppression under Solomon and Rehoboam.

Later, King Jeroboam disguised his queen and sent her to the aging and nearly blind prophet to ask whether their sick child would recover. Ahijah prophesied that because of Jeroboam's wickedness the child would die (1 Kin. 14:1–18). His prophecies were also put into writing (2 Chr. 9:29).

AHIKAM [a HIGH kumm] (my brother has risen)

A son of Shaphan and an officer in King Josiah's court. He was a member of the delegation sent by Josiah to the prophetess Huldah (2 Kin. 22:12–14). He helped protect the prophet Jeremiah from the persecutions of King Jehoiakim (Jer. 26:24).

AHIMAAZ [a HIM a az] *(powerful brother)*

A son of Zadok the high priest, Ahimaaz kept David informed of Absalom's revolt after the king was forced to flee Jerusalem (2 Sam. 15:27). This "spy" system worked well at first, but it was later discovered, and Ahimaaz and Jonathan fled for their lives (2 Sam. 17:18).

AHITHOPHEL [a HITH oh fell] *(brother of folly)*

One of David's counselors who assisted Absalom in his revolt. When Absalom rebelled against David, Ahithophel apparently believed his own popularity would bring success to Absalom's revolt. Possibly sensing a chance to rise to power himself, Ahithophel advised Absalom to take David's harem (2 Sam. 15:12; 16:21)—an act equivalent to claiming the throne.

Ahithophel also advised Absalom to pursue David, who had fled Jerusalem. But Absalom chose to listen to Hushai, who advised the prince not to pursue his father. Sensing that Absalom's rebellion was doomed, Ahithophel put his household in order and hanged himself (2 Sam. 17:23)—one of the few cases of suicide in the Bible.

AI [A eye] *(the ruin)*

A Canaanite city (Josh. 10:1) located east of Bethel (Gen. 12:8), "beside Beth Aven" (Josh. 7:2), and north of Michmash (Is. 10:28). Many years before Joshua's time, Abraham pitched his tent at Ai before journeying to Egypt (Gen. 12:8).

Ai figures prominently in the story of Israel's conquest of Canaan. After Joshua conquered Jericho, he sent men to spy out Ai and the surrounding countryside. Because Ai was small, the spies assured Joshua that he could take Ai with only a handful of soldiers.

Joshua dispatched about 3,000 soldiers to attack Ai. This army was soundly defeated, due to Achan's sin of taking spoils from Jericho contrary to God's commandment. When God singled out Achan and his family, the people stoned them to death. Joshua then sent 30,000 soldiers against Ai and captured the city by a clever military tactic—an ambush (Josh. 7–8).

Although Ai has been identified with modern et-Tell, situated southeast of Bethel, recent archaeological discoveries conflict with this placement and make this identification uncertain. Nearby Khirbet Nisya is another possible location for Ai. Ai is also called Aiath (Is. 10:28, KJV), Aija (Neh. 11:31, KJV), and Hai (Gen. 12:8; 13:3, KJV).

AIJALON [A juh lon] *(place of deer)*

A city in the Shephelah, the lowlands west of Jerusalem. It belonged to the tribe of Dan (Josh. 19:42) and was assigned to the Kohathite Levites. The area surrounding Aijalon was the scene of the famous battle between Joshua and the five Amorite kings. This was the battle where Joshua made the sun stand still, while the Israelites destroyed their enemies (Josh. 10:12–14). After the Ten Tribes seceded to form the northern kingdom of Israel, Aijalon was fortified by Rehoboam (1 Chr. 8:13; 2 Chr. 11:10). In the days of King Ahaz, the city was captured by the Philistines (2 Chr. 28:18).

Aijalon is identified with Yalo, a village situated about 14 miles (23 kilometers) northwest of Jerusalem (Josh. 10:12; 19:42; 2 Chr. 28:18; Ajalon, KJV).

AKELDAMA [ah kell DA mah] *(field of blood)*

A field located outside the walls of Jerusalem. According to Matthew, this field was purchased by the chief priests with the 30 pieces of silver they paid to Judas for betraying Jesus. Remorseful at having betrayed innocent blood, Judas flung the 30 pieces of silver on the floor of the temple and went out and hanged himself. The priests would not put the coins in the temple treasury because they were tainted with "the price of blood." So they took the money and bought the potter's field, in which to bury strangers (Matt. 27:3–10).

According to Luke, however, the field was purchased by Judas himself with the 30 pieces of silver. Apparently it was this field that became known as "Akel Dama, or Field of Blood" (Acts 1:18–19; Aceldama in KJV)—the place where Judas died. Apparently, Judas did not personally buy the field; he "bought" it only in the sense that his own money, thrown down on the temple floor, was used by the chief priests to purchase the field.

A tradition from the fourth century places this plot of ground on the Hill of Evil Counsel, a level plot overlooking the Valley of Hinnom.

ALEXANDER THE GREAT [eh leg ZAN dur] *(defender of men)*

Founder of the Hellenistic (Greek) Empire. He was born in 356 B.C. and ascended the Macedonian throne in 336 B.C. Advised by his teacher Aristotle that he could rule the world if he could make people adopt the Greek culture, Alexander extended his empire east from Greece, around the Mediterranean Sea to Egypt, and then to the borders of India. He died in Babylon in 323 B.C. at the age of 33.

Although Alexander the Great is not mentioned directly in the Bible, many scholars think that "the large horn that is between [the] eyes . . . of the male goat" (Dan. 8:21) and the "mighty king" in the vision of Daniel 11:3–4 may refer to him.

ALEXANDRIA [eh leg ZAN drih uh]

The capital of Egypt during the Greek and Roman periods. Situated on the Mediterranean Sea at the western edge of the Nile River delta, the city was established by Alexander the Great when he conquered Egypt in 331 B.C. After Alexander's death, the capital of Egypt was moved from Memphis to Alexandria, and it became one of the most significant cities of the Greek Empire. The population of Alexandria included native Egyptians, learned Greeks, and many Jews. The commercial strength of the city was aided by the famous towering lighthouse (one of the seven wonders of the ancient world) that guided ships into port. Paul himself sailed in an Alexandrian ship on his way to Rome (Acts 27:6; 28:11).

As a cultural center, Alexandria had a large museum and a library that attracted many scholars and writers. These learned people carried out research to establish accurate versions of the important Greek myths and epics as well as scientific investigations in astronomy, botany, and mathematics. One of the results of these interests was the commissioning of 70 (or 72) Jewish scholars to translate the Old Testament from Hebrew to Greek. The translation they produced is known as the Septuagint.

Philo and other learned Jews in Alexandria wrote many books in defense of the Jewish faith to show that their beliefs were consistent with Greek philosophical thinking. This sometimes resulted in unusual methods of interpretation because the literal understanding of Scripture often was mixed with fanciful explanations—a type of interpretation known as allegory. A Christian school of thought that used the allegorical method grew up in Alexandria, led by such great church fathers as Clement and Origen.

Apollos, a believer from Alexandria,

who worked with the church at Corinth after it was founded by the apostle Paul, may have attended one of these early schools. The Book of Acts describes Apollos as one who was well versed in the Scriptures (Acts 18:24). Because the Book of Hebrews reflects thinking that is similar to writings from Alexandria, some scholars believe Apollos may have written the book.

The early church father Eusebius recorded the tradition that John Mark was one of the first missionaries who brought the message of Christ to the people of Alexandria. Years earlier, prominent Jews from Alexandria who gathered in Jerusalem strongly opposed Stephen's preaching about Christ (Acts 6:9).

Of the many Alexandrias that Alexander the Great founded and named after himself, the one in Egypt outshines them all. It remains a thriving city to this day.

ALGUM

A large leguminous tree native to India and Ceylon. While its identity is uncertain, many consider it to be the red sandalwood. Its blossoms were pea-like, and its wood was close grained, dark outside, and red inside. It was highly scented, making it resistant to insects. Most authorities believe that algum and almug are two names for the same wood.

Solomon ordered the algum wood from Ophir and Lebanon (1 Kin. 10:11–12; 2 Chr. 9:10–11). The wood was well-suited for making musical instruments, cabinet work, and pillars for the temple.

ALLELUIA [al e LOO yuh] (praise the Lord)

A Greek form of the Hebrew word *Hallelujah* used to express joy, praise, and thanksgiving. The words "Praise the Lord," found often in the Psalms, are a translation of the Hebrew *Hallelujah* (Pss. 104:35; 116:19; 147:1)

ALLIANCE

An agreement or treaty among two or more individuals or nations for the purpose of providing mutual trading privileges or military protection. Alliances between the patriarchs and foreigners were common—for example, Abraham with Abimelech of Gerar (Gen. 21:22–34) and Jacob with Laban (Gen. 31:43–55). At Sinai Israel was forbidden to make alliances with the Canaanites (Ex. 23:32). This was to keep Israel's loyalties from being divided between God and pagan powers.

During the conquest of the land of Canaan, the Israelites were tricked into an alliance with the Gibeonites (Josh. 9). Later, during the period of the judges, the individual Hebrew tribes apparently made alliances with one another for their common defense (Judg. 4:10; 6:35).

King David entered into several foreign treaties—for example, with Achish of Gath (1 Sam. 27:1–12) and Hiram of Tyre (1 Kin. 5:1–12). Solomon's many marriages probably included alliances with other nations (1 Kin. 3:1; 9:16; 11:1–3). Other Hebrew kings formed many alliances, such as Asa with Ben-Hadad of Syria (1 Kin. 15:18–20; 2 Chr. 16:1–6). Judah's attempts to make alliances with Egypt were responsible for the attacks of Nebuchadnezzar of Babylon on Jerusalem in 597 B.C. and 586 B.C. (2 Kin. 24:1, 20; Ezek. 17:12–21).

The prophets warned the nation of Israel against forming alliances that sought to replace dependence on God with reliance on a foreign power (Jer. 2:18, 36; Ezek. 23:11–21).

ALLOTMENT

In the Old Testament, a system of land tenure used in Israel to distribute the land to the tribes, clans, and families. Joshua 13–19 describes the division of the land on both sides of the Jordan

River among the tribes of Israel, with each tribe except the Levites receiving a specific territory.

How the allotment was determined is not explained, but many scholars believe the "lot" involved the use of the Urim and Thummim (Ex. 28:30; Lev. 8:8; Deut. 33:8; Ezra 2:63; Neh. 7:65), which were stones kept in the breastplate (or pouch) on the high priest's ephod and used in determining God's will.

Over a period of time, a reallotment or redistribution of the land was necessary. This explains the provision for a "Year of Jubilee" (Lev. 25:8–55; 27:17–24; Num.

36:4). Every fiftieth year, the allotments were to be restored to their original owners—a practice that helped prevent drastic inequalities of wealth and poverty. Because the Lord himself was the "lot" (allotment, portion, or inheritance) of the Levites (or priests), the tribe of Levi received no allotment of land (Num. 18:20; Deut. 10:9; Josh. 13:14). They were allowed, however, to live among all the tribes.

ALMOND

A large tree resembling the peach tree in both size and fruit. The almond was

ALMS

chiefly valued for the nuts it produced, which were used for making oil used in the home and as medicine. The Hebrew word for almond means "awakening," an allusion to the almond blossom, which is first to bloom in the spring. The almond's pinkish-white blossoms always appear before its leaves.

The almond played an important role in the history of Israel. Jacob included almond nuts in his gifts to Joseph in Egypt (Gen. 43:11). The decorations on the lampstands were modeled after the almond blossom (Ex. 25:33), and Aaron's rod was an almond twig (Num. 17:8). The almond also symbolized the dependability of God (Jer. 1:11–12). Many scholars think the hazel of Genesis 30:37 (KJV) is the almond tree.

ALMS

Money given out of mercy for the poor. The Israelites were commanded to be generous in opening their hands wide to the poor and needy (Deut. 15:11). Gleanings from vineyards, orchards, olive groves, and fields should be made available to the poor (Lev. 19:9–10; Ruth 2:2, 7–8). Blessings were promised to those who were generous in aiding the poor (Prov. 14:21; 19:17). Eventually, the notion developed that almsgiving had power to atone for the giver's sins.

By Jesus' time, the word *righteousness* was tied closely to the word *alms*. Thus, when Jesus taught about "charitable deeds" (or almsgiving; Matt. 6:2–4), prayer (Matt. 6:5–15), and fasting (Matt. 6:16–18), he prefaced his teachings by saying, "Beware of practicing your piety [literally, righteousness] before men in order to be seen by them" (Matt. 6:1). In this way he taught that the giving of alms to the poor must not become a theatrical display to win people's applause; the praise that comes from God is more important.

The Book of Acts comments favorably on several instances of almsgiving. A certain disciple at Joppa—a woman named Tabitha, or Dorcas—was full of good works and charitable deeds (Acts 9:36). A God-fearing man named Cornelius "gave alms generously to the people, and prayed to God always" (Acts 10:2). Then, as now, God acknowledges those who give gifts of food to the hungry and in other ways show compassion to the needy (Is. 58:6–8; 1 John 3:17).

ALPHA AND OMEGA [AL fuh, oh MAY guh]

The first and last letters of the Greek alphabet. This title is given to God the Father and God the Son (Rev. 1:8; 21:6). The risen Christ says, "I am the Alpha and the Omega, the Beginning and the End, the First and the Last" (Rev. 22:13). By calling Jesus Christ the Alpha and the Omega, the writer of the Book of Revelation acknowledged that He is the Creator, the Redeemer, and the final Judge of all things.

ALTAR

A table, platform, or elevated place on which a priest placed a sacrifice as an offering to God. The nature of altars changed considerably during the several centuries of Bible history. In addition to describing altars dedicated to God, the Bible speaks frequently also of pagan altars, particularly those associated with the false worship of the Canaanites.

The first altar in the Bible was the one built by Noah after the Flood (Gen. 8:20). The next several altars mentioned appear in connection with the patriarch Abraham and his wanderings. His first altar, at Shechem, seemed to serve as a symbol of his possession of the land (Gen. 12:7). At his altars between Bethel and Ai (Gen. 12:8) and at Hebron (Gen. 13:18), he sacrificed animals and called upon the name of the Lord. Abraham built his last altar on top of a mountain in the land of Moriah (Gen. 22:9). To these altars, his son Isaac added one at Beersheba (Gen. 26:25). Isaac's son Jacob built no new altars; but he restored those that Abraham had built at Shechem (Gen. 33:20) and Bethel (Gen. 35:1, 3).

The Hebrew word for altar means "a place of slaughter or sacrifice." But the altars of the Old Testament were not restricted to offerings of animals as sacrifices. Joshua 22:26–29 indicates that altars were occasionally used to remind the Israelites of their heritage or to call attention to a major event. Sometimes an altar might even be used as a place for refuge (1 Kin. 1:50–51; 2:28).

During the days of Moses, two priestly altars assumed important roles in the ritual of the tabernacle in the wilderness. These were the altar of burnt offering and the altar of incense.

The altar of burnt offering (Ex. 27:1–8) was placed in front of the entrance to the tabernacle (Ex. 40:6), where it was used for the daily burnt offering and meal offering. This altar declared that entry into the presence of God must be preceded by sacrificial atonement for sin. The altar of burnt offering was made of acacia wood, overlaid with bronze. The corners of the altar extended at the

ALTAR

top into projections that looked like horns.

The golden altar of incense (Ex. 30:1–10) stood just before the veil inside the tabernacle that separated the most holy place from the rest of the worship area (Ex. 40:26–27). Priests burned incense on this altar every day so its fragrance would fill the tabernacle.

As the first king of Israel, Saul built an altar during his conquest of the Philistines for the sacrifice of sheep, oxen, and calves (1 Sam. 14:35). Later David erected an altar on a threshing floor of natural stone that he bought from Araunah the Jebusite (2 Sam. 24:15–25). This site became the central place of sacrifice in the temple after it was constructed by Solomon, David's son and successor. Some have identified this site with the large rock structure in the city of Jerusalem now seen under the famous building known as the Dome of the Rock.

After building the temple in Jerusalem, Solomon constructed an altar (2 Chr. 4:1) larger than the one Moses had built, probably adapting it to the size of the temple. This was the altar restored later by King Asa (2 Chr. 15:8). Still later, King Ahaz had Solomon's altar moved to the northern part of the temple courtyard (2 Kin. 16:14–15). This was also the same altar cleansed by Hezekiah (2 Chr. 29:18) and rebuilt by Manasseh (2 Chr. 33:16) at later times in Old Testament history.

The incense altar of the tabernacle was also replaced by Solomon's altar made of cedar and overlaid with gold (1 Kin. 6:20, 22; 7:48). Incense was burned every morning and evening on this altar. The priest also sprinkled the blood of a sacrificial animal on the incense altar to make atonement for his sins and the sins of the people. The incense altar was also symbolic of prayer. It is the only altar that appears in the heavenly temple (Is. 6:6; Rev. 8:3).

When the captives returned to Jerusalem following their years of captivity in Babylon, one of their first acts was to build an altar (Ezra 3:3).

In addition to the temple of the Jewish people with its altars, the New Testament refers to the altar in Athens that was dedicated "TO THE UNKNOWN GOD" (Acts 17:23). No physical Christian altar appears in the New Testament. The statement "we have an altar" (Heb. 13:10) refers to the sacrifice of Christ. The altar of incense mentioned in Revelation 8:3 belongs to the heavenly temple. In this heavenly temple there is no need for an altar of burnt offering since atonement for our sins is now complete through the death of Jesus Christ.

Archaeology has turned up many Canaanite altars from all periods of Old Testament history. A kind of table or altar built into the rear wall of a temple in ancient Megiddo has been dated at about 2000 B.C. Also uncovered at Megiddo was a large round altar from an even earlier period.

Canaanite altars were constructed of earth, stone, or metal. Stone altars have been preserved in Israel. Their form ranges from unworked, detached rocks to carefully cut natural stone. Altars of earth are mentioned in the ancient records, but none have been preserved. These were the simplest altars, probably built by the common people.

References to altars dedicated to pagan gods other than the one true God appear throughout the Old Testament. They were devoted to the Baals (2 Chr. 33:3) and various other Canaanite gods and goddesses (Deut. 12:3)—Chemosh the god of Moab, Ashtoreth of the Sidonians, and Molech of the Ammonites (1 Kin. 11:5–7). The Lord gave specific instructions that these pagan altars should be torn down and destroyed before altars dedicated to His worship were built (Deut. 12:2–3).

AMALEKITES [AM uh leck ites]

An ancient wandering tribe descended from Esau's grandson Amalek (Gen. 36:12, 16; 1 Chr. 1:36). The main territory of the Amalekites was in the Sinai peninsula and in the Negev, the southern part of present-day Israel. But they roamed widely throughout the territory later settled by the people of Israel. Throughout the Old Testament period the Amalekites were bitter foes of the Israelites.

The Amalekites are first mentioned in the time of Abraham, when a group of kings under the leadership of Chedorlaomer defeated Amalek (Gen. 14:7). At the time of Israel's journey through the wilderness, the Amalekites lived in the southern part of the land promised to Israel. The Amalekites attacked the Israelites, but Joshua later defeated them in a battle at Rephidim (Ex. 17:8–16). Because of their treacherous attacks, Moses declared that God would continually wage war against them (Ex. 17:14–16).

During the period of the judges, the Amalekites joined forces with the Ammonites and Eglon, king of Moab, to attack and capture Jericho (Judg. 3:13). Along with the Midianites and the people of the East, they were defeated in the Valley of Jezreel by Gideon's army (Judg. 6:3, 33; 7:12–22).

Eventually the Amalekites gained a mountain in the land of Ephraim. King Saul of Israel won this area back and then chased the Amalekites from the land (1 Sam. 14:48; 15:1–9). But Saul did not destroy the rich booty of livestock as God commanded, so he was rebuked by the prophet Samuel (1 Sam. 15:10–33).

The Amalekites continued to raid Israel. David attacked and defeated them (1 Sam. 27:8–10), but they countered by raiding Ziklag and carrying off two of David's wives. He pursued and defeated them (1 Sam. 30:1–31), executing one of them for claiming to have killed Saul in battle (2 Sam. 1:1–16).

In the days of King Hezekiah, 500 men of the tribe of Simeon defeated the Amalekites. Consequently, the Simeonites took their land and the Amalekites became a dispossessed people (1 Chr. 4:39–43).

AMARNA, TELL EL- [a MAR nuh]

The modern name of the site of Akhetaten, capital of Egypt during the reign of Amunhotep IV (about 1375–1358 B.C.), and the site of important archaeological finds.

In 1887 a peasant woman discovered some clay tablets in the ruins of Akhetaten. Archaeologists carefully examined the area and found fragments of about 350 documents in the wedge-shaped (cuneiform) script that was popular in ancient Mesopotamia. These tablets provide firsthand geographical and historical information about political events and important people during the fourteenth century B.C.

AMASA [AM ah sah] *(burden-bearer)*

David's nephew, the son of Jether and Abigail (1 Chr. 2:17). Amasa was also the cousin of Joab, a captain in David's army (2 Sam. 17:25). When Absalom rebelled against his father David, he appointed Amasa commander of the rebel army. After Absalom was defeated and killed by Joab (2 Sam. 18:14), David forgave Amasa and appointed him commander of the royal army in place of Joab (2 Sam. 19:13).

AMAZIAH [am ah ZIE uh] *(the Lord is mighty)*

The son of King Joash (2 Kin. 14:1–20; 2 Chr. 25:1). Amaziah was 25 years old when he began his reign as the ninth king of Judah. He followed in the steps of his father, doing "what was right in the sight of the Lord" (2 Kin. 14:3). However, he permitted the high places of false worship to stand (2 Kin. 14:4). After becoming king, Amaziah built up an army in Judah, adding to these ranks 100,000 mercenaries, or paid troops, from Israel to war against Edom (2 Chr. 25:6). Warned by a "man of God" that if he used the mercenaries he was inviting certain defeat (2 Chr. 25:7), he sent them home. He incurred their wrath for this action (2 Chr. 25:10).

Following a stunning victory over the Edomites, Amaziah embraced the gods of Edom (2 Chr. 25:14). The folly of his action was exposed by the ironic question of a godly priest, "Why have you sought the gods of the people, which could not rescue their own people from your hand?" (2 Chr. 25:15). Meanwhile, the mercenaries he had dismissed attacked several towns in Judah, killing 3,000 and taking much spoil (2 Chr. 25:13).

Apparently filled with pride over his victory, Amaziah challenged the king of Israel, Joash (or Jehoash), to war and suffered defeat at Beth Shemesh. The Bible notes that this was God's punishment for Amaziah's sin of idolatry (2 Chr. 25:20). King Joash destroyed a large section of the wall of Jerusalem and claimed spoil from the temple and the king's treasury. He also took hostages back to Samaria, possibly even King Amaziah (2 Chr. 25:23–24). Amaziah outlived Joash by 15 years. Learning of a conspiracy against him in Jerusalem, he fled to Lachish. However, his enemies followed and assassinated him there, ending a reign of 29 years (2 Chr. 25:25–28).

AMBASSADOR

An official representative of kings and rulers. In ancient times many kings and rulers spoke to other nations through official representatives who congratulated (1 Kin. 5:1), sought favors (Num. 20:14), made treaties (Josh. 9:4–6), and regis-

tered protests (Judg. 11:12). How the other nations treated the ambassador represented how they related to the ruler. If one treated the ambassador rudely, it was an insult to the ruler and could lead to war (2 Sam. 10:4–6). In the New Testament, the apostle Paul called himself Christ's ambassador (Eph. 6:20)—an idea that he applied to all Christian ministers (2 Cor. 5:20). An ambassador is sometimes called an envoy.

AMEN [A min] *(so be it)*

A solemn word by which a person confirms a statement, an oath, or a covenant (Num. 5:22; Neh. 5:13). It is also used in worship to affirm an address, psalm, or prayer.

In Isaiah 65:16 the Lord is called "the God of truth"; the original Hebrew means, "the God of amen." This is Isaiah's way of saying that the Lord is the One who remains eternally true, the One who can always be relied on. In the New Testament, our Lord Jesus Christ is given the same title: "the Amen, the Faithful and True Witness" (Rev. 3:14). He, too, is eternally true and reliable.

AMMON [AM muhn] *(kinsman* or *people)*

The land of Ammon, settled by those who were descended from Ben-Ammi, Lot's son. Ben-Ammi was born in a cave near Zoar (Gen. 19:30–38), a city near the southern end of the Dead Sea. The land of the Ammonites generally was located in the area north and east of Moab, a region between the river Arnon and the river Jabbok. Its capital city was Rabbah (Deut. 3:11; 2 Sam. 11:1). Amman, the name of the capital of the modern Hashemite kingdom of Jordan, is a continuing use of this ancient name.

AMMONITES [AM muhn ites]

A nomadic race descended from Ben-Ammi, Lot's son, who became enemies of the people of Israel during their later history. During the days of the Exodus, the Israelites were instructed by God not to associate with the Ammonites (Deut. 23:3). No reason is given in the Bible for such hostility, but the rift between the two peoples continued across several centuries.

In the days of the judges, Eglon, king of Moab, enlisted the aid of the Ammonites in taking Jericho from the Hebrew people (Judg. 3:13). In Saul's time, Nahash, the Ammonite king, attacked Jabesh Gilead. Saul responded to the call for help and saved the people of Jabesh Gilead from being captured by Nahash (1 Sam. 11:1–11).

Later in the history of the Israelites, Ammonites were among the armies allied against King Jehoshaphat; God caused confusion among them, and they destroyed themselves (2 Chr. 20:1–23). The prophets of the Old Testament often pronounced God's judgment against the Ammonites (Jer. 9:26; Amos 1:13–15). Archaeological evidence suggests that Ammonite civilization continued from about 1200 B.C. to 600 B.C.

AMNON [AM nun] *(faithful)*

The oldest son of David, born at Hebron while that city was still capital of the nation of Israel (2 Sam. 3:2; 1 Chr. 3:1). Amnon raped Tamar, his half sister, incurring the wrath of Absalom, Tamar's full brother. After two years, Absalom had Amnon murdered.

AMON [A mun]

A son of Manasseh and a king of Judah (2 Kin. 21:18–26; 2 Chr. 33:20–25). Amon became king at the age of 22 and reigned for only two years. His reign was characterized by idolatry. His wicked father may have deliberately named him after the Egyptian god Amun.

Finally, Amon's own servants conspired to kill him, possibly because his corruption and idolatry had made him

a weak king and they hoped to claim the throne for themselves. However, after Amon was assassinated, the people of Judah killed the conspirators and set Amon's eight-year-old son, Josiah, on the throne. Amon is mentioned in the New Testament as an ancestor of Jesus (Matt. 1:10).

AMORITES [AM oh rites] *(Westerners)*

The inhabitants of the land west of the Euphrates River, which included Canaan, Phoenicia, and Syria. The Amorites were one of the major tribes, or national groups, living in Canaan. The Old Testament frequently uses "Amorites" as a synonym for Canaanites in general. The Book of Genesis cites Canaan as the ancestor of the Amorites (Gen. 10:16).

Shortly before 2000 B.C., the Amorites lived in the wilderness regions of what today is western Saudi Arabia and southern Syria. In the court records of Accad and Sumer they were known as barbarians, or uncivilized people. Beginning about 2000 B.C., Amorites migrated eastward to Babylonia in large numbers. There they captured major cities and regions from the native Mesopotamians. "Abram" is an Amorite name, and Abraham himself may have been an Amorite.

Throughout Old Testament times, other Amorites remained in Syria, Phoenicia, and the desert regions to the south (Josh. 13:4). A significant number, however, settled in the land of Canaan itself, eventually occupying large areas both east and west of the Jordan River (Judg. 11:19–22). These Amorites spoke a dialect that was closely related to Canaanite and Hebrew. Occasionally, the Amorites were identified as a Canaanite tribe (Gen. 10:16). At other times they were called the people of Canaan (Deut. 1:27).

When Israel invaded Canaan under Joshua, the first Israelite victories came against the Amorite kings Sihon and Og, who ruled much of the Promised Land east of the Jordan River (Josh. 12:1–6). Various cities west of the Jordan—Jerusalem, Hebron, Jarmuth, Lachish, and Eglon—also were called "Amorite" cities (Josh. 10:5), even though Jerusalem was also known as a Jebusite city.

While conquering Canaan, the Israelites frequently fought with the Amorites. After the Israelites prevailed, the Amorites who had not been killed remained in Canaan and became servants to the Israelites (1 Kin. 9:20–21).

Much of our knowledge about the Amorites and their culture comes from clay tablets discovered at Mari, a major Amorite city situated on the Euphrates River in western Mesopotamia.

AMOS [AIM us] *(burden bearer)*

The famous shepherd-prophet of the Old Testament who denounced the people of the northern kingdom of Israel for their idol worship, graft and corruption, and oppression of the poor. He was probably the earliest of the writing prophets. His prophecies and the few facts known about his life are found in the Book of Amos.

Although he prophesied to the northern kingdom, Amos was a native of Judah, Israel's sister nation to the south. He came from the village of Tekoa (Amos 1:1), situated about 10 miles (16 kilometers) south of Jerusalem.

On one occasion, Amos's authority in Israel was questioned by a priest who served in the court of King Jeroboam II, and Amos admitted he was not descended from a line of prophets or other religious officials. By vocation, he claimed to be nothing but "a herdsman and a tender of sycamore fruit" (Amos 7:14), but he pointed out that his right to speak came from the highest authority of all: "The Lord took me as I followed the flock, and the Lord said to me, 'Go, prophesy to My people Israel' " (Amos 7:15).

Amos spoke because the Lord had called him to deliver His message of judgment. This is one of the clearest statements of the compulsion of the divine call to be found in the Bible.

The theme of Amos's message was that Israel had rejected the one true God in order to worship false gods. He also condemned the wealthy class of the nation for cheating the poor through oppressive taxes (Amos 5:11) and the use of false weights and measures (Amos 8:5). He urged the people to turn from their sinful ways, to acknowledge God as their Maker and Redeemer, and to restore justice and righteousness in their dealings with others.

Amaziah the priest, who served in the court of King Jeroboam, made a report to the king about Amos and his message (Amos 7:10–13). This probably indicates that the prophet's stern warning created quite a stir throughout the land. But there is no record that the nation changed its ways as a result of Amos's message. About 40 years after his prophecies, Israel collapsed when the Assyrians overran their capital city, Samaria, and carried away the leading citizens as captives.

After preaching in Israel, Amos probably returned to his home in Tekoa. No facts are known about his later life or death. He will always serve as an example of courage and faithfulness.

AMPHIPOLIS [am FIP oh liss] *(surrounded city)*

A city of Macedonia through which the apostle Paul passed on his second missionary journey (Acts 17:1). Amphipolis was situated about 30 miles (50 kilometers) southwest of Philippi. It was almost completely surrounded by a bend in the river Strymon.

Situated on a terraced hill, the city was highly visible from land and sea. A large monument, the Lion of Amphipolis, commemorating a military victory, stands guard today at the ancient site, as it did in Paul's time.

ANAKIM [AN uh kim]

A race of fierce giants (Deut. 1:28; 2:10–11; Josh. 14:12, 15) descended from Anak. So gigantic were they that the spies sent out by Moses considered themselves as mere grasshoppers compared to the Anakim (Num. 13:33). Under Joshua, however, the Israelites destroyed many of the Anakim. A remnant of these giants took refuge among the Philistines.

ANANIAS [an uh NYE us] *(the Lord is gracious)*

1. A Christian disciple living in Damascus at the time of Paul's conversion (Acts 9:10–18; 22:12–16). In a vision the Lord told Ananias of Paul's conversion and directed him to go to Paul and welcome him into the church. Aware of Paul's reputation as a persecutor of Christians, Ananias reacted with alarm. When the Lord informed him that Paul was "a chosen vessel of Mine" (Acts 9:15), Ananias went to Paul and laid his hands upon him. Paul's sight was restored immediately, and he was baptized (Acts 9:18).

ANANIAS [an uh NYE us] *(the Lord is gracious)*

2. A Christian in the early church at Jerusalem (Acts 5:1–11). With the knowledge of his wife, Sapphira, Ananias sold a piece of property and brought only a portion of the proceeds from its sale to Peter, claiming this represented the total amount realized from the sale. When Peter rebuked him for lying about the amount, Ananias immediately fell down and died. Sapphira later repeated the same falsehood, and she also fell down and died. Apparently, their pretense to be something they were not caused God to strike Ananias and Sapphira dead.

ANANIAS [an uh NYE us] *(the Lord is gracious)*

3. The Jewish high priest before whom Paul appeared after his arrest in Jerusalem following his third missionary journey, about A.D. 58 (Acts 23:2). Ananias was also one of those who spoke against Paul before the Roman governor Felix (Acts 24:1). Ananias was appointed high priest about A.D. 48 by Herod. In A.D. 52 the governor of Syria sent Ananias to Rome to be tried for the Jews' violent treatment of the Samaritans. Ananias was acquitted of the charges through Agrippa's influence, and he was returned to his office in Jerusalem. About A.D. 59 Ananias was deposed by Agrippa. Known to the Jews as a Roman collaborator, Ananias was murdered by a Jewish mob at the beginning of the Jewish-Roman War of A.D. 66–73.

ANATHEMA [ah NATH a mah] *(accursed)*

The transliteration of a Greek word that means "accursed" or "separated" (Luke 21:5; Rom. 9:3; Gal. 1:8–9). In the Greek translation of the Old Testament (Septuagint, LXX), the word is applied to the images, altars, and sacred objects of the Canaanites (Deut. 7:23–26). The gold and silver images of their gods were "accursed" (Deut. 7:26); they were not to be kept by the Israelites but were to be destroyed with fire.

To act greedily and take what was "devoted to destruction" brought the curse on the taker as well as the entire congregation of Israel, as in the case of Achan (Josh. 7:1, 11–12, 20–26).

With a self-condemning oath (Mark 14:71), Peter denied that he knew Jesus. Paul pronounced a curse on preachers of a false gospel (Gal. 1:8–9). In Romans 9:3–4 Paul said, "I could wish that I myself were accursed from Christ for my brethren, my kinsmen according to the flesh, who are Israelites." The phrase "accursed from Christ" means to be separated from all benefits of Jesus' life, death, and resurrection.

Early in church history, the term *anathema* took on an ecclesiastical meaning and was applied to a person expelled from the church because of moral offenses or heresy. The person who continued in stubborn rebellion against the church was considered "devoted to destruction." Today the Roman Catholic Church often uses the term *anathema* in declarations against what it considers false beliefs.

ANATHOTH [AN uh thoth]

A city in the tribe of Benjamin given to the Levites (1 Kin. 2:26). Anathoth was the birthplace of the prophet Jeremiah (Jer. 1:1; 29:27). During a time of siege, the Lord instructed Jeremiah to purchase a field in Anathoth. This was to serve as a sign of God's promised redemption of Israel (Jer. 32:7–9). Anathoth was located about 3 miles (5 kilometers) northeast of Jerusalem.

ANCESTOR WORSHIP

A form of superstitious religion in which the living seek to deify the spirits of their departed relatives. It is likely that ancestor worship occurred among the Canaanites and other pagan neighbors of Israel, particularly the Syrians. No conclusive evidence exists, however, to indicate that ancestor worship or a cult of the dead was ever a part of the religion of Israel. Although prohibitions against such practices were given (Lev. 19:28; Deut. 14:1; 26:14), these commands were probably given to warn Israel not to begin ancestor worship rather than to command that it be stopped.

ANDREW [AN droo] *(manly)*

Brother of Simon Peter and one of Jesus' first disciples. Both Andrew and Peter were fishermen (Matt. 4:18; Mark 1:16–18) from Bethsaida (John 1:44), on the northwest coast of the Sea of Galilee. They also had a house at Capernaum in this vicinity (Mark 1:29).

According to the Gospel of John, Andrew and an unnamed friend were among the followers of John the Baptist (John 1:35–40). When John the Baptist identified Jesus as the Lamb of God, both he and Andrew followed Jesus (John 1:41). Andrew then brought his brother Simon to meet the Messiah (John 1:43–51)—an action that continues to be a model for all who bring others to Christ.

At the feeding of the 5,000, Andrew called Jesus' attention to the boy with five barley loaves and two fish (John 6:5–9). Later Philip and Andrew decided to bring to Jesus the request of certain Greeks for an audience with Him (John 12:20–22). Andrew is mentioned a final time in the Gospels, when he asked Jesus a question concerning last things in the company of Peter, James, and John (Mark 13:3–4).

All lists of the disciples name Andrew among the first four (Matt. 10:2–4; Mark 3:16–19; Luke 6:14–16; Acts 1:13). According to tradition, Andrew was martyred at Patrae in Achaia by crucifixion on an X-shaped cross. According to Eusebius, Andrew's field of labor was Scythia, the region north of the Black Sea. For this reason he became the patron saint of Russia. He is also considered the patron saint of Scotland.

ANGEL

A member of an order of heavenly beings who are superior to human beings in power and intelligence. By nature angels are spiritual beings (Heb. 1:14). Their nature is superior to human nature (Heb. 2:7), and they have superhuman power and knowledge (2 Sam. 14:17, 20; 2 Pet. 2:11). They are not, however, all-powerful and all-knowing (Ps. 103:20; 2 Thess. 1:7).

Artistic portrayals of angels as winged beings are generally without basis in the Bible. Rarely is an angel so described. (For exceptions, compare the cherubim and seraphim and the living creatures— Ex. 25:20; Is. 6:2, 6; Ezek. 1:6; Rev. 4:8.)

Angels were created by God (Ps. 148:2, 5) and were present to rejoice when He created the world (Job. 38:4–7). In their original state they were holy, but before the creation of the world some of them rebelled against God and lost this exalted position. The leading angel in this revolt became the devil, also known as Satan (Gen. 3:4, 14; Rev. 12:4, 7–9). Another of the fallen angels is named Abaddon or Apollyon (Rev. 9:11), "the angel of the bottomless pit" (abyss in NASB, NIV; bottomless pit in NRSV).

Two of the vast company of unfallen angels are named in the Bible. They are the archangels Michael (Dan. 10:13, 21; 12:1; Jude 9; Rev. 12:7) and Gabriel (Dan. 8:16; 9:21; Luke 1:19, 26). Michael has the special task of caring for Israel, and Gabriel communicates special messages to God's servants.

The vast army of unfallen angels delights in praising the Lord continually (Ps. 103:21; 148:1–2). Large numbers of them remain at God's side, ready to do His every command (1 Kin. 22:19). Angels in God's presence include the cherubim, seraphim, and living creatures (or living beings) (Ex. 25:20; Is. 6:2; Ezek. 1:5–6; Rev. 4:6).

Unfallen angels are known for their reverence for God and their obedience to His will. Angels represent God in making significant announcements of good news (Gen. 18:9–10; Luke 1:13, 30; 2:8–15). On His behalf they also warn of coming dangers (Gen. 18:16–19:29; Matt. 2:13). In some cases they are God's agents in the destruction and judgment of evil (Gen. 19:13; 2 Sam. 24:16).

Of special importance in the Old Testament is the angel of the Lord (Gen. 16:7; 22:11; 31:11). This angel is depicted as a visible manifestation of God Himself. He has powers and characteristics that belong only to God, such as the power to forgive sins (Ex. 23:20–21). His similarities to Jesus lead many scholars to conclude that He is the pre-incarnate Word present with God at the creation of the world (John 1:1, 14).

When visible to human beings, angels consistently appear in human form (Gen. 18:2; Dan. 10:18; Zech. 2:1). Sometimes, however, their appearance inspires awe (Judg. 13:6; Matt. 28:3–4; Luke 24:4).

Angels are never known to appear to wicked people—only to those whom the Bible views as good, such as Abraham, Moses, David, Daniel, Jesus, Peter, and Paul. They are charged with caring for such people and serving them in times of need (Ps. 91:11–12; Heb. 1:14). They also guide and instruct good people (Gen. 24:7, 40; Ex. 14:19). This task is illustrated by the role the angels played in God's giving of the Law to Moses (Acts 7:38, 53; Heb. 2:2). Sometimes their guidance comes through human dreams (Gen. 28:12; 31:11).

Angels also protect the people of God (Ex. 14:19–20; Dan. 3:28; Matt. 26:53). They meet a wide variety of human needs, including relieving hunger and thirst (Gen. 21:17–19; Mark 1:13) and overcoming loneliness and dread (Luke 22:43). They sometimes deliver the people of God from danger (Acts 5:19; 12:6–11).

Although they are not the objects of salvation, angels are interested in the salvation of human beings (Luke 15:10; 1 Cor. 4:9). They also were particularly active in the events surrounding the birth and resurrection of Jesus (Matt. 1:20; 2:13, 19; 28:2; Luke 1:11–38; 2:9–15; 22:43; 24:23; John 20:12). The frequency with which angels participate in human affairs has diminished since Pentecost, probably because of the larger role played by the Holy Spirit in the lives of Christians since then.

Jesus spoke frequently of angels, both good and bad (Matt. 13:41; 26:53; Mark 8:38; Luke 12:8–9). Angels are quite real, and they play a vital part in God's plan for the world.

ANGEL OF THE LORD

A mysterious messenger of God, sometimes described as the Lord Himself (Gen. 16:10–13; Ex. 3:2–6; 23:20; Judg. 6:11–18), but at other times as one sent by God. The Lord used this messenger to appear to human beings who otherwise would not be able to see Him and live (Ex. 33:20).

The angel of the Lord performed actions associated with God, such as revelation, deliverance, and destruction; but he can be spoken of as distinct from God (2 Sam. 24:16; Zech. 1:12). This special relationship has led many to conclude that the angel of the Lord was Jesus in a pre-incarnate form.

ANKLETS

Rings of precious metals worn around the ankle. Anklets were popular in the ancient world, and archaeologists have unearthed many different types. They varied greatly in size and design. Apparently, some people who wore them even attached small bells to the anklets to make them jingle (Is. 3:16). Some anklets were hollow. This design increased the sound when they were struck together. Some scholars think the sound of anklets joined with an ankle chain may have announced the approach of Jeroboam's wife (1 Kin. 14:6).

ANNA [AN ah] *(favor)*

A widow, daughter of Phanuel of the tribe of Asher (Luke 2:36). She was at the temple in Jerusalem when Mary and Jo-seph brought Jesus to be dedicated (Luke 2:27). Anna recognized Jesus as the long-awaited Messiah (Luke 2:37–38).

ANNAS [AN us] *(grace of the Lord)*

One of the high priests at Jerusalem, along with Caiaphas, when John the Baptist began his ministry, about A.D. 26 (Luke 3:2). Quirinius, governor of Syria, appointed Annas as high priest about A.D. 6 or 7. Although Annas was deposed by Valerius Gratus, the procurator of Judea, about A.D. 15, he was still the most influential of the priests and continued to carry the title of high priest (Luke 3:2; Acts 4:6).

After his removal, Annas was officially succeeded by each of his five sons, one grandson, and his son-in-law Caiaphas, the high priest who presided at the trial of Jesus (Matt. 26:3, 57; John 18:13–14). During His trial, Jesus was first taken to Annas, who then sent Jesus to Caiaphas (John 18:13, 24). Both Annas and Caiaphas were among the principal examiners when Peter and John were arrested (Acts 4:6).

ANOINTING

To authorize, or set apart, a person for a particular work or service (Is. 61:1). The anointed person belonged to God in a special sense. The phrases, "the Lord's anointed," "God's anointed," "My anointed," "Your anointed," or "His anointed" are used of Saul (1 Sam. 26:9, 11), David (2 Sam. 22:51), and Solomon (2 Chr. 6:42). In the New Testament, all who are Christ's disciples are said to be anointed; they are God's very own, set apart and commissioned for service (2 Cor. 1:21).

Priests, kings, and prophets were anointed. Oil was poured on the head of the person being anointed (Ex. 29:7). Kings were set apart through the ritual of anointing, which was performed by a prophet who acted in God's power and

authority (1 Sam. 15:1). The Old Testament also records two instances of the
anointing of a prophet (1 Kin. 19:16; Is.
61:1).

Jesus the Messiah is described as
"anointed." This description is found in
the psalms of the Old Testament that
prophesy the coming of Christ and in
the preaching of the apostle Peter in
the Book of Acts. "Messiah" comes
from the Hebrew word for "anointed"
and "Christ" comes from the Greek
word.

In the New Testament, anointing was
frequently used in connection with healing. The Holy Spirit's activities in a believer's life are pictured in terms associated
with anointing. Jesus' disciples anointed
the sick (Mark 6:13), and James instructed the elders of the church to
anoint the sick with oil (James 5:14). This
anointing was for healing.

Anointing in the New Testament also
refers to the anointing of the Holy Spirit,
which brings understanding (1 John
2:20, 27). This anointing is not only for
kings, priests, and prophets; it is for
everyone who believes in the Lord Jesus
Christ. The anointing occurs physically
with a substance such as oil, myrrh, or
balsam. But this is also a spiritual anointing, as the Holy Spirit anoints a person's
heart and mind with the love and truth
of God.

ANT

Approximately 100 species of ants live
in the Holy Land. Harvester ants are the
ones meant in Proverbs 6:6–8 and 30:25.
These tiny insects settle near grain fields,
carrying seed after seed into their private
storehouses. In cold weather these ants
cluster together and hibernate. When
winter comes, they have food stored up
until the next harvest.

God has provided ants with such
amazing instincts that they appear to
reason and plan ahead. If stored grain

gets wet, they haul it out into the sun to
dry. Their hard work was considered a
worthy example for human beings by the
writer of Proverbs (Prov. 6:6–8; 30:25).

ANTEDILUVIANS

The people who lived before the Flood.
They possessed some skills that compare
with modern technology. For example,
Cain built cities (Gen. 4:17), Jubal was a
musician (Gen. 4:21), and Tubal-Cain
was an "instructor of every craftsman in
bronze and iron" (Gen. 4:22). Such crafts
imply the skills to mine, smelt, and purify
brass and iron. That Noah could construct his huge ark is witness to the engi-
neering skills and tools that were
available. The antediluvians also lived
long lives (Gen. 5:5–31).

Before the Flood, sin was rampant.
Life was marked by disobedience, murder, and immorality: "The earth also was
corrupt before God, and the earth was
filled with violence" (Gen. 6:11). Humanity's spiritual condition was appalling.

Both Noah and Enoch preached to the
antediluvians (2 Pet. 2:5; Jude 14–15).
Their preaching, however, was not
heeded; and the sinful world was destroyed by the Flood. Noah was the only
righteous man whom God could find on
the entire earth at the time: "Noah was
a just man, perfect in his generations.
Noah walked with God" (Gen. 6:9).

In the New Testament, Jesus compared the antediluvians—who were
"eating and drinking, marrying and giving in marriage"—to the people who will
be living in the end times (Matt. 24:37–
41). His words point to the need for
watchfulness, for "as it was in the days
of Noah, so it will be in the days of the
Son of Man" (Luke 17:26).

ANTHROPOMORPHISM

The practice of describing God in human terms, as if He had feet (Ex. 24:10),
hands (John 10:29), a face (Matt. 18:10),

a heart (Hos. 11:8), and so forth. Although the Old and New Testaments deny any literal similarity of form between God and His creatures (Job 9:32; John 4:24), the Bible frequently uses such human language to affirm that God is personal and active in His creation.

ANTICHRIST, THE

A False Prophet and evil being who will set himself up against Christ and the people of God in the last days before the Second Coming. The term is used only in the writings of John in the New Testament. It refers to one who stands in opposition to all that Jesus Christ represents (1 John 2:18, 22; 4:3; 2 John 7). John wrote that several antichrists existed already in his day—false teachers who denied the Deity and the Incarnation of Christ—but that the supreme Antichrist of history would appear at some future time.

The Antichrist's primary work is deception, which also characterizes Satan in his attempts to undermine the work of God in the world. Satan's deception began in the Garden of Eden (Gen. 3) and will continue until the end of time. The dragon (or serpent) of Revelation 12 is Satan, the serpent mentioned in Genesis 3. Thus the thread of Satan's deceptive work may be traced from Genesis through Revelation. That work reaches its climax in the Antichrist, who receives his authority and power from the dragon, Satan (Rev. 13:4).

The work of Satan through the Antichrist is clearly rooted in the prophecies of Daniel. Daniel spoke of a dreadful beast with ten horns and one little horn (Dan. 7:7–8). The Ancient of Days will kill the beast and throw it in the fire (Dan. 7:11). Then, according to Daniel, one like the Son of Man will receive the everlasting kingdom (Dan. 7:13–14).

The Antichrist will be the sum total of the beasts referred to in Daniel 7 (Rev. 13:1–4). He will speak arrogant, boastful words; and he will be aided by a False Prophet, who will make the entire earth worship him (Rev. 13:11–12) and receive his mark (Rev. 13:16–17). The number of the Beast, says John, is 666—a mysterious code name.

Those who worship the Antichrist will experience certain doom through the wrath of God (Rev. 14:9–11). The Antichrist makes war against Christ and His army, but he is captured and is "cast alive into the lake of fire burning with brimstone" (Rev. 19:20). He is later joined by the devil; together they "will be tormented day and night forever and ever" (Rev. 20:10). The devil, the Beast (or Antichrist), and the False Prophet form a kind of unholy Trinity, counterfeiting Father, Son, and Holy Spirit. After much wickedness and suffering has been loosed against Christ and His people, the satanic rebellion will be crushed by the power of God.

Although the apostle Paul does not use the term *Antichrist*, he surely had the Antichrist in mind when he wrote of the great apostasy, or falling away, that would occur before the return of Christ (2 Thess. 2:1–12). The Antichrist is also called the lawless one (v. 9) who, empowered and inspired by Satan, will lead the final rebellion against God (v. 3, REB), but will be destroyed at the coming of the Lord. Paul urges believers to stand firm in the faith and not be deceived by the Antichrist, who will display "all kinds of counterfeit miracles, signs and wonders" (2 Thess. 2:9, NIV).

The main reason the Bible discusses the Antichrist is not to encourage idle speculation, but to warn believers not to be misled by his deceit (Matt. 24:4–5, 23–24). The times when the Antichrist will appear will be very hard for the faithful. They need to be prepared with special instructions on how to deal with this unsettling event.

ANTIOCH OF PISIDIA [AN tih ock, pih SID ih uh]

A city of southern Asia Minor in Phrygia, situated just north of the territory of Pisidia. Antioch was an important first-century commercial center and an important center for the spread of the gospel. Founded by Seleucus I Nicator (about 300 B.C.) and named for his father Antiochus, it became a great center for commerce and was inhabited by many Jews.

The apostle Paul preached in this city's synagogue and founded a church there during his first missionary journey (Acts 13:14–49). Just as Antioch exerted great cultural and political influence over the surrounding area, so also it became a strong base from which to launch the church's evangelistic outreach (Acts 13:42–49). In reaction to Paul's success, the Jews at Antioch caused some influential women to turn against the gospel and had Paul driven out of the city (Acts 13:50).

ANTIOCH OF SYRIA [AN tih ock, SIHR ih uh]

The capital of the Roman province of Syria that played an important part in the first-century expansion of the church. Antioch was situated on the east bank of the Orontes River, about 16.5 miles (27 kilometers) from the Mediterranean Sea and 300 miles (485 kilometers) north of Jerusalem. The city was founded about 300 B.C. by Seleucus I Nicator, one of the three successors to Alexander the Great, and named for his father Antiochus.

The early history of the church is closely connected with Antioch of Syria. One of the first seven "deacons," Nicolas, was a "proselyte from Antioch" (Acts 6:5). After the stoning of Stephen (Acts 7:54–60), great persecution caused certain disciples to flee from Jerusalem to Antioch, where they preached the gospel to the Jews (Acts 8:1; 11:19). Others arrived later and had success preaching to the Gentiles (Acts 11:20–21).

When the church leaders at Jerusalem heard of this success in Antioch, they sent Barnabas to visit the church there (Acts 11:25–26).

Apparently, Paul and Barnabas used Antioch as the base for their missionary journeys into Asia Minor (Acts 13:1–3; 15:36–41; 18:22–23). Following the first missionary journey, Antioch became the scene of an important dispute. Certain men from Judea taught that Gentile converts must be circumcised and follow other rules for converts to Judaism before becoming Christians (Acts 15:1–2). This theological disagreement led to a church council at Jerusalem. Paul and Barnabas were sent here to report how God had given them success in bringing the gospel to the Gentiles. The council decided that Gentile converts did not have to be circumcised. Antioch is now known as Antakya, in modern-day Turkey.

ANTIOCHUS [an TIE oh kus] IV EPIPHANES (withstander)

Antiochus IV (175–164 B.C.), surnamed Epiphanes ("God manifest") but called by his Jewish enemies Epimanes ("madman"). Antiochus IV was one of the cruelest rulers of all time. Like his father, Antiochus III the Great, he was enterprising and ambitious; however, he had a tendency to cruelty that bordered on madness. His primary aim—to unify his empire by spreading Greek civilization and culture—brought him into direct conflict with the Jews. This conflict broke into open rebellion in 167 B.C. Accounts of these conflicts are found in the apocryphal book of 2 Maccabees.

The revolt began with Antiochus's edict that sought to unite all the peoples of his kingdom in religion, law, and custom. The Jews were the only people who would not adhere to this edict. Antiochus issued regulations against observing the Sabbath, practicing circumcision, and keeping all food laws. These regulations were followed by the "Abomination of Desolation" (Dan. 11:31)—the desecration of the altar of the burnt offering in the temple in Jerusalem. Jews were forced to participate in heathen festivities and were put to death if they were caught with the Book of the Law in their possession.

As the revolt, led by the pious priest Mattathias and his sons, gained momentum, the Jews united to overthrow Seleucid domination of their land. The Syrians were routed and the temple was cleansed on the twenty-fifth of Chislev, 165 B.C. This cleansing is now observed by the Jews as the Feast of Lights (Hanukkah), around December 25. According to ancient writers, Antiochus IV withdrew into the East following his defeat. He died in Persia a madman. The "little horn" of Daniel 8:9 is a reference to Antiochus IV Epiphanes.

ANTIPATRIS [an TIP uh tris] *(belonging to Antipater)*

A city built on the Plain of Sharon by Herod the Great and named in honor of his father, Antipater. Located on the Roman military road between Jerusalem and Caesarea, Antipatris was the lodging place for the apostle Paul and the Roman soldiers who were transporting him as a prisoner to Felix, the governor of Judea (Acts 23:31). The city was the site of the Old Testament Aphek (Josh. 12:18; 1 Sam. 4:1; 29:1).

ANTONIA, TOWER OF [an TONE ih ah]

A fortress-palace rebuilt by Herod the Great and situated at the northwest corner of the temple area. Herod named the rebuilt tower after his friend, Mark Antony.

The fortress was rectangular in shape,

measuring about 490 feet (165 meters) by 260 feet (87 meters), with walls about 60 feet (19 meters) high. Each corner had a high tower, three of which were 75 feet (24 meters) high. The tower in the northwest corner, which overlooked the temple area, however, was about 100 feet (32 meters) high. Stairs connected the Antonia with the temple area (see Acts 21:35, 40).

Soldiers from the Antonia ("the barracks") rescued the apostle Paul from enraged crowds on several occasions (Acts 21:27–36; 22:24; 23:10). Paul was held in the fortress in protective custody until a military escort took him to Caesarea (Acts 23:12–24, 31–35).

APIS [A pis]

The sacred bull-god of Memphis (the biblical Noph) worshiped by the ancient Egyptians (Jer. 46:15; REB, NRSV). Apis was thought to be the reincarnation of Ptah, a creator god. Some scholars believe the Apis bull served as the model for the golden calf the Israelites made at Mount Sinai (Ex. 32).

APOCALYPTIC LITERATURE [a pock uh LIP tik]

A certain type of Jewish and Christian literature written in Egypt and Palestine during the period from 200 B.C. to A.D. 200. The word *apocalypsis* is a Greek word meaning "revelation." Therefore, apocalyptic literature is a special kind of writing that arose among the Jews and Christians to reveal certain mysteries about heaven and earth, humankind and God, angels and demons, the life of the world today, and the world to come.

Two books in the Bible—the Book of Daniel in the Old Testament and the New Testament Book of Revelation—are good examples of the apocalyptic literary form.

Most of the apocalyptic books were

written by Jews in reaction to the oppression of their people by foreign powers. Often they wrote to explain why evil seemed to prosper while the righteous suffered. The Christian apocalyptic writings were influenced by these earlier Jewish works.

Each of the apocalyptic books is rich in symbolism. The events of the time, evil rulers, and pagan nations are symbolized by distorted animals and beasts, horrible signs from heaven, or a chaotic flowing of waters. But the people who are faithful to God are portrayed as majestic animals, like lions, or well-kept plants. The purpose of this symbolism was to make the contrast between good and evil obvious to the reader.

APOCRYPHA, THE [A POCK rih fuh]

A group of books written during a time of turmoil in the history of the Jewish people, from about 190 B.C. to about A.D. 210. These books fall into two main divisions, Old Testament apocryphal books and New Testament apocryphal books.

The Old Testament books, 15 in number, were written during the period from about 190 B.C. to about A.D. 70, when the Jewish people were in rebellion against the repression of foreign military rulers. These books were excluded from some early versions of the Old Testament but included in others. This explains why Bibles used by Roman Catholics contain the Old Testament Apocrypha, while they are not included in most Protestant editions of the Bible.

The books known as the New Testament Apocrypha were written during the second and third centuries A.D., long after the death of the apostles and other eyewitnesses to the life and ministry of Jesus. None of these books were included in the New Testament because they were judged as unworthy and not authoritative by officials of the early church.

Books of the Old Testament Apocrypha are Baruch; Bel and the Dragon; Ecclesiasticus, or the Wisdom of Jesus, Son of Sirach; 1 and 2 Esdras; Additions to Esther; Epistle of Jeremiah; Judith; 1 and 2 Maccabees; Prayer of Azariah and the song of the Three Young Men; Prayer of Manasseh; Susanna; Tobit; and the Wisdom of Solomon.

The books of the New Testament Apocrypha were greatly influenced by the philosophies and religions of the cities or nations out of which they came. Some of the apocryphal gospels were written to replace the Gospels of the New Testament but were declared false writings by officials of the early church.

Often the apocryphal books from the early history of the church present stories and legends meant to fill in information about the apostles and Jesus that is lacking in the New Testament. For example, some New Testament apocryphal works claim to give details on the childhood of Jesus (Protevangelium of James, The Gospel of Thomas) as well as a description of how Jesus was raised from the dead (The Gospel of Peter). These writings expand on the accounts found in the New Testament.

The Acts of the Apostles in the New Testament is also paralleled by several apocryphal books. These include stories about the apostles themselves written in the second and third century. Titles of some of these books are The Acts of John, The Acts of Peter, The Acts of Paul, The Acts of Andrew and The Acts of Thomas.

APOLLONIA [ap oh LONE ih ah] (place of Apollo)

A Greek city on the Egnatian Way of Macedonia about 28 miles (45 kilometers) west of Amphipolis. Paul and Silas passed through Apollonia on their way from Philippi to Thessalonica (Acts 17:1) on Paul's second missionary journey.

APOLLOS [a POL lus] *(destroyer)*

A learned and eloquent Jew from Alexandria in Egypt and an influential leader in the early church. Well-versed in the Old Testament, Apollos was a disciple of John the Baptist and "taught accurately the things of the Lord" (Acts 18:25). However, while Apollos knew some of Jesus' teaching, "he knew only the baptism of John" (Acts 18:25). When Priscilla and Aquila, two other leaders in the early church, arrived in Ephesus, they instructed Apollos more accurately in the way of God (Acts 18:26).

In Corinth, Apollos publicly contended with the Jewish leaders and refuted their objections to Christian teaching. He was apparently quite popular in Corinth. In 1 Corinthians 1:12 Paul wrote of four parties into which the church at Corinth had become divided: one "following" Apollos, one Paul, one Cephas [Peter], and one Christ. In dealing with this division, Paul compared himself to the one who planted and Apollos to the one who watered what was already planted (1 Cor. 3:6).

APOSTASY

A falling away from the faith. Apostasy is generally defined as the determined, willful rejection of Christ and His teachings by a Christian believer (Heb. 10:26–29; John 15:22). This is different from false belief, or error, which is the result of ignorance. Some Christian groups teach that apostasy is impossible for those persons who have truly accepted Jesus as Savior and Lord.

APOSTLE

A special messenger of Jesus Christ; a person to whom Jesus delegated authority for certain tasks. The word *apostle* is used of those twelve disciples whom Jesus sent out, two by two, during His ministry in Galilee to expand His own ministry of preaching and healing. It was on that occasion, evidently, that they were first called "apostles" (Mark 3:14; 6:30).

These same disciples, with the exception of Judas Iscariot, were recommissioned by Jesus after His resurrection to be His witnesses throughout the world (Luke 24:46–49; Acts 1:8). After Jesus' ascension, the apostles brought their number to twelve by choosing Matthias (Acts 1:23–26).

The word *apostle* is sometimes used in the New Testament in a general sense of "messenger." For instance, when delegates of Christian communities were charged with conveying those churches' contributions to a charitable fund, they were described by Paul as "messengers [apostles] of the churches" (2 Cor. 8:23). Jesus also used the word this way when He quoted the proverb, "A servant is not greater than his master, nor he who is sent [literally, "an apostle"] greater than he who sent him" (John 13:16). Jesus Himself is called "the Apostle . . . of our confession" (Heb. 3:1), a reference to His function as God's special messenger to the world.

The word *apostle* has a wider meaning in the letters of the apostle Paul. It includes people who, like himself, were not included in the Twelve, but who saw the risen Christ and were specially commissioned by Him. Paul's claim to be an apostle was questioned by others. He based his apostleship, however, on the direct call of the exalted Lord, who appeared to him on the Damascus Road and on the Lord's blessing of his ministry in winning converts and establishing churches (1 Cor. 15:10).

Apparently, Paul also counted James, the Lord's brother, as an apostle (Gal. 1:19). This James was not one of the Twelve; in fact, he was not a believer in Jesus before the crucifixion (John 7:5). It was the resurrected Lord who "appeared to James" (1 Cor. 15:7) and presumably commissioned him for his ministry. When Paul says Jesus was seen not only by James but also by "all the apostles" (1 Cor. 15:7), he seems to be describing a wider group than "the Twelve" to whom Jesus appeared earlier (1 Cor. 15:5).

In 1 Corinthians 12:28 and Ephesians 4:11, apostles are listed along with prophets and other saints as part of the foundation of the household of God. In this strictly New Testament sense, apostles are confined to the first generation of Christians.

At an early stage in the church's history it was agreed that apostles to the Jews and Gentiles should be divided into separate camps. Paul and Barnabas were to concentrate on the evangelization of Gentiles; Peter, John, and James (the Lord's brother) were to continue evangelizing Jews (Gal. 2:7–9).

As pioneers in the work of making converts and planting churches, apostles were exposed to special dangers. When persecution erupted, they were the primary targets for attack (1 Cor. 4:9–13). Paul, in particular, welcomed the suffering he endured as an apostle because it was his way of participating in the suffering of Christ (Rom. 8:17; 2 Cor. 1:5–7).

The authority committed to the apostles by Christ was unique. It could not be transmitted to others. The apostles could install elders or other leaders and teachers in the churches, and they could authorize them to assume special responsibilities; but apostolic authority could not be transferred. Their authority has not come to us through their successors; it has come through their writings, which are contained in the New Testament.

APPIAN WAY [AP pih un]

An ancient Roman road built by Appius Claudius. It ran from Rome to Brundisium on the Adriatic Sea. Paul traveled this road from near the city of Puteoli to Rome, where he was imprisoned (Acts 28:13–16).

APPII FORUM [AP ih eye] *(marketplace of Appius)*

A town in Italy located about 40 miles (64 kilometers) southeast of Rome on the Appian Way where the apostle Paul was welcomed by Christians from Rome (Acts 28:15).

AQUEDUCT

A channel for transporting water from a remote source to a city. Israel's climate provides abundant rainfall in the winter months, but there is seldom any rain from May to October. This, along with the scarcity of good water supplies, made it necessary to build artificial storage areas to catch the winter rains. Elaborate systems of stone and masonry aqueducts and storage pools were sometimes constructed to bring water from the hill country to the cities and larger towns.

The best-known biblical accounts of the building of an aqueduct occur in 2 Kings 20:20 and 2 Chronicles 32:30. King Hezekiah of Judah had a tunnel dug under the city of Jerusalem to bring water from the spring outside the city to the Siloam reservoir inside the city wall. Across part of the course the workmen cut a tunnel through solid rock to complete the aqueduct. "Hezekiah's Tunnel" is still a major tourist attraction in Jerusalem.

"Solomon's Pools" near Bethlehem are part of an ancient aqueduct system that brought water from the hills south of Jerusalem into the temple area. During his administration, Pontius Pilate, Roman prefect of Judea, built an aqueduct to bring water to Jerusalem. Some scholars suggest that the Tower of Siloam (Luke 13:4) that fell and killed 18 people may have been part of that building project.

AQUILA [A kwil uh] *(eagle)*

A Jewish Christian living in Corinth with his wife Priscilla at the time of Paul's arrival from Athens (Acts 18:2). Aquila was born in Pontus (located in Asia Minor) but lived in Rome until Claudius commanded that all Jews leave the city. He and Priscilla moved to Corinth, where Aquila took up his trade—tentmaking.

When Paul left Corinth, Aquila and Priscilla traveled with him as far as Ephesus (1 Cor. 16:19), where they met Apollos and instructed him more thoroughly in the Christian faith (Acts 18:24–26). Apparently, they returned to Rome, because Paul sent them greetings in his letter to the Romans (Rom. 16:3).

ARABAH [AIR ah bah] *(plain, desert)*

A major region of the land of Israel, referring usually to the entire valley region between Mount Hermon in the north to the Red Sea in the south (Num. 22:1; Deut. 1:7). The Arabah is more than 240 miles (390 kilometers) long, varying in width from 6 to 25 miles (10 to 40 kilometers).

The Arabah includes the Sea of Galilee, the Jordan River valley, the Dead Sea, and the area between the Dead Sea and the Red Sea. Much of this region lies below sea level. The Dead Sea, which lies at approximately 1,292 feet (394 meters) below sea level, is the lowest spot on the earth's surface. The NKJV refers several times to the "Sea of the Arabah," meaning the Salt Sea or the Dead Sea (Deut. 3:17; Josh. 3:16; 2 Kin. 14:25).

Before their entry into the Promised Land, the people of Israel camped in the Arabah, in an area called "the plains of Moab" (Num. 22:1), just north of the Dead Sea. While the Israelites were camped there, God turned Balaam's curses to blessings (Num. 22:1–24:25), Israel committed idolatry and immorality (Num. 25), Moses renewed the covenant, and Joshua sent out spies to prepare for the invasion of Canaan (Josh. 1:1–3:17).

ARABIA [uh RAY bih uh]

The large peninsula east of Egypt, between the Red Sea and the Persian Gulf. About 800 miles (1,300 kilometers) wide and 1,400 miles (2,300 kilometers) long, Arabia is nearly one-third the size of the United States. It has almost no rainfall except along the coast, where it measures about 20 inches (51 centimeters) per year. There is only one river and one lake in the entire peninsula. Although a sudden shower may create a short-lived stream, most of the water in Arabia comes from deep wells or desert oases. Consequently, there is little agricultural activity on the peninsula.

The Arabian peninsula is a sandy, rocky desert with high mountain ranges on the western and southern coasts. The western mountains reach a height of 12,000 feet (3,660 meters) and show some evidence of past volcanic activity. Because of this volcanic activity, a few scholars have suggested that Mount Sinai was located in the western region of this mountain range. However, the traditional site at the southern end of the Sinai Peninsula is much more likely. Much of the sandy interior of Arabia is uninhabited, although there is barely enough grass on the lower mountain slopes to support its nomadic population. In addition to its lack of water, the desert was known for its sandstorms driven by violent winds (Job 1:19; 27:20–21).

The queen of Sheba came from Arabia, bringing gold, spices, and precious stones to Solomon (1 Kin. 10:2, 10, 14; 2 Chr. 9:1, 9, 14). Solomon and other kings sent their ships to Ophir in Arabia to bring back gold (1 Kin. 9:28; 2 Chr. 9:10). Ophir, Raamah, and Sheba were famous for their gold, silver, and precious stones (Job 22:24; Is. 13:12; Ezek. 27:22).

The people who lived in Arabia included the children of Joktan (Gen. 10:26–30), Cush (Gen. 10:7), the sons of Abraham and Keturah (Gen. 25:1–6), and Esau (Gen. 36). The "country of the east" (Gen. 25:6) is probably a reference to Arabia. The early history of many of these peoples is unknown. Israel's earliest contacts with the inhabitants of Arabia probably came through their camel caravans. Some of them oppressed the Israelites during the time of the judges, but God delivered Israel from them by raising up the judge Gideon (Judg. 6:11).

David subdued some of the Arabian tribes that were close to Israel (2 Sam. 8:3–14), and Solomon established extensive trade relations with more distant tribes in Arabia to obtain their gold for his building projects (1 Kin. 9:28; 10:2, 11). Jehoshaphat, king of Judah, received rams and goats from the Arabians as tribute (2 Chr. 17:10–12), but after his death they revolted and refused to pay tribute to his son Jehoram. Instead, they invaded Jerusalem and carried away Jehoram's wealth, his wives, and all but his youngest son (2 Chr. 21:16–17).

Most of the tribes of southern and eastern Arabia were not well-known to Israel. Joel referred to the slave-trading Sabeans [Shebaites] as a people who lived far away (Joel 3:8). Isaiah pictured the Arabians wandering as far east as Babylon (Is. 13:19, 20). Tribes that lived closer—those at Tema, Dedan, and Kedar—were included in Isaiah's prophecies of judgment against the foreign nations (Is. 21:13–17). Jeremiah also announced God's judgment upon Dedan, Tema, Buz, Kedar, Hazor, and all the kings of Arabia (Jer. 25:23–24; 49:28–33).

Although most of Israel's knowledge of the Arabians and their habits (Jer. 3:2) was due to a passing association with their caravan traders (Ezek. 27:21), some Arabians eventually settled in Palestine. While attempting to rebuild the walls of Jerusalem, Nehemiah struggled against Geshem the Arab, who scorned and despised the Jews (Neh. 2:19). When this tactic failed to discourage the work on Jerusalem's walls, the Arabs, Ammonites, Ashdodites, and others planned to attack the city by force (Neh. 4:7–13). When this strategy also failed, Sanballat, Tobiah, and Geshem the Arab set a trap to lure Nehemiah out of the city to kill him (Neh. 6:1–7). Nehemiah prayed for guidance, and God delivered him from this plot.

It is likely that Job was from Arabia. Uz, the home of Job (Job 1:1), appears to be named after a descendant of Esau and the Edomites (Gen. 36:28; Lam. 4:21). Eliphaz, one of Job's comforters, was from Teman, a city in Arabia (Job 2:11). Bands of Sabeans [Shebaites] and Chaldeans were close enough to attack Job's cattle (Job 1:15, 17). A great desert wind destroyed the house of Job's children (Job 1:19). The dialogue between Job and his comforters is filled with desert imagery and animals (Job 39).

ARAMAIC LANGUAGE

Spoken from at least about 2000 B.C., Aramaic eventually replaced many of the languages of the ancient world in popularity and usage. Parts of the books of Ezra (4:8–6:18; 7:12–26) and of Daniel (2:46–7:28) were written in Aramaic. Aramaic was the language spoken in Palestine in the time of Jesus. While the New Testament was written in the Greek language, the language Jesus spoke was probably Aramaic.

ARAMEANS [AIR ah mee unz]

An ancient desert people who flourished along with the Israelites during much of their history, sometimes as enemies and sometimes as friends.

The region of the Arameans, the land of Aram, extended from the Lebanon Mountains on the west eastward to the Euphrates River and from the Taurus Mountains on the north southward to Damascus. Arameans were among the ancient peoples who settled the Near East as early as 2250 B.C. They were fully established as a separate kingdom by the twelfth century B.C., which made their history parallel with Israel's.

The Arameans made their presence felt internationally during the time of the judges, when they existed in large numbers in the region east of the Jordan River. An Aramean ruler, Cushan-Rishathaim, overran the land of Israel and oppressed it for eight years (Judg. 3:8–10).

In later years, David extended the boundary of Israel to the Euphrates River by subduing the Aramean rulers Hadadezer of Zobah and Toi of Hamath (2 Sam. 8:1–13). But a third Aramean official, Rezon, fled to Damascus and founded a strong Aramean city-state there (1 Kin. 11:23–24). This city-state was Israel's bitter foe for many generations.

Between quarrels and hostilities, there were times when either the nation of Judah or the nation of Israel was allied with Aram against a common foe. Judah and Aram were allied with each other against Israel (1 Kin. 15:18–20); Israel and Aram were allies against Judah (2 Kin. 16:5). Judah also joined with Assyria against Israel and Aram.

The result of this strong alliance was the downfall of Damascus and the end of the Aramean power, about 732 B.C. (2 Kin. 16:7–18). Many Arameans were taken as hostages to other lands, in keeping with the foreign policy of the conquering Assyrians.

ARARAT [AIR uh rat]

The mountainous region between the Black Sea and the Caspian Sea where Noah's ark rested when the Flood subsided (Gen. 8:4). From this region streams converge to form the Tigris and the Euphrates rivers. Originally called Urartu, Ararat referred to the whole mountainous area; its use, however has gradually come to be restricted to the huge volcanic mountain at the borders of Turkey, Iran, and the Soviet Union.

This volcanic mountain includes two peaks, 17,000 feet (5,600 meters) and 13,000 feet (4,200 meters) above sea level. The taller peak rises 3,000 feet (920 meters) above the line of perpetual snow. Some people believe that Noah's ark still rests on Mount Ararat, and occasional expeditions have been launched to find it. However, shifting glaciers, avalanches, hidden crevices, and sudden storms make the mountain so difficult to climb that it is referred to by the native inhabitants of that region as "the Painful Mountain."

ARAUNAH [a ROW nah]

A Jebusite who owned a threshing floor on Mount Moriah in Jerusalem. King David purchased the threshing floor on which to build an altar to the Lord (2 Sam. 24:16–24). Later, this land was the site on which Solomon's temple was built (2 Chr. 3:1). Araunah was also called Ornan.

ARCHANGEL

In the celestial hierarchy, a spiritual being next in rank above an angel. The word *archangel* occurs several times in the Bible. In the New Testament, the voice of an archangel and the sounding of the trumpet of God will signal the coming of Christ for His people (1 Thess.

4:16). Michael the archangel disputed with the devil about the body of Moses (Jude 9). In the Old Testament, Michael is described as having great power and authority (Dan. 10:13) and is the guardian of Israel (Dan. 10:21), especially in the "time of trouble" in the last days (Dan. 12:1).

AREOPAGUS [air ee OP ah gus] (hill of the god Ares)

A limestone hill in Athens situated between the Acropolis and the Agora; by association, also the council which often met on or near the hill. The apostle Paul addressed the Areopagus in his "philosophical sermon" that attempted to meet the objections of the Epicurean and Stoic philosophers to the gospel (Acts 17:16–34).

Paul's speech before the Areopagus (Acts 17:22–31) is a good example of the council meeting to discuss and evaluate a philosophical issue. Paul argued about the nature of God and the way God relates to human beings, especially through Jesus Christ. Paul's argument must have made an impact in the council. "Dionysius the Areopagite" was among those who joined Paul and believed in Christ (Acts 17:34).

Paul's argument on the Areopagus is extremely important. It identifies the decisive difference between Greek philosophy and the Christian faith. Apparently the philosophers were not greatly troubled by Paul's talking about God or God's relationship to people. But when he spoke of the resurrection of Jesus, they mocked him, although some apparently gave his words careful thought (Acts 17:32). The resurrection of Jesus was, and continues to be, a decisive element in Christian theology. It always provokes controversy among unbelievers.

Today Paul's speech is affixed in Greek on a tablet at the entrance to the Areopagus. With the benches carved into the rock and the worn steps to the summit, it stands as a monument to a time when the Athenians deliberated before the gods and missed the significance of the One whom Paul identified with the "unknown God" (Acts 17:23).

ARIMATHEA [air ih mah THEE ah] (height)

A city in the Judean hills northwest of Jerusalem. It was the home of Joseph, a member of the Jewish Sanhedrin in Jerusalem, who placed the body of Jesus in his new tomb (Luke 23:50).

ARISTARCHUS [air ihs TAR kus] (best ruler)

A Macedonian of Thessalonica who traveled with the apostle Paul on his third missionary journey through Asia Minor (Acts 19:29; 20:4; 27:2). He was with Paul during the riot at Ephesus (Acts 19:29); later, he preceded Paul to Troas (Acts 20:4–6). A faithful companion and friend, Aristarchus accompanied Paul to Rome (Acts 27:2), where he attended the apostle and shared his imprisonment.

ARK, NOAH'S

A vessel built by Noah to save him, his family, and animals from the Flood (Gen. 6:14–9:18). God commanded Noah to make the ark of gopherwood (Gen. 6:14). Many scholars believe gopherwood is cypress, which was noted for its lightness and durability and therefore was used extensively in shipbuilding by the Phoenicians.

Noah's ark was 300 cubits long, 50 cubits wide, and 30 cubits high (Gen. 6:15)—about 450 feet long, 75 feet wide, and 45 feet high. The ark was constructed with three "decks," or stories (Gen. 6:16). When Noah and his family and all the animals entered the ark, God himself shut its door to insure their safety against the raging flood (Gen. 7:16). In this way God sealed the judgment against the ungodly who had refused to heed Noah's warnings. When the waters subsided after the Flood, the ark rested on the mountains of Ararat (Gen. 8:4).

In the New Testament, Jesus spoke of the Flood and of Noah and the ark, comparing "the days of Noah" with the time of "the coming of the Son of Man" (Matt. 24:37–38; Luke 17:26–27). The ark is a striking illustration of salvation through Christ, who preserves us from the flood of divine judgment.

ARK OF MOSES

A small basket-like container in which Moses was hidden by his mother to save him from the slaughter of Hebrew children by the Egyptian pharaoh (Ex. 2:3–6). The basket was made of woven papyrus reeds and sealed with a tar-like pitch. The lid on the basket kept insects and the sun off the child so he could sleep. The ark was discovered by the daughter of Pharaoh when she came to bathe at the river.

ARK OF THE COVENANT

A sacred portable chest, which—along with its two related items, the mercy seat and cherubim—was the most important sacred object of the Israelites during the wilderness period. It was also known as

ARK, NOAH'S

the ark of the Lord (Josh. 6:11), the ark of God (1 Sam. 3:3), and the ark of the Testimony (a synonym for covenant; Ex. 25:22).

The ark of the covenant was the only article of furniture in the innermost room, or Most High Place, of Moses' tabernacle and of Solomon's temple. From between the two cherubim that were on the ark of the Testimony, God spoke to Moses. Once a year, on the Day of Atonement, the high priest could enter the Most High Place, but only with sacrificial blood that he sprinkled on the mercy seat for the atonement of sin (Lev. 16).

The Hebrew word translated as "ark" is also translated as "coffin." In the last verse of the Book of Genesis, this word is used of the coffin in which Joseph's embalmed body was placed after he died in Egypt (Gen. 50:26). The ark of the covenant was also a "coffin," or chest 2.5 cubits long, 1.5 cubits wide, and 1.5 cubits deep (or, in inches, about 45 by 27 by 27). The builder of the ark was a man named Bezaleel (Ex. 37:1).

The ark was made of acacia wood (shittim wood in KJV) overlaid with gold. It had four rings of gold through which carrying poles were inserted (Ex. 37:1–9). These poles were never removed from the rings, apparently to show that the ark was a portable sanctuary. Even when the ark was placed in Solomon's temple, the poles stayed in place, and they could be seen from a certain point outside the inner sanctuary (1 Kin. 8:8).

The ark had a gold cover known as the "mercy seat" (Ex. 25:17–22) because the blood of a sacrificial animal was applied to it on the Day of Atonement, signifying the mercy of God to forgive sin. The ark had a gold molding or "crown" surrounding the top edge. The mercy seat was a slab of pure gold that fit exactly within the crown of the ark, so the mercy seat could not slide around during transportation.

Of one piece with the mercy seat were two angelic statues called cherubim. They stood at opposite ends of the mercy seat, facing each other with wings outstretched above and their faces bowed toward the mercy seat. They marked the place where the Lord sat enthroned (1 Sam. 4:4; 2 Sam. 6:2) as well as the place where He communicated with Moses.

Within the ark were the two stone tablets containing the Ten Commandments (Ex. 25:16, 21), considered to be the basis of the covenant between God and His people Israel. Thus the ark was often called the ark of the Testimony. The golden pot of manna, which God miraculously preserved as a testimony to future generations (Ex. 16:32–34), was also deposited in the ark. The third item in the ark was Aaron's rod that budded to prove that Aaron was God's chosen (Num. 17:1–11).

While the New Testament states that the ark contained these three items (Heb. 9:4), the ark must have lost two of them through the years. At the dedication of Solomon's temple, Aaron's rod and the golden pot of manna were gone: "There was nothing in the ark except the two tablets of stone which Moses put there at Horeb" (1 Kin. 8:9).

The ark was carried by the sons of Levi during the wilderness wanderings (Deut. 31:9). Carried into the Jordan River by the priests, the ark caused the waters to part so Israel could cross on dry ground (Josh. 3:6–4:18). During the conquest of the land of Canaan, the ark was carried at the fall of Jericho (Josh. 6:4–11); later it was deposited at Shiloh, which had become the home of the tabernacle (Josh. 18:1).

Trusting the "magic power" of the ark rather than God, the Israelites took the ark into battle against the Philistines and suffered a crushing defeat (1 Sam. 4:1–11). The Philistines captured the ark, only to send it back when disaster struck their camp (1 Sam. 5–6). It remained at Kirjath Jearim until David brought it to Jerusalem (1 Chr. 13:3–14; 15:1–28). Solomon established it in the Most High Place of the temple that he built.

Nothing is known of what became of the ark. It disappeared when Nebuchadnezzar's armies destroyed Jerusalem in 586 B.C., and was not available when the second and third temples were built. Synagogues today continue the centuries-old tradition of providing a special place for a chest or ark containing the Torah (scrolls of the Law).

ARMAGEDDON [ar mah GED un]
(mountain of Megiddo)

The site of the final battle of this age in which God intervenes to destroy the armies of Satan and to cast Satan into the bottomless pit (Rev. 16:16). Scholars disagree about the exact location of this place, but the most likely possibility is the valley between Mount Carmel and the city of Jezreel. This valley (known as the Valley of Jezreel and sometimes referred to as the Plain of Esdraelon) was the crossroads of two ancient trade routes and thus was a strategic military site and the scene of many ancient battles.

Because of this history, Megiddo became a symbol of the final conflict between God and the forces of evil. According to the Book of Revelation, at Armageddon "the cup of the wine of the fierceness of His [God's] wrath" (Rev. 16:19) will be poured out, and the forces of evil will be overthrown and destroyed.

See also JEZREEL.

ARMORBEARER

A servant who carried additional weapons for commanders. Abimelech (Judg. 9:54), Jonathan (1 Sam. 14:6–17), and Joab (2 Sam. 18:15) had armorbearers. David was once Saul's armorbearer (1 Sam. 16:21). Armorbearers were also responsible for killing enemies slain by their masters. After enemy soldiers were wounded with javelins or bows and arrows, armorbearers finished the job by using clubs and swords. After the time of David, commanders fought from chariots and armorbearers are no longer mentioned.

ARMY

A large body of warriors organized and trained for warfare. The nation of Israel developed a regular standing army at a relatively late time in its history. One reason for this is that the nation lacked political unity until the time of the united kingdom under David and Solomon. The sense that God was the divine warrior and would protect His people regardless of their military strength may have been another reason why they were slow to develop an army.

Thus, from the time of Abraham to the beginning of Saul's reign there was no regular army, continually prepared to respond to foreign attacks. Instead, the call would go out at the moment of crisis; and able-bodied, nonexempt males would gather in response. The first example comes from Genesis 14, when Abraham's nephew Lot was kidnapped by Chedorlaomer, king of Elam, and his allies. Abraham rallied to Lot's aid by gathering 318 trained men of his household and defeating the foreign forces.

During the years of the Exodus, wilderness wanderings, and conquest of the land of Canaan, the whole nation was temporarily changed into an army. All the men from every tribe participated in the warfare. Numbers 2 pictures the nation of Israel camped as an army in battle, with their heavenly commander in the center and the various divisions (individual tribes) dwelling under their battle banners. The same chapter describes the position of each tribe marching behind the ark of the covenant as they traveled toward Canaan and holy war. At this time the army was under the command of Moses, and later of Joshua; but each tribal division had its own leader as well.

The period of the judges that followed was characterized by lack of unity and purpose. This was true militarily as well as politically and religiously. At times of military crisis, God would raise up a military leader, called a judge, who would then seek the aid of the tribes in order to gather an army. Judges 5 (particularly vv. 15–18) shows that Deborah, one of these judges, met with reluctance or indifference from some of the tribes.

The development of a regular standing army in Israel came only after a strong, centralized political system had developed. This came with kings Saul, David, and Solomon. Although Saul began his reign as a type of gifted leader, as were the earlier judges, he soon began to form a permanent army (1 Sam. 13:2; 24:2; 26:2). Nevertheless, the army had to be supported by food and other supplies from the homes of individual soldiers (1 Sam. 17:17–19).

What Saul began, David continued. He increased the army, brought in hired troops from other regions who were loyal to him alone (2 Sam. 15:19–22), and turned over the direct leadership of his armies to a commander-in-chief (Joab). Under David Israel also became more aggressive in its offensive military policies, absorbing neighboring states like Ammon (2 Sam. 11:1; 1 Chr. 20:1–3). David established a system of rotating troops with 12 groups of 24,000 men serving one month of the year (1 Chr. 27). Although Solomon's reign was peaceful, he further expanded the army, adding chariots and horsemen (1 Kin. 10:26).

The standing army came into existence with these three kings. It contin-

ued (though divided along with the kingdom after the death of Solomon) until 586 B.C., when Israel ceased to exist as a political entity.

The most important army to the faithful Israelite was not a human army; it was God's holy army. The human army could not succeed unless the Lord of Hosts led his troops into battle. Thus Joshua conferred with the "commander of the army of the Lord" before the battle of Jericho (Josh. 5:13). David awaited the movement of God's army in the balsam trees before attacking the Philistines (2 Sam. 5:24). The prophet Elisha prayed that God would open the eyes of Gehazi so he might be comforted by seeing the power of God's army (2 Kin. 6:8–23).

ARNON [AR none]

A swift river that runs through the mountains of Transjordan and empties into the Dead Sea. It served as the boundary between Moab and Ammon (Num. 21:24). Now known as the Wadi el-Mojib, it flows through the rugged sandstone ravine that rises more than 1,650 feet (503 meters) above the river.

ARTAXERXES [ar tuh ZERK sees]

A king of Persia in whose court Ezra and Nehemiah were officials (Ezra 7:1, 7). Known as Artaxerxes I Longimanus (long-handed), he temporarily halted the rebuilding program at Jerusalem that Cyrus, his predecessor, had encouraged (Ezra 4:7–23), but later allowed it to continue (Ezra 6:14). In the seventh year of his reign (458 B.C.), he authorized the mission of Ezra to lead a large number of Israelites back from the captivity to Jerusalem (Ezra 7:1–28).

ASA [AY sah]

The third king of Judah (911–870 B.C.) and the son of Abijam, king of Judah. Asa was the grandson of King Rehoboam and Maachah (1 Kin. 15:8–24). The first ten years of Asa's reign were peaceful and prosperous. He led many religious reforms, "banished the perverted persons from the land" (1 Kin. 15:12), and tore down pagan images and idols.

When he received further direction and encouragement from the prophet Azariah, Asa became more zealous in his call for revival. He restored the temple altar and called upon the tribes of Judah and Benjamin to renew their covenant with God at Jerusalem. When Israelites from the tribes of Ephraim, Manasseh, and Simeon saw how God had blessed Asa, they joined him in renewing their loyalty to the covenant. He was one of the four most godly kings of Judah.

Asa had two major confrontations with foreign nations. When the Ethiopian king Zerah attacked Asa with superior forces, Asa put his trust in God and dealt the Ethiopians a humiliating blow (2 Chr. 14:11–12). But his second confrontation did not yield such glorious results. When Baasha, king of Israel, fortified Ramah in an attempt to blockade Asa and prevent anyone from traveling to or from Jerusalem, Asa hired Ben-Hadad, king of Syria, to thwart Baasha's plans (2 Chr. 16:1–6). Ben-Hadad invaded northern Israel and forced Baasha to withdraw from Ramah. When the prophet ("seer") Hanani rebuked him for relying on Ben-Hadad instead of the Lord, Asa was enraged and put Hanani into prison (2 Chr. 16:7–10).

When Asa contracted a disease in his feet in the thirty-ninth year of his reign, he did not seek the Lord, but he consulted physicians instead (2 Chr. 16:12). Shortly thereafter, he died and was buried in Jerusalem.

ASAPH [AY saf] (God has gathered)

A Levite and the son of Berachiah the Gershonite (2 Chr. 20:14). Asaph sounded cymbals before the ark of the covenant when it was moved from the house of Obed-Edom to Jerusalem (1 Chr. 15:16–

19). Asaph's family became one of the three families given responsibility for music and song in the temple (1 Chr. 25:1–9). Following the captivity, 128 singers from this family returned from Babylon and conducted the singing when the foundations of Zerubbabel's temple were laid (Ezra 2:41; 3:10). Twelve psalms (Pss. 50; 73–83) are attributed to the family of Asaph.

ASCENSION OF CHRIST

The dramatic departure of the risen Christ from His earthly, bodily ministry among His followers. Since His birth in Bethlehem by the miracle of the Incarnation, Christ had lived physically on earth. But 40 days after the Resurrection, His earthly ministry ceased with His ascension into heaven (Mark 16:19; Luke 24:50–51; Acts 1:9–11). To a large extent the Ascension was for the benefit of Jesus' followers. They could no longer expect His physical presence. They must now wait for the promised Holy Spirit through whom the work of Jesus would continue.

Jesus' departure into heaven was a bodily ascension in His resurrection body. Stephen and Paul both reported seeing Jesus in bodily form after His ascension (Acts 7:56; 9:27; 1 Cor. 15:8).

The Ascension marked the beginning of Christ's intercession for His followers at the right hand of God. There He makes continual intercession for all believers (Rom. 8:34; Heb. 4:14; 6:20; 7:25). Although Christ is not physically present with His people today, He is no less concerned for them or less active on their behalf. Christians enjoy peace, hope, and security because Christ is their advocate with the Father (1 John 2:1).

The Ascension set in motion the coming of the Holy Spirit with His gifts for believers (John 14:16–18, 26; 16:7–15; Acts 2:23; Eph. 4:11–12). God determined that the presence of Jesus would be replaced by the presence of the Holy Spirit, who could be everywhere at the same time. Jesus' followers now enjoy the presence of the Spirit and the operation of the Spirit's gifts through them.

One additional result of the Ascension is that Jesus began His heavenly reign at the right hand of the Father (1 Cor. 15:20–28). This reign will last until His Second Coming, when He will return to the earth as the reigning Messiah (Acts 3:20–21).

Finally, the ascension of Christ is the pledge of His Second Coming: "This same Jesus, who was taken up from you into heaven, will so come in like manner as you saw Him go into heaven" (Acts 1:11). Jesus will return to earth in bodily form just as He ascended into heaven.

ASENATH [AS ih nath]

The Egyptian wife of Joseph and the mother of Manasseh and Ephraim (Gen. 41:45, 50–52; 46:20). Asenath was the daughter of Poti-Pherah, priest of On. Pharaoh himself may have arranged the marriage between Joseph and Asenath to help Joseph adjust to life in Egypt.

ASHDOD [ASH dahd]

One of the five principal Philistine cities (1 Sam. 6:17), situated 3 miles (5 kilometers) from the Mediterranean coast and 20 miles (32 kilometers) north of Gaza. The city's military and economic significance was enhanced by its location on the main highway between Egypt and Syria.

ASCENSION OF CHRIST

Joshua and the Israelites drove the Canaanites out of the hill country of Judah, but the Anakim—a group of Canaanites—remained in Ashdod, Gaza, and Gath (Josh. 11:22). During the time of Eli and Samuel, the ark of the covenant accompanied Israel's army (1 Sam. 4:3). When the Philistines defeated Israel, they took the ark to the temple of Dagon in Ashdod (1 Sam. 5:1–7).

Uzziah, the powerful king of Judah, captured Ashdod (2 Chr. 26:6). The prophet Amos predicted the destruction of the city because of its inhumane treatment of Israelites (Amos 1:8; 3:9). When Sargon II, king of Assyria, destroyed Ashdod in 711 B.C., he fulfilled this prophecy (Is. 20:1).

In New Testament times, Ashdod was renamed Azotus. Philip the evangelist preached in all the cities from Azotus to Caesarea (Acts 8:40).

ASHER [ASH err] (happy)

The eighth son of Jacob, the second by Leah's maidservant, Zilpah (Gen. 30:13). On his deathbed Jacob blessed Asher: "Bread from Asher shall be rich, and he shall yield royal dainties" (Gen. 49:20).

ASHER, TRIBE OF

A tribe descended from Asher and that part of Canaan where the tribe of Asher lived (Josh. 19:24, 31–34). The territory of Asher extended to the northern boundary of Canaan; its southern border was the tribe of Manasseh and the mountains of Mount Carmel. Asher was bounded on the west by the Mediterranean Sea and on the east by the tribe of Naphtali. The Asherites never succeeded in expelling the inhabitants of the Phoenician strongholds—such as Tyre, Sidon, and Acco (Judg. 1:31–32)—which were in their territory.

ASHKELON [ASH kuh lon]

One of the five principal cities of the Philistines (Josh. 13:3). Situated on the seacoast 12 miles (19 kilometers) north of Gaza, Ashkelon and her sister cities (Ashdod, Gath, Gaza, and Ekron) posed a serious threat to the Israelites during the period of the judges. Shortly after Joshua's death, Ashkelon was captured and was briefly controlled by the tribe of Judah (Judg. 1:18). A few years later Samson killed 30 men from this city (Judg. 14:19). During most of the Old Testament era, however, Ashkelon remained politically and militarily independent of Israel.

In the eighth century B.C. Ashkelon was denounced by the prophet Amos (Amos 1:8). Shortly before the Babylonian captivity, Zephaniah prophesied that the Jews would return from Babylonia and occupy the ruins of Ashkelon (Zeph. 2:4, 7). Zechariah also prophesied the destruction of Ashkelon (Zech. 9:5).

ASHTAROTH [ASH tah rahth]

The plural form of Ashtoreth, a pagan goddess. First Samuel 31:10 connects her with the Philistines, and 1 Kings 11:5 connects her with the Sidonians. She was often considered the companion or partner of the male god Baal (Judg. 2:13).

Apparently the worship of these goddesses was practiced by the Israelites from time to time. Solomon compromised his faith by worshiping at the altar of Ashtaroth (1 Kin. 11:5, 33). Along with the Baalim (the plural of Baal), the Ashtaroth were thought by the Philistines to be responsible for fertility and the growth of crops and herds.

The Ashtaroth were worshiped by other peoples under such names as Astarte (Phoenicians), Inanna (Sumerians), Ishtar (Babylonians), Aphrodite (Greeks), and Venus (Romans). All these were goddesses of sensual love and fertility.

ASHURBANIPAL [a shoor BAN ih pal]
(Asshur is creating an heir)

The last of the great kings of Assyria (668–626 B.C.). He was the son and successor of the Assyrian king Esarhaddon. Most scholars now identify him with the "great and noble" Osnapper of Ezra 4:10. Apparently, Ashurbanipal was the monarch who made King Manasseh of Judah, along with 21 other kings, pay tribute to him and kiss his feet.

A large part of Ashurbanipal's reign was spent in a tug-of-war with his own brother, Shamash-shum-ukin, who was viceroy of Babylon. Outright rebellion against Ashurbanipal broke out in 652 B.C. and ended in 648 B.C. following a two-year siege of Babylon by the Assyrians that resulted in famine.

The mighty Assyrian Empire disintegrated under Ashurbanipal's son, Sinsharishkun (627[?]–612 B.C.). Upon his death Babylon fell immediately to Nabopolassar, founder of a new Babylonian Empire; and the Medes and Babylonians destroyed Nineveh, the capital city of Assyria.

ASHURNASIRPAL [ash er NAS ir pal]
(Asshur is guarding an heir)

A king of Assyria who reigned early in the ninth century B.C., when Assyria was at the height of its power (about 884–860 B.C.). King Jehoshaphat of Judah (873–848 B.C.) and King Ahab of Israel (874–853 B.C.) were his contemporaries.

ASIA [AY zyuh]

A Roman province in western Asia Minor which included Mysia, Lydia, Caria, and the coastal islands as well as western Phrygia. The borders of this province were, for the most part, those of the earlier kingdom of Pergamos.

The kingdom of Pergamos gained its independence from the Seleucids with help from the Romans. By the time of

Augustus, the first Roman emperor (27 B.C.–A.D. 14), Asia had become a senatorial province (a Roman political division governed by a proconsul), with Pergamos as its capital.

Three cities continued to compete for the role of principal city: Ephesus, Smyrna, and Pergamos—the first three cities mentioned in the Book of Revelation (see Rev. 1:11; 2:1–17). Eventually, Ephesus became the chief commercial center and was known as the most prominent city of the province. The Roman Senate granted both Ephesus and Pergamos the right to have three imperial temples for the worship of the emperors.

Although scholars disagree on the time when Ephesus became the capital, it probably occurred after the death of the apostle Paul and perhaps as late as the time of the emperor Hadrian (about A.D. 129). The fact that the martyr Antipas is mentioned in connection with Pergamos (Rev. 2:13) argues for the capital's being at Pergamos during the time the Book of Revelation was written.

The governor of a senatorial province was called a proconsul, and the proconsulship of Asia became one of the most prized among all in the Roman Empire. The wealth and culture of Asia was legendary. When the New Testament mentions the officers of Ephesus, the term used is asiarchs (local elected authorities), or "officials of Asia" (Acts 19:31).

The seven cities mentioned in the Book of Revelation follow two principal north-south roads of Asia, beginning with Ephesus, the largest city, and ending inland with Laodicea. John must have known these cities of Asia fairly well, because each of the letters (Rev. 2–3) alludes to some important fact about that city.

At the beginning of his second missionary journey, the apostle Paul was "forbidden by the Holy Spirit to preach the word in Asia" (Acts 16:6). Thus, he made his way to Troas, the northwestern seaport of Asia, and entered Europe (Acts 16:6–10). On his return trip, however, he visited Ephesus (Acts 18:9). On his third missionary journey, he spent more than two years in ministry in this region. During this time, "all who dwelt in Asia heard the word of the Lord Jesus, both Jews and Greeks" (Acts 19:10).

ASIA MINOR

A peninsula, also called Anatolia, situated in the extreme western part of the continent of Asia. Asia Minor was bounded on the north by the Black Sea, the Sea of Marmara, and the Dardanelles; the Aegean Sea on the west; and Syria and the Mediterranean Sea on the south.

Roughly identical with the modern nation of Turkey, Asia Minor was a high plateau crossed by mountains, especially the Taurus Mountains near the southern coast. In the Old Testament period, it was the home of the Hittites. In the New Testament, the term *Asia* is ambiguous, sometimes referring to the peninsula of Asia Minor as a whole (Acts 19:26–27), but more often referring to proconsular Asia, situated in the western part of the peninsula (Acts 2:9; 6:9). The writer of Acts appears to use the term *Asia* to describe the region of the province of Asia around Ephesus. He refers to other regions of the province as Phrygia and Mysia (Acts 2:9–10; 16:6–7).

See also SEVEN CHURCHES OF ASIA.

ASSASSINS

A fanatical group of Jewish nationalists in the first century A.D. Four thousand of them followed an Egyptian who promised to lead them in a rebellion against the Romans (Acts 21:38; terrorists, NIV). The Roman commander at Jerusalem wondered whether the apostle Paul was a member of this group (Acts 21:38).

ASSHUR [AS shoor]

The chief god of the Assyrians. Asshur was a god of war, conquest, and military strength. The ancient ideas about the ordering and governing of the universe was taken over by this god and his Babylonian counterpart, Marduk. In contrast, the Bible makes it clear that the forces of nature are not pagan gods that war with one another annually to bring about an established order ot the universe. They are part of the Lord's creation (Gen. 1).

ASSOS [AS ohs]

A seaport of the Roman province of Mysia in Asia Minor, not far from Troas. While on his third missionary journey, the apostle Paul walked overland from Troas to Assos while Luke and the others took the longer trip around the cape (Acts 20:13–14).

ASSURANCE

The state of being assured; freedom from doubt and uncertainty. As a theological concept, assurance refers to the believers' full confidence and conviction that the penalty of their sins has been paid and that heaven has been secured as their eternal destiny by Christ's death and resurrection.

The basis of assurance must never be our own subjective experience, which can waver with fear, doubt, and uncertainty. True assurance is founded on the Word of God alone—the Holy Spirit bearing witness to our spirits that the Word of God is true and reliable. Believers have been forgiven by God in Christ and are now free to forgive others, to love as they have first been loved by God.

ASSYRIA [as SIHR ih ah]

A kingdom between the Tigris and Euphrates rivers that often dominated the ancient world. After defeating the northern kingdom of Israel in 722 B.C., the Assyrians carried away thousands of Israelites and resettled them in other parts of the Assyrian Empire. This was a blow from which the nation of Israel never recovered.

The early inhabitants of Assyria were ancient tribesmen (Gen. 10:22) who probably migrated from Babylonia. They grew powerful enough around 1300 B.C. to conquer Babylonia. For the next 700 years they were the leading power in the ancient world, with their leading rival nation, Babylonia, constantly challenging them for this position.

Tiglath-Pileser I (1120–1100 B.C.) built the Assyrian kingdom to the most extensive empire of the age. But under his successors, it declined in power and influence. This decline offered the united kingdom of Judah, under the leadership of David and Solomon, the opportunity to reach its greatest limits. If the Assyrians had been more powerful at that time, they probably would have interfered with the internal affairs of Israel, even at that early date.

After the Assyrians had languished in weakness for an extended period, Ashurnasirpal (844–860 B.C.) restored much of the prestige of the empire. His son, Shalmaneser III, succeeded him, and reigned from about 860 to 825 B.C. Shalmaneser was the first Assyrian king to come into conflict with the northern kingdom of Israel.

In an effort to halt the Assyrian expansion, a group of surrounding nations formed a coalition, of which Israel was a part. Ahab was king of Israel during this time. But the coalition eventually split up, allowing the Assyrians to continue their relentless conquest of surrounding territories.

During the period from 833 to 745 B.C., Assyria was engaged in internal struggles as well as war with Syria. This allowed Israel to operate without threat from the Assyrian army. During this time, Jeroboam II, king of Israel, was able to raise the northern kingdom to the status of a major nation among the countries of the ancient Near East.

The rise of Tiglath-Pileser III (745–727 B.C.) marked the beginning of a renewed period of Assyrian oppression for the nation of Israel. Tiglath-Pileser, known also in the Bible as Pul (2 Kin. 15:19), set out to regain territories previously occupied by the Assyrians. He was resisted by a coalition led by Rezin of Damascus and Pekah of Israel. These rulers tried to force Ahaz, king of Judah, to join them. When Ahaz refused, Rezin and Pekah marched on Jerusalem, intent on destroying the city. Against the counsel of the prophet Isaiah, Ahaz enlisted the aid of Tiglath-Pileser for protection. This protection cost dearly. From that day forth, Israel was required to pay tribute to Assyria. Israel also was forced to adopt some of the religious practices of the Assyrians (2 Kin. 16).

Tiglath-Pileser was succeeded by his son, Shalmaneser V (727–722 B.C.). When Hoshea, king of Israel, who had been placed on the throne by Tiglath-Pileser, refused to pay the required tribute, Shalmaneser attacked Samaria, the capital of Israel. After a long siege, Israel fell to Assyria in 722 B.C., perhaps to Sargon II; and 27,000 inhabitants of Israel were deported to Assyrian territories. This event marked the end of the northern kingdom of Israel. Most of the deported Israelites never returned to their homeland.

Israel's sister nation, the southern kingdom of Judah, also felt the power of the Assyrian Empire. In 701 B.C., Sennacherib, king of Assyria (705–681 B.C.), planned an attack on Jerusalem. However, the Assyrian army was struck by a plague, which the Bible referred to as "the angel of the Lord" (2 Kin. 19:35). Sennacherib was forced to retreat from his invasion when 185,000 Assyrian soldiers died. Thus, Jerusalem was saved from Assyrian oppression by divine intervention.

The religion of the Assyrians, much like that of the Babylonians, emphasized worship of nature. They believed every object of nature was possessed by a spirit. The chief god was Asshur. All other primary gods whom they worshiped were related to the objects of nature. These included Anu, god of the heavens; Bel, god of the region inhabited by people, animals, and birds; Ea, god of the waters; Sin, the moon-god; Shamash, the sun-god; and Ramman, god of the storms. These gods were followed by five gods of the planets. In addition to these primary gods, lesser gods also were worshiped. In some cases, various cities had their own patron gods. The pagan worship of the Assyrians was soundly condemned by several prophets of the Old Testament (Is. 10:5; Ezek. 16:28; Hos. 8:9).

The favorite pursuits of the Assyrian kings were war and hunting. Archaeologists have discovered that the Assyrians were merciless and savage people. The Assyrian army was ruthless and effective. Its cruelty included burning cities, burning children, impaling victims on stakes, beheading, and chopping off hands. But, like Babylonia, which God used as an instrument of judgment against Judah, Assyria became God's channel of punishment and judgment against Israel because of their sin and idolatry.

Because of the cruelty and paganism of the Assyrians, Israel harbored deep-seated hostility against this nation. This attitude is revealed clearly in the Book of Jonah. When God instructed Jonah to preach to Nineveh, the capital of Assyria, Jonah refused and went in the opposite direction. After he finally went to Nineveh, the prophet was disappointed with God because He spared the city.

ASTROLOGY

The study of the sun, moon, planets, stars, and constellations in the belief that they influence individuals and the course of human events. Astrology attempts to predict the future by analyzing the movements of these heavenly bodies.

Although the word *astrology* does not appear in the Bible, the word *astrologers* does. The prophet Isaiah taunted the Babylonians to go to the powerless "astrologers, the stargazers, and the monthly prognosticators" (Is. 47:13) for their salvation. The word is found eight times in the Book of Daniel, in association with "magicians," "sorcerers," "Chaldeans," "wise men," and "soothsayers" (Dan. 1:20; 2:2, 10, 27; 4:7; 5:7, 11, 15). Some Bible scholars believe the "wise men" or Magi who saw the star of the infant Jesus (Matt. 2:1–12) were astrologers. We do know that the earliest records of astrology have come from Mesopotamia—the land between the Tigris and Euphrates rivers where the ancient Babylonians flourished.

The attempt to forecast the future from the stars probably arose very naturally in the ancient world. These beliefs would have come from observing that the signs in the heavens and events on earth are sometimes related. For instance, it is evident that the winter season begins at the same time when the sun begins to set low in the sky. It takes only one step of logic to conclude that when the sun begins to dip low in the sky, it causes winter to come. Given the lack of scientific thought in the ancient Near East, it required only one further step of logic to conclude that other movements of the sun, moon, or stars affect historical events. An example of this kind of reasoning is found in a letter addressed to the Assyrian king Esarhaddon. "If the planet Jupiter is present during an eclipse," the letter stated, "it is good for the king because an important person in court will die in his stead."

The close association in Babylonian thought between the stars and the gods led ancient skywatchers to stress their impact on human affairs. This association may be seen clearly in the unique script used to write their language. The sign used to distinguish a god's name was the sign of the star.

The Bible classes astrology with other techniques for predicting the future. Going to the stars for guidance was the same as idolatry to biblical writers. Samuel equated the two in his denunciation of Saul (1 Sam. 15:23).

The Bible's contempt for astrology is most clearly seen in its prohibition of any technique to aid in predicting the future. Astrology assumes that God does not control history. It assumes that history is governed by the affairs of the pagan gods as revealed in the movement of the planets. The believer knows that a Sovereign God rules this world. He also knows that resorting to astrology is a denial of the life of faith by which one trusts God and not his lucky stars for the future.

See also MAGIC, SORCERY, AND DIVINATION.

ATHALIAH [ath ah LIE ah] *(the Lord is strong)*

The queen of Judah for six years (2 Kin. 11:1–3). Athaliah was the daughter of King Ahab of Israel. Presumably, Jezebel was her mother.

Athaliah married Jehoram (or Joram), son of Jehoshaphat, king of Judah. Jehoram reigned only eight years and was succeeded by his son Ahaziah, who died after reigning only one year. Desiring the throne for herself, Athaliah ruthlessly killed all her grandsons—except the infant Joash, who was hidden by his aunt (2 Kin. 11:2).

Athaliah apparently inherited Jezebel's ruthlessness. She was a tyrant whose every whim had to be obeyed. As her mother had done in Israel, Athaliah introduced Baal worship in Judah and in so doing destroyed part of the temple.

Joash was hidden in the house of the Lord for six years (2 Kin. 11:3), while Athaliah reigned over the land (841–835 B.C.). In the seventh year, the high priest Jehoiada declared Joash the lawful king of Judah. Guards removed Athaliah from the temple before killing her, to avoid defiling the temple with her blood (2 Kin. 11:13–16; 2 Chr. 23:12–15).

Athaliah reaped what she sowed. She gained the throne through murder and lost her life in the same way. She also failed to thwart God's promise, because she did not destroy the Davidic line, through which the Messiah was to be born.

ATHENS [ATH ins]

The capital city of the ancient Greek state of Attica and the modern capital of Greece. It was the center of Greek art, architecture, literature, and politics during the golden age of Greek history (the fifth century B.C.) and was visited by the apostle Paul on his second missionary journey (Acts 17:15–18:1).

Even today the visitor to Athens is impressed by the city's ancient glory. The Acropolis (the great central hill)—with its Parthenon (the temple dedicated to the virgin Athena, the goddess of wisdom and the arts), its Erechtheion (the unique double sanctuary dedicated to Athena and Neptune), its Propylaea (the magnificent entrance), and its small temple to Wingless Victory (symbolizing the Athenian hope that victory would never leave them)—stand as monuments to the city's glorious past.

The history of Athens goes back before 3000 B.C., when a small village grew up on the slopes of the Acropolis. As it developed, Athens became a sea power with its port at Piraeus about 5 miles (8 kilometers) distant and its navy stationed at Phaleron. Its government developed in stages, and in about 509 B.C. Cleisthenes provided a new constitution that became the basis of Athenian democracy.

Athens' history involved a number of battles with other city-states, such as Sparta, and with the Persians, who were led by Darius and Xerxes. In the sea battle with the Persians at Salamis (480 B.C.), the Athenians won decisively, but the retreating Persians burned Athens.

The rebuilding of Athens began under Themistocles, and Athens started its golden age under Pericles (about 495–429 B.C.). Learning was stimulated and philosophers found Athens a congenial home (with the exception of Socrates, whom the Athenians put to death in 399 B.C.). Plato founded his famous school, the Academy, in 388 B.C.

As one visits the museum in Athens filled with statues and the theater of Dionysus with the heads of the gods removed, one recalls Paul's assessment of Athens as a city "given over to idols" (Acts 17:16). As one walks through the Agora (marketplace) and visits the reconstructed porch of Attalus, one remembers that in porches like these the ancient Greek philosophers used to debate. Acts 17:18, for instance, describes Paul's encounter with "certain Epicurean and Stoic philosophers." In fact, the Stoics, the followers of Zeno (324?–270? B.C.), took their name from these porches. In this area, between the Acropolis and the Agora, lies the hill known as the Areopagus (Mars' Hill), where Paul may have made his defense before the council of Athens (Acts 17:22–31).

ATONEMENT

The act by which God restores a relationship of harmony and unity between Himself and human beings. Because of Adam's sin (Rom. 5:18; 1 Cor. 15:22) and our own personal sins (Col. 1:21), no one

is worthy of relationship with a holy God (Eccl. 7:20; Rom. 3:23). Since we are helpless to correct this situation (Prov. 20:9) and can do nothing to hide our sin from God (Heb. 4:13), we all stand condemned by sin (Rom. 3:19).

God's gracious response to the helplessness of His chosen people, the nation of Israel, was to give them a means of reconciliation through Old Testament covenant Law. This came in the sacrificial system where the death or "blood" of the animal was accepted by God as a substitute for the death (Ezek. 18:20) the sinner deserved (Lev. 17:11).

The Lord Jesus came according to God's will (Acts 2:23; 1 Pet. 1:20) "to give His life a ransom for many" (Mark 10:45). Christ "has loved us and given Himself for us, an offering and a sacrifice to God" (Eph. 5:2), so that those who believe in Him (Rom. 3:22) might receive atonement through "the precious blood of Christ" (1 Pet. 1:19).

ATONEMENT, DAY OF

A holy feast day to the Israelites. The tenth day of the seventh month was set aside as a day of public fasting and humiliation. On this day the nation of Israel sought atonement for its sins (Lev. 23:27; 16:29; Num. 29:7). This day fell in the month equivalent to our August, and it was preceded by special Sabbaths (Lev. 23:24). The only fasting period required by the law (Lev. 16:29; 23:31), the Day of Atonement was a recognition of people's inability to make any atonement for their sins. It was a solemn, holy day accompanied by elaborate ritual (Lev. 16; Heb. 10:1–10).

The high priest who officiated on this day first sanctified himself by taking a ceremonial bath and putting on white garments (Lev. 16:4). Then he had to make atonement for himself and other priests by sacrificing a bullock (Num. 29:8). God was enthroned on the mercy seat in the sanctuary, but no person could approach it except through the mediation of the high priest, who offered the blood of sacrifice.

After sacrificing a bullock, the high priest chose a goat for a sin offering and sacrificed it. Then he sprinkled its blood on and about the mercy seat (Lev. 16:12, 14, 15). Finally the scapegoat bearing the sins of the people was sent into the wilderness (Lev. 16:20–22). This scapegoat symbolized the pardon for sin brought through the sacrifice (Gal. 3:12; 2 Cor. 5:21).

ATTALIA [at ah LIE ah]

A city on the seacoast of Pamphylia in modern Turkey. Attalia derived its name from Attalus Philadelphus, the king of Pergamos (159–138 B.C.). At the end of Paul's first missionary journey, he preached in Attalia (Acts 14:25). From there he sailed to Antioch, where the journey had begun (Acts 14:26). Known today by the name Adalia, Attalia is the main seaport on the Gulf of Adalia.

AUGUSTAN REGIMENT

One of five cohorts, or regiments, of the Roman army stationed at or near Caesarea. While the apostle Paul was being transported to Rome as a prisoner, he was put in the charge of "one named Julius, a centurion of the Augustan Regiment" (Acts 27:1). A regiment, or cohort, was made up of about 600 infantrymen.

AUGUSTUS [aw GUS tus] (consecrated, holy, sacred)

A title of honor bestowed upon Octavian, the first Roman emperor (27 B.C.–A.D. 14). Luke refers to him as "Caesar Augustus" (Luke 2:1). A nephew of Julius Caesar, Octavian was born in 63 B.C. In 43 B.C., Octavian, Lepidus, and Mark Antony were named as the Second Triumvirate, the three rulers who shared the office

of emperor. Octavian eventually became the sole ruler of Rome and reigned as emperor for more than 44 years, until his death in A.D. 14. It was during his reign that Jesus was born (Luke 2:1).

Augustus reigned during a time of peace and extensive architectural achievements. After his death, the title "Augustus" was given to all Roman emperors. The "Augustus Caesar" mentioned in Acts 25:21, 25, for instance, is not Octavian but Nero.

AVA [AY vah]

A city (or perhaps a district or province) of the Assyrian Empire. Sargon II, king of Assyria, brought settlers from Ava to colonize Samaria after the nation of Israel fell to his forces (2 Kin. 17:24). The province is also identified as Ivah (2 Kin. 18:34). Ava is spelled Avva in some translations.

AVENGER OF BLOOD

A relative responsible for avenging an injury to a member of his family or clan—especially murder (Deut. 19:6, 12; 2 Sam. 14:11).

A kind of primitive justice existed among the various families, clans, and tribes of the ancient Hebrews in the Old Testament. Being related by blood, each of these groups was responsible for the care and protection of its own members, even to the point of avenging wrongs inflicted upon the clan. This responsibility fell to the victim's closest relative, who would seek to find and kill the murderer (Judg. 8:18–21). The trouble with this primitive system of justice is that the avenger of blood, having killed the murderer of his kinsman, might himself be killed by a member of the opposing clan, thus setting in motion a vicious blood feud.

Plainly, vengeance could not be allowed to flourish, or it would lead to chaos. The Law of Moses established certain guidelines or limits concerning the avenger of blood. Six cities of refuge were established to which the slayer could flee for protection: Kedesh, Shechem, Kirjath Arba (also called Hebron), Bezer, Ramoth in Gilead, and Golan (Josh. 20:1–9). If someone killed another by accident, he was not necessarily liable to punishment (Deut. 19:4–6). The community would decide if the crime was murder or manslaughter (Num. 35:24). If it was manslaughter, the slayer could stay safely in one of these cities of refuge, where the avenger of blood could not hurt him (Deut. 4:41–43; Josh. 20:1–9).

But if a person was guilty of murder, he could not be saved by fleeing to a city of refuge (Ex. 21:14). Even if he were to flee to the tabernacle (or temple) and take "hold of the horns of the altar" (1 Kin. 1:50–51; 2:28)—both an appeal for mercy and a claim to the protection of the sanctuary—he could be put to death by the avenger (1 Kin. 2:25, 34).

In contrast to these provisions of the Old Testament law, Jesus taught us to love our enemies (Matt. 5:44). We must forgive one another, not merely "up to seven times, but up to seventy times seven" (Matt. 18:22). Only by love, forgiveness, and mercy can the vicious cycle of hatred and revenge be broken.

See also CITIES OF REFUGE.

AZEKAH [a ZEE kah]

A fortified city of Judah near Socoh, situated in the lowland country between Lachish and Jerusalem (Josh. 15:35; Neh. 11:30). Azekah is mentioned in connection with Joshua's pursuit of the Canaanites (Josh. 10:10–11), with the Philistine camp in Goliath's time (1 Sam. 17:1), with Rehoboam, who fortified it (2 Chr. 11:9), and with Nebuchadnezzar king of Babylon, who beseiged the city (Jer. 34:7).

AZMAVETH [az MAH veth] *(strong as death)*

A village near the border of Judah and Benjamin, about 5 miles (8 kilometers) northeast of Jerusalem. Forty-two men of Azmaveth returned from the captivity with Zerubbabel (Ezra 2:24). Musicians and singers from this village helped dedicate the rebuilt wall of Jerusalem (Neh. 12:29). This village was also called Beth Azmaveth (Neh. 7:28).

B

BAAL [BAY uhl] *(lord, master)*

A fertility and nature god of the Canaanites and Phoenicians. Baal was considered the god who brought rain and fertility (especially good harvests and animal reproduction). In a number of passages in Canaanite literature, he is identified as Hadad, another god believed to bring the rains, storms, and fertility.

Archaeologists have discovered rock carvings of Baal holding a club in his right hand and a lightning flash with a spearhead in his left. These identify him as the god of rain and storm. Baal is also known as the "rider of the clouds," a term showing his power over the heavens. Psalm 68:4, "Extol Him who rides on the clouds," gives this title to the God of Israel—a declaration that the Lord and not the false god Baal is ruler over the heavens.

During the history of the Israelites, a rivalry developed between Baalism and the true worship of the Lord (Jer. 23:37).

Perhaps the best example of this rivalry was the conflict between Elijah and the prophets of Baal on Mount Carmel (1 Kin. 18). Elijah's challenge to them to bring down fire from heaven was appropriate, because the Canaanites believed that Baal could shoot lightning flashes from the sky. Elijah's mocking of Baal struck at the heart of their claims; he knew that Baal was powerless, that the prophets of Baal had misled the people, and that only the Lord God of Israel was alive and able to answer.

BAASHA [BAY uh shah]

The son of Ahijah, of the tribe of Issachar, and the third king of the northern kingdom of Israel. Baasha succeeded Nadab, the son of Jeroboam I, as king by assassinating him. Then he murdered every member of the royal house, removing all who might claim his throne (1 Kin. 15:27–29).

Baasha's 24-year reign (909–885 B.C.) was characterized by war with Asa, king of Judah (1 Kin. 15:32; Jer. 41:9). He fortified Ramah (2 Chr. 16:1), 4 miles (6 kilometers) north of Jerusalem, to control traffic from the north to Jerusalem during a time of spiritual awakening under Asa (2 Chr. 15:1–10). When the Syrian king, Ben-Hadad, invaded Israel, Baasha withdrew to defend his cities (1 Kin. 15:16–21).

Baasha's dynasty ended as it began; his son Elah was murdered by a servant, and the royal household of Baasha came to an end (1 Kin. 16:8–11).

BABEL, TOWER OF [BAY buhl]

An ancient tower symbolizing human pride and rebellion. It was built during the period after the Flood.

The narrative of the Tower of Babel appears in Genesis 11:1–9 as the climax to the account of early mankind found in Genesis 1–11. The geographical setting is a plain in the land of Shinar (Gen. 11:2).

In the light of information contained in Genesis 10:10, Shinar probably refers to Babylonia.

The tower was constructed of brick because there was no stone in southern Mesopotamia. It corresponds in general to a notable feature of Babylonian religion, the Ziggurat or temple tower. The one built at Ur in southern Mesopotamia about 2100 B.C. was a pyramid consisting of three terraces of diminishing size as the building ascended, topped by a temple. Converging stairways on one side led up to the temple. Its surviving lower two terraces were about 70 feet (21 meters) high. The outside of the structure was built of fired bricks and bituminous mortar, just like the tower described in Genesis 11:3.

The narrative in Genesis 11 is told with irony and with a negative attitude toward the people involved. Human beings delight in bricks, but the narrator and readers know that these are an inferior substitute for stone (Is. 9:10). To people the tower is a skyscraper (Deut. 1:28), but to God it is so small that He must come down from heaven to catch a glimpse of this tiny effort. The construction of the tower and city is described as an act of self-glorification by the builders (Gen. 11:4). People seek for their own security in community life and culture, independent of God. This is human initiative apart from God (Ps. 127:1). As such, the activity is evil and sinful.

The account moves from a description of the sin to a narration of the punishment. God has to step in to prevent mankind from seizing yet more power for themselves and going beyond the limits of their creaturehood (Gen. 3:22; 11:5–8). Their communication with one another to advance their efforts is frustrated because they begin to speak different languages. Finally, they abandon the building of the city and go their own way, becoming scattered over the earth.

The climax of the story occurs when the city is identified with *Babel,* the Hebrew name for Babylonia. This nation's sophisticated culture and power deliberately excluded God. Just as the Old Testament prophets foresaw the future downfall of Babylonia in spite of its glory (Is. 13:19; Rev. 18), this downfall is anticipated in Genesis 11: The end corresponds to the beginning. *Babel* derives ultimately from an Akkadian word that means "gateway to God." A similar Hebrew word, *balal,* means "confuse" and provides the author with a useful wordplay that emphasizes God's confusing of the builders' languages and His scattering of them throughout the earth (Gen. 11:9).

God's rejection of the nations symbolized by the Tower of Babel is reversed in Genesis 12:1–3 by the call of Abraham, through whom all nations would be blessed. Ultimately the sinful and rejected condition of mankind, which is

BABEL, TOWER OF

MODERN DAY TOWER OF BABEL
BABBLE

clearly shown by the diversity of human language and territory described in this account, needed Pentecost as its answer. On this day the Holy Spirit was poured out on all people so they understood one another, although they spoke different languages (Acts 2:1–11; Eph. 2:14–18). The barriers that divide people and nations were thus removed.

BABYLON, CITY OF [BAB uh lon]

Ancient walled city between the Tigris and Euphrates rivers and capital of the Babylonian Empire. The leading citizens of the nation of Judah were carried to this city as captives in 586 B.C. after Jerusalem fell to the invading Babylonians. Biblical writers often portrayed this ancient capital of the Babylonian people as the model of paganism and idolatry (Jer. 51:44; Dan. 4:30).

Babylon was situated along the Euphrates River about 300 miles (485 kilometers) northwest of the Persian Gulf and about 30 miles (49 kilometers) southwest of modern Baghdad in Iraq. Its origins are unknown. According to Babylonian tradition, it was built by the god Marduk. The city must have been built some time before 2300 B.C., because it was destroyed about that time by an invading enemy king. This makes Babylon one of the oldest cities of the ancient world. Genesis 10:10 mentions Babel (the Hebrew spelling of Babylon) as part of the empire of Nimrod.

Some time during its early history, the city of Babylon became a small independent kingdom. Its most famous king was Hammurapi (about 1792–1750 B.C.), who conquered southern Mesopotamia and territory to the north as far as Mari. He was known for his revision of a code of law that showed concern for the welfare of the people under his rule. But the dynasty he established declined under his successors. It came to an end with the conquest of Babylon by the Hittite king

Murshilish I about 1595 B.C. Then the Kassites took over for a period, ruling southern Mesopotamia from the city of Babylon as their capital. The Assyrians attacked and plundered Babylon about 1250 B.C., but it recovered and flourished for another century until the Assyrians succeeded in taking over the city with their superior forces about 1100 B.C.

After Tiglath-Pileser I of Assyria arrived on the scene, the city of Babylon became subject to Assyria by treaty or conquest. Tiglath-Pileser III (745–727 B.C.) declared himself king of Babylon with the name Pulu (Pul, 2 Kin. 15:19), deporting a number of its citizens to the subdued territory of the northern kingdom of Israel (2 Kin. 17:24).

In 721 B.C. a Chaldean prince, Marduk-apal-iddina (Heb. Merodach-Baladan), seized control of Babylon and became a thorn in Assyria's side for a number of years. He apparently planned a large-scale rebellion of eastern and western parts of the Assyrian Empire (2 Kin. 20:12). In retaliation against this rebellion, Sennacherib of Assyria (704–681 B.C.) attacked Babylon in 689 B.C., totally destroying it, although it was rebuilt by his successor Esarhaddon (680–669 B.C.). After this, Assyrian power gradually weakened, so the city and kingdom of Babylonia grew stronger once again.

In 626 B.C. Nabopolassar seized the throne of Babylon. He was succeeded by Nebuchadnezzar II (605–562 B.C.), the greatest king of Babylon, who enlarged the capital city to an area of six square miles and beautified it with magnificent buildings. This period of the city's development has been the focal point of all archaeological research done in ancient Babylon. The city's massive double walls spanned both sides of the Euphrates River. Set into these walls were eight major gates. One of the numerous pagan temples in the city was that of the patron god Marduk, flanked by a Ziggurat or temple-tower. To this temple a sacred processional way led from the main gate, the Ishtar Gate. Both the gate and the walls facing the way were decorated with colored enameled bricks picturing lions, dragons, and bulls.

The city of Babylon also contained a palace complex, or residence for the king. On the northwest side of this palace area, the famous terraced "hanging gardens" may have been situated. They were one of the seven wonders of the ancient world. According to tradition, Nebuchadnezzar built these gardens for one of his foreign wives to remind her of the scenery of her homeland.

Babylon's glory reflected the king's imperial power. Captured kings were brought to his court at Babylon. These included Jehoiachin (2 Kin. 24:15) and Zedekiah (2 Kin. 25:7), kings of Judah. During the reign of Nabonidus (555–539 B.C.), while Belshazzar was co-regent (Dan. 5), the city surrendered to the Persians without opposition.

Eventually the balance of power passed from the Persians to Alexander the Great, to whom Babylon willingly submitted in 331 B.C. Alexander planned to refurbish and expand the city and make it his capital, but he died before accomplishing these plans. The city later fell into insignificance because one of Alexander's successors founded a new capital at Seleucia, a short distance away.

The books of Isaiah and Jeremiah predicted the downfall of Babylon. This would happen as God's punishment of the Babylonians because of their destruction of Jerusalem and their deportation of the citizens of Judah (Is. 14:22; 21:9; 43:14; Jer. 50:9; 51:37). Today, the ruins of this city stand as an eloquent testimony to the passing of proud empires and to the providential Hand of God.

BABYLONIA [bab i LOW nih uh]

Ancient pagan empire between the Tigris and Euphrates rivers in southern Mesopotamia. The Babylonians struggled with the neighboring Assyrians for domination of the ancient world during much of their history. At the height of their power, the Babylonians overpowered the nation of Judah, destroyed Jerusalem, and carried God's covenant people into captivity in 586 B.C.

The fortunes of the Babylonians rose and fell during the long sweep of Old Testament history—from about 2000 B.C. to about 500 B.C. References to these people—their culture, religion, and military power—occur throughout the Old Testament.

Babylonia was a long, narrow country about 40 miles (65 kilometers) wide at its widest point and having an area of about 8,000 square miles. It was bordered on the north by Assyria, on the east by Elam, on the south and west by the Arabian desert, and on the southeast by the Persian Gulf.

Among the earliest inhabitants of this region were the Sumerians, whom the Bible refers to as the people of the "land of Shinar" (Gen. 10:10). Sargon I (the Great), from one of the Sumerian cities, united the people of Babylonia under his rule about 2300 B.C. Many scholars believe Sargon was the same person as Nimrod (Gen. 10:8).

In 1792 B.C. Hammurapi emerged as the ruler of Babylonia. He expanded the borders of the empire and organized its laws into a written system, referred to by scholars as the Code of Hammurapi. Abraham had earlier left Ur, one of the ancient cities in lower Babylonia, and moved to Haran, a city in the north. Abraham eventually left Haran and migrated into the land of Canaan under God's promise that he would become the father of a great nation (Gen. 12:1–20).

Any account of Babylonia must also mention Assyria, which bordered Babylonia on the north. Assyria's development was often intertwined with the course of Babylonian history. About 1270 B.C., the Assyrians overpowered Babylonia. For the next 700 years, Babylonia was a second-rate power as the Assyrians dominated the ancient world.

In 626 B.C., Babylonian independence was finally won from Assyria by a leader named Nabopolassar. Under his leadership, Babylonia again became a great empire. In 605 B.C., Nebuchadnezzar, the son of Nabopolassar, became ruler and reigned for 44 years. Under him the Babylonian Empire reached its greatest strength. Using the treasures he took from other nations, Nebuchadnezzar built Babylon, the capital city of Babylonia, into one of the leading cities of the world. The famous "hanging gardens" of Babylon were known as one of the seven wonders of the ancient world.

In 586 B.C., the Babylonians destroyed Jerusalem and carried the leading citizens of the nation of Judah as captives to Babylon. During this period of captivity, the Persians conquered Babylonia, and the Babylonians passed from the scene as a world power.

During its long history, Babylonia attained a high level of civilization that was influential beyond its borders. Sumerian culture was its basis, which later Babylonians regarded as traditional. In the realm of religion, the Sumerians already had a system of gods, each with a main temple in a particular city. The chief gods were Anu, god of heaven; Enlil, god of the air; and Enki or Ea, god of the subterranean ocean. Others were Shamash, the sun-god; Sin, the moon-god; Ishtar, goddess of love and war; and Adad, the storm-god. The Amorites promoted the god Marduk at the city of Babylon, so that he became the chief god of the Babylonian religion, beginning about 1100 B.C.

Babylonian religion was temple-centered, with elaborate festivals and many different types of priests, especially the exorcist and the diviner, whose function was to drive away evil spirits.

Babylonian literature was dominated by mythology and legends. Among these was a "creation" myth called Enuma Elish, written to glorify a god known as Marduk. According to this myth, Marduk created heaven and earth from the corpse of the goddess Tiamat. Another work was the Gilgamesh Epic, which includes a flood story and was written about 2000 B.C. Scientific literature of the Babylonians included treatises on astronomy, mathematics, medicine, chemistry, botany, and zoology.

An important aspect of Babylonian culture was a codified system of law. Hammurapi's code was the successor of earlier collections of laws going back several centuries. The Babylonians used art for the celebration of great events and glorification of the gods. It was marked by stylized and symbolic representations, but it expressed realism and spontaneity in the depiction of animals.

The Old Testament contains many references to Babylonia. Genesis 10:10 mentions four Babylonian cities: Babel (Babylon), Erech (Uruk), Accad (Agade) and Calneh. These, along with Assyria, were ruled by Nimrod.

See also CHALDEA.

BACKSLIDE

To revert to sin or wrongdoing; to lapse morally or in the practice of religion. "Backsliding" is a term found mainly in the Book of Jeremiah (2:19; 31:22; 49:4). It refers to the lapse of the nation of Israel into paganism and idolatry.

BAHURIM [bah HOO rim] *(young men)*

A village near the Mount of Olives, located east of Jerusalem in the territory of Benjamin (2 Sam. 3:16). During Absalom's rebellion, King David fled along the old Jerusalem-to-Jericho road and passed through Bahurim. Later Jonathan and Ahimaaz hid themselves in a well at Bahurim when they were fleeing the forces of Absalom (2 Sam. 17:18–21).

BALAAM [BAY lum]

A magician or soothsayer (Josh. 13:22) who was summoned by the Moabite king Balak to curse the Israelites before they entered Canaan (Num. 22:5–24:25; Deut. 23:4–5). Recently, a plaster inscription concerning Balaam that dates to the eighth century B.C. has been found at Tell Deir Alla in Jordan.

Balaam lived in Aram in the town of Pethor on the Euphrates River. A curious mixture of good and evil, Balaam wavered when he was asked by Balak to curse the Israelites. But he finally agreed to go when the Lord specifically instructed him to go to Balak (Num. 22:20).

The exact meaning of the account of Balaam's "stubborn" donkey is not clear. After telling Balaam it was all right to go, God either tried to forbid him from going or wanted to impress upon him that he should speak only what he was told to say. When the angel of the Lord blocked their way, the donkey balked three times and was beaten by Balaam, who had not seen the angel. Finally, after the third beating, the donkey spoke, reproving Balaam.

When the angel told Balaam, "Your way is perverse before Me" (Num. 22:32), Balaam offered to return home. The angel told him to go on, however, and reminded him to speak only the words God gave him to speak.

Balaam and Balak met at the river Arnon and traveled to "the high places of Baal" (Num. 22:41). From there they could see part of the Israelite encampment at Acacia Grove (Num. 25:1). After sacrificing on seven altars, Balaam went off alone. When he heard the word of God, he returned to Balak and blessed the people whom Balak wanted him to curse.

The New Testament mentions Balaam in three passages. Peter speaks of false teachers who "have forsaken the right way and gone astray, following the way of Balaam" (2 Pet. 2:15). Jude speaks of backsliders who "have run greedily in the error of Balaam for profit" (Jude 11). Balaam's error was greed or covetousness; he was well paid to bring a curse upon the people of Israel.

The nature of Balaam's curse is made clear by John in the Book of Revelation. It refers to some members of the church in Pergamos who held "the doctrine of Balaam, who taught Balak to put a stumbling block before the children of Israel" (Rev. 2:14).

Before leaving Balak, Balaam apparently told the Moabite leader that Israel could be defeated if its people were seduced to worship Baal, "to eat things sacrificed to idols and to commit sexual immorality" (Rev. 2:14). Indeed, this was exactly what happened: "The people [of Israel] began to commit harlotry with the women of Moab. They invited the people to the sacrifice of their gods, and the people ate and bowed down to their gods. So Israel was joined to Baal of Peor, and the anger of the Lord was aroused against Israel" (Num. 25:1–3).

In condemning "the way of Balaam," the New Testament condemns the greed of all who are well paid to tempt God's people to compromise their moral standards.

BALAK [BAY lack]

The king of Moab near the end of the wilderness wanderings of the Israelites.

Because Balak feared the Israelites, he hired Balaam the soothsayer to curse Israel (Num. 22–24; Josh. 24:9). But Balaam blessed Israel instead.

BALANCES

Devices to measure weight. At the time of the Exodus and following, the Israelites probably used the common balances of Egypt. These balances consisted of a vertical stand and a horizontal crossbeam, from each end of which a pan was suspended.

In the Bible, "balances" are often used in a figurative way. The Lord told the Israelites, "You shall have just balances, just weights" (Lev. 19:36; Ezek. 45:10). The "just balances" symbolize honesty, righteousness, justice, and fair dealing (Job 31:6; Ps. 62:9; Prov. 16:11). "False balances" symbolize evil and bring the displeasure and judgment of God (Prov. 11:1; Mic. 6:11). "A pair of scales" (Rev. 6:5), used in connection with the sale of wheat and barley (v. 6), symbolize famine.

BALDNESS

Because the Israelites regarded the hair as a special ornament and glory, the condition of baldness carried a stigma of shame. This way of thinking probably expressed Israel's disgust for the practices of certain pagans, who customarily shaved their heads. To shave one's head was to behave like a Canaanite—a person associated with idolatrous and immoral practices.

Baldhead was a term of contempt and derision hurled by some youths at the prophet Elisha (2 Kin. 2:23). The prophets mention baldness as a sign of mourning (Is. 15:2; Jer. 7:29). Baldness is also used symbolically to indicate the barrenness of Philistia after the judgment of God (Jer. 47:5).

BALM OF GILEAD

A plant product of Gilead exported to such nations as Egypt and Phoenicia. After Joseph's brothers cast him into a pit, they saw an Ishmaelite caravan "coming from Gilead with their camels, bearing spices, balm, and myrrh on their way to carry them down to Egypt" (Gen. 37:25).

Apparently, the balm of Gilead was an aromatic resin used as an incense and a medical ointment used for the healing of wounds. Its identity, however, has not been clearly established. The prophet Jeremiah asked, "Is there no balm in Gilead, / Is there no physician there?" (Jer. 8:22). The New Testament declares that there is a Balm in Gilead: Jesus Christ, the Great Physician.

BALSAM

A thorny tree growing 10 to 15 feet (3 to 5 meters) tall with clusters of green flowers, also known as the Jericho balsam. Some think the lentisk or mastic tree, a shrubby evergreen growing 3 to 10 feet (1 to 3 meters) tall, is meant.

Balsam was highly valued during Bible times (Gen. 37:25; 43:11; Jer. 8:22; 46:11; 51:8; Ezek. 27:17). It produced a fragrant, resinous gum called balm.

This was an article of export (Gen. 37:25) and was given as a gift by Jacob (Gen. 43:11). Balm was used as a symbol in Jeremiah 8:22 to refer to spiritual healing.

BAN

A vow or pledge under which property or persons devoted to pagan worship were destroyed. The Levitical law stated, "No person under the ban [devoted to destruction, NIV] shall be redeemed, but shall surely be put to death" (Lev. 27:29). This was probably the authority under which Joshua destroyed many of the settlements throughout Canaan as the

Hebrew people conquered the land (Josh. 6:17–21).

See also ANATHEMA.

BANNER

A flag, ensign, streamer, or emblem attached to the end of a standard. Banners served as rallying points for military, national, or religious purposes. Four large banner-bearing standards (one on each of the four sides of the tabernacle of meeting) were used by the twelve tribes of Israel during their wilderness journeys (Num. 1:52; 2:2–3). A smaller standard, or banner, was used by each separate tribe (Num. 2:2, 34).

The most common use of banners was for military campaigns. A large signal flag usually was erected on a hill or other high place; it served as a signal for the war trumpets to be blown (Is. 5:26; 18:3; Jer. 4:6).

When the Israelites fought the Amalekites at Rephidim, Moses held up his hand, thus becoming a living banner symbolizing God's presence to help His people win the victory (Ex. 17:8–16). After the battle, Moses built an altar and called it "Jehovah-nissi" (Ex. 17:15, KJV; The Lord Is My Banner; NKJV).

BANQUET

An elaborate meal, frequently given in honor of an individual or for some other special occasion.

Notable Old Testament banquets include that of Ahasuerus (Xerxes I), at which Vashti refused to allow herself to be displayed (Esth. 1); the two banquets of Esther, at which she exposed the plot of Haman to destroy the Jews (Esth. 5:4; 7:2); and that of Belshazzar, at which the gold and silver vessels stolen from the temple by Nebuchadnezzar were used and at which the handwriting appeared on the wall (Dan. 5).

The New Testament speaks of the messianic banquet—a banquet at the end of this age—at which the patriarchs and all the righteous will be guests, but from which the wicked will be excluded (Matt. 8:11; Luke 13:29). The Book of Revelation concludes with all people invited to one or the other of the two banquets. At "the supper of the great God" (Rev. 19:17), the scavenger birds are invited to devour the defeated kings of the earth and their armies; at "the marriage supper of the Lamb" (Rev. 19:9), Christ will have fellowship with the faithful.

BAPTISM

A ritual practiced in the New Testament church that is still used in various forms by different denominations and branches of the Christian church. Baptism involves the application of water to the body of a person. It is frequently thought of as an act by which the believer enters the fellowship of a local congregation or the universal church. Widely differing interpretations of the act exist among Christian groups.

According to the sacramental view of this rite, baptism is a means by which God conveys grace. By undergoing this rite, the person baptized receives remission of sins, and is regenerated or given a new nature and an awakened or strengthened faith.

Other Christian groups think of baptism not as a means by which salvation is brought about, but as a sign and seal of the covenant. The covenant is God's pledge to save humankind. Because of what He has done and what He has promised, God forgives and regenerates. On the one hand, baptism is a sign of the covenant. On the other, it is the means by which people enter into that covenant.

The symbolic view of baptism emphasizes the symbolic nature of the rite by emphasizing that baptism does not cause an inward change or alter a person's relationship to God in any way. Baptism is a sign, or an outward indication, of the inner change that has already occurred in the believer's life. It serves as a public identification of the person with Jesus Christ, and thus also as a public testimony of the change that has occurred. It is an act of initiation. It is baptism *into* the name of Jesus.

Another issue over which Christian groups disagree is the question of who should be baptized. Should only those who have come to a personal, conscious decision of faith be baptized? Or, should children be included in this rite? And if children are proper subjects, should all children, or only the children of believing parents, be baptized?

Groups that practice baptism of infants baptize not only infants but also adults who have come to faith in Christ. One of the arguments proposed in favor of baptizing infants is that entire households were baptized in New Testament times (Acts 16:15, 33). Certainly such households or families must have included children. Consequently, groups who hold this position believe this practice should be extended to the present day.

Groups that hold to the view of believer's baptism insist that baptism should be restricted to those who actually exercise faith. This approach excludes infants, who could not possibly have such faith. The proper candidates for baptism are those who already have experienced the new birth on the basis of their personal faith and who give evidence of this salvation in their lives.

Another major issue about baptism is its method or form—whether by immersion, pouring, or sprinkling. On this issue, Christian groups organize into two major camps—those that insist upon the exclusive use of immersion, and those that permit and practice other forms.

The immersionist group insists that immersion is the only valid form of baptism. One of their strongest arguments revolves around the Greek word for baptism in the New Testament. Its predominant meaning is "to immerse" or "to dip," implying that the candidate was plunged beneath the water.

Holders of the pluralist view of baptism believe that immersion, pouring, and sprinkling are all appropriate forms of baptism. They point out that the Greek word for baptism in the New Testament is sometimes ambiguous in its usage. While its most common meaning in classical Greek was to dip, to plunge, or to immerse, it also carried other meanings as well. Thus, the question cannot be resolved upon linguistic grounds.

BARABBAS [buh RAB bas]

A "robber" (John 18:40) and "notorious prisoner" (Matt. 27:16) who was chosen by the mob in Jerusalem to be released instead of Jesus. Barabbas had been imprisoned for insurrection and murder (Luke 23:19, 25; Mark 15:7). Pilate offered to give the crowd either Jesus or Barabbas. The mob demanded that he release Barabbas and crucify Jesus. Ironically, the name Barabbas probably means "son of the father." There is no further mention of Barabbas after he was released.

BARAK [BAR ack] *(lightning)*

A son of Abinoam of the city of Kedesh. Barak was summoned by Deborah, a prophetess who was judging Israel at that time. Deborah told Barak to raise a militia of 10,000 men to fight Jabin, king of Canaan, who had oppressed Israel for 20 years. The commander-in-chief of Jabin's army was Sisera.

Apparently during the battle, the Lord sent a great thunderstorm. The rain swelled the Kishon River and the plain surrounding the battle area, making Sisera's 900 iron chariots useless (Judg. 5:21). The Israelites routed the Canaanites. The victory is described twice: in prose (Judg. 4) and in poetry, the beautiful "Song of Deborah" (Judg. 5). Barak is listed in the New Testament among the heroes of faith (Heb. 11:32).

BARBARIAN

A person who is different from the dominant class or group. Originally, this term *(barbaros)* had no negative connotation. The Greeks used it to describe anyone who did not speak the Greek language. Later, when Rome conquered Greece and absorbed its culture, the word *barbarian* signified those whose lives were not ordered by Greco-Roman culture.

When the apostle Paul used the phrase "Greeks and barbarians" (Rom. 1:14), he was speaking of all mankind. The "barbarians" (Acts 28:4, KJV) who aided the apostle Paul on the island of Melita do not appear to have been uncivilized. In this instance the word meant something very similar to the word *foreigner.* It is good to remember the apostle Paul's declaration that in Christ all human distinctions disappear (Gal. 3:26–29).

BAR-JESUS [bar GEE zus] *(son of Jesus)*

A false prophet who opposed Barnabas and Paul at Paphos, a town on the island of Cyprus (Acts 13:4–12). He is also called Elymas, which means "magician" or "sorcerer." Bar-Jesus was temporarily struck blind because of his opposition to the gospel.

BARLEY

A grain known since early times. It was well adapted to varied climates, ripening quickly and resistant to heat; it usually was harvested before wheat. Because barley was considered a food for slaves and the very poor, however, it was held in low esteem as a grain.

In the Bible barley was first associated with Egypt (Ex. 9:31). It was used as an offering of jealousy (Num. 5:15), for fodder (1 Kin. 4:28), and for food (Judg. 7:13; John 6:5, 13).

BARNABAS [BAR nuh bus] *(son of encouragement)*

An apostle in the early church (Acts 4:36–37; 11:19–26) and Paul's companion on his first missionary journey (Acts 13:1–15:41). A Levite from the island of Cyprus, Barnabas's given name was Joseph, or Joses (Acts 4:36). When he became a Christian, he sold his land and gave the money to the Jerusalem apostles (Acts 4:36–37).

Early in the history of the church, Barnabas went to Antioch to check on the growth of this early group of Christians. Then he journeyed to Tarsus and brought Saul (as Paul was still called) back to minister with him to the Christians in Antioch (Acts 11:25). At this point Barnabas apparently was the leader of the church at Antioch, because his name is repeatedly mentioned before Paul's in the Book of Acts. But after Saul's name was changed to Paul, Barnabas' name is always mentioned after Paul's (Acts 13:43).

Because of his good reputation, Barnabas was able to calm the fear of Saul among the Christians in Jerusalem (Acts 9:27). He and Saul also brought money from Antioch to the Jerusalem church when it was suffering a great famine (Acts 11:27–30). Shortly thereafter, the Holy Spirit led the Antioch church to commission Barnabas and Paul, along with John Mark, Barnabas's cousin (Col. 4:10), to make a missionary journey (Acts 13:1–3) to Cyprus and the provinces of Asia Minor.

A rift eventually developed between Barnabas and Paul over John Mark (Col. 4:10). Barnabas wanted to take John Mark on their second missionary journey. Paul, however, felt John Mark should stay behind because he had left the first mission at Cyprus (Acts 13:13). Paul and Barnabas went their separate ways, and Barnabas took John Mark with him on a second mission to Cyprus (Acts 15:36–39). A pseudepigraphic epistle named after Barnabas is falsely attributed to him.

BARRENNESS

The condition of being unable to bear children. In the Bible, the term is also applied figuratively to anything that is unproductive, such as land (2 Kin. 2:19) or a nation (Is. 54:1). In the Old Testament, barrenness was looked on as a curse or punishment from God (Gen. 16:2; 20:18; 1 Sam. 1:5–7). Old Testament women who are described as barren include Sarah, Rebekah, Rachel, and Hannah (Gen. 11:30; 25:21; 29:31; Judg. 13:2–3; 1 Sam. 2:5).

BARTHOLOMEW [bar THOL oh mew] (son of Tolmai)

One of the twelve apostles of Jesus, according to the four lists given in the New Testament (Matt. 10:3; Mark 3:18; Luke 6:14; Acts 1:13). Many scholars equate Bartholomew with Nathanael (John 1:45–49), but no proof of this identification exists, except by inference. According to church tradition, Bartholomew was a missionary to various countries, such as Armenia and India. He is reported to have preached the gospel along with Philip and Thomas. According to another tradition, he was crucified upside down after being flayed alive.

BARTIMAEUS [bar tih MEE us] (son of Timaeus)

A blind man of Jericho healed by Jesus (Mark 10:46–52). As he sat by the road begging, Bartimaeus cried out, "Jesus, Son of David, have mercy on me!" (v. 47).

Jesus replied, "Go your way; your faith has made you well" (v. 52).

BARUCH [bah RUKE] (blessed)

The scribe or secretary of Jeremiah the prophet (Jer. 32:12–16; 36:1–32; 45:1–5). A son of Neriah, Baruch was a member of a prominent Jewish family. In the fourth year of the reign of Jehoiakim, king of Judah (605 B.C.), Baruch wrote Jeremiah's prophecies of destruction from the prophet's dictation (Jer. 36:1–8). Baruch read Jeremiah's words publicly on a day of fasting, then read them to the officials of the king's court. A clay seal inscribed "Baruch son of Neriah the scribe," dating from Jeremiah's time and clearly belonging to his secretary (see Jer. 36:32), was recently discovered in a burned archive in Israel.

BARZILLAI [bar ZILL ay eye] (made of iron)

A member of the tribe of Gilead from Rogelim who brought provisions to David and his army at Mahanaim, where they had fled from Absalom (2 Sam. 17:27–29). On his deathbed, David remembered Barzillai's kindness and reminded Solomon to care for his children (1 Kin. 2:7).

BASHAN [BAY shan]

The territory east of the Jordan River and the Sea of Galilee. At the time of the Exodus, King Og ruled Bashan. His kingdom included 60 cities (Num. 21:33; Deut. 3:4; 29:7). His capital was at Ashtaroth. When Og was defeated at Edrei (Deut. 3:1–3), the territory was given to the half-tribe of Manasseh (Deut. 3:13), except for the cities of Golan and Be Eshterah, which were given to the Levites (Josh. 21:27). In the days of Jehu, the region was captured by the Aramean king, Hazael (2 Kin. 10:32–33).

A rich, fertile tableland about 1,600 to 2,300 feet (490 to 700 meters) above sea

B

level, with abundant rainfall and volcanic soil, Bashan became the "breadbasket" of the region. Wheat fields and livestock were abundant. But in the Old Testament, the prosperity of Bashan became a symbol of selfish indulgence and arrogant pride. Evil persons who attacked the righteous were compared to "strong bulls of Bashan" (Ps. 22:12). The pampered, pleasure-seeking women of Samaria were called "cows of Bashan" (Amos 4:1).

BASKET

A container made of woven cane or other fibers. Baskets were fashioned out of various materials: willow, rush, palmleaf twigs, and even a mixture of straw and clay. Some had handles and lids. They were used for carrying bread (Gen. 40:17), for grape-gathering (Jer. 6:9), for holding the offered firstfruits (Deut. 26:2), for carrying various fruits (Jer. 24:1), for carrying clay to the brickyard (Ps. 81:6), or for holding bulky articles (2 Kin. 10:7). The most ingenious use of these containers was when Paul was lowered in a basket over a wall to escape his foes (Acts 9:25; 2 Cor. 11:33).

BATHING

A washing or soaking of the body in water for cleansing. Water was scarce in Bible times, but laws of ritual demanded much washing. The Israelites washed their hands after returning from the market, before meals, and at many other times; and they immersed their bodies before entering the synagogue or temple courts. Archaeologists have discovered such ritual baths close to the broad steps leading up to Herod's temple, as well as many other archaeological sites.

Bathing for the purpose of physical cleansing or hygiene is seldom mentioned in the Bible. Bathsheba was bathing when David spied her from his rooftop (2 Sam. 11:2). Pharaoh's daughter was on her way to the river to bathe when she found the baby Moses (Ex. 2:5, NRSV). At Masada, Herod had splendid Greco-Roman baths with hot and cold water rooms. Archaeologists have discovered a swimming pool in Herod's palace at Jericho. According to the Jewish historian Josephus, it was the scene of Herod's murder of a young priest by drowning.

Even before Abraham's time, the homes of Ur in ancient Mesopotamia had a tile drain in the entryway. A servant met visitors, removed their sandals, and washed their feet. Jesus taught the lesson of becoming a servant by washing the disciples' feet (John 13:3–17). If the home had no servant, it was the wife's duty to perform this task. Therefore, Paul describes the faithful widow as one who has "brought up children . . . lodged strangers . . . washed the saints' feet" (1 Tim. 5:10).

BATHSHEBA [bath SHE buh] (daughter of oath)

A wife of Uriah the Hittite and of King David (2 Sam. 11; 12:24). Standing on the flat roof of his palace in Jerusalem one evening, David saw the beautiful Bathsheba bathing on the roof of a nearby house. With his passion aroused, David committed adultery with Bathsheba. Out of that union Bathsheba conceived a child.

When David discovered her pregnancy, he hurriedly sent for Uriah, who was in battle with the Ammonites. But Uriah refused to engage in marital relations with his wife while his companions were involved in battle. When David's attempt to trick Uriah failed, he sent him back into battle. This time, David ordered that Uriah be placed at the front of the battle and that his fellow soldiers retreat from him, so that he might be killed. After a period of mourning, Bathsheba became David's wife (2 Sam.

11:27). But the child conceived in adultery died.

When Nathan the prophet confronted David with the enormity of his sin, David repented (2 Sam. 12:13). God blessed them with four more children—Shammua (or Shimea), Shobab, Nathan, and Solomon (1 Chr. 3:5). The New Testament mentions Bathsheba indirectly in the genealogy of Jesus (Matt. 1:6). Bathsheba is also called Bathshua (1 Chr. 3:5).

BATTERING RAM

A war machine used to destroy a city's walls (Ezek. 26:9; engine of war in KJV). Although the battering ram was made in many shapes and sizes, a typical one featured a long, pointed pole that was driven with great force against a fortified city's massive stone walls. It took a crew of several men to operate the battering ram. Many models provided extensive protection for the crew, since the city's defenders usually fired upon them as they worked. The whole machine was mounted on wheels for easy movement. The prophet Ezekiel showed a knowledge of the use of battering rams (Ezek. 4:2; 21:22).

BATTLEMENT

A protective wall surrounding the flat roofs of houses in Bible times. This wall was required by law (Deut. 22:8, KJV) to prevent accidental injuries by falling. "Battlements" (Jer. 5:10, KJV) on a city wall protected soldiers from enemy attack (Song 8:9, NKJV, NRSV).

BDELLIUM

A substance found in Havilah in Arabia, a land noted for its precious stones and aromatic gum. With the same color as manna, bdellium was considered to be a gum resin (Num. 11:7). In the Numbers passage, the word for bdellium is rendered as bdellium (REB) and resin (NIV) by some translations. But in Genesis 2:12, bdellium was associated with gold and therefore it was considered a precious stone. Some scholars suggest that bdellium jewels were pearls from the Persian Gulf.

BEAR

In Old Testament times, bears were a threat to other animals as well as people. They ate honey, fruit, and livestock; so they harmed both crops and herds. Bears are easily angered, and the Asian black bear is exceptionally fierce. This bear is prone to attack people, with or without provocation, as did the two female bears that mauled the boys who taunted the prophet Elisha (2 Kin. 2:24). It was a mark of David's courage that he killed a bear that stole from his father's flock (1 Sam. 17:34–37).

A bear "robbed of her cubs" (2 Sam. 17:8) was legendary because of her fierceness. Since bears are rather clumsy, they sometimes lie in ambush, waiting for prey to come to them (Lam. 3:10). The era of peace will arrive when, as Isaiah 11:7 predicts, "the cow and the bear shall graze" side by side.

BEATITUDES, THE

The eight declarations of blessedness made by Jesus at the beginning of the Sermon on the Mount (Matt. 5:3–12), each beginning with "Blessed are . . ." The Greek word translated *blessed* means "having spiritual well-being and prosperity," the deep joy of the soul (see also Luke 6:20–22). The blessed have a share in salvation, and have entered the kingdom of God, experiencing a foretaste of heaven.

The Beatitudes describe the ideal disciple, and his rewards, both present and future. The person whom Jesus describes in this passage has a different quality of character and lifestyle than those still "outside the kingdom." As a literary form, the beatitude is also found often in the Old Testament, especially in the Psalms (1:1; 34:8; 65:4; 128:1), and often in the New Testament also (John 20:29; Rom. 14:22; James 1:12; Rev. 14:13).

See also SERMON ON THE MOUNT.

BED, BEDROOM

A place for reclining and sleeping. Even the best beds in Bible times would be considered uncomfortable by modern standards. Most people slept on a mat spread on the floor. During the day, the mats were rolled up and stored. Sometimes the mats were placed on a raised platform, above cold drafts during the winter time.

The wealthier classes often had an actual bed to sleep on. The simplest bed was a rectangular wooden frame on legs. Ropes or webs of cloth were stretched across the frame, on which a mat was placed. Some of the wealthy had very elaborate bed frames with gold and silver trim and ivory inlay. Amos, in speaking of beds of ivory (Amos 6:4), probably referred to the ivory trim that decorated their beds.

Poor people usually slept in their clothes with a cloak or cover to ward off the cold. Most people of this class had a single cloak that served as both their coat and also as their cover at night. The Mosaic Law forbade the Israelites from keeping a cloak, taken to secure a debt, beyond sunset to make sure the person had a cover to sleep under (Ex. 22:26–27; Deut. 24:13).

In the summer, it was common for people to move onto the roof and sleep in the open. Roofs were usually flat, serving as living quarters when the weather allowed. The houses of the wealthy would frequently have separate sleeping quarters. If the house had two floors, the second story was the preferred location for a bedroom. A Shunammite woman provided Elisha with his own separate room on the roof because he frequently stayed with the woman and her elderly husband. The room was furnished with a bed, a table, a chair, and a lampstand (2 Kin. 4:10). This represented well-equipped sleeping quarters in that day. This is in keeping with the description of the lady as "a notable woman" (v. 8), one of social prominence and wealth.

In the Bible the bed is seen not only as a place to sleep, but also as a place of meditation and prayer. For instance, David meditated on his bed late at night (Ps. 63:6); and the prophets received revelations from God while lying on their beds (1 Sam. 3:3). A bed was also a place of ease and luxury (Amos 6:4), laziness (Prov. 26:14), and scheming (Ps. 36:4).

BEER LAHAI ROI [BEE ear lah HIGH roy] (the well of the Living One who sees me)

A well in the wilderness between Kadesh Barnea and Bered in the Desert of Shur (Gen. 16:14). It received its name when an angel appeared to Hagar in this place. Hagar's son Ishmael lived here both before and after the death of Abraham his father (Gen. 24:62; 25:11).

BEERSHEBA [BEE ur SHE buh] (well of the seven or well of the oath)

The chief city of the Negev. Beersheba was situated in the territory of Simeon (Josh. 19:1–2) and was "at the limits of the tribe of the children of Judah, toward the border of Edom in the South" (Josh. 15:21, 28). Midway between the Mediterranean Sea and the southern end of the Dead Sea, Beersheba was considered the southern extremity of the Promised Land, giving rise to the often-used expression, "from Dan [in the north] to Beersheba" (Judg. 20:1) or "from Beersheba to Dan" (1 Chr. 21:2).

In Beersheba Abraham and Abimelech, king of Gerar (in Philistia), made a covenant and swore an oath of mutual assistance (Gen. 21:31). Abraham pledged to Abimelech seven ewe lambs to bear witness to the sincerity of his oath; from this transaction came the name Beersheba. It was in the Wilderness of Beersheba that Hagar wandered as she fled from Sarah (Gen. 21:33). Abraham dug a well and also planted a tamarisk tree here (Gen. 21:33), and he returned to Beersheba after God prevented him from offering Isaac as a sacrifice on Mount Moriah (Gen. 22:19).

At Beersheba a number of important encounters took place between God and various people. Here God appeared to Hagar (Gen. 21:17), Isaac (Gen. 26:23–33), and Jacob (Gen. 46:1–5). Ancient Beersheba has been identified with a large tract known as Tell es-Saba, situated about 2 miles (3 kilometers) east of the modern city.

BEGGAR

A person who begged for a living. There are very few biblical references to beggars and no term in biblical Hebrew to describe the professional beggar. A person was reduced to begging by divine judgment or wickedness (1 Sam. 1:7–8; Ps. 109:10; Luke 16:3), a physical handicap (Mark 10:46; Luke 18:35; John 9:8), or laziness (Prov. 20:4). God commanded Israel to care for the poor and handicapped, so the presence of beggars indicated Israel's disobedience (Deut. 15:1–11; 8:4, 6–10). In New Testament times, beggars were commonplace. Almsgiving—giving to beggars—was praised as good work contributing to a person's righteousness.

BEHEMOTH

This word could refer to the elephant, hippopotamus, water buffalo, or a mythological monster. The word appears in Job 40:15, where God humbles Job by praising two of His creations, behemoth and Leviathan. Hippopotamus is the best

choice for the precise meaning of behemoth. Hippos submerge themselves in rivers and bask in cool marshes. Yet they can climb up riverbanks and hillsides, devouring vegetation. An angered hippo can bite a man in half or crush a canoe with his enormous jaws.

BELIEVE, BELIEVER

To place one's trust in God's truth; one who takes God at His word and trusts in Him for salvation. Mere assent to God's truth is not saving faith, according to the Bible (John 8:31–46; James 2:14–26). Neither is total commitment of oneself to Jesus as Lord a form of saving faith.

A belief that saves is one that rests in the finished work of Christ; it trusts God alone for salvation (John 3:16). Believers are those who have trusted God with their will as well as their mind (Rom. 1:16; 3:22; 1 Thess. 1:7).

BELSHAZZAR [bell SHAZ zur] (Bel, protect the king)

The oldest son of Nabonidus and the last king of the Neo-Babylonian Empire (Dan. 5:1–2; 7:1; 8:1). According to Daniel 5, Belshazzar was a king given to sensual pleasure. He held a drunken banquet involving his wives, concubines, and a thousand of his lords, or "nobles" (Dan. 5:1, NASB, NIV, REB). At the banquet Belshazzar and his guests drank from the sacred vessels that his "father" (Dan. 5:2)—or grandfather—Nebuchadnezzar had brought from the temple in Jerusalem, thus insulting the captive Jews and their God.

In the midst of the revelry, the fingers of a hand began writing these words on the wall: "MENE, MENE, TEKEL, UPHARSIN" (Dan. 5:25). Daniel tells us that upon seeing these words Belshazzar became troubled "so that the joints of his hips loosened and his knees knocked against each other" (Dan. 5:6).

At the queen's advice, Belshazzar sent

for Daniel, who interpreted the writing as a signal of doom for the Babylonian Empire: "MENE: God has numbered your kingdom, and finished it; TEKEL: You have been weighed in the balances, and found wanting; PERES: Your kingdom has been divided, and given to the Medes and Persians" (Dan. 5:26–28). That very night, the soldiers of Darius the Mede—possibly another name for Cyrus the Persian—captured Babylon, and Belshazzar was killed.

BELT

The belt, made of leather, cloth, or cord, was worn around the waist, much like the belt of today. The Bible mentions belts worn by Elijah (2 Kin. 1:8) and John the Baptist (Matt. 3:4). The rich man's leather belt might hold his sword, dagger, knife, or an inkhorn for writing. The scribe's reed or pen was also carried in the belt (Ezek. 9:2, 11).

When Elijah "girded up his loins" (1 Kin. 18:46), he was probably tucking up the loose ends of his cloak, or outer garment, into his belt. Peter urged the early Christians to "gird up the loins of your mind" (1 Pet. 1:13)—to open themselves to Jesus' message. Agabus bound Paul's hands and feet with his own belt (Acts 21:11).

The sash was longer than the belt. It consisted of a piece of folded cloth wound two or three times around the waist. When made into a pouch, it might serve as a pocket for carrying money, other valuables (Matt. 10:9; Mark 6:8), or even food. Shepherds might even carry a lamb in their sash.

BEN [ben] (son)

A Hebrew word that means "son." Usually it referred to a male descendant, as a prefix in proper names, such as Ben-Ammi, "son of my people" (Gen. 19:38); and Ben-Oni, "son of my sorrow" (Gen. 35:18).

BENEDICTION

A prayer that God may bestow certain blessings on His people. In Old Testament times, a regular part of the temple service was pronouncing the benediction. The form of the priestly benediction was prescribed in the law: "The LORD bless you and keep you; / The LORD make His face shine upon you, / And be gracious to you; / The LORD lift up his countenance upon you, / And give you peace" (Num. 6:24–26).

The so-called apostolic benediction is often used at the conclusion of a Christian worship service: "The grace of the Lord Jesus Christ, and the love of God, and the communion of the Holy Spirit be with you all. Amen" (2 Cor. 13:14).

BEN-HADAD [ben HAY dad] (son of [the god] Hadad)

1. Ben-Hadad I (900–860? B.C.), "the son of Tabrimmon, the son of Hezion, king of Syria" (1 Kin. 15:18). Ben-Hadad I was king of Damascus during the reign of Israel's King Baasha (909–886 B.C.). These two kings joined in an alliance to invade Judah, but King Asa of Judah persuaded Ben-Hadad to change sides by paying him to invade Israel instead (1 Kin. 15:19–20; 2 Chr. 16:1–4). This forced Baasha to withdraw from Judah to protect his own interests. This Ben-Hadad is also known from the famous stone monument he erected after making a treaty with King Pygmalion of Tyre about 860 B.C.

BEN-HADAD [ben HAY dad] (son of [the god] Hadad)

2. Ben-Hadad II (860–843? B.C.), the son of Ben-Hadad I. Ben-Hadad I may have reigned as long as 57 years (900–843 B.C.). If so, the information given here about Ben-Hadad II would properly refer to Ben-Hadad I. However, it is likely that Ben-Hadad I died sometime during the

reign of King Ahab of Israel (874–852 B.C.) and was succeeded by a son, Ben-Hadad II. The Bible does not mention this transition, but Assyrian records from 853 B.C. do mention Hadadezer as king of Damascus. This was probably the throne name used by a new king, Ben-Hadad II.

This Ben-Hadad also continued to invade and oppress the northern kingdom of Israel each year during the reign of King Ahab. Finally, Ahab defeated the Syrians in two successive years and captured Ben-Hadad (1 Kin. 20:1–33). As a price for releasing Ben-Hadad, Ahab received the right for Israelite merchants to trade in the marketplaces of Damascus (1 Kin. 20:34).

In 853 B.C. Ben-Hadad II led a coalition of neighboring nations, including Israel, in a major battle at Qarqar in Syria against the forces of Shalmaneser III, king of Assyria. Shalmaneser, who had been exacting tribute from Syria and Israel under the threat of military destruction, was driven out of Israel. Some time later, Ahab of Israel and King Jehoshaphat of Judah joined forces to attack Ben-Hadad II. Their object was to regain Ramoth Gilead, originally part of Israel. Ahab and Jehoshaphat ignored the unpleasant warning of defeat spoken by Micaiah, a true prophet of the Lord, and were defeated by Ben-Hadad II. Ahab also lost his life in the battle (1 Kin. 22:1–38).

Ben-Hadad II is probably the unnamed "king of Syria" whose officer Naaman was healed of leprosy by the Lord through the prophet Elisha (2 Kin. 5:1–19). Ben-Hadad himself also sent a servant, Hazael, to inquire of Elisha concerning his own illness (2 Kin. 8:7–10). Hazael later murdered Ben-Hadad and became king of Damascus (Syria), just as Elisha had prophesied (2 Kin. 8:12–15). Hazael also oppressed Israel during his reign (2 Kin. 10:32; 13:22). Hazael reigned

as king of Syria from about 843 B.C. to about 798 B.C.

BEN-HADAD [ben HAY dad] *(son of* [the god] *Hadad)*

3. Ben-Hadad III, the son of Hazael. He succeeded his father as king of Damascus about 798 B.C. When the Israelite king Joash (798–782 B.C.) came to power, he won back Israelite territory from Ben-Hadad III, defeating him in battle three times (2 Kin. 13:25). Joash's son, King Jeroboam II, also was successful in battle against Ben-Hadad III and expanded Israel to its full borders (2 Kin. 14:13–28).

Having failed in his battles against Israel, Ben-Hadad III led a coalition of Syrian kings against Zakir, the king of Hamath, who had attempted to expand his kingdom at the expense of the other kings. Ben-Hadad lost this war also. An Aramaic stone monument mentions Ben-Hadad III by name. Eventually, "the palaces of Ben-Hadad" (Amos 1:4) in Damascus were destroyed by invading Assyrian armies, just as the prophet Amos had predicted.

BENAIAH [beh NIE yuh] *(the Lord has built)*

A loyal supporter of David and Solomon (1 Kin. 1:8; 4:4; 1 Chr. 27:5). Benaiah commanded the Cherethites and the Pelethites, David's bodyguard (2 Sam. 8:18; 20:23; 1 Chr. 18:17; 27:5–6). A Levite, Benaiah remained loyal to David when David's son Absalom rebelled. When another of David's sons, Adonijah, tried to seize the king's throne and prevent Solomon from becoming king, Benaiah escorted Solomon to Gihon, where he was anointed king (1 Kin. 1:32–45). Benaiah carried out Solomon's orders to execute Adonijah (1 Kin. 2:25) and Joab (1 Kin. 2:34). Solomon then made Benaiah commander in chief over the army (1 Kin. 2:35; 4:4). Benaiah was famous for three courageous deeds: (1) climbing down into a pit and killing a lion; (2) killing two lion-like warriors of Moab; and (3) killing an Egyptian giant with the giant's own weapon (2 Sam. 23:20–22; 1 Chr. 11:22–24).

BENJAMIN [BEN juh mun] *(son of the right hand* or *son of the south)*

Jacob's youngest son, born to his favorite wife, Rachel (Gen. 35:18, 24). After giving birth to Benjamin, the dying Rachel named him Ben-Oni (Gen. 35:18), which means "son of my pain." But Jacob renamed him Benjamin. When Jacob lost his beloved son Joseph, he became very attached to Benjamin because Benjamin was the only surviving son of Rachel. When his sons went to Egypt in search of food to relieve a famine, Jacob was reluctant to let Benjamin go with them (Gen. 43:1–17).

It is apparent that Joseph also loved Benjamin, his only full brother (Gen. 43:29–34). During this trip Joseph ordered that his silver cup be planted in Benjamin's sack. The reaction of Jacob and Benjamin's brothers shows the great love they had for Benjamin (Gen. 44). Benjamin had five sons and two grandsons, and he became the founder of the tribe that carried his name (Gen. 46:21; Num. 26:38–41; 1 Chr. 7:6–12; 8:1–40).

BENJAMIN, TRIBE OF

The tribe descended from Benjamin (Num. 1:36–37; Judg. 1:21). Its northern boundary ran westward from the Jordan River through Bethel and just south of Lower Beth Horon; its western boundary picked up at this point to Kirjath Jearim; its southern border ran eastward to the northern point of the Dead Sea; and its easternmost limit was the Jordan River (Josh. 18:11–20). The chief towns in this hilly, fertile region were Jerusalem, Jericho, Bethel, Gibeon, Gibeah, and Mizpah (Josh. 18:21–28).

Saul, Israel's first king, was a Benjamite, and the Benjamites supported Saul over David (2 Sam. 2:9, 15; 1 Chr. 12:29). Although the Benjamites continued to show some unrest throughout David's reign (2 Sam. 20:1; Ps. 7), most of the tribe remained loyal to the house of David and became part of the southern kingdom of Judah when Israel divided into two nations (1 Kin. 12:21; Ezra 4:1). Saul of Tarsus, who later became known as the apostle Paul, was a Benjamite (Phil. 3:5).

BEREA [beh REE ah]

A city of Macedonia about 45 miles (73 kilometers) west of Thessalonica (modern Salonika). On his first missionary journey, the apostle Paul preached at Berea (Acts 17:10) with much success. The Bereans were "more fair-minded than those in Thessalonica," because they "searched the Scriptures daily to find out whether these things were so" (Acts 17:11).

BERNICE [ber NIECE] *(victorious)*

The oldest daughter of Herod Agrippa I, who ruled Palestine A.D. 37–44 (Acts 25:13). According to the historian Josephus, she was first married to a man named Marcus and later to her uncle Herod, king of Chalcis, who soon afterward died. She later married Polemo, king of Cilicia, but deserted him shortly after their wedding. Then she made her way to Jerusalem, where she lived with Agrippa II. She was with Agrippa II when the apostle Paul made his defense before him (Acts 25:13, 23; 26:30).

Bernice eventually became a mistress of the Roman emperor Vespasian, then of his son Titus. Bernice and her sister Drusilla (Acts 24:24) were two of the most corrupt and shameless women of their time.

BETH [beth] *(house)*

A prefix used in many compound words, such as Beth Anath (house of Anath) or Beth Arabah (house of the desert). Dozens of place names retained *Beth* as the first half of a two-part name (as Beth Aven, below). In other instances the two parts were merged, yielding such familiar names as Bethel (house of God), Bethlehem (house of bread), and Bethsaida (house of fishing). *Beth* is also the second letter of the Hebrew alphabet.

See Acrostic

BETH AVEN [beth A ven] *(house of idols)*

A town in the hill country of Benjamin east of Bethel and west of Michmash (Josh. 7:2). Some scholars believe Beth Aven was an older name for Ai. The prophet Hosea used the name symbolically to say that Bethel ("house of God") had become Beth Aven ("house of idols") because of the golden calf set up at Bethel by Jeroboam, the first king of the northern kingdom of Israel (1 Kin. 12:28–29).

BETH HORON [beth HOE run] *(house of [the god] Horon)*

Twin towns named after Horon, the Canaanite god of the underworld. The two towns, Upper and Lower Beth Horon (Josh. 16:3, 5), were separated by only a few miles. The towns were situated at the west end of the Ephraimite mountains on the boundary line between the territories of Benjamin and Ephraim. They were assigned to Ephraim and given to the Kohathites (Josh. 21:20–22).

These twin towns were called Upper and Lower because of the great difference in elevation between them. Upper Beth Horon was approximately 2,000 feet (615 meters) above sea level, while Lower Beth Horon was only 1,200 feet (369 meters) above sea level. The steep descent between them provided the best pass through the mountains from Jerusalem to Joppa (modern Jaffa) and the Mediterranean Sea. For this reason both towns became heavily fortified at various pe-

riods in history as a means of defense for Jerusalem.

The historical record of these cities reads like a page out of a war manual. When Joshua overcame the Amorites, in the battle where the sun stood still, "the Lord routed them before Israel, killed them with a great slaughter at Gibeon, [and] chased them along the road that goes to Beth Horon" (Josh. 10:10). When the Philistines fought against King Saul at Michmash, they sent a company of soldiers along the "road to Beth Horon" (1 Sam. 13:18).

BETH SHAN [BETH shan]

A city at the junction of the Jezreel and Jordan valleys. Beth Shan shows evidence of occupation from prehistoric times throughout the biblical period. Archaeologists unearthed 18 separate levels of occupation. This continuous occupation probably was due to natural and geographic factors. The many springs in the area, combined with the intense heat that is characteristic of the Jordan valley, made Beth Shan a garden paradise.

Beth Shan's location at the crossroads of Canaan's two great valleys meant that all traffic through Canaan—from Egypt to Damascus and from the Mediterranean coast to the East—had to pass by the city.

After the Egyptian pharaoh Thutmose III's victory at Megiddo (about 1482 B.C.), the fortress at Beth Shan passed into Egyptian hands for three centuries. Joshua was unable to capture Beth Shan; his infantry could not cope with its iron chariots (Josh. 17:16). Later, the Philistines occupied the city; and after Saul's tragic last battle near Mount Gilboa, the Philistines "put his armor in the temple of Ashtaroth as an offering and "fastened his body to the wall of Beth Shan" (1 Sam. 31:10). That Israel eventually gained control of the city is evidenced by the garrison that Solomon kept here (1 Kin. 4:12). In some places the name occurs as Beth Shean (Josh. 17:11, 16; Judg. 1:27).

During the intertestamental period, the name of Beth Shan was changed to Scythopolis (city of Scythians), which Josephus called the largest of the Decapolis, perhaps meaning it was the capital. In spite of its importance, this city is not mentioned in the New Testament.

BETH SHEMESH [beth SHEH mesh] (house of the sun-god)

A town in the valley of Sorek, 15 miles (24 kilometers) west of Jerusalem. It was situated northwest of Judah's territory near the Philistine border (Josh. 15:10). It was probably the same city as Ir Shemesh (Josh. 19:41), which was allotted to the tribe of Dan. Later, Judah gave Beth Shemesh to the Levites (Josh. 21:16).

After their victory at Aphek (1 Sam. 4), the Philistines took the ark of the covenant to Ashdod and Ekron, cities upon which God's judgment quickly fell (1 Sam. 5). The ark was removed then to Beth Shemesh (1 Sam. 6:10–7:2), where it remained until it was taken to Kirjath Jearim. Later, Beth Shemesh was in the second administrative district of Solomon (1 Kin. 4:9). At Beth Shemesh Israel's king, Jehoash, and Judah's king, Amaziah, met in battle (2 Kin. 14:11–14).

BETHANY [BETH ah nih]

A village on the southeastern slopes of the Mount of Olives about 2 miles (3 kilometers) east of Jerusalem near the road to Jericho (Mark 11:1). Bethany was the scene of some of the most important events of Jesus' life. It was the home of Martha, Mary, and Lazarus and the place where Jesus raised Lazarus from the dead (John 11). During Jesus' final week, He spent at least one night in Bethany (Matt. 21:17). At Bethany Jesus was anointed by Mary in the home of Simon the leper (Matt. 26:6–13). From a site near Bethany, He ascended into heaven (Luke 24:50).

BETHEL [BETH uhl] (house of God)

A city of Canaan about 12 miles (19 kilometers) north of Jerusalem. Bethel is mentioned more often in the Bible than any other city except Jerusalem. It is first mentioned in connection with Abraham, who "pitched his tent with Bethel on the west and . . . built an altar to the Lord" (Gen. 12:8; 13:3). The region around Bethel is still suitable for grazing by livestock.

Jacob, Abraham's grandson, had a lifechanging experience at this site. He had a vision of a staircase reaching into the heavens with the angels of God "ascending and descending on it" (Gen. 28:12). Jacob called the name of that place Bethel, "the house of God" (Gen. 28:19). He erected a pillar at Bethel to mark the spot of his vision (Gen. 28:22; 31:13). Jacob later built an altar at Bethel, where he worshiped the Lord (Gen. 35:1–16).

During Israel's war with the Benjamites in later years (Judg. 20), the children of Israel suffered two disastrous defeats (Judg. 20:21, 25). They went to Bethel (the house of God, NKJV) to inquire of the Lord, since the ark of the covenant was located there (Judg. 20:26–27). At Bethel they built an altar and offered burnt offerings and peace offerings before the Lord. The third battle ended in disaster for the Benjamites. At the end of the war the Israelites returned to Bethel (the house of God, NKJV), built an altar, and again offered burnt offerings and peace offerings (Judg. 21:1–4).

After the death of Solomon and the division of his kingdom, Jeroboam, the king of Israel (the northern kingdom), set up two calves of gold, one in Bethel and

B

one in Dan (1 Kin. 12:29, 32–33). Thus, Bethel became a great center of idolatry (1 Kin. 13:1–32; 2 Kin. 10:29) and the chief sanctuary of Israel (Amos 7:13), rivaling the temple in Jerusalem.

The prophets Jeremiah and Amos denounced Bethel for its idolatries (Jer. 48:13; Amos 5:5–6). Hosea, deploring its great wickedness (Hos. 10:5, 15), called it Beth Aven ("house of idols"), because of the golden calf set up there. Bethel, the house of God, had deteriorated into Beth Aven, the house of idols.

In a religious reformation that sought to restore the true worship of God, King Josiah broke down the altar at Bethel (2 Kin. 23:15). Still later in Israel's history, Bethel was occupied by Jewish people who returned from the captivity in Babylon with Zerubbabel (Ezra 2:28; Neh. 7:32). The place again reverted to the Benjamites (Neh. 11:31). The city was destroyed about 540 B.C. by a great fire. This destruction may have been the work of Nabonidus of Babylon or of the Persians in the period just before Darius. Today the site of Bethel is occupied by a small village called Beitin.

The New Testament does not refer to Bethel, but Jesus must have gone through this area on His trips. The city was situated on the main road from Shechem to Jerusalem.

BETHESDA [buh THEZ duh] *(house of grace)*

A pool in the northeastern part of Jerusalem, near the Sheep Gate. At this pool Jesus healed the man "who had an infirmity thirty-eight years" (John 5:5). Archaeologists have discovered two pools in this vicinity, 55 and 65 feet (16.5 and 19.5 meters) long respectively. The shorter pool had five arches over it with a porch beneath each arch, corresponding to the description given in John 5:2.

The Crusaders later built a church on this site to commemorate the healing miracle that took place.

The man who had been lame for 38 years came to the pool hoping to be cured by its miraculous waters; instead he was healed by the word of Jesus (John 5:1–15).

BETHLEHEM [BETH luh hem] *(house of bread* or *house of* [the god] *Lahmu)*

The birthplace of Jesus Christ. Bethlehem was situated about 5 miles (8 kilometers) south of Jerusalem in the district known as Ephrathah in Judah (Mic. 5:2), a region known for its fertile hills and valleys.

Bethlehem was the burial place of Rachel, the wife of Jacob (Gen. 35:19). The original home of Naomi and her family, it was also the setting for much of the Book of Ruth. Bethlehem also was the ancestral home of David (1 Sam. 17:12) and was rebuilt and fortified by King Rehoboam (2 Chr. 11:6).

The most important Old Testament figure associated with Bethlehem was David, Israel's great king. At Bethlehem Samuel anointed David as Saul's successor (1 Sam. 16:1, 13). Although David made Jerusalem his capital city, he never lost his love for Bethlehem. Second Samuel 23:14–17 is a warm story about David's longing for a drink of water from the well of Bethlehem, which was a Philistine garrison at the time. But when three of David's mighty men broke through the Philistine lines to draw a drink of water, David refused to drink it because it symbolized "the blood of the men who went in jeopardy of their lives" (2 Sam. 23:17).

The prophet Micah predicted that Bethlehem would be the birthplace of the Messiah (Mic. 5:2), a prophecy quoted in Matthew 2:6. It is significant that the King of kings, who was of the house of David, was born in David's ancestral home. According to Luke 2:11, Jesus was born in "the city of David," Bethlehem. Christ, who is the Bread of Life, was cradled in a town whose name means "house of bread."

The Church of the Nativity, which marks the birthplace of the Savior, is one of the best authenticated sites in the Holy Land. The present structure, built over the cave area that served as a stable for the inn, goes back to the time of the Roman emperor Justinian (sixth century A.D.). This church replaces an earlier building, built in A.D. 330 by Helena, the mother of the Roman emperor Constantine.

BETHPHAGE [beth FAY jeh]

A village near Bethany, on or near the road from Jerusalem to Jericho. It has been described as a "suburb" of Jerusalem. The site is mentioned only in connection with Jesus' Triumphal Entry (Matt. 21:1). From Bethphage Jesus sent two of His disciples into the next village to obtain a colt for Him to ride on the Sunday before His crucifixion.

BETHSAIDA [beth SAY ih duh] (house of fishing)

1. Later called Julias, this city was situated 2 miles (3 kilometers) north of the Sea of Galilee and east of the Jordan River. The name Julias was given to it by the tetrarch Philip (Luke 3:1), after Julia, the daughter of Caesar Augustus. In the wilderness near Bethsaida, Jesus fed the 5,000 and healed the multitudes (Luke 9:10–17). It was also in Bethsaida that He restored sight to a blind man (Mark 8:22).

BETHSAIDA [beth SAY ih duh] (house of fishing)

2. The Gospels of Mark, Luke, and John seem to speak of another Bethsaida which was the home of Philip, Andrew, and Peter (John 1:44) and perhaps of James and John (Luke 5:10). This city

was situated northwest of the Sea of Galilee in the fertile plain of Gennesaret (Mark 6:45, 53) near Capernaum (John 6:17) in the province of Galilee (John 12:21).

Some scholars argue that there was only one city called Bethsaida. The Jewish historian Josephus identified the Bethsaida developed by Philip as being near the Jordan in "Lower Gaulanitis." Yet, the Gospels seem to indicate that there was another Bethsaida west of the Jordan River (for example, see Mark 6:45, 53). Philip, Peter, and Andrew were from "Bethsaida of Galilee" (John 12:21). Bethsaida-Julias could not be considered to be "of Galilee." The close connection of Bethsaida with Chorazin (Matt. 11:21) and Capernaum (Matt. 11:23) as the center of Jesus' ministry in Galilee is strong evidence for another Bethsaida situated closer to them.

BETROTHAL

A mutual promise or contract for a future marriage (Deut. 20:7; Jer. 2:2; Luke 1:27).

The selection of the bride was followed by the betrothal, not to be entirely equated with the modern concept of engagement. A betrothal was undertaken by a friend or agent representing the bridegroom and by the parents representing the bride. It was confirmed by oaths and was accompanied with presents to the bride and often to the bride's parents.

The betrothal was celebrated by a feast. In some instances, it was customary for the bridegroom to place a ring, a token of love and fidelity, on the bride's finger. In Hebrew custom, betrothal was actually part of the marriage process. A change of intention by one of the partners after he or she was betrothed was a serious matter, subject in some instances to penalty by fine.

The most important instance of

betrothal in the Bible is the one between Joseph and Mary (Matt. 1:18–19). A Jewish betrothal could be dissolved only by the man's giving the woman a certificate of divorce. A betrothal usually lasted for one year. During that year the couple were known as husband and wife, although they did not have the right to be united sexually.

Betrothal was much more closely linked with marriage than our modern engagement. But the actual marriage took place only when the bridegroom took the bride to his home and the marriage was consummated in the sexual union.

BIBLE, CANON OF THE

The word *canon* means a "rod"—specifically, a rod with graduated marks used for measuring length. This word refers to the list of individual books that were eventually judged as authoritative and included in the Old Testament and the New Testament.

The "Bible" Jesus used was the Hebrew Old Testament, consisting of the Law, the Prophets, and the Writings. He left no instructions about forming a new collection of authoritative writings to stand beside the books that He and His disciples accepted as God's Word. The Old Testament was also the Bible of the early church, but it was the Old Testament as fulfilled by Jesus. Early Christians interpreted the Old Testament in the light of His person and work.

The works and words of Jesus were first communicated in spoken form. The apostles and their associates proclaimed the gospel by word of mouth. Paul taught the believers orally in the churches he founded when he was present. But when he was absent, he communicated through his letters.

Quite early in its history, the church felt a need for a written account of the teachings of Jesus. His teachings did provide the basis for the new Christian way of life. But the church grew so large that many converts were unable to rely on the instructions of those who had heard and memorized the teachings of Jesus. From about A.D. 50 onward, probably more than one written collection of sayings of Jesus circulated in the churches. The earliest written Gospel appears to have been the Gospel of Mark, written about A.D. 64.

When officials of the early church sought to make a list of books about Jesus and the early church that they considered authoritative, they retained the Old Testament, on the authority of Jesus and His apostles. Along with these books they recognized as authoritative the writings of the new age—four Gospels, or biographies on the life and ministry of Jesus; the 13 letters of Paul; and letters of other apostles and their companions. The Gospel collection and the apostolic collection were joined together by the Book of Acts, which served as a sequel to the gospel story, as well as a narrative background for the earlier epistles. The whole was concluded by the Book of Revelation.

The primary standard applied to a book was that it must be written either by an apostle or by someone close to the apostles. This guaranteed that their writing about Jesus and the early church would have the authenticity of an eyewitness account.

BIBLE, INTERPRETATION OF THE

The science and art of biblical interpretation is called hermeneutics. Correct Bible interpretation should answer the question, "How can I understand what this particular passage means?" Several basic principles are at the heart of a sound method of biblical interpretation.

1. Because Scripture is a divine Book, and because of our limitation as humans, prayer is an absolute necessity as

we study the Bible. We must pray that God will bridge the gap that separates us from understanding spiritual things, by having the Holy Spirit teach us (John 14:26; 16:13).

2. The primary rule of biblical interpretation is "context." Many times we approach a passage thinking we already understand it. In the process we read our own meaning into the passage. But interpreting the Bible correctly demands that we listen to what the text itself is saying, and then draw the meaning out of the passage. Only by watching the context carefully and by letting the passage speak for itself do we give Scripture the respect it deserves.

3. Interpreting the Bible correctly is a two-step process. We must first discover what the passage meant in the day and age of the author. Then we must discover its message for us in today's culture. These steps force us to *understand* the meaning of the passage before we *apply* it to our lives.

BIBLE, MAJOR DIVISIONS

The Bible contains two major sections known as the Old Testament and the New Testament. The books of the Old Testament were written over a period of about 1,000 years in the Hebrew language, except for a few selected passages, which were written in Aramaic. The Old Testament tells of the preparation that was made for Christ's coming.

The New Testament was written over a period of about 60 years. The original language in which it was written was Greek. This portion of the Bible tells of Christ's coming, His life and ministry, and the growth of the early church.

The meaning of *testament* from both the Hebrew and the Greek languages is "settlement," "treaty," or "covenant." Of these three English words, covenant best captures the meaning of the word. Thus, the two collections that make up the

Bible can best be described as the books of the old covenant and the books of the new covenant.

The old covenant is the covenant sealed at Mount Sinai in the days of Moses. By this covenant, the living and true God, who had delivered the Israelites from slavery in Egypt, promised to bless them as His special people. The new covenant was announced by Jesus as He spoke to His disciples in the upper room in Jerusalem the night before His death. When He gave them a cup of wine to drink, Jesus declared that this symbolized "the new covenant in My blood" (Luke 22:20). The second covenant is the fulfillment of what was promised in the first.

The Old Testament, or Hebrew Bible, contains three divisions: the Law, the Prophets, and the Writings. The Law consists of Genesis, Exodus, Leviticus, Numbers, and Deuteronomy; this section of the Old Testament is also known as the Pentateuch. The Prophets fall into two subdivisions: the former prophets (Joshua, Judges, 1 and 2 Samuel, and 1 and 2 Kings) and the latter prophets (Isaiah, Jeremiah, Ezekiel, and the Book of the Twelve Prophets—Hosea through Malachi). The rest of the books are gathered together in the Writings: Psalms, Proverbs, Job, Song of Solomon, Ruth, Lamentations, Ecclesiastes, Esther, Daniel, Ezra-Nehemiah (counted as one book), and 1 and 2 Chronicles.

The New Testament opens with five narrative books—the four Gospels and the Acts of the Apostles. The Gospels deal with the ministry, death, and resurrection of Jesus. The Book of Acts continues the story of the development of the early church across the next 30 years. Acts serves as a sequel to the Gospels in general; originally it was written as a sequel to the Gospel of Luke in particular.

Twenty-one letters, or epistles, follow the historical narratives. Thirteen of these letters bear the name of the apostle Paul as writer, while the remaining eight are the work of other apostles or of authors associated with apostles. The last book in the New Testament, the Revelation of John, portrays through visions and symbolic language the accomplishment of God's purpose in the world and the ultimate triumph of Christ.

BIBLE, VERSIONS AND TRANSLATIONS

The Bible was written across a period of several centuries in the languages of Hebrew and Aramaic (Old Testament) and Greek (New Testament). With the changing of nations and cultures across the centuries, these original writings have been translated many times to make the Bible available in different languages. Just as God inspired people to write His Word, He also has preserved the Bible by using human instruments to pass it on to succeeding generations.

The oldest Bible translation in the world was made in Alexandria, Egypt, where the Old Testament was translated from Hebrew into Greek for the benefit of the Greek-speaking Jews of that city. This version (completed some time before 200 B.C.) is commonly called the Septuagint, from *septuaginta* the Latin word for 70 (LXX). This name was selected because of a tradition that the Pentateuch was translated into Greek by about 70 elders of Israel who were brought to Alexandria especially for this purpose.

The Septuagint was based on a Hebrew text much older than most surviving Hebrew manuscripts of the Old Testament. Occasionally, this Greek Old Testament helps scholars to reconstruct the wording of a passage where it has been lost or miscopied by scribes as the text was passed down across the centuries.

The need for a Latin Bible first arose during the second century A.D., when Latin began to replace Greek as the dominant language of the Roman Empire. The first Old Testament sections of the Latin Bible were considered unreliable, since they were actually a translation of a translation. They were based on the Septuagint, which, in turn, was a translation of the Hebrew Bible into Greek. Since the New Testament was written originally in Greek, it was translated directly into the Latin language. Several competing New Testament translations were in use throughout the Latin-speaking world as early as about A.D. 250.

The task of producing one standard Latin Bible to replace these competing translations was entrusted by Damasus, bishop of Rome (366-384), to his secretary Jerome, who completed this work in A.D. 405. Jerome's translation of the Bible is known as the Latin Vulgate. This translation is especially important because it was the medium through which the gospel arrived in Western Europe. It remained the standard version in this part of the world for centuries.

Until the beginning of the sixteenth century, all Bible versions in the languages of the masses of Western Europe were based on the Latin Vulgate. But in the early Middle Ages, parts of the Bible were translated from Latin into several of the dialects of Western Europe. These included versions in the Bohemian, Czech, and Italian languages, as well as the Provencal dialect of southeastern France. But none of these compare in importance with the work of John Wycliffe, pioneering reformer who translated the entire Bible from Latin into the English language in 1384.

More than 200 years passed from the time that Wycliffe's English version was issued until the historic King James Version was published in 1611. These were fruitful years for new versions of the Bible. The stage was set for the monumental King James Bible by several different English translations that were issued during these years: Tyndale's translation of the Bible (1525), Coverdale's English translation (1535), the Great Bible (1539), and the Geneva Bible (1560).

Shortly after James VI of Scotland ascended the throne of England as James I (1603), he convened a conference to settle matters under dispute in the Church of England. The only important result of this conference was an approval to begin work on the King James Version of the English Bible (KJV).

A group of 47 scholars, divided into six teams, was appointed to undertake the work of preparing the new version. When the six groups had completed their task, the final draft was reviewed by a committee of 12. The King James Version was published in 1611.

The new version won wide acceptance among the people of the English-speaking world. Nonsectarian in tone and approach, it did not favor one shade of theological or ecclesiastical opinion over another. The translators had an almost instinctive sense of good English style; the prose rhythms of the version gave it a secure place in the popular memory. Never was a version of the Bible more admirably suited for reading aloud in public.

Although there was resistance to the King James Version at first, it quickly made a place for itself. For more than three centuries it remained "The Bible" throughout the English-speaking world.

During the eighteenth century and the earlier part of the nineteenth century, several private attempts were made at revising the King James Version. The reasons for revision included the outdated English of the KJV, the progress made by scholars in understanding the original languages of the Bible, and the availability of better texts in the original biblical

languages, especially the Greek text of the New Testament.

In 1870 the Church of England initiated plans for a revision. Two groups of revisers were appointed, one for the Old Testament and one for the New. Before long, parallel companies of revisers were set up in the United States. The three installments of the British revision (RV) appeared in 1881, in 1885, and in 1894. The American revision, or American Standard Version (ASV), was released in 1901.

The RV and ASV were solid works of scholarship. The Old Testament revisers had a much better grasp of Hebrew than the original translators of the King James Bible. The New Testament revision was based on a much more accurate Greek text than had been available in 1611. Although the RV and ASV were suitable for Bible study, they did not gain popular acceptance, mainly because their translators paid little attention to style and rhythm as they rendered the biblical languages into English.

The first half of the twentieth century was marked by a succession of brilliant private enterprises in translation. Translations in this category included the Twentieth Century New Testament and the Weymouth, Moffatt, and Goodspeed translations. During this time, several Catholic translations of the Bible were also completed. These included the Knox translation, the Jerusalem Bible, and the New American Bible.

The Revised Standard Version (RSV) is one of the last versions in the long line of English Bible translations that stem from William Tyndale. Although it is a North American production, it has been widely accepted in the whole English-speaking world.

The RSV was launched as a revision of the KJV (1611), RV (1885), and ASV (1901). Authorized by the International Council of Religious Education, it is copyrighted by the Division of Christian Education of the National Council of Churches in the USA. The New Testament first appeared in 1946, the two Testaments in 1952, and the Apocrypha in 1957. The newest version of this Bible is the New Revised Standard Version, issued during the 1990s.

In recent years several prominent and popular English translations have appeared. These include the Revised English Bible, New Living Translation, New American Standard Bible, New International Version, New King James Version, New Century Version, and the Contemporary English Version.

BIBLICAL CRITICISM

The application of one or more techniques in the scientific study of the Bible. Biblical criticism examines the Greek and Hebrew texts (textual criticism), the historical setting of the various parts of the Bible (historical criticism), and various literary questions regarding how, when, where, and why the books of the Bible were first written (literary criticism). These methods of study, when done with reverence for Scripture, should assist a student's appreciation for the inspiration of the Bible.

BIBLICAL ETHICS

Living righteously—doing what is good and refraining from what is evil—in accordance with the will of God. The term refers not to human theories or opinions about what is right and wrong but to God's revealed truth about these matters. Questions of human conduct prevail throughout the Bible. God's revelation through His written Word narrates the story of ethical failure on the part of human beings, God's redeeming grace, and the ethical renewal of His people.

God's people are called to holiness because they are God's people: "You shall therefore be holy, for I am holy" (Lev. 11:45). The New Testament counterpart

to this principle is found in Matthew 5:48: "Therefore you shall be perfect, just as your Father in heaven is perfect."

For the Christian the ultimate standard of ethics is Jesus Christ and His teachings. The Christian is not under the Law of the Old Testament (Eph. 2:14–16). But since the ethical teachings of Jesus sum up the true meaning of the Old Testament Law, following His teachings fulfills the Law. So there is a direct relationship between the concept of righteousness as revealed in the Old Testament and later in the New.

Jesus' commandment to love is the essence of Christian ethics (see Matt. 22:37–40). The apostle Paul also declared that all the commandments are "summed up in this saying, namely, 'You shall love your neighbor as yourself'" (Rom. 13:9–10).

While love is the summary of Christian ethics, the New Testament contains many specific ethical instructions. A basic pattern for this ethical teaching is the contrast between our old existence before faith in Christ and our new existence in Him. Christians are called to leave behind their old conduct and to put on the new (Eph. 4:22–24), to walk in newness of life (Rom. 6:4), and to exhibit the fruit of the Spirit (Gal. 5:22–23).

BIBLICAL THEOLOGY

Theology as it is understood from the perspective of the biblical writers themselves. This category of theology must be carefully distinguished from systematic theology, which systematizes and re-expresses the teachings of the Bible through the use of modern concepts and categories. Biblical theology is *biblical* because it states the theology of the Bible by limiting itself to the language, categories, and perspectives of the biblical writers.

Biblical theologians seek to find the best organizing principle or idea that

B

serves as the center of a biblical theology. Old Testament theologians have suggested such ideas as the covenant, the Lordship of God, the presence of God, and the people of God. New Testament theologians have mentioned the kingdom of God, grace, salvation, resurrection, and kerygma (a summary of the main points in the preaching of the earliest Christians in the Book of Acts).

Any of these concepts can be used as an organizing principle, for all the central concepts of the Bible are related. But certainly one of the most helpful suggestions to come from biblical theologians is the idea of "salvation history." This refers to the saving acts of God in history. It is an ideal organizing principle for both Old and New Testaments.

The history of salvation begins with the call of Abraham and the covenant between Abraham and God (Gen. 12:1–3). This story reaches its conclusion in the coming of Jesus Christ. The election of the nation of Israel as God's special people is not for their sake alone, but for the sake of all the peoples of the world ("in you all the families of the earth shall be blessed," Gen. 12:3). This blessing is ultimately experienced by the church through faith in Jesus Christ.

The New Testament announced the ministry of Jesus as the turning point of the ages, the beginning of the great fulfillment proclaimed by the prophets of the Old Testament. The message of Jesus was that the kingdom of God had arrived. The kingdom was expressed in both the words and deeds of Jesus. The presence of the kingdom depends directly on the presence of the Messianic King.

The death of Jesus was important as the basis of the kingdom. The rule of God in the human heart cannot be experienced in any age, present or future, without the atoning sacrifice that reconciles sinners with a holy God. Thus the death of Jesus became central for the theology of the New Testament. But the resurrection was equally important. In this event, the new order of the new creation broke directly into the present age. The resurrection of Christ was assurance of the truths He had proclaimed, as well as the resurrection of the dead at the end of time.

The pouring out of the Holy Spirit at Pentecost depended on the finished work of Christ in His death and resurrection. This was a certain sign of the new age brought by Christ and the mark of the new people of God, the church. The ministry of the Spirit guarantees that the results of Christ's work are experienced in the believer's life until Jesus returns to earth.

BILDAD [BILL dad]

The second of the "friends" or "comforters" of Job. In his three speeches to Job (Job 8:1–22; 18:1–21; 25:1–6), Bildad expressed the belief that all suffering is the direct result of one's sin. He had little patience with the questionings and searchings of Job. He is called "Bildad the Shuhite" (Job. 2:11), which means he belonged to an Aramean nomadic tribe that lived in the Transjordan area southeast of Canaan.

BINDING AND LOOSING

A phrase describing the authority and power that Jesus assigned to His disciples, allowing them to forbid or allow certain kinds of conduct.

This phrase occurs only twice in the New Testament. In the first instance (Matt. 16:19), Jesus gave Peter "the keys of the kingdom of heaven" and told him, "Whatever you bind on earth will be bound [literally, "shall have been bound"] in heaven, and whatever you loose on earth will be loosed ["shall have been loosed"] in heaven." This means that Peter was granted the authority to pronounce the freedom or condemnation of a person, based on that person's response to the gospel. The tense of the verbs "shall have been" indicates that this fact was already established in the will of the Father.

In Matthew 18:18 the same words were spoken by Jesus to all the disciples, granting them authority in matters of church discipline.

BIRTHRIGHT

A right, privilege, or possession to which a person, especially the firstborn son, was entitled by birth in Bible times. In Israel, as in the rest of the ancient world, the firstborn son enjoyed a favored position. His birthright included a double portion of his father's assets upon his death (Deut. 21:17). Part of the firstborn's benefits also were a special blessing from the father (Gen. 27:27) and the privilege of leadership of the family (Gen. 43:33).

The inheritance rights of the firstborn were protected by law, so the father could not give his benefits to a younger son (Deut. 21:15–17). The firstborn himself, however, could lose the birthright. Because he committed incest with his father's concubine (Gen. 35:22), Reuben lost his favored position (1 Chr. 5:1–2), while Esau sold his birthright to his younger brother Jacob for a stew of lentils (Gen. 25:29–34), or for "one morsel of food" (Heb. 12:16).

Jesus was both the firstborn of his heavenly Father (John 3:16), and his earthly mother, Mary (Luke 2:7); so he enjoyed the rights and privileges of the Jewish birthright. All Christians are His brothers, sharing in His spiritual inheritance (Rom. 8:17). They are counted as "firstborn" by God's grace (Heb. 12:23).

BISHOP

An overseer, elder, or pastor charged with the responsibility of spiritual leadership in a local church in New Testament times. Jesus is called the "Overseer of your souls" (1 Pet. 2:25). In this passage the word is associated with the term *shepherd.* It is also used to identify the leader of a Christian community or the one who filled the office of overseer. In Acts 20:28 the elders of the church at Ephesus summoned to meet Paul are identified as overseers. Their responsibility, given by the Holy Spirit, was "to shepherd the church of God." In Philippians 1 bishops are associated with deacons, and the qualifications are outlined in 1 Timothy 3:2–7 and Titus 1:7–9. Included are standards for his personal and home life, as well as the bishop's relationships with nonbelievers.

In Acts 20:17, 28 and Titus 1:5, 7, the terms *bishop* and *elder* are used synonymously. Also the word *bishop,* or its related words, appears to be synonymous with the word *shepherd,* or its equivalents (Acts 20:28; 1 Pet. 2:25; 5:2).

In his work, the bishop was to oversee the flock of God, to shepherd his people, to protect them from enemies, and to teach, exhort, and encourage. He was to accomplish this primarily by being an example to his people. He was to do this willingly and with an eager spirit, not by coercion or for financial gain. To desire a position as bishop, the apostle Paul declared, was to desire a good work (1 Tim. 3:1).

BITHYNIA [bih THIN ih uh]

A coastal province in northwestern Asia Minor. Bithynia was bounded on the north by the Black Sea, on the south and east by Phrygia and Galatia, and on the west by Mysia. While at Mysia, Paul and Silas decided to go into Bithynia, "but the Spirit did not permit them" (Acts 16:7). Later, however, the gospel reached the province; and many of the citizens of Bithynia became Christians (1 Pet. 1:1–2).

The experience of Paul and Silas illustrates that God's delays are not always denials.

BITTER HERBS

Herbs eaten by the Israelites during the celebration of Passover. Those herbs helped them remember their bitter experience as an enslaved people in Egypt (Ex. 1:14; 12:8; Num. 9:11). These herbs may have included such plants as sorrel, dandelions, and horseradish.

BITUMEN

A mineral substance consisting chiefly of hydrogen and carbon. Mineral pitch and asphalt are forms of bitumen. Highly flammable, its consistency varies from solids to semi-liquids (Is. 34:9). Large deposits of bitumen have been known to exist around the Dead Sea, and in Egypt and Mesopotamia since ancient times.

Bitumen was used as caulking to waterproof Noah's ark (Gen. 6:14) and the basket in which Moses was hidden (Ex. 2:3). It was also used as mortar (Gen. 11:3). The pits into which the kings of Sodom and Gomorrah fell were bitumen pits (Gen. 14:10, NRSV). Various English versions of the Bible translate the word for bitumen as asphalt, slime, tar, or pitch.

BLASPHEMY

The act of cursing, slandering, reviling or showing contempt or lack of reverence for God. In the Old Testament, blaspheming God was a serious crime punishable by death (Lev. 24:15–16). It was a violation of the third commandment, which required that the name and reputation of the Lord be upheld (Ex. 20:7).

The unbelieving Jews of Jesus' day charged Him with blasphemy because they thought of Him only as a man while He claimed to be God's Son (Matt. 9:3). Actually, the lawlessness of the Jews themselves was causing God's name to be blasphemed among the Gentiles (Rom. 2:24). By their bitter opposition to Jesus and His gospel, they themselves were guilty of blasphemy (Acts 18:6). Jesus condemned as blasphemy their attributing the work of the Holy Spirit to Satan (Matt. 12:31–32).

Christians are commanded to avoid behavior that blasphemes the Lord's name and His teaching (1 Tim. 6:1).

BLESS, BLESSING

The act of declaring, or wishing, favor and goodness upon others. The blessing is not only the good effect of words; it also has the power to bring them to pass. In the Bible, important persons blessed those with less power or influence. The patriarchs pronounced benefits upon their children, often near their own deaths (Gen. 49:1–28). Even if spoken by mistake, once a blessing was given it could not be taken back (Gen. 27:33).

Leaders often blessed people, especially when getting ready to leave them. These included Moses (Deut. 33), Joshua (22:6–7), and Jesus (Luke 24:50). Equals could bless each other by being friendly (Gen. 12:3). One can also bless God, showing gratitude to Him (Deut. 8:10) in songs of praise (Ps. 103:1–2).

God also blesses people by giving life, riches, fruitfulness, or plenty (Gen. 1:22, 28). His greatest blessing is turning us from evil (Acts 3:25–26) and forgiving our sins (Rom. 4:7–8).

Cases of the opposite of blessing, or cursing, are often cited in the Bible (Deut. 27:11–26). Although the natural reaction to a curse is to curse back, Christians are called to bless—to ask for the person's benefit (Matt. 5:44).

BLINDNESS

Three types of blindness are mentioned in the Bible: sudden blindness caused by flies and aggravated by dirt, dust, and glare; the gradual blindness caused by old age; and chronic blindness. Paul suffered temporary blindness on the road to Damascus (Acts 9:8). Scripture often refers to old people whose eyes "grew dim" (Gen. 27:1; 48:10; 1 Sam. 4:15). But the Bible more often refers to chronic blindness.

The Israelites had compassion for the blind. In fact, God placed a curse upon those who made the blind wander out of their way (Deut. 27:18). Jesus ministered to many people who were blind. He said, "[God] has anointed me to preach the gospel to the poor. He has sent me to heal the broken-hearted, to preach deliverance to the captives, and recovering of sight to the blind" (Luke 4:18). Jesus healed a man born blind (John 9:1–41); a blind man whose healing was gradual (Mark 8:22–24); two blind men sitting by the wayside (Matt. 20:30–34); and a great number of others (Mark 10:46–52; Luke 7:21).

Blindness was often understood to be a punishment for evildoing. We find examples of this at Sodom (Gen. 19:11); in the Syrian army (2 Kin. 6:18); and in the case of Elymas at Paphos (Acts 13:6–11).

BLOOD

The red fluid circulating in the body that takes nourishment to the body parts and carries away waste. The word *blood* is often used literally in Scripture. Sometimes the word refers to the blood of animals (Gen. 37:31); at other times it refers to human blood (1 Kin. 22:35). The word is also used figuratively in the Bible. It may mean "blood red" (Joel 2:31) or murder (Matt. 27:24). The phrase "flesh and blood" means humanity (Heb. 2:14).

But the most important biblical concept in regard to blood is the spiritual significance of the blood of sacrificial animals. Although some scholars believe the blood primarily means the animal's *life*, most agree that blood refers to the animal's *death*. Most of the Old Testament passages that discuss sacrifices mention the death of the animal, not its life (Lev. 4:4–5). The Bible makes it clear that the satisfaction or payment for human sins was made by the death of a specified animal substitute: "For the life of the flesh is in the blood, and I have given it to you upon the altar to make atonement for your souls; for it is the blood that makes atonement for the soul" (Lev. 17:11).

In the New Testament, this Old Testament idea of sacrifice is applied to Christ's blood. References to the "blood of Christ" always mean the sacrificial death of Jesus on the cross. References to the blood of Christ were made by Paul (Rom. 3:25); Peter (1 Pet. 1:19); John (Rev. 1:5) and the author of Hebrews (Heb. 9:14). Although all have sinned, "we have redemption through His blood, the forgiveness of sins" (Eph. 1:7).

BOAT

A small vessel propelled by oars or a sail; a fishing boat. In the NKJV the word *boat* is found only in the New Testament, in the four Gospels. The boats mentioned are usually associated with the ministry of Jesus and His disciples in the area around the Sea of Galilee. At least four of Jesus' disciples were fishermen—Simon Peter, Andrew, James, and John (Matt. 4:18–22; Mark 1:16–20). On one occasion, when the multitude pressed too closely to Him, Jesus got into a boat and taught the people (Matt. 13:2; Mark 4:1).

BOAZ [BOE az] *(in him is strength)*

A wealthy and honorable man of Bethlehem from the tribe of Judah. He was a kinsman of Elimelech, Naomi's husband, and he became the husband of Ruth, Naomi's widowed daughter-in-law (Ruth 2–4). Through their son Obed, Boaz and Ruth became ancestors of King David and of the Lord Jesus Christ (Matt. 1:5; Booz, KJV).

BODY

The material or physical part of a person, whether alive or dead. Some religions consider the body evil or inferior to the soul, but the Bible teaches that the body is God's good gift to us (Gen. 1:31). It is a necessary ingredient for a fully human existence (Gen. 2:7).

Paul teaches that the body is often the instrument of sin (1 Cor. 6:18); that the body must die as a penalty for sin (Rom. 7:24); and that sin dishonors a person's body (Rom. 1:24). On the other hand, believers in Christ may "put to death the deeds of the body" (Rom. 8:13) and present their bodies as holy sacrifices that please God (Rom. 12:1).

BOILS

This term probably refers to anthrax, a disease that can be transmitted to humans by cattle, sheep, goats, and horses. The disease is caused by a rod-shaped bacterium that forms spores. These spores, in turn, can infect humans, who develop a boil-like lesion with a pustule (blain). In the infectious stage, the blain is called a malignant pustule. God inflicted boils on the Egyptians when the pharaoh refused to let the Hebrews go to the Promised Land (Ex. 9:9–10; blains in KJV). This was also one of the afflictions God threatened to bring upon the Hebrew people because of their grumbling after the Exodus from Egypt (Deut. 28:27; botch in KJV).

Satan was permitted to afflict Job with boils from the top of his head to the tip of his toes (Job 2:7). King Hezekiah also was afflicted with boils (2 Kin. 20:7), which Isaiah cured by applying a poultice of figs. A fresh fig poultice has a drawing effect. Before the advent of antibiotics, this type of treatment for boils was common. Other words for boils

used by different translations of the Bible are sores and scabs.

BOOK

A collection of written sheets, bound together along one edge and protected by a cover. In Bible times a book was almost anything in written form, usually preserved on a scroll, a roll of papyrus, leather, or parchment. Book and scroll were used interchangeably until the second century A.D., when the Codex was introduced. The codex was the first attempt to stack sheets, fasten them together, and bind them on one edge. This forerunner of today's book eliminated the problem of rolling and unrolling several bulky scrolls in order to read a written document.

The Bible sometimes uses the idea of book in a figurative manner. To "eat a book" (Jer. 15:16; Ezek. 2:8–3:3) refers to the need to absorb the Word of God into one's system, just as the body digests food. The Hebrew nation understood exactly what this meant; on their first day of school six-year-old boys were given small cakes with Old Testament verses written on them to eat. They also licked honey off their slates and were admonished to absorb the teachings of the Old Testament just as they had eaten these cakes and honey.

BOOK OF LIFE

A heavenly book in which the names of the righteous (the redeemed or saved) are written. The concept of God's having a "Book of Life" was probably first enunciated by Moses, who prayed that God would blot him out of God's book rather than dooming his fellow Israelites (Ex. 32:32–33). This concept likely arose from the practice of registering people by genealogy (Jer. 22:30; Neh. 7:5, 64) and keeping a record of priests and Levites (Neh. 12:22–23).

At the end of time (Rev. 20:11–15),

those whose names are not written in the Book of Life will be "cast into the lake of fire" (Rev. 20:15). But those whose names appear there (Rev. 21:27) will be allowed to enter the New Jerusalem.

BOOTH

A temporary shelter made of shrubs and tree branches, which protected cattle against the weather (Gen. 33:17). Booths were used also by keepers of vineyards (Is. 1:8) and soldiers on the battlefield (2 Sam. 11:11).

During the Feast of Tabernacles (or Feast of Booths), the Israelites made booths and lived in them for seven days. This was to remind them of their temporary dwellings in the wilderness, when God delivered them from Egyptian bondage (Neh. 8:13–18). The Book of Job uses "booth" as a symbol of the transitory, impermanent security of the wicked (Job 27:18).

BOOTHS, FEAST OF (see

TABERNACLES, FEAST OF).

BOTTLE

A container for carrying liquids (Jer. 13:12). Bottle is actually a mistranslation, since glass bottles as we know them were not in use in Old Testament times. Liquid-carrying containers were made of pottery or leather.

Large pottery jugs were used to carry water from the village well and to store it in the house. Job 38:37 describes the storm clouds as the "bottles of heaven."

As pottery was breakable and unsuitable for many uses, some "bottles" were animal skins (usually goatskins) sewn together and sealed to make them watertight. The Bible contains many references to these skins containing wine (Josh 9:4), water (Ps. 33:7), or milk (Judg. 4:19).

Jesus recognized that wineskins, once they had been used, tend to become brittle. When subjected to the increasing pressure caused by the fermenting process of winemaking, they would burst, causing the loss of the wine (Luke 5:37–38). New skins were more resilient and flexible, able to take the pressure of such fermentation.

Small pottery flasks were used for oil (1 Kin. 17:12) or honey (1 Kin. 14:3). The prophet Jeremiah spoke of one of these honey jars in his object lesson about God's certain destruction of the nation of Judah (Jer. 19:1, 10).

BOW

Bows were the most characteristic weapons of warfare in the Old Testament period, serving often as the decisive element in a battle. Simple bows were used in the prehistoric period, mostly for hunting.

Simple bows, composed of a piece of wood and string, were easy to make. Bows like this did not have much power or range; so the composite bow was developed early in the history of the Near East. The composite bow was a combination of wood and animal horn. This combination of materials provided the bow with the flexibility and strength needed for effective combat. But a composite bow was difficult to use. Thus certain units within an army were specially trained to shoot the bow.

The bow was usually the first weapon fired in an open-field battle, because the archers of the hostile armies could send arrows from long distances. Chariot troops often were equipped with bows. This combination of mobility and firepower made the army a potent war machine. When attacking a city, the archers of the attacking army would try to pick city defenders off the walls. Archers of the defending city would use their bows to try to keep the army from getting close enough to break down the city's defenses.

The destructive agent of a bow was the arrow, a long, slender shaft of wood with a tip of sharp stone or metal. The archer was also equipped with a quiver, a deep, narrow basket constructed especially for arrows.

Bows, arrows, and archers are mentioned often in the Old Testament, beginning with the boy Ishmael, who "became an archer" (Gen. 21:20; expert with the bow in NRSV). Another term for bow used by some translations is "battle bow" (Zech. 9:10, NKJV, NRSV, NIV).

BOWING

The practice of bowing down or bending the knee. In a more pronounced form, it involved prostration, the practice of falling upon the knees, gradually inclining the body, and touching the forehead to the ground. In Bible times such practices were intended to convey an attitude of reverence, respect, humility, and homage toward others. When he met Esau, Jacob "bowed himself to the ground seven times" (Gen. 33:3).

BRACELET

A piece of jewelry, usually of gold or silver, worn on the wrist of women in Bible times (Gen. 24:22; Is. 3:19). King Saul is also described as wearing a bracelet (2 Sam. 1:10), but this was probably an armband worn by the Israelite warriors of his day.

BRASS

True brass is an alloy of copper and zinc. However, when "brass" is mentioned in the Bible, it refers to either copper or bronze (1 Cor. 13:1; Rev. 1:15; 2:18; 9:20). The three words—brass, bronze, and copper—are often used interchangeably in various English translations of the Bible. Copper was in general use relatively early in human history. Numerous refineries have been discovered

in Sinai, Armenia, Syria, and many other places in the ancient world.

Many articles in the ancient world were fashioned from bronze, or brass. These included cooking utensils, shovels, spoons, musical instruments, weapons, and tools. Solomon used copper and bronze in many of the items in the temple (1 Kin. 7:14).

BREAD

A staple food made from flour or meal and mixed with a liquid, usually combined with leaven and kneaded into dough, then shaped into loaves and baked.

Bread played an important role in Israel's worship. During the celebration of Pentecost, "two wave loaves of two-tenths of an ephah . . . of fine flour . . . baked with leaven" were offered with the animal sacrifices (Lev. 23:17). A type of ritualistic bread known as showbread consisted of 12 loaves baked without leaven by the Levites and placed weekly in the tabernacle, and later in the temple (Ex. 25:30). When removed at the end of the week, the loaves were eaten by the priests. The purpose of the showbread was to symbolize God's presence with His people.

When fleeing from bondage in Egypt, the Israelites made unleavened bread, or bread without yeast (Ex. 12:8; 13:6–7). For that reason, the Exodus was remembered annually by eating unleavened bread for a period of seven days (Lev. 23:6). This celebration was called "the Days of Unleavened Bread" (Acts 12:3).

In the New Testament, Satan tempted Jesus by saying, "If You are the Son of God, command that these stones become bread." But Jesus answered, "It is written, 'Man shall not live by bread alone, but by every word that proceeds from the mouth of God'" (Matt. 4:3–4).

In the Lord's Prayer, Jesus taught his disciples to pray, "Give us this day our daily bread" (Matt. 5:11). In the Gospel of John, Jesus called Himself "the true bread from heaven" (5:32), "the bread of God" (5:33), "the bread of life" (5:34), and "the bread which came down from heaven" (5:41). The Old Testament background for these references is the manna that fell miraculously from heaven to sustain God's people during the Exodus (Ex. 16). Symbolically, Jesus is the heavenly manna, the spiritual or supernatural bread given by the heavenly Father to those who ask, seek, and knock (Rev. 2:17).

On the night before His crucifixion, Jesus instituted the Lord's Supper: "And as they were eating, Jesus took bread, blessed it and broke it, and gave it to the disciples and said, 'Take, eat; this is My body'" (Matt. 26:26). By His sacrifice, Christ became the Bread of Life for His people, that they may eat of Him and find forgiveness of sin and eternal life.

Bread is also spoken of often in figurative language in the Bible. "The bread of tears" (Ps. 80:5) and "the bread of sorrows" (Ps. 127:2) refer to food eaten in grief and distress. The "bread of mourners" (Hos. 9:4) is bread eaten at the time of death. The "bread of adversity" symbolizes hardship (Is. 30:20). The virtuous woman does not eat "the bread of idleness" (Prov. 31:27); she is diligent, hardworking, and productive.

Securing bread "without money and without price" (Is. 55:1) is finding that free gift of God that not only satisfies spiritual needs, but also bestows abundant life.

BREATH

Since breathing is the most obvious sign of life, the phrase "breath of life" is used frequently in the Bible to mean "alive" or "living" (Gen. 2:7; 6:17). Breath is recognized as the gift of God to His creatures (Job 12:10). The word *breath* may be used figuratively, as when Jesus "breathed" the Holy Spirit upon His disciples (John 20:22).

BRICK

A common building material in the ancient world, usually rectangular in shape and composed of clay or mud, along with other ingredients such as straw (Ex. 5:7–9) or sand. Bricks were usually baked by the sun; but they could also be fired in a kiln, or oven, to produce greater strength and hardness. Fired bricks were most common in Roman times, although they were made earlier, especially in Mesopotamia. An allusion to the process of firing bricks is found in the story of the Tower of Babel (Gen. 11:3).

The earliest bricks were shaped by hand; later, they were formed with wooden molds. Brickmaking involved several stages. A good clay source was absolutely necessary; then the clay was sifted and mixed to the desired consistency by adding water. Generally, a temper, often straw, was added; this temper acted as a binder for poor clays and prevented warping and cracking during the drying process. Following this, the bricks were shaped and then dried. Bricks were often inscribed with an official's name, the name of a building, or a dedicatory inscription.

The Bible contains a few references to brickmaking. David forced the defeated Ammonites to labor at the brickworks (2 Sam. 12:31). The pharaoh in Egypt withheld straw from the Israelite brickmakers while demanding that they maintain the daily quota of brick production (Ex. 5:7–9).

BRIDE

In biblical times, it was customary for fathers to select wives for their sons (Gen. 38:6). In the Old Testament, the word *marriage* is used to describe God's spiritual relationship with His chosen people, Israel (Ps. 45; Is. 54:6). When

God's people fell into sin, especially idolatry, the sin was likened to adultery on the part of a wife (Jer. 3:1–20).

In the New Testament, the analogy is continued: Christ is the Bridegroom (John 3:29), and the church is His bride (Eph. 5:25–33; Rev. 21:2). The apostle Paul counsels husbands and wives to imitate the spiritual closeness and love that Christ has for His bride, the church (Eph. 5:22–33).

BRIMSTONE

A bright yellow mineral usually found near active volcanoes. Large deposits of this substance are found in the Dead Sea region. Highly combustible, it burns with a very disagreeable odor. Brimstone (burning stone) is often associated with fire (Rev. 9:17–18; 20:10; 21:8), and with barrenness and devastation (Deut. 29:23; Job 18:15). Brimstone was considered an agent of God's judgment (Gen. 19:24). In the New Testament, it is used symbolically to represent God's wrath and the future punishment of the wicked (Rev. 9:17–18; 14:10; 20:10).

BRONZE SEA

A huge basin made of cast bronze near the entrance of the temple and in front of the altar (1 Kin. 7:23–26). The bronze sea, about 15 feet (4.5 meters) in diameter, was cast by Hiram, a bronze worker employed by Solomon (1 Kin. 7:13–14). The bronze sea was supported by 12 oxen—or bulls—consisting of three animals pointing toward each of the four points of the compass. According to 2 Chronicles 4:6, the purpose of the sea was "for the priests to wash in." The Babylonians broke the bronze sea and carried the pieces to Babylon (2 Kin. 25:13).

BRONZE SERPENT

A metal image that Moses raised on a pole in the wilderness at God's command to save the Israelites from death (Num. 21:4–9).

Israel's unbelief and rebellion during the Exodus from Egypt resulted in God's judgment. God sent "fiery serpents" (Num. 21:6; poisonous or venomous snakes in REB, NIV), and many Israelites were bitten. Because they repented and begged for deliverance, God instructed Moses to make a bronze serpent (serpent of brass in KJV) and place it on a pole. All who looked at the bronze serpent were saved from death.

When the Israelites entered the land of Canaan, they carried the bronze serpent with them and preserved it until the time of Hezekiah, king of Judah (715–686 B.C.). During his religious reform, Hezekiah destroyed the image because it had been turned into an idol that the people regarded with superstitious reverence (2 Kin. 18:4).

Jesus compared His coming crucifixion to this saving event in the wilderness: "As Moses lifted up the serpent in the wilderness, even so must the Son of man be lifted up, that whoever believes in Him should not perish but have eternal life" (John 3:14–15). Just as the bronze serpent brought deliverance from poisonous snakes, so the Son of Man would be raised to deliver His people from sin. Just as the Israelites had to look in faith at the bronze serpent to be saved from death, so we must look in faith at the crucified Christ to have eternal life.

BROTHERLY LOVE

The love of brothers (or sisters) for one another; the love of fellow Christians for one another, all being children of the same Father in a special sense.

In the Old Testament, Israelites were taught not to hate their brothers: "You shall not hate your brother in your heart . . . but you shall love your neighbor as yourself" (Lev. 19:17–18). This emphasis is continued and is made even more positive in the New Testament. Believers are exhorted to "be kindly affectionate to one another with brotherly love" (Rom. 12:10), to "let brotherly love continue" (Heb. 13:1), to "love the brotherhood" (1 Pet. 2:17), and to "love as brothers" (1 Pet. 3:8).

BURIAL

The interment of the dead. Due to the hot climate of Canaan, dead bodies decayed rapidly, so burial usually took place within a few hours after death. If someone died late in the day, burial took place the next day, but always within 24 hours after death.

When death occurred, the oldest son or nearest of kin closed the eyes of the dead (Gen. 46:4), and the mouth was closed and the jaws bound up (John 11:44). After the body was washed (Acts 9:37), it was usually wrapped in cloth. The wealthy used linen with spices placed between the folds (John 19:40).

The Hebrews did not follow the Greek custom of cremation, except in an emergency, such as in the case of Saul and his sons, who were killed by the Philistines (1 Sam. 31:12). After the valiant men had burned the bodies of Saul and his sons, however, they buried their bones (1 Sam. 31:13).

Neither did the Israelites generally use coffins or embalm their dead. The only biblical mention of a coffin (KJV) is in the Egyptian context of Genesis 50:26, where

BRONZE SERPENT

it may refer to a sarcophagus made of limestone. After it was wrapped, the body was placed on a bier and taken to the burial place (2 Sam. 3:31–32).

Depending upon economic and social status, burial was either in a shallow grave covered with stones or in a cave or tomb hewn out of stone. A tomb was made secure by rolling a circular stone over the entrance and sealing it (Mark 16:3–4). This was done to secure the body from animals. Graves were often marked with a large, upright stone.

For a body not to be buried was considered a great shame and a sign of God's judgment (1 Kin. 14:11; 2 Kin. 9:36–37). Unburied bodies polluted the land (Ezek. 39:11–16).

The Egyptians and the Babylonians took great pains to prepare their dead for the afterlife. Personal belongings, as well as food and drink, were often placed in the graves. The Egyptians perfected the intricate process of mummification, which included embalming. In the interiors of the pyramids, the mummified bodies of Egyptian royalty were buried. Babylonians, Greeks, and Romans often cremated their dead and deposited their ashes in ornate funeral urns.

See also EMBALMING.

BURNING BUSH

The flaming shrub at Mount Horeb through which Moses became aware of the presence of God (Ex. 3:2–4). Attracted by the phenomenon, Moses turned aside to see why the bush did not burn. Some scholars believe the burning bush symbolized Israel, which had endured and survived the "fiery trial" of Egyptian bondage. The bush may have been a thornbush.

BURNT OFFERING

This kind of offering was described as "that which goes up (to God)." It was termed "whole" (Lev. 6:22) because the entire offering was to be burnt upon the altar. It was termed "continual" (Ex. 29:38–42) to teach the nation of Israel that their sinfulness required a complete and continual atonement and consecration. This sacrifice, offered every morning and evening, pointed to Christ's atoning death for sinners (2 Cor. 5:21) and His total consecration to God (Luke 2:49). The burnt offering spoke of Christ's passive obedience and His submission to the penalty required by human sinfulness. It also refers to His perfect obedience to God's law by which He did for us what we are unable to do for ourselves.

C

CAESAREA [sess uh REE uh]
(pertaining to Caesar)

An important biblical seaport located south of modern Haifa. Built at enormous expense by Herod the Great between 25 and 13 B.C., and named in honor of Caesar Augustus, the city was sometimes called Caesarea of Palestine to distinguish it from Caesarea Philippi.

Herod spent 12 years building his sea-

port jewel on the site of an ancient Phoenician city named Strato's Tower. He constructed a huge breakwater. The enormous stones he used in this project were 50 feet (15.25 meters) long, 18 feet (5.5 meters) wide, and 9 feet (2.75 meters) deep. Some of them still can be seen extending 150 feet (45.75 meters) from the shore.

Caesarea frequently was the scene of

disturbances as cities of mixed Jewish-Gentile population tended to be. When Pilate was prefect (governor) of Judea, he lived in the governor's residence at Caesarea. In 1961, a stone inscribed with his name was found in the ruins of an ancient amphitheater there. Philip the evangelist preached there (Acts 8:40), and Peter was sent to Caesarea to minister to the Roman centurion Cornelius (Acts 10:1, 24; 11:11). Herod Agrippa I died at Caesarea, being "eaten of worms" (Acts 12:19–23).

Caesarea was prominent in the ministry of the apostle Paul as well. After Paul's conversion, some brethren brought him to the port at Caesarea to escape the Hellenists and sail to his hometown of Tarsus (Acts 9:30). Paul made Caesarea his port of call after both his second and third missionary journeys (Acts 18:22; 21:8). Felix sent Paul to Caesarea for trial (Acts 23:23, 33) and the apostle spent two years in prison before making his celebrated defense before Festus and Agrippa (Acts 26). Paul sailed from the harbor in chains to appeal his case before the emperor in Rome (Acts 25:11; 26:1–13).

CAESAREA PHILIPPI [sess uh REE uh FILL uh pie] *(Caesar's city of Philip)*

A city on the southwestern slope of Mount Hermon and at the northernmost extent of Jesus' ministry (Matt. 16:13; Mark 8:27). In New Testament times the city was known as Paneas, although Philip the tetrarch renamed the city Caesarea Philippi, in honor of the Roman emperor Augustus Caesar. Agrippa II later changed its name to Neronias, in honor of Nero. The present-day village of Baniyas is built on the same site. It was near Caesarea Philippi that Jesus asked His disciples who He was and received the inspired answer from Simon Peter: "You are the Christ, the Son of the living God" (Matt. 16:16).

CAIAPHAS [KY uh fuhs]

The high priest of Israel appointed about A.D. 18 by the Roman procurator, Valerius Gratus. Caiaphas and his father-in-law, Annas, were high priests when John the Baptist began his preaching (Matt. 26:3, 57; Luke 3:2). Caiaphas also was a member of the Sadducees.

After Jesus raised Lazarus from the dead, the Jewish leaders became alarmed at Jesus' increasing popularity. The Sanhedrin quickly called a meeting, during which Caiaphas called for Jesus' death. As high priest, Caiaphas's words carried great authority, and his counsel was followed (John 11:49–53). Subsequently, Caiaphas plotted the arrest of Jesus (Matt. 26:3–4) and was a participant in the illegal trial of Jesus (Matt. 26:57–68).

The final appearance of Caiaphas in the New Testament was at the trial of Peter and John. He was one of the leaders who questioned the two disciples about the miraculous healing of the lame man "at the gate of the temple which is called Beautiful" (Acts 4:6–7). In 1990, an ornate ossuary bearing the name of Caiaphas and containing the bones of a 60-year-old man was found outside Jerusalem. The bones may be those of Caiaphas himself.

CAIN [kane] *(metalworker)*

The oldest son of Adam and Eve and the brother of Abel (Gen. 4:1–25). Cain was the first murderer. A farmer by occupation, Cain brought fruits of the ground as a sacrifice to God. His brother Abel, a shepherd, sacrificed a lamb from his flock. The Lord accepted Abel's offering but rejected Cain's (Gen. 4:7). The proof of Cain's wrong standing before God is seen in his impulse to kill his brother, Abel, when his own offering was rejected (Gen. 4:8). Cain was the ancestor of a clan of metalworkers (Gen. 4:18–19, 22).

The New Testament refers to Cain in three places. Abel's offering to God was "a more excellent sacrifice" than Cain's because Abel was "righteous." His heart was right with God, and Cain's was not (Heb. 11:4). John calls Cain "the wicked one" and asks why he murdered his brother; the answer was, "Because his works were evil, and his brother's righteous" (1 John 3:12). Jude warns his readers to beware of those who have "gone in the way of Cain" (Jude 11).

CALAH [KAY luh]

A city of Assyria that, according to Genesis 10:8–12, was built by Nimrod. Located where the Tigris and Zab rivers come together, Calah was rebuilt and fortified by Shalmaneser I (about 1274–1245 B.C.) and was made the place where the Assyrian king lived by Ashurnasirpal (about 884–859 B.C.). The ruins of this city, now called Nimrud, are situated approximately 18 miles (29 kilometers) south of Nineveh.

CALEB [KAY lubb] (dog)

One of the 12 spies sent by Moses to investigate the land of Canaan (Num. 13:6, 30; 14:6, 24, 30, 38). Ten of the 12 spies frightened the Israelites with reports of fortified cities and gigantic peoples. Compared to the giants in the land, they saw themselves as "grasshoppers" (Num. 13:33).

Joshua and Caleb also saw the fortified cities in the land, but they reacted in faith rather than fear. They advised Moses and Aaron and the Israelites to attack Canaan immediately (Num. 13:30). The Israelites listened to the spies rather than the two, and the Lord viewed their fear as a lack of faith and judged them for their spiritual timidity. Of all the adults alive at that time, only Caleb and Joshua would live to possess the land (Josh. 14:6–15).

Caleb was also part of the group selected by Moses to help divide the land among the tribes. He was 85 years old when Canaan was finally conquered. Hebron was given to Caleb as a divine inheritance.

CALL, CALLING

God's call of individuals to salvation, made possible by the sacrifice of Jesus Christ on the cross (Rom. 8:28–30; 1 Thess. 2:12). God's call to salvation also involves believers in the high calling of living their lives in service to others (1 Cor. 7:20).

CALNEH [KAL neh]

A city in Mesopotamia whose exact location is unknown. In Genesis 10:10 it is included among the cities of the kingdom of Nimrod, the mighty hunter. This suggests a location in southern Mesopotamia. However, Amos 6:1–2 includes Calneh in a list of cities in northern Mesopotamia. There may have been two places with this name, or perhaps the northern town was later named after the earlier settlement. Calno (Is. 10:9) may be identical with Calneh.

CALNO [KAL no]

A city conquered by the Assyrians (Is. 10:9). Isaiah the prophet reported the arrogant boast of the Assyrians, who said that just as Calno had fallen, so would Jerusalem. Calno is probably the same place as Calneh (Gen 10:10; Amos 6:2).

CALVARY [KAL vuh rih] (from the Latin word calvaria, "the skull")

The name used in the KJV and NKJV for the place outside Jerusalem where the Lord Jesus was crucified (Luke 23:33; the Skull in NIV). No one knows for sure why this place was called "the skull." The most likely reason is that the site was a place of execution; the skull is a widely recognized symbol for death. The site may have been associated with a cemetery, although its location near Jerusalem makes it improbable that skulls could be viewed there. Perhaps the area was an outcropping of rock that in some way resembled a skull.

Mark 15:40 and Luke 23:49 indicate that some people viewed Jesus' crucifixion from a distance. John 19:20 says the place was "near the city" of Jerusalem; and Hebrews 13:12 reports that our Lord "suffered outside the gate," which means outside the city walls. From Matthew's reference to "those who passed by" (27:39), it seems the site was close to a well-traveled road. It also is reasonable to think that Joseph's tomb (John 19:41) was quite close. But the Bible does not clearly indicate exactly where Jesus died.

Sites of the crucifixion have been proposed on every side of Jerusalem. One factor that makes it difficult to pinpoint the site is that Jerusalem was destroyed in A.D. 70 by the Romans, and another Jewish revolt was crushed in a similar manner in A.D. 135. Many geographical features and the location of the city walls were greatly changed because of these and a series of conflicts that continued for centuries.

Except in areas that have been excavated, Jerusalem's present walls date from more recent times. The presence of modern buildings prevents digging to find where the walls were located during New Testament times. Some groups claim to have found the very place where Jesus died, but these complicating factors make it unlikely.

At present, Christian opinion is divided over two possible sites for Calvary. One is on the grounds of the Church of the Holy Sepulcher. The other, called "Gordon's Calvary," is about 250 yards (229 meters) northeast of the Damascus Gate in the old city wall.

A tradition going back to the fourth century says that a search was initiated by the Christian historian Eusebius and that the site was found by Bishop Macarius. Later the Roman emperor Constantine built a church on the site. Previously the place was the location of a temple to Aphrodite. Tradition also has it that while looking for Jesus' tomb, Constantine's mother Helena found part of "the true cross" on which Jesus died. These traditions are very old, but their historical value is uncertain. The Church of the Holy Sepulcher is now inside what is called "the old city," but supporters claim the location was outside the walls of the city in New Testament times.

Following an earlier lead, a British general, Charles Gordon, in 1885 strongly advocated the other major site, which is outside the present existing city walls. The place is a grass-covered rocky knoll that, due to excavations (perhaps mining) some time during the past three centuries, now looks something like a skull when viewed from one direction. Beside the hill is what has been called "Jeremiah's Grotto," where an ancient tomb has been recently landscaped to produce a garden setting. This area is sometimes called the "Garden Tomb."

The site known as "Gordon's Calvary" has commended itself especially to some Protestant groups, while the location at the Church of the Holy Sepulcher is highly regarded by the Roman Catholic and Orthodox churches.

For Christians, it is the fact of our Lord's self-sacrifice—"that Christ died for our sins according to the Scriptures, and that He was buried, and that He rose again" (1 Cor. 15:3–4)—not the location, that should concern us. At "Calvary," Golgotha's cross—"the emblem of suffering and shame"—became the symbol of love, blessing, and hope.

The Aramaic name for the place where Jesus was crucified is Golgotha (Matt. 27:33; Mark 15:22; John 19:17), which like Calvary, also means "the skull."

CAMEL

Although it is an ugly beast, the camel is prized as the "ship of the desert." From the time of Abraham, the Bible mentions camels frequently, mostly in lists of possessions. Large herds of camels were a sign of wealth.

Jeremiah spoke of the "swift dromedary" (Jer. 2:23), a camel raised for riding and racing. Jesus talked of "blind guides, who strain out a gnat and swallow a camel!" (Matt. 23:24), and declared, "It is easier for a camel to go through the eye of a needle than for a rich man to enter the kingdom of God" (Matt. 19:24).

Camels are bad-tempered, prone to spit and grumble when they take on a load. But they are well suited for harsh desert life. With a heavy coat as insulation, this animal perspires little; and his well-balanced system does not require much liquid. He can go for weeks or even months without water. When he does drink, he takes only enough to replace lost moisture. Each one of his three stomachs can hold 23 liters (5 gallons) of water. In the hump on his back the camel stores fat for times when food is scarce. Then the hump shrinks when his body draws on that reserve.

The camel stands 6 feet (20 meters) or higher at the shoulder. He is trained to kneel on his leathery knees to take on a load. He holds his head high with what seems to be a haughty air, but he is merely peering out from under bushy eyebrows. Like his tightly closing lips and nostrils, his eyebrows protect him against desert sandstorms. His tough feet are ideal for walking through sharp rocks and hot sands.

The Hebrew people used camels as pack animals. They were indispensable for traveling the desert routes, carrying several hundred pounds on their backs.

The Israelites also rode camels and milked them, although they considered camels unclean and did not eat them (Lev. 11:4).

The Arabs, however, let no part of a camel go to waste. They ate camel meat and wove the soft fur into warm, durable cloth. John the Baptist was clothed in a garment of camel's hair (Matt. 3:4). The tough hide made good leather for sandals and water bags, and camel-dung chips served as fuel. Even the dried bones of camels were carved like ivory. Desert tribes rode camels to war (Judg. 7:12), and camels were seized as spoils of war.

CAMEL'S HAIR

Hair taken from the back, hump, and underside of a camel. It was woven into a coarse cloth used for tent covers and coats for camel drivers and shepherds. A "robe of coarse hair" (Zech. 13:4) was an appropriate article of clothing for a prophet. John the Baptist wore a garment of camel's hair in the wilderness (Matt. 3:4; Mark 1:6). Jesus contrasted John's dress with the "soft garments" of those who live in king's houses (Matt. 11:8; Luke 7:25).

CAMP, ENCAMPMENT

A temporary dwelling place. The sites where the Hebrew people stopped during their escape from Egypt and the period of the wilderness wandering are called camps.

As the 12 tribes journeyed toward the land of Canaan, their temporary camps were to be set up in a specific manner. The tabernacle of meeting was erected in the center, surrounded by the Levites in their own encampment. The next circle consisted of the 12 tribes themselves, three tribes on each side of the tabernacle (Num. 1:50–2:34). The Book of Numbers also contains specific instructions for breaking camp and the order of their march (Num. 2:1–3:51; 10:21–28). In later times some of the language from the Book of Numbers was used to describe the service of the Levites at the temple (1 Chr. 9:18–19).

Acts 21:34 uses the common Greek word for camp, although most modern English versions translate the word as barracks (NIV, NKJV, NRSV, NASB). Hebrews 13:11–13 uses the figure of the Hebrew camp to compare the death of Jesus "outside the gate" with the burning of the carcasses of sacrificial animals "outside the camp" in Old Testament times (Ex. 29:14; Num. 19:3, 7). In Revelation 20:9 the reference to "the camp of the saints" symbolizes the triumphant church at the end of time.

CANA [KANE nuh] *(place of reeds)*

A village of Galilee where Jesus performed his first miracle—turning water

CAMEL'S HAIR

into wine (John 2:1, 11). Cana was the home of Nathanael, one of the Twelve (John 21:2). Its probable location, Kfar Kanna, is about 8 miles (13 kilometers) northeast of Nazareth.

CANAAN [KANE un]

The fourth son of Ham and the grandson of Noah (Gen. 9:18–27; 10:6, 15). Ham's descendants were dispersed into several distinctive tribes, such as the Jebusites and the Zemarites. These people became known collectively in later years as the Canaanites, pagan inhabitants of the land that God promised to Abraham and his descendants. Under the leadership of Joshua, the people of Israel occupied the land of Canaan and divided it among the twelve tribes.

CANAAN [KANE un] *(land of purple)*

The region along the Mediterranean Sea occupied by the Canaanites before it was taken and settled by the Israelite people (Gen. 11:31; Josh. 5:12). The land of Canaan stretched from the Jordan River on the east to the Mediterranean Sea on the west. From south to north, it covered the territory between the Sinai Peninsula and the ancient coastal nation of Phoenicia. Much of this territory was dry, mountainous, and rocky, unfit for cultivation. But it also contained many fertile farmlands, particularly in the river valleys and the coastal plains along the sea. While leading the people of Israel toward the land of Canaan, Moses sent scouts, or spies, into the territory on a fact-finding mission. They returned with grapes, pomegranates, and figs to verify the fertility of the land (Num. 13:2, 17, 23).

The land of Canaan was ideally situated on the trade routes that stretched from Egypt in the south to Syria and Phoenicia in the north and the ancient Babylonian Empire to the east. This location gave the small region a strategic po-

sition in the ancient world. After the Israelites captured the land of Canaan, they developed a thriving commercial system by trading goods with other nations along these routes. The finest royal purple dye was manufactured in Canaan, giving the territory its name.

CANAANITES [KANE un ites]

An ancient tribe that lived in the land of Canaan before they were displaced by the nation of Israel. The Canaanites, along with the Amorites, settled the land well before 2000 B.C. Archaeological exploration of their native land and adjacent territories has provided information on many aspects of their culture. Among the numerous sites excavated in ancient Canaan, or the present-day Holy Land, are Hazor, Megiddo, Beth Shan, Jericho, Jebus (Jerusalem), Debir, Lachish, and Arad. Sites in the northern part of ancient Canaan include Byblos and Ras Shamra (Ugarit) along the coast of the Mediterranean Sea and Hamath on the Orontes River.

Although both Canaanites and Amorites were established in Canaan before 2000 B.C., the Canaanites established their civilization as dominant during the Middle Bronze age (about 2100 to 1550 B.C.). Their society had several classes, ranging from the ruling nobility to the peasants. The northern Canaanites used a particular Cuneiform script, featuring a wedge-shaped alphabet. Their land was also dotted with walled cities. Several of these served as the centers of city-states, each having its own king, or mayor, and army.

The Canaanites, therefore, were a highly civilized people in many ways when Joshua led the Israelites across the Jordan River to conquer the people and settle the land. Canaanite history ended with the Israelite conquest. But certain segments of Canaanite culture remained to make both positive and negative impacts on the life of God's covenant people.

Knowledge of Canaanite language and literature was enhanced by the discovery of the Ugaritic texts at Ras Shamra (ancient Ugarit), a site on the Mediterranean coast in modern Syria. Accidental discovery of a vaulted room by a farmer while plowing his field on the top of Ras Shamra led to several full-scale excavations by Claude F. A. Schaeffer, the first in 1929. These excavations resulted in the recovery of a store of religious texts and other documents on clay tablets. These writings have yielded a great deal of knowledge about Canaanite life, particularly their form of religion.

The Canaanite language in written form, as revealed by the Ugaritic texts of Ras Shamra, is an alphabetic cuneiform (wedge-shaped) type of writing. This form contrasts markedly with the syllabic cuneiform of the ancient Babylonian and Assyrian languages. It does have many similarities to other ancient languages of the Middle Eastern world during this period, but it also has many significant differences. These differences are so significant that archaeologists can say with certainty that the Canaanites developed a language all their own.

The Ugaritic texts from Ras Shamra are by far the most significant literary sources of the Canaanite language in the alphabetic cuneiform script. These texts go back to the fourteenth century B.C. or earlier. Most of them are of a religious nature, providing valuable details on both the literature and the religion of the Canaanites. These texts have also given Bible scholars a better understanding of Old Testament writings and background. They also show that the Israelites' faith in their one Redeemer God was a dramatic contrast to the pagan religion of the Canaanites.

The religion of the Canaanites fea-

tured many gods. These gods were worshiped with elaborate ritual. Various kinds of cultic personnel, or priests, officiated at these pagan ceremonies. Their religious system also featured many different places of worship, varying from simple outdoor altars to massive stone temples.

The Old Testament refers frequently to Baal (Num. 22:41), Baals (Hos. 2:13, 17), or a Baal of a particular place, such as Baal of Peor (Num. 25:3, 5). The Old Testament also refers to Asherah (1 Kin. 18:19), Ashtoreth (1 Kin. 11:5, 33), and the Ashtoreths (Judg. 2:13). References to these Canaanite gods and goddesses always carry strong denunciations by the biblical writers. But these names mentioned in the Old Testament are only a few of the many additional names for Canaanite gods that appear in the Ugaritic texts.

The highest of all the Canaanite gods was El, as shown clearly by the Ugaritic texts. But El chose to remain in the background, conferring power and authority upon his brood of gods and goddesses. The main goddess by whom El fathered children was Asherah. She and El were the parents of more than 70 other deities. The Baal mentioned frequently in the Old Testament was lord among the gods because of authority granted by El. Baal was known chiefly as the god of fertility and as god of the storm. Temples were built in his name at a number of sites, including one at Ugarit.

Three Canaanite goddesses mentioned frequently in the Ugaritic texts are Anath (Judg. 3:31), Asherah, and Astarte (Ashtoreth of the Old Testament). Among the many other deities of the Canaanites were Resheph, god of pestilence, and Mot, god of drought and death.

Canaanite religion had a number of features that were similar to certain practices of the religious system of the Israelites. Like the Israelites, the Canaanites offered various kinds of offerings to their gods. Animals offered included sheep, cattle, and certain wild animals. A high priest among the Canaanites served as the head of 12 priestly families. Other important worship leaders who served in the Canaanite temples included singers, who used liturgy or a form of psalmody; consecrated persons (in effect, male and female prostitutes); vestment makers and sculptors; and priest-scribes, who were responsible for preserving important literary traditions. Like the Hebrew feasts and festivals, the celebrations of the Canaanites also paralleled the seasons or cycles of the agricultural year.

But in other important ways, Canaanite and Hebrew religion were poles apart. The religion of these pagan people was basically a fertility cult. At temples scattered throughout their land, Canaanite worshipers actually participated in lewd, immoral acts with "sacred" prostitutes. Theirs was a depraved form of worship that appealed to the base instincts of sinful human nature. They also practiced human sacrifice, and their religion sanctioned unbelievable cruelty in warfare. In contrast, the Hebrews worshiped a holy God who insisted on purity and righteousness among His people.

Although the Israelites were called to a high ethical plane in their worship, at times the sensual appeal of the Canaanite cults enticed them into sin and idolatry. This explains the strong appeal Joshua made to the people of Israel in his farewell speech. Joshua had led them to take the land, but many of the Canaanites still remained. The aging warrior knew their form of pagan worship would be a strong temptation to the people. Thus he declared, "Put away the foreign gods which are among you, and incline your heart to the LORD God of Israel" (Josh. 24:23).

CANDLE

A mass of tallow or wax containing a linen or cotton wick that is burned to give light. The people of biblical times did not use candles as such. The NKJV translates as "lamp" (Job 18:6; Prov. 20:27; Luke 8:16). The lamps of the ancient world were shallow bowls with a pinched rim. A wick was laid in these grooves, with one end extending above the lip of the lamp while the other end rested in the olive oil, which provided fuel.

CAPERNAUM [kuh PURR nay uhm]
(village of Nahum)

The most important city on the northern shore of the Sea of Galilee in New Testament times and the center of much of Jesus' ministry. Capernaum is not mentioned in the Old Testament, and the Nahum after whom it was named is probably not the prophet Nahum. In all likelihood, Capernaum was founded some time after the Jews returned from captivity.

By the New Testament era, Capernaum was large enough that it always was called a "city" (Matt. 9:1; Mark 1:33). It had its own synagogue, in which Jesus frequently taught (Mark 1:21; Luke 4:31–38; John 6:59). Apparently the synagogue was built by the Roman soldiers garrisoned in Capernaum (Matt. 8:8; Luke 7:1–10). The synagogue was a center for the Roman system of taxation. Capernaum had a permanent office of taxation (Matt. 9:9; Mark 2:14; Luke 5:27), and itinerant tax collectors operated in the city (Matt. 17:24). Ruins of a later synagogue cover those of the one where Jesus worshiped, although sections of the latter can still be seen today.

After being rejected in His hometown, Nazareth, Jesus made Capernaum the center of His ministry in Galilee. He performed many miracles here, including the healing of the centurion's paralyzed servant (Matt. 8:5–13), a paralytic carried by four friends (Mark 2:1–12), Peter's mother-in-law (Matt. 8:14–15; Mark 1:29–31), and the nobleman's son (John 4:46–54).

As Jesus walked by the Sea of Galilee near Capernaum, He called the fishermen Simon, Andrew, James, and John to be His disciples (Mark 1:16–21, 29). It was also in "His own city" (Capernaum) that Jesus called the tax collector Matthew (Matt. 9:1, 9; Mark 2:13–14). Immediately following the feeding of the five thousand, Jesus delivered His discourse on the Bread of Life near this city (John 6:32).

Although Jesus centered His ministry in Capernaum, the people of that city did not follow Him. Jesus pronounced a curse on the city for its unbelief (Matt. 11:23–24), predicting its ruin (Luke 10:15). So strikingly did this prophecy come true that only recently has Tell Hum been identified confidently as ancient Capernaum.

CAPHTOR [KAF tawr]

The island or maritime area from which the Philistines originally came (Deut. 2:23; Jer. 47:4; Amos 9:7). Scholars are divided concerning the location of Caphtor. The most probable location is the island of Crete, together with the nearby Aegean isles. The Septuagint, however, reads Cappadocia, a province in eastern Asia Minor, instead of Caphtor (Deut. 2:23; Amos 9:7). The Caphtorim (Gen. 10:14; Deut. 2:23; 1 Chr. 1:12) were people who came from Caphtor.

CAPPADOCIA [kap uh DOH shih uh]

A large Roman province in eastern Asia Minor. It was bounded on the north by Pontus and the mountains along the Halys River, on the east by Armenia and the Euphrates River, on the south by Cilicia and the Taurus Mountains, and on the west by Lycaonia and Galatia. Visitors from Cappadocia were at Jerusalem on the Day of Pentecost (Acts 2:1, 9), and the apostle Peter included this province in his first letter to the converts of the Dispersion (1 Pet. 1:1). Christianity apparently spread northward into Cappadocia from Tarsus of Cilicia, through the Cilician Gates (a gap in the Tarsus Mountains), and then on to Pontus and Galatia.

CAPTIVITY

Two periods when the nations of Israel (722 B.C.) and Judah (605 B.C. and later) were taken away from their native lands and into exile.

The captivity of Israel, the ten northern tribes, occurred in 722 B.C. when the Assyrians overran the nation and carried away the most prominent citizens as captives to the Assyrian capital. The Hebrew prophets interpreted this event as God's punishment for Israel's idolatry (2 Kin. 17:7–23) and rejection of covenant spirituality (Amos 5:1–15). There is no record of the people of the northern tribes of Israel ever returning to the land in large numbers.

The captivity of Judah, the southern kingdom, occurred in 597 B.C. when powerful Babylonian armies conquered Jerusalem and took "three thousand and twenty-three Jews" captive to Mesopotamia (Jer. 52:28). Additional deportations in 586 B.C. and 581 B.C. involved hundreds more captives (Jer. 52:29, 30) and ended the kingdom of Judah.

Little is known about Israel and Judah's life during the captivity. Captivity meant a shameful and humiliating punishment for this disobedient, idolatrous people. The royal court of Judah was taken into captivity, along with the priests, skilled workers, and anyone else who might ever lead a revolt against Babylon. The captives realized that God had finally brought the long-standing covenant curses (Deut. 28:15–68) to bear upon them. Torn from their homes and familiar surroundings, they were forced to travel across a hot desert to a strange land. Many of them had to work for their conquerors.

The punishment of captivity lasted 70 years for Judah (Jer. 25:11–12; Dan. 9:2), after which the penitent were allowed to return to their homeland under the leadership of Zerubbabel and others (Ezra 2:1–2). Israel's tribes, however, never returned and became lost to history.

CARAVAN

A company of people, often merchants with pack animals such as donkeys and camels, traveling together, especially through desert or hostile regions (Job 6:19). Genesis 37:25 mentions "a company of Ishmaelites, coming from Gilead with their camels, bearing spices, balm, and myrrh, on their way to carry them down to Egypt." The main trade routes connecting Egypt and Arabia with Syria and Babylonia passed through Canaan. Arab caravans carrying all sorts of spices and incense regularly traveled through Canaan on these routes; their presence was a natural part of life in Israel.

CARCHEMISH [KAHR kem ish] *(city of [the god] Chemosh)*

A city west of the Euphrates River in northwest Mesopotamia (2 Chr. 35:20; Is. 10:9; Jer. 46:2). Carchemish was the ancient capital of the Hittites; later it became a fortified city of the Assyrians. It was the site of one of the most important battles of ancient history.

In 605 B.C., the army of Pharaoh Necho of Egypt and the army of Nebuchadnezzar II of Babylon collided at Carchemish, and the Egyptians suffered a crushing defeat. This victory allowed the Babylonians to assume control of the Syrian-Palestinian region. Before the battle of Carchemish, King Josiah of Judah tried

to block the advance of Pharaoh Necho in his march northward. He was fatally wounded in the Valley of Megiddo (2 Chr. 35:20–24).

CARMEL [KAHR muhl] *(garden/orchard of God)*

1. A town in the hill country of Judah (Josh. 15:55; 1 Sam. 25:2, 5, 7, 40). It has been identified as present-day Khirbet el-Kermel, about 8 miles (13 kilometers) southeast of Hebron. Carmel, near Maon, was the home of a very rich and very foolish man named Nabal. This man was a stubborn, churlish fellow who insulted David by refusing to show hospitality to David's servants. The Lord struck Nabal so that "his heart died within him, and he became like a stone" (1 Sam. 25:37). After Nabal's death, David sent for Abigail the Carmelitess, widow of Nabal, to take her as his wife. Abigail, "a woman of good understanding and beautiful appearance" (1 Sam. 25:3), became one of David's wives. Hezrai (2 Sam. 23:35), or Hezro (1 Chr. 11:37), one of David's mighty men, also came from Carmel.

CARMEL [KAHR muhl] *(garden/orchard of God)*

2. A mountain range stretching about 13 miles (21 kilometers) from the Mediterranean coast southeast to the Plain of Dothan. At the Bay of Accho (Acre), near the modern city of Haifa, this mountain range juts out into the Mediterranean Sea in a promontory named Mount Carmel. It rises sharply from the seacoast to a height of 470 feet (143 meters) near Haifa. The mountain range as a whole averages over 1,000 feet above sea level, with 1,742 feet (530 meters) being the summit.

The Canaanites built sanctuaries to pagan deities on this mountain. Thus, Carmel was an appropriate site for a confrontation between Elijah, the prophet of the Lord, and the "prophets of Baal" (1 Kin. 18:19–20), the idolatrous Canaanite priests. It was also from the top of Mount Carmel that Elijah saw a sign of the coming storm: "a cloud, as small as a man's hand, rising out of the sea" (1 Kin. 18:44), a cloud that signaled the end of a prolonged drought. The prophet Elisha also visited Mount Carmel (2 Kin. 2:25; 4:25).

CASTLE

A large fortified building. Fortified towers were often situated on a country's borders, or in other strategic places such as mountain passes, to guard against invading armies (2 Chr. 27:4). They served as the first line of Israel's defense. First Chronicles 11:5, 7 refers to the castle, or stronghold, of Jerusalem. Larger cities in biblical times often had an upper and a lower city. The upper city was usually on an elevated site where the earlier town had been situated; it was called the castle or fortress. With its own wall system, the upper city served as a second line of defense if the outer wall protecting the lower city was broken or scaled.

The word *castle* also appears in the Book of Acts, referring to the fortress of Antonia in Jerusalem. This fortress overlooked the temple area. Roman troops were stationed here to curb any outbreaks of violence. When the apostle Paul was threatened by a mob in Jerusalem, soldiers from Antonia rescued him and took him into the fortress, or castle, for protection (Acts 21:34; 22:24; 23:10, KJV; barracks in NKJV, NIV).

CEDARS OF LEBANON

Huge evergreen trees that grew on the mountains of Lebanon, a region along the coast of the Mediterranean Sea northwest of Jerusalem. King Solomon of Judah purchased logs from these magnificent trees for use in building the temple in Jerusalem (1 Kin. 5:8–10).

CENSER

A container, probably a ladle or shovel-like device, used for carrying live coals of fire, in which incense was burned (Num. 16:6, 17–18, 37–39, 46). The censers of the tabernacle were of bronze (Ex. 27:3; Lev. 16:12); those of the temple were "of pure gold" (1 Kin. 7:50; 2 Chr. 4:22). The censer was used in the purification ritual on the Day of Atonement (Lev. 16:12–14).

CENSUS

An official counting and registration of citizens; a property evaluation for tax purposes in early Rome.

The first numbering of the people in the Old Testament occurred at the time of the Exodus. All men 20 years of age or older who were able to go to war were counted (Num. 1:2–46). One purpose of this census was to help in the distribution of the land (Num. 26:52–56). After the Babylonian captivity, there was another census (Ezra 2) of men to show how many had returned from captivity and also as an aid for the distribution of the land.

In New Testament times the Roman government conducted periodic countings of the people to assess the amount of tax their country should pay to the treasury of the Roman Empire. The New Testament mentions two censuses. At the time of Jesus' birth, Joseph and Mary went to Bethlehem to be registered (Luke 2:1–5). This was probably a census required of all nations under the rule of Rome. All citizens were required to return to their places of birth for an official registration of their property for tax purposes.

The second Roman census was conducted to make an assessment of the property of Judea in A.D. 6. At this time

Judea came under direct Roman rule. Because of this, Judas of Galilee incited a revolt, stating that the Jews should be ruled by God rather than by a foreign power (Acts 5:37).

The Roman system of taking census began in 10–9 B.C. Such a registration took place every 14 years.

CHASTISEMENT

Punishment or discipline brought by God for the purpose of (1) education, instruction, and training (Job 4:3); (2) corrective guidance (2 Tim. 2:25); and (3) discipline, in the sense of corrective physical punishment (Prov. 22:15; Rev. 3:19).

One marvelous passage that does not fit into any of these three categories is Isaiah's portrait of the Suffering Servant: "He was wounded for our transgressions, He was bruised for our iniquities; the chastisement for our peace was upon Him, and by His stripes we are healed" (Is. 53:5). Christians believe that Isaiah was speaking of Jesus Christ, who died in our place, and for us.

CHAFF

The fine, dry material, such as husks (seed coverings) and other debris, that is separated from the seed in the process of threshing grain. In the Bible, chaff

CENSUS

symbolizes worthless, evil, or wicked persons (or things) that are about to be destroyed (Ps. 1:4; Matt. 3:12; Luke 3:17). It is a fitting figure of speech to describe complete destruction by judgment. "The ungodly," said the psalmist, "are like the chaff which the wind drives away" (Ps. 1:4).

CHALDEA [kal DEE uh]

Originally, the lower Tigris and Euphrates valley, or the southern portion of Babylonia. Later, beginning with the reign of Nebuchadnezzar II (king of Babylonia from 605 to 562 B.C.), the term Chaldea came to include practically all of Babylonia and was virtually synonymous with the Neo-Babylonian Empire.

In the NKJV the term Chaldea is found only in the books of Jeremiah and Ezekiel. Jeremiah prophesied the fall of Babylon by saying, "Chaldea shall become plunder" (Jer. 50:10) and "I will repay Babylon, and all the inhabitants of Chaldea for all the evil they have done" (Jer. 51:24). In a vision, the Spirit of God took Ezekiel into Chaldea to his fellow Jews in captivity (Ezek. 11:24). Ezekiel later referred to "the Babylonians of Chaldea" (Ezek. 16:29; 23:15–16).

See also BABYLONIA.

CHAMBERLAIN

A person responsible for guarding the king's bedroom and harem. This man, usually a eunuch to remove all possibility of unfaithfulness, was employed by ancient kings. He was a highly trusted and influential official (Acts 8:27).

CHARIOT

Chariots were introduced in Mesopotamia (the land between the Tigris and Euphrates rivers) about 2800 B.C. These machines of war served as mobile firing platforms. The advantage of the chariot is that it can bring great firepower quickly to the key point of the battle.

Chariots came in many different forms. They could be two-wheeled or four-wheeled, drawn by two to four horses. Some chariots would carry as many as four warriors.

In combat a chariot usually carried two soldiers—a driver who controlled the reins and a warrior who needed both arms free to fire his bow. In some cases, depending on the nation and the period of history, a third person might serve as a shield-bearer to protect both the warrior and the driver. The warrior was usually equipped with a bow, as well as a medium-range weapon, such as the javelin or spear.

The first chariots mentioned in the Bible belonged to Egypt. Joseph rode in a chariot behind the pharaoh (Gen. 41:43). A later pharaoh pursued Moses and the Israelites with his chariot corps (Ex. 14:6–9).

At first, the nation of Israel rejected chariots as tools of warfare (Josh. 11:4–9). Most of Canaan was not suitable for chariot warfare because of its high hills and deep ravines. Also, the spirit of conquest under Joshua was such that the use of a powerful weapon like the chariot might have led Israel to boast in their own power rather than God's. Solomon, however, developed a chariot corps in his army (1 Kin. 4:26; 9:19). But the chariots in the armies of Judah and Israel had radically diminished by a later time in the history of God's people (2 Kin. 13:7).

CHEBAR [KEE bahr] (great)

A "river" of Chaldea. The Jewish captives, including the prophet Ezekiel, lived along the banks of this river at the village of Tel Abib (Ezek. 1:1, 3; 3:15, 23). It was here that Ezekiel saw several of his remarkable visions (Ezek. 10:15, 20, 22; 43:3; Kebar in NIV). The Chebar was most likely not a river at all, but the famous Grand Canal of Nebuchadnezzar that connected the Tigris and Euphrates rivers.

CHEDORLAOMER [ked awr LAY oh muhr] *(servant of* [the Elamite God] *Lagamar)*

A king of Elam, a country east of Babylonia, in Abraham's day (Gen. 14:1, 4–5, 9, 17; Kedorlaomer in NIV). Allied with three other Mesopotamian kings—Amraphel of Shinar, Arioch of Ellasar, and Tidal of "nations"—Chedorlaomer led a campaign against southern Canaan and defeated the inhabitants in the Valley of Siddim near the Dead Sea. The conquered people served Chedorlaomer for twelve years, but in the thirteenth year they rebelled (Gen. 14:4).

Chedorlaomer came again with his allies and conquered the region east of the Jordan River from Bashan southward to the Red Sea as well as the plain around the Dead Sea, thus gaining control of the lucrative caravan routes from Arabia and Egypt through Canaan. In making this conquest, Chedorlaomer captured Lot, Abraham's nephew. Aided by his allies and numerous servants, Abraham launched a night attack on Chedorlaomer at Dan, defeating him and recovering Lot and the spoils. Although Chedorlaomer has not been identified in references outside the Old Testament, the elements of his name are typically Elamite.

CHEESE

A food produced from curdled milk (1 Sam. 17:18; 2 Sam. 17:29; Job 10:10). In the desert climate of Canaan, cheesemaking preserved surplus milk for future use without refrigeration. Although the word occurs only three times in the Bible, cheese was probably more common in ancient Israel than this might indicate. The Tyropoeon [literally, cheesemakers] Valley of Jerusalem ap-

parently was the center of the cheesemaking industry.

Jewish tradition prohibited the eating of cheese made by a Gentile because it may have been made from the milk of an animal offered to idols. Modern orthodox Jews still require rigid controls over cheesemaking.

CHEMOSH [KEE mahsh]

The national god of the Moabites (Judg 11:24; 2 Kin. 23:13). This deity was apparently compounded with *Athtar,* the Venus star, and so is thought to be a pagan god associated with the heavenly bodies. Chemosh has been identified with Baal of Peor, Baal-Zebub, Mars, and Saturn, as the star of ill-omen. Dibon (Num. 21:30), a town in Moab north of the river Arnon, was the chief seat of its worship.

Like Molech, Chemosh was worshiped by the sacrifice of children as burnt offerings, but scholars believe it is incorrect to identify Chemosh directly with Molech. Solomon sanctified Chemosh as a part of his tolerance of pagan gods (1 Kin. 11:7), but Josiah abolished its worship (2 Kin. 23:13). Human sacrifice was made to Chemosh, according to 2 Kings 3:27, which reports that Mesha, king of Moab, offered his oldest son as a burnt offering on the wall of Kir Hareseth, the ancient capital of Moab.

CHERUBIM [CHAIR oo beam]

Winged angelic beings, often associated with worship and praise of God. The cherubim are first mentioned in the Bible in Genesis 3:24. When God drove Adam and Eve from the Garden of Eden, He placed cherubim at the east of the garden, "and a flaming sword which turned every way, to guard the way to the tree of life." They were similar in appearance to the statues of winged sphinxes that flanked the entrances to palaces and temples in ancient Babylonia and Assyria.

Symbolic representations of cherubim were used in the tabernacle in the wilderness. Two cherubim made of gold were stationed at the two ends of the mercy seat, above the ark of the covenant in the Most High Place (Ex. 25:17–22; 1 Chr. 28:18; Heb. 9:5). Artistic designs of cherubim decorated the ten curtains (Ex. 26:1; 36:8) and the veil (Ex. 26:31; 2 Chr. 3:14) of the tabernacle.

When Solomon built the temple, he ordered that two cherubim be made of olive wood and overlaid with gold. Each measured 10 cubits (15 feet or 4.6 meters) high with a wingspread of 10 cubits (1 Kin. 6:23–28; 8:6–7; 2 Chr. 3:10–13; 5:7–8). These gigantic cherubim were placed inside the inner sanctuary, or in the Most Holy Place in the temple. Their wings were spread over the ark of the covenant. Cherubim functioned as the armrests of the throne of the invisible Lord God of Israel, the true ruler and king of His people (1 Sam. 4:4; 2 Sam. 6:2). The woodwork throughout the temple was decorated with engraved figures of cherubim, trees, and flowers (1 Kin. 6:29–35; 7:29, 36; 2 Chr. 3:7).

A careful comparison of the first and tenth chapters of the Book of Ezekiel shows clearly that the "four living creatures" (Ezek. 1:5) were the same beings as the cherubim (Ezek. 10). Each had four faces—that of a man, a lion, an ox, and an eagle (Ezek. 1:10; also 10:14)—and each had four wings. In their appearance, the cherubim "had the likeness of a man" (Ezek. 1:5). These cherubim used two of their wings for flying and the other two for covering their bodies (Ezek. 1:6, 11, 23). Under their wings the cherubim appeared to have the form, or likeness, of a man's hand (Ezek. 1:8; 10:7–8, 21).

The imagery of Revelation 4:6–9 seems to be inspired, at least in part, by the prophecies of Ezekiel. The "four living creatures" described here, as well as the cherubim of Ezekiel, served the purpose of magnifying the holiness and power of God. This is one of their main responsibilities throughout the Bible. In addition to singing God's praises, they also served as a visible reminder of the majesty and glory of God and His abiding presence with His people.

In some ways, the cherubim were similar to the seraphim, another form of angelic being mentioned in the Bible. Both were winged beings, and both surrounded God on His throne (Is. 6:2–3). But the seraphim of the prophet Isaiah's vision were vocal in their praise of God, singing "holy, holy, holy is the LORD of hosts" (Is. 6:3). Nowhere else in the Bible do the seraphim break forth in such exuberant praise. They apparently played a quieter, more restrained role in worship.

CHIOS [KYE ahs]

An island in the Aegean Sea—between Greece and Asia Minor—at the entrance to the Gulf of Smyrna (modern Izmir). On his return to Jerusalem during his third missionary journey, the apostle Paul "sailed . . . opposite Chios" (Acts 20:15; Kios in NIV). Situated between the islands of Lesbos and Samos, Chios rests about 5 miles (8 kilometers) from the mainland of Asia Minor. The island was famous for its wine, wheat, figs, and gum mastic.

CHORAZIN [koh RAY zin]

A city north of the Sea of Galilee where Jesus performed many "mighty works" (Matt. 11:21; Luke 10:13; Korazin in NIV). It has been identified as present-day Khirbet Kerazeh, about 2 miles (3 kilometers) north of Capernaum (present-day Tell Hum). Jesus pronounced judgment upon Chorazin because it did not repent and believe.

CHOSEN PEOPLE

A name for the people of Israel, whom God chose as His special instruments. As a holy people set apart to worship God, they were to make His name known throughout the earth (Ex. 19:4–6; Ps. 105:43). In the New Testament, Peter describes Christians as members of a "chosen generation" (1 Pet. 2:9; chosen people, NIV).

CHRIST (*anointed one*)

A name for Jesus that showed He was the long-awaited king and deliverer. For centuries the Jewish people had looked for a prophesied Messiah, a deliverer who would usher in a kingdom of peace and prosperity (Ps. 110; Amos 9:13). Jesus was clearly identified as this Messiah in Peter's great confession, "You are the Christ, the Son of the living God" (Matt. 16:16).

CHURCH

A local assembly of believers as well as the redeemed of all the ages who follow Jesus Christ as Savior and Lord. In the four Gospels of the New Testament, the term *church* is found only in Matthew 16:18 and 18:17. This scarcity of usage in those books that report on the life and ministry of Jesus is perhaps best explained by the fact that the church as the body of Christ did not begin until the day of Pentecost after the ascension of Jesus (Acts 2:1–4).

The Greek word for church is *ekklesia*. This word is used 115 times in the New Testament, mostly in the Book of Acts and the writings of the apostle Paul and the general epistles. At least 92 times this word refers to a local congregation. The other references are to the church general, or all believers everywhere for all ages. The greatest emphasis in the New Testament is placed upon the idea of the local church. The local church is the visible operation of the church general in a given time and place.

When the church general is implied, "church" refers to all who follow Christ, without respect to locality or time. The most general reference to the church occurs in Ephesians 1:22; 3:10–21; 5:23–32. Since the church general refers to all believers of all ages, it will not be complete until after the judgment, and the assembly of all the redeemed in one place will become a reality only after the return of Christ (Heb. 12:23; Rev. 21–22).

Speaking to His followers after His resurrection, Jesus commissioned the church to make disciples and teach them what He had taught (Matt. 28:16–20). The Book of Acts is the story of the early church's struggle to be loyal to this commission. Christ, through the presence of the Holy Spirit, continued to direct His church as it carried out its commission.

At first, church organization was flexible to meet changing needs. As the church became more established, however, church officers came into existence. These included the apostles; bishops; elders; evangelists; ministers; prophets or teachers, deacons, and deaconesses. Although church organization varies from denomination to denomination today, the pattern and purpose of the New Testament remain a model for churches as they pursue their mission in the world.

CIRCUMCISION

The surgical removal of the foreskin of the male sex organ. This action served as a sign of God's covenant relation with His people.

Circumcision was widely practiced in the ancient world, including the Egyptian and Canaanite cultures. But among these people the rite was performed at the beginning of puberty, or about 12 years of age, for hygienic reasons or as a sort of initiation ceremony into manhood. In contrast, the Hebrew people performed circumcision on infants. This rite had an important ethical meaning to them. It signified their responsibility to serve as the holy people whom God had called as His special servants in the midst of a pagan world.

In the Bible's first mention of circumcision, God instructed Abraham to circumcise every male child in his household, including servants, "in the flesh of your foreskins" (Gen. 17:11). The custom was performed on the eighth day after birth (Gen. 17:12; 21:4; Phil. 3:5). At this time a name was given to the son (Luke 1:59; 2:21). In the early history of the Hebrew people circumcision was performed by the father. But the surgical task was eventually taken over by a specialist.

Circumcision of the Jewish male was required as a visible, physical sign of the covenant between the Lord and His people (Gen. 17:11). Any male not circumcised was to be "cut off from his people" (Gen. 17:14) and regarded as a covenant-breaker (Ex. 12:48).

Although circumcision was required by the Mosaic Law, the rite was neglected during the days when the people of Israel wandered in the wilderness. Perhaps this was a sign that the nation had broken their covenant with God through their disobedience. The rite was resumed when they entered the land of Canaan, with Joshua performing the ritual on the generation born in the wilderness.

The Hebrew people came to take great pride in circumcision; in fact, it became a badge of their spiritual and national superiority. This practice fostered a spirit of exclusivism instead of a missionary zeal to reach out to other nations as God intended. A daily prayer of strict Jewish males was to thank God that he was nei-

ther a woman, a Samaritan, nor a Gentile.

Gentiles came to be regarded by the Jews as the "uncircumcision," a term of disrespect implying that non-Jewish peoples were outside the circle of God's love. The terms *circumcised* and *uncircumcised* became emotionally charged symbols to Israel and their Gentile neighbors. This issue later brought discord into the fellowship of the New Testament church.

Moses and the prophets used the term *circumcised* as a symbol for purity of heart and readiness to hear and obey. Through Moses the Lord challenged the Israelites to submit to "circumcision of the heart," a reference to their need for repentance. "If their uncircumcised hearts are humbled, and they accept their guilt," God declared, "then I will remember My covenant" (Lev. 26:41–42; also Deut. 10:16). Jeremiah characterized rebellious Israel as having "uncircumcised" ears (6:10) and being "uncircumcised in the heart" (9:26).

In the New Testament, circumcision was faithfully practiced by devout Jews as recognition of God's continuing covenant with Israel. Both John the Baptist (Luke 1:59) and Jesus (Luke 2:21) were circumcised. But controversy over circumcision divided the early church (Eph. 2:11), which included believers from both Jewish and Gentile backgrounds. Gentile believers regarded their Jewish brethren as eccentric because of their dietary laws, Sabbath rules, and circumcision practices. Jewish believers tended to view their uncircumcised Gentile brothers as unenlightened and disobedient to the Law of Moses (Acts 15:5).

A crisis erupted in the church at Antioch when believers from Judea (known as Judaizers) taught the brethren, "Unless you are circumcised according to the custom of Moses, you cannot be saved" (Acts 15:1–2). In effect, the Judaizers insisted that a believer from a non-Jewish background (Gentile) must first become a Jew ceremonially (by being circumcised) before he could be admitted to the Christian brotherhood.

A council of apostles and elders was convened in Jerusalem to resolve the issue (Acts 15:6–29). Among those attending were Paul, Barnabas, Simon Peter, and James, pastor of the Jerusalem church. To insist on circumcision for the Gentiles, Peter argued, would amount to a burdensome yoke (Acts 15:10, 19). This was the decision handed down by the council, and the church broke away from the binding legalism of Judaism.

Years later, reinforcing this decision, the apostle Paul wrote the believers at Rome that Abraham, "the father of circumcision" (Rom. 4:12), was saved by faith rather than by circumcision (Rom. 4:9–12). He declared circumcision to be of no value unless accompanied by an obedient spirit (Rom. 2:25, 26).

Paul also spoke of the "circumcision of Christ" (Col. 2:11), a reference to His atoning death, which "condemned sin in the flesh" (Rom. 8:3) and nailed legalism "to the cross" (Col. 2:14). In essence, Paul declared that the New Covenant of Christ's shed blood has provided forgiveness to both Jew and Gentile and has made circumcision totally unnecessary (Rom. 2:28–29; Gal. 5:6). All that ultimately matters for both Jew and Gentile, Paul says, is a changed nature—a new creation that makes them one in Jesus Christ (Eph. 2:14–18).

CISTERN

An artificial reservoir for storing liquids (especially water); specifically, an underground tank for catching and storing runoff rainwater. For about half the year, rainfall in Israel is scarce, falling mainly during the winter months. As a result, it was important that water be stored during the rainy months for the long dry season.

Before about 1200 B.C., cisterns were dug out of the soft limestone rock found in many parts of Canaan. Because of the porous nature of limestone, however, these cisterns often broke and became unsatisfactory for holding rainwater. About the time of Israel's conquest of the land of Canaan, a remarkable advance in cistern construction allowed the bottom and walls of the cistern to be sealed with plaster. This made it possible to build cisterns virtually anywhere and opened up many dry areas to permanent settlement.

In most cities, each house generally had its own cistern. Rain falling on the roof was collected and channeled to the cistern, usually situated beneath the house. Cisterns were of great importance to fortified cities, enabling them to withstand a long military siege by an enemy.

CITADEL [SIT uh dell]

The inner or final defensive system of a walled city. Protected by its own wall within the city's outer wall, the citadel was usually built on a hill for even greater protection. Here is where the residents would make their last stand if the enemy should break through the outer defenses. In capital cities like Jerusalem and Samaria, the king's palace was situated within the citadel (2 Kin. 15:25; palace in KJV).

CITIES OF REFUGE

Six Levitical cities set aside to provide shelter and safety for those guilty of manslaughter. Of the 48 cities assigned to the Levites, 6 were designated as cities of refuge, three on either side of the Jordan River (Num. 35:6–7; Josh. 20:7–8). The 3 cities of refuge west of the Jordan were Kedesh in Galilee, in the mountains of Naphtali (Josh. 20:7; 21:32); Shechem, in the mountains of Ephraim (Josh. 20:7; 21:21; 1 Chr. 6:67); and Hebron, also known as Kirjath Arba, in the mountains of Judah (Josh. 20:7).

The three cities east of the Jordan River were Bezer, in the wilderness on the plateau, or plain, of Moab, and assigned to the tribe of Reuben (Deut. 4:43; Josh. 20:8; 21:36); Ramoth Gilead, or Ramoth in Gilead, from the tribe of Gad (Deut. 4:43; Josh. 20:8; 21:38); and Golan, in Bashan, from the half-tribe of Manasseh (Deut. 4:43; Josh. 20:8; 21:27).

In the ancient Near East if a person were killed, it was the custom that the nearest relative became the "avenger of blood" (Num. 35:19, 21–27; Deut. 19:12). It became his duty to slay the slayer. However, if a person killed another accidentally or unintentionally, the cities of refuge were provided as an asylum, "that by fleeing to one of these cities he might live" (Deut. 4:42).

The regulations concerning these cities are found in Numbers 35, Deuteronomy 19:1–13, and Joshua 20. If the manslayer reached a city of refuge before the avenger of blood could slay him, he was given a fair trial and provided asylum until the death of the high priest. After that the manslayer was permitted to return home; but if he left the city of refuge before the death of the high priest, he was subject to death at the hands of the avenger of blood.

In the New Testament, the cities of refuge apparently became a type, or symbolic illustration, of the salvation found in Christ: "We . . . have fled for refuge to lay hold of the hope set before us" (Heb. 6:18). In other words, when the sinner flees to Christ Jesus for refuge he is safe from the divine Avenger of Blood. The apostle Paul wrote, "Having now been justified by his [Christ's] blood, we shall be saved from wrath through Him" (Rom. 5:9) and "There is therefore now no condemnation to those who are in Christ Jesus" (Rom. 8:1). Regardless of his sin, the sinner may find asylum and sanctuary in Christ; all who flee to Him find refuge: "The one who comes to Me I will by no means cast out" (John 6:37). The believer is safe forever in the heavenly city of refuge because the great High Priest, Jesus Christ, will never die: "He ever lives to make intercession for him" (Heb. 7:25).

See also AVENGER OF BLOOD.

CITY OF DAVID (see BETHLEHEM; JERUSALEM).

CLAUDIUS [CLAW dih us]

The fourth emperor of the Roman Empire (A.D. 41–54), Tiberius Claudius Nero Germanicus, who suppressed the worship activities of the Jewish people in the city of Rome.

Early in his reign as emperor, Claudius was favorable toward the Jews and their practice of religion. But he later forbade their assembly and eventually "commanded all the Jews to depart from Rome" (Acts 18:2). This edict may have extended also to Christians, who were considered a sect of the Jews at that time.

Aquila and Priscilla, who became friends of the apostle Paul, were refugees from Italy because of this order of the Roman emperor (Acts 18:1–2). The Book of Acts also refers to a great famine that "happened in the days of Claudius Caesar" (Acts 11:28).

CLAY

Soil that consists of extremely fine particles of sand, flint, or quartz. Some clays were formed of soft limestone with much grit and flint, while others included quartz, which formed a much harder clay. Clay was used widely in the ancient world. Among its many uses, it was an important building material. The Tower of Babel was constructed of clay bricks (Gen. 11:3). The poorest quality clay was used in making bricks. Both sun-baked and kiln-fired bricks were known (2 Sam. 12:31). Mortar was also usually made of clay.

Impressions were made into wet clay with signet rings or cylinder seals to prove ownership (Job 38:14; Dan. 6:17). Clay seals were placed on houses, vessels of various kinds, and perhaps on Christ's tomb (Matt. 27:66). Clay tablets were used in Mesopotamia for cuneiform writing. Letters were inscribed in soft clay with a stylus. The tablet was then sun-baked or kiln-fired to increase its strength. Various kinds of pottery were made of clay. These included lamps, cooking utensils, pots, vases, jars, dishes, and idols.

CLEOPAS [KLEE uh pus]

One of the two disciples with whom Jesus talked on the Emmaus Road on the day of His resurrection (Luke 24:18). Cleopas is apparently not the same person as Cleophas—or Clopas (NRSV)—of John 19:25.

CLOPAS [KLOE puhs]

The husband of Mary, one of the women who was present at the crucifixion of Jesus (John 19:25; Cleophas in KJV). According to tradition, Clopas was the same person as Alphaeus, the father of James the Less and of Joses (Matt. 10:3; Mark 15:40). Most scholars agree that Clopas is not the same person as Cleopas (Luke 24:18).

COLOSSE [kuh LAH see]

A city in the Roman province of Asia (western Turkey), situated in the Lycus River Valley about 100 miles (160 kilometers) east of Ephesus. The apostle Paul wrote a letter to the church at Colosse (Col. 1:2; Colossae in NASB, REB, NRSV). The Christian community at Colosse apparently grew up under the leadership of Epaphras (Col. 1:7; 4:12) and Archippus

(Col. 4:17; Philem. 2). Philemon and Onesimus lived at Colosse (Col. 4:9).

Colosse formed a triangle with two other cities of the Lycus Valley, Hierapolis and Laodicea, both of which are mentioned in the New Testament. As early as the fifth century B.C., Colosse was known as a prosperous city; but by the beginning of the Christian Era it was eclipsed by its two neighbors. Thereafter its reputation declined to that of a small town.

Shortly after the apostle Paul sent his Epistle to Colosse, the cities of the Lycus Valley suffered a devastating earthquake in A.D. 61. They were soon rebuilt, even Laodicea, which had suffered the greatest damage. Although Colosse was increasingly overshadowed by Laodicea and Hierapolis, it retained considerable importance into the second and third centuries A.D. Later, the population of Colosse moved to Chonai (modern Honaz), three miles to the south. The mound that marks the site of Colosse remains uninhabited today.

CONCUBINE [CON cue bine]

In Old Testament times, a female slave or mistress with whom a man was lawfully permitted to have sexual intercourse.

The first mention of a concubine occurs in Genesis 22:24, where Reumah is described as the concubine of Nahor, Abraham's brother. Other men in the Old Testament who had these female slaves included Abraham (Gen. 25:6), Jacob (Gen. 35:22), Eliphaz (Gen. 36:12), Gideon (Judg. 8:31), and Saul (2 Sam. 3:7).

Sarai presented Hagar, her Egyptian maidservant, to Abram as a concubine so he could father children through Hagar (Gen. 16:2–3). This apparently was a common practice during the patriarchal period in Israel's history. The ancient Hebrews placed great value on having many children. If a couple remained childless after several years of marriage, the husband would often father children through a concubine.

By the time of the monarchy in Israel, the practice of keeping concubines apparently became a privilege of kings only. King Solomon is especially remembered for his many concubines (1 Kin. 11:3). Most of these concubines were foreign women. They led to Solomon's downfall, because they brought their pagan religions, which introduced idolatry into the land (1 Kin. 11:1–13; Neh. 13:25–27).

In the ancient world, concubines were protected by law; so they could not be sold if they were no longer of interest to the man. The Law of Moses also recognized the rights of concubines and guarded them from inhumane and callous treatment (Ex. 21:7–11; Deut. 10–14).

CONFESSION

An admission of sins (1 John 1:9); the profession of belief in the doctrines of a particular faith. In the Bible most of the uses of the word *confession* fall into one of these two categories. Examples of confession of sin may be found in Joshua's words to Achan (Josh. 7:19), in the confession during the Passover during Hezekiah's reign (2 Chr. 30:22), and in Ezra's call to the people to admit wrongdoing in marrying pagan wives (Ezra 10:11).

The Bible also uses the word confession to describe an open, bold, and courageous proclamation of one's faith (see Rom. 10:9–10).

CONGREGATION

A gathering or assembly of persons for worship and religious instruction; a religious community, such as the people of Israel or the Christian church.

In the Old Testament the English word "congregation" is the translation of several Hebrew words that carry the idea of "an appointed meeting" or "an assembly called together." These words point to Israel as the community of the Law, a "sacred assembly" gathered together by God and appointed to be His covenant people.

In the New Testament the term *congregation* is used only three times in the NKJV (Acts 7:38; 13:43; Heb. 2:12 assembly, NIV). The two Greek words translated as congregation, however, occur often elsewhere in the New Testament. Originally these words—*ekklesia* and *synagoge*—were virtually interchangeable. But they began to take on separate and specialized meanings as the rift between the Christian church (*ekklesia*) and the Jewish synagogue (*synagoge*) became more antagonistic. The words soon referred to rival religious faiths.

CONSCIENCE

A person's inner awareness of conforming to the will of God or departing from it, resulting in either a sense of approval or condemnation. David was smitten in his heart because of his lack of trust in the power of God (2 Sam. 24:10). But his guilt turned to joy when he sought the Lord's forgiveness (Ps. 32).

In the New Testament, the term *conscience* is found most frequently in the writings of the apostle Paul. Some people argue erroneously that conscience takes the place of the external law in the Old Testament. However, the conscience is not the ultimate standard of moral goodness (1 Cor. 4:4). The conscience must be formed by the will of God. The law given to Israel was inscribed on the hearts of believers (Heb. 8:10; 10:16); so the sensitized conscience is able to discern God's judgment against sin (Rom. 2:14–15).

The conscience of the believer has been cleansed by the work of Jesus Christ; it no longer accuses and condemns (Heb. 9:14; 10:22). To act contrary to the urging of one's conscience is wrong, for actions that go against the conscience cannot arise out of faith (1 Cor. 8:7–13; 10:23–30).

CONSECRATION

The act of setting apart, or dedicating, something or someone for God's use. In the Old Testament, the temple and its trappings were the most important objects consecrated to God (2 Chr. 7:5–9; Ezra 6:16–17); and Aaron and his sons were consecrated to the priesthood (Ex. 29; Lev. 8). Before the beginning of the priesthood in Israel's history, the first-born of men and animals alike were consecrated (Ex. 13:2).

In the New Testament, the supreme example of consecration is Christ Himself (John 17:19; Heb. 7:28; 10:10). But believers are also consecrated by Christ (John 17:17; 1 Pet. 2:9), and are urged to consecrate themselves as well (Rom. 12:1; 2 Tim. 2:21). One of the results of our consecration by Christ is that we are now a priesthood of believers (1 Pet. 2:9) with direct access to our heavenly Father (Eph. 3:11–12).

CONVERSION

The initial change of attitude and will that brings a person into right relationship with God. Conversion involves turning away from evil deeds and false worship and turning toward serving and worshiping the Lord. Conversion marks a person's entrance into a new relationship with God, forgiveness of sins, and new life as a part of the fellowship of the people of God.

The experience of conversion may differ with various individuals. Paul's conversion was sudden and radical (Acts 9:1–6), while the conversion of Lydia (Acts 16:14–15) was gradual and gentle. But the results of conversion are always a clear change of attitude and a new direction for life.

CONVICTION

The process of being condemned by one's own conscience as a sinner because of God's demands. The idea of conviction is a major theme of Scripture, although the word is rarely used (Rom. 7:7–25). The agent of conviction is the Holy Spirit (John 16:7–11); and the means of conviction is either the Word of God (Acts 2:37) or God's general revelation of His demands through nature and people's inborn consciousness of a sense of right and wrong (Rom. 1:18–20; 2:15). The purpose of conviction is to lead people to repent of their sins (Rom. 2:1–4) and to turn to God for salvation and eternal life.

COPPER

A reddish-brown metal derived from many kinds of ores. One of the oldest metals known to humankind, copper was the first to be used for making tools. Gold and meteoric iron were probably used before copper. Pure copper was used until it was alloyed with tin to form bronze sometime between 4500 and 3000 B.C. Ancient copper refineries were located in Sinai, Egypt, Syria, Persia, the Phoenician coast, and Palestine. During Solomon's reign (about 970–931 B.C.), enormous amounts of bronze were used in the temple furnishings (1 Kin. 7:13–47).

Many useful articles were made from copper and its alloys, including tools of all kinds, utensils (Lev. 6:28), weapons (2 Sam. 21:16; 22:35; 2 Chr. 12:10), idols, and musical instruments.

CORBAN [KAWR bahn] (an offering brought near)

A word applied to a gift or offering in the temple that declared that gift dedicated to God in a special sense. Once a gift was offered under the special declaration of *corban*, it could not be withdrawn or taken back; it was considered totally dedicated for the temple's special use.

Jesus condemned the Pharisees for encouraging the people to make such gifts to the temple while neglecting their responsibility to care for their parents (Mark 7:11–13). According to Jesus, this was a clear violation of a higher commandment, "Honor your father and your mother" (Mark 7:10).

CORINTH [KAWR inth]

Ancient Greece's most important trade city (Acts 18:1; 19:1; 1 Cor. 1:2; 2 Cor. 1:1, 23; 2 Tim. 4:20). Ideally situated on the Isthmus of Corinth between the Ionian Sea and the Aegean Sea, Corinth was the connecting link between Rome, the capital of the world, and the East. At Corinth the apostle Paul established a flourishing church, made up of a cross section of the worldly minded people who had flocked to Corinth to participate in the gambling, legalized temple prostitution, business adventures, and amusements available in a first-century navy town (1 Cor. 6:9–11).

Although the apostle Paul did not establish the church in Corinth until about A.D. 51 (Acts 18:1–18), the city's history dates back to prehistoric times, when ancient tribesmen first settled the site. Always a commercial and trade center, Corinth was already prosperous and famous for its bronze, pottery, and shipbuilding more than 800 years before Christ. The Greek poet Homer mentioned "wealthy Corinth" in 850 B.C.

In the following centuries Corinth competed for power with Athens, its stronger neighbor across the isthmus to the north. And in 146 B.C. invading Roman armies destroyed Corinth, killing the men and enslaving the women and children. Only a token settlement remained until 44 B.C., when Julius Caesar ordered the city rebuilt. Not only did he restore it as the capital city of the Roman province of Achaia; he also repopulated it with freed Italians and slaves from every nation. Soon the merchants flocked back to Corinth, too.

The city soon became a melting pot for the approximately 500,000 people who lived there at the time of Paul's arrival. Merchants and sailors, anxious to work the docks, migrated to Corinth. Professional gamblers and athletes, betting on the Isthmian games, took up residence. Slaves, sometimes freed but with no place to go, roamed the streets day and night. And prostitutes (both male and female) were abundant. People from Rome, the rest of Greece, Egypt, Asia Minor—indeed, all of the Mediterranean world—relished the lack of standards and freedom of thought that prevailed in the city.

These were the people who eventually made up the Corinthian church. They had to learn to live together in harmony, although their national, social, economic, and religious backgrounds were very different.

Perched on a narrow strip of land connecting the Peloponnesus, a peninsula of southern Greece, with central Greece and the rest of Europe, Corinth enjoyed a steady flow of trade. The city had two splendid harbor cities—Cenchreae, the eastern port on the Saronic Gulf; and Lechaeum, the western port on the Corinthian Gulf.

In the outlying areas around Corinth, farmers tended their grain fields, vineyards, and olive groves. But the pulse of Corinth was the city itself, enclosed by walls 6 miles (10 kilometers) in circumference. Most of the daily business was conducted in the marble-paved agora, or marketplace, in the central part of the city. Although only one percent of the ancient city has been excavated by archaeologists, some interesting discoveries give ideas of what the city was like when Paul arrived.

A marble lintel or crosspiece of a door was found near the residential section of Corinth. It bore part of the inscription, "Synagogue of the Hebrews." This may have been on the same site of the earlier synagogue in which Paul first proclaimed the gospel message to Corinth, accompanied by his newfound Jewish friends, Aquila and Priscilla (Acts 18:2).

Not far from the synagogue excavation site was the magnificent judgment seat, covered with ornate blue and white marble. There, the Roman proconsul of Achaia, Gallio, dismissed Paul's case (Acts 18:12–17). In the pavement of an amphitheater is inscribed the name Erastus, perhaps the official of Corinth mentioned in Romans 16:23 and 2 Timothy 4:20.

South of the marketplace were the butcher stalls (shambles in KJV; meat market in NKJV, NASB, NIV, REB, NRSV) that Paul mentioned in 1 Corinthians 10:25. Corinthians purchased their meat from these stalls. The meat was often dedicated to pagan idols before being sold. This presented a cultural problem for the Christians in Corinth (1 Cor. 8).

Today the temple of Apollo, partially in ruins, towers above the ancient marketplace. Each fluted Doric column, almost 24 feet (about 7 meters) tall, was cut from a single piece of stone in one of several quarries outside Corinth's walls.

Rising 1,500 feet (457 meters) above the city itself and to the south is the Acrocorinth, the acropolis or citadel. From there, the acropolis at Athens, about 45 miles (73 kilometers) away, can be seen. Also, the infamous temple of Aphrodite (or Venus) was located on top of this fortified hill. This pagan temple and its 1,000 "religious" prostitutes poisoned the city's culture and morals. For this reason, the apostle Paul sometimes had to deal harshly with the converts in the Corin-

thian church. Most of the Corinthians had lived in this godless society all their lives, and the idea of tolerating even incest had not seemed so terrible to them (1 Cor. 5).

In spite of Corinth's notorious reputation, God used the apostle Paul to establish a vigorous church in the city about A.D. 51 (Acts 18:1–18). Later, Paul wrote at least two letters to the church at Corinth. Both deal with divisions in the church, as well as immorality and the abuse of Christian freedom.

The Corinth that Paul knew was partially destroyed by an earthquake in A.D. 521, then totally devastated by another in 1858. Modern Corinth, rebuilt about 2.5 miles (4 kilometers) from the ancient site, is little more than a town. It is certainly not a thriving trade center, but the inhabitants only need to look at the ancient ruins to recall the former glory of their city. The success of the gospel at Corinth—bittersweet though it was—illustrates that the grace of God comes not so much to the noble as to the needy (1 Cor. 1:26–31).

CORNELIUS [kor NEEL yus]

A Roman soldier stationed in Caesarea who was the first recorded Gentile convert to Christianity (Acts 10:1–33).

Cornelius was a God-fearing man strongly attracted to the Jewish teaching of monotheism (the belief in one God), as opposed to pagan idolatry and immorality, and to the concern expressed in the Law of Moses concerning helping the poor and needy (Acts 10:2). He is introduced in the Book of Acts as a representative of thousands in the Gentile world who were weary of paganism and who were hungry for the coming of the Messiah—the Christ who would deliver them from their sins and lead them into an abundant, Spirit-filled life.

God sent a heavenly vision both to Cornelius and to Simon Peter. Obeying his vision, Cornelius sent some of his men to Joppa, about 36 miles (58 kilometers) south of Caesarea, to find Peter. Peter, in turn, obeyed his own vision (which he interpreted to mean that Gentiles were to be included in Christ's message) and went to Cornelius. While Peter was still preaching to Cornelius and his household, "the Holy Spirit fell upon all those who heard the word" (Acts 10:44). Peter commanded them to be baptized in the name of the Lord.

This incident marked the expansion of the early church to include Gentiles as well as Jews (Acts 10:34–35; 11:18). Peter alluded to Cornelius's conversion at the Jerusalem Council (Acts 15:7–11).

COURT OF THE GENTILES

The outermost court of Herod's temple in Jerusalem. The temple consisted of a series of courts. As one entered the temple precincts and proceeded toward the interior, each court was higher than the previous one. Non-Jews could enter the Court of the Gentiles but were prohibited from going farther. At Jesus' death, the veil that separated the inner court from the outer court was split, showing that all people had equal access to God through Jesus Christ, the great mediator and redeemer (Matt. 27:51; Eph. 2:14).

COVETOUSNESS

An intense desire to possess something (or someone) that belongs to another person. The Ten Commandments prohibit this attitude (Ex. 20:17). Covetousness springs from a greedy self-centeredness and an arrogant disregard of God's law. The Bible repeatedly warns against this sin (2 Pet. 2:10).

The best way to avoid a self-centered, covetous attitude is to trust the Lord and to face one's responsibilities (2 Thess. 3:6–15). To those tempted by "covetousness" and "worthless things" (Ps.

119:36), Jesus declares, "Take heed and beware of covetousness, for one's life does not consist in the abundance of the things he possesses" (Luke 12:15).

COVENANT

An agreement between two people or two groups that involves promises on the part of each to the other. The Hebrew word for *covenant* probably means "betweenness," emphasizing the relational element that lies at the basis of all covenants. Human covenants or treaties were either between equals or between a superior and an inferior. Divine covenants, however, are always of the latter type, and the concept of covenant between God and His people is one of the most important theological truths of the Bible. Indeed, the word itself has come to denote the two main divisions of Christian Scripture: Old Covenant and New Covenant (traditionally, Old Testament and New Testament).

By making a covenant with Abraham, God promised to bless His descendants and to make them His special people. Abraham, in return, was to remain faithful to God and to serve as a channel through which God's blessings could flow to the rest of the world (Gen. 12:1–3). God's covenant with Abraham was made (Gen. 15:18) and confirmed (Gen. 17:2) to guarantee that Abraham's descendants would be innumerable and that they would receive the Promised Land. The Abrahamic covenant sign is circumcision (Gen. 17:11).

Even before Abraham's time, God also made a covenant with Noah. It illustrates three important principles: (1) All divine covenants originate with God (Gen. 9:9); (2) all of them are everlasting (Gen. 9:16); (3) all of them are memorialized with a visible sign, in this case the rainbow (Gen. 9:13). The purpose of the Noahic covenant was the divine promise that

God would never again destroy all sinful humanity by a flood (Gen. 9:11).

Another famous covenant was between God and David, in which David and his descendants were established as the royal heirs to the throne of the nation of Israel (2 Sam. 7:12; 22:51). This covenant agreement reached its highest fulfillment when Jesus the Messiah, a descendant of the line of David, was born in Bethlehem about a thousand years after God made this promise to David the king (Matt. 1:1; 2:4–6; Luke 1:29–33).

God's covenant with Israel through Moses is the "old" or "first" covenant as contrasted with the "new" (Jer. 31:31–34; 2 Cor. 3:6–17; Gal. 4:24–31; Heb. 8:3–9:22). Its establishment (Ex. 19:3–25), stipulations (Ex. 20:1–17), exposition (Ex. 20:22–23:33), and confirmation (Ex. 24:1–12) constituted the formal basis of the redemptive relationship between the Lord and His chosen people until it was superseded by the New Covenant (Heb. 8:3). The Mosaic covenant sign is the Sabbath (Ex. 31:13, 16–17). Israel's pledge to obey the Lord (Ex. 19:8; 24:3, 7), on the basis of which Moses sprinkled the "blood of the covenant" on them (Ex. 24:8), was broken soon (Ex. 32:1–31) and often (Jer. 31:32).

All biblical covenants were solemnized by killing one or more animals and shedding their blood (Gen. 8:20; 15:9–10; Ex. 24:5; Jer. 34:18–20), the importance of which is reflected in the Hebrew idiom "cut a covenant" (Gen. 15:18; Jer. 34:18), uniformly translated "made a covenant." The blood-bought ratification of the earlier covenants prefigured the "new covenant in [Jesus'] blood" (Luke 22:20; 1 Cor. 11:25), shed as the sign and seal of our redemption once for all people and for all time (Heb. 10:5–19).

A covenant, in the biblical sense, implies much more than a contract or simple agreement. A contract always has an end date, while a covenant is a permanent arrangement. Another difference is that a contract generally involves only one part of a person, such as a skill, while a covenant covers a person's total being.

The Old Testament contains many examples of covenants between people who related to each other as equals. For example, David and Jonathan entered into a covenant because of their love for each other. This agreement bound each of them to certain responsibilities (1 Sam. 18:3). The striking thing about God's covenants with His people is that God is holy, all-knowing, and all powerful; but He consents to enter into covenants with people who are weak, sinful, and imperfect.

The New Testament makes a clear distinction between covenants of law and covenants of promise. The apostle Paul spoke of these "two covenants," one originating "from Mount Sinai," the other from "the Jerusalem above" (Gal. 4:24–26). Paul also argued that the covenant established at Mount Sinai, the law, is a "ministry of death" and "condemnation" (2 Cor. 3:7, 9)—a covenant that cannot be obeyed because of human weakness and sin (Rom. 8:3).

But the "covenants of promise" (Eph. 2:12) are God's guarantees that He will provide salvation in spite of people's inability to keep their side of the agreement because of sin. The provision of a chosen people through whom the Messiah would be born is the promise of the covenants with Adam and David (Gen. 3:15; 2 Sam. 7:14–15). The covenant with Noah is God's promise to withhold judgment on nature while salvation is occurring (Gen. 8:21–22; 2 Pet. 3:7, 15). In the covenant with Abraham, God promised to bless Abraham's descendants because of his faith (Gen. 12:1–3).

These many covenants of promise may be considered one covenant of grace, which was fulfilled in the life and ministry of Jesus. His death ushered in the New Covenant under which we are justified by God's grace and mercy rather than by our human attempts to keep the law. And Jesus Himself is the Mediator of this better covenant between God and humankind (Heb. 9:15).

Jesus' sacrificial death served as the oath, or pledge, that God made to us to seal this New Covenant. He is determined to give us eternal life and fellowship with Him, in spite of our unworthiness. As the Book of Hebrews declares, "The word of the oath, which came after the law, appoints the Son who has been perfected forever" (Heb. 7:28). This is still God's promise to any person who turns to Him in repentance and faith.

See also COVENANT, NEW.

COVENANT, BOOK OF THE

A name for the code of laws in Exodus 20:22–23:33, given to Moses at Mount Sinai as an expansion and exposition of the Ten Commandments (Ex. 24:7). The Book of the Covenant discovered in the temple during the reign of King Josiah of Judah (640–609 B.C.), who used it in his restoration of true worship (2 Kin. 23:2–3, 21; 2 Chr. 34:30–31), may have included also some additional sections of Exodus as well as most or all of the Book of Deuteronomy.

COVENANT, NEW

The new agreement God has made with mankind, based on the death and resurrection of Jesus Christ. The concept of a New Covenant originated with the promise of the prophet Jeremiah that God would accomplish for His people what the Old Covenant had failed to do (Jer. 31:31–34). Under this New Covenant, God would write His law on human hearts. This promised action suggested a new level of obedience, a

new knowledge of the Lord, and a new forgiveness of sin.

The New Testament, which itself means "new covenant," interprets the work of Jesus Christ as bringing this promised New Covenant into being. In Luke 22:20, when Jesus ate the Passover meal at the Last Supper with His disciples, He spoke of the cup as "the new covenant in My blood." When the apostle Paul recited the tradition he had received concerning the Last Supper, he quoted these words of Jesus about the cup as "the new covenant in My blood" (1 Cor. 11:25).

But the Epistle to the Hebrews gives the New Covenant more attention than any other book in the New Testament. It includes a quotation of the entire passage from Jeremiah 31:31–34 (Heb. 8:8–12; see also 10:16–17). Jesus is also referred to by the writer of Hebrews as "the Mediator of the new covenant" (Heb. 9:15; 12:24). The New Covenant, a "better covenant . . . established on better promises" (Heb. 8:6), rests directly on the sacrificial work of Christ, according to Hebrews. The New Covenant accomplished what the Old Covenant could not: removal of sin and cleansing of the conscience (Jer. 31:34; Heb. 10:2, 22). The work of Jesus Christ on the cross thus makes the Old Covenant "obsolete" (Heb. 8:13) and fulfills the promise of the prophet Jeremiah.

CREATION

God's action in bringing the natural universe into being. The writer of the Epistle to the Hebrews in the New Testament declared, "By faith we understand that the world was framed by the word of God, so that the things which are seen were not made of things which are visible" (Heb. 11:3).

People of the pagan nations of the ancient world believed that matter was eternal and that the gods evolved out of natural processes. But the Bible teaches that God existed before creation and called the physical world into existence out of nothing. The main account of His acts of creation is found in the first two chapters of the Book of Genesis, although God as Creator is a prominent theme in Isaiah 40–48 as well.

The phrase "God created" (Gen. 1:1, 21, 27) in Genesis 1 is eclipsed by another: "God said" (Gen. 1:3, 6–7, 11, 14, 20, 24, 26, 29). Its frequency attests to its significance in emphasizing the way in which God created—simply by speaking a word (Ps. 33:6, 9; Heb. 11:3).

God's first act of creation was to bring into being the great watery chaos described in Genesis 1:2: "The earth was without form and void; and darkness was on the face of the deep." His next creative act was to bring order out of chaos—to separate the land from the water. This set the stage for the creation of plant and animal life.

First God created inanimate life: grass, other vegetation, trees, and fruit trees. Then the sea was filled with living creatures, the air with flying things, and the earth with creeping things. Then God moved on in orderly fashion to create land animals.

The creation of man was left for the sixth and final day of creation because man was special and was to rule over the rest of creation. "Then God said, 'Let Us make man in Our image, according to Our likeness'" (Gen. 1:26). This statement has fascinated thinkers for centuries. Just what does the image of God mean? Since God is spirit—not a material substance—it must mean more than physical resemblance. To be created in God's image means that men and women, though creatures, are akin to God.

God is Creator—the only being capable of making something from nothing. The Hebrew verb for "create" always has God as its subject. Yet, on a lesser level, people also have the capacity to be creative. This is one distinct meaning of the truth that we are created in God's image. God is speaker and a ruler. People were also told to have dominion over the creation. God is holy, a moral and ethical God who is righteous. People are also morally and ethically responsible and must make moral choices. God has revealed that He is a social being (Father, Son, and Holy Spirit). People also are social beings who need relationships with others. Human experience and the biblical record suggest that these are some ways in which we reflect the image of God.

The Genesis writer also declared that God created humanity as "male and female" (Gen. 1:27). This account of creation does not give priority to either male or female. Both are needed to reflect the image of God. The most fundamental difference in humanity is not race but sex. The Greeks said that people once were androgynous—both male and female. Somehow they lost the female half and ever since have been looking for their other half. But the writer of Genesis pointed out that sex is an order of creation that is good and proper in God's sight.

Genesis 2 contains what some scholars call a second creation account. But others point out that it focuses on specific events relating to creation as they unfolded in the Garden of Eden. It thus sets the stage for what follows in the accounts of human temptation and sin. A major emphasis of chapter 2 is the creation of woman as a companion for man. Man's incompleteness apart from woman is shown in his loneliness and frustration. None of the animals could meet Adam's need. Then the Lord created woman from Adam's rib.

Bible students have long seen symbolic truth in this rib imagery. Woman was taken from under man's arm to symbolize his protection of her. She was taken from near his heart that he might love and cherish her. She was not made from a head bone to rule over man, nor from his foot to be trampled on and degraded. Like the man, she reflects God's image. Together they formed the blessed pair needed to replenish and subdue the earth.

Many Bible students wonder about the six days of creation. Were these 24-hour days or indefinite periods of time? It may help us in our interpretation if we remember that we use the word "day" in several ways, even as the ancient Hebrews did. We speak of the "day of reckoning," the "day of opportunity," and the "day of trouble." These may signify more than a 24-hour day. In similar fashion, the biblical writers spoke of the "day of the Lord" and "day of visitation."

Skeptics have ridiculed the creation story in Genesis because it reports that the creation occurred in six days. But the indefinite meaning of "day" takes care of this objection. Besides, Scripture says that with the Lord, "A day is as a thousand years and a thousand years as a day" (2 Pet. 3:8). The biblical writer was not writing a scientific journal. He was moved by God's Spirit to give a revelation of spiritual reality. His primary emphasis was not on the process by which the world was created but on the Creator and His purpose.

Many of the pagan nations of the ancient world had their own creation stories. But in these stories, their gods evolved out of natural processes connected with the world itself. Ancient people believed the material universe was eternal, and it brought their gods into being. But Genesis declares that God existed before creation and is in full control of the physical universe. He called the world into being by His word. His power is absolute. He does not have to

conform to nature and cannot be threatened by it. God is sovereign and does not have to share His power with other supernatural beings.

Since God created the universe out of nothing, it is His and will always serve His purpose. As He shaped creation without any interference from anyone, He will bring creation to its desired end. No power can frustrate God in His purpose to complete the process started in creation and revealed in Scripture. Our hope rests in the sovereign power of Him who created the world and then re-created us through the saving power of His Son, Jesus Christ.

CRETANS [KREET uhns]

Inhabitants of the island of Crete in the Mediterranean Sea. The Book of Acts records that Cretans were among those present in Jerusalem on the Day of Pentecost (Acts 2:11). Cretan lifestyle was known for its excesses. In writing to Titus, Paul quoted from the Greek poet Epimenides of Knossos (about 600 B.C.) that "Cretans are always liars, evil beasts, lazy gluttons" (Titus 1:12). This must have presented a real challenge for Titus, who was assigned the responsibility to "set in order the things that are lacking" in the Cretan church (Titus 1:5).

CRETE [kreet]

An island in the Mediterranean Sea where a ship on which the apostle Paul was sailing was struck by a storm. Crete is about 160 miles (258 kilometers) long and varies between 7 and 30 miles (11 and 49 kilometers) wide (Acts 27:7, 12–13, 21). It is probably to be identified with Caphtor (Deut. 2:23; Amos 9:7), the place from which the Philistines (Caphtorim) originated. A number of legends are associated with Crete, particularly those involving King Minos and the Minotaur (the half-bull, half-man monster). The is-

C

land was captured by the Romans in 68–66 B.C. and made a Roman province.

During his voyage to Rome, Paul's ship touched at Fair Havens, a harbor on the south coast of Crete (Acts 27:8). Not heeding Paul's advice about the weather, the Roman soldier who held Paul in custody agreed with the captain and set sail for Crete's large harbor at Phoenix. The result was a shipwreck at Malta (Acts 27:9–28:1).

CROSS

An upright wooden stake or post on which condemned people were executed. Before the manner of Jesus' death caused the Cross to symbolize the very heart of the Christian faith, the Greek word for cross referred primarily to a pointed stake used in rows to form the walls of a defensive stockade.

It was common in the biblical period for the decapitated bodies of executed persons to be publicly displayed by impaling them on stakes to discourage civil disobedience and to mock defeated military foes (Gen. 40:19; 1 Sam. 31:8–13). This gruesome practice may explain how the stake eventually came to be used as an instrument of civil and military punishment. Such stakes eventually came to be fitted with crossbeams as instruments of humiliation, torture, and execution for persons convicted as enemies of the state (foreign soldiers, rebels and spies, for example) or of civil criminals (such as robbers).

During the Old Testament period, there is no evidence that the Jews fastened people to a stake or a cross as a means of execution. The law directed death by stoning (Lev. 20:2; Deut. 22:24). But the law did permit the public display (or "hanging") of a lawbreaker's body "on a tree" (Deut. 21:22), strictly commanding that the "body shall not remain overnight on the tree, but you shall surely bury him that day" (Deut. 21:23; also see John 19:31).

Grisly as such a practice seems today, it did set Israel apart from other nations. The degrading practice most often used throughout the ancient world was to allow the victim to rot in public. Persons so displayed (or "hanged") after execution by stoning for breaking Israel's law were said to be "accursed of God" (Deut. 21:23). This helps explain the references to Jesus' being killed "by hanging on a tree" (Acts 5:30; 10:39) and the statement that Jesus was "cursed" in Galatians 3:13. Although Jesus died in a different manner, He was publicly displayed as a criminal and enemy of the state.

Excavated relief sculptures show that the Assyrians executed their captured enemies by forcing their living bodies down onto pointed stakes. This barbaric cruelty was not crucifixion as we think of it today but impalement. Scholars are not certain when a crossbeam was added to the simple stake. Jeremiah's mention of princes being "hung up by their hands" (Lam. 5:12) by the Babylonians may refer to the use of a crossbeam. But there is no way of knowing whether the prophet speaks of a method of execution or the dishonoring of bodies killed in battle. The classical Greek historians Herodotus and Thucydides refer to the stake or cross as a method of execution during the time of the Persians. But it is not clear whether the victim was tied or nailed to the wood or impaled.

Crucifixion on a stake or cross was practiced by the Greeks, notably Alexander the Great, who hung 2,000 people on crosses when the city of Tyre was destroyed. During the period between Greek and Roman control of Palestine, the Jewish ruler Alexander Jannaeus crucified 800 Pharisees who opposed him at Bethome. But these executions were condemned as detestable and abnormal by decent-minded people of

Jannaeus's day as well as by the later Jewish historian, Josephus.

From the early days of the Roman Republic, death on the cross was used for rebellious slaves and bandits, although Roman citizens were rarely subjected to this method of execution. The practice continued well beyond the New Testament period as one of the supreme punishments for military and political crimes such as desertion, spying, revealing secrets, rebellion, and sedition. Following the conversion of the emperor Constantine to Christianity, the cross became a sacred symbol and its use by Romans as a means of torture and death was abolished.

Those sentenced to death on a cross in the Roman period were usually beaten with leather lashes—a procedure that often resulted in severe loss of blood. Victims were then generally forced to carry the upper crossbeam to the execution site, where the central stake was already set up.

After being fastened to the crossbeam on the ground with ropes—or, in rare cases, nails through the wrist—the naked victim was then hoisted with the crossbeam against the standing vertical stake. A block or peg was sometimes fastened to the stake as a crude seat. The feet were then tied or nailed to the stake. Death by suffocation or exhaustion normally followed only after a long period of agonizing pain.

In time the simple pointed stake first used for execution was modified. The four most important of the resulting crosses are: (1) the Latin cross (shaped like a lower case "t"), on which it seems likely that Jesus died, because of the notice placed above His head (Matt. 27:37); (2) the St. Anthony's cross, which has the crossbeam at the top (shaped like a capital "T"); (3) the St. Andrew's cross, which is shaped like a capital "X"; and (4) the so-called Greek cross which has the crossbeam in the center (shaped like a plus sign).

The authors of the Gospels tell us that the Lord Jesus spoke of the Cross before His death (Matt. 10:38; Mark 10:21; Luke 14:27) as a symbol of the necessity of full commitment (even unto death) for those who would be His disciples. But the major significance of the Cross after Jesus' death and resurrection is its use as a symbol of Jesus' willingness to suffer for our sins (Phil. 2:8; Heb. 12:2) so that we might be reconciled (2 Cor. 5:19; Col. 1:20) to God and know His peace (Eph. 2:16).

Thus the Cross symbolizes the glory of the Christian gospel (1 Cor. 1:17): the fact that through this offensive means of death (1 Cor. 1:23; Gal. 5:11), the debt of sin against us was "nailed to the cross" (Col. 2:14), and we, having "been crucified with Christ" (Gal. 2:20), have been freed from sin and death and made alive to God (Rom. 6:6–11).

See also CRUCIFIXION OF CHRIST.

CROWN

Special headgear used to symbolize a person's high status and authority. Several different words in the Hebrew and Greek languages of the Bible are translated as "crown." Persons in the Bible who are described as wearing crowns include Vashti (Esth. 1:11) and Esther (Esth. 2:17). The high priest and the king in the early history of the nation of Israel also apparently wore crowns as a mark of their office and authority (Lev. 8:9; 2 Sam. 1:10).

The wreath of leaves awarded the winner of an athletic competition in the Grecian games was also described by the apostle Paul as a crown (1 Cor. 9:25; 2 Tim. 4:8). The Roman soldiers mocked Jesus on the cross by placing a crown of thorns on His head, taunting Him as "King of the Jews" (Matt. 27:29; also Mark 15:17; John 19:2, 5).

The Book of Revelation portrays Christ with many crowns on His head, signifying His kingly authority (Rev. 19:12). Our inheritance as Christians who follow the will of our Lord is also described symbolically as a crown. As a reward for our faithfulness, we will receive an imperishable crown (1 Cor. 9:25), one that will not wither or fade away, and a crown of eternal life (James 1:12; 1 Pet. 5:4).

CRUCIFIXION OF CHRIST

The method of torture and execution used by the Romans to put Christ to death. At a crucifixion the victim usually was nailed or tied to a wooden stake and left to die.

Crucifixion involved attaching the victim with nails through the wrists or with leather thongs to a crossbeam attached to a vertical stake. Sometimes blocks or pins were put on the stake to give victims some support as they hung suspended from the crossbeam. At times the feet were also nailed to the vertical stake. As the victim hung dangling by the arms, the blood could no longer circulate to the vital organs. Only by supporting themselves on the seat or pin could victims gain relief.

But gradually exhaustion set in, and death followed, although usually not for several days. If victims had been severely beaten, they would not live this long. To hasten death, the executioners sometimes broke the victims' legs with a club. Then they could no longer support their bodies to keep blood circulating, and death quickly followed. Usually bodies were left to rot or to be eaten by scavengers.

To the Israelites, impalement was the most disgusting form of death: "He who is hanged is accursed of God" (Deut. 21:23). Yet the Jewish Sanhedrin sought and obtained Roman authorization to have Jesus crucified (Mark 15:13–15). As was the custom, the charge against Jesus was attached to the cross; He was offered a brew to deaden His senses, but He refused (Mark 15:23). There was no need for the soldiers to break His legs to hasten death. By the ninth hour (Mark 15:25, 34, 37), probably 3:00 P.M.—in only six hours—Jesus was already dead (John 19:31–33). Jesus' body was not left to rot; the disciples were able to secure Pilate's permission to give Him a proper burial.

The Cross has been a major stumbling block in the way of the Jews, preventing the majority of them from accepting Jesus as the Messiah. The apostle Paul summed up the importance of the Crucifixion best: "We preach Christ crucified, to the Jews a stumbling block and to the Greeks foolishness, but to those who are called, both Jews and Greeks, Christ the power of God and the wisdom of God" (1 Cor. 1:23–24). Out of the ugliness and agony of crucifixion, God accomplished the greatest good of all—the redemption of sinners.

See also CROSS.

CUPBEARER

A person who tasted and served wine to the king. Ancient kings had to be very cautious about what they ate and drank. They used trusted servants to taste everything before they consumed it. If the servant lived or did not get sick, the king and queen then ate or drank. The "chief butler" in the Joseph account (Gen. 40) headed the king's cupbearers. Nehemiah held this highly trusted position under King Artaxerxes (Neh. 1:11), influencing the king politically. King Solomon also employed cupbearers (1 Kin. 10:5).

CURSE

A prayer for injury, harm, or misfortune to befall someone. Noah, for instance, pronounced a curse on Canaan (Gen. 9:25). Isaac pronounced a curse on anyone who cursed Jacob (Gen. 27:29). The soothsayer Balaam was hired by

Balak, king of Moab, to pronounce a curse on the Israelites (Num. 22–24). Goliath, the Philistine giant of Gath, "cursed David by his gods" (1 Sam. 17:43).

In Bible times, a curse was considered to be more than a mere wish that evil would befall one's enemies; it was believed to possess the power to bring about the evil the curser spoke.

In the account of the temptation and Fall, God Himself is described as cursing the serpent (Gen. 3:14–15), as well as the ground (Gen. 3:17). Although the word *curse* is not used directly of Adam and Eve, the woman is sentenced to pain in childbirth and the man is condemned to earn his living by the sweat of his face. In the New Testament, Jesus cursed the fig tree, saying, " 'Let no fruit grow on you ever again.' And immediately the fig tree withered away" (Matt. 21:19; Mark 11:14). He also taught Christians how to deal with curses: "Bless those who curse you" (Luke 6:28).

The apostle Paul spoke of the law as a curse because it pronounces a curse upon everyone "who does not continue in all things which are written in the book of the law, to do them" (Gal. 3:10). By the grace of God, however, "Christ has redeemed us from the curse of the law, having become a curse for us (for it is written, 'Cursed is everyone who hangs on a tree')" (Gal. 3:13). John promised that the day is coming when "there shall be no more curse" (Rev. 22:3); all those whose names are written in the Lamb's Book of Life will enjoy the abundant blessings of God.

CUSH [kush]

The land south of Egypt, also called Nubia, which includes part of Sudan. Cush began just beyond Syene (modern Aswan; Ezek. 29:10). The Persian Empire of Ahasuerus (Xerxes, 486–465 B.C.) extended to this point, "from India to Ethiopia" (Esth. 1:1; 8:9). Precious stones came from Cush, "the topaz of Ethiopia" (Job 28:19), and the people were tall with smooth skin (Is. 18:2, 7) that could not be changed (Jer. 13:23). The prophets predicted that the distant land of Cush would be judged by God (Is. 18:1–6; Zeph. 2:12). Other texts indicate, however, that some from Cush will bring gifts to God and worship Him as their king (Ps. 68:31; Is. 11:11; 18:7). Its ancient Greek name was Ethiopia, not to be confused with the modern nation of Ethiopia (Abyssinia).

CYPRUS [SIGH prus]

A large island in the northeastern corner of the Mediterranean Sea, about 60 miles (97 kilometers) off the coast of Syria and about 41 miles (66 kilometers) off the coast of Cilicia (modern Turkey). Although Cyprus is a rocky island, many nations sought its rich copper deposits and timber reserves (especially the cypress tree). Consequently, in the course of its history, Cyprus frequently was conquered by many powerful nations, including the Mycenaeans, Phoenicians, Assyrians, and Persians.

After Alexander the Great, the Egyptian Ptolemies controlled Cyprus until the Romans took it in 58 B.C. During the Roman period it was joined to the province of Cilicia, then made an independent imperial province; and in 22 B.C. it became a senatorial province, with a proconsul in charge at the capital city of Paphos.

The name Cyprus is not found in the Old Testament; but because extrabiblical texts refer to Alashiya as a primary source of copper, many believe that Elishah (Gen. 10:4; 1 Chr. 1:7; Ezek. 27:7) is Cyprus. Kittim is another Old Testament name that may refer to Cyprus (Gen. 10:4; 1 Chr. 1:7). Another spelling is Chittim (Num. 24:24; Is. 23:1; Jer. 2:10, KJV).

The New Testament contains several references to Cyprus—all in the Book of Acts. Barnabas was a native "of the country of Cyprus" (Acts 4:36). The first Christians fled to Cyprus because of the persecution of the early church after the death of Stephen (Acts 8:1–4; 11:19–20). Barnabas, Mark, and Paul began their first missionary journey by stopping at Salamis, the largest city of Cyprus on the east coast of the island (Acts 13:4–5).

After the split between Paul and Barnabas, Barnabas took John Mark and returned to Cyprus to do missionary work there (Acts 15:39). Mnason, an early Christian, was from Cyprus (Acts 21:16). Later Paul sailed past the island (Acts 21:3; 27:4).

CYRENE [sigh REE neh]

A city on the north coast of Africa founded by Dorian Greeks about 630 B.C. Cyrene was later the capital of the Roman province of Cyrenaica (ancient and modern Libya). Midway between Carthage and Alexandria—about 100 miles (160 kilometers) northeast of modern Benghazi—the city was built on a beautiful tableland nearly 2,000 feet (610 meters) above sea level.

Less than 10 miles (16 kilometers) from the sea, Cyrene attracted travelers and commerce of every kind. The city was renowned as an intellectual center; Carneades, the founder of the new Academy at Athens, and Aristippus, the Epicurean philosopher and friend of Socrates, were among its distinguished citizens. The city surrendered to Alexander the Great in 331 B.C. and passed into the hands of Rome in 96 B.C.

Although Cyrene is not mentioned in the Old Testament, it was an important city in New Testament times because of its large Jewish population. A Cyrenian named Simon was pressed into service to carry the cross of Jesus (Matt. 27:32; Mark 15:21; Luke 23:26). Cyrenians were

present at Pentecost (Acts 2:10) and were converted and subsequently scattered in the persecution that followed Stephen's death (Acts 11:19–20).

Once a very populous city, Cyrene declined for several reasons. In a Jewish revolt in A.D. 115–116, over 200,000 inhabitants of the city were killed in the rioting. A disastrous earthquake in A.D. 365 contributed to its further decline. With the Arab invasion of A.D. 642, the city came to an end. The site is now a wasteland occupied by Bedouins.

CYRUS [SIGH russ]

The powerful king of Persia (559–530 B.C.), sometimes called Cyrus the Great, who allowed the Jewish captives to return to their homeland in Jerusalem after he led the Persians to become the dominant nation in the ancient world. Within 20 years after becoming king of Persia, Cyrus had conquered the Medes, Lydians, and Babylonians (549, 547, and 539 B.C., respectively). He is praised most highly, in the Old Testament, in Isaiah 44:28 and 45:1, where he is called God's "shepherd" and His "anointed." He is the only pagan ruler to be honored with the latter title.

Cyrus first appears in the Old Testament in connection with the release of the Jewish captives (taken in the Babylonian captivity of Judah), when he proclaimed their return from captivity (2 Chr. 36:22–23; Ezra 1:1–4). This restoration, which was highlighted by the rebuilding of the temple in Jerusalem, had been prophesied by Jeremiah (Jer. 29:10–14; also see Is. 44:28). The Book of Ezra contains a number of reports on the progress of the work related to the decree of Cyrus (Ezra 3:7; 4:3, 5; 5:13–14, 17; 6:3, 14). The prophet Daniel was a member of his court (Dan. 1:21; 6:28; 10:1).

Cyrus was known in Persia as a wise and tolerant ruler. He was able to gain the goodwill of the varied ethnic and religious groups within his large empire, which extended from India to the western edge of Asia Minor (modern Turkey). The Old Testament describes him as chosen by the Lord God of Israel as the deliverer of His people. It was not that Cyrus became a follower of Israel's God; rather, he described himself as the one who received "all the kingdoms of the earth." He declared that God "commanded me to build Him a house at Jerusalem" (2 Chr. 36:23). The famous Cyrus Cylinder, containing records of Cyrus's reign, revealed that Babylon's chief god, Marduk, had accepted Cyrus as "righteous prince," and had appointed him ruler "over the whole world."

Ezra 6:1–12 gives some idea of the careful organization carried out by Cyrus in relation to the rebuilding of the Jewish temple in Jerusalem. Its dimensions and the materials and supplies required are carefully described, along with the specification of severe penalties for anyone who would change his orders regarding its construction.

Cyrus's reign ended in 530 B.C., when he was killed in battle. His tomb still stands at Pasargadae in southwestern Iran. He was succeeded by his son, Cambyses II.

D

DAMASCUS [duh MASS cuss]

The oldest continually-inhabited city in the world and capital of Syria (Is. 7:8), located northeast of the Sea of Galilee.

Damascus was situated on the border of the desert at the intersection of some of the most important highways in the ancient Near Eastern world. Three major caravan routes passed through Damascus. Major roads extended from the city to the southwest into Canaan and Egypt, straight south to Edom and the Red Sea, and east to Babylonia. Because of its ideal location, the city became a trade center. Its major exports (Ezek. 27:18) included a patterned cloth called "damask." Egypt, Arabia, and Mesopotamia, as well as Canaan, were some of the trade neighbors that made Damascus the "heart of Syria."

Damascus owed its prosperity to two rivers, the Abana and the Pharpar (2 Kin. 5:12). These rivers provided an abundant source of water for agriculture. The Syrian people were so proud of these streams that Naaman the Syrian leper almost passed up his opportunity to be healed when the prophet Elisha asked him to dip himself in the waters of the Jordan River in Israel. He thought of the Jordan as an inferior stream in comparison with these majestic rivers in his homeland (2 Kin. 5:9–14).

The Bible first mentions the city as the hometown of Eliezer, Abraham's faithful servant. Early Egyptian texts refer to Egypt's control over Damascus, but this influence did not last long. By the time of David's reign, Syria (Aram) was a powerful state with Damascus as its capital. David defeated the Syrians and stationed his own troops in Damascus (2 Sam. 8:5–6; 1 Chr. 18:5–6). During Solomon's reign, however, God allowed Rezon (1 Kin. 11:23–25), Solomon's enemy, to take Syria from Israel's control because of Solomon's sins. Rezon founded a powerful dynasty based in Damascus that lasted more than 200 years.

Shortly after Solomon's death, the king of Damascus formed a powerful league with other Aramean states. This alliance resulted in many years of conflict between Israel and Damascus. First, Ben-Hadad I of Damascus defeated King

Baasha of Israel (1 Kin. 15:16–20; 2 Chr. 16:1–4). Later, God miraculously delivered King Ahab of Israel and his small army from the superior Syrian forces (1 Kin. 20:1–30).

Even after this miraculous deliverance, Ahab made a covenant with Ben-Hadad II against God's will (1 Kin. 20:31–43). Ahab was killed a few years later in a battle with Syria (1 Kin. 22:29–38).

In the midst of these wars, the prophet Elijah was instructed by God to anoint Hazael as the new king of Damascus (1 Kin. 19:15). King Joram of Israel successfully opposed Hazael for a time (2 Kin. 13:4–5), but the situation was eventually reversed. Hazael severely oppressed both Israel and Judah during later years (2 Kin. 13:3, 22).

Much later, God sent Rezin, king of Syria, and Pekah, king of Israel, against wicked King Ahaz of Judah (2 Kin. 16:1–6). Ahaz called on the Assyrians, who had become a powerful military force, for help (2 Kin. 16:7). The Assyrian king Tiglath-Pileser responded by conquering Syria, overthrowing the Aramean dynasty, killing Rezin, and destroying Damascus (732 B.C.), just as the prophets Amos and Isaiah had prophesied (Is. 17:1; Amos 1:4–5). This marked the end of Syria as an independent nation. The city of Damascus was also reduced to a fraction of its former glory.

The exact date of the reconstruction of Damascus is unknown, but such an excellent location could not long remain weak and insignificant. Damascus was the residence of Assyrian and Persian governors for five centuries after its conquest by Tiglath-Pileser. Still later, the city was conquered by Alexander the Great, who made it a provincial capital. In 64 B.C. the Romans invaded Syria, making it a province with Damascus as the seat of government.

All references to Damascus in the New Testament are associated with the apostle Paul's conversion and ministry. During this time, the city was part of the kingdom of Aretas (2 Cor. 11:32), an Arabian prince who held his kingdom under the Romans. The New Testament reports that Paul was converted while traveling to Damascus to persecute early Christians who lived in the city (Acts 9:1–8). After his dramatic conversion, Paul went to the house of Judas, where God sent Ananias, a Christian who lived in Damascus, to heal Paul of his blindness (Acts 9:10–22).

Paul preached boldly in the Jewish synagogues in Damascus, but eventually he was forced to flee the city because of the wrath of those to whom he preached. The governor of Damascus tried to capture Paul, but the apostle escaped in a large basket through an opening in the city wall (Acts 9:25; 2 Cor. 11:32–33).

Little physical change has taken place in the city of Damascus since biblical times. The long streets are filled with open-air markets that sell the same type of ancient wares. But modern Damascus does show the strong influence of Muslim culture. The most important building in Damascus is the Great Mosque, a Muslim shrine built during the eighth century A.D. on the site of a former Christian church.

DAN [dan] (a judge)

The fifth son of Jacob and the first born to Rachel's handmaid Bilhah (Gen. 30:1–6). Dan had one son—Hushim (Gen. 46:23), or Shuham (Num. 26:42). Jacob's blessing of Dan predicted: "Dan shall judge his people as one of the tribes of Israel. Dan shall be a serpent by the way, a viper by the path, that bites the horse's heels, so that its rider shall fall backward" (Gen. 49:16–17). Nothing else is known of Dan himself.

DAN, TRIBE OF

This tribe never lived up to its promise. The area allotted to Dan included the towns of Aijalon, Ekron, Eltekeh, and Zorah in the west central part of Canaan (Josh. 19:40–46; 21:5, 23–24) and stretched to Joppa on the Mediterranean Sea. The Danites, however, were unable to conquer much of the territory assigned to them. The original inhabitants, the Amorites, kept the Danites confined to the hill country of Ephraim and Benjamin. Unable to conquer their allotted territory, some members of the tribe of Dan migrated far to the northernmost area of the Promised Land and conquered the isolated city of Laish, which they renamed Dan. The tribe's one glorious moment occurred when the mighty Danite Samson judged Israel (Judg. 13–16).

Apparently, Dan was among the tribes that were the least supportive of the Israelite tribes. The Song of Deborah, which celebrates the Israelite victory over the Canaanite king Jabin and his mighty general Sisera, reproves the tribes of Gilead, Dan, and Asher. Of Dan, Deborah asked: "And why did Dan remain on ships?" (Judg. 5:17). Dan's apparent lack of interest in assisting the other tribes suggests that Dan, situated on Israel's northernmost border, had more in common with its foreign neighbors to the north than with Israel's other tribes.

The exclusion of the tribe of Dan from the sealing of the Twelve Tribes (Rev. 7:5–8) should not be overlooked. It appears that Dan had been cut off from the other tribes of Israel. However, Ezekiel prophesied a "portion for Dan" (Ezek. 48:1).

DANIEL [DAN yuhl] (God is my judge)

A prophet during the period of the captivity of God's covenant people in Babylon and Persia (Dan. 1:6–12:9; Matt.

24:15). Daniel also wrote the book in the Old Testament that bears his name.

Daniel was a teenager when he was taken from Jerusalem into captivity by the Babylonians in 605 B.C. He was in his 80s when he received the vision of the prophecy of the 70 weeks (Dan. 9). In more than 60 years of his life in Babylon, Daniel faced many challenges. But in all those years, he grew stronger in his commitment to God.

We know very little about Daniel's personal life. His family history is not mentioned, but he was probably from an upper-class family in Jerusalem. It seems unlikely that Nebuchadnezzar, the king of Babylon, would have selected a trainee for his court from the lower classes. Neither do we know whether Daniel married or had a family. As a servant in Nebuchadnezzar's court, he may have been castrated and made into a eunuch, as was common in those days. But the text does not specify that this happened. It does indicate that Daniel was a person of extraordinary abilities.

We tend to think of Daniel as a prophet because of the prophetic dimension of his book. But he also served as an advisor in the courts of foreign kings. Daniel remained in governmental service through the reigns of the kings of Babylon and into the reign of Cyrus of Persia after the Persians became the dominant world power (Dan. 1:21; 10:1).

Daniel was also a person of deep piety. His book is characterized not only by prophecies of the distant future but also by a sense of wonder at the presence of God. From his youth Daniel was determined to live by God's law in a distant land (see Dan. 1). In moments of crisis, Daniel turned first to God in prayer before turning to the affairs of state (2:14–23). His enemies even used his regularity at prayer to trap him and turn the king against him. But the grace of God protected Daniel (ch. 6).

After one of his stunning prophecies (ch. 9), Daniel prayed a noble prayer of confession for his own sins and the sins of his people. This prayer was based on Daniel's study of the Book of Jeremiah (Dan. 9:2). He was a man of true devotion to God.

The Book of Daniel is more than a treasure of prophetic literature. It also paints a beautiful picture of a man of God who lived out his commitment in very troubled times. We should never get so caught up in the meanings of horns and beasts that we forget the human dimension of the book—the intriguing person whose name means "God Is My Judge."

DARIUS [duh RYE us]

1. Darius I, the Great, who reigned from about 522 to 485 B.C. He was one of the most able Persian kings, and is also known as Darius Hystaspis, or Darius, son of Hystaspis.

Darius spent the first three years of his reign putting down rebellions in the far-flung regions of his empire. After he had secured his power, he divided the empire into 29 satrapies, or provinces, each ruled by Persian or Median nobles. He made Shushan, or Susa, his new capital and created a code of laws similar to the Code of Hammurapi; this code of Darius was in effect throughout the Persian Empire.

An effective organizer and administrator, Darius developed trade, built a network of roads, established a postal system, standardized a system of coinage, weights, and measures, and initiated fabulous building projects at Persepolis, Ecbatana, and Babylon.

Darius continued Cyrus the Great's policy of restoring the Jewish people to their homeland. In 520 B.C., Darius's second year as king (Hag. 1:1; Zech. 1:1), the Jews resumed work on the still unfinished temple in Jerusalem. Darius as-

sisted with the project by ordering it to continue and even sending a generous subsidy to help restore worship in the temple (Ezra 6:1–12). The temple was completed in 516–515 B.C., in the sixth year of Darius's reign (Ezra 6:15).

The final years of Darius's reign were marked by clashes with the rising Greek Empire in the western part of his domain. He led two major military campaigns against the Greeks, both of which were unsuccessful.

DARIUS [duh RYE us]

2. Darius II Ochus, the son of Artaxerxes I, who ruled over Persia from about 424 to 405 B.C. He was not popular or successful, and he spent much time putting down revolts among his subjects. His rule was marked by incompetence and misgovernment. Darius II may be the ruler referred to as "Darius the Persian" (Neh. 12:22).

DARIUS [duh RYE us]

3. Darius III Codomannus, the king of Persia from 336 to 330 B.C. This Darius is probably the "fourth" king of Persia mentioned by the prophet Daniel (Dan. 11:2). Darius III underestimated the strength of the army of Alexander the Great when the Macedonians invaded Persia. He was defeated by Alexander in several major battles. He attempted to rally the eastern provinces of his empire, but he was hunted down in 330 B.C. and assassinated by his own followers. For all practical purposes, these events brought the Persian Empire to an end and marked the beginning of the period of Greek dominance in the ancient world.

DARIUS [duh RYE us]

4. Darius the Mede, successor of Belshazzar to the throne of Babylon (Dan. 5:31). He is called the "son of Ahasuerus, of the lineage of the Medes" (Dan. 9:1). Darius the Mede has not been identified

with certainty; he is not mentioned by Greek historians or in any Persian literature.

Darius the Mede was the Persian king who made Daniel a governor, or ruler, of several provincial leaders (Dan. 6:1–2). Daniel's popularity with his subjects caused the other governors and the satraps under them to become jealous of Daniel and to plot against him. It was Darius the Mede who had Daniel thrown into the den of lions (Dan. 6:6–9), but who ultimately issued a decree that all in his kingdom "must tremble and fear before the God of Daniel" (Dan. 6:26).

DATHAN [DAY thun]

A chief of the tribe of Reuben who, along with Korah and others, tried to overthrow Moses and Aaron (Num. 16; Deut. 11:6; Ps. 106:17). He and his conspirators and their households were swallowed up by the earth (Num. 16:31–33).

DAVID [DAY vid] *(beloved)*

Second king of the united kingdom of Israel, ancestor of Jesus Christ, and writer of numerous psalms. The record of David's life is found in 1 Samuel 16–

DAVID

AT HOME WITH YOUNG DAVID

31; 2 Samuel 1–24; 1 Kings 1–2; and 1 Chronicles 10–29.

David's youth was spent in Bethlehem. The youngest of eight brothers (1 Sam. 16:10–11; 17:12–14), he was the son of Jesse, a respected citizen of the city. As the youngest son, David was the keeper of his father's sheep. In this job he showed courage and faithfulness by killing both a lion and a bear that attacked the flock.

As a lad, he displayed outstanding musical talent with the harp, a fact that figured prominently in his life. When Saul was rejected by God as king, the prophet Samuel went to Bethlehem to anoint David as the future king of Israel. Apparently, there was no public announcement of this event, although David and his father surely must have been aware of it.

King Saul, forsaken by God and troubled by an evil spirit, was subject to moods of depression and insanity. His attendants advised him to secure a harpist, whose music might soothe his spirit. David was recommended for this task. As harpist for Saul, David was exposed to governmental affairs, a situation that prepared him for his later service as king of Israel.

King Saul led the army of Israel to meet the enemy. Three of David's brothers were in Saul's army, and Jesse sent David to the battle area to inquire about their welfare. While on this expedition, David encountered and killed the Philistine giant, Goliath. For this feat, he became a hero in the eyes of the nation. But it aroused jealousy and animosity in the heart of Saul. Saul's son, Jonathan, however, admired David because of his bravery, and they soon became good friends. This friendship lasted until Jonathan's death, in spite of Saul's hostility toward David.

Perhaps Saul realized that Samuel's prediction that the kingdom would be taken from him could reach fulfillment in David. On two occasions, he tried to kill David with a spear; he also gave his daughter, whom he had promised as David's wife, to another man. As David's popularity grew, Saul's fear increased until he could no longer hide his desire to kill him. David was forced to flee with Saul in pursuit.

David gathered a handful of fugitives as his followers and fled from Saul. On at least two occasions, David could have killed Saul while the king slept, but he refused to do so. Perhaps David hesitated to kill Saul because he realized that he would be king one day, and he wanted the office to be treated with respect. If he had killed Saul, David also would have entered the office of king through his own personal violence.

When the Philistines battled Saul and his army at Gilboa, they were victorious, killing Saul and his son, Jonathan, whom David loved as a dear friend. When David heard this news, he mourned their fate (2 Sam. 1).

At Saul's death the tribe of Judah, to whom David belonged, elected him as king of Judah and placed him on the throne in Hebron. The rest of the tribes of Israel set up Ishbosheth, Saul's son, as king at Mahanaim. For the next two years civil war raged between these two factions. It ended in the assassination of Ishbosheth, an event that saddened David.

On the death of Ishbosheth, David was elected king over all the people of Israel. He immediately began work to establish a united kingdom. One of his first acts as king was to attack the fortified city of Jebus. Although the inhabitants thought it was safe from capture, David and his army took it. He then made it the capital city of his kingdom and erected his palace there. Also known as Jerusalem, the new capital stood on the border of the southern tribe of Judah and the other tribal territories to the north. This location tended to calm the jealousies between the north and the south, contributing greatly to the unity of the kingdom.

After establishing his new political capital, David proceeded to reestablish and strengthen the worship of God. He moved the ark of the covenant from Kirjath Jearim (Josh. 15:9) and placed it within a tabernacle that he pitched in Jerusalem. Next, he organized worship on a magnificent scale and began plans to build a house of worship. But God brought a halt to his plans, informing David that the building of the temple would be entrusted to his successor.

Although David was a righteous king, he was subject to sin, just like other human beings. On one occasion when his army went to battle, David stayed home. This led to his great sin with Bathsheba. While Uriah, the Hittite, Bathsheba's husband, was away in battle, David committed adultery with her. Then in an effort to cover his sin, he finally had Uriah killed in battle. David was confronted by the prophet Nathan, who courageously exposed his wrongdoing. Faced with his sin, David repented and asked for God's forgiveness. His prayer for forgiveness is recorded in Psalm 51.

Although God forgave David of this act of adultery, the consequences of the sin continued to plague him. The child born to David and Bathsheba died. The example he set as a father was a bad influence on his sons. One son, Amnon, raped and humiliated his half sister. Another son, Absalom, rebelled against David and tried to take away his kingdom by force. David died when he was 71 years old, having been king for a total of over 40 years, including both his reign in Hebron and his kingship over the united kingdom.

Early in his life David distinguished himself as the "sweet psalmist of Israel"

(2 Sam. 23:1). Many of the psalms in the Book of Psalms are attributed to him. His fondness for music is recorded in many places in the Bible. He played skillfully on the harp (1 Sam. 16:18–23). He arranged worship services in the sanctuary (1 Chr. 6:31). He composed psalms of lament over Saul and Jonathan (2 Sam. 1:17–27). His musical activity was referred to by Amos (Amos 6:5), Ezra (Ezra 3:10), and Nehemiah (Neh. 7:24, 46).

Jesus was referred to as the "Son of David." The genealogy of Jesus as recorded in the Gospels of Matthew and Luke traced Jesus back through the ancestry of David. God promised David a kingdom that would have no end. This prophecy was fulfilled in Jesus (Luke 1:31–33), who came to establish the kingdom of God. Jesus was born in Bethlehem because this was the "city of David" (Luke 2:4), David's birthplace and boyhood home.

The Jewish historian Josephus praised David by saying, "This man was of an excellent character, and was endowed with all the virtues that were desirable in a king." David was truly a man after God's own heart (1 Sam. 13:14; Acts 13:22).

DAY OF THE LORD, THE

A special day at the end of time when God's will and purpose for mankind and His world will be fulfilled. Amos 5:18–20 is probably the earliest occurrence in Scripture of the phrase. According to Amos, that day would be a time of great darkness for any in rebellion against God, whether Jew or Gentile. The day would be a time of judgment (Is. 13:6, 9; Jer. 46:10), as well as restoration (Is. 14:1; Joel 2:28–32; Zeph. 1:7, 14–16; 1 Thess. 5:2; 2 Peter 3:10).

DEAD SEA

A large lake in southern Israel at the lowest point on earth. In the Old Testament, it is called the Salt Sea (Gen. 14:3; Josh. 3:16); the Sea of the Arabah (Deut. 3:17); and the Eastern Sea (Ezek. 47:18; Joel 2:20). Josephus, the Jewish historian, referred to this buoyant body as Lake Asphaltitis. The Arabic name is Bahr Lut, meaning, "Sea of Lot." But from the second Christian century onward, Dead Sea has been the most common name for this unusual body of water.

The topography of the Middle East is dominated by a geologic fault that extends from Syria south through Palestine, all the way to Nyasa Lake in east-central Africa. The Dead Sea is located at the southern end of the Jordan valley at the deepest depression of this geologic fault. With a water level approximately 1,300 feet (390 meters) below sea level, the surface of the Dead Sea is the lowest point on earth. At the deepest point of the sea, on the northeast corner at the foot of the Moab mountains, the bottom is 1,300 feet (390 meters) deeper still.

The dimensions of the sea change from year to year. Many factors, such as rainfall and irrigation, contribute to this. In general, however, the Dead Sea measures approximately 50 miles (80 kilometers) in length and averages 9 to 10 miles (15 to 16 kilometers) in breadth, yielding a surface area of from 350 to 400 square miles (600 to 640 square kilometers).

A large peninsula known as el-Lisan ("the Tongue") protrudes into the sea from the southeast shore. It extends to within 2 miles (3 kilometers) of the western shore and is located some 15 miles (24 kilometers) from the southern tip. Throughout the centuries this tongue separated the sea into two parts with a channel of water flowing between them on the west. From the depths of the northeast corner, the bottom of the sea quickly shelves and rises southward. Thus the area of the sea south of el-Lisan

is extremely shallow. It is at the entrance to el-Lisan that the destroyed cities of Sodom and Gomorrah most probably lie (Gen. 19:24–29).

Except on the north where the Jordan River enters, the Dead Sea is nearly surrounded by hills and cliffs. From these hills, streams feed fresh water to the Salt Sea. In addition to these year-round streams and the Jordan River, waters flow into the sea from the winter torrents of several seasonal streams.

These water sources pour millions of gallons of water each day into the Dead Sea. However, the extreme hot temperatures and sparse rainfall (about two inches a year) cause an enormous evaporation rate that has kept the water level constant over the years. Due to increased irrigation by the Israeli government, the volume of water flowing into the Dead Sea from the Jordan River is decreasing each year. Thus the level of the sea goes down proportionately.

Because the Dead Sea has several watercourse entrances but no exits, it is indeed a "dead" sea. Although lush vegetation can be found at the mouths of these tributaries, the water itself is very salty. This is because it flows through nitrous soil and is fed by sulphurous springs. With the absence of an outlet, the water from the Dead Sea is left to evaporate, leaving behind most of its minerals. Thus it contains a very large supply of potash, bromine, magnesium chloride, salt, and other minerals.

Although the value of these chemicals is enormous, making the Dead Sea the richest mineral deposit on earth, the cost of retrieving these minerals is also high. Potash extraction has been one of the most successful operations. But as technology increases, the interest in "mining" the Dead Sea will also increase.

The Dead Sea formed part of Israel's eastern border (Num. 34:12; Ezek. 47:18). In addition to the destruction of Sodom and Gomorrah, many other historical and biblical events occurred along its shores. The springs of En Gedi provided a refuge for David in his flight from King Saul (1 Sam. 24:1). In the Valley of Salt south of the sea, David and Amaziah won victories over the Edomites (1 Chr. 18:12; 2 Kin. 14:7). Here, too, Jehoshaphat encountered the Edomites (2 Chr. 20:1–2; 2 Kin. 3:8–9). The last days of Herod the Great were spent on the eastern shore of the Dead Sea at the hot sulphur springs of Callirhoe. At Machaerus, just to the southeast, his son Herod Antipas imprisoned John the Baptist.

The prophet Ezekiel (Ezek. 47:1–12) saw a vision of a river issuing from the temple sanctuary in Jerusalem and flowing to the desert sea, the Dead Sea. And the prophet Zechariah wrote: "And in that day it shall be that living waters shall flow from Jerusalem, half of them toward the eastern sea [the Dead Sea] and half of them toward the western sea [the Mediterranean Sea]" (Zech. 14:8). Prophetically this is apparently a reference to the "pure river of water of life" said to flow from the throne of God in John's vision (Rev. 22:1–2).

The discovery of the Dead Sea Scrolls in caves on the northwest shore of the Dead Sea near Qumran has mustered renewed historical interest in this area. The remains of the Essene community at Qumran and the search for scrolls in the more than 250 surrounding caves focused the eyes of the world on a tiny sea devoid of marine life but bristling with mineral potential and archaeological promise.

DEAD SEA SCROLLS

The popular name for about 800 scrolls and fragments of scrolls that were found in 11 caves near Khirbet ("ruin of") Qumran on the northwest shore of the Dead Sea in 1947 and shortly thereafter. Taken together, these leather and papyrus (primitive paper) manuscripts were a find without precedent in the history of modern archaeology. The Dead Sea Scrolls have helped scholars to: (1) establish the date of a Hebrew Bible no later than A.D. 70; (2) reconstruct various details of the history of the Holy Land from the fourth century B.C. to A.D. 135; and (3) clarify the relationship between Jewish religious traditions and early Christianity.

The Dead Sea Scrolls were discovered when a Bedouin shepherd, who was looking for a stray goat, discovered several large clay pots containing ancient scrolls on the floor of a cave above Wadi Qumran. After some delay, several scholars were shown the manuscripts by dealers in antiquities. When it was determined that these manuscripts were extremely old, scholars began their search in earnest. Slowly other valuable scrolls were found, gathered, carefully unrolled, and published. It took 20 years (1947–1967) to bring together the various texts of the Dead Sea Scrolls.

Because the Scrolls were written between 250 B.C. and A.D. 68, they offer an invaluable source for understanding the beliefs, community life, and use of the Bible of one group of Jews, probably the Essenes, who were active during the time Jesus lived. Some scholars believe that some of the early followers of Jesus or John the Baptist may have come from the Qumran community. However, there is no evidence that the followers of John or Jesus joined the Qumran group.

Not all of the Dead Sea Scrolls have been translated or published. Probably the most interesting ones were found in Cave I not far from Qumran. Seven scrolls were found preserved in fairly good condition. They had been carefully stored in large clay jars and include:

1. A complete manuscript of the Book of Isaiah in Hebrew.

2. A partial manuscript of Isaiah in

Hebrew. (The two Isaiah scrolls are easy to read, even after more than 2,000 years, and are the earliest copies of Isaiah in existence.)

3. *The Community Rule*, or *The Manual of Discipline*, containing the laws that governed the life of the Qumran community.

4. *The Thanksgiving Psalms* are similar to the biblical psalms. They praise God the Creator for His protection against evil: "I give thanks unto Thee, O Lord, for Thou hast put my soul in the bundle of life and hedged me against all the snares of corruption."

5. *The War Scroll* is an interesting collection of plans for the final battle between the "sons of light" and the "sons of darkness," or between the "army of God" and the "army of Belial" (the Evil One). Such information as that of religious offices during wartime, recruitment, the sequence of campaigns, and the order of deploying battle squadrons is included.

6. A commentary on the Book of Habakkuk known as the *Pesher on Habakkuk* was written to demonstrate how the prophet Habakkuk, who lived in the seventh century B.C., was actually writing for the battle of the last days, when the wicked would be defeated by the righteous. The author of the *Pesher on Habakkuk* made direct references from

DEAD SEA SCROLLS

Habakkuk to his own day. One section has the following commentary: "And God told Habakkuk to write down that which would happen to the final generation, but He did not make known to him when time would come to an end. And as for that which He said, 'That he who reads may read it speedily' (Hab. 2:2); interpreted, this concerns the Teacher of Righteousness, to whom God made known all the mysteries of the words of His servants the prophets."

7. *The Genesis Apocryphon,* a "commentary" on the Book of Genesis, is only partially preserved. Written around 50 B.C. in Aramaic, the common language of the Jews, it begins with the birth of Noah and documents the life and adventures of Abraham.

These seven manuscripts are typical of the scrolls found in the other caves on the west side of the Dead Sea. The material discovered includes various kinds of literature. There are numerous biblical fragments, such as commentaries on Isaiah, Hosea, Micah, Nahum, Habakkuk, Psalm 37, Psalm 45, and Genesis. Except for Esther, all the books of the Old Testament were found in part or in full.

DEBIR [duh BEER]

A town in Judah's hill country (Josh. 10:38–39), in the Negev, or southland, and designated a city for the Levites (Josh. 21:15; 1 Chr. 6:57–58). In Joshua's time the town, also called Kirjath Sannah (Josh. 15:49) and Kirjath Sepher (Josh. 15:15–16; Judg. 1:11–12), was inhabited by the giant people, the Anakim, and was captured by Joshua (Josh. 10:38–39). Debir had to be recaptured later by the judge Othniel (Josh. 15:15–17; Judg. 1:11–13).

DEBORAH [DEB uh rah] *(bee)*

The fifth judge of Israel, a prophetess and the only female judge (Judg. 4–5). The Bible tells us nothing about her fam-

ily except that she was the wife of Lapidoth. Deborah's home was in the hill country of Ephraim between Bethel and Ramah. The palm tree under which she sat and judged Israel was a landmark; it became known as "the palm tree of Deborah" (Judg. 4:5).

Deborah summoned Barak (Judg. 4; 5:1; Heb. 11:32) and told him it was God's will that he lead her forces against the mighty warrior, Sisera. Sisera was the commander of the army of Jabin, king of Canaan, who had terrorized Israel for 20 years. Barak accepted on one condition: Deborah must accompany him. Deborah and Barak's army consisted of only 10,000, while Sisera had a multitude of fighters and 900 chariots of iron.

God was on Israel's side, however. When the battle ended, not a single man of Sisera's army survived, except Sisera himself, who fled on foot. When Sisera took refuge in the tent of Heber the Kenite, Jael (the wife of Heber) killed him by driving a tent peg through his temple (Judg. 4:21).

The "Song of Deborah" (Judg. 5) is one of the finest and earliest examples of Hebrew poetry.

DECAPOLIS [dih CAP oh liss] *(ten cities)*

A district of northern Palestine, with a large Greek population, mostly on the east side of the Jordan River and embracing ten cities. Early in His ministry, Jesus was followed by "great multitudes," including people from Decapolis (Matt. 4:25). When Jesus healed the demon-possessed man from Gadara, he "began to proclaim in Decapolis all that Jesus had done for him" (Mark 5:20). Later, Jesus traveled through the midst of the region (Mark 7:31).

Pliny, the Greek historian, identified the ten cities of the Decapolis as: Damascus, Dion, Gadara, Gerasa (or Galasa), Hippos (or Hippo), Canatha (or Kanatha), Pella, Philadelphia (the Old Testament

Rabbah or Rabbath Ammon and present-day Amman, the capital of Jordan), Raphana (or Rephana), and Scythopolis (Beth Shan). Later other towns, such as Abila and Edrei, were added to this district.

DECREE

An official order, command, or edict issued by a king or other person of authority. The decrees of kings were often delivered to distant towns or cities by messengers and publicly announced at city gates or other public places (Ezra 1:1; Amos 4:5). The Bible also refers to God's decrees, universal laws, or rules to which the entire world is subject (Ps. 148:6).

DEDICATION, FEAST OF

This feast, also known as Hanukkah and the Feast of Lights, is mentioned only once in the Bible (John 10:22). It developed in the era of the Maccabees and celebrated the cleansing of the temple after its desecration by Antiochus Epiphanes. The Feast of Dedication is observed on the twenty-fifth day of the ninth month.

DEHAVITES [dih HAY vites]

One of the tribes that colonized Samaria after Israel was carried away into captivity (Ezra 4:9). Herodotus, the fifth-century Greek historian, mentions that these people, known as Dai or Daoi, were among the nomadic tribes of Persia.

DELILAH [dih LIE lah]

The woman loved by Samson, the mightiest of Israel's judges. She was probably a Philistine. She betrayed Samson to the lords of the Philistines for 1,100 pieces of silver (Judg. 16:5). Deluding Samson into believing she loved him, Delilah persuaded him to tell her the secret of his strength—his long hair, which was the symbol of his Nazirite vow. While

Samson slept at her home in the Valley of Sorek, the Philistines entered and cut his hair. With his strength gone, Samson was easily captured and imprisoned, then blinded.

No biblical evidence supports the popular belief that Delilah was deeply repentant over her actions. She even may have been one of the 3,000 Philistines buried beneath the temple of Dagon that Samson destroyed when his God-given strength returned (Judg. 16:27–30).

DEMETRIUS [dih ME tree us]

A silversmith at Ephesus (Acts 19:24, 38) who made and sold silver models of the city's famed temple of the goddess Diana (Artemis). Alarmed at what the spread of the gospel would do to his business, Demetrius incited a riot against the apostle Paul. For two hours, the mob cried, "Great is Diana of the Ephesians!" (Acts 19:28, 34). The mob was quieted by the city clerk (Acts 19:35–40). Later, Paul left Ephesus for Macedonia (Acts 20:1).

DEMON POSSESSION

An affliction of persons in the New Testament who were possessed or controlled by demons (Matt. 4:24; 8:33).

The New Testament gives graphic descriptions of the effect of demons on people. Some of the diseases which they caused included muteness (Matt. 12:22; Mark 9:17, 25), deafness (Mark 9:25), blindness (Matt. 12:22), and bodily deformity (Luke 13:10–17). But demons were not responsible for all physical ailments. The Gospel writers frequently distinguished between sickness and demon possession (Matt. 4:24; Mark 1:32; Luke 6:17–18). Sometimes a problem caused by demons appears to have another cause in another situation (Matt. 12:22; 15:30).

In New Testament times, demons were also responsible for some mental problems (Matt. 8:28; Acts 19:13–16). The ranting and raving that they produced probably should be included with mental disorders (Mark 1:23–24; John 10:20). Uncontrolled fits were another form of demonic affliction (Luke 9:37–42; Mark 1:26). Sometimes a demon also caused a person to behave in an antisocial manner (Luke 8:27, 35).

The method of Jesus and His disciples in casting out demons differed radically from the magical methods so often used in that time. Through His simple command Jesus expelled them (Mark 1:25; 5:8; 9:25). His disciples simply added the authority of His name to the command (Luke 10:17; Acts 16:18). Even some people who were not His followers invoked His power (Luke 9:49; Acts 19:13). In some instances prayer was necessary before a demon could be cast out (Mark 9:29).

By casting out demons, Jesus showed that the kingdom of God—God's rule in the affairs of mankind—was a present reality. This was also a clear demonstration of His power over Satan and the demonic forces of sin and evil in the world.

DEMONS

Another name for fallen angels who joined the kingdom of Satan in rebellion against God. The origin of demons is not explicitly discussed in the Bible. But the New Testament speaks of the fall and later imprisonment of a group of angels (1 Pet. 3:19–20; 2 Pet. 2:4; Jude 6). The group that participated in the fall apparently followed one of their own number, Satan. The fall left Satan and his angels free to contaminate the human race with wickedness (Gen. 3; Matt. 25:41; Rev. 12:9).

A symbolic view of this "initial" fall appears in Revelation 12:3–4 where the dragon (a symbol for Satan) "drew a third of the stars of heaven" (a symbol for angels) and "threw them to the earth."

Thus, Satan has his own angels, presumably these demons (Matt. 25:41; Rev. 12:9).

Because the Israelites believed God's power was unlimited, the Old Testament contains little information about demons. The primitive status of the understanding of demons during this time is perhaps reflected in the way the Old Testament relates the fallen angels to God. It was a "distressing (or evil) spirit from God" (1 Sam. 16:15–16, 23) that brought great distress to Saul the king. It was a "lying spirit" from the Lord about whom Micaiah, the prophet of the Lord, spoke (1 Kin. 22:21–23).

Pagan worship is also related to demon activity in the Old Testament (Lev. 17:7; Ps. 106:37). Demons delight in making heathen idols the focus of their activities.

The New Testament accepts the Old Testament teaching about demons and advances the doctrine significantly. Demons are designated in a number of different ways in the New Testament. Quite frequently they are called "unclean spirits" (Matt. 10:1; Mark 6:7). Another descriptive phrase for them is "wicked (or evil) spirits" (Luke 7:21; Acts 19:12–13). In his writings Paul calls them "deceiving spirits" (1 Tim. 4:1). John refers to "spirits of demons" (Rev. 16:14). Luke describes one demon as a "spirit of divination" (Acts 16:16).

The only individual demon named in the New Testament (Satan himself is never referred to as a demon) is the one called Abaddon in Hebrew and Apollyon in Greek (Rev. 9:11). Some scholars believe this is another name for Satan or that this is an unfallen angel. But stronger evidence suggests he was a fallen angelic leader who is subject to the kingly authority of Satan. Legion (Mark 5:9; Luke 8:30) is probably a collective name for a group of demons rather than the name of a single demon.

A prime purpose of Jesus' earthly ministry was to overcome the power of Satan. This included His conquest of the demonic realm (Matt. 12:25–29; Luke 11:17–22; John 12:31; 1 John 3:8). This explains the fierce conflict between Jesus and these evil spirits while He was on earth.

Yet Jesus' enemies accused Him of being in alliance with Satan's kingdom, including his demons (Mark 3:22; John 8:48). This same accusation was made against His forerunner, John the Baptist (Matt. 11:18; Luke 7:33). But Jesus' works of goodness and righteousness showed that these claims were not true (Matt. 12:25–29; Luke 11:17–22).

Following the resurrection of Jesus and His return to heaven, these demonic principalities and powers have continued their warfare against those who are His followers (Rom. 8:38–39; Eph. 6:12). Yet Satan and his allies will finally be overthrown by God. After Christ returns, the devil and his angels will be defeated and thrown into the lake of fire and brimstone (Matt. 25:41; Rev. 20:10). This is a doom with which demons are quite familiar (Matt. 8:29). God will achieve the ultimate victory in this conflict, which has been going on since the beginning of time.

DEN OF LIONS

The lair (Job 38:40), thicket (Ps. 10:9), or cave (Nah. 2:12) where lions live. The most famous den of lions in the Bible is that into which Daniel was thrown (Dan. 6). This apparently was a deep cavern, either natural or artificial, sealed with a large stone (Dan. 6:17). The kings of Assyria kept lions in captivity, releasing them periodically for the royal sport of lion hunting. The lions of the Daniel story probably were kept by King Darius for this purpose. Daniel's preservation from the lions is an inspiring example of God's control of His world and His power to protect His people.

DENARIUS [dih NAIR e us]

The basic unit of Roman coinage was the silver denarius, probably equal to a laborer's daily wage, as in the parable of the vineyard workers (Matt. 20:9–10, 13). It was also used for paying tribute, or taxes, to the Roman emperor, whose image it carried. Jesus was shown a denarius, in a ploy by the Pharisees to trick him into opposing the Roman taxation authority. But he replied, "Render therefore to Caesar the things that are Caesar's, and to God the things that are God's" (Matt. 22:15–22).

DERBE [DUR bih]

A city in the southeastern part of Lycaonia, a province of Asia Minor, to which Paul and Barnabas retreated when driven from Lystra (Acts 14:6–20), while on their first missionary journey. Paul also visited Derbe on his second missionary journey (Acts 16:1). Derbe is twice mentioned with Lystra; it was situated southeast of that city (Acts 14:6; 16:1). One of Paul's travel companions, Gaius, was a native of Derbe (Acts 20:4).

DESCENT INTO HADES BY JESUS

Traditionally, Christ's journey to the place of the dead on our behalf following His crucifixion. Some interpreters see this descent in Paul's reference to "lower parts of the earth" (Eph. 4:9). Both Peter (Acts 2:27) and Paul (Acts 13:35) quote Psalm 16:10, declaring that Jesus experienced death, but that He was kept from the corruption of the grave. God did not abandon His Son in hell, but raised Him from the dead (Acts 2:27). From the heights of heaven's throne Jesus descended to earth and even to death itself to provide for our redemption.

DEVIL *(accuser, slanderer)*

The main title for the fallen angelic being who is the supreme enemy of God and humankind. Satan is his most common name, and devil is what he is—the accuser or deceiver. The title "devil" appears 35 times in the New Testament of the NKJV. In every case it is preceded by the article "the," indicating a title rather than a name. The term comes from a Greek word that means "a false witness" or "malicious accuser."

Several descriptive phrases applied to the devil in the New Testament point out the nature of his wicked personality and the extent of his evil deeds.

That Serpent of Old (Rev. 12:9; 20:2). The devil worked through the serpent to tempt Eve (Gen. 3:1–6).

The Wicked or Evil One (Matt. 6:13; 13:19, 38; 1 John 2:13). This phrase depicts the devil's fundamental nature. He is in direct opposition to everything God is or all he wishes to do. He is the source

DEVIL

WHERE DEVILED EGGS COME FROM

of all evil and wickedness. While the KJV reads, "Deliver us from evil," the NKJV more accurately reads, "Deliver us from the evil one." Humanity needs this deliverance, because the devil "walks about like a roaring lion, seeking whom he may devour" (1 Pet. 5:8).

Enemy (Matt. 13:25, 28, 39). The devil is our worst enemy. This is one enemy Jesus does not want us to love. He is an enemy of Christ, the church, and the gospel; and he is tireless in his efforts to uproot good and sow evil.

Murderer (John 8:44). "He was a murderer from the beginning" are strong words from the lips of Jesus. The devil killed Abel and the prophets, and he wanted to kill Jesus before His time (8:40).

Deceiver (Rev. 20:10). Starting with Eve, the devil has attempted to deceive every human being. Evil people operating under the power of the evil one will continue to deceive (2 Tim. 3:13).

Beelzebub, the Ruler of the Demons (Matt. 9:34; 12:24). Beelzebub (see also 2 Kin. 1:2–3, 6, 16) means literally "lord of flies" and is a title of ridicule. The religious leaders of Jesus' time were guilty of blasphemy against the Holy Spirit because they claimed the miracles of Jesus were actually conducted by the devil. The KJV and some other versions incorrectly translate "demons" as "devils." There are many demons but only one devil. His name is Beelzebub, the chief leader of the fallen angels known as demons.

Belial (2 Cor. 6:15). This name means "worthlessness."

Ruler of This World (John 12:31; 14:30; 16:11). Three times Jesus called the devil the "ruler of this world." The devil offered the world to Jesus if He would worship him (Luke 4:5–7), but the Lord refused with these words, "Get behind me, Satan" (4:8). At Calvary God dealt a death blow to this world ruler. It is only

a matter of time before God will win the final victory at the end of time (1 John 3:8; Matt. 25:41; Rev. 12:7).

The devil is strong, but Christians are stronger through the Lord (Eph. 6:11). They have the protection needed to withstand his assaults. The devil tempts, but God provides a way of escape (1 Cor. 10:13); the devil tries to take advantage of people (2 Cor. 2:11), but he will flee if fought (James 4:7). The devil should not be feared, for Jesus is more powerful than this deceiving prince of the demons (1 John 4:4).

See also SATAN.

DIANA [die ANN uh]

In Roman mythology, Diana was the goddess of the moon, hunting, wild animals, and virginity. Diana is the same as the Greek goddess *Artemis* (NRSV, NIV, NASB), virgin goddess of the hunt and the moon. When Paul preached in Ephesus, the Ephesians were in an uproar because the gospel threatened to destroy the profit of the artisans who crafted silver shrines of Diana (Acts 19:24, 27–28, 34–35).

The temple of Artemis at Ephesus ranked as one of the seven wonders of the ancient world. As the twin sister of Apollo and the daughter of Zeus, Artemis was known variously as the moon goddess, the goddess of hunting, and the patroness of young girls. The temple at Ephesus housed the image of Artemis that was reputed to have come directly from Zeus (Acts 19:35). The temple of Artemis in Paul's day was supported by 127 columns, each of them 197 feet (60 meters) high. The Ephesians took great pride in this grand edifice. During the Roman period, they promoted the worship of Artemis by minting coins with the inscription, "Diana of Ephesus."

DINAH [DIE nah] *(one who judges)*

Jacob's daughter by Leah (Gen. 30:21; 34:1). When she was raped by Shechem, the son of Hamor the Hivite, her brothers were enraged. Later, when Shechem wanted Dinah for his wife, he asked his father to make arrangements for him to marry her. Dinah's brothers consented on the condition that all the Hivites be circumcised.

The Hivites agreed; but after they had been circumcised, Simeon and Levi, two of Dinah's brothers, suddenly attacked them "on the third day, when they were in pain" (Gen. 34:25) and killed all the males. Jacob did not condone the deed; in fact, upon his deathbed he denounced it (Gen. 49:5–7).

DIONYSIUS THE AREOPAGITE [die oh NISS e us; air e OP uh ghyte]

A member of the Areopagus, the supreme court of Athens. Dionysius became a Christian after hearing the gospel preached by the apostle Paul (Acts 17:34). Nothing else is known about him except by tradition. One tradition says he was martyred in Athens during the reign of the Roman emperor Domitian.

DOG

In ancient Israel, the dog was not "man's best friend." In fact, calling someone a dog was one of the most offensive ways of insulting that person. The Bible mentions dogs frequently; most of the references are derogatory. Even in New Testament times, Jews called Gentiles "dogs" (Matt. 15:26). The term "dog" also referred to a male prostitute (Deut. 23:18). Unbelievers who were shut out of the New Jerusalem were also termed "dogs" (Rev. 22:15)—probably a reference to their sexual immorality. Moslems later applied the insult to Christians.

The dog may have been the first animal in the ancient world to be tamed.

Ancient Egyptians raced greyhounds, mentioned in Proverbs 30:31 (NKJV), and the Greeks raised mastiffs. But dogs in Palestine were more wild than tame. They often banded together in packs and lived off the refuse and food supplies of a village. Some dogs were useful as watchdogs or guardians of sheep, but even they were not altogether reliable (Is. 56:10).

DONKEY

One of the first animals tamed by people, the donkey was a necessity in Bible times. It is mentioned frequently in the Bible. Wild donkeys (referred to as the onager in Job 39:5, NKJV) also roamed the land. "Like a wild donkey" (Hos. 8:9) described a headstrong, untamed nature. But the domesticated donkey was an obedient servant.

Donkeys stand about 4 feet (1.3 meters) high. They are usually gray, reddish-brown, or white. The longsuffering donkey often won the affection of the household and was decorated with beads and bright ribbons. But his true role was to serve as a work animal. He trampled seed, turned the millstone to grind grain, and pulled the plow.

Donkey caravans were the freight trains and transport trucks of ancient times. These animals could carry great weight in spite of their small size. Since they required only a fraction as much fodder as a horse, they were more economical to own. The donkey was also a safe and comfortable animal to ride. They were ridden by rich and poor alike. When Jesus entered Jerusalem, he signaled his peaceful intentions by riding a young donkey rather than a prancing warhorse.

The offspring of a male donkey (jack) and female horse (mare) was a mule. The mule had the sure-footedness and endurance of the donkey, coupled with the greater size and strength of the horse.

Crossbreeding like this was outlawed among the Jewish people (Lev. 19:19), but from David's time mules were imported and increasingly used by the Israelites (2 Sam. 18:9; 1 Kin. 1:33; 18:5). Ezra 2:66 records that the Israelites brought 245 mules with them when they returned from captivity.

DOORPOSTS

The two sides of a doorway, similar to a doorframe. The Hebrews were ordered by the Lord to spread the blood of a sacrificial lamb on the doorposts of their houses during the Passover while in captivity in Egypt. This was a sign of their loyalty to the Lord; it also was a sign for the destroying angel to pass over the houses of the Hebrews when the firstborn of Egypt were killed in the tenth and final plague that struck the land (Ex. 12:7). The Hebrews were later told to write sacred words on the doorposts of their houses as a reminder of God's commands (Deut. 6:9; 11:20).

DORCAS [DOR cuss] *(gazelle)*

A Christian woman from Joppa known for befriending and helping the poor (Acts 9:36–43); Tabitha was her Aramaic name (it also means "gazelle"). She was raised from the dead by the apostle Peter. The Bible tells us little about her background, but it is possible that she was a woman of some wealth, or at least had connections with the wealthy. Dorcas may well have been one of the early converts of Philip the evangelist, who established a Christian church at Joppa.

DOTHAN [DOE thun]

A city of the tribe of Manasseh situated west of the Jordan River and 12 miles (19 kilometers) northeast of Samaria near Mount Gilboa. It was here that Joseph found his brothers tending their sheep. They put him in a pit and later sold him into slavery (Gen. 37:17). At Dothan the Syrians were blinded by God in the time of Elisha (2 Kin. 6:8–23). Dothan's modern name is Tell Dotha.

DOVE

Doves and pigeons belong to the same family. They are often mentioned in the Bible as if they are the same bird. The rock dove found in Palestine is the wild ancestor of our common street pigeon. Turtledoves are migrants. They spend the months of April to October in the Holy Land, filling the air with soft cooing when they arrive each spring (Song 2:11–12).

Doves come in several colors, from pure white to the chestnut-colored palm turtledove. Even the plain gray pigeon has a silver sheen. Solomon waxed poetic over doves' eyes. David longed for "wings like a dove" (Ps. 55:6) so he could fly away from his enemies.

Pigeons were probably the first domesticated bird. When people realized doves could travel long distances and always find their way home, they used them to carry messages. Homing pigeons have keen eyes with which they spot landmarks to help them stay on the right route.

Hebrews ate pigeons and, from Abraham's time, used them in sacrifice. Even a poor man could provide a pigeon or two for worship, as Joseph and Mary did at Jesus' circumcision (Luke 2:21–24; Lev. 12:8).

Doves appear to express affection, stroking each other, and "billing and cooing." They mate for life, sharing nesting and parenting duties. They are gentle birds that never resist attack or retaliate against their enemies. Even when her young are attacked, a dove will give only a pitiful call of distress.

Because of its innocence and gentle nature, the dove is a common religious symbol. The Holy Spirit took the form of a dove at Jesus' baptism (Matt. 3:16; Mark

1:10; Luke 3:22). The dove also symbolizes peace, love, forgiveness, and the church.

DRUSILLA [droo SILL uh]

Youngest daughter of Herod Agrippa I by his wife Cypros. Drusilla was the wife of Felix, the governor of Judea. While he was a prisoner, the apostle Paul pleaded his case before Felix and Drusilla: "Now as he [Paul] reasoned about righteousness, self-control, and the judgment to come, Felix was afraid" (Acts 24:25). The Scriptures do not record Drusilla's reaction.

According to the Jewish historian, Josephus, Drusilla was a Jewess who married Azizus, king of Emesa, who then converted to Judaism. Because of Drusilla's great beauty, Felix desired her for his wife. Drusilla then left Azizus and married the Gentile Felix in defiance of Jewish law (Acts 24:24).

DULCIMER

This musical instrument is mentioned only in the Book of Daniel. It was one of the Babylonian instruments that signaled the time for Daniel's three friends—Shadrach, Meshach, and Abed-Nego—to bow down before a golden image of King Nebuchadnezzar (Dan. 3:5, 7, 10, 15, KJV). Other English versions translate the Hebrew word for dulcimer as bagpipes (NASB) or pipes (NIV, NRSV).

The exact nature of the dulcimer is unknown. Some scholars believe it may have been similar to a Greek instrument known as the symphonia, which consisted of two pipes thrust through a leather sack. The pipes gave out a plaintive sound. The Scottish bagpipes of later centuries may have developed from this instrument. However, other scholars believe the dulcimer was similar to the flute in its construction and the sound it produced.

E

EAGLE

Eagles are included among the unclean birds mentioned in the Bible (Lev. 11:13, NKJV), but they were admired as majestic birds. The golden eagle, which is really dark brown with sprinkles of gold, has an 8-feet (26-meter) wingspread. It nests in high places that are inaccessible (Jer. 49:16). There, in a nest that the eagle makes larger each year, the eagle hatches two eggs. Usually only one eaglet survives to adulthood.

An eagle has keen eyesight. He can spot his prey while soaring hundreds of feet in the air. Like a lightning bolt, he drops to seize it, killing it quickly with his powerful claws. Then he swoops back to his nest to rip the meat apart and share it with his young.

A mother eagle carries her eaglet on her back until it masters the art of flying. Moses used this familiar picture from nature to describe God's care for His people. God stirred up Jacob (the nation of Israel), and carried His people on His wings (Deut. 32:11–12) as He delivered them from slavery in Egypt.

Agur marveled at "the way of an eagle in the air" (Prov. 30:19). An eagle can stay aloft for hours, rarely moving his wings and riding wind currents. But many passages in the Bible also speak of the swiftness of the eagle's flight (Deut. 28:49). The belief that an eagle renews its strength and youthful appearance after shedding its feathers gave rise to Psalm 103:5 and Isaiah 40:31. Eagles do have a long lifespan, living 20 to 30 years in the wild, and longer in captivity.

In the Old Testament, prophets spoke

of the eagle as a symbol of God's judgment (Jer. 48:40; Ezek. 17:3, 7). In Revelation 12:14, "two wings of a great eagle" portray God's intervention to deliver His people from persecution.

EARRINGS

Pieces of jewelry worn on the earlobe in Bible times (Gen. 35:4). While these were generally worn only by Hebrew women, the men among the ancient Ishmaelites apparently wore earrings (Judg. 8:24–25). Earrings were generally fashioned from silver or gold.

EARTHQUAKE

A trembling or convulsion of the earth, often accompanied by volcanic erup-tions. Earthquakes may cause fissures in the earth, avalanches, loud rumbling noises, and destructive fires (Num. 16:32; 1 Kin. 19:11).

A notable earthquake occurred during the reigns of Uzziah, king of Judah (792–740 B.C.), and Jeroboam II, king of Israel (793–753 B.C.). Amos dates his prophecy "two years before the earthquake" (Amos 1:1), and Zechariah writes about "the earthquake in the days of Uzziah king of Judah" (Zech. 14:5). Earthquakes were common in ancient Israel. A notable earthquake took place in 31 B.C. during the reign of Herod the Great.

An earthquake occurred at the crucifixion of Jesus (Matt. 27:51–54), and an-

EARTHQUAKE

VIBRATING IN PHILIPPI

other occurred at His resurrection (Matt. 28:2). A great earthquake occurred in Macedonia when Paul and Silas were in jail at Philippi, "so that the foundations of the prison were shaken" (Acts 16:26).

The Bible uses earthquakes as symbols of God's power (2 Sam. 22:8), presence (Ps. 68:8), revelation (Ex. 19:18), and judgments (Ezek. 38:19–23).

Jesus said that "famines, pestilences, and earthquakes in various places . . . are the beginning of sorrows" (Matt. 24:7–8). All these events are only "the beginning" (Matt. 24:8) that will end in the catastrophic disasters of the last days. The Book of Revelation uses earthquakes as a symbol of the upheavals in the religious and political realms that will precede and accompany the Second Coming of Christ (Rev. 6:12).

EASTER

A feast or festival of the Christian church that commemorates the resurrection of Christ. It is celebrated on the first Sunday following the full moon that occurs on or after March 21—or one week later if the full moon falls on Sunday. In other words, Easter falls between March 22 and April 25. As early as the eighth century, the word was used to designate the annual Christian celebration of the resurrection of Christ.

EBAL [EE buhl]

A mountain north of Shechem and opposite Mount Gerizim (Deut. 11:29). Moses gave instructions to the Israelites about a religious ceremony they should observe after they crossed the Jordan River into the Promised Land. Moses also instructed that stones be set up on Mount Ebal, and an altar built to the Lord (Deut. 27:4–5).

At a later time, Joshua and the other leaders of the Israelites did all these things as Moses had commanded (Josh. 8:30–35). Joshua renewed the covenant

by building "an altar to the Lord God of Israel in Mount Ebal" (v. 30), by offering "burnt offerings" and "peace offerings" to the Lord (v. 31), by writing on the stones the Law of Moses (v. 32), and by reading the words of the law to the assembled multitude (vv. 33–35).

When Joshua read the blessings of the Law, the people on Mount Gerizim responded with an "Amen"; when he read the curses, the people on Mount Ebal responded with an "Amen." Hence, Mount Ebal became known as the "Mount of Cursing." Ebal is somewhat higher than Gerizim. The tops of the two mountains are about 2 miles (3 kilometers) distant from each other. The modern name of Mount Ebal is Jebel Eslamiyeh.

EBENEZER [ebb un EE zur] (stone of help)

A stone erected by Samuel to commemorate Israel's victory over the Philistines. It may have been named after the place where the Israelites were defeated by the Philistines 20 years before to show that this defeat had been reversed (1 Sam. 7:12).

EDEN [EE den] (delight)

The first home of Adam and Eve, the first man and woman. The concept "Garden of Delight" fits perfectly the setting of Genesis 2–3, a place of God's blessing and prosperity.

Suggestions offered about the location of Eden include Babylonia (in Mesopotamia), Armenia (north of Mesopotamia), and an island in the Indian Ocean. The statement in Genesis 2:10 that four "riverheads" divided from the river that flowed out of the Garden of Eden (Gen. 2:10–14) supports a location somewhere in Mesopotamia.

Two of the rivers are clearly identified: the Tigris, which ran along the east side of Asshur (Assyria), and the Euphrates.

The Pishon ("Spouter") and Gihon ("Gusher") rivers are hard to identify. The Gihon may have been in Mesopotamia, since Genesis 2:13 says it encompassed the whole land of "Cush" (possibly southeast Mesopotamia). Some think Pishon and Gihon represent the Indus and the Nile, respectively, suggesting that Eden included the whole of the Fertile Crescent from India to Egypt.

The Garden of Eden included many kinds of beautiful and fruitbearing trees, including "the tree of life" and "the tree of the knowledge of good and evil" (Gen. 2:9). Man was to tend and keep the garden (Gen. 2:15), which, in addition to trees, could have contained other vegetation such as grain crops and vegetables (Gen. 1:11–12). The garden was also filled with all kinds of birds and land animals (Gen. 2:19–20), probably including many of the animals created on the sixth day of creation (Gen. 1:24–25). It was well-watered (Gen. 2:10), insuring lush vegetation and pasture.

After Adam and Eve sinned against God (Gen. 3:1–19), the Lord banished them from the garden. Cain, the son of Adam and Eve, is said to have lived "east of Eden" (Gen. 4:16).

In several Old Testament passages, Eden is used as a symbol of beauty and fruitfulness, the place blessed by God (Is. 51:3). Revelation 22:1–2 alludes to the Garden of Eden by picturing a "river of water of life" and "the tree of life" in the heavenly Jerusalem.

EDOM [EE dum] *(red)*

The land inhabited by the descendants of Edom, or Esau (Gen. 32:3; 36:8). Ancient Edom included the region beginning in the north at the river Zered, a natural boundary also for southern Moab, and extending southward to the Gulf of Aqabah. At times it included mountain ranges and fertile plateaus on the east and west of the Arabah, the desert valley south of the Dead Sea.

The most significant area of ancient Edom was the mountain-encircled plain on the east of the Arabah. Mount Seir, the highest of this range, rises to an elevation of nearly 3,500 feet (1,200 meters) above the Arabah. Edom's capital during the days of Israel's monarchy was Sela, situated at the southern end of a secluded valley that became the location of the city of Petra in later times. Other important Edomite cities were Bozrah and Teman (Is. 34:6; Amos 1:12). In New Testament times, Edom was known as Idumea.

EDOMITES [EE dum ites]

Descendants of Edom, or Esau—an ancient people who were enemies of the Israelites. During the days of Abraham, the region which later became the home of the Edomites was occupied by more than one tribe of non-Israelite peoples. When Esau moved to this region with his family and possessions, the Horites already lived in the land (Gen. 36:20).

After the years of wilderness wandering, Moses wanted to lead Israel northward to Canaan across Edom into Moab. The king of Edom, however, refused them passage (Num. 20:14–21), forcing them to bypass Edom and Moab through the desert to the east (Judg. 11:17, 18). Later in the journey northward to Abel Acacia Grove in the plains of Moab across from Jericho (Num. 33:48–49), Balaam prophesied that Israel would one day possess Edom (Num. 24:18).

In dividing the land of Canaan after the conquest, Joshua established Judah's border to the west of the Dead Sea and to the border of Edom (Josh. 15:1, 21). During the reign of Saul, Israel fought against Edom (1 Sam. 14:47). But Edomites at times served in Saul's army (1 Sam. 21:7; 22:9). David conquered

Edom, along with a number of other adjacent countries, and stationed troops in the land (2 Sam. 8:13–14). In later years, Solomon promoted the building of a port on the northern coast of the Red Sea in Edomite territory (1 Kin. 9:26–27).

During the time of the divided kingdom, a number of hostile encounters occurred between the nations of Judah or Israel and Edom. During Jehoshaphat's reign, Edomites raided Judah but were turned back (2 Chr. 20:1, 8). An attempt to reopen the port at Ezion Geber failed (1 Kin. 22:48), and the Edomites joined forces with those of Judah in Jehoshaphat's move to put down the rebellion of Mesha of Moab (2 Kin. 3:4–5). During the reign of Joram, Edom freed herself from Judah's control (2 Kin. 8:20–22), but again became subject to Judah when Amaziah captured Sela, their capital city. Edom became a vassal state of Assyria, beginning about 736 B.C. So antagonistic were relationships between Israel and Edom that Edom is pictured as Israel's representative enemy (Is. 34:5–17). The entire Book of Obadiah is a prophecy against Edom.

After the downfall of Judah in 586 B.C., Edom rejoiced (Ps. 137:7). Edomites settled in southern Judah as far north as Hebron. Nabateans occupied old Edom beginning in the third century B.C., continuing their civilization well into the first century A.D. Judas Maccabeus subdued the Edomites, and John Hyrcanus forced them to be circumcised and then made them a part of the Jewish people. The Herod family of New Testament times was of Idumean (Edomite) stock.

EGLON [EGG lahn] *(young bull)*

An overweight Moabite king who reigned during the period of the judges (Judg. 3:12–25). Allied with the Ammonites and the Amalekites, Eglon invaded the land of Israel. His army captured Jer-

icho, and he exacted tribute from the Israelites.

After 18 years of Eglon's rule, the Lord raised up Ehud the Benjamite, a left-handed man, to deliver Israel. Ehud stabbed Eglon in the belly with a dagger. Because Eglon was a very fat man, "even the hilt went in after the blade, and the fat closed over the blade, for (Ehud) did not draw the dagger out of his belly" (Judg. 3:22).

EGYPT [EE jipt]

The country in the northeast corner of Africa that extended from the Mediterranean Sea on the north to the first waterfall on the Nile River in the south—a distance of about 540 miles (880 kilometers). The Israelites spent 430 years in this land (Ex. 12:40) between the time of Joseph and Moses. Jesus lived temporarily in Egypt during His infancy (Matt. 2:13–15).

Around 3100 B.C., some 1,000 years before Abraham, all of Egypt was joined together under one king at Memphis. The land was divided into districts called "nomes." Irrigation and the plow were introduced to increase the nation's agricultural productivity. Shortly thereafter, the Old Kingdom period of Egypt's history began. During this era, the famous pyramids of Egypt were built. Djoser's step pyramid at Saqqara and the three great pyramids at Giza are a testimony to the power and prosperity of the nation, as well as evidence of the people's belief in the divine character of the pharaoh, the Egyptian ruler.

The arts of painting, sculpturing, and architecture excelled in Egypt. One group of texts known as the "Memphite Theology" probably dates back to this era. They describe how the god Ptah spoke and created all things, indicating that the pharaoh was considered divine. Wisdom writings from Imhotep and Ptahhotep reveal something of the moral values and ideals of the nation and the high literary achievements of the educated classes.

As the government of Egypt expanded, noblemen from various parts of the nation began to gain greater power. This led to a decentralization of power and ultimately to the First Intermediate Period of weakness around 2200 B.C. The time was described as an epic of chaos, instability, poverty, and despair.

The Middle Kingdom era of Egypt's history (2000–1800 B.C.) parallels the time of Abraham's journey into Egypt (Gen. 12:10–20). Wisdom texts, one supposed prophecy, and stories about fishing and hunting depict life at this time. During this era, the new kings centralized the government, expanded agricultural production through new irrigation projects, established the security of the nation by defeating the Nubians from Cush, and set up a series of defensive fortresses on the southern and western borders.

Trade with Phoenicia, mining in the Sinai desert, and at least one military raid into Palestine to Shechem indicate that Egypt had close relationships with Palestine when the patriarchs such as Abraham and his descendants first came to the land. The "Story of Sinuhe" describes an Egyptian's trip to Palestine and the fertility of the land. A painting in a tomb from the time of Sesostris III (1890 B.C.) shows 37 people from Canaan who traveled to Egypt. Texts containing magical curses (the Execration Texts) on Egypt's enemies contain the names of the kings of Tyre, Beth-Shemesh, and Jerusalem. These indicate that Egypt's stability was weakening and that the Second Intermediate Period of weakness (1750–1570 B.C.) was about to begin.

During this time of weakness, many non-Egyptians entered the country. A group called the Hyksos ("rulers from a foreign land") took control of the nation. Joseph's rise to an important position in the house of Potiphar (Gen. 39) and his appointment to the task of collecting grain during the years of plenty (Gen. 41) may have been made possible because other foreigners had significant places in the Hyksos government.

Some scholars once thought the Hyksos were the people of Israel, but few accept this view today. The Hyksos used the bow, body armor, the horse and chariot, and a new defensive wall system for Egyptian cities. But in spite of their military power, they were driven out of Egypt when the New Kingdom began.

The New Kingdom period (1570–1100 B.C.) parallels the biblical period before the birth of Moses until the time of Samuel. The New Kingdom began when the Egyptians managed to drive out the Hyksos and reunite Egypt. This new dynasty was made of kings "who did not know Joseph" (Ex. 1:8). They began to persecute the Hebrews, forcing them to build the stone cities of Pithom and Rameses (Ex. 1:11). The Hebrews were seen as foreigners who were a threat to the security of the nation (Ex. 1:10), so they were enslaved.

Egyptian texts do not mention the ten plagues, the Exodus of Israel from Egypt, or the defeat of Pharaoh and his army in the Red Sea (Ex. 7–15). But this would hardly be expected since the Egyptians seldom recorded any of their defeats. Before the Exodus, Egypt was at the height of its power; but God humbled the nation and taught its people that He was God— not Pharaoh or any of the other gods of Egypt (Ex. 7:5; 8:10, 22; 9:14, 29; 10:2; 12:12).

No one knows how the Exodus affected Egypt's religious beliefs. However, several years later King Akhenaten rejected the worship of Amon at Thebes and proclaimed that Aten, the solar disk of the sun, was the only god. A beautiful hymn of praise to Aten has been discovered. This shows clearly that Akhenaten was pushing the Egyptians to adopt belief in one god. Religious tension was very high because Akhenaten dismissed the priests at the other temples and moved his capital to El-Amarna.

After the New Kingdom came the Late Period of Egyptian history (1100–330 B.C.). The fragmentation of Egyptian power allowed David and Solomon to establish Israel as a strong nation. Egypt was not a strong military power during this period. Emphasis was placed on trying to form peaceful trade relations with neighboring states.

Solomon married the daughter of an Egyptian pharaoh (1 Kin. 3:1), another sign of Egypt's weakness. But later in his reign a new king (probably Shishak) provided refuge for two of Solomon's enemies (1 Kin. 11:17, 40). A few years after Solomon's death (930 B.C.), Shishak, a Libyan who had become Pharaoh, attacked Rehoboam and plundered the gold from the king's palace and the temple in Jerusalem (1 Kin. 14:25–28). Later Zerah, an Ethiopian general or pharaoh (2 Chr. 14:9–15; 16:8), led an Egyptian army against Asa, king of Judah; but God miraculously gave victory to Asa.

Ethiopian and Saite dynasties controlled Egypt for several hundred years until the destruction of Israel by the Babylonian king Nebuchadnezzar in 587 B.C. These pharaohs were not particularly powerful because of the political supremacy of the Assyrians and the Babylonians. The Israelite king Hoshea sought the help of Pharaoh So around 725 B.C. (2 Kin. 17:4) to fight against the Assyrians, but the Egyptians were of little help.

Around 701 B.C. King Hezekiah of Judah was attacked by the Assyrian king Sennacherib. Tirhakah, the Ethiopian king of Egypt, came to Hezekiah's aid (2 Kin. 19:9; Is. 37:9). The Assyrians marched into Egypt in 671 and 664 B.C., destroying the Egyptian forces as far south as Thebes. The Egyptians hired Greek mercenaries to fight in their army; but this still did not give them any great strength. Josiah, king of Judah, was killed by the Egyptian pharaoh Necho in 609 B.C. because Josiah tried to interfere with the Egyptian efforts to help the Assyrians who were under attack by the Babylonians (2 Kin. 23:29).

After Josiah's death, Judah came under the control of Egypt; but in 605 B.C. the Egyptians were crushed by the Babylonians at Carchemish on the Euphrates. Many Jews fled to Egypt after the destruction of Jerusalem. Many Jews lived in Alexandria during this period. The Greek translation of the Old Testament from Hebrew to Greek was completed during this time so the Greek-speaking Jews would have a Bible in their language. The Romans took control of Egypt around 30 B.C.

The Egyptians were polytheists, believing in many gods. Many of their gods were the personification of nature, such as the Nile, the sun and the earth. But other gods stood for abstract concepts such as wisdom, justice, and order. Some gods were worshiped on a national level, but others were local deities. Many cities had their favorite deity, which was the patron god of that locality (Ptah at Memphis or Amon at Thebes). But the cosmic gods like Nut (the goddess of the sky), Geb (the god of the earth), and Re (the sun god) were known throughout the nation.

The pharaoh himself was one of the most important Egyptian gods. While ruling, he was the incarnation of the god Horus and the son of Re. After his death, he was identified with the god Osiris. The pharaoh was a mediator between the people and the cosmic gods of the universe. Thus the pharaoh was a key factor in determining the fate of the nation. Israel's kings were never considered gods, because God was the true King of Israel (1 Sam. 8:7). Originally only the Egyptian kings had the possibility of eternal life after death, but later the same hope was opened to all people. This possibility was dependent on one's character in this life.

EHUD [EE hud]

One of the judges of Israel (Judg. 3:15–4:1). A left-handed man from the tribe of Benjamin, he assassinated Eglon, king of Moab, who was Israel's oppressor. He then fled to the hill country of Ephraim, where he summoned the Israelites. Under Ehud's leadership the Israelites descended into the Jordan valley and captured the river crossing. They then killed 10,000 Moabites who attempted to cross the Jordan. After the victory, Ehud judged Israel the remainder of his life.

EKRON [ECK ron]

The northernmost of the five chief cities of the Philistines, near the Mediterranean Sea and about 35 miles (66 kilometers) west of Jerusalem (1 Sam. 6:16–17). Ekron was apportioned first to the tribe of Judah (Josh. 15:45–46), then given to the tribe of Dan (Josh. 19:40–43). After David killed Goliath, the Israelites pursued the Philistines to the very gates of Ekron, their fortified stronghold (1 Sam. 17:52).

The prophets pronounced God's judgment upon Ekron, along with her sister cities (Amos 1:8).

ELAH [EE la] (oak)

The fourth king of Israel. Elah was the son and successor of Baasha (1 Kin. 16:6–14). His wicked two-year reign ended when Zimri, one of his captains, murdered him while he was in a drunken stupor.

ELAM [EE lum] (highland)

A geographical region east of the Tigris River. It was bounded on the north by Media and Assyria, on the east and southeast by Persia, and on the south by the Persian Gulf. In the time of Abraham, "Chedorlaomer, king of Elam" is described as the overlord of three other Mesopotamian kings (Gen. 14:1–17). The prophet Isaiah lists Elam as one of the places to which the Israelites were exiled (Is. 11:11). Elam is described as a people who "bore the quiver" (bow and arrow) and who had "chariots of men and horsemen" (Is. 22:6). Jeremiah lists Elam as one of the peoples who would be forced to drink from the cup of God's fury (Jer. 25:15, 25).

Ezekiel prophesied of a time when a funeral dirge would be chanted over the grave of Elam; the once-mighty nation would be consigned to the Pit (Ezek. 32:24–25). When the Assyrians transported people from the east to settle them in Samaria, the Elamites were among those resettled (Ezra 4:9). Cyrus the Great, the founder of the Persian Empire who conquered Babylon and assisted the Jews, was from Anshan (a designation that apparently refers to eastern Elam with Susa, or Shushan, as its capital). The Book of Esther records events that took place in Shushan (Esth. 1:2; 8:14–15). Daniel wrote, "I was in Shushan, the citadel, which is in the province of Elam" (Dan. 8:2). Among the foreigners present in Jerusalem on the Day of Pentecost were "Parthians and Medes and Elamites" (Acts 2:9).

ELAMITES [EE lum ites]

Descendants of Elam; an ancient people who lived in the area east of the Tigris and Euphrates rivers. During their history, the Elamites struggled with the Babylonians, Assyrians, and Persians for domination of the Mesopotamian region of the ancient world.

The great Babylonian dynasty of Ur was brought to an end about 1950 B.C. by the Elamites, who destroyed the city and took its king prisoner. The capital of Elam during its entire history was

Shushan (Susa). To it the Persian king, Darius I, transferred the Persian capital about 520 B.C. The city is therefore mentioned several times in the books of Nehemiah, Esther, and Daniel, since these books deal with events during the time of the Persian Empire (Neh. 1:1; Esth. 1:2; Dan. 8:2).

From about 2000 to 1800 B.C., the Elamites expanded their kingdom at the expense of the Mesopotamian states, until Hammurapi (about 1792–1750 B.C.) put an end to Elamite expansion. Elam was a virtual province of Babylon until about 1200 B.C. Then from about 1200 to 1130 B.C. Babylon was ruled by Elam. Under the leadership of a succession of strong kings, the Elamites raided and defeated Babylon. In 1130 B.C., however, Nebuchadnezzar I of Babylon captured Elam. For almost three centuries thereafter the Elamites were again under Babylonian domination.

From about 740 B.C. onward, Assyria's power created a more serious threat to the Elamites. Finally, Ashurbanipal, king of Assyria, conquered Elam about 645 B.C. The Persians had already taken the part of Elam called Anshan; after the Assyrian Empire was destroyed (609 B.C.), the Medes annexed most of Elam. When the Persians, in turn, began to control Media, all of Elam became a Persian administrative district. After the sixth century B.C., Elam was never again an independent nation.

Genesis 10:22 identifies Elam, the ancestor of the Elamites, as a son of Shem. Chedorlaomer, who led a group of eastern kings on raids to Palestine about 2000 B.C., also was an Elamite. These kings defeated several cities in the Jordan River plain, including Sodom and Gomorrah. Abraham and his allies finally defeated Chedorlaomer and his fellow kings and rescued Lot, regaining the wealth the easterners had captured

(Gen. 14). Chedorlaomer himself was driven back to Elam.

After the Assyrians captured the northern kingdom of Israel in 722 B.C., they followed their usual practice of deporting the population as a means of strengthening their control over them. Elamites were among the national groups deported to Samaria. Some Samaritan Israelites were in turn deported to Elam (Ezra 4:9). Some of the Israelites returned from Elam when the Persians allowed the Jews to go back to Palestine after the captivity.

Isaiah prophesied that Elam would be involved in the defeat of Babylon (Is. 21:2). By its connection with the Persians during their conquest of the Babylonian Empire, they fulfilled Isaiah's prophecy (Dan. 8:1–4). Elamites serving in the Assyrian army also took part in the siege of Jerusalem (Is. 22:6) in 701 B.C. The prophets Jeremiah and Ezekiel prophesied that Elam itself would eventually be destroyed (Jer. 49:34–39; Ezek. 32:24–25).

Elamites were among the pilgrims at Jerusalem on the Day of Pentecost (Acts 2:9). They probably were Jews from Elam, or descendants of those who had been exiled there in 722 B.C. This group may also have included native Elamites who had converted to Judaism.

ELATH [EE lath] *(palm grove)*

A seaport town on the northeast corner of the Gulf of Elath, or Aqaba, on the Red Sea. King David captured the city, where he established an extensive trade. King Solomon built a fleet at Ezion Geber, which is near Elath on the shore of the Red Sea, in the land of Edom (1 Kin. 9:26; Eloth in KJV, NRSV). Subsequently the town was conquered by Rezin, king of Syria, and then held by the Syrians until it became a border station for the Roman legion (2 Kin. 16:6). During the Greek and Roman period the town was called Aila or Aelana.

ELDER

A term used throughout the Bible but designating different ideas at various times in biblical history. The word may refer to age, experience, and authority, as well as specific leadership roles.

In ancient times authority was given to older people with wider experience. These were often considered the most qualified to hold places of leadership. The basic meaning of the Hebrew and Greek words for elder is "old age."

In the Old Testament, those leaders associated with Moses in governing the nation of Israel were called "the elders of Israel" (Ex. 3:16; 24:1), "the elders of the people" (Ex. 19:7), or the "seventy elders" (Ex. 24:1). Moses called the elders together to give them instructions for the observance of the Passover before the Exodus from Egypt.

Later, after the years of wandering in the wilderness, bodies of elders ruled in each city. They were viewed as the representatives of the nation and its people. The term *elder* eventually came to be applied to those who governed in the local communities, the rulers of the various tribes, and those who ruled all of Israel. These leaders were responsible for legal, political, and military guidance and supervision.

During the years of Israel's captivity in Babylon and the following centuries, elders again appeared as leaders who were responsible for governing in the

ELDER

Jewish communities. They became the upper class, forming a type of ruling aristocracy. Later in this period, a council of elders of 71 members, called the Sanhedrin, emerged. It had both religious and political authority among all the Jewish people in Palestine, particularly in New Testament times. The high priest was the chairman of the Sanhedrin. Local Jewish synagogues, which emerged in the period between the Old and New Testaments, were also governed by a council of elders.

A governing structure similar to the ruling elders among the Jews was followed in the early church. The title "elder" was continued, but the significance of the office changed. Thus the term *elder* is used in the New Testament to refer to the Jewish elders of the synagogue, to the members of the Sanhedrin, and to certain persons who held office in the church. It also implied seniority by reason of age (1 Tim. 5:2; 1 Pet. 5:5).

The presence of elders in the church in the New Testament indicates that this office was taken over from the synagogue. Elders were associated with James in Jerusalem in the local church's government (Acts 11:30; 21:18) and, with the apostles, in the decisions of the early church councils (Acts 15). Elders were also appointed in the churches established during Paul's first missionary journey (Acts 14:23). Paul addressed the elders at Ephesus (Acts 20:17–35). Elders played an important role in church life through their ministry to the sick (James 5:14, 15). They were apparently the teachers also in a local congregation. Additional duties consisted of explaining the Scriptures and teaching doctrine (1 Tim. 5:17; 1 Pet. 5:5).

ELECTION

The gracious and free act of God by which He calls those who become part of His kingdom and special beneficiaries of His love and blessings. The Bible describes the concept of election in three distinct ways. Election sometimes refers to the choice of Israel and the church as a people for special service and privileges. Election may also refer to the choice of a specific individual to some office or to perform some special service. Still other passages of the Bible refer to the election of individuals to be children of God and heirs of eternal life.

Throughout the history of redemption, election has characterized God's saving activity. He chose and called Abraham from Ur to Canaan, making an everlasting covenant with him and his offspring (Gen. 11:31–12:7). God also called Moses to lead His people out of bondage (Ex. 2:24–3:10). He chose Israel from among the nations of the world to be His special covenant people (Is. 44:1–2).

Election to salvation takes place "in Christ" (Eph. 1:4; 2:10) as a part of God's purpose for the human race. As part of His eternal plan, God allows us to use our freedom to rebel against Him. Thus it is gracious of God to save those who find salvation through Jesus Christ. It is not unjust of Him not to save everyone, since no one deserves to be saved (Rom. 9:15). Election is gracious; it is also unconditional and unmerited (1 Pet. 1:2). It is an expression of the eternal, sovereign will of God who cannot change (Rom. 8:29). Therefore the salvation of the elect is certain (Rom. 8:28, 33).

Election is not to be a source of complacency (2 Pet. 1:12) or presumption (Rom. 11:19–22) on the part of Christians. They are to make their calling and election certain by growing in godliness (2 Pet. 1:2–11) as they respond with gratitude to God's electing love (Col. 3:12–17). The ultimate goal of our election is that we might bring praise and glory to God (Rom. 11:33; 2 Thess. 2:13).

See also PREDESTINATION.

ELEAZAR [el e A zur] *(God is helper)*

Aaron's third son by his wife, Elisheba (Ex. 6:23). Eleazar was the father of Phinehas (Ex. 6:25). Consecrated a priest, he was made chief of the Levites after his elder brothers, Nadab and Abihu, were killed for offering unholy fire (Lev. 10:1–7). Before Aaron died, Eleazar ascended Mount Hor with him and was invested with Aaron's high priestly garments (Num. 20:25–28). Eleazar served as high priest during the remainder of Moses' life and throughout Joshua's leadership. He helped in the allotment of Canaan among the twelve tribes of Israel (Josh. 14:1), and was buried "in a hill that belonged to Phinehas his son . . . in the mountains of Ephraim" (Josh. 24:33). Phinehas succeeded him as high priest (Judg. 20:28).

ELI [EE lie] *(the Lord is high)*

A judge and high priest with whom the prophet Samuel lived during his childhood (1 Sam. 1–4; 14:3).

The first mention of Eli occurs when the childless Hannah poured out to him her unhappiness over her barren condition. Later, her prayers for a son were answered when Samuel was born. True to her word, she brought her son to the tabernacle and dedicated him to God. There the future prophet lived with the high priest Eli.

Eli was a deeply pious man whose service to the Lord was unblemished. However, he was a lax father who had no control over his two sons. Phinehas and Hophni took meat from sacrificial animals before they were dedicated to God. They also "lay with the women that assembled at the door of the tabernacle" (1 Sam. 2:22). God pronounced judgment on Eli because of his failure to discipline his sons.

God's judgment was carried out through the Philistines. Hophni and Phinehas carried the ark of the covenant into battle to help the Israelites. Both were killed, and the ark was captured. When Eli, 98 years old and nearly blind, heard the news, he fell backward and broke his neck. God's final judgment against Eli and his descendants occurred when Solomon removed Abiathar, Eli's descendant, and installed Zadok in his place as high priest of the nation (1 Kin. 2:35).

ELIAKIM [e LIE uh kim] *(God is setting up)*

A son of Hilkiah and overseer of the household of King Hezekiah of Judah (2 Kin. 18:18; 19:2). When the invading Assyrian army approached Jerusalem (701 B.C.), Eliakim was one of three men sent by Hezekiah to confer with Sennacherib's forces. Hezekiah then sent these men to report the Assyrians' answer to the prophet Isaiah, who praised Eliakim highly (Is. 22:20–23).

ELIHU [eh LIE hew] *(He is my God)*

The youngest of Job's "comforters." Elihu spoke to Job after the three friends—Bildad, Eliphaz, and Zophar—failed to give convincing answers to Job's questions. Elihu is called "the son of Barachel the Buzite of the family of Ram" (Job 32:2). Like Job's other friends, Elihu was probably from the Transjordan area southeast of Israel.

ELIJAH [ee LIE juh] *(the Lord is my God)*

An influential prophet who lived in the ninth century B.C. during the reigns of Ahab and Ahaziah in the northern kingdom of Israel. Elijah shaped the history of his day and dominated Israelite thinking for centuries afterward.

Elijah's prophetic activities emphasized the unconditional loyalty to God required of the nation of Israel. His strange dress and appearance (2 Kin. 1:8), his fleetness of foot (1 Kin. 18:46), his rugged constitution that resisted famine (1 Kin. 19:8), and his cave-dwelling habits (1 Kin. 17:3; 19:9)—all these suggest that he was a robust, outdoors-type person.

Elijah was opposed to the accepted standards of his day, when belief in many gods was normal. He appears in the role of God's instrument of judgment upon a wayward Israel because of the nation's widespread idolatry. The miracles that Elijah performed occurred during the period when a life-or-death struggle took place between the religion of the Lord and Baal worship.

Elijah's views were in conflict with those of King Ahab, who had attempted to cultivate economic ties with Israel's neighbors, especially Tyre. One of the consequences was that he had married Jezebel, a daughter of Ethbaal, king of Tyre. Ahab saw no harm in participating in the religion of his neighbors, particularly the religion of his wife. Therefore, he established a center of Baal worship at Samaria. Influenced by Jezebel, Ahab gave himself to the worship of Baal. Suddenly Elijah appeared on the scene.

As punishment against Ahab for building the temple for Baal worship at Samaria, Elijah predicted that a drought would grip the land. Then he fled to the eastern side of the Jordan River and later to Zarephath on the Mediterranean coast to escape Ahab's wrath. At both sites he was kept alive through miraculous means. While staying at a widow's home, he performed a miracle by bringing her son back to life (1 Kin. 17:1–24).

After the drought had lasted three years, the Lord instructed Elijah to present himself before Ahab with the message that the Lord would provide rain. Elijah then challenged the 850 prophets of Baal and Asherah to a contest on Mount Carmel (1 Kin. 18:21). Each side would offer sacrifices to their God without building a fire. The ignition of the fire was left to the strongest god, who would thereby reveal himself as the true God.

The best efforts of the pagan prophets through the better part of a day failed to evoke a response from Baal. Elijah poured water over his sacrifice to remove any possibility of fraud or misunderstanding about the offering. After Elijah prayed briefly to the Lord, his sacrifice was consumed by fire from heaven. The people of Israel responded strongly in favor of God (1 Kin. 18:39). Then the prophets of Baal were slaughtered at Elijah's command (1 Kin. 18:40), and God sent rain to end the drought (1 Kin. 18:41–46).

Queen Jezebel was furious over the fate of her prophets. She vowed that she would take revenge on Elijah. He was forced to flee to Mount Horeb—the mountain where Moses had received the Ten Commandments. Like Moses, Elijah was sustained for 40 days and nights in the wilderness.

While Elijah was at Mount Horeb, the Lord revealed Himself in a low, murmuring sound. The prophet received a revelation of the coming doom on Ahab and Israel (1 Kin. 19:14). Then Elijah was given a threefold charge: He was instructed to anoint Hazael as king of Syria, Jehu as the future king of Israel, and Elisha as the prophet who would take his place (1 Kin. 19:16). These changes would bring to power those who would reform Israel in the coming years.

In the years of war that followed between Ahab and Ben-Hadad of Syria, Elijah did not appear (1 Kin. 20). But he did appear after Jezebel acquired a family-owned vineyard for Ahab by having its owner, Naboth, falsely accused and executed (1 Kin. 21:1–29). Elijah met the king in the vineyard and rebuked him for the act (1 Kin. 21:1–24). Ahab repented, and Elijah brought him word from the Lord that the prophesied ruin on his house would not come during his lifetime, but would occur in the days of his son.

The prophet Elijah did not die. He was carried bodily to heaven in a whirlwind (2 Kin. 2:1–11). This was an honor previously bestowed only upon Enoch (Gen. 5:24). Elisha, the only witness to this event, picked up Elijah's mantle which fell from him as he ascended. He carried it during his ministry as a token of his continuation of Elijah's ministry (2 Kin. 2:13–14).

Elijah's impact on the prophetic movement among the Hebrew people was extensive. He stands as the transitional figure between Samuel (the adviser and anointer of kings) and the later writing prophets. Like the prophets who followed him, Elijah emphasized Israel's responsibility for total commitment to their God and the covenant responsibilities that God and His people had sworn to each other. Both ideas are more fully developed in later prophets, such as Amos and Hosea.

In later Jewish thought, the messianic age was frequently associated with Elijah's return. The Old Testament spoke of the reappearance of Elijah. The prophet Malachi prophesied that the Lord would send Elijah before the day of the Lord arrived. This prophecy was fulfilled in the coming of John the Baptist (Matt. 11:4; 17:10–13; Luke 1:17). John the Baptist was similar to Elijah in his preaching as well as his dress and physical appearance (Matt. 11:7–8; Luke 7:24–28). During Jesus' earthly ministry, some identified him with Elijah (Matt. 16:14; Luke 9:8).

ELIMELECH [e LIM uh leck] *(my God is king)*

The husband of Naomi and the father-in-law of Ruth (Ruth 1:2–3; 2:1). An Ephrathite of Bethlehem of Judah, he moved his family to Moab to escape famine. His two sons, Chilion and Mahlon, married Moabite women, Orpah and Ruth, re-

spectively. After the death of Elimelech and his two sons, Ruth chose to return to Bethlehem with Naomi (Ruth 1:16–17).

ELIPHAZ [EL ih faz]

The chief and oldest of Job's three "friends" or "comforters" (Job 2:11). A very religious man, Eliphaz sought to uphold the holiness, purity, and justice of God; he became uneasy when Job questioned this understanding of God.

ELISHA [ee LIE shuh] *(my God saves)*

An early Hebrew prophet who succeeded the prophet Elijah when Elijah's time on earth was finished (1 Kin. 19:16). Elisha ministered for about 50 years in the northern kingdom of Israel, serving God during the reigns of Jehoram, Jehu, Jehoahaz, and Joash. The period of his ministry dates from about 850 to 800 B.C. Elisha's work consisted of presenting the Word of God through prophecy, advising kings, anointing kings, helping the needy, and performing several miracles.

The prophet Elijah found Elisha plowing with a team of oxen. As Elijah walked past Elisha, he threw his mantle over the younger man's shoulders. Elisha "arose and followed Elijah, and became his servant" (1 Kin. 19:21). Before taking his leave, Elijah fulfilled the final request of Elisha by providing him with a double portion of his prophetic spirit (2 Kin. 2:9–10), making him his spiritual firstborn. Upon receiving Elijah's mantle, Elisha demonstrated this gift by parting the waters of the Jordan River, allowing him to cross on dry land (2 Kin. 2:14). In this way, Elisha demonstrated that he had received God's blessings on his ministry as Elijah's successor.

Elisha cultivated a different image from his predecessor. Instead of following Elijah's example as a loner and an outsider, Elisha chose to work within the established system. He assumed his rightful place as the head of the "official" prophetic order in Israel, where his counsel and advice were sought out by kings. In contrast to Elijah's strained relationship with the king and his officials, Elisha enjoyed the harmonious role of trusted advisor. This is not to say that Elisha never had a word of criticism for the government, as for example in the part he played in the overthrow of Jezebel and the dynasty of Ahab (2 Kin. 9:1–3).

Elisha's appearance was much more typical and average than Elijah's. He was bald (2 Kin. 2:23), while Elijah had been an extremely hairy man (2 Kin. 1:8). Elisha did not wander as extensively as Elijah. Instead, he had a house in Samaria (2 Kin. 6:32). Much tension had existed between Elijah and his audience. Elisha's ministry provided a strong contrast as he was welcomed into virtually all levels of society.

In perhaps the most important part of his ministry, however, Elisha followed in Elijah's footsteps. This consisted of his performance of miracles, which answered a wide variety of needs in every level of society. He sympathized with the poor and the oppressed. Elisha's activities and miracles as a prophet were often focused on those who were abused by officials in positions of power.

In one miracle, Elisha helped the widow of one of the sons of the prophets. To help her pay off creditors who intended to take the widow's two sons, Elisha multiplied the amount of oil in one jar to fill all available containers. This brought in enough money to pay off the debts and provided a surplus on which the widow and her sons could live (2 Kin. 4:1–7).

Elisha became a friend of a wealthy family in Shunem. The Shunammite woman displayed hospitality toward the prophet by feeding him and building a room onto her home where he could lodge. Elisha repaid the childless couple by promising them a son (2 Kin. 4:8–17).

Later, when tragedy struck the child, Elisha raised him from the dead (2 Kin. 4:18–37). When Elisha learned that a famine would strike Israel, he warned the family to flee the land. When the family returned seven years later, the king restored their property because of their relationship with Elisha (2 Kin. 8:1–6).

Elisha ministered to all people, regardless of their nationalities. He cured Naaman, the commander of the Syrian army (2 Kin. 5:1–14), of leprosy, but he also advised the kings of Israel of the plans (2 Kin. 6:8–10) of their Assyrian enemies. Even the bones of the dead Elisha had miraculous powers. When a corpse was hidden in Elisha's tomb, it came back to life as it touched the prophet's bones (2 Kin. 13:21).

ELIZABETH [ee LIZ uh buth] *(God is my oath)*

The mother of John the Baptist (Luke 1). Of the priestly line of Aaron, Elizabeth was the wife of the priest Zacharias. Although both "were . . . righteous before God, they had no child, because Elizabeth was barren" (Luke 1:6–7). But God performed a miracle, and Elizabeth conceived the child who was to be the forerunner of the Messiah.

Elizabeth was privileged in another way. When her cousin Mary visited her, Elizabeth, six months pregnant, felt the child move as if to welcome the child whom Mary was carrying. Elizabeth recognized the significance of this action and acknowledged the Messiah before He had been born.

ELYMAS [EL ih mas]

A false prophet who was temporarily struck blind for opposing Paul and Barnabas at Paphos on Cyprus (Acts 13:8). Described as "a Jew whose name was Bar-Jesus" (Acts 13:6), he apparently had some influence with Sergius Paulus, the Roman governor of the island. Elymas was jealous of the gospel that Paul preached and tried to turn the governor away from accepting the Christian faith.

EMBALMING

A method of preparing the dead for burial and preserving the body from decay. The practice of treating a corpse to preserve it dates back more than 3,500 years. Mummification was invented by the Egyptians, who believed that the preservation of the body insured the continuation of the person after death.

The most elaborate method of embalming required the removal of the brain and all internal organs except the heart. The inner cavity of the body was then washed and filled with spices. The corpse was soaked in natron, then washed and wrapped in bandages of linen soaked with gum. Finally, the embalmed body was placed in a wooden coffin.

The Bible mentions embalming only once, in reference to Joseph and his father Jacob (Gen. 50:2–3, 26). Even this single reference is surprising, since the ancient Israelites did not generally embalm their dead because of laws concerning the touching of dead bodies (Num. 5:1–4; 19:11–22). But both Joseph and Jacob died in Egypt. They were apparently embalmed so their bodies could be taken back to Israel for burial.

See also BURIAL.

EMERALD

A precious stone of deep green color. The emerald was found in Egypt, Cyprus, and Ethiopia. It was the third jewel in the first row of Aaron's breastplate (Ex. 28:17; 39:10). Emeralds were also an article of trade between Tyre and Syria (Ezek. 27:16). The emerald was the fourth foundation stone of the New Jerusalem (Rev. 21:19), and was used to describe the rainbow around the throne (Rev. 4:3).

EMMAUS [em MAY us] (warm wells)

A village in Judea where Jesus revealed Himself to two disciples after His resurrection. The disciples, Cleopas and an unidentified companion, encountered Jesus on the road to Emmaus, but they did not recognize Him. Jesus accompanied them to Emmaus, and they invited Him to stay there with them. As He blessed and broke bread at the evening meal, the disciples' "eyes were opened and they knew Him" (Luke 24:31). The modern location of ancient Emmaus is uncertain. Luke reported the village was 7 miles (11 kilometers) from Jerusalem, but he did not specify in which direction.

EMPEROR WORSHIP

A pagan custom of ancient times in which a ruler claimed for himself the qualities of a god and was so treated by those whom he ruled.

Many nations of the ancient world followed the custom of worshiping their rulers. The Egyptians, for example, claimed their pharaohs had descended from the sun god. The Greek conquerer Alexander the Great established a cult of such worship in Alexandria. The rulers of Syria and Egypt followed this tradition, calling themselves gods who ruled on earth.

The Book of Daniel records two actual instances of emperor worship. King Nebuchadnezzar had a statue made. Then he ordered everyone to bow down to it. Those who refused were thrown into a fiery furnace (Dan. 3). Later, the prophet Daniel was thrown to the lions for his refusal to pray to King Darius (Dan. 6).

When the Roman Empire conquered ancient nations, the worship of the Roman state naturally replaced other pagan forms of worship. The conquered peoples began to worship outstanding

Roman leaders, such as Mark Antony and Julius Caesar.

Under Augustus Caesar as emperor of Rome, emperor worship grew in intensity. In the various Roman provinces, the subjects worshiped the Roman state and the emperor as a sign of their loyalty to Rome. Throughout the empire, Roman subjects incorporated emperor worship into their local religions. Leading citizens became priests in the emperor worship cult as evidence of their loyalty to the Roman Empire.

Although the New Testament never speaks directly of emperor worship, passages that refer to Jesus as the only Lord (Rom. 10:9) and God as the only ruler (1 Tim. 6:15) condemn it by implication. Secular history records that the Roman emperor Caligula (A.D. 37–41) proclaimed himself as a god, built temples for himself, and required his subjects to worship him. In A.D. 40, some Jews destroyed a statue that had been erected to him. Caligula retaliated by threatening to place a statue in the Jewish temple, but the plan was never carried out because of Jewish opposition.

Open conflict between Christians and the Roman Empire over emperor worship came long after the close of the New Testament. Under Emperor Trajan, Christians who would not renounce their allegiance to Christ and pledge their worship of the emperor often were executed.

Emperor worship continued as the official religion of the Roman Empire until Christianity was recognized under the emperor Constantine (A.D. 305–337).

EN GEDI [en GEH dee] *(spring of a kid)*

An oasis on the barren western shore of the Dead Sea about 35 miles (54 kilometers) southeast of Jerusalem. It lay on the eastern edge of the rugged Wilderness of Judah, which contained many hideouts where David sometimes hid when he was fleeing from King Saul (1 Sam. 23:29–24:1).

En Gedi was watered by a hot spring, yielding an abundance of fresh water that burst forth hundreds of feet above the base of a large cliff. Its ancient name was Hazezon Tamar or Hazazon Tamar ("pruning of palms"), indicating the presence of date palms there. Vineyards also prospered at En Gedi (Song 1:14). In Abraham's day, Chedorlaomer conquered the Amorites who occupied this spot (Gen. 14:7).

ENOCH [EE nuck] *(initiated or dedicated)*

A son of Jared and the father of Methuselah (Gen. 5:18–24; Henoch, 1 Chr. 1:3, KJV). After living for 365 years, Enoch was "translated," or taken directly into God's presence without experiencing death (Gen. 5:24; Heb. 11:5–6).

EPAPHRAS [EP uh frus] *(charming)*

A Christian preacher who spread the gospel to his fellow Colossian citizens (Col. 1:7; 4:12). When Paul was a prisoner in Rome, Epaphras came to him with a favorable account of the church at Colosse. He remained with Paul in Rome and was, in a sense, his "fellow prisoner" (Philem. 23).

EPAPHRODITUS [ih paf ruh DIE tus] *(charming)*

A messenger sent by the church at Philippi with a gift for the apostle Paul, who was under house arrest in Rome (Phil. 2:25; 4:18). While in Rome Epaphroditus became ill and word of his sickness spread to Philippi. As soon as Epaphroditus was well enough, Paul sent him back home to relieve the church's anxiety and to deliver Paul's letter to the Philippians.

EPHESUS [EFF uh sus]

A large and important city on the west coast of Asia Minor where the apostle Paul founded a church. A number of factors contributed to the prominence that Ephesus enjoyed.

The first factor was economics. Situated at the mouth of the river Cayster, Ephesus was the most favorable seaport in the province of Asia and the most important trade center west of Tarsus. Today, because of silting from the river, the ruins of the city lie in a swamp 5 to 7 miles (8 to 11 kilometers) inland.

Another factor was size. Although Pergamum was the capital of the province of Asia in Roman times, Ephesus was the largest city in the province, having a population of perhaps 300,000 people.

A third factor was culture. Ephesus contained a theater that seated an estimated 25,000 people. A main thoroughfare, some 105 feet (35 meters) wide, ran from the theater to the harbor, at each end of which stood an impressive gate. The thoroughfare was flanked on each side by rows of columns 50 feet (15 meters) deep. Behind these columns were baths, gymnasiums, and impressive buildings.

The fourth, and perhaps most significant, reason for the prominence of Ephesus was religion. The temple of Artemis (or Diana, according to her Roman name) at Ephesus ranked as one of the seven wonders of the ancient world. As the twin sister of Apollo and the daughter of Zeus, Artemis was known variously as the moon goddess, the goddess of hunting, and the patroness of young girls. The temple at Ephesus housed the image of Artemis that was reputed to have come directly from Zeus (Acts 19:35).

The temple of Artemis in Paul's day was supported by 127 columns, each of them 197 feet (60 meters) high. The Ephesians took great pride in this grand edifice. During the Roman period, they promoted the worship of Artemis by minting coins with the inscription, "Diana of Ephesus."

The history of Christianity at Ephesus began about A.D. 50, perhaps as a result of the efforts of Priscilla and Aquila (Acts 18:18). Paul came to Ephesus in about A.D. 52, establishing a resident ministry for the better part of three years (Acts 20:31). During his Ephesian ministry, Paul wrote 1 Corinthians (1 Cor. 16:8).

The Book of Acts reports that "all who dwelt in Asia heard the word of the Lord Jesus" (Acts 19:10), while Paul taught during the hot midday hours in the lecture hall of Tyrannus (Acts 19:9). Influence from his ministry undoubtedly resulted in the founding of churches in the Lycus River valley at Laodicea, Hierapolis, and Colosse.

So influential, in fact, was Paul's ministry at Ephesus that the silversmiths' league, which fashioned souvenirs of the temple, feared that the preaching of the gospel would undermine the great temple of Artemis (Acts 19:27). As a result, one of the silversmiths, a man named Demetrius, stirred up a riot against Paul.

During his stay in Ephesus, Paul encountered both great opportunities and great dangers. He baptized believers who apparently came to know the gospel through disciples of John the Baptist (Acts 19:1–5), and he countered the strong influence of magic in Ephesus (Acts 19:11–20).

After Paul departed from Ephesus, Timothy remained to combat false teaching (1 Tim. 1:3; 2 Tim. 4:3; Acts 20:29). Many traditions testify that the apostle John lived in Ephesus toward the end of the first century. In his vision from the island of Patmos off the coast of Asia Minor, John described the church of Ephesus as flourishing, although it was troubled with false teachers and had lost its first love (Rev. 2:1–7). In the sixth century A.D. the Roman emperor Justinian (A.D. 527–565) raised a magnificent church to John's memory in this city.

Ephesus continued to play a prominent role in the history of the early church. A long line of bishops in the Eastern Church lived there. In A.D. 431 the Council of Ephesus officially condemned the Nestorian heresy, which taught that there were two separate persons, one divine and one human, in the person of Jesus Christ.

EPHOD OF HIGH PRIEST [EE fod]

A vest worn by the high priest when he presided at the altar (Ex. 28:4–14; 39:2–7). Worn over a blue robe (Ex. 28:31–35), the ephod was made of fine linen interwoven with threads of pure gold and other threads that were blue, purple, and scarlet in color. The ephod consisted of two pieces joined at the shoulders and bound together at the bottom by a woven band of the same material as the ephod.

Upon the shoulders of the ephod, in settings of gold, were two onyx stones, upon which were engraved the names of the twelve tribes of Israel. The front of the vest, or the breastplate, was fastened to the shoulder straps by two golden chains (Ex. 28:14) and by a blue cord (Ex. 28:28).

In later years, ephods were worn by associate priests as well as the high priest (1 Sam. 22:18). Even the boy Samuel, dedicated to serve in the Shiloh sanctuary, wore an ephod (1 Sam. 2:18). David, although not a priest, wore an ephod when he brought the ark of the covenant to Jerusalem (2 Sam. 6:14; 1 Chr. 15:27).

EPHRAIM [EE freh em] (doubly fruitful)

The second son of Joseph by Asenath. When Ephraim was born to Joseph in Egypt, he gave him his name meaning "fruitful" because "God has caused me to be fruitful in the land of my affliction" (Gen. 41:52). Even though Joseph was a foreigner (a Hebrew) in Egypt, he had been blessed by God as he rose to a high position in the Egyptian government and fathered two sons.

Later this same theme of fruitfulness

and blessing was echoed by Joseph's father, Jacob, as he accepted Ephraim as his grandson (Gen. 48:5). Eventually Ephraim's thousands of descendants settled in the land of Canaan as one of the most numerous of the tribes of Israel (Gen. 48:19; Num. 1:10).

EPHRAIM, TRIBE OF

Descendants of Ephraim who settled the land of Canaan as one of the twelve tribes of Israel. Their territory was bounded on the north by Manasseh (west of the river Jordan) and on the south by Dan and Benjamin (Josh. 16:5–10).

From the early days, the tribe of Ephraim was an influential force in Israel, being highly commended by Gideon (Judg. 8:2), and including such key religious and political centers as Bethel and Shechem. At the time of the first census in their new land, the tribe contained 40,500 men eligible for military service (Num. 1:33).

Following the revolt of the ten tribes after Solomon's rule, Ephraim became a leader in the northern kingdom of Israel (1 Kin. 12:25–33). Often the name Ephraim was used for Israel because of its size and its leadership role. The Hebrew prophets, especially Hosea, chastised Ephraim for idolatry (Hos. 4:17), spiritual unfaithfulness (8:9–10), and relationships with pagan nations (12:1). Ephraim was involved in an alliance with Syria against Judah and King Ahaz (2 Chr. 28:5–8; Is. 7:3–9).

In 722 B.C., the northern kingdom of Israel was taken into captivity in Assyria. This seemed to be the end of the tribe of Ephraim, but the Lord would not forget them. Through the prophet Jeremiah, He declared that these people were still His "dear son" and He would have mercy on them (Jer. 31:20). Years later, after God's people returned to their homeland following a long period of captivity in

Babylon, "children of Ephraim" settled in Jerusalem (1 Chr. 9:3).

EPHRON [EE fron]

A Hittite from whom Abraham purchased a field containing the cave of Machpelah. It became the burial place of the patriarchs Abraham, Isaac, and Jacob (and also of their wives, Sarah, Rebekah, and Leah; Gen. 23:8–17; 25:9; 49:29–30; 50:13).

EPICUREANS [epp uh cue REE anz]

Greek philosophers who belonged to a school founded by Epicurus about 306 B.C. The Epicureans were concerned with the practical results of philosophy in everyday life. Their chief aim in life was pleasure. They believed they could find happiness by seeking what brought physical and mental pleasure, and by avoiding what brought pain.

Only one reference to the Epicureans occurs in Scripture—in the New Testament account of the apostle Paul's encounter with "certain Epicurean and Stoic philosophers" at Athens (Acts 17:16–34). In contrast to these philosophers, Paul believed that true happiness was found in following the will of Jesus Christ.

ERASTUS [ih RAS tus] *(beloved)*

The "treasurer of the city" (Rom. 16:23) in Corinth who sent greetings to Rome. If an inscription found in the pavement of the amphitheater at ancient Corinth and bearing the name "Erastus" refers to this man, Erastus is the earliest Christian name attested outside of the Bible.

ESARHADDON [eh sar HAD un]

The favorite, though not the oldest, son of Sennacherib, who succeeded his father as king of Assyria. Sennacherib's favoritism toward Esarhaddon so enraged two other brothers, Adrammelech

and Sharaezer, that they assassinated their father about 681 B.C., then escaped into Armenia (2 Kin. 19:36–37; 2 Chr. 32:21; Is. 37:37–38). At the time of the assassination, Esarhaddon was conducting a military campaign, probably in Armenia. He returned to Nineveh, the Assyrian capital, ended the civil strife, and assumed the Assyrian throne.

Esarhaddon was a wise ruler, both militarily and politically. He restored the city of Babylon, which his father had destroyed in an earlier campaign against Babylonia; and he successfully waged war against numerous groups that had been persistent in creating problems for the Assyrian Empire. Among his most notable military achievements was his conquest of Egypt, Assyria's competitor for world domination. In 677 B.C. Esarhaddon captured Memphis and then conquered the rest of Egypt. He then used native rulers and Assyrian advisors to rule the distant country.

Egypt rebelled in 669 B.C. On his way to Egypt to put down the rebellion, Esarhaddon became ill and died. As his father before him had done, Esarhaddon had provided for an orderly succession in the affairs of Assyria. His younger son, Ashurbanipal, ascended to the Assyrian throne.

Esarhaddon participated in the resettling of Samaria with foreigners long after this capital city of the northern kingdom of Israel fell to Assyrian forces in 722 B.C. (Ezra 4:2). This was an example of the Assyrian policy of intermingling cultures in the nations that they conquered to make them weak and compliant.

ESAU [EE saw]

A son of Isaac and Rebekah and the twin brother of Jacob. Also known as Edom, Esau was the ancestor of the Edomites (Gen. 25:24–28; Deut. 2:4–8). Most of the biblical narratives about

Esau draw a great contrast between him and his brother, Jacob. Esau was a hunter and outdoorsman who was favored by his father, while Jacob was not an outdoors type and was favored by Rebekah (Gen. 25:27–28).

Even though he was a twin, Esau was considered the oldest son because he was born first. By Old Testament custom, he would have inherited most of his father's property and the right to succeed him as family patriarch. But in a foolish, impulsive moment, he sold his birthright to Jacob in exchange for a meal (Gen. 25:29–34). This determined that Jacob would carry on the family name in a direct line of descent from Abraham and Isaac, his grandfather and father.

The loss of Esau's rights as firstborn is further revealed in Genesis 27. Jacob deceived his blind father by disguising himself as Esau in order to receive his father's highest blessing. Esau was therefore the recipient of a lesser blessing (Gen. 27:25–29, 38–40; Heb. 11:20). He was so enraged by Jacob's actions that he determined to kill him once his father died. But Jacob fled to his uncle Laban in Haran and remained there for 20 years. Upon Jacob's return to Canaan, Esau forgave him and set aside their old feuds (Gen. 32:1–33:17). Years later, the two brothers together buried their father in the cave at Machpelah without a trace of their old hostilities (Gen. 35:29).

Esau in many ways was more honest and dependable than his scheming brother Jacob. But he sinned greatly by treating his birthright so casually and selling it for a meal (Heb. 12:16–17). To the ancient Hebrews, one's birthright actually represented a high spiritual value. But Esau did not have the faith and farsightedness to accept his privileges and responsibilities. Thus, the right passed to his younger brother.

ESDRAELON [ez dra EE lon] *(God sows)*

The great plain loosely identified as the Plain of Jezreel, about 55 miles (89 kilometers) north of Jerusalem. The word *Esdraelon* is the Greek form of the Hebrew word *Jezreel*. Esdraelon is a triangular plain approximately 15 by 15 by 20 miles (24 by 24 by 32 kilometers) in size, bounded along the southwest by the Carmel Mountain range and on the north by the hills of Nazareth.

The Plain of Esdraelon contains rich farmland because of the soil washed down into it from the mountains of Galilee and the highlands of Samaria. It is also the only east-west valley that divides the north-south mountain ranges and provides easy access to them.

Esdraelon has been the scene of numerous battles. There Deborah and Barak were victorious over Sisera (Judg. 4–5). Here, too, the Philistines were victorious over King Saul (1 Sam. 31:1–3). In this valley the Egyptians mortally wounded Josiah, king of Judah, when he attempted to intercept the army of Pharaoh Necho (2 Kin. 23:29).

But the greatest battle of this valley is yet to happen. The great Battle of Armageddon will be fought here (Rev. 16:16). In this battle, the lord of glory, Jesus Christ, will triumph over the forces of Satan, and "the kingdoms of this world [will] become the kingdoms of the Lord and of His Christ, and He shall reign forever and ever!" (Rev. 11:15).

ESTHER [ESS ter] *(star)*

The Jewish queen of the Persian king Ahasuerus (Xerxes). Esther saved her people, the Jews, from a plot to eliminate them. A daughter of Abihail (Esth. 2:15; 9:29) and a cousin of Mordecai (Esth. 2:7, 15), Esther was raised by Mordecai as his own daughter after her mother and father died. Esther was a member of a family carried into captivity in Babylon that later chose to stay in Persia rather than return to Jerusalem. Her Jewish name was Hadassah, which means "myrtle" (Esth. 2:7).

The story of Esther's rise from an unknown Jewish girl to become the queen of a mighty empire illustrates how God used events and people as instruments to fulfill His promise to His chosen people. Following several days of revelry, the drunken king Ahasuerus—identified with Xerxes I (reigned 486–465 B.C.)—asked his queen, Vashti, to display herself to his guests. When Vashti courageously refused, she was banished from the palace. Ahasuerus then had "all the beautiful young virgins" (Esth. 2:3) of his kingdom brought to his palace to choose Vashti's replacement.

Scripture records that "the young woman [Esther] was lovely and beautiful" (Esth. 2:7). The king loved Esther more than all the other women. He appointed her queen to replace Vashti (Esth. 2:17).

At the time, Haman was Ahasuerus's most trusted advisor. An egotistical and ambitious man, Haman demanded that people bow to him as he passed—something that Mordecai, a devout Jew, could

ETERNAL LIFE

not do in good conscience. In rage, Haman sought revenge not only on Mordecai but also on the entire Jewish population of the empire. He persuaded the king to issue an edict permitting him to kill all the Jews and seize their property.

With great tact and skill, Esther exposed Haman's plot and true character to the king. As a result, Ahasuerus granted the Jews the right to defend themselves and to destroy their enemies. With ironic justice, "they hanged Haman on the gallows that he had prepared for Mordecai (Esth. 7:10).

Even today Jews celebrate their deliverance from Ahasuerus's edict at the Feast of Purim (Esth. 9:26–32), celebrated on the fourteenth and fifteenth days of the month of Adar.

ETERNAL LIFE

A person's new and redeemed existence in Jesus Christ that is granted by God as a gift to all believers. Eternal life refers to the quality or character of our new existence in Christ as well as the unending character of that life.

The majority of references to eternal life in the New Testament are oriented to the future. The emphasis, however, is upon the blessed character of the life that will be enjoyed endlessly in the future. Jesus made it clear that eternal life comes only to those who make a total commitment to Him (Matt. 19:16–21; Luke 18:18–22). Paul's letters refer to eternal life relatively seldom, and again primarily with a future rather than a present orientation (Rom. 5:21; 6:22; Gal. 6:8).

ETHIOPIAN EUNUCH [YOU nuck]

A person baptized by Philip who held a responsible position as the royal treasurer in the court of Candace, queen of Ethiopia (Acts 8:26–40). The word *eunuch* refers to an emasculated servant who could rise to positions of power and influence in ancient times. The Ethiopian eunuch had apparently been a convert to Judaism. A keen student of the Bible, he was probably a proselyte who had come to Jerusalem to participate in worship at the temple. On his return to his own country, he encountered Philip. On Philip's explanation of Isaiah 53, he confessed his faith in Christ and was baptized.

EUNUCH [YOU nuck]

A male servant of a royal household in Bible times. Such servants were often emasculated by castration as a precautionary measure, especially if they served among the women in a ruler's harem (2 Kin. 9:32; Esth. 2:15). The New Testament reported the conversion of a eunuch from Ethiopia under the ministry of Philip the evangelist (Acts 8:26–38).

EUPHRATES [you FRAY tease]

The longest river of western Asia and one of two major rivers in Mesopotamia. The river begins in the mountains of Armenia in modern-day Turkey. It then heads west toward the Mediterranean Sea, turns to the south, swings in a wide bow through Syria, and then flows some 1,000 miles southeast to join the Tigris River before it empties into the Persian Gulf.

The Euphrates is about 1,780 miles (2,890 kilometers) long and is navigable for smaller vessels for about 1,200 miles (1,950 kilometers). The ruins of many ancient cities are located along the river in Iraq. Among them are Babylon, Eridu, Kish, Larsa, Nippur, Sippar, and Ur.

In the Bible the Euphrates is referred to as "the River Euphrates," "the great river, the River Euphrates," or simply as "the River." It was one of the four rivers that flowed from the Garden of Eden (Gen. 2:14). The Euphrates formed the northern boundary of the territories promised by God to Israel (Gen. 15:18; Josh. 1:4).

The biblical writer declared that the fathers of Israel had lived on "the other side of the River" (Josh. 1:2–3, 14–15; "beside the Euphrates," REB), where they served other gods. But God took Abraham "from the other side of the River" (v. 3) and brought him to the land of Canaan. David attempted to expand the boundaries of his kingdom to this river (2 Sam. 8:3). The Euphrates also was the site of the great battle at Carchemish (605 B.C.) that led to the death of King Josiah (2 Chr. 35:20–24). "The great river Euphrates" is also mentioned in Revelation 9:14 and 16:12.

EUROCLYDON [you ROCK lih dun] *(east wind)*

A fierce, tempestuous wind often experienced by navigators, especially in the spring, in the eastern Mediterranean. Sometimes of hurricane or typhoon force, this tremendous wind (Acts 27:14; the Northeaster in NRSV; Euraquilo in NASB) is so called because it blows from the northeast or east-northeast. The ship in which the apostle Paul was being transported to Rome was caught in this tempest (Acts 27:13–44).

EUTYCHUS [YOU tih cuss] *(fortunate)*

A young man of Troas who fell asleep while listening to a sermon by the apostle Paul and "fell down from the third story." When his friends reached him, he was "taken up dead." Paul miraculously brought Eutychus back to life (Acts 20:9–10).

EVE [eev] *(life-giving)*

The first woman (Gen. 3:20; 4:1), created from one of Adam's ribs to be "a helper comparable to him" (Gen. 2:18–22). Adam and Eve lived together in innocence and happiness, enjoying sexual union ("one flesh") without guilt and sin (Gen. 2:25). However, the serpent tempted Eve to eat the forbidden fruit (Gen. 2:17).

Eve succumbed to the serpent's temptation and ate the fruit. Then "she also gave to her husband with her, and he ate" (Gen. 3:6). The result of this disobedience was losing innocence and receiving the disturbing knowledge of sin and evil. "Then the eyes of both of them were opened, and they knew that they were naked; and they sewed fig leaves together and made themselves coverings" (Gen. 3:7) to conceal their shame.

In falling into temptation (Gen. 3:6), Eve learned about sin and death (Gen. 2:17). She and her descendants experienced the animosity between Satan and Christ—the "offspring of the serpent" and "the seed of the woman" (Gen. 3:15). Her pain in childbirth and Adam's authority over her were other results of her sin (Gen. 3:16).

The apostle Paul referred to Eve twice. By saying "the serpent deceived Eve by his craftiness," Paul gave an example of how easily a person can be led into temptation and sin, with disastrous consequences (2 Cor. 11:3; 1 Tim. 2:12–14).

EVIL

A force that opposes God and His work of righteousness in the world (Rom. 7:8–19). The ultimate source of evil in the world is Satan, also called "the devil" (Luke 8:12) and "the wicked one" (Matt. 13:19). The Christian believer can rest assured that Jesus will triumph at the end of time, when Satan will be cast into a lake of fire and brimstone and evil will be overcome (Rev. 20:10).

Evil also comes from the hearts of people (Mark 7:20–23). It does not come from God, "for God cannot be tempted by evil, nor does He Himself tempt anyone" (James 1:13).

EVIL-MERODACH [EE vil MARE uh dak]
(man of [the god] *Marduk)*

King of the Neo-Babylonian Empire (562–560 B.C.) and son of Nebuchadnezzar II. When Evil-Merodach (Awil-Marduk) became king, he released King Jehoiachin of Judah, whom Nebuchadnezzar had kept imprisoned for 37 years (2 Kin. 25:27–30; Jer. 52:31–34). Evil-Merodach's brother-in-law, Nergal-shar-usur (Neriglissar), formed a conspiracy against him and put him to death. Neriglissar then became king.

EXCOMMUNICATION

The expulsion of a member from the church because of a serious doctrinal or moral lapse. The concept of the curse or the ban in the Old Testament is similar to excommunication (see also John 9:22). The curse signified divine judgment on sin (Num. 5:21;). It was considered God's agent in cleansing sin from the land (Deut. 27:11–26). To be under a curse meant to be excluded from society—thus removing a cancerous agent from the people (Lev. 20:17).

The process of excommunication from the church was spelled out by Jesus (Matt. 18:15–18). The errant Christian should first be confronted about his behavior. If he refuses to heed the warnings, a representative of the church should return with witnesses. If that, too, is ineffective, the person should be brought before the church, which is to excommunicate him (see Matt. 18:17). The apostle Paul often used the phrase "deliver to Satan" to speak of excommunication. This idea implies that God has removed His presence from the person's life and therefore Satan is free to afflict him (1 Cor. 5:5; 1 Tim. 1:20).

Several purposes stood behind this disciplinary tool. Primarily excommunication was to protect the church from blatant evil in its midst (1 Cor. 5:6). It also had a redemptive function—to force the member to realize the seriousness of his offense and to return to Christ (1 Cor. 5:5).

EXILE IN BABYLONIA

The period of captivity of the Israelites by the nation of Babylonia. The end of national life in Judah began with the first attack on Jerusalem by the Babylonians in 597 B.C. The final attack in 581 B.C. marked the end completely. By the end of this period, a total of some 4,600 prominent persons had been deported from Judah to Babylonia (Jer. 52:28–30). This number probably did not include family members or servants. The total may well have been many times the number recorded by Jeremiah.

Little is known about Israel and Judah's life during the captivity. Captivity meant a shameful and humiliating punishment for this disobedient, idolatrous people. The royal court of Judah was taken into captivity, along with the priests, skilled workers, and anyone else who might ever lead a revolt against the Babylonians. The captives realized that God had finally brought the long-standing covenent curses (Deut. 28:15–68) to bear upon them. Torn from their homes and familiar surroundings, they were forced to travel across a hot desert to a strange land. Many of them had to work for their conquerors.

The punishment of captivity lasted 70 years for Judah (Jer. 25:11–12; Dan 9:2), after which the penitent were allowed to return to their homeland under the leadership of Zerubbabel and others (Ezra 2:1–2). Israel's tribes, however, never returned and became lost to history.

EXODUS, THE

The departure of the Israelites from captivity in Egypt under the leadership of Moses. The actual Exodus was the final event in a series of miracles by which God revealed Himself to His people in bondage, humbled the pride of the pharaoh who opposed the Israelites, and enabled Jacob's descendants to live in freedom once again.

The precise date of the Exodus from Egypt is uncertain, because the information in the Bible can be interpreted to support more than one date. Archaeological discoveries also present a confused picture. The result is that some scholars date the Exodus as early as 1446 B.C., while others place it later, about 1290 B.C.

The promise of the Exodus began with God's revelation of Himself to Moses at the burning bush (Ex. 3:2). This was followed by the commissioning of Moses and Aaron to stand before Pharaoh and demand the release of the Israelites. When he refused, a series of ten plagues began. Nine of these involved partially natural occurrences that were miraculously concentrated within a short time, affecting the Egyptians only and leaving the Israelites untouched. Each plague involved an Egyptian god in some manner, showing how powerless such deities were in comparison to Israel's God.

The final, tenth, plague resulted in the death of all the Egyptian firstborn male children and animals. Only then did Pharaoh agree to release the Hebrew people. They were spared from death by remaining in their houses and putting sacrificial blood on the doorposts before they ate the newly-instituted Passover meal (Ex. 12:6–13). The Egyptians were so glad to be relieved of what had become a great burden to them that they gave the departing Israelites gifts of gold, silver, and clothing (Ex. 12:35).

Then the Exodus from Egypt began, with the whole company under Moses being directed away from the northerly road (Ex. 13:17) leading from Egypt to Gaza in Canaan. From Rameses, probably near Qantir, they moved to Succoth, perhaps the ancient Tell el-Maskhuta situated in the Wadi Tumilat in the southeastern region of the Nile delta. Then the Hebrews camped at Etham, on the edge of the Wilderness of Shur (Ex. 13:20), at a site still unknown but probably north of Lake Timsah close to the fortifications guarding Egypt's northeastern frontier. They were directed by a pillar of cloud during the day. At night they were guided by a pillar of fire, which led them away from Etham, probably in a northwesterly direction, to a site opposite Baal Zephon and Pi Hahiroth.

At this site a body of water stood in the way (Ex. 14:2). To the Egyptians this spelled the doom of a group of runaway slaves that had become thoroughly confused about their location as they struggled to get out of the Goshen area. This misunderstanding was part of God's plan to destroy the Egyptian armies (Ex. 14:3–4). They closed in on the Israelite camp, eager to recapture their escaped slaves. While the Hebrews assembled and rushed to the edge of the water, the pillar of cloud moved to the rear of the fleeing Hebrews, preventing the movement of the Egyptian armies.

A strong east wind from the desert began to blow on the surface of the water. The concentrated, hot winds miraculously parted the marsh waters and dried the bottom so the Israelites could flee across it. As the Egyptians followed, the winds stopped and the waters drowned the pursuers. The miracles of the Exodus were thus completed by the destruction of the Egyptian armies. The jubilant Israelites sang a victory song with Moses to celebrate the event (Ex. 15:1–18). The women, led by Miriam the sister of Aaron and Moses, also danced and sang (Ex. 15:20–21) as they praised God for His deliverance.

Then the Israelites began to journey into the Wilderness of Shur (Ex. 15:22), known in Numbers 33:8 as the Wilderness of Etham. They had traveled in a circular manner, except that now they were east of the body of water. Being free from the threat of capture, they traveled east and south into the Sinai peninsula in order to meet with God at Mount Sinai (Horeb). Here they would establish a covenant that would make them God's chosen nation. Etham contained very little water. But after God enabled Moses to locate a supply, the Hebrews arrived at an oasis named Elim.

The Exodus became for the Israelites the supreme occasion when God acted to deliver His people from harsh captivity, binding them to Himself by a solemn covenant. Even today when the Jews celebrate the Passover, they are reminded of God's mighty deliverance in that long-ago time.

EZEKIEL [ih ZEEK e uhl] *(God will strengthen)*

A prophet of a priestly family carried captive to Babylon in 597 B.C. when he was about 25 years old. His call to the prophetic ministry came five years later. Ezekiel prophesied to the captives who dwelt by the river Chebar at Tel Abib. He is the author of the Book of Ezekiel.

In his book, Ezekiel identifies himself as a priest, the son of Buzi (1:3). He was married to a woman who was "the desire of his eyes" (24:16). One of the saddest events of his life was the death of his wife. The prophet was told that on the very day he received this revelation, his wife would die as the armies of Babylon laid siege against the Holy City of Jerusalem. Ezekiel's sadness at the death of his wife was to match the grief of the people at the destruction of Jerusalem. Ezekiel was commanded not to grieve her death; he was to steel himself for this tragedy even as God's people were to prepare themselves for the death of their beloved city (24:15–22). Perhaps no other event in the lives of the Old Testament prophets is as touching as this.

Ezekiel shows us just how ugly and serious our sin is. Perhaps this is why God acted so dramatically in dealing with the human condition—by sending His Son Jesus to die in our place and set us free from the bondage of sin.

EZION GEBER [EE zih on GHEE bur] *(backbone of a man)*

A site between the modern city of Eilat in Israel and the modern city of Aqaba in Jordan where King Solomon built a port. Situated on the northern shore of the Gulf of Aqaba—the eastern arm of the Red Sea—Ezion Geber was first mentioned in the Bible as the last stopping place for the people of Israel before they reached Kadesh (Num. 33:35–36; Deut. 2:8).

Ezion Geber's prominence came about during the golden age of Israel under Solomon. At this site Solomon built a port from which fleets of ships sailed to foreign ports along the coasts of Africa and Arabia (1 Kin. 9:26; 10:22; 2 Chr. 8:17). To the docks of Ezion Geber came gold from Ophir, silver, ivory, spices, precious stones, wood, apes, and baboons (1 Kin. 10:11, 22).

EZRA [EZ ruh] *([God is] a help)*

A scribe and priest who led the returned captives in Jerusalem to make a new commitment to God's law. A descendant of Aaron through Eleazar, Ezra was trained in the knowledge of the law while living in captivity in Babylon with other citizens of the nation of Judah. Ezra gained favor during the reign of Artaxerxes, king of Persia. This king commissioned him to return to Jerusalem about 458 B.C. to bring order among the people of the new community. Artaxerxes even gave Ezra a royal letter (Ezra 7:11–16), granting him civil as well as religious authority, along with the finances to furnish the temple, which had been rebuilt by the returned captives.

Ezra was a skilled scribe and teacher with extensive training in the Books of the Law (Genesis, Exodus, Leviticus, Numbers, and Deuteronomy). After his return to Jerusalem, he apparently did a lot of work on the Hebrew Bible of that time, modernizing the language, correcting irregularities in the transmitted text, and updating and standardizing expressions in certain passages. References to this work by Ezra are found in 2 Esdras, one of the apocryphal books of the Old Testament. He also refers to himself in his own book as a skilled scribe (Ezra 7:6, 12), whose task was to copy, interpret, and transmit the Books of the Law.

When he arrived in Jerusalem, Ezra discovered that many of the Hebrew men had married foreign wives from the surrounding nations (Ezra 9:1, 2). After a period of fasting and prayer (Ezra 9:3, 15), he insisted that these men divorce their wives (Ezra 10:1, 17). He feared that intermarriage with pagans would lead to worship of pagan gods in the restored community of Judah.

In addition to these marriage reforms, Ezra also led his countrymen to give attention to the reading of the law. Several priests helped Ezra read the law, translating and interpreting it for the people's clear understanding in their new language (Aramaic). This reading process went on for seven days as the people focused on God's commands (Neh. 7:73–8:18).

During this period, they also celebrated one of their great religious festivals, the Feast of Tabernacles, to commemorate their sustenance by God in the wilderness following their miraculous escape from Egyptian bondage (Neh. 8). The result of this week of concentration on their heritage was a religious revival. The people confessed their sins and renewed their covenant with God (Neh. 9–10).

Ezra must have been a competent scribe and priest, since he found favor with the ruling Persians. But he was also devoted to his God and the high standards of holiness and righteousness that the Lord demanded of His people.

As he communicated God's requirements to the captives in Jerusalem, Ezra also proved he was a capable leader who could point out shortcomings while leading the people to a higher commitment to God's law at the same time. Through it all, Ezra worked with a keen sense of divine guidance, "according to the good hand of his God upon him" (Ezra 7:9).

F

FAITH

A belief in or confident attitude toward God, involving commitment to His will for one's life. According to Hebrews 11, faith was already present in the experience of many people in the Old Testament as a key element of their spiritual lives. In this chapter, the various heroes of the Old Testament (Abel, Enoch, Noah, Abraham, Sarah, Isaac, Jacob, Joseph, and Moses) are described as living by faith.

Genuine saving faith is a personal attachment to Christ, best thought of as a combination of two ideas—reliance on Christ and commitment to Him. Saving faith involves personally depending on the finished work of Christ's sacrifice as the only basis for forgiveness of sin and entrance into heaven. But saving faith is also a personal commitment of one's life to following Christ in obedience to His commands (2 Tim. 1:12).

FALL, THE

The disobedience and sin of Adam and Eve that caused them to lose the state of innocence in which they had been created. This event plunged them and all of mankind into a state of sin and corruption. The account of the Fall is found in Genesis 3.

Adam and Eve were created by God in a state of sinless perfection so they could glorify God, reflecting His righteousness on the earth, and enjoy fellowship and communion with Him. Their calling was to exercise dominion, or control, over God's creation through their own labors and those of their offspring in faithful response to the word of God. As a specific test of this loyalty, God commanded them not to eat the fruit of "the tree of the knowledge of good and evil" (Gen. 2:17). Adam and Eve were to demonstrate their willingness to live "by every word that proceeds from the mouth of the Lord" (Deut. 8:3; Matt. 4:4). God warned them clearly that their disobedience would result in death.

The fall from their original state of innocence occurred when Satan approached Eve through the serpent, who tempted her to eat of the forbidden fruit. Satan called into question the truthfulness of what God had spoken about the tree and its significance. He urged Eve to discover, through trial and error, whether it was in her best interest to do what God had forbidden. Eve's sin did not consist of being tempted but in believing and acting on Satan's lie. Her rejection of God's command occurred when she ate the forbidden fruit and persuaded her husband to do the same thing. The term *Fall* should not be interpreted to suggest that their sin was accidental. The temptation was purposeful,

and their submission to it involved their willing consent.

The immediate consequence of the Fall was ultimately death, symbolized by their loss of fellowship with God. For the first time, Adam and Eve experienced fear in the presence of the Lord God; they hid when He approached (Gen. 3:8–10). Because of their unbelief and rebellion, they were driven from the garden that God had provided as their home. From that time on, people would experience pain and encounter resistance as they worked at the task of earning their daily bread. Physical death, with the decay of the body, is not a natural process. It entered the human experience as God's curse upon sin.

Adam and Eve did not sin simply as private persons but as the representatives of all members of the human race. Their sin is the sin of all, and all persons receive from them a corrupt nature. It is this nature that stands behind all personal violations of the Lord's commandments. For this reason, the fall of Adam is the fall of the human race. The apostle Paul thought of Christ as the last Adam (1 Cor. 15:45), who would rebuild the old, sinful Adam through His plan of redemption and salvation: "As in Adam all die, even so in Christ all shall be made alive" (1 Cor. 15:22).

FAMINE

The lack of a supply of food or water. Since the line between famine and plenty in Palestine depends mainly on the rains coming at the right time and in the proper supply, famine was an ever-present threat. In the face of famine, Abraham migrated to Egypt (Gen. 12:10), Isaac went to Gerar in Philistine territory (Gen. 26:1), and Jacob moved to Egypt (Gen. 41–47).

The most famous famine recorded in the Bible is the seven-year famine in Egypt foretold by Joseph in interpreting

Pharaoh's dream. Extending even into Canaan, it eventually brought the rest of Joseph's family to Egypt (Gen. 41–47; Ps. 105:16). During another famine Elijah was kept alive by the widow of Zarephath (1 Kin. 17:8; Luke 4:25–26).

Drought and conditions of war brought famine to besieged cities (1 Kin. 18:2; Ezek. 6:12). Pathetic descriptions of famine conditions include people's resorting to cannibalism (2 Kin. 6:28–29), cries of hungry children (Lam. 4:4), and the fainting of people in the streets (Is. 51:20).

Famine was also one of the punishments sent by the Lord upon His people because of their sins (Is. 51:20; Ezek. 14:21). A famine in the time of David was caused by Saul's mistreatment of the Gibeonites (2 Sam. 21:1). A striking description of famine conditions was given by the prophet Amos in his phrase, "cleanness of teeth" (Amos 4:6)—clean because there was no food to foul them.

A famine is one of the signs of the approaching fall of Jerusalem (Matt. 24:7), and one of the plagues coming upon "Babylon," as recorded in Revelation 18:8.

Using figurative language, the prophet Amos described a famine of an entirely different sort—not one of lack of food or water, but a famine of hearing the word of the Lord (Amos 8:11). Those who had refused to hear the prophets would have no prophets to guide them in the perilous days when God's judgment would fall upon His people.

FAN

The fan mentioned in the Old Testament was probably a type of long-handled fork used to toss threshed grain into the air. The wind blew the chaff away, allowing the heavier grain to fall into a separate pile (Is. 30:24; Jer. 15:7). Some versions translate this tool as fork or winnowing fork. John the Baptist's de-

scription of the Messiah as one who would separate good from evil in the last days uses this illustration (Matt. 3:12; Luke 3:17).

FASTING

Going without food or drink voluntarily, generally for religious purposes. Fasting, however, could also be done for other reasons. It was sometimes done as a sign of distress, grief, or repentance. The Law of Moses specifically required fasting for only one occasion—the Day of Atonement. This custom resulted in calling this day "the day of fasting" (Jer. 36:6) or "the Fast" (Acts 27:9).

Moses did not eat bread or drink water during the 40 days and 40 nights he was on Mount Sinai receiving the law (Ex. 34:28). Voluntary group fasts (not specified in the law) were engaged in during time of war, such as when the Benjamites defeated the other Israelites (Judg. 20:26), and when Samuel gathered the people to Mizpah during the Philistine wars (1 Sam. 7:6). It was at a called fast that witnesses accused Naboth, setting the stage for his death (1 Kin. 21:9, 12).

In times of grief, people fasted. A seven-day fast was held when the bones of Saul and his sons were buried (1 Sam. 31:13; 1 Chr. 10:12). Fasting was practiced during the 70 years of the exilic period on the fifth and the seventh months, the date the siege of Jerusalem began and the date when Jerusalem fell to the Babylonians (Zech. 7:5).

Fasting was practiced by individuals in times of distress. David fasted after hearing that Saul and Jonathan were dead (2 Sam. 1:12). Nehemiah fasted and prayed upon learning that Jerusalem had remained in ruins since its destruction (Neh. 1:4). Darius, the king of Persia, fasted all night after placing Daniel in the lions' den (Dan. 6:18).

Going without food or water was not automatically effective in accomplishing the desires of those who fasted. In the prophet Isaiah's time, people complained that they had fasted and that God had not responded favorably (Is. 58:3–4). The prophet declared that the external show was futile. The fast that the Lord requires is to loose the bonds of wickedness, undo the heavy burdens, feed the hungry, shelter the poor, and clothe the naked (Is. 58:5–7).

In the New Testament, Anna at the temple "served God with fastings and prayers night and day" (Luke 2:37). John the Baptist led his disciples to fast (Mark 2:18). Jesus fasted 40 days and 40 nights before His temptation (Matt. 4:2). Using a marriage-feast comparison, however, Jesus insisted that fasting was not suitable for His disciples as long as He, the Bridegroom, was with them (Matt. 9:14–15; Mark 2:18–20; Luke 5:33–35).

Cornelius was fasting at the time of his vision (Acts 10:30). The church in Antioch fasted (Acts 13:2) and sent Paul and Barnabas off on the first missionary journey with fasting and prayer (Acts 13:3). Paul and Barnabas prayed with fasting at the appointment of elders in the churches (Acts 14:23). Paul suggested that husbands and wives might abstain from sexual intercourse for a while to give themselves to fasting and prayer (1 Cor. 7:5).

FELIX [FEE lix] *(happy)*

Roman governor of Judea before whom the apostle Paul appeared. Felix was an unscrupulous ruler. In addition to having three wives, he considered himself capable of committing any crime and avoiding punishment because of his influence with the courts.

Felix is best known for his encounter with the apostle Paul (Acts 23:23). Arrested in Jerusalem as a disturber of the peace, Paul was sent to Caesarea for judgment by Felix. Paul was accused of committing rebellion against the Ro-

mans, being the ringleader of a trouble-making religious sect, and profaning the Jewish temple. The purpose of these accusations was to persuade Felix to surrender Paul to the Jewish courts, in which case he would have been assassinated.

When Felix gave Paul permission to speak, Paul refuted each of these charges; and Felix postponed his judgment. Several days later, Paul was brought before Felix a second time. On this occasion Paul gave his testimony as a Christian. Felix was visibly moved; and he dismissed Paul, indicating he would talk with him again on a more convenient day.

Felix kept Paul in suspense about his judgment because he hoped Paul would give him a bribe. He sent for Paul on several occasions. But his hopes for a bribe were unfulfilled, and he kept Paul a prisoner for two years.

Felix was eventually removed as procurator by the Roman authorities. Because the Jews were making numerous accusations against Felix, Paul was left in prison in Caesarea for two years in an effort to appease the Jewish officials (Acts 24:27). Paul appealed to Rome, which was his right as a Roman citizen, and finally was released from prison and taken to Rome.

FELLOWSHIP

Sharing things in common with others. Believers have fellowship with the Father, Son, and Holy Spirit (John 17:21–26; 1 John 1:3), as well as with other believers (1 John 1:3, 7). The only reason why we dare to have fellowship with God, in the sense of sharing things in common with Him, is that He has raised our status through the death and resurrection of Christ (Eph. 2:4–7).

What believers share in common with God is a relationship as well as God's own holy character (1 Pet. 1:15). Those who have fellowship with Christ should enjoy fellowship with other believers, a communion that ought to illustrate the very nature of God Himself (John 13:35; 1 John 1:5–10).

FESTUS, PORCIUS [FESS tuss POUR shih us]

The successor of Felix as Roman procurator, or governor, of Judea (Acts 24:27). After Festus arrived at Caesarea, he went to Jerusalem and met with the high priest and other Jewish leaders. They informed him of Paul's confinement in prison. Paul had been left in prison when Felix was removed as procurator by the Roman authorities.

The Jewish leaders requested that Paul be brought from Caesarea to Jerusalem so he could be tried before the Jewish Sanhedrin (Acts 25:3). Their real intent, however, was to have Paul killed along the way. Festus refused and told the Jewish leaders they must meet with Paul in Caesarea.

A few days later, Paul was summoned before Festus, who asked if he would be willing to go to Jerusalem. Paul, knowing that danger awaited him on such a trip, used his right as a Roman citizen to appeal to Rome for trial (Acts 25:11).

About this time, Herod Agrippa, with his sister, Bernice, came to Caesarea to visit Festus. The result was a meeting between the three and Paul in which Paul was declared innocent. But because Paul had appealed to Caesar, he had to be sent to Rome (Acts 26:32).

FIG

A fruit-producing plant that could be either a tall tree or a low-spreading shrub. The size of the tree depended on its location and soil. The blooms of the fig tree always appear before the leaves in spring. When Jesus saw leaves on a fig tree, He expected the fruit (Mark 11:12–14, 20–21). There were usually two crops of figs a year.

Figs were eaten fresh (2 Kin. 18:31), pressed into cakes (1 Sam. 25:18), and used as a poultice (Is. 38:21). Jeremiah used the fig tree as a symbol of desolation (Jer. 8:13). It also signified security and hope for Adam and Eve (Gen. 3:7), the 12 spies (Num. 13:23), and the poets and prophets. Sycamore figs were similar to the fig but were smaller and of poorer quality (Amos 7:14). They were eaten by poor people who could not afford the better variety.

FIRMAMENT

The expanse of sky and space in which the stars and planets are set. God made the firmament on the second day of creation to divide the waters that covered the earth from those that were above it (Gen. 1:7). But the firmament includes more than the atmospheric region between the seas of earth and the rain clouds of the sky; it is far more vast. In fact, on the fourth day of creation God placed the stars, the sun, and the moon in the "firmament of the heavens" (Gen. 1:15–18).

It is this vastness that the Hebrew writers tend to emphasize about the firmament. The writer of Psalm 150 pointed out that the firmament is "mighty" (v. 1). The prophet Ezekiel envisioned the firmament "like the color of an awesome crystal, stretched out over . . . [people's] heads" (Ezek. 1:22). What the firmament reflects, then, is the greatness of the God who created it. We are urged to praise God because "the firmament shows His handiwork" (Ps. 19:1). God's people can look forward to a day when they will "shine like the brightness of the firmament" (Dan. 12:3).

FIRSTFRUITS

The firstborn of the flocks and the first vegetables and grains to be gathered at harvest time. The Hebrew people thought of these as belonging to God in a special sense. They were dedicated or presented to God on the day of the firstfruits, a part of the celebration of Pentecost (Num. 28:26; 2 Chr. 31:5). In the New Testament, Christ is described as "the firstfruits of those who have fallen asleep" (1 Cor. 15:20)—the first who rose from the dead.

FLINT

A very hard variety of quartz. Dark gray or brown in color, it is usually found in chalk or limestone rock. A form of silica, it sparks when struck by steel or another flint (2 Macc. 10:3). Because flint has a sharp edge when broken, tools such as knives, weapons, saws, sickles, and many other implements were made from flint by prehistoric people throughout the Stone Age.

Archaeologists have found many flint objects, especially knives, in Palestine. These were dated from the Neolithic or Late Stone Age (about 7000–4500 B.C.). Zipporah used a "sharp stone" to circumcise her children (Ex. 4:25). The Bible refers to "rocks of flint" (Deut. 8:15) or "flinty rock" (Deut. 32:13).

Flint is also spoken of in a figurative manner in the Bible, denoting strength and determination (Is. 5:28; 50:7; Ezek. 3:9). This mineral is still abundant in the limestone rock of Syria, Palestine, and Egypt.

FLOOD, THE

The divinely-sent deluge that destroyed all sinful humankind by water during the time of Noah. The inspired writer of Genesis took two chapters to tell of the creation of the world and one chapter to portray the Fall, but he devoted four chapters to the Flood. Since the concern of the writer was to reveal the nature of God and His dealings with humankind, he evidently saw this story

as a good vehicle for this truth. The Flood reveals both the judgment and the mercy of God.

Archaeologists have discovered a number of flood stories among pagan nations in the ancient world. One Sumerian and two Babylonian stories have survived. A comparison of these stories with the Flood account in Genesis is both interesting and significant.

In one of the Babylonian stories, the gods became irritated with the people because they grew too numerous and became too noisy; so they considered several different ways to get rid of these bothersome people. Finally, they decided on a flood. But the flood apparently got out of hand. For a while the gods were afraid they would be destroyed. They began to quarrel among themselves, shrinking in fear from the rising waters and crowding around a sacrifice like flies.

In stark contrast to such pagan stories, the Book of Genesis presents the holy and Sovereign God who acted in judgment against sin and yet mercifully saved Noah and his family because of their righteousness.

The Flood was not simply a downpour of ordinary rain. The text indicates a cosmic upheaval. "The fountains of the great deep" were broken up (Gen. 7:11). Perhaps there were earthquakes and the ocean floors may have been raised up until the waters covered the earth. By a supernatural upheaval, God returned the earth to the primitive chaos described in Genesis 1:2.

The Flood was a drastic judgment, but the condition that brought it to pass was also serious. Society degenerated to the point that "every intent" of the thoughts of man's heart "was only evil continually" (Gen. 6:5). Violence raged upon earth. Instead of living responsibly as persons created in the image and likeness of God, people existed as beasts.

God chose to destroy that generation and make a new start with the family of righteous Noah.

In stark contrast to the degenerate people among whom he lived, "Noah was a just man" who "walked with God" (Gen. 6:9). God's righteous judgment is seen in the destruction of the wicked, but His mercy and care are seen in His saving of Noah and, through him, the human race. God's judgment was accompanied by grief, but His grace was freely given to Noah and his family.

Noah could save himself and his family by building an ark of wood. The ark was to be large enough to hold Noah, his wife, his three sons, and their wives. In addition, it must provide room for two of every kind of animal and bird. Plenty of time was allowed for this massive building project by Noah and his sons.

The dimensions of the ark were 450 feet (140 meters) long, 75 feet (23 meters) wide, and 45 feet (14 meters) high. There were three levels—lower, middle, and upper decks. The displacement or capacity of a vessel of these dimensions has been estimated as 43,300 tons.

F

FLOOD, THE

The raging waters kept rising for 40 days, and the ark floated high above the hills and mountains. When the waters finally stopped rising, Noah and his passengers faced a long wait for the waters to go down. The total time spent in the ark was about one year and ten days. The ark came to rest on "the mountains of Ararat" (Gen. 8:4) in what is now Turkey.

Noah released a raven and a dove to determine whether the waters were low enough to allow them to leave the ark. When the dove returned to the ark, he knew it had been unable to survive outside the ark. After seven days, he again released the dove. This time it came back with an olive leaf. This was good news, indicating that the waters had dropped further and the time when the people and animals could leave the ark was near. Finally the earth dried, and they left the ark (Gen. 8:7–19).

The first act of the grateful Noah was to build an altar and worship God, thanking Him for deliverance from the Flood. Then the Lord made a covenant with Noah. Never again would He destroy the world by water. The rainbow was given as a covenant sign. The bow was an instrument of war, but the rainbow represents a bow with the string on the ground—a symbol of peace.

The Flood came upon the earth as a severe judgment of God against wickedness. But God's grace and mercy were also revealed in the preservation of Noah and, through him, the human race. The covenant was granted to reassure humanity about God's care. References to the Flood are found in Matthew 24:38; Luke 17:26, 27; Hebrews 11:7; 1 Peter 3:20; and 2 Peter 2:5. The Flood was used to illustrate the holy God's wrath against human wickedness and the salvation of His people.

See also NOAH.

FLUTE

A wind instrument that produced a high, shrill sound. Because of its unique sound, the flute was associated with fertility cults and was considered appropriate only in a secular setting to show both ecstatic joy and deep sorrow. The flute is mentioned in connection with the temple only in the Psalms (Ps. 150:4). However, the Hebrew word *nehiloth* in the title of Psalm 5 means "[with] flutes." Some flutes were made of silver, while others were made of reeds, wood, or bone. Other words for flute used in various translations of the Bible are organ (Gen. 4:21, KJV); fife (1 Sam. 10:5, REB); pipe (Job 21:12, NRSV); and reed-pipe (Jer. 48:36, REB).

FOOT-WASHING

An expression of hospitality extended to guests in Bible times. People traveling dusty roads in Palestine needed to wash their feet for comfort and cleanliness. Foot-washing was generally performed by the lowliest servant in the household (Luke 7:44). Guests were often offered water and vessels for washing their own feet (Gen. 18:4; Judg. 19:21).

At the Last Supper, Jesus washed His disciples' feet. He explained that this act was an example of the humble ministry that they must always be ready to perform for one another (John 13:5–17). First Timothy 5:10 suggests that the early church followed Christ's example in observing the ritual of foot-washing. But many churches reject this because the other duties mentioned in the verse are household tasks. Churches of some denominations continue to practice foot-washing today.

FORGIVENESS

The act of excusing or pardoning others in spite of their slights, shortcomings, and errors. As a theological term, forgiveness refers to God's pardon of the sins of human beings. No religious book except the Bible teaches that God completely forgives sin (Heb. 10:17). The initiative comes from Him (Col. 2:13) because He is ready to forgive (Luke 15:11–32). He is a God of grace and pardon (Dan. 9:9).

Sin deserves divine punishment because it is a violation of God's holy character (Rom. 1:18–32; 1 Pet. 1:16), but His pardon is gracious (Rom. 5:6–8). In order for God to forgive sin, two conditions are necessary. A life must be taken as a substitute for that of the sinner (Heb. 9:22), and the sinner must come to God's sacrifice in a spirit of repentance and faith (Acts 10:43; James 5:15).

Forgiveness in the New Testament is directly linked to Christ (Col. 1:14), His sacrificial death on the cross (Rom. 4:24), and His resurrection (2 Cor. 5:15). He was the morally perfect sacrifice (Rom. 8:3), the final and ultimate fulfillment of all Old Testament sacrifices (Heb. 9:11–10:18). Since He bore the law's death penalty against sinners (Gal. 3:10–13), those who trust in His sacrifice are freed from that penalty. By faith sinners are forgiven—"justified" in Paul's terminology (Gal. 3:8–9). Those who are forgiven sin's penalty also die to its controlling power in their lives (Rom. 6:1–23).

Christ's resurrection was related in a special way to His forgiveness. Christ's resurrection was an act by which God wiped out the false charges against Him; it was God's declaration of the perfect righteousness of His Son, the last Adam, and of His acceptance of Christ's sacrifice (1 Tim. 3:16). Because He has been acquitted and declared righteous, this is also true for those whom He represents. Thus, Christ's resurrection was a necessary condition for the forgiveness of human sin (1 Cor. 15:12–28). To be forgiven is to be identified with Christ in His crucifixion and resurrection.

God's forgiveness of us demands that we forgive others, because grace brings responsibility and obligation (Luke 6:37). Jesus placed no limits on the extent to which Christians are to forgive others (Matt. 18:22, 35). A forgiving spirit shows that one is a true follower of Christ (Matt. 5:43–48).

FORTIFICATION

The practice of erecting defensive walls around a city to protect it from enemy attacks. Such fortifications were not used widely by Israel until the period of the united kingdom under David and Solomon. Before that time, the Israelites hid from roving enemy bands in caves and mountain strongholds (Judg. 6:2). The first Israelite city to be fortified was Saul's capital at Gibeah. His successor David used fortifications extensively, especially at the capital city of Jerusalem.

The first fortifications were massive walls around cities. Material for these walls was plentiful in rocky Palestine. Usually they were from 15 to 25 feet (5 to 8 meters) thick, and about 25 feet (8 meters) high. Sometimes several walls were built around a city for even greater protection.

The massive walls were strengthened at regular intervals by supporting balconies and embankments. Towers were erected on the corners and at obvious points of attack (2 Chr. 14:7; Zeph. 1:16). The tops of these towers often looked like rows of teeth with gaps between them. The protective towers were placed at regular intervals along the wall to give the city's defending archers a good vantage point for turning back an attack.

The walls were protected outside the city by a dry moat or an earthen ramp heaped against the wall to make direct assault almost impossible. Most towns had only one or two gates. For even greater security, these massive gates were often reinforced with metal, usually bronze (Ps. 107:16; Is. 45:2).

Fortified cities were most often overcome by a prolonged siege from the enemy army. The enemy stationed their forces outside the walls so nothing could get in or out of the fortress. The greatest danger to a city under such a siege was a shortage of water. For this reason a city needed to be situated close to an abundant supply of water. If the water supply was not situated inside the walls, long underground tunnels were sometimes built to provide convenient access during times of siege.

Several methods were used by the attacking army to weaken a city's walls. The Assyrians built earthen causeways so their siege machines, or battering rams, could be rolled up to the wall to break it down. Attackers sometimes tunneled underneath to weaken the walls. Once the walls were weakened, a direct attack was made on the city.

Walled cities that served as Israelite defense posts included Lachish, Beth Horon, Samaria, Jezreel, Geba, and Mizpah. Solomon built fortresses around Jerusalem, Megiddo, Hazor, and Gezer (1 Kin. 9:15) as well as defense outposts across the kingdom for his army. His son Rehoboam fortified 15 more cities (2 Chr. 11:5–12).

See also RAMPART.

FOWLER

A person who hunts and captures birds. The Egyptians were especially known for their taste for bird meat. Ancient fowlers used all kinds of implements and devices such as decoys, traps, nets, bait, bows and arrows, slings, lures, setting dogs, and bird lime smeared on branches to catch their prey. The Mosaic Law forbade taking a mother bird and her young together; only the young were to be taken (Deut. 22:6–7). Wicked, scheming enemies of the righteous are called fowlers (Ps. 91:3; 124:7).

FOX

Foxes were common predators in Bible times. Since they fed on small rodents such as rats and mice, they helped to protect the grain crops. But their fondness for grapes caused farmers much grief. Sometimes they even tunneled under protective walls to feast on grapevines (Song 2:15). Foxes also settle in holes and burrows, often those abandoned by other animals. Jesus pointed out that foxes have holes, but the Son of Man had nowhere to lay His head (Matt. 8:20).

Foxes have a keen sense of sight, smell, and hearing. They are also clever enough to lie in wait for prey. They may even play dead to attract a bird within striking range. When hunted, they are cunning and devious, misleading their pursuers. Jesus compared Herod, the Roman tetrarch of Galilee and Perea, to a fox, because of his crafty, devious nature (Luke 13:32).

FRANKINCENSE

An aromatic gum resin obtained from the Boswellia tree. These trees are large with small, white, star-shaped flowers and leaves resembling the mountain ash. The gum is obtained by cutting into the bark and collecting the resin from the tree. When this substance hardens, it is gathered and used as incense.

Frankincense was part of the sacred anointing oil (Ex. 30:34). It was used in sacrificial offering (Lev. 2:1), as a fumigant during animal sacrifices (Ex. 30:7), and as perfume (Song 3:6). It was a gift to the baby Jesus (Matt. 2:11).

The trees are native to India, Arabia, and Africa. Palestine probably obtained this product through foreign trade.

FREEDOM

The absence of slavery; the ability to do and go as one desires. Only God has absolute freedom. He is not controlled from the outside. Human beings, while not totally free, can experience a measure of freedom in different areas of life: social, economic, political, and spiritual.

When the apostle Paul spoke of a free man (Col. 3:11), he referred to rights of citizenship. Politically, in Paul's day, one might be either a citizen of Rome, a free person (Acts 22:28), or a non-citizen, one who was not free under the Roman law. As a free person, Paul had certain rights, especially the right of a fair trial. In Christ, distinctions between citizens and non-citizens—"slave" and "free"—disappear (Gal. 3:28). In Christ, all have the glorious freedom of the children of God.

In the spiritual realm, Jesus explained that when people know the truth, the truth will set them free (John 8:32). He Himself is the Truth (John 14:6). Jesus also declared that if He, the Son of God, set persons free, they would be truly free (John 8:36). Sin enslaves; Christ sets free. Set free from sin, the believer is able to choose service for God (Rom. 6:22). The spiritual freedom of others becomes the concern of those who have been set free by Christ.

FULLER

A person who cleans, shrinks, thickens, and sometimes dyes newly cut wool or cloth. The Hebrew word rendered as "fuller" means "to trample" or "to tread," suggesting that action as a major part of the craft. The fuller removed the oily and gummy substances from material before it could be used by washing it in some alkaline such as white clay, putrid urine, or nitre, as there was no soap in those days. The alkaline was washed out by treading on the material repeatedly in running or clean water. The material was then dried and bleached by the sun.

The fuller's process created an unpleasant odor. Therefore, it was usually done outside the city gates in an area named Fuller's Field (2 Kin. 18:17; Is. 7:3). God is compared to fuller's "soap" (Mal. 3:2). Jesus' garments at His transfiguration were described as whiter than any human fuller could make them (Mark 9:3; launderer in NASB; bleacher in REB).

FURNACE

Many tradesmen needed the fiery heat provided by the furnace to perfect their goods. Furnaces made of stone or brick were used mostly by potters and metalsmiths. The word used for household furnaces or stoves in Bible times is usually translated as "oven."

Clay pots and jars were of limited use unless they had been "fired" by being raised to a very high temperature. The heat changed the chemical makeup of the clay, leaving it very strong but brittle. By carefully controlling the amount of fuel and the air supply, the proper temperature was reached and maintained until the clay was cured.

Special furnaces were also necessary for smelting metal ores. Finely ground ores were mixed with charcoal and fluxes of limestone or crushed seashells, and placed into the fire. Bellows kept the fire hot enough to melt the ore. As it melted, the liquid metal sank to the bottom of the furnace, allowing the waste slag to float to the top. This waste was removed through a small pipe. The metal was allowed to cool and then remelted in a crucible for purification. It was then cast into molds to be shaped into many useful items.

Large furnaces big enough for several people to walk into were used in Babylon to make bricks. This is probably the "burning fiery furnace" of Daniel 3:15–30.

GABBATHA [GAB ah thah] *(elevated place)*

The Aramaic name of the place from which Pontius Pilate—the Roman prefect, or governor, of Judea—pronounced the formal sentence of death by crucifixion against Jesus (John 19:13). Gabbatha was probably a raised platform. It has been excavated and identified with the Roman pavement of the courtyard of the Tower of Antonia, at the northwest corner of the temple area.

GABRIEL [GAY brih el] *(God is great)*

An archangel who acts as the messenger of God; he appeared to Daniel (Dan. 8:16), Zacharias (Luke 1:19), and the Virgin Mary (Luke 1:26–38).

All appearances of Gabriel recorded in the Bible are connected with the promise about the coming of the Messiah. But one passage may link Gabriel with Christ's return. In Christian tradition, Gabriel is sometimes identified as the archangel whose voice is heard at the Second Coming of Christ (1 Thess. 4:16). Although Gabriel is not mentioned by name in this passage, he is sometimes depicted as the trumpeter of the Last Judgment.

GAD [gad] *(good fortune)*

The seventh of Jacob's twelve sons. Gad was the firstborn of Zilpah (Leah's maid) and a brother of Asher (Gen. 30:11). Moses praised Gad for his bravery and faithfulness to duty (Deut. 33:20–21). With the possible exception of Ezbon, Gad's seven sons all founded tribal families (Num. 26:15–18).

GAD, TRIBE OF

The tribe that sprang from Gad and the territory this tribe inhabited, often referred to as Gilead (Num. 1:14). The territory of Gad lay east of the Jordan River between the half-tribe of Manasseh to the north and the tribe of Reuben to the south. Its western boundary was the Jordan River; on the east it faced the territory of the Ammonites. Gad had few major towns.

When Moses assigned the territory east of the Jordan River to the Gadites, he stipulated that they must cross over the river to help the other tribes in the conquest of Canaan (Num. 32:20–32). They did not always do this, however, most likely because the tribe experienced a great deal of trouble holding its own territory.

GADARA [GAD ah ruh] *(walls)*

A city of Transjordan about 6 miles (10 kilometers) southeast of the Sea of Galilee. Gadara was primarily a Greek city, one of the cities of the Decapolis. It also was the capital city of the Roman province of Perea. The ruins of Gadara, present-day Um Qeis, include two theaters, a basilica, baths, and a street lined with columns. They indicate that at one time Gadara was a large and beautiful city.

Matthew 8:28–34 records that two demon-possessed men of the area of Gadara were healed by Jesus. Mark 5:1–20 and Luke 8:26–39 refer to only one man possessed by unclean spirits. He may have been the more violent of these two.

GALATIA [guh LAY shih uh]

A region in central Asia Minor (modern Turkey) bounded on the east by Cappadocia, on the west by Asia, on the south by Pamphylia and Cilicia, and on the north by Bithynia and Pontus. The northern part of the region was settled in the third century B.C. by Celtic tribes that had been driven out of Gaul (France). From these tribes, the region derived its name, Galatia.

In 64 B.C. the Roman general Pompey defeated the king of Pontus, Mithradates

VI, and established a foothold for Rome in the region. When the last Galatian king, Amyntas, died in 25 B.C., the Romans inherited the kingdom. Caesar Augustus then created the Roman province of Galatia, making Ancyra the capital and annexing a number of districts to the south and west, including Pisidia, Isauria, Phrygia, and Lycaonia. The term *Galatia*, consequently, is somewhat ambiguous. It may refer to the older ethnic region in north-central Asia Minor (north Galatia), or to the later and larger Roman province (including south Galatia).

On his first missionary journey (about A.D. 46–48), the apostle Paul and Barnabas evangelized the Galatian cities of Pisidian Antioch, Iconium, Lystra, and Derbe (Acts 13–14). Paul revisited the area on his second and third missionary journeys.

Although the point is debated, it appears that Paul's Epistle to the Galatians (Gal. 1:2; 3:1) was addressed to the churches founded by him in the southern part of the province of Galatia (south Galatian theory). No evidence exists to show that Paul visited the region of Galatia in north-central Asia Minor. Although Acts 16:6 and 18:23 are sometimes thought to refer to this more remote northern region, the context of these passages seems to point to southern Galatia (Acts 13–14).

GALILEE [GAL ih lee] (circle or circuit)

A Roman province of Palestine during the time of Jesus. Measuring roughly 50 miles (80 kilometers) north to south and about 30 miles (58 kilometers) east to west, Galilee was the most northerly of the three provinces of Palestine—Galilee, Samaria, and Judea. Covering more than a third of Palestine's territory, Galilee extended from the base of Mount Hermon in the north to the Carmel and Gilboa ranges in the south. The Mediter-

ranean Sea and the Jordan River valley were its western and eastern borders, respectively.

Originally a district in the hill country of Naphtali (2 Kin. 15:29; 1 Chr. 6:76), Galilee was inhabited by a "mixed race" of Jews and heathen. The Canaanites continued to dominate Galilee for many years after Joshua's invasion (Judg. 1:30–33; 4:2). It was historically known among the Jews as "Galilee of the Gentiles" (Is. 9:1; Matt. 4:15).

Galilee had such a mixed population that Solomon could award unashamedly to Hiram, king of Tyre, 20 of its cities in payment for timber from Lebanon (1 Kin. 9:11). After conquest by Tiglath-Pileser, king of Assyria (about 732 B.C.), Galilee was repopulated by a colony of heathen immigrants (2 Kin. 15:29; 17:24). Thus the Galilean accent and dialect were very distinct (Matt. 26:69, 73). For this and other reasons, the pure-blooded Jews of Judea, who were more orthodox in tradition, despised the Galileans (John 7:52). Rather contemptuously Nathanael asked, "Can anything good come out of Nazareth?" (John 1:46).

Galilee consisted essentially of an upland area of forests and farmlands. An imaginary line from the plain of Acco (Acre) to the north end of the Sea of Galilee divided the country into Upper and Lower Galilee. Since this area was actually the foothills of the Lebanon mountains, Upper and Lower Galilee had two different elevations.

The higher of the elevations, Upper Galilee, was more than 3,000 feet (1,000 meters) above sea level; and in the days of the New Testament it was densely forested and thinly inhabited. The lower elevation, Lower Galilee, averaged between 1,500 to 2,000 feet (500 to 700 meters) above sea level; it was less hilly and enjoyed a milder climate than Upper Galilee. This area included the rich plain of Esdraelon and was a "pleasant" land

G

(Gen. 49:15). Chief exports of the region were olive oil, grains, and fish.

Galilee was the boyhood home of Jesus Christ. He was a lad of Nazareth, as it was prophesied: "He shall be called a Nazarene" (Matt. 2:23). Here He attempted to begin His public ministry, but was rejected by His own people (Luke 4:16–30).

All the disciples of Jesus, with the exception of Judas Iscariot, came from Galilee (Matt. 4:18; John 1:43–44; Acts 1:11; 2:7). In Cana of Galilee Jesus performed His first miracle (John 2:11); in fact, most of His 33 great miracles were performed in Galilee. Capernaum in Galilee became the headquarters of His ministry (Matt. 4:13; 9:1). Of His 32 parables, 19 were spoken in Galilee. The first three gospels concern themselves largely with Christ's Galilean ministry. Most of the events of our Lord's life and ministry are set against the backdrop of the Galilean hills.

When Herod the Great died in 4 B.C.,

Galilee fell to the authority of Antipas; Herod, who governed until A.D. 39. He built his capital city at Tiberias on the Sea of Galilee and was succeeded by Herod I who took the title of "king." After Agrippa's death in A.D. 44 (Acts 12:23), Galilee became a Zealot stronghold until the Romans crushed Jewish resistance in Palestine between A.D. 66 and 73.

GALILEE, SEA OF

A freshwater lake, fed by the Jordan River, which was closely connected with the earthly ministry of Jesus. This "sea" is called by four different names in the Bible: the Sea of Chinnereth [or Chinneroth] (the Hebrew word for "harp-shaped," the general outline of the lake; Num. 34:11; Josh. 12:3; 13:27); the "Lake of Gennesaret" (Luke 5:1), taking the name from the fertile Plain of Gennesaret that lies on the northwest (Matt. 14:34); the "Sea of Tiberias" (John 6:1; 21:1), because of its association with the capital of Herod Antipas; and the "Sea of Galilee" (Matt. 4:18; Mark 1:16).

Situated some 60 miles (98 kilometers) north of Jerusalem, the Sea of Galilee contains fresh water since it is fed by the Jordan River. The lake itself is the deepest part of the northern Jordan Rift and thus the water collects there before it flows on its way. The surface of Galilee is about 700 feet (230 meters) below the Mediterranean Sea. The floor of the lake is another 80 to 160 feet (25 to 50 meters) lower. The lake itself is nearly 13 miles (21 kilometers) long and 8 miles (13 kilometers) wide at Magdala, the point of its greatest width.

The lake is surrounded, except on the southern side, by steep cliffs and sharply rising mountains. On the east these mountains rise to the fertile Golan Heights as high as 2,700 feet (900 meters). As a result of this formation, cool winds frequently rush down these slopes and unexpectedly stir up violent storms on the warm surface of the lake. Waves such as these were easily calmed at the command of Jesus (Mark 4:35–41).

A fishing industry thrived on the Sea of Galilee. Jesus called His first disciples— Peter, Andrew, James, and John—from that industry (Mark 1:16–20). In spite of the steep hillsides around the lake, nine cities of 15,000 population or more thrived in the first century as part of an almost continuous belt of settlements around the lake. Of these cities, Bethsaida, Tiberias, and Capernaum were the most important. On and around the Sea of Galilee Jesus performed most of His 33 recorded miracles and issued most of His teachings to His disciples and the multitudes that followed Him.

GALLIO [GAL ih oh]

The Roman proconsul of Achaia before whom the apostle Paul appeared during his first visit to Corinth (Acts 18:12–17). When Gallio discovered that Paul's Jewish enemies had a religious grievance against him, he threw them out of his court. He also refused to take action when the mob took the synagogue ruler Sosthenes and beat him before the tribunal.

GAMALIEL [guh MAY lih el] (God is my recompense)

A famous member of the Jewish Sanhedrin and a teacher of the law. Gamaliel, who had taught the apostle Paul (Acts 22:3), advised the Sanhedrin to treat the apostles of the young Christian church with moderation. Gamaliel's argument was simple. If Jesus was a false prophet, as many others had been, the movement would soon fade into obscurity. If, however, the work was "of God," he pointed out, "you cannot overthrow it" (Acts 5:39).

GATH [gath] *(wine press)*

One of the five chief cities of the Philistines (Judg. 3:3). Gath was known as the residence of the Anakim, men of great stature (Josh. 11:22). Goliath and other giants belonged to this race and the city of Gath (1 Sam. 17:4). David captured Gath during his reign (1 Chr. 13:1). The residents of Gath, known as Gittites, were still subject to Israel during Solomon's reign, although they still had their own king (1 Kin. 2:39, 42).

Solomon's son, Rehoboam, later fortified Gath (2 Chr. 11:8), but the city returned to the hands of the Philistines. Later, it was recaptured by Hazael (2 Kin. 12:17), and Uzziah broke down its walls (2 Chr. 26:6).

GAZA [GAY zuh] *(stronghold)*

One of the five principal cities of the Philistines. The southernmost city of Canaan, Gaza was situated on the great caravan route between Mesopotamia and Egypt, at the junction of the trade route from Arabia. This location made Gaza an ideal rest stop and a commercial center for merchants and travelers.

Gaza was originally inhabited by the Avvim, a people who were replaced by the Caphtorim (Deut. 2:23). Gaza was allotted to the tribe of Judah by Joshua (Josh. 15:47); but it was not immediately occupied (Judg. 1:18) because the Anakim were still present in the city (Josh. 11:22; 13:3). Soon afterwards the Philistines recovered Gaza (Judg. 13:1). Here the mighty Samson was humiliated by being forced to grind grain as a blinded prisoner (Judg. 16:21). In a final victorious performance, Samson brought down the house of the pagan god Dagon, destroying many Philistines (Judg. 16:23–31).

Although Solomon ruled over Gaza, not until the reign of Hezekiah, king of Judah, was the decisive blow dealt to the Philistines (2 Kin. 18:8). Through the prophet Amos, God threatened Gaza with destruction by fire for its sins (Amos 1:6–7). This prophecy was fulfilled by the army of Alexander the Great in 332 B.C., when Gaza was destroyed and her inhabitants massacred (Zeph. 2:4; Zech. 9:5).

In the New Testament, the evangelist Philip was directed by God to preach the gospel along the road from Jerusalem to Gaza (Acts 8:26). On this road the Ethiopian eunuch professed faith in Jesus and was baptized.

GEDALIAH [gad uh LIE ah] *(The Lord is great)*

A person of high birth appointed governor of Judah by Nebuchadnezzar (2 Kin. 25:22–25). Gedaliah governed Judah from Mizpah, where after ruling for only two or three months he was assassinated by Jewish nationalists led by Ishmael. Gedaliah's father had protected the prophet Jeremiah, and Gedaliah probably did the same.

GEHAZI [geh HAH zih] *(valley of vision)*

A servant of the prophet Elisha (2 Kin. 4:8–5:27). Gehazi is first mentioned when Elisha asked how he could reward the Shunammite woman who had welcomed him into her home. Gehazi suggested that the childless woman and her husband might be given a child. A son was eventually born to the couple, but after a few years he died. The Shunammite woman sought Elisha's help. In an attempt to show Gehazi that faith healed, and not magic, Elisha sent him to lay the prophet's staff on the dead child's head. Nothing happened. But when Elisha himself went to the child, the child revived.

Gehazi's true character came out in the story of Naaman the Syrian, whom Elisha cured of a skin disease. Elisha refused any reward, but Gehazi ran after

Naaman to claim something for himself. He told Naaman that Elisha wanted a talent of silver and two changes of clothing for the needy. Because of his greed, lying, and misuse of the prophetic office, Elisha cursed Gehazi with the same disease from which Naaman had been cured.

GENTILES

A term used by Jewish people to refer to foreigners, or any other people who were not a part of the Jewish race.

The Jews were the chosen people of God who had entered a covenant with God. God initiated the covenant with Abraham (Gen. 12:1–7) and affirmed it repeatedly through Israel's leaders and prophets.

Because of this covenant relationship, a feeling of exclusivism gradually developed among the Jews over a period of several centuries. In early Hebrew history, Gentiles were treated cordially by the Israelites (Deut. 10:19; Num. 35:15; Ezek. 47:2). Men of Israel often married Gentile women, including Rahab and Ruth. However, after the Jews returned from their period of captivity in Babylon, the practice of intermarriage was discouraged (Ezra 9:12; 10:2–44; Neh. 10:30). Separation between Jews and Gentiles became increasingly strict; by the New Testament period the hostility was complete. The persecution of the Jews by the Greeks and Romans from the third century B.C. to the New Testament era caused the Jews to retaliate with hatred for all Gentiles and to avoid all contact with foreigners.

The life and teachings of Jesus set the ideal for positive relationships between Jews and Gentiles, as recorded in the apostle Paul's writings (Rom. 1:16; Eph. 2:14; Col. 3:11). But the process of such idealism becoming a reality was a struggle for the early church.

The Book of Acts pictures the struggle of the church to include the Gentiles in its life. When Peter, taught by the vision at Joppa, broke with Jewish tradition by visiting and eating with the Gentile Cornelius, it gave offense even to the Christian Jews (Acts 10:28; 11:3).

The apostle Paul became an effective missionary to the Gentiles (Acts 13:46–49; 15:14). At first the early church was composed of converted Jews who accepted Jesus as the Messiah, God's Anointed One. But more and more Gentiles came to accept the teaching of the gospel. Some Jewish leaders warned that they could not enter the church unless they also submitted to the Jewish ritual of circumcision (Acts 15:1–31). But Paul fought against this requirement as a denial of the gospel and ultimately convinced the churches. The only condition of salvation is repentance from sin and faith in Christ Jesus (Acts 20:21). "There is neither Jew nor Greek . . . for you are all one in Christ Jesus" (Gal. 3:28).

GERAR [GEE rar]

An ancient Philistine city in the Negev, in southern Palestine, between Kadesh Barnea and Shur (Gen. 10:19; 20:1). A wealthy city, Gerar probably controlled an important caravan route between Egypt and Palestine. Gerar was ruled by Abimelech, "king of the Philistines" (Gen. 26:1). During a famine, Abraham and his wife Sarah journeyed to Gerar. Fearing for his life, Abraham concealed the truth that Sarah was his wife, calling her his "sister." Abraham was reprimanded by Abimelech for his deception; eventually the two men concluded a treaty.

GERIZIM, MOUNT [GEH ruh zim]

A mountain in the district of Samaria. Mount Gerizim is located southwest of Mount Ebal. The main north-south road through central Palestine ran between these two mountains. Thus, Gerizim was of strategic military importance.

When the Hebrew people reached the Promised Land, Moses directed them to climb Mount Gerizim and Mount Ebal. Six tribes stood on each mountain (Deut. 27:11–14). Then Moses pronounced the blessings for keeping the law from Mount Gerizim and the curses for not keeping it from Mount Ebal (Deut. 11:29; 27:4–26). A ledge halfway to the top of Gerizim is called "Jotham's pulpit" (see Judg. 9:7). The characteristics of the two mountains make it possible to speak from either mountain and be heard easily in the valley below.

When the Israelites returned from their years of captivity in Babylon, they refused to allow the Samaritans, the residents of this mountain region, to assist in rebuilding Jerusalem (Ezra 4:1–4; Neh. 2:19–20; 13:28). In the days of Alexander the Great, a Samaritan temple was built on Mount Gerizim. Although it was destroyed by the Hasmonean king John Hyrcanus in 128 B.C., the Samaritans still worshiped on Mount Gerizim in Jesus' day (John 4:20–21). The small Samaritan community in Israel continues to celebrate the Passover on Mount Gerizim to this day.

Jacob's Well is situated at the foot of Mount Gerizim, today called Jebel et-Tor. This is the well where Jesus met the woman of Samaria, discussed Samaritan worship practices on Mount Gerizim, and told her of Himself—"a fountain of water springing up into everlasting life" (John 4:14).

GETHSEMANE [geth SEMM uh nee]
(olive press)

The garden where Jesus often went alone or with His disciples for prayer, rest, or fellowship, and the site where He was betrayed by Judas on the night before His crucifixion (Luke 21:37; John 18:1–2).

Gethsemane was situated on the Mount of Olives just east of Jerusalem, across the Kidron Valley and opposite the temple (Mark 13:3; John 18:1). From its name scholars conclude that the garden was situated in an olive grove that contained an olive press. Attempts to locate the exact site of the garden have been unsuccessful. Many Christians have agreed on one site—the place that Constantine's mother Helena designated about A.D. 325. But at least two other sites are also defended by tradition and have their supporters. The Gospel accounts do not provide enough details to show the exact site of the garden.

The four Gospel writers focus special attention on Jesus' final visit to Gethsemane just before His arrest and crucifixion. After the Last Supper, Jesus returned there with His disciples for final instructions and a period of soul-searching prayer. All the disciples were instructed; but only Peter, James, and John went to Gethsemane with Jesus to pray (Mark 14:26–32). Jesus urged them to stand watch while He prayed. Then He pleaded with God to deliver Him from the coming events (Mark 14:32–42). But His prayer was not an arrogant attempt to resist God's will or even to change God's plan. His pleas clearly acknowledged His obedience to the will of the Father: "O My Father, if this cup cannot pass away from Me unless I drink it, Your will be done" (Matt. 26:42).

An important lesson can be learned from a study of Gethsemane. Jesus, no less than His disciples then and since, faced the temptation of Satan. He "was in all points tempted as we are, yet without sin" (Heb. 4:15). No wonder He cried, "My soul is exceedingly sorrowful, even to death" (Matt. 26:38). But He won the victory over Satan as He declared to His Father, "Your will be done."

Because Jesus has faced such powerful temptation Himself, we can relate to Him as a personal Lord and Savior: "For in that He Himself has suffered, being tempted, He is able to aid those who are tempted'' (Heb. 2:18).

GEZER [GEZ ur] *(portion, division)*

An ancient Canaanite city 20 miles (17 kilometers) west of Jerusalem that was conquered by Joshua (Josh. 10:33; 12:12). Because the Israelites never fully obeyed God's command to destroy the Canaanites in this city (Josh. 21:21; 1 Chr. 6:67), they eventually lost it to the Philistines (2 Sam. 5:25; 1 Chr. 20:4).

During the reign of Solomon, an Egyptian pharaoh conquered Gezer, burned the city, and killed its inhabitants. Pharaoh gave the city and his daughter to Solomon to establish peace between Egypt and Israel. Solomon rebuilt Gezer and turned it into a strategic military and economic center (1 Kin. 9:15, 17–19). Many years later, Gezer was destroyed by the Assyrian king, Tiglath-Pileser (2 Kin. 16:5–7) when he came to rescue Ahaz, king of Judah, from the attack of the Syrians and Israelites.

In the Jewish wars just before the time of Christ, Gezer was an important military fortress (1 Macc. 9:52; 13:53). The city is not mentioned in the New Testament because it was destroyed earlier by the Romans.

Major archaeological excavations at

GIANTS

Gezer were conducted by R. A. S. Macalister from 1902–1909 and by G. E. Wright, W. G. Dever, and J. D. Seger from 1964–1973. The city covered an area of about 30 acres and was first established before the time of Abraham. Some of the most significant discoveries at Gezer were: (1) a Palestinian calendar based on the agricultural seasons. This inscription in the ancient Hebrew script is one of the oldest Hebrew documents (from the time of Solomon); (2) a four-entryway gate that was characteristic of the construction methods of Solomon at Hazor and Megiddo; (3) an impressive sloping tunnel about 150 feet (50 meters) long that leads down to a large cistern under the city. This water supply was important to ancient walled cities if the people hoped to withstand an extended enemy siege; and (4) a row of ten huge stones standing on end. These stones may be a part of a high place where heathen gods were worshiped.

GIANTS

Human beings of abnormal size and strength. Races of giants are first mentioned in the Old Testament in Genesis 6:4, where giant godlike beings were produced by the union of "the sons of God" and "the daughters of men." These abnormal unions displeased God (Gen. 6:5–6). The giants, or Nephilim, became "mighty men . . . men of renown," perhaps a reference to their great height.

Rephaim were primitive giants who lived in Canaan, Edom, Moab, and Ammon. They were also known as Emim (Deut. 2:11) and Zamzummim (Deut. 2:20). King Og of Bashan (Deut. 3:11) was the last of these giants. His iron bed was 9 cubits long and 4 cubits wide (about 13 feet by 6 feet).

When Moses sent 12 men to spy out the land of Canaan, they returned with the frightening report that they saw "giants" who made them feel like "grass-hoppers" (Num. 13:33). These giants were descendants of Anak, "a people great and tall" (Deut. 9:2). This negative report by 10 of the spies caused the children of Israel to spend a night in murmuring and weeping. Only Joshua and Caleb urged the people to claim the land (Num. 14:38).

Goliath is the most famous giant in the Bible (1 Sam. 17:4), measuring six cubits and a span, which is more than 9 feet (3 meters) tall. Goliath taunted the Israelites and demanded a warrior to meet him in combat. David, the shepherd boy, with his sling and stone, dared to accept the challenge of the Philistine giant in full armor because he knew that God would direct him in the battle (1 Sam. 17:45). David's stone struck Goliath in the forehead, and Goliath fell facedown. David then cut off the giant's head, and the Philistines were put to flight (1 Sam. 17:49, 51).

GIBEAH, GIBEATH [GIB ee ah, GIB ee ath] (hill)

A city belonging to Benjamin (Judg. 19:14). Scholars disagree over whether this is the same city called Gibeath in Joshua 18:28. Gibeah has been excavated at the modern site of Tell el-Ful, 3 miles (5 kilometers) north of Jerusalem. This city figured prominently in two separate periods of Old Testament history. It first appeared in Judges 19–20 as the site of a crime of lewdness and obscenity. All the children of Israel came together to punish Gibeah for its crimes. After a prolonged and mostly unsuccessful war against the Benjamites, the Israelites completely destroyed Gibeah (Judg. 20:40). The Tell el-Ful excavations have uncovered the remains of a village completely destroyed by fire.

Gibeah was apparently rebuilt after the fire. The birthplace of Saul, it became the capital of his kingdom (1 Sam. 14:16; 15:34). In many passages, it is even called

"Gibeah of Saul" (1 Sam. 11:4; Is. 10:29). At Tell el-Ful, the remains of Saul's fortress, built around 1015 B.C., have been found. The fortress walls, 8 to 10 feet (2.5 to 3.5 meters) thick, enclosed an area of 170 x 155 feet (52 x 47 meters). The stronghold was made up of two stories joined by a stone staircase.

GIBEON [GIBB eh un] *(pertaining to a hill)*

A city in the territory of Benjamin about 6 miles (10 kilometers) northwest of Jerusalem. It was the chief city of the Hivites.

The first reference to Gibeon in the Bible is Joshua 9:3. After the Israelites destroyed the cities of Jericho and Ai (Josh. 6–8), Gibeon's inhabitants, fearing the same fate, made a covenant with the Israelites. Although they established the treaty by deceit and thus were made slaves by the Israelites, the Gibeonites were still protected from the alliance of five Amorite kings. In a battle over Gibeon between Joshua and the Amorite alliance (Josh. 10:1–11), the sun stood still for a day and hailstones rained down on the fleeing Amorites.

Gibeon does not appear again in Scripture until about 1000 B.C. Then, in a gruesome contest of strength, 12 of David's men and 12 of the men of Ishbosheth (Saul's son) killed one another with their swords. The place was named "the Field of the Sharp Swords" (2 Sam. 2:16) because of this event. There followed a great battle in which David's forces were victorious (2 Sam. 2:12–17).

The prophet Jeremiah mentioned a "great pool that is in Gibeon" (Jer. 41:12). This pool was discovered in an excavation of the site, beginning in 1956. Archaeologists discovered a large open pit about 35 feet (11 meters) deep that had been dug into the solid rock. A large stone stairway descended into the pit, then continued another 11 meters down to a water chamber. Gibeon was the center of a winemaking industry during the seventh century B.C. The lower chamber of the "great pool" provided water for the wine and also served as the city's main water supply.

GIBEONITES [GIB ee un ites]

The Canaanite inhabitants of the city of Gibeon, probably also including the people of its three dependent towns (2 Sam. 21:1–9). When the Gibeonites heard of Joshua's victories at Jericho and Ai, they pretended to be ambassadors from a far country in order to make a peace treaty with the invading Israelites (Josh. 9:4–5). When the deception was discovered, the Israelites permitted the Gibeonites to live, according to their agreement. However, they were made slaves, "woodcutters and water carriers for all the congregation and for the altar of the Lord" (Josh. 9:21).

Apparently King Saul broke this covenant of peace with the Gibeonites in later years. During the reign of David, when a three-year famine blighted the land, it was discovered that the Lord was angry with the "bloodthirsty house" of Saul, who had "killed the Gibeonites" (2 Sam. 21:1) in a frenzy of patriotic zeal. To make up for this wrong, David allowed the Gibeonites to execute seven of Saul's descendants (2 Sam. 21:9).

GIDEON [GIDD ee un]

A military hero and spiritual leader who delivered Israel from the oppression of the Midianites. As a young lad, Gideon had seen the land oppressed by the Midianites and Amalekites for seven years (Judg. 6:1). Like invading locusts, the roving bands camped on the land of the Israelites. At harvest time, they destroyed the crops and animals and plundered the farmers' houses. Israel's misfortune was apparently caused by their spiritual relapse into Baal worship (Judg. 6:1).

As young Gideon was threshing wheat, the angel of the Lord appeared with strong words of encouragement: "The Lord is with you, you mighty man of valor . . . Surely, I will be with you, and you shall defeat the Midianites as one man" (Judg. 6:12, 16).

Gideon then asked the messenger for a sign that God had selected him for divine service. He prepared an offering and placed it on an altar. The angel touched the offering with his staff, and fire consumed it (6:19–21). Gideon then recognized his personal call to serve God.

Gideon's first assignment was to destroy his father's altar of Baal in the family's backyard (Judg. 6:25). This act required great courage because Gideon feared his father's house and the men of the city who must have worshiped at the altar. For this reason, Gideon and ten servants destroyed the altar of Baal and a wood idol by night and erected an altar to the Lord. Gideon immediately presented an offering to the Lord on the altar (6:27–28).

When Gideon's fellow citizens discovered that the altar to Baal had been destroyed, they were outraged. When it was learned that "Gideon the son of Joash has done this thing" (6:29), Joash was called to account for his son's behavior. To his credit, Joash defended Gideon by implying that an authentic god should require no defense. "If he [Baal] is a god, let him plead for himself" (6:31). So that day Gideon was called Jerubbaal, meaning "Let Baal plead" (6:25–32).

As the oppression of the Midianites intensified, Gideon sent out messengers to all Manasseh and the surrounding tribes to rally volunteers to Israel's cause (Judg. 6:35). When Gideon's volunteers assembled, about 32,000 citizen soldiers stood in the ranks (Judg. 7:1). Although there were 135,000 Midianites camped in a nearby valley, God directed Gideon to thin out the ranks. After dismissing the fearful and afraid, only 10,000 remained. Gideon's band was now outnumbered about 13 to 1.

"There are still too many," God told Gideon. "Bring them down to the water, and I will test them for you there" (7:4). Those who scooped up the water with their hands, never taking their eyes from the horizon, were retained in Gideon's army; those who got down on their knees to drink, forgetting to keep watch for the enemy, were dismissed. Now only 300 soldiers remained (Judg. 7:5–7). The Midianites outnumbered Gideon's band 450 to 1. But God and Gideon had a secret plan.

Gideon divided the army into three companies. Then he gave each man a trumpet, a pitcher, and a torch. At the appointed time, 300 trumpets blasted the air, 300 hands raised their pitchers and smashed them to bits, 300 burning torches pierced the darkness, and 300 warriors cried, "The sword of the Lord and of Gideon" (Judg. 7:19–21).

The Midianites were thrown into panic. In the confusion, some committed suicide or killed their comrades. The remaining soldiers fled. The enemies of Israel were completely routed, and Israel's homeland was secure (Judg. 7:22; 8:10). It was a glorious victory for God and for Gideon, who became an instant hero (8:22).

Gideon and his men pursued the fleeing enemy. Many of them were killed or captured by Gideon's allies. Two Midianite kings, Zebah and Zalmunna, were captured and killed for their murderous deeds (Judg. 8).

As a conquering warrior, Gideon was invited to become king (Judg. 8:22), but he declined. Modest and devout, he was careful not to grasp at the power and glory that belonged to God. After he retired to his home, Israel was blessed with 40 years of peace (Judg. 8:28).

Through the life and exploits of Gideon, God reveals much about Himself and the preparation that His leaders need for divine service. Gideon shows that God calls leaders from unlikely situations. Gideon was a poor farmer's son who worked with his hands, and his father was an idol worshiper (Judg. 6:15, 25). Still, Gideon was an effective leader in God's service.

The story of Gideon also reminds us that God prefers a few dedicated and disciplined disciples to throngs of uncommitted workers. God can win victories with a fully committed minority (Judg. 7:2, 4, 7).

Another leadership lesson from Gideon's life is that a leader's spiritual life is sustained by regular worship. Devout Gideon appears to have worshiped frequently—in times of personal crisis as well as celebration (Judg. 6:18–21; 7:15).

GIHON SPRING [GIH hon] *(gusher)*

A spring outside the walls of Jerusalem where the city obtained part of its water supply (2 Chr. 32:30). The Canaanite inhabitants of ancient Jerusalem, or Jebus, had used and protected the spring in their fortifications, too. When David and his soldiers conquered Jebus, they entered it through the water shaft that led from the spring into the city (2 Sam. 5:8). Israel continued to use Gihon and its water channel. King Hezekiah channeled the water more elaborately when he constructed the famous Siloam tunnel in 701 B.C. as part of the city's preparation against the siege of the Assyrians (2 Kin. 20:20).

Gihon was the site where Solomon was anointed and proclaimed king (1 Kin. 1:33, 38, 45). Some scholars believe it later became customary for the new king to drink from the waters of Gihon during his coronation ceremony (Ps. 110:7).

GILEAD [GILL ee ad]

A mountain region east of the Jordan River 3,000 feet (915 meters) above sea level. Extending about 60 miles (97 kilometers) from near the south end of the Sea of Galilee to the north end of the Dead Sea, Gilead is about 20 miles (32 kilometers) wide. It is bounded on the

west by the Jordan River, on the south by the land of Moab, on the north by the Yarmuk River, and on the east by the desert.

The Jabbok River divides Gilead into two parts: northern Gilead, the land between the Jabbok and the Yarmuk, and southern Gilead, the land between the Jabbok and the Arnon (Josh. 12:2). The term *Gilead*, however, came to be applied to the entire region of Israelite Transjordan (Deut. 34:1).

This lush region receives an annual rainfall of from 28 to 32 inches (71 to 81 centimeters). Thus, much of it is thickly wooded today, as it was in Absalom's day (2 Sam. 18:6–9). Many fugitives fled to this region for safety. Jacob fled to Gilead from Laban his father-in-law (Gen. 31:21). The Israelites who feared the Philistines in King Saul's day fled here (1 Sam. 13:7), as did Ishbosheth (2 Sam. 2:8–9) and David (2 Sam. 17:22, 26) during Absalom's revolt. Gilead also contains rich grazing land (1 Chr. 5:9–10).

The balm of Gilead, an aromatic resin used for medical purposes (Jer. 8:22), was exported to Tyre and elsewhere (Ezek. 27:17). The Ishmaelites who carried Joseph into Egyptian bondage also traded in Gilead's balm (Gen. 37:25).

When Canaan was being allocated to the Israelite tribes, Gilead fell to the Reubenites and Gadites because of its suitability for grazing cattle (Deut. 3:12–17). The half-tribe of Manasseh also shared in the land of Gilead.

GILGAL [GILL gal] *(circle)*

The first campsite of the people of Israel after they crossed the Jordan River and entered the Promised Land (Josh. 4:19–20). They took stones from the Jordan and set them up at Gilgal as a memorial to God's deliverance. Many important events in Israel's history are associated with this city. The first Passover in Canaan was held at Gilgal (Josh.

5:9–10). It also became the base of military operations for Israel during the conquest of Canaan. From Gilgal Joshua led Israel against the city of Jericho (Josh. 6:11, 14) and conducted his southern campaign (Josh. 10). It was there that he began allotting the Promised Land to the tribes.

In later years, Gilgal was the site of King Saul's coronation as well as his rejection by God as king (1 Sam. 11:15; 13:4–12; 15:12–33). After Absalom's revolt, the people of Judah gathered at Gilgal to welcome David back as their king (2 Sam. 19:15, 40). But during the days of later kings, Gilgal became a center of idolatry. Like Bethel, it was condemned by the prophets (Hos. 4:15; Amos 5:5). The presumed site of Gilgal is about 1 mile (2 kilometers) northeast of Old Testament Jericho (Josh. 4:19).

GLEANING

The process of gathering grain or other produce left in the fields by reapers (Judg. 8:2; Is. 17:6). The Old Testament law required that property owners leave the gleanings of their produce in the fields so they might be gathered by "the poor and the stranger" (Lev. 19:9–10; 23:22). The story of Ruth reflects this custom. When Boaz, the wealthy kinsman of Naomi's departed husband, saw Ruth in his field, he told his reapers to leave grain for her to gather. At noon he invited her to share his parched grain (Ruth 2:14).

See also REAPING.

GLORY

Beauty, power, or honor; a quality of God's character that emphasizes His greatness and authority. While God's glory is not a substance, at times God does reveal His perfection to humans in a visible way. Such a display of the presence of God is often seen as fire or dazzling light, but sometimes as an act of power. Some examples from the Old Testament are the pillar of cloud and fire (Ex. 13:21), the Lord's deliverance of the Israelites at the Red Sea (Ex. 14), and especially His glory in the tabernacle (Lev. 9:23–24) and temple (1 Kin. 8:11).

Since the close of the Old Testament, the glory of God has been shown mainly in Christ (Luke 9:29–32; John 2:11) and in the members of His church. Christ now shares His divine glory with His followers (John 17:5–6, 22), so that in their lives Christians are being transformed into the glorious image of God (2 Cor. 3:18). Believers will be fully glorified at the end of time in God's heavenly presence (Rom. 5:2; Col. 3:4). There the glory of God will be seen everywhere (Rev. 21:23).

GNOSTICISM [NOS tuh siz em]

A system of false teachings that existed during the early centuries of Christianity. Its name came from gnosis, the Greek word for knowledge. The Gnostics believed that knowledge was the way to salvation. For this reason, Gnosticism was condemned as false and heretical by several writers of the New Testament.

The Gnostics accepted the Greek idea of a radical dualism between God (spirit) and the world (matter). According to their world view, the created order was evil, inferior, and opposed to the good. God may have created the first order, but each successive order was the work of anti-gods, archons, or a demiurge (a subordinate deity).

The Gnostics also taught that every human being is composed of body, soul, and spirit. Since the body and the soul are part of people's earthly existence, they are evil. Enclosed in the soul, however, is the spirit, the only divine part of this triad. This "spirit" is asleep and ignorant; it needs to be awakened and liberated by knowledge.

According to the Gnostics, the aim of salvation is for the spirit to be awakened by knowledge so the inner person can be released from the earthly dungeon and return to the realm of light where the soul becomes reunited with God. As the soul ascends, however, it needs to penetrate the cosmic spheres that separate it from its heavenly destiny. This, too, is accomplished by knowledge. One must understand certain formulas that are revealed only to the initiated.

Ethical behavior among the Gnostics varied considerably. Some sought to separate themselves from all evil matter in order to avoid contamination. Paul may be opposing such a view in 1 Timothy 4:1–5. For other Gnostics, ethical life took the form of libertinism. For them knowledge meant freedom to participate in all sorts of activities. Many reasoned that since they had received divine knowledge and were truly informed as to their divine nature, it did not matter how they lived.

Such an attitude is a misunderstanding of the gospel. Paul, on a number of occasions, reminded his readers that they were saved from sin to holiness. They were not to have an attitude of indifference toward the law. They had died to sin in their baptism into Christ (Rom. 6:1–11) and so were to walk "in newness of life." John reminded the Christians that once they had been saved they were not to continue living in sin (1 John 3:4–10).

These Gnostic teachings also had a disruptive effect on fellowship in the church. Those who were "enlightened" thought of themselves as being superior to those who did not have such knowledge. Divisions arose between the spiritual and the fleshly. This attitude of superiority is severely condemned in the New Testament. Christians are "one body" (1 Cor. 12) who should love one another (1 Cor. 13; 1 John). Spiritual gifts are for the Christian community rather than individual use; they should promote humility rather than pride (1 Cor. 12–14; Eph. 4:11–16).

GOAT

In Bible times shepherds treasured the goat because it was such a useful animal. They wove its hair into a type of rough cloth. They drank the goat's milk which is sweet and more nutritious than cow's milk—ideal for making cheese. They even used goatskin bottles to transport water and wine. When the hide of these containers wore thin, they leaked and had to be patched (Josh. 9:4; Matt. 9:17).

Goats often grazed with sheep in mixed flocks. Unlike their gentle and helpless cousins, goats were independent, willful, and curious. Bible writers sometimes used goats to symbolize irresponsible leadership (Jer. 50:8; Zech. 10:3). In Jesus' parable of the Great Judgment (Matt. 25:32–33), the goats represented the unrighteous who could not enter His kingdom.

Goats were often sacrificed in the worship system of ancient Israel. On the Day of Atonement the Israelites used two goats. One was sacrificed, and the other was sent into the wilderness, symbolically bearing the sins of the people (Lev. 16:10).

GOD

The creator and sustainer of the universe who has provided humankind with a revelation of Himself through the natural world and through His Son, Jesus Christ. The Bible does not seek to prove the existence of God; it simply affirms His existence (Gen. 1:1). God has revealed Himself through the physical universe (Rom. 1:19–20). By observing the universe, one can find positive indications of God's existence.

The greatest revelation of God, however, comes through the Bible. Through the inspired written record, both the existence of God and the nature of God are revealed in and through Jesus Christ (John 14:9). Although the full revelation of God was in Jesus Christ, the human mind cannot fully understand God because of the limitation of the human mind. Although we cannot fully understand God, we still can know Him. We know Him through a personal relationship of faith and through a study of what the Bible teaches about His nature.

God may be described in terms of attributes. For example, He is holy, changeless, all-knowing, and wise. God's wisdom is revealed in His doing the best thing, in the best way, at the best time, for the best purpose.

Some people have knowledge, but little wisdom, while the most wise at times have little knowledge. But God is "the only wise God" (1 Tim. 1:17). In creation, history, human lives, redemption, and Christ, His divine wisdom is revealed. Human beings, lacking wisdom, can claim God's wisdom simply by asking (James 1:5).

Another attribute of God is love. Love is the essential, self-giving nature of God. God's love for humankind seeks to awaken a responsive love of people for God. Divine love runs like a golden thread through the entire Bible. Nature is eloquent with the skill, wisdom, and power of God. Only in the Bible, however, do we discover God giving Himself and all He possesses to His creatures, in order to win their response and to possess them for Himself.

GOG [gog]

The leader of a confederacy of armies that attacked the land of Israel. Described as "the prince of Rosh, Meshech, and Tubal," Gog is also depicted as being "of the land of Magog" (Ezek. 38:2–3), a "place out of the far north" of Israel. Ezekiel prophetically describes Gog and his allies striking at Israel with a fierce and sudden invasion (Ezek. 38–39). According to Ezekiel's prophecy, Gog will be crushed on the mountains of Israel in a slaughter so great it will take seven months to bury the dead (Ezek. 39:12).

In the Book of Revelation, Gog and Magog reappear as symbols of the nations of the world that will march against God's people in the end times (Rev. 20:7–8).

GOLD

A soft, bright yellow metal, gold was one of the first metals known to humankind. It could be used in its pure state without smelting. It never tarnishes—a property that makes it ideal for jewelry. This metal was extremely mallable; it could be hammered into thin strips and delicate objects: "And they beat the gold into thin sheets and cut it into threads, to work it in with the blue and purple and scarlet and fine linen thread, into artistic designs" (Ex. 39:3).

Gold is mentioned over 500 times in the Bible, more than any other metal. Rich deposits of gold were in Havilah (Gen. 2:11), Ophir (1 Kin. 22:48; 2 Chr. 8:18), Sheba (1 Kin. 10:1–2), Egypt, Armenia, Asia Minor, and Persia.

Gold was at first hammered into desired shapes and sizes. In later periods it was refined and cast. Some scholars believe gold was not refined in Palestine until about 1000 B.C. Many objects were made of gold, including the high priest's vest (Ex. 28:5), crowns (Ps. 21:3), chains (Gen. 41:42), rods (Song 5:14; rings, KJV), and coins (1 Chr. 21:25; Acts 3:6). Hiram brought gold to Israel for Solomon's palace (1 Kin. 10:16–21) and for furnishings for the temple (1 Kin. 6:20; 10:2, 10). Gold was also taken as plunder in war (2 Kin. 24:13).

GOLDEN CALF

An idolatrous image of a young bull, probably made of wood and overlaid with gold, which the Israelites worshiped in the wilderness while Moses was on Mount Sinai receiving the Ten Commandments (Ex. 32). Another instance of this form of idolatry occurred years later in the history of God's people when King Jeroboam I of Israel set up golden calves at Bethel and Dan (1 Kin. 12:26–33).

GOLIATH [goe LIE ahth]

A Philistine giant whom David felled with a stone from his sling (1 Sam. 17:4–51). Goliath, who lived in the Philistine city of Gath, was probably a descendant of a tribe of giants known as the Anakim, or descendants of Anak (Num. 13:33). These giants probably served in a capacity similar to that of a foreign mercenary or soldier of fortune.

Based on the figures in the Bible (1 Sam. 17:4), Goliath was over nine feet tall. The magnificence of Goliath's armor and weapons—his bronze coat of mail, bronze greaves, bronze javelin, spear with an iron spearhead, and huge sword—must have made him appear invincible.

For 40 days this enormous man challenged Saul's army to find one man willing to engage in hand-to-hand combat. The winner of that one battle would determine the outcome of the war. The young David, chosen by God as Israel's next king, accepted the challenge, felling Goliath with a single stone to the forehead from his sling. When David beheaded the fallen giant, the Philistines fled in panic.

GOMER [GOAM ur]

A prostitute who became the wife of the prophet Hosea (Hos. 1:1–11). When Gomer left Hosea and became the slave of one of her lovers, Hosea bought her back at God's command for the price of a slave. Gomer's unfaithfulness and Hosea's forgiveness symbolized God's forgiving love for unfaithful Israel.

GOMORRAH [guh MOR ruh]
(submersion)

One of the five "cities of the plain" located in the Valley of Siddim (Salt Sea or Dead Sea). The other cities were Sodom, Admah, Zeboiim, and Zoar (Gen. 14:2–3). Gomorrah is associated closely with its twin city, Sodom. Because these cities became the site of intolerable wickedness, they were destroyed by fire (Gen. 19:24, 28). The destruction of Sodom and Gomorrah is often referred to in the Bible as a clear example of divine judgment against the vilest of sinners (Is. 13:19; Jer. 49:18; Amos 4:11; Matt. 10:15; 2 Pet. 2:6; Jude 7).

The exact location of the "cities of the plain" has been a subject of much debate. The current consensus, however, places them near Bab edh-Dhra, the entrance to the "tongue" (Lisan) of land that juts out into the Dead Sea on its eastern shore.

GOSHEN [GOE shun]

The northeastern territory of the Nile Delta in Egypt, known today as the area of the Wadi Tumilat. Jacob and his family were granted permission to settle in this fertile section during Joseph's rule as prime minister of Egypt (Gen. 46:28). During the time of the Exodus, Goshen was protected from the plagues of flies (Ex. 8:22) and hail (Ex. 9:26) that engulfed the rest of Egypt. The district was not large, containing perhaps 900 square miles, and it had two principal cities: Rameses and Pithom.

GOSPELS

The four accounts at the beginning of the New Testament about the saving work of God in His Son Jesus Christ. The writers of the four Gospels introduced a new category into literature. The Gospels are not true biographies, because apart from certain events surrounding His birth (Matt. 1–2; Luke 1–2) and one from His youth (Luke 2:41–52), they record only the last two or three years of Jesus' life.

Moreover, the material included is not written as an objective historical survey of Jesus' ministry. The Gospels present Jesus in such a way that the reader realizes that God acted uniquely in Him. The authors of the Gospels wrote not only to communicate knowledge about Jesus as a person, but also to call us to commitment to Him as Lord.

If one sets the four Gospels side by side, it becomes apparent that Matthew, Mark, and Luke have much in common. Each Gospel arranges its material in a similar fashion, and each Gospel casts the life of Jesus within the framework of a Galilean ministry that extended from Jesus' baptism to His death, with emphasis on His final days.

The similarity of the Gospels also includes their content. The first three Gospels recount many of the same incidents or teachings, and often in the same or related wording. Because of this similarity in arrangement, content, and wording, the first three Gospels are called synoptic Gospels (from the Greek *synopsis*, "a seeing together").

The Gospel of John presents a more independent account of Christ. In the Synoptics, Jesus' ministry lasts less than a year, and is conducted mainly in Galilee; in John it extends to three or more years and centers more often in Judea.

The Synoptics present Jesus as a man of action who paints word pictures for His hearers; John, however, portrays longer, less picturesque, and more speculative discourse coming from Jesus, and comparatively little action. In the

Synoptics, Jesus teaches in parables—nearly 60 in all—but in John no parables exist. In the Synoptics, Jesus teaches mainly about the kingdom of God, whereas in John He teaches about Himself. In the Synoptics, Jesus often demands silence of those who behold His miracles, but in John miracles are signs revealing Jesus and His mission.

These facts are sufficient to indicate that the Synoptics present basically one perspective on the life of Jesus and that the Gospel of John presents another perspective, achieved most probably by profound meditation on the meaning of Jesus Christ.

The importance of the Gospels for the early church may be indicated by noting that these four, which were collected perhaps as early as A.D. 125, were the first books of the New Testament to be accepted as authoritative by the early church. Today the four Gospels remain our only reliable source of information about the central figure of the human race.

GOVERNOR

A regional agent or officer for the Roman emperor during New Testament times. This office gradually developed across a period of many years. The primary function of the governor was to serve as a financial officer. In a senatorial province the governor was in charge of the emperor's properties within the province. In an imperial province he acted as the treasurer, collecting taxes and paying the troops in the Roman army. Later, in A.D. 53, Claudius gave governmental powers to governors in the third-class provinces such as Judea. They had auxiliary troops to maintain order and were responsible to the Roman ruler based in Syria.

Before A.D. 53 the governor was officially called "prefect" as in the case of Pilate. After A.D. 53 he was called "procurator" as in the cases of Felix and Festus. There was much confusion at the time because after A.D. 53 the Jewish historian Josephus calls the ruler of Judea prefect, procurator, and governor. In the New Testament the political ruler of Judea was always called by the more general term "governor." The governors of Judea included Pilate (Matt. 27:2), Felix (Acts 23:24), and Festus (Acts 26:30–32).

GRACE

Favor or kindness shown without regard to the worth or merit of the one who receives it and in spite of what that person deserves. Grace is one of the key attributes of God. The Lord God is "merciful and gracious, long-suffering, and abounding in goodness and truth" (Ex. 34:6). Therefore, grace is almost always associated with mercy, love, compassion, and patience.

In the Old Testament, the supreme example of grace was the redemption of the Hebrew people from Egypt and their establishment in the Promised Land. This did not happen because of any merit on Israel's part, but in spite of their unrighteousness (Deut. 7:7–8; 9:5–6). Although the grace of God is always free and undeserved, it must not be taken for granted. Grace is only enjoyed within the covenant—the gift is given by God, and the gift is received by people through repentance and faith (Amos 5:15). Grace is to be humbly sought through the prayer of faith (Mal. 1:9).

The grace of God was supremely revealed and given in the person and work of Jesus Christ. Jesus was not only the beneficiary of God's grace (Luke 2:40), but was also its very embodiment (John 1:14), bringing it to humankind for salvation (Titus 2:11). By His death and resurrection, Jesus restored the broken fellowship between God and His people, both Jew and Gentile. The only way of salvation for any person is "through the grace of the Lord Jesus Christ" (Acts 15:11).

The theme of grace is especially prominent in the letters of Paul. He sets grace radically over against the law and the works of the law (Rom. 3:24, 28). Paul makes it abundantly clear that salvation is not something that can be earned; it can be received only as a gift of grace (Rom. 4:4). Grace, however, must be accompanied by faith; a person must trust in the mercy and favor of God, even while it is undeserved (Rom. 4:16; Gal. 2:16).

GRAPES

A luscious fruit cultivated on vines. Large clusters of grapes weighing about five kilograms (12 pounds) each (Num. 13:23) have been reported in Palestine. Grapes were used in a variety of ways. They were eaten fresh or dried and were made into wine or vinegar. Dried grapes were called raisins. The first suggestion of grapes in Scripture was in connection with Noah's vineyard (Gen. 9:20).

The soil and climate of Palestine was well suited for vineyards, where grapes were grown. They were cultivated here long before the Israelites occupied the land (Gen. 14:18). The vineyards of Palestine produced immense clusters of grapes (Num. 13:20, 23–24). Vineyards were hedged or fenced as protection from wild animals (Song 2:15). In each vineyard a tower was erected and a guard placed to protect the vines from robbers (Matt. 21:33).

Vinedressers were hired to care for the vines and prune them yearly (Lev. 25:3; Is. 61:5). The grapes were gathered in baskets in September and October with much festivity (Judg. 9:27; Is. 16:10). Provision was made for the poor to glean the fields (Lev. 19:10; Deut. 24:21). The

choicest grapes were dried or eaten fresh and the rest were placed in presses to extract the juice (Is. 61:5; Hos. 9:2–4). This was drunk fresh or fermented.

Jesus alluded to His relationship with His followers by referring to Himself as the Vine and to them as the branches (John 15:5). The fruit of the vine symbolized Jesus' shed blood (Matt. 26:27–29). He also referred to vineyards in many of His parables (Matt. 9:17; 20:1–6; 21:28–32; Luke 13:6–9).

GRASSHOPPER

Numerous references to grasshoppers and locusts in the Bible show what an impact these insects had in the hot, dry lands of the ancient world. Some of these references are literal (Ex. 10:4–19) while others are symbolic (Num. 13:33).

The terms grasshopper and locust are often used interchangeably. A locust is one kind of grasshopper. Another term used rarely for these insects is katydid (Lev. 11:22, NIV). It has a brown-colored body two to three inches long. Airborne, with two sets of wings, the locust was dreaded because of its destructive power as a foliage-eating insect in the ancient world.

The eighth plague that God sent upon the Egyptians was an invasion of locusts. Millions of these insects may be included in one of these swarms, which usually occur in the spring. Locusts in such numbers speedily eat every plant in sight, totally destroying the crops. A locust plague is practically unstoppable. Water does not work; for when enough locusts drown, the survivors use their bodies as a bridge. They have also been known to smother fires that had been set to destroy them. Even modern farmers wrestle with this problem, often resorting to poisoning the adults and harrowing fields in the fall to destroy the eggs before they can hatch in the spring.

Chapter 9 of the Book of Revelation presents a nightmarish prospect: locusts with special powers will be unleashed upon mankind for five months.

Locusts do not always appear in swarms. Hot weather normally brings a few solitary grasshoppers and locusts to the Holy Land. But scientists have learned that under certain conditions of climate and food scarcity, chemical changes take place in the female locust. These cause more eggs to hatch, sending millions of locusts into the air at the same time in search of food.

GREECE

A region or country of city-states in southeastern Europe between Italy and Asia Minor. Greece was bounded on the east by the Aegean Sea, on the south by the Mediterranean Sea, on the west by the Adriatic Sea and Ionian Sea, and on the north by Mount Olympus and adjacent mountains. The Old Testament name for Greece was Javan (Gen. 10:2, 4; Is. 66:19).

In the early years of its history, Greece was a country of self-governing city-states. Politically and militarily, the Greek city-states were weak. Their varied backgrounds led to frictions and rivalries that kept them from becoming one unified nation.

In 338 B.C., Philip II, king of Macedon, conquered the southern peninsula of Greece. Under Philip's son, Alexander the Great (336–323 B.C.), the Greek Empire was extended from Greece through Asia Minor to Egypt and the borders of India. Alexander's military conquests and his passion to spread Greek culture contributed to the advancement of Greek ideas throughout the ancient world. This adoption of Greek ideas by the rest of the ancient world was known as Hellenism. So thoroughly did Greek ideas penetrate

the other nations that the Greek language became the dominant language of the known world.

Greek learning and culture eventually conquered the ancient Near East and continued as dominant forces throughout the New Testament era. Even after the rise of the Romans, about 146 B.C., the influence of Greek language, culture, and philosophy remained strong, even influencing the Jewish religion.

Greek religion included many gods. The religions of Egypt, Asia Minor, and Persia were more appealing than the old Greek gods because they promised immortality. However, the Greeks did not abandon their former gods; they simply adopted new gods and gave them old names. A renewed interest in astrology among the Greeks also led to widespread belief that the planets governed the lives and fates of human beings. The Greeks sought to control any turn of fate through worship. They even erected an altar inscribed "to the unknown god" in their capital city of Athens (Acts 17:23).

The peninsula of Greece fell to the Romans in 146 B.C. and later became the senatorial province of Achaia with Corinth as its capital. The apostle Paul visited this area on his second missionary journey, delivering his famous sermon to the Athenian philosophers (Acts 17:22–34). Later he appeared before the proconsul Gallio at Corinth (Acts 18:12–17). On his third missionary journey, he visited Greece for three months (Acts 20:2–3).

Greece is important to Christianity because of its language. In New Testament times Greek was the language spoken by the common people of the ancient world, as far west as Rome and the Rhone Valley in southeastern France. Most of the New Testament was written originally in Greek, a precise and expressive language.

HABAKKUK [huh BAK uhk]

A courageous Old Testament prophet and author of the Book of Habakkuk. The Scriptures say nothing of his ancestry or place of birth. A man of deep emotional strength, Habakkuk was both a poet and a prophet. His hatred of sin compelled him to cry out to God for judgment (Hab. 1:2–4). His sense of justice also led him to challenge God's plan to judge the nation of Judah by the pagan Babylonians (Hab. 1:12–2:1). His deep faith led him to write a beautiful poem of praise in response to the mysterious ways of God (Hab. 3).

HAGAR [HAY gahr]

The Egyptian bondwoman of Sarah who bore a son, Ishmael, to Abraham (Gen. 16:1–16). After waiting ten years for God to fulfill his promise to give them a son, Sarah presented Hagar to Abraham so he could father a child by her, according to the custom of the day. Sarah's plan and Abraham's compliance demonstrated a lack of faith in God.

When Hagar became pregnant, she mocked Sarah, who dealt with her harshly. Hagar then fled into the wilderness, where, at a well on the way to Shur, she encountered an angel of the Lord. The angel revealed Ishmael's future to Hagar—that his descendants would be a great multitude. Tradition has it that Hagar is the ancestress of all the Arab peoples and of the prophet Muhammad. Hagar called the well Beer Lahai Roi, "The well of the Living One who sees me."

When Hagar returned to Abraham's camp, Ishmael was born and accepted by Abraham as his son. But when Ishmael was 14 years old, Isaac, the promised son, was born. The next year Ishmael mocked Isaac at the festival of Isaac's weaning. At Sarah's insistence and with God's approval, Hagar and Ishmael were expelled from Abraham's family. Abraham grieved for Ishmael, but God comforted him by revealing that a great nation would come out of Ishmael.

Hagar and Ishmael wandered in the wilderness until their water was gone. When Hagar laid her son under the shade of a bush to die, the angel of the Lord appeared to Hagar and showed her a well. This is a beautiful picture of God's concern for the outcast and helpless.

In Paul's allegory in Galatians 4, Hagar stands for Mount Sinai and corresponds to the earthly Jerusalem, while Isaac stands for the children of promise who are free in Christ.

HAGGAI [HAG eye] *(festive)*

An Old Testament prophet and author of the Book of Haggai. As God's spokesman, he encouraged the captives who had returned to Jerusalem to complete the reconstruction of the temple. This work had started shortly after the first exiles returned from Babylon in 538 B.C. But the building activity was soon abandoned because of discouragement and oppression. Beginning in 520 B.C., Haggai and his fellow prophet, Zechariah, urged the people to resume the task. The temple was completed five years later, about 515 B.C. (Ezra 5:1).

HALF-TRIBE

A term used in the Old Testament to refer to the two separate settlements of the tribe of Manasseh—one east of the Jordan River and the other in central Palestine west of the Jordan. During the days of Moses, half of the people of the tribe of Manasseh requested permission to settle the territory east of the Jordan after the land was conquered. Moses agreed to this request, on the condition that the entire tribe assist in the conquest of Canaan (Num. 32:33–42; Deut. 3:12–13; Josh. 1:12–18).

HAM [hamm]

The youngest of Noah's three sons (Gen. 9:18, 24). Ham, along with the rest of Noah's household, was saved from the great Flood by entering the ark (Gen. 7:7). After the waters went down and Noah's household left the ark, Ham found his father, naked and drunk, asleep in his tent. Ham told his brothers, Shem and Japheth, who covered their father without looking on his nakedness. Noah was furious because Ham had seen him naked, and he placed a prophetic curse on Canaan, the son of Ham (Gen. 9:18, 25). The Canaanites were to serve the descendants of Shem and Japheth (Gen. 9:26–27; Josh. 9:16–27).

Ham had four sons: Cush, Mizraim, Put, and Canaan (Gen. 10:6). The tribe of Mizraim settled in Egypt, while the tribes of Cush and Put settled in other parts of Africa. The tribe of Canaan populated Phoenicia and Palestine.

HAMAN [HAY mun]

The evil and scheming prime minister of Ahasuerus (Xerxes I), king of Persia (485–464 B.C.). When Mordecai refused to bow to Haman, Haman plotted to destroy Mordecai and his family, as well as all of the Jews in the Persian Empire. But Esther intervened and saved her people. Haman was hanged on the very gallows he had constructed for Mordecai (Esth. 3:1–9:25). This shows that God is always in control of events, even when wickedness and evil seem to be winning out.

HAMATH [HAY math]

The territory that surrounded the city of Hamath in ancient Syria. In the days of David, the King of Hamath, Toi (or Tou), was friendly to Israel. He congratulated David for defeating their common enemy, King Hadadezer of Damascus (2 Sam. 8:9–10; 1 Chr. 18:9–10). King Solomon later controlled Hamath, where he

built storage depots (2 Chr. 8:4). Archaeological sources reveal that numerous kings of Syria-Palestine—including the king of Hamath, Ahab of Israel, and Ben-Hadad of Damascus—formed an alliance to stop the advance of King Shalmaneser III of Assyria in 853 B.C. at the battle of Qarqar.

About 780 B.C., Jeroboam II, king of Israel, took Hamath for Israel (2 Kin. 14:28). About 722 B.C., Syria-Palestine fell to Assyria. Sargon, king of Assyria, settled colonists from Hamath in cities of Samaria (2 Kin. 17:24; Is. 36:18–20; 37:13, 18–20). The colonists worshiped an idol called Ashima (2 Kin. 17:30), which brought the Lord's anger upon them (2 Kin. 17:25). Likewise, some Israelites were deported from Samaria and settled in Hamath (Is. 11:11).

HAMMURAPI, CODE OF [hah muhr RAH pee]

An ancient law code named after a king who ruled Babylonia from about 1792 to 1750 B.C. These laws from the ancient world are valuable to Bible students because they are so similar to the law as revealed to Moses in the first five books of the Old Testament.

The Code of Hammurapi was discovered in 1901–1902 by the archaeologist V. Scheil at Susa, an early city of the ancient Babylonians. It was written on a seven-foot-high stone monument (called a stele) with the upper part picturing Hammurapi receiving a scepter and a ring, symbols of justice and order, from Shamash, the Babylonian sun-god and divine lawgiver. The rest of the monument contains the code. Hammurapi's law dates from about 300 years after Abraham and some 300 years before the events described in the books of Exodus, Leviticus, and Deuteronomy. This law code was written for a complex urban culture, in contrast to the simple agricultural culture of Palestine.

The contents of Hammurapi's Code are listed as follows:

1. Various offenses and crimes, including false witness, sorcery, corrupt judgment, theft, and kidnapping.

2. Property, with special reference to crown tenants, tenant farmers, and loans of money or seed. The king of Babylon owned crownland in the Old Babylonian period, as did the God of Israel. According to the code, land owned by the king could not be sold.

3. Commercial law, related to partnerships and agencies.

4. Marriage law, including dowry settlements, bridal gifts, divorce, and matrimonial offenses.

5. The firstborn, who had special rights and privileges (compare Deut. 15:19).

6. Special cases involving women and priestesses, whose support was weakened by an increase in state and private ownership of land.

7. Adoption, as it relates to Genesis 17:17–18.

8. Assault and damage to persons and property, including pregnant women, a surgeon's liability in an eye operation, and the hire of boats.

9. Agricultural work and offenses, including goring by an ox (compare Ex. 21:28–32).

10. Rates and wages for seasonal workers, hire of beasts, carts and boats, and so forth.

11. An appendix concerning slaves, including their purchase and sale.

The contents of the Code of Hammurapi and the Law of Moses are similar in many ways. This may be a result of the common cultural background the Babylonians and Israelites shared. Both were ancient peoples of the Near East who inherited their customs and laws from common ancestors. Yet it should be noted that much is different in the Old Testament revelation. For example, the law given at Mount Sinai reflects a unique and high view of the nature of God, and the Old Testament law is presented as an expression of His holy nature, as Leviticus 19:2 clearly shows. Also, when compared with the Code of Hammurapi, the Old Testament law is usually less harsh.

HANDS, LAYING ON OF

The placing of hands upon a person by a body of believers in ceremonial fashion to symbolize that person's authority or his appointment to a special task.

The practice of laying hands on someone or something occurs frequently in the Old Testament—particularly the laying of hands on the head of an animal intended for sacrifice. In the account of the ritual of the Day of Atonement, the priest laid his hands on the scapegoat (Lev. 16:21). This symbolized the transferral of the sins and guilt of the people to the goat, which was taken away into the wilderness. The act of laying on of hands in the Old Testament was also associated with blessing (Gen. 48:18), installation to office (Deut. 34:9), and the setting apart of Levi (Num. 8:10). These passages seem to express the idea of transferral of authority and quality.

In the New Testament, Jesus laid his hands on children (Matt. 19:13, 15) and on the sick when he healed them (Matt. 9:18). In the early church, the laying on of hands was also associated with healing, the reception of the Holy Spirit (Acts 9:17), the setting apart of persons to particular offices and work in the church (Acts 6:6), the commissioning of Barnabas and Paul as missionaries (Acts 13:3), and the setting apart of Timothy (1 Tim. 4:14; 2 Tim. 1:6). The ritual was accompanied by prayer (Acts 6:6).

The laying on of hands was not a magical or superstitious rite that gave a person special power. It expressed the idea of being set apart by God's people for a special task.

HANNAH [HAN nuh] (gracious)

A wife of Elkanah, a Levite of the Kohathite branch of the priesthood (1 Sam. 1:1–2:21). Unable to bear children, Hannah suffered ridicule from Elkanah's other wife Peninnah, who bore him several children. Hannah vowed that if she were to give birth to a son, she would devote him to the Lord's service. The Lord answered her prayers, and to her was born the prophet Samuel.

Hannah was faithful to her promise. Making what must have been a heart-rending sacrifice, Hannah took Samuel to the temple after he was weaned, there to "remain forever" (1:21). God rewarded Hannah's piety and faithfulness with three more sons and two daughters. Hannah's beautiful thanksgiving prayer (2:1–10) is similar to the song that Mary sang when she learned she would be the mother of Jesus (Luke 1:46–55).

HARAN [HAIR uhn] (crossroads)

A city of northern Mesopotamia. Abraham and his father Terah lived there for a time (Gen. 11:31–32; 12:4–5). The family of Abraham's brother Nahor also lived in this city for a time, as did Jacob and his wife Rachel (Gen. 28:10; 29:4–5). The city was on the Balikh, a tributary of the Euphrates River, 240 miles (386 kilometers) northwest of Nineveh and 280 miles (450 kilometers) northeast of Damascus. Haran lay on one of the main trade routes between Babylonia and the Mediterranean Sea. Like the inhabitants of Ur of the Chaldeans, Haran's inhabitants worshiped Sin, the moon-god. Second Kings 19:12 records that the city was captured by the Assyrians. Today Haran is a small Arab village, Harran. The city name is also spelled Charran (Acts 7:2, 4; KJV).

HARLOT

A prostitute. The term *harlot* is often used in a symbolic way in the Old Testament to describe the wicked conduct of the nation of Israel in worshiping false gods (Is. 1:21; Jer. 2:20; Ezek. 16).

In the New Testament, harlots were objects of Jesus' mercy (Matt. 21:31–32; Luke 15:30). The apostle Paul used the term in a warning to the Corinthian church against the prevailing sexual immorality that had made Corinth a byword (1 Cor. 6:15–16). In the Book of Revelation, the term *harlot* is used symbolically of "Babylon the Great"—an apocalyptic image of great moral corruption (Rev. 17:1, 5, 15–16; 19:2).

When the spies entered the Promised Land and came to Jericho, they hid in the house of Rahab the harlot (Josh. 2:1). She made them promise that when the Lord gave Israel the land, she would be spared (Josh. 6:17–25). The New Testament records: "By faith the harlot Rahab did not perish with those who did not believe, when she had received the spies with peace" (Heb. 11:31). Placed among the heroes of faith (Heb. 11:1–40), Rahab brings into bold relief the power of God's love and mercy to transform a person's life. She is listed as one of the ancestors of Jesus (Matt. 1:1–16).

HARP

A stringed musical instrument, also called a lyre. Scholars believe these two instruments were similar in function and design, but the harp was probably a larger version.

The harp is the instrument that David used to soothe the "distressing spirit" that troubled King Saul (1 Sam. 16:16, 23). This smaller lyre was used for sacred ((2 Chr. 29:25) and secular (Is. 23:16) purposes. Although David apparently plucked the strings with his fingers, the harp was usually played by stroking the strings with a pick, much as a guitar is played. The harp had from three to twelve strings. Considered an aristocratic instrument, it was often made of silver or ivory.

HARVEST

The period at the end of the growing season, when crops were gathered. Harvest was one of the happiest times of the year in Palestine (Ps. 126:5–6; Is. 9:3), marked with celebrations and religious festivals (Ex. 23:16). There were two grain harvests. Barley was gathered from mid-April onwards, and wheat from mid-May. The harvest of fruit from trees and vines took place in the fall.

Cutting with a sickle began the process of harvesting grain (Deut. 16:9; Mark 4:29). Then it was gathered into sheaves (Deut. 24:5). Next the grain was taken to the threshing floor, an important local site with a hard surface and often situated on higher ground. Various tools, such as metal-toothed sledges drawn by oxen, were used for threshing (Is. 28:28; 41:15). Then the grain was winnowed, or tossed into the air, with a pitchfork. The wind blew the chaff away, but the heavier kernels and straw fell to the ground (Matt. 3:12). Finally, the kernels were shaken in a sieve, made of a wooden hoop with leather thongs (Is. 30:28; Amos 9:9). Then the grain was stored.

Harvest became a picture of God's judgment (Jer. 51:33; Joel 3:13), and Jesus compared the Last Judgment with the harvest (Matt. 13:30, 39; Rev. 14:14–20). However, Jesus used the same metaphor for the gathering together of those who believed in Him (Matt. 9:37–38; Luke 10:2), indicating that the final harvest has already begun with His first coming (John 4:35).

HAURAN [HOHR uhn]

A region in Transjordan east of the Sea of Galilee, north of the Yarmuk River, and south of Damascus and Mount Hermon. According to Ezekiel's prophetic vision (Ezek. 47:16, 18), Hauran marked the northeastern limits of the land of Israel. Hauran had roughly the same boundaries as the Old Testament Bashan (Num. 21:33). Noted for its rich and fertile volcanic soil, this region became the breadbasket of the land because of its wheat production.

HAZAEL [HAZ a el] (God has seen)

A Syrian official whom the prophet Elijah anointed king over Syria at God's command (1 Kin. 19:15). Some time between 845 and 843 B.C., Ben-Hadad, king of Syria, sent Hazael to the prophet Elisha to ask whether the king would recover from an illness. Elisha answered that Hazael himself was destined to become king. The next day Hazael assassinated Ben-Hadad and took the throne (2 Kin. 8:7–15). Hazael immediately attacked Ramoth Gilead, seriously wounding King Joram of Israel (2 Kin. 8:28–29).

At the end of Jehu's reign over Israel, Hazael attacked the Israelites east of the Jordan River (2 Kin. 10:32). During the reign of Jehu's successor, Jehoahaz, Hazael oppressed Israel because "the anger of the Lord was aroused against Israel" (2 Kin. 13:3). A gift of the dedicated treasures of the temple from King Jehoash of Judah prevented Hazael from attacking Jerusalem (2 Kin. 12:17–18). When Hazael died, his son Ben-Hadad II succeeded him.

HAZOR [HAH zohr] (enclosure)

An ancient Canaanite fortress city in northern Palestine, situated about 10 miles (16 kilometers) northwest of the Sea of Galilee. When Joshua and the Israelites invaded Palestine, Hazor was one of the most important fortresses in the land (Josh. 11:10). This was due to its enormous size, its large population, and its strategic location on the main road between Egypt and Mesopotamia.

When the Israelites approached Palestine, Jabin, the king of Hazor, and several other kings formed an alliance against them. Through God's power the Israelites defeated these armies, killed all the people of Hazor, and burned the city (Josh. 11:1–14). The city regained its strength during the time of the judges. Because of Israel's sinfulness, God allowed the armies of Hazor to oppress the Israelites for 20 years (Judg. 4:1–3). Sisera, the captain of the armies of Hazor, and his 900 chariots were miraculously defeated by God through the efforts of Deborah and Barak (Judg. 4:4–24).

Solomon later chose Hazor as one of his military outposts (1 Kin. 9:15). The rebuilt city continued to play an important part in the northern defenses of Israel until it was destroyed by the Assyrian king, Tiglath-Pileser (2 Kin. 15:29), about ten years before the collapse of the northern kingdom in 722 B.C.

HEART

The inner self that thinks, feels, and decides. In the Bible the word *heart* has a much broader meaning than it does to the modern mind. The heart is that which is central to a person.

H

HARVEST

Nearly all the references to the heart in the Bible refer to some aspect of human personality.

In the Bible all emotions are experienced by the heart: love and hate (Ps. 105:25; 1 Pet. 1:22); joy and sorrow (Eccl. 2:10; John 16:6); peace and bitterness (Ezek. 27:31; Col. 3:15); courage and fear (Gen. 42:28; Amos 2:16). The thinking processes are said to be carried out by the heart. This intellectual activity corresponds to what would be called "mind" in English.

HEAVEN

The dwelling place of God (Gen. 28:17; Rev. 12:7–8). It is the source of the New Jerusalem (Rev. 21:2, 10). Because of the work of Christ on the Cross, heaven is, in part, present with believers on earth as they obey God's commands (John 14:2, 23). At the end of time a new heaven will be created to surround the new earth. This new heaven will be the place of God's perfect presence (Is. 65:17; 66:22; Rev. 21:1). Then there will be a literal fulfillment of heaven on earth.

HEAVENS, NEW

The perfected state of the created universe and the final dwelling place of the righteous. The phrase is found in Isaiah 66:22, 2 Peter 3:13, and in a slightly modified form in Revelation 21:1.

Rooted deep in Jewish thought was the dream of a new heaven and a new earth, a recreation of the universe that would occur following the Day of the Lord (Is. 13:10–13; Joel 2:1–2, 30–31). The concept of a recreated universe is closely related to the biblical account of the creation and the Fall and the sin of Adam and Eve in the Garden of Eden (Gen. 1–3). Because of their sin, "the creation was subjected to futility . . . [and] the bondage of corruption" (Rom. 8:19, 21). The need for a new heaven and a new earth arises from human sin and God's judgment,

not from some deficiency or evil in the universe (Gen. 3:17).

The apostle Paul referred to the Old Testament doctrine of the Day of the Lord and applied it to the events that will occur at the Second Coming of Christ (2 Pet. 3:10, 13). When Christ returns, this present evil age will give way to the age to come. The universe will be purified and cleansed by the power of God. This will be reminiscent of the purging of the earth in the days of Noah, but on a universal scale.

HEBRON [HEE bruhn] (alliance)

A city situated 19 miles (31 kilometers) southwest of Jerusalem on the road to Beersheba. Although it lies in a slight valley, the city is 3,040 feet (927 meters) above sea level, which makes it the highest town in Palestine. Originally Hebron was called Kirjath Arba (Gen. 23:2). Numbers 13:22 speaks of Hebron being built seven years before Zoan in Egypt. This probably refers to the rebuilding of the city by the Hyksos rulers of Egypt. The 12 Hebrew spies viewed Hebron on their mission to explore the Promised Land.

The area surrounding Hebron is rich in biblical history. Abram spent much of his time in Mamre in the area of Hebron (Gen. 13:18). He was living in Mamre when the confederacy of kings overthrew the Cities of the Plain and captured Lot (Gen. 14:1–13). Here, too, Abram's name was changed to Abraham (Gen. 17:5). At Hebron the angels revealed to Abraham that he would have a son who would be called Isaac (Gen. 18:1–15). Later, Sarah died at Hebron (Gen. 23:2); Abraham bought the cave of Machpelah as her burial place (Gen. 23:9). The present mosque built over the cave is called Haran el-Khalil, "the sacred precinct of the friend (of God)," reminiscent of a title given to Abraham in 2 Chronicles 20:7; Isaiah 41:8; James 2:23.

During the period of the conquest of the land of Canaan, Joshua killed the king of Hebron (Josh. 10:3–27). Later, Caleb drove out the Anakim and claimed Hebron for his inheritance (Josh. 14:12–15). Hebron was also designated as one of the cities of refuge (Josh. 20:7). David ruled from Hebron the first seven years of his reign (2 Sam. 2:11), after which he established Jerusalem as his capital.

When Absalom rebelled against his father David, he made Hebron his headquarters (2 Sam. 15:7–12). King Rehoboam fortified the city to protect his southern border (2 Chr. 11:10–12). The discovery of five jar handles stamped with the royal seal dating from the eighth century B.C. testifies that Hebron was a key storage city, perhaps for rations of Uzziah's army (2 Chr. 26:10).

HELL

The place of eternal punishment for the unrighteous. The NKJV and KJV use this word to translate Sheol and Hades, the Old and New Testament words, respectively, for the abode of the dead.

Hell also translates *Gehenna,* the Greek form of the Hebrew phrase that means "the vale of Hinnom"—a valley west and south of Jerusalem. In this valley the Canaanites worshiped Baal and the god Molech by sacrificing their children in a fire that burned continuously. Even Ahaz and Manasseh, kings of Judah, were guilty of this terrible, idolatrous practice (2 Chr. 28:3; 33:6).

The prophet Jeremiah predicted that God would visit such destruction upon Jerusalem that this valley would be known as the "Valley of Slaughter" (Jer. 7:31–34; 19:2, 6). In his religious reforms, King Josiah put an end to this worship. He defiled the valley in order to make it unfit even for pagan worship (2 Kin. 23:10).

In the time of Jesus, the Valley of Hinnom was used as the garbage dump of Jerusalem. Into it were thrown all the filth and garbage of the city, including the dead bodies of animals and executed criminals. To consume all this, fires burned constantly. Maggots worked in the filth. When the wind blew from that direction over the city, its awfulness was quite evident. At night wild dogs howled as they fought over the garbage.

Jesus used this awful scene as a symbol of hell. In effect he said, "Do you want to know what hell is like? Look at Gehenna." So hell may be described as God's "cosmic garbage dump." All that is unfit for heaven will be thrown into hell.

The Book of Revelation describes hell as "a lake of fire burning with brimstone" (Rev. 19:20; 20:10, 14–15; 21:8). Into hell will be thrown the Beast and the False Prophet (Rev. 19:20). At the end of the age the devil himself will be thrown into it, along with death and Hades and all whose names are not in the Book of Life. "And they will be tormented day and night forever and ever" (Rev. 20:10b).

Because of the symbolic nature of the language, some people question whether hell consists of actual fire. Such reasoning should bring no comfort to the lost. The reality is greater than the symbol. The Bible exhausts human language in describing heaven and hell. The former is more glorious, and the latter more terrible, than language can express.

See also SHEOL.

HELLENISM [HELL un is em]

A style of Greek civilization associated with the spread of Greek language and culture to the Mediterranean world after the conquests of Alexander the Great. On the advice of Aristotle, his teacher, Alexander sought to instill a love for the Greek way of life within those whom he conquered. His generals adopted the same pattern of operation. Conflict soon arose between the Jews and his successors in Israel, the Seleucids. The history of this conflict is detailed in the books of the Maccabees.

HERALD

A person responsible for bearing a message, often in preparation for the appearance of a king or other royal figure. The heralds ran before the king's chariot to announce his coming. Heralds also were responsible for announcing the king's messages (Dan. 3:4). The Aramaic word for herald is sometimes translated "to preach" (Matt. 3:1; 4:17). Hence, New Testament preachers are heralds of the King. Heralds are also sometimes referred to as messengers.

HERESY

False doctrine, or teaching that denies one of the foundational beliefs of the church, such as the lordship or deity of Jesus. In the Book of 2 Corinthians, Paul condemned certain "false apostles" and "deceitful workers" who claimed to be "apostles of Christ" (2 Cor. 11:13). These may have been the Judaizers, who tried to force believers to observe the Jewish ritual of circumcision before they could be accepted as members of the church.

HERMES [HUR meez] (interpreter)

The Greek god of commerce who served as the messenger of the other gods. He corresponded to the Roman god Mercury (Acts 14:12; Mercurius, KJV).

HERMON, MOUNT [HUR mon] (sacred place)

The northern boundary of the land east of the Jordan River that Israel took from the Amorites (Deut. 3:8; Josh. 12:1). The mountain is the southern end of the Anti-Lebanon range and is about 20 miles (32 kilometers) long. It has three peaks (Ps. 42:6), two of which rise over 9,000 feet (2,750 meters) above sea level.

Hermon was regarded as a sacred place by the Canaanites, who inhabited the land before the Israelites (Judg. 3:3). Snow covers the mountain during most of the year. Patches of snow remain even through the summer in shaded ravines. The beautiful snow-covered peaks of Mount Hermon can be seen from the region of the Dead Sea, over 120 miles (196 kilometers) distant. The glaciers of Mount Hermon are a major source of the Jordan River, and water from its slopes ultimately flows into the Dead Sea.

The psalmist speaks of the "dew of Hermon" (Ps. 133:3). The snow condenses to vapor during the summer, so that a heavy dew descends on the mountain while the areas surrounding Hermon are parched.

Mount Hermon probably was the site of Jesus' transfiguration (Matt. 17:1–9; Mark 9:2–9; Luke 9:28–37). Jesus traveled with His disciples from Bethsaida, on the Sea of Galilee, to the area of Caesarea Philippi to the north and from there to a "high mountain." There, in the presence of His disciples, Jesus was transfigured.

HEROD [HEHR ud]

1. Herod the Great (37–4 B.C.), a Roman ruler in Palestine. The title Herod the Great refers not so much to Herod's greatness as to the fact that he was the eldest son of Antipater, procurator of Judea. Nevertheless, Herod did show some unusual abilities. He was a ruthless fighter, a cunning negotiator, and a subtle diplomat. The Romans appreciated the way he subdued opposition and maintained order among the Jewish people. These qualities, combined with an intense loyalty to the emperor, made him an important figure in the life of Rome and the Jews of Palestine.

After Herod became governor of Galilee, he quickly established himself in the entire region. For 33 years he remained a loyal friend and ally of Rome. He was appointed as king of Judea, where he was in direct control of the Jewish people. This required careful diplomacy because he was always suspect by the Jews as an outsider (Idumean) and thus a threat to their national right to rule.

At first Herod was conscious of Jewish national and religious feelings. He moved slowly on such issues as taxation, Hellenism, and religion. He did much to improve his relationship with the Jews when he prevented the temple in Jerusalem from being raided and defiled by invading Romans.

Herod the Great established his authority and influence through a centralized bureaucracy, well-built fortresses, and foreign soldiers. To assure his continued rule, he slaughtered all male infants who could possibly be considered legal heirs to the throne. His wife Mariamne also became a victim.

The territories under Herod's rule experienced economic and cultural growth. His business and organizational ability led to the erection of many important buildings. Hellenistic (Greek) ideas were introduced into Palestine through literature, art, and athletic contests. His major building project was the temple complex in Jerusalem, which, according to John 2:20, had taken 46 years to build up to that time. From the Jewish perspective, this was his greatest achievement.

At times Herod implemented his policies with force and cruelty. His increasing fear of Jewish revolt led to suppression of any opposition. His personal problems also increased, and by 14 B.C. his kingdom began to decline. This decline was brought on mainly by his personal and domestic problems.

Herod's murder of his wife Mariamne apparently haunted him. This was compounded when his two sons from that marriage, Alexander and Aristobulus, re-

alized that their father was responsible for their mother's death. By 7 B.C., Herod had both of these sons put to death. Of Herod it was said, "It is better to be Herod's pig (hys) than to be his son (huios)."

As Herod became increasingly ill, an intense struggle for succession to his throne emerged within the family. His 10 marriages and 15 children virtually guaranteed such a struggle. One son, Antipater, poisoned Herod's mind against two other eligible sons, Archelaus and Philip. This resulted in his initial choice of a younger son, Antipas, as sole successor. However, he later changed his will and made Archelaus king. Antipas and Philip received lesser positions as Tetrarchs, or rulers, over small territories.

After Herod died, his will was contested in Rome. Finally Archelaus was made ethnarch over Idumea, Judea, and Samaria—with a promise to be appointed king if he proved himself as a leader. Antipas became tetrarch over Galilee and Perea. Philip was made tetrarch over Gaulanitis, Trachonitis, Batanea, and Paneas in the northern regions.

Jesus was born in Bethlehem during the reign of Herod the Great. The wise men came asking, "Where is he that is born King of the Jews?" This aroused Herod's jealous spirit. According to Matthew's account, Herod tried to eliminate Jesus by having all the male infants of the Bethlehem region put to death (Matt. 2:13–16). But this despicable act failed. Joseph and Mary were warned by God in a dream to take their child and flee to Egypt. Here they hid safely until Herod died (Matt. 2:13–15).

HEROD [HEHR ud]

2. Herod Archelaus (4 B.C.–A.D. 6). Archelaus inherited his father Herod's vices without his abilities. He was responsible for much bloodshed in Judea

and Samaria. Jewish revolts, particularly those led by the Zealots, were brutally crushed. Antipas and Philip did not approve of Archelaus's methods; so they complained to Rome. Their complaints were followed by a Jewish delegation that finally succeeded in having Archelaus stripped of power and banished to Rome.

The only biblical reference to Archelaus occurs in Matthew 2:22. Matthew recorded the fear that Mary and Joseph had about going through Judea on their way from Egypt to Galilee because Archelaus was the ruler.

HEROD [HEHR ud]

3. Herod Philip the Tetrarch (4 B.C.–A.D. 30). Philip, who inherited the northern part of his father Herod the Great's kingdom (Luke 3:1), must have been the best of Herod's surviving sons. During his long and peaceful rule, he was responsible for a number of building projects, including the city of Caesarea Philippi. He also rebuilt Bethsaida into a Greek city and renamed it Julias in honor of Augustus Caesar's daughter, Julia.

HEROD [HEHR ud]

4. Herod Antipas (4 B.C.–A.D. 39). Antipas, another of Herod the Great's sons, began as tetrarch over Galilee and Perea. He was the ruling Herod during Jesus' life and ministry. Herod Antipas was first married to the daughter of Aretas, a Nabatean king. But he became infatuated with Herodias, the wife of his half brother, Philip I. The two eloped, although both were married at the time. This scandalous affair was condemned severely by John the Baptist (Matt. 14:4; Mark 6:17–18; Luke 3:19).

Although Antipas apparently had some respect for John the Baptist, he had John arrested and imprisoned for his outspokenness. Later, at a royal birthday party,

Antipas granted Salome, the daughter of Herod Philip, a wish. Probably at the prodding of Herodias (Mark 6:19), Salome requested the head of John the Baptist (Matt. 14:6–12; Mark 6:21–29). Since he was under oath and did not want to lose face before his guests, Herod ordered John's execution.

Antipas's contacts with Jesus occurred at the same time as the ministry of John the Baptist. Because of Jesus' popularity and miraculous powers, Antipas may have been haunted by the possibility that Jesus was John the Baptist come back to life.

The New Testament record shows that the relationship between Jesus and Antipas must have been strained. Jesus' popularity and teachings may have threatened Antipas who, according to the Pharisees, sought to kill Him (Luke 13:31). By calling Herod a fox "Go, tell that fox," (Luke 13:32), Jesus showed His disapproval of his cunning and deceitful ways.

The next encounter between Antipas and Jesus occurred at the trial of Jesus (Luke 23:6–12). Luke indicated that Herod could not find anything in the charges against Jesus that deserved death; so he sent Jesus back to Pilate for a final decision.

During this time of his rule, Antipas was experiencing political problems of his own. Aretas, the Nabatean king whose daughter had been Antipas's wife before he became involved with Herodias, returned to avenge this insult. Antipas's troops were defeated. This, together with some other problems, led to his political downfall. Antipas was finally banished by the Roman emperor to an obscure section of France.

HERODIANS [heh ROW dee uns]

Jews of influence and standing who were favorable toward Greek customs and Roman law in New Testament times.

Although the Herodians should not be equated with the Sadducees, they sided with the Sadducees in their pro-Roman sympathies and opposed the Pharisees, who were anti-Roman. The Herodians joined forces with the Pharisees, however, in their opposition to Jesus.

In Galilee, the Herodians and the Pharisees plotted against Jesus' life (Mark 3:6). At Jerusalem, the Herodians and the Pharisees again joined forces, seeking to trap Jesus on the issue of paying tribute to Caesar (Matt. 22:16; Mark 12:13). Jesus warned his disciples, "Take heed, beware of the leaven [evil influence] of the Pharisees and . . . of Herod" (Mark 8:15).

HERODIAS [heh ROE dee uhs]

The queen who demanded John the Baptist's head on a platter (Matt. 14:1–12). The granddaughter of Herod the Great, Herodias first married her father's brother, Herod Philip I. One child was born to this union. Philip's half brother, the tetrarch Herod Antipas, wanted Herodias for his own wife, so he divorced his wife and married Herodias while Philip was still living.

When John the Baptist denounced their immorality, Herodias plotted John's death. She had her daughter Salome gain Herod's favor by dancing seductively for him at a banquet. As a result, Herod promised her anything she wanted. Following her mother's wishes, Salome asked for the head of John the Baptist.

HEZEKIAH [hez uh KIGH uh] *(the Lord is my strength)*

The thirteenth king of Judah. Born the son of Ahaz by Abi, daughter of Zechariah, Hezekiah became known as one of Judah's godly kings. That an ungodly man like Ahaz could have such a godly son can only be attributed to the grace of God. Hezekiah's father had given the

kingdom over to idolatry; but upon his accession to the throne, Hezekiah courageously initiated religious reforms (2 Kin. 18:4).

In the first month of his reign, Hezekiah reopened the temple doors that his father had closed. He also assembled the priests and Levites and commissioned them to sanctify themselves for service and to cleanse the temple. Appropriate sacrifices were then offered with much rejoicing (2 Chr. 29:3–36).

Hezekiah faced a golden opportunity to reunite the tribes spiritually. In the north Israel had fallen to Assyria in 722 B.C. Hezekiah invited the remnant of the people to come to Jerusalem to participate in the celebration of the Passover. Although some northern tribes scorned the invitation, most responded favorably (2 Chr. 30:1–27).

Hezekiah's reformation reached beyond Jerusalem to include the cleansing of the land, extending even to the tribes of Benjamin, Ephraim, and Manasseh. High places, images, and pagan altars were destroyed. The bronze serpent that Moses had made in the wilderness centuries earlier (Num. 21:5–9) had been preserved, and people were worshiping it. Hezekiah had it destroyed also (2 Kin. 18:4; 2 Chr. 31:1). The land had never undergone such a thorough reform.

When Hezekiah experienced a serious illness, the prophet Isaiah informed the king that he would die. In response to Hezekiah's prayer for recovery, God promised him 15 additional years of life. God also provided a sign for Hezekiah as evidence that the promise would be fulfilled. The sign, one of the most remarkable miracles of the Old Testament, consisted of the sun's shadow moving backward ten degrees on the Sundial of Ahaz (Is. 38:1–8).

Shortly after he recovered from his illness (Is. 39:1), Hezekiah received visitors from the Babylonian king, Merodach-Baladan (2 Kin. 20:12). They came with letters to congratulate Hezekiah on his recovery and to inquire about the sign (2 Chr. 32:31) in the land. But their real reason for visiting may have been to gain an ally in their revolt against Assyria. When they lavished gifts upon Hezekiah, he in turn showed them his wealth—an action that brought stiff rebuke from Isaiah (2 Kin. 20:13–18).

There is no evidence to indicate that Hezekiah formed an alliance with Babylon. Neither is there any indication that he joined the rebellion in 711 B.C. led by Ashdod, the leading Philistine city. However, Scripture does reveal that he finally did rebel. Sargon II had died in 705 B.C.; and his successor, Sennacherib, was preoccupied with trying to consolidate the kingdom when Hezekiah rebelled. With that accomplished, however, Sennacherib was ready to crush Hezekiah's revolt.

Anticipating the Assyrian aggression, Hezekiah made extensive military preparations. He strengthened the fortifications of Jerusalem, produced weapons and shields for his army, and organized his fighting forces under trained combat commanders. Realizing the importance of an adequate water supply, Hezekiah constructed a tunnel that channeled water from the Spring of Gihon outside the city walls to the Pool of Siloam inside the walls (2 Kin. 20:20). This waterway (now known as Hezekiah's Tunnel) was cut through solid rock, extending more than 1,700 feet (520 meters).

As Sennacherib captured the fortified cities of Judah, Hezekiah realized that his revolt was a lost cause and he attempted to appease the Assyrian king. To send an apology and tribute, he emptied the palace treasuries and the temple, even stripping the gold from the doors and pillars. But this failed to appease Sennacherib's anger.

At the height of the Assyrian siege, the angel of the Lord struck the Assyrian camp, leaving 185,000 dead (2 Kin. 19:35). In humiliation and defeat, Sennacherib withdrew to his capital city of Nineveh.

Little more is said about Hezekiah's remaining years as king, but his achievements are recorded in 2 Chronicles 32:27–30. When he died, after reigning for 29 years, the people of Jerusalem "buried him in the upper tombs of the sons of David" (2 Chr. 32:33), a place of honor.

HIERAPOLIS [HIGH uh rap uh lis]
(priestly city)

A city of the district of Phrygia in southwest Asia Minor (modern Turkey). One of the three major cities of the Lycus River Valley, it was about 10 miles (16 kilometers) northwest of Colossae (Col. 4:13). According to tradition, Philip the evangelist was the first Christian messenger to Hierapolis. Christianity apparently flourished in the city.

HIGH PLACES

Elevated or hilltop sites dedicated to worship of pagan gods. Ancient peoples often built their shrines on hilltops. In Mesopotamia, where the land is flat, they built artificial mountains in the shape of step pyramids called ziggurats. The Tower of Babel (Gen. 11:1–9) was probably such a ziggurat.

Most of the Old Testament references to high places imply a form of pagan worship forbidden to the Israelites. But sometimes the Lord's people, with His approval, worshiped Him at elevated altars. This happened between the time Shiloh was destroyed and before the ark of the covenant was installed in Solomon's temple. For instance, Samuel blessed the offerings made at a high place that perhaps was Ramah, a word that itself means "high place" (1 Sam. 9:12–14). At nearby Gibeon there was a high place. During the reign of David the tabernacle was there (1 Chr. 16:39; 21:29; 2 Chr. 1:3–4). At this high place Solomon made many sacrifices, had his dream, and asked God for wisdom (1 Kin. 3:4–15).

After this early period in Israel's history, all high places mentioned in the Bible were off limits to God's people. In Leviticus 26:30 God promised to destroy the high places, which He knew His people would later build. They probably got the idea for such shrines of worship from the native Canaanites.

In his waning years, Solomon established high places for his pagan wives (1 Kin. 11:7–8). After Solomon's death, the rebellious northern kingdom had its high places. The two major ones, containing golden calves, were at Dan and Bethel (1 Kin. 12:28–33). Then as evil kings came to the throne in Judah they inaugurated high places, and successive good kings abolished them. During Rehoboam's reign, high places appeared (1 Kin. 14:23), but Hezekiah broke them down (2 Kin. 18:4). Wicked Manasseh built them again (2 Kin. 21:3), but righteous Josiah dismantled them (2 Kin. 23:8). Eventually, "high place" became a general term for a pagan shrine, whether or not it was established in an elevated site.

The prophets condemned the high places (Jer. 17:1–3; 32:35; Ezek. 6:3; Amos 7:9). God is not found on a mountaintop or at a hilltop shrine. He is everywhere, always ready to listen to the prayers of those who call on him (John 4:21–24).

HINNOM, VALLEY OF [HIN nahm]

A deep, narrow ravine west and south of Jerusalem. At the high places of Baal in the Valley of Hinnom, parents sacrificed their children as a burnt offering to Molech (2 Kin. 23:10). Ahaz and Manasseh, kings of Judah, were both guilty of this awful wickedness (2 Chr. 28:3;

33:6). But good King Josiah destroyed the pagan altars to remove this temptation from the people of Judah.

The prophet Jeremiah foretold that God would judge this awful abomination of human sacrifice and would cause such a destruction that "the Valley of the Son of Hinnom" would become known as "the Valley of Slaughter" (Jer. 7:31–32; 19:2, 6; 32:35). The place was also called "Tophet."

Apparently, the Valley of Hinnom was used as the garbage dump for the city of Jerusalem. Refuse, waste materials, and dead animals were burned here. Fires continually smoldered, and smoke from the burning debris rose day and night. Hinnom thus became a graphic symbol of woe and judgment and of the place of eternal punishment called hell.

Translated into Greek, the Hebrew "Valley of Hinnom" becomes *Gehenna,* which is used 12 times in the New Testament (11 times by Jesus and once by James), each time translated as "hell" (Matt. 5:22; Mark 9:43, 45, 47; Luke 12:5; James 3:6).

See also Tophet.

HIRAM [HIGH rum] *(my brother is exalted)*

A king of Tyre and friend of both David and Solomon (2 Sam. 5:11; 1 Kin. 10:11, 22; 2 Chr. 8:2, 18). The Jewish historian Josephus records that Hiram succeeded his father, Abibaal, and reigned for 34 years. Hiram greatly enhanced the city of Tyre, building an embankment on its east side and a causeway to connect the city with the island where the temple of Baal-Shamem stood.

Hiram appears throughout the reigns of David and Solomon. He sent representatives to David after David captured Jerusalem. When David built a palace, Hiram furnished cedar from Lebanon and workmen to assist with the project. In later years, when Solomon built the temple in Jerusalem, Hiram again sent cedar and skilled laborers—this time in return for wheat and olive oil. Hiram also supplied ships and sailors for Solomon's trade interests, probably for a share of the profits.

HITTITES [HIT tights]

A people of the ancient world who flourished in Asia Minor between about 1900 and 1200 B.C. The name Hittite comes from Hatti, another name for Anatolia, the capital of which was Hattusha. Later the Hittites spread into northern Syria and populated such cities as Aleppo, Carchemish, and Hamath. The Old Testament contains many references to the Hittites (Gen. 15:20; Num. 13:29; 1 Kin. 10:29; Ezra 9:1; Ezek. 16:3, 45).

When Sarah died, Abraham purchased the field of Machpelah with a burial cave from Ephron the Hittite (Gen. 23:10–20). This incident between a patriarch and a Hittite was followed later by Esau's act of taking two Hittite women as wives (Gen. 26:34).

Hittites were included among the peoples dwelling from the river of Egypt to the river Euphrates—the region promised to Abraham. Hittites also occupied the land of Canaan while the Israelites were in Egypt. They were among the people who had to be driven out when Israel conquered Canaan under Joshua (Ex. 3:8, 17; Deut. 7:1; Judg. 3:5).

After the dissolution of the Hittite empire, remnants of the Hittites were particularly visible in Palestine during the reign of David. Ahimelech the Hittite was among the close associates and trusted companions of David during his flight from Saul (1 Sam. 26:6). The most famous of these later Hittites was Uriah, Bathsheba's husband, whom David sent to his death to conceal his adultery with Uriah's wife (2 Sam. 11:15). The northern border of Israel during David's time was extended to the river Euphrates (2 Sam.

8:3) to include Syrian city-states. It is highly possible that "Hittites" of the Syrian region served in David's administration (2 Sam. 8:17; 1 Kin. 4:3).

Solomon had a Hittite wife (1 Kin. 11:1), apparently from a royal marriage to seal an alliance with a foreign power. After Solomon's time, the "kings of the Hittites" were powerful rulers in Syria during the time when Judah and Israel existed as separate kingdoms (2 Kin. 7:6; 2 Chr. 1:17).

The Hittites themselves described their array of pagan gods as "the thousand gods." Among this diversity of deities, there were many names that were Hattic, Hurrian, Sumerian, and Canaanite in origin. The names of many gods occur in treaties of the Hittite people as guardian deities over the parties bound by treaty commitments. Each god was worshiped in its own native language. A storm god was the chief male god, and a solar goddess was his mistress.

The Hittites may have been one of the pagan influences that pulled the nation of Israel away from worship of the one true God during its long history. Students of the Old Testament point out that the Hittites formed treaties with other countries long before the Hebrew people developed the consciousness of being a nation governed directly by God. Some scholars believe these treaties were used as a model for the covenant that God established with the Hebrews at Mt. Sinai.

HIVITES [HIGH vights]

A people descended from Canaan (Gen. 10:17) who lived in the land before and after Israel's conquest of the land of Canaan (Ex. 13:5; Deut. 7:1; Josh. 11:3; Judg. 3:5; 1 Kin. 9:20). No reference to the Hivites exists outside the Bible. Many scholars think the name "Hivite" is an early scribal error for "Horite" (Hurrian). Other scholars suggest that the Hivites were a smaller group within the Horites.

The Bible indicates that the Hivites lived near Tyre and Sidon (2 Sam. 24:7), in the hill country of Lebanon (Judg. 3:3), in Mizpah near Mount Hermon (Josh. 11:3), in central Palestine at Shechem (Gen. 34:2), and in the town of Gibeon north of Jerusalem (Josh. 9:7; 11:19).

Many Hivites were murdered by Simeon and Levi, sons of Jacob, after a member of a Hivite clan assaulted their sister Dinah (Gen. 34). Later, the Israelites were commanded to take Canaan from various groups of Canaanites, including Hivites (Ex. 13:5; 23:23, 28).

Hivites from Gibeon tricked Joshua and the Israelites into making a covenant with them (Josh. 9). Joshua spared the Hivites and made them servants (Josh. 9:27). Hivites were also among those Canaanites whom Solomon used as slave laborers for his building projects (1 Kin. 9:20–21; 2 Chr. 8:7–8).

HOLY

Moral and ethical wholeness or perfection; freedom from moral evil. Holiness is one of the essential elements of God's nature required of His people. The Hebrew word for "holy" denotes that which is "sanctified" or "set apart" for divine service.

While "holy" is sometimes used in a ceremonial sense, the main use is to describe God's righteous nature or the ethical righteousness demanded of His followers (Is. 1:10–14). Originating in God's nature, holiness is a unique quality of His character. The Bible emphasizes this divine attribute. "Who shall not fear You, O Lord . . . For You alone are holy" (Rev. 15:4). God's high expectations of His people flow out of His own holy nature: "You shall be holy, for I the LORD your God am holy" (Lev. 19:2).

Jesus was the personification of holiness; He reinforced God's demands for holiness by insisting that His disciples have a higher quality and degree of righteousness than that of the scribes and Pharisees (Matt. 5:20). Like Amos and Hosea, Jesus appealed for more than ceremonial holiness: "I desire mercy and not sacrifice" (Hos. 6:6; Matt. 12:7).

The theme of sanctification, or growing into God's likeness and being consecrated for His use, is prominent throughout the Bible. Like Jesus, the apostles taught that sanctification, or true holiness, expressed itself in patient and loving service while awaiting the Lord's return.

HOLY PLACE

KJV term for the most sacred inner room in the tabernacle and the temple, where only the high priest was allowed to go. This room, separated from the rest of the worship area by a sacred veil, represented the presence of God in all His power and holiness. In this room was the ark of the covenant, covered by the sacred mercy seat (Ex. 25:10–22). Once a year on the Day of Atonement, the high priest entered the Holy Place with sacrificial blood and made atonement before God for the sins of the people (Lev. 16).

HOLY SPIRIT

The Third Person of the Trinity who exercises the power of the Father and the Son in creation and redemption. Because the Holy Spirit is the power by which believers come to Christ and see with new eyes of faith, He is closer to us than we are to ourselves. Like the eyes of the body through which we see physical things, He is seldom in focus to be seen directly because He is the one through whom all else is seen in a new light. This explains why the relationship of the Father and the Son is more prominent in the gospels, because it is through the eyes of the Holy Spirit that the Father-Son relationship is viewed.

The Holy Spirit appears in the Gospel of John as the power by which Christians are brought to faith and helped to understand their walk with God. He brings a person to New Birth: "That which is born of the flesh is flesh, and that which is born of the Spirit is spirit" (John 3:6); "It is the Spirit who gives life" (John 6:63). The Holy Spirit is the Paraclete, or Helper, whom Jesus promised to the disciples after His ascension. The Trinity of Father, Son, and Holy Spirit are unified in ministering to believers (John 14:16, 26). It is through the Helper that Father and Son abide with the disciples (John 15:26).

This unified ministry of the Trinity is also seen as the Spirit brings the world under conviction of sin, righteousness, and judgment. He guides believers into all truth with what He hears from the Father and the Son (John 15:26). It is a remarkable fact that each of the Persons of the Trinity serves the others as all defer to one another: The Son says what He hears from the Father (John 12:49–50); the Father witnesses to and glorifies the Son (John 8:16–18, 50, 54); the Father and Son honor the Holy Spirit by commissioning Him to speak in their name (John 14:16, 26); the Holy Spirit honors the Father and Son by helping the community of believers.

Like Father and Son, the Holy Spirit is

HOLY SPIRIT

WRITING PROPHECY IS EASY WHEN THE HOLY GHOSTWRITER TELLS ME WHAT TO SAY.

JONNY HAWKINS

at the disposal of the other Persons of the Trinity, and all three are one in graciously being at the disposal of the redeemed family of believers. The Holy Spirit's attitude and ministry are marked by generosity; His chief function is to illumine Jesus' teaching, to glorify His person, and to work in the life of the individual believer and the church.

During His ministry, Jesus referred to the Spirit of God (Matt. 12:28–29; Luke 11:20) as the power by which He was casting out demons, thereby invading the stronghold of Beelzebub and freeing those held captive. Accordingly, the Spirit works with the Father and Son in realizing the redeeming power of the kingdom of God. God's kingdom is not only the reign of the Son but also the reign of the Spirit, as all share in the reign of the Father.

The person and ministry of the Holy Spirit in the Gospels is confirmed by His work in the early church. The baptism with the Holy Spirit (Acts 1:5) is the pouring out of the Spirit's power in missions and evangelism (Acts 1:8). This prophecy of Jesus (and of Joel 2:28–32) began on Pentecost (Acts 2:1–18). Many of those who heard of the finished work of God in Jesus' death and resurrection (Acts 2:32–38) repented of their sins. In this act of repentance, they received the gift of the Holy Spirit (Acts 2:38), becoming witnesses of God's grace through the Spirit.

Paul's teaching about the Holy Spirit harmonizes with the accounts of the Spirit's activity in the gospels and Acts. According to Paul, it is by the Holy Spirit that one confesses that Jesus is Lord (1 Cor. 12:3). Through the same Spirit varieties of gifts are given to the body of Christ to ensure its richness and unity (1 Cor. 12:4–27). The Holy Spirit is the way to Jesus Christ the Son (Rom. 8:11) and to the Father (Rom. 8:14–15). He is the person who bears witness to us that we are children of God (8:16–17). He

"makes intercession for us with groanings which cannot be uttered" (Rom. 8:26–27).

The Holy Spirit also reveals to Christians the deep things of God (1 Cor. 2:10–12) and the mystery of Christ (Eph. 3:3–5). The Holy Spirit acts with God and Christ as the pledge or guarantee by which believers are sealed for the day of salvation (2 Cor. 1:21–22), by which they walk and live (Rom. 8:3–6) and abound in hope with power (Rom. 15:13). Against the lust and enmity of the flesh Paul contrasts the fruit of the Spirit: "Love, joy, peace, longsuffering, kindness, goodness, faithfulness, gentleness, self-control" (Gal. 5:22–23).

Although the phrase "Holy Spirit" occurs only three times in the Old Testament (Ps. 51:11; Is. 63:10–11), the Spirit's work is everywhere evident. The Spirit is the energy of God in creation (Gen. 1:2; Job 26:13; Is. 32:15). God endows human beings with personal life by breathing into their nostrils the breath of life (Gen. 2:7). The Spirit strives with fallen humankind (Gen. 6:3) and comes upon certain judges and warriors with charismatic power (Joshua, Num. 27:18; Othniel, Judg. 3:10; Gideon, Judg. 6:34; Samson, Judg. 13:25; 14:6). However, the Spirit departs from Saul because of his disobedience (1 Sam. 16:14).

In the long span of Old Testament prophecy, the Spirit played a prominent role. David declared, "The Spirit of the Lord spoke by me, and His word was on my tongue" (2 Sam. 23:2). Ezekiel claimed that "the Spirit entered me when He spoke to me" (Ezek. 2:2). The Spirit also inspired holiness in the Old Testament believer (Ps. 143:10). It also promised to give a new heart to God's people: "I will put My Spirit within you, and cause you to walk in My statutes" (Ezek. 36:27).

This anticipates the crucial work of the Spirit in the ministry of the Messiah.

H

The prophecy of Isaiah 11:1–5 is a Trinitarian preview of the working of the Father, the Spirit, and the Son, who is the Branch of Jesse. Looking forward to the ministry of Jesus Christ, the Holy Spirit inspired Isaiah to prophesy: "The Spirit of the Lord shall rest upon Him" (Is. 11:2). The Holy Spirit inspired Jesus with wisdom, understanding, counsel, might, knowledge, fear of the Lord, righteousness, and faithfulness. Thus we come full cycle to the New Testament where Jesus claims the fulfillment of this prophecy in Himself (Is. 61:1–2; Luke 4:18–19).

HOPE

Confident expectancy. Hope does not arise from the individual's desires or wishes but from God, who is Himself the believer's hope (Ps. 39:7). Genuine hope is not wishful thinking, but a firm assurance about things that are unseen and still in the future (Heb. 11:1, 7).

Hope distinguishes the Christian from the unbeliever, who has no hope (1 Thess. 4:13). Indeed, a Christian is one in whom hope resides (1 Pet. 3:15). In contrast to Old Testament hope, the Christian hope is superior (Heb. 7:19). Christian hope comes from God (Rom. 15:13) and especially His calling (Eph. 1:18), His grace (2 Thess. 2:16), His Word (Rom. 15:4) and His gospel (Col. 1:23).

HOPHNI [HOFF nigh] *(tadpole)*

A son of Eli the high priest who, along with his brother Phinehas, proved unworthy of priestly duties (1 Sam. 1:3; 2:34; 4:4–17). Their behavior was characterized by greed (1 Sam. 2:13–16) and lust (1 Sam. 2:22). Eli made only a halfhearted attempt to control his sons' scandalous behavior. Consequently, God's judgment was pronounced upon Eli and his household. Hophni and Phinehas were killed in a battle, and the ark of the covenant was captured by the Philistines (1 Sam. 4:1–11). When Eli heard the news, he fell backward and died of a broken neck (1 Sam. 4:12–18).

See also PHINEHAS.

HOPHRA [HOFF ruh]

A king of Egypt who reigned 589–570 B.C. Early in his reign, Hophra marched against Babylonia's Nebuchadnezzar II, who had besieged Jerusalem in 589 B.C. When the Babylonians turned from Jerusalem to challenge him, Hophra retreated to Egypt. Hophra's overthrow was foretold by the prophet Jeremiah (Jer. 44:30).

HOR, MOUNT [hoer]

The mountain on the border of the Edomites where Aaron died and was buried (Num. 20:22–29; Deut. 32:50). Numbers 20:23 indicates that Mount Hor was situated by the border of the land of Edom. This was the place where the Hebrew people stopped after they left Kadesh (Num. 20:22; 33:37).

Early tradition established Jebel Harun, meaning "Aaron's Mountain," as the site of Mount Hor. It is a conspicuous mountain about 4,800 feet (1,440 meters) high on the eastern side of the Arabah, midway between the southern tip of the Dead Sea and the northern end of the Gulf of Aqaba. However, this peak is far from Kadesh. In recent years Jebel Madurah northeast of Kadesh on the northwest border of Edom has been suggested as the more likely site for Mount Hor.

HORSE

Horses are mentioned often in the Bible. But they were of little importance to the average Hebrew, who found it more practical to keep a donkey to ride or an ox to pull the plow. Horses were traded for food when money failed during a famine in Egypt (Gen. 47:17). Some kings used swift horses rather than camels to carry messages (Esth. 8:10, 14). But for the most part, Hebrews thought of horses in terms of war.

Pharaoh's horses and chariots pursued when Moses led the Israelites out of Egypt (Ex. 14:9). Their Canaanite enemies met them with many horses and chariots, but they still fell before the Israelites (Josh. 11:4–9). Repeatedly God warned the Hebrews not to place their faith in the strength and speed of horses (Ps. 20:7) or to "multiply" horses (Deut. 17:16). In spite of these warnings, David and Solomon did multiply horses, even importing them from other countries. Solomon had a sizeable cavalry as well as horses to draw war chariots.

The prophet Jeremiah used the word *stallion* in speaking of horses (Jer. 8:16; 47:3; 50:11, NRSV, NIV). He warned the nation of Judah that it would fall to a conquering army that would be riding prancing stallions. He also used the symbol of a "well-fed, lusty stallion" (Jer. 5:8, NKJV) to describe the idolatry and unfaithfulness of God's people.

The New Testament tells of the "Four Horsemen of the Apocalypse," who ride out to ravage the earth in the end times (Rev. 6:1–8). But even more dramatic than this is the entrance of a white horse bearing the "King of kings and Lord of lords" (Rev. 19:11–16).

HOSEA [hoe ZAY uh] *(deliverance)*

An Old Testament prophet and author of the Book of Hosea. The son of Beeri (Hos. 1:1), Hosea ministered in the northern kingdom of Israel during the chaotic period just before the fall of this nation in 722 B.C. The literary features within Hosea's book suggest he was a member of the upper class. The tone and contents of the book also show he was a man of deep compassion, strong loyalty, and keen awareness of the political events taking place in the world at that time. As a prophet, he was also deeply committed to God and His will as it was being revealed to His covenant people.

Hosea is one of the most unusual prophets of the Old Testament, since he was commanded by God to marry a prostitute (Hos. 1:2–9). His wife Gomer eventually returned to her life of sin, but Hosea bought her back from the slave market and restored her as his wife (Hos. 3:1–5). His unhappy family experience was an object lesson of the sin or "harlotry" of the nation of Israel in rejecting the one true God and serving pagan gods. Although the people deserved to be rejected because they had turned their backs on God, Hosea emphasized that God would continue to love them and use them as His special people.

In his unquestioning obedience of God, Hosea demonstrated he was a prophet who would follow his Lord's will, no matter what the cost. He was a sensitive, compassionate spokesman for righteousness whose own life echoed the message that God is love.

HOSHEA [hoe SHEE ah] *(salvation)*

The last king of Israel (2 Kin. 15:30; 17:1–6; 18:1, 9–10). Hoshea became king after he assassinated the former king, Pekah. Hoshea did evil in God's sight, but not to the extent of former kings. While he did not wipe out idolatrous worship, he at least did not give official approval to the practice. When Hoshea took the throne, he served as a puppet king under Assyria. But he eventually quit sending tribute money to Assyria and began negotiating an alliance with Egypt. When the Assyrian king, Shalmaneser V, learned of Hoshea's rebellion and conspiracy, he advanced toward Israel. The capital city of Samaria was besieged, and Hoshea was captured and imprisoned. After two years, Assyria finally captured Samaria, and its inhabitants were carried away to new locations in the Assyrian Empire (2 Kin. 17:18–23).

HOSPITALITY

The practice of entertaining strangers graciously. Hospitality was a very important trait in Bible times. Hospitality was specifically commanded by God (Lev. 19:33–34; Luke 14:13–14; Rom. 12:13). It was to be characteristic of all believers (1 Pet. 4:9), especially bishops (Titus 1:7–8; 1 Tim. 3:2). Jesus emphasized the importance of hospitality by answering the question of who should inherit the kingdom: "I was a stranger and you took Me in" (Matt. 25:35).

HULDAH [HUHL duh]

A prophetess consulted when the lost Book of the Law was found (2 Chr. 34:22–28). An indication of the esteem in which Huldah was held can be seen in Josiah's action. When the Book of the Law was found, he consulted her rather than the prophet Jeremiah. Huldah prophesied Jerusalem's destruction but added that because Josiah had done what was right in God's sight, it would not happen before Josiah died.

HUMAN SACRIFICE

A pagan rite in which a human being, often the firstborn child, was offered to a god to atone for sin or secure the god's favor. God distinctly prohibited the Hebrew people from imitating their heathen neighbors by offering up human beings as sacrifices (Lev. 20:2–5; Deut. 18:10). God's command to Abraham to sacrifice Isaac was no exception, because this was done to test Abraham and his faith (Gen. 22:1–19).

In times of rebellion and idolatry, the Israelites sometimes copied their neighbors in sacrificing children to Molech and other gods. The Valley of Hinnom was often the scene of these activities (Jer. 19:5–6; 32:35). Specific instances of human sacrifice mentioned in the Bible include the burning of his son on the city wall by the king of Moab (2 Kin. 3:26–27), and Kings Ahaz and Manasseh making their sons "pass through the fire" (2 Kin. 16:3; 21:6). Jephthah's offering of his daughter is another example (Judg. 11:29–40).

HUMILITY

A freedom from arrogance that grows out of the recognition that all we have and are comes from God. Jesus is the supreme example of humility (John 13:4–17; Phil. 2:5–8), and He is completely adequate and of infinite dignity and worth. Biblical humility is not a belittling of oneself (Rom. 12:3), but an exalting or praising of others, especially God and Christ (Phil. 2:3). Humble people focus more on God and others than on themselves.

Biblical humility is also a recognition that by ourselves we are inadequate, without dignity, and worthless. Yet, because we are created in God's image and because believers are in Christ, we have infinite worth and dignity (1 Pet. 1:18–19).

HUSHAI [HOO shigh]

A friend and wise counselor of King David (2 Sam. 15:32, 37). During Absalom's revolt, Hushai remained faithful to David and became a spy for him in Jerusalem. He probably was the father of Baana, one of Solomon's 12 officers (1 Kin. 4:16).

HYPOCRISY

Pretending to be what one is not. The New Testament meaning of "hypocrisy" and "hypocrite" reflects its use in Greek drama. In the Greek theater, a hypocrite was one who wore a mask and played a part on the stage, imitating the speech, mannerisms, and conduct of the character portrayed.

Throughout His ministry, Jesus vigorously exposed and denounced the hypocrisy of many who opposed Him, especially the scribes and Pharisees. They paraded their charitable deeds, praying and fasting as a theatrical display to win the praise of people (Matt. 6:1–2, 5, 16). They sought to give the appearance of being godly, but they were actually blind to the truth of God (Luke 20:19–20).

HYSSOP

A species of marjoram and a member of the mint family of plants. Hyssop was an aromatic shrub under 3 feet (1 meter) tall with clusters of yellow flowers. It grew in rocky crevices and was cultivated on terraced walls: "From the cedar tree of Lebanon even to the hyssop that springs out of the wall" (1 Kin. 4:33). Bunches of hyssop were used to sprinkle blood on the doorposts in Egypt (Ex. 12:22), and in purification ceremonies (Lev. 14:4, 6, 51–52). David mentioned it as an instrument of inner cleansing (Ps. 51:7). It was used at the crucifixion to relieve Jesus' thirst (John 19:29).

I

IBZAN [IB zan]

A judge who ruled over Israel, or a portion of it (Judg. 12:8–10). He had 30 sons and 30 daughters and was a man of wealth and influence.

ICONIUM [eye KOE nih uhm]

The capital of the province of Lycaonia in central Asia Minor. Iconium was visited by Paul and Barnabas when they were expelled from Antioch of Pisidia (Acts 13:51). Paul's ministry at Iconium was blessed by the salvation of many Jews and Gentiles (Acts 14:1). But persecution overtook them, and they had to flee for their lives (Acts 14:6, 19, 21). Iconium is known today as Konya, or Konia.

IDOLATRY

The worship of something created as opposed to the worship of the Creator Himself. Scores of references to idolatry appear in the Old Testament. This shows that idolatry probably was the greatest temptation our spiritual forefathers faced. While we find bowing down to a statue no temptation, they apparently slipped into idolatry constantly. So serious was this sin that the prohibition against the making and worshiping of images was included near the beginning of the Ten Commandments (Ex. 20:4–6).

Israel's ancient neighbors believed there were many gods. They worshiped whatever gods were necessary at a given time. An equally erroneous notion was that these gods either were the idols themselves or were represented by idols. Some people probably insisted that the idol was only an aid to worship and not the object of worship itself. But this distinction must have been hard to keep in mind. That is why the Bible strictly forbids the making of images of any kind—because they themselves receive the worship that God jealously reserves for Himself.

Archaeologists have discovered idols of most of the pagan gods mentioned in the Bible, in addition to many unidentified ones. Since the Romans began emperor worship late in the New Testament period, some of the elegant statues of the Caesars discovered by archaeologists may have been idols to be worshiped.

Idolatry can take many forms, and it has persisted from the earliest times. Joshua 24:2 states that Abraham's father served idols. Perhaps the earliest reference in the Bible to idols is the "household idols" or teraphim (small figurines) that Rachel stole from her father Laban when she and Leah fled with Jacob (Gen. 31:34).

The next noteworthy instance of idolatry was Aaron's making of the golden calf at the foot of Mount Sinai. This happened when the Israelites lost their patience while waiting for Moses to return with the revelation of the true and living God (Ex. 32:1–4). The incident at Baal of Peor (Num. 25:1–3) also involved the worship of an idol.

The conquest of Canaan by the Hebrews brought new temptations to worship the object created rather than the Creator. Joshua 24:15 poses the classic question: Whom will you serve? The gods of Egypt where you have lived? The gods of the Amorites where you now dwell? Or Yahweh the God of Israel? As always, some made the wrong choices (Judg. 17–18). A man made an idol for his personal use, but the tribe of Dan took it over for their own use. The Bible does not indicate what form that statue took or what god it represented.

Others tried the route of compromise: the mixing of idolatry with worship of the true God. So Gideon's ephod was made an object of worship (Judg. 8:24–27). Much later there was another instance of an otherwise good symbol of God's deliverance turned into an idol. In King Hezekiah's time, the people worshiped Moses' bronze snake (Num. 21:9; 2 Kin. 18:4).

While idolatry was held in check during most of the period of the united kingdom under David and Solomon, it burst forth again after the separation of Israel into two nations in 931 B.C. In fact, Jeroboam I made two calf idols and installed them at the major cities in the north and the south (Dan and Bethel) for the purpose of keeping his people's religious allegiance within the borders of the new kingdom (1 Kin. 12:27–30). He was afraid that if they returned to Jerusalem they might also return to the Lord, and that would spell political disaster for him.

All the successive monarchs in the northern kingdom of Israel were bad. Invariably their sin involved idolatry. Although there were some good kings in the southern kingdom of Judah, the bad ones invariably fell to idolatry. This prompted the major prophets—Isaiah, Jeremiah, and Ezekiel—and most of the minor prophets as well to ridicule, condemn, and warn against idolatry.

The captivity of the people of Israel at the hands of the Babylonians produced a permanent cure for the sin of idolatry. Never again, even to the present time, has Judaism succumbed to idolatry.

In the Gospels there is virtually nothing about idolatry, but in the letters of Paul and the other New Testament books Christians are frequently warned against idolatry. The Christians lived in a world filled with idols. Both the Romans and the Greeks used them. Paul's observation about Athens in Acts 17:16 tells it well: "He saw that the city was given over to idols."

In the New Testament period, the term *idolatry* began to be used as an intellectual concept. Idolatry became not bowing down before a statue but the replacement of God in the mind of the worshiper. Colossians 3:5 points in this direction: "Put to death . . . covetousness, which is idolatry" (see also Eph. 5:5). While we may not make or bow down to a statue, we must be constantly on guard that we let nothing come between us and God. As soon as anything does, that thing is an idol.

ILLYRICUM [ih LIHR ih kuhm]

A Roman province in the Balkan Peninsula, stretching along the east coast of the Adriatic Sea from Italy to Macedonia. Paul preached the gospel of Christ "from Jerusalem and round about to Illyricum" (Rom. 15:19). Dalmatia (2 Tim.

4:10) was one of the two major divisions of Illyricum. This region is known today as Yugoslavia and Albania.

IMAGE OF GOD

The characteristics of humankind with which God endowed them at creation, distinguishing them from the rest of God's creatures.

The expression, "image of God," appears in Genesis 1:26–27; 9:6, and 1 Corinthians 11:7. Some also see a reference to this image in Romans 8:29, 2 Corinthians 3:18, and allusions to it in Psalm 8:5, 1 Corinthians 15:49, Ephesians 4:24, and Colossians 3:10. Jesus is referred to as being "the image of the invisible God" (Col. 1:15) and "the express image of His [God's] person" (Heb. 1:3).

One understanding of the image of God is that it refers to qualities or attributes present in the person. Thus, the image of God is identified as human reason, will, or personality. Others believe the image is something present when the person is in a relationship to God, and in fact, is that relationship. The image is present like a reflection in a mirror, rather than like a photo—a permanent image printed on paper. Still others believe the image is something a person does. Immediately after God made people in His image, He gave them dominion or authority over the whole earth (Gen. 1:28). According to this view, this active tending and caring for God's creation constitutes the image of God in people.

The Bible does not indicate exactly what the image of God in humankind is. It may involve all these ideas. Human beings alone have personal, conscious fellowship with God (Gen. 1:29–30; 2:15–16; 3:8). Man is to take God's place in ruling over and developing the creation (Gen. 1:26, 28). Yet these are possible only because of certain qualities of personality that people alone have (Ps. 139:14).

To be created in the image of God means that we humans have the ability and the privilege of knowing, serving, and loving God, and that we are most fully human when fulfilling our spiritual potential. Every human life is precious to God, and this is exactly how we should treat the people with whom we share the world.

IMMANUEL [im MAN you ell] *(with us is God)*

A symbolic name from the prophecy of Isaiah applied in later years to Jesus the Messiah.

In the time of the prophet Isaiah, Syria and Israel were attacking Judah in an attempt to force King Ahaz of Judah to join a coalition against Assyria. Isaiah called on Ahaz to put his trust in the word of the Lord so the threat of Syria and Israel would come to nothing (Is. 7:1–9). Then the prophet announced God's intention to give Ahaz a sign that His word was true. Syria and Israel would lose their capacity to be a threat to Judah. But before this peace and prosperity became a reality, Isaiah announced there would be a drastic purging judgment at the hands of the king of Assyria. Only a remnant would experience the good future that God had intended for his people (Is. 7:10–25).

The sign that God promised to provide to Ahaz was the birth of a child within whose childhood years these events of promise and judgment would take place. The child would be given the name Immanuel, meaning "God with us," as a symbol of Judah's hope in the midst of adversity (Is. 8:8, 10). God would be with His people, in spite of the devastation wrought by the forces of the Assyrians (Is. 8:7–8). Immanuel offered a future and a hope for those who would place their trust in God.

The identity of this child and the circumstances of his birth are much disputed. This remarkable prophecy achieved its full meaning with the coming of Jesus. But there may have been an initial fulfillment in the eighth century B.C. when Hezekiah was born to the wicked King Ahaz. When Hezekiah took over the throne, he did lead many moral reforms that brought the people of Judah closer to God. Some scholars believe this may have been the child Isaiah had in mind when he announced this prophecy. Others think the child may have been a son born to Isaiah and "the prophetess" (Is. 8:3). In that case, "Immanuel" would have been another name for Maher-Shalal-Hash-Baz.

Regardless of Isaiah's understanding, Matthew rightly recognized that hope for restoration through the house of David reached its ultimate fulfillment only with Jesus (Matt. 1:23). With the coming of Jesus, God is with us in the most profound sense. With the virgin birth God's pattern of working out His purposes through special births (Gen. 3:15; 1 Sam. 2:1–10; 2 Sam. 7:12–16) reaches its climax. And in Jesus God is with us always, even to the end of the age (Matt. 28:20).

IMMORTALITY

Exemption from death; the state of living forever. The biblical concept of immortality is rooted in our creation in God's image and likeness (Gen. 1:26–27). God is spirit. So the reference in Genesis is not to bodily form but to spiritual nature. As the Eternal, God is also immortal (1 Tim. 6:16). God made people to live forever, physically and spiritually. At death the body returns to dust (Gen. 3:19), but the spirit lives on.

The ancient Hebrews believed in the survival of the spirit, although they thought of the afterlife as a shadowy existence. But the idea of bodily resurrection gradually developed (Job 19:26; Dan. 12:2). In Jesus' time the Sadducees denied bodily resurrection, while the Phar-

isees believed in it. Jesus clearly taught that the dead rise (Matt. 22:31–32).

In Jesus we have God's full revelation about immortality of both body and spirit (John 11:23–26; 2 Tim. 1:10). His bodily resurrection is proof of our immortality (1 Cor. 15:12–16).

The nature of the resurrection body is not clear. Some see it as like that of Jesus—a real body, but not subject to time, space, or density (John 20:19–20, 26–29). But the matter should not be pressed too far. As our present bodies are fitted to conditions on earth, so will our resurrection bodies be suitable for conditions in heaven (1 Cor. 15:38–44).

Although death is an enemy (1 Cor. 15:26), Paul thought of death as necessary in order that believers may receive immortal, incorruptible bodies (1 Cor. 15:50–57). Those living at the Lord's return will receive transformed bodies (1 Cor. 15:51–54). Jesus spoke of "the resurrection of life" and "the resurrection of condemnation" (John 5:29). Thus, we may assume that both believers and unbelievers will receive resurrection bodies—but their eternal destiny will be different (Dan. 12:2).

IMPUTATION

Charging or reckoning something to a person's account. Three distinct theological truths in the Bible are directly related to the concept of imputation:

1. *The Imputation of Adam's Sin to His Descendants.* Romans 5:12–19 declares that God imputes the guilt of Adam's sin to all other members of the human race: "By one man's disobedience many were made sinners." "Through one man's offense judgment came to all men, resulting in condemnation." "By the one man's offense death reigned through the one." This concept, also called "original sin," is touched on as well in 1 Corinthians 15:21–22.

2. *The Imputation of the Believer's Sin*

to Christ. In addition to guilt imputed from Adam's sin, all people are also charged with guilt for their personal sins. This Paul describes as "imputing their trespasses to them" (2 Cor. 5:19). The Lord Jesus, whose supernatural conception and birth freed Him from guilt from Adam's sin and who committed no personal sin, had no sin counted against Him. But when He died as our substitute, God "made Him who knew no sin to be sin for us" (2 Cor. 5:21) so that He "bore our sins in His own body on the tree" (1 Pet. 2:24).

3. *The Imputation of Christ's Righteousness to the Believer.* "The blessedness of the man to whom God imputes righteousness" is the theme of the fourth chapter of Romans (also 1 Cor. 1:30; Phil. 3:9). Jesus became the Holy and Just One (Acts 3:14) through His perfect obedience to God's Law (Rom. 5:19). These qualities are imputed in turn "to us who believe in Him who raised up Jesus our Lord from the dead" (Rom. 4:24). Because of this the believer will appear before God "faultless" (Jude 24). We can stand in God's presence because Jesus has imputed His righteousness and holiness to us through His sacrificial death on the Cross.

INCARNATION

A theological term for the coming of God's Son into the world as a human being. The term itself is not used in the Bible, but it is based on clear references in the New Testament to Jesus as a person "in the flesh" (Rom. 8:3; Col. 1:22).

Jesus participated fully in all that it means to live a human life. But if Jesus were merely a man, no matter how great, there would be no significance in drawing attention to His bodily existence. The marvelous thing is that in Jesus, God Himself began to live a fully human life. The capacity of Jesus to reveal God to us and to bring salvation depends upon His being fully God and fully man at the same time (Col. 2:9). Our human minds cannot understand how Jesus can be both fully God and fully man. But the Bible gives clear indication of how this works out in practice.

No person may see God and live (Ex. 33:20). He dwells in unapproachable light (1 Tim. 6:16). Can we, therefore, only know Him from a distance? No, because God has come near in the person of Jesus (Matt. 1:23). He has taken on a form in which He can be seen, experienced, and understood by us as human beings (John 1:14, 18). Jesus reveals God to us perfectly since in His human life He is the image of God (2 Cor. 4:4), exhibiting full likeness with the Father (John 1:14). Jesus' godhood in His manhood is the key to our intimate knowledge of God.

This does not mean, however, that Jesus' humanity is only a display case for His divinity. Jesus lived out His human life by experiencing all the pressures, temptations, and limitations that we experience (Heb. 2:18; 4:15; 5:2, 7–8). That is why Jesus' life really is the supreme human success story (Heb. 5:8). Jesus was a pioneer (Heb. 2:10, NRSV), showing in practical terms the full meaning and possibility of human life, lived in obedience to God. In this respect, Jesus is a kind of second Adam (Rom. 5:14–15), marking a new beginning for the human race.

Jesus would have performed a great work if He had done no more than set a perfect example. But His full humanity is also the basis on which it is possible for Him to represent us—indeed, take our place—in dying for us. The Bible makes this clear when it speaks of "one Mediator between God and men, the Man Christ Jesus, who gave Himself a ransom for all" (1 Tim. 2:5–6).

When He ascended to His Father after His resurrection, Jesus left behind some of the human restrictions experienced during His earthly life. He received at that time His original divine glory (John 17:5). But the joining together of deity and humanity that marks His incarnation did not come to an end with His ascension. Jesus took His resurrected body with Him back to heaven (Luke 24:51; Acts 1:9). In heaven now He is our divine Lord, our human leader, and the great High Priest who serves as a mediator between God and humankind (Heb. 3:1).

INCENSE

A sweet-smelling substance that was burned as an offering to God on the altar in the tabernacle and the temple. The purpose of this incense offering was to honor God. Incense symbolized and expressed the prayers of the Hebrew people, which were considered a pleasant aroma offered to God.

The incense used in Israelite worship was of a specific composition, considered very sacred. The four substances from which it was made were stacte, onycha, galbanum, and pure frankincense (Ex. 30:34–35). Some of this was to be ground into powder and placed in front of the Testimony in the tabernacle of meeting (Ex. 30:36). The use of any other composition of incense or of this particular compound for any other purpose was regarded as sin; this incense alone was to be considered holy (Ex. 30:36–38).

According to the law, only the priests descended from Aaron could offer in-

INCENSE

cense (Lev. 2:2). The priest offered holy incense morning and evening on the altar of incense in front of the veil in the Holy Place in the tabernacle or temple.

This incense formula specified for use in public ritual was not to be allowed for private use (Ex. 30:37, 38). Apparently some wealthy individuals were tempted to make their own private supply for personal use.

Incense is also mentioned in connection with certain pagan worship practices of the Israelites. The worship of Baal, the queen of heaven, and other foreign gods by means of incense was condemned in the Old Testament (1 Kin. 11:8). The Lord warned that he would destroy the pagan incense altars (Lev. 26:30; 2 Chr. 30:14). The burning of incense at the pagan shrines on "high places" and to other gods was strongly denounced (2 Kin. 22:17; 2 Chr. 34:25). The use of incense appeared widespread in connection with Israelite lapses into pagan worship (Jer. 11:12, 17; 48:35).

Another misuse of incense is mentioned in 2 Chronicles 26:16–21. This passage describes how King Uzziah was afflicted by the Lord, who caused leprosy to break out on his forehead because Uzziah had attempted to burn incense in the temple. This duty was reserved for the priestly descendants of Aaron.

The New Testament church did not adopt the use of incense in worship. In fact, the use of it was considered a work of paganism and was banned by the first Christian emperors. However, later in church history incense was again widely used.

In a figurative use of the word, the psalmist requested that his prayer might be brought before the Lord as incense (Ps. 141:2). Incense possibly was also a symbol of a godly life, offered up to God as a pleasant aroma before him.

INHERITANCE

The receipt of property as a gift or by legal right, usually upon the death of one's father.

In ancient Israel the property of a deceased person was usually distributed according to law or tribal custom. Written wills were rarely used. The real and personal property of a father was normally divided among his sons. A larger amount, usually a double portion, went to the oldest son, who assumed the care of his mother and unmarried sisters.

The birthright of the firstborn son could be denied only because of a serious offense against the father, as in the case of Reuben (Deut. 21:15–17; 1 Chr. 5:1). The sons of concubines normally received presents of personal property. If there were no surviving sons, the inheritance went to daughters. The daughters had to marry within the tribe, however, or lose their inheritance. If a man died childless, his estate was received by his brothers or his father's brothers (Num. 27:9–11).

To the Hebrew mind, the term *inheritance* had strong spiritual and national associations extending far beyond the family estate. The land of Canaan was regarded as an inheritance from the Lord because God had promised the land to Abraham and his descendants (Num. 33:53). Both Moses and Joshua were told by the Lord to divide the land of Canaan among the tribes "as an inheritance" (Num. 26:52–53; Josh. 13:6). God directed that the land be distributed to each tribe by lot according to its population.

Each family, in turn, was assigned a parcel that was to remain in the family's possession. This sense of sacred birthright probably accounted for Naboth's refusal to sell his vineyard to King Ahab: "The Lord forbid that I should give the inheritance of my fathers to you!" (1 Kin. 21:3).

The apostle Paul's concept of a spiritual inheritance for Christians is primarily of Jewish origin. But the doctrine was strongly influenced by Greek and Roman inheritance practices. Three of these influences were: (1) inheritance was regarded as immediate as well as ultimate, (2) all legitimate heirs usually shared the inheritance equally and jointly rather than a division favoring a firstborn son, and (3) legally adopted children enjoyed full inheritance rights along with natural offspring.

According to Paul, the Christian's spiritual inheritance is based strictly on our relationship to Christ. "For you are all sons of God through faith in Jesus Christ. . . . And if you are Christ's, then you are Abraham's seed, and heirs according to the promise" (Gal. 3:26, 29). This spiritual birthright cannot be inherited by sinners (1 Cor. 6:9–11).

Paul also declared that the Spirit's indwelling power is both the sign and seal that we are heirs of God's promise: "Having believed, you were sealed with the Holy Spirit of promise, who is the guarantee of our inheritance" (Eph. 1:13–14). Those who are redeemed, including the Gentiles, become God's adopted sons with full inheritance rights (Gal. 4:1–7).

Other New Testament passages present the Christian's spiritual inheritance as a reward for faithfulness and Christlikeness. Jesus invited those showing kindness in His name to "inherit the kingdom prepared for you from the foundation of the world" (Matt. 25:34). Peter counseled suffering saints in the Roman world to be patient in their trials, "That you may inherit a blessing" (1 Pet. 3:9). James declared that the poor of this world have been chosen "to be rich in faith and heirs of the kingdom" that God promised to those who love Him (James 2:5).

In a burst of joy, Peter celebrated the "living hope" all Christians have of their heavenly inheritance: "To an inheritance incorruptible and undefiled and that does not fade away, reserved in heaven for you" (1 Pet. 1:3–4).

INN

A lodging place for travelers. Hospitality was a religious duty in Bible times, so most travelers were guests in private residences. Inns were usually primitive shelters or enclosures for travelers and their animals.

In the Old Testament (Gen. 42:27, KJV), the word *inn* referred to a place to rest for the night or the act of pitching a tent. In New Testament times inns were usually built along trade routes. Pilgrims or merchants traveling together for safety would spend the night at these inns. A host or innkeeper provided basic lodging and some necessities such as food for the animals. Bazaars and markets offering provisions and entertainment for the weary traveler were usually located nearby.

Some synagogues had an adjacent inn where needy travelers could receive free food and a night's lodging. Joseph's brothers stayed at an inn near the Egyptian border (Gen. 42:27). A place called the "Three Inns" is mentioned by Luke (Acts 28:15; Three Taverns, NIV, NRSV).

In the New Testament, two inns were the settings for very significant events.

Joseph and Mary were turned away by the innkeeper at Bethlehem, requiring them to seek refuge in a nearby cave where the Son of God was born (Luke 2:7). As Mary laid her Son in a cattle trough for a cradle, the Son of God was displayed in humiliation, identifying Him with all humanity.

The Good Samaritan carried a Jewish traveler who had been robbed and beaten by thieves to an inn where provision was made for his future care (Luke

10:33–37). The Samaritan displayed a spirit of compassion and brotherhood that overcame the prejudices that usually separated Jews from Samaritans.

INSPIRATION

A technical term for the Holy Spirit's supernatural guidance of those who received special revelation from God as they wrote the books of the Bible. The end result of this inspiration is that the Bible conveys the truths that God wanted His people to know and to communicate to the world.

Two terms often used in discussion of the inspiration of the Bible are "plenary" and "verbal." "Plenary," a term meaning full or complete, means that each book, chapter, and paragraph of the Bible is equally derived from God. "Verbal" inspiration emphasizes the truth that the wording of the text, as well as the ideas conveyed, is supernaturally inspired by God through the Holy Spirit.

"Inerrancy" is a term used along with plenary verbal inspiration to convey the view that the Bible's teaching is true on everything of which it speaks. The words of Scripture, in the original writings, teach the truth without any admixture of error. The Bible is not just a useful body of human ideas. It makes clear the mind of God Himself.

"Infallibility" is a term often used as a synonym for inerrancy. However, the root meaning of infallibility is "not liable to fail in achieving its purpose." Truth, or inerrancy, is affirmed of the content of the Bible; infallibility refers to the effectiveness of the wording in conveying reliable ideas, as well as the effectiveness of those ideas when used by the all-powerful Holy Spirit (Is. 55:11).

Important as biblical infallibility is, it is not enough without inerrancy. The reason why the Spirit can use Scripture so effectively is that He directed its production from the beginning so that all of it is God's reliable information.

Inspiration, then, is a statement about God's greatness. God is intelligent and able to communicate with human beings, whom He created in His image. God knows everything about all reality in creation and is absolutely faithful and true (Rev. 3:7; 21:5). It follows that ideas communicated by divine revelation are true and conform to reality as God knows it. God overruled human limitations and sinful biases so that His human agents were able to write what He wanted written. God guided the thought conveyed so that it was without error, accomplishing the objectives He intended.

Although the Bible does not tell exactly how God inspired its writers, it was certainly not in a mechanical way. God the Holy Spirit is the third person of the Trinity who is working with persons. How does one person influence another person? Why do some have a more powerful impact upon people than others? Many factors are involved. We do know for certain that the Scriptures originated with God and that the writers were "moved" or carried along by the Holy Spirit (2 Pet. 1:20–21) as they recorded God's message.

INTERCESSION

The act of petitioning God or praying on behalf of another person or group. The sinful nature of this world separates human beings from God. It has always been necessary, therefore, for righteous individuals to go before God to seek reconciliation between Him and His fallen creation.

One of the earliest and best examples of intercession of this type occurs in Genesis 18, where Abraham speaks to God on behalf of Sodom. His plea is compassionate; it is concerned with the well-being of others rather than with his own needs. Such selfless concern is the mark of all true intercession. Jesus Christ is the greatest intercessor. He prayed on behalf of Peter (Luke 22:32) and His disciples (John 17). Then in the most selfless intercession of all, He petitioned God on behalf of those who crucified Him (Luke 23:34).

But Christ's intercessory work did not cease when He returned to heaven. In heaven He intercedes for His church (Heb. 7:25). His Holy Spirit pleads on behalf of the individual Christian (Rom. 8:26–27). Finally, because of their unique relationship to God through Christ, Christians are urged to intercede for all people (1 Tim. 2:1).

ISAAC [EYE zik] ([God] *laughs)*

The only son of Abraham by his wife Sarah; father of Jacob and Esau. God promised to make Abraham's descendants a great nation that would become God's chosen people. But the promised son was a long time in coming. Isaac was born when Abraham was 100 years old and Sarah was 90 (Gen. 17:17; 21:5).

Isaac's birthright was an important part of his life. The blessings that God gave to Abraham were also given to his descendants. Thus, to inherit this covenant with God was of far greater value than to inherit property or material goods. Isaac's life gave evidence of God's favor. His circumcision was a sign of the covenant with God. Isaac was in a unique position historically because he would carry on the covenant.

When Isaac was a young man, God tested Abraham's faith by commanding him to sacrifice Isaac as an offering. But when Abraham placed Isaac upon the altar, an angel appeared and stopped the sacrifice, providing a ram instead (Gen. 22). This showed clearly that Isaac was God's choice to carry on the covenant.

Isaac married Rebekah when he was 40 years old. She became Isaac's wife when God directed one of Abraham's servants to her. The Bible reveals that Isaac loved Rebekah and that she was a comfort to him after his mother Sarah's death (Gen. 24:67). Isaac and Rebekah had twin sons, Jacob and Esau, who were born when Isaac was 60 years old (Gen. 25:20–26).

The older twin, Esau, was Isaac's favorite son, although God had declared that the older should serve the younger (Gen. 25:23). Jacob was Rebekah's favorite. Disagreement arose over which of the twins would receive the birthright and carry on the covenant that God had made with Abraham. Rebekah conspired with Jacob to trick the aging, blind Isaac into giving his blessing to Jacob rather than Esau.

Shortly thereafter, Isaac sent Jacob to Laban in Padan Aram to find a wife and to escape Esau's wrath. Esau soon left his father's household. Many years passed before the two brothers were at peace with each other. But they were united at last in paying last respects to their father after his death. Isaac lived to be 180 years old. He was buried alongside Abraham, Sarah, and Rebekah in the cave of Machpelah (Gen. 35:28–29; 49:30–31).

The Bible contains many references to Isaac's good character. The Scripture gives evidence of his submission (Gen. 22:6, 9), meditation (Gen. 24:63), trust in God (Gen. 22:6, 9), devotion (Gen. 24:67), peaceful nature (Gen. 26:20–22), and his life of prayer and faith (Gen. 26:25; Heb. 11:11–17).

In the New Testament, Isaac is called a "child of promise" (Gal. 4:22–23). The Book of Acts points to his significance as one who received circumcision on the eighth day (Acts 7:8). His position as the channel of the Abrahamic blessing is also emphasized (Rom. 9:7). In a famous passage, Paul used Isaac and his mother as historical examples when discussing those who are justified by faith in God's promise (Gal. 4:21–31).

ISAIAH [eye ZAY uh] *(the Lord has saved)*

A famous Old Testament prophet who predicted the coming of the Messiah; the author of the Book of Isaiah. Isaiah was probably born in Jerusalem of a family related to the royal house of Judah. He recorded the events of the reign of King Uzziah of Judah (2 Chr. 26:22). When Uzziah died (740 B.C.), Isaiah received his prophetic calling from God in a stirring vision of God in the temple (Is. 6). The king of Judah had died; now Isaiah had seen the everlasting King in whose service he would spend the rest of his life.

Isaiah was married to a woman described as "the prophetess" (Is. 8:3). They had two sons whom they named Shear-Jashub, "A Remnant Shall Return" (Is. 7:3), and Maher-Shalal-Hash-Baz,

ISAIAH

FALSE PROPHETS PREDICT A ROSY FUTURE.

"Speed the Spoil, Hasten the Booty" (Is. 8:3). These strange names portray two basic themes of the Book of Isaiah: God is about to bring judgment upon His people, hence Maher-Shalal-Hash-Baz; but after that there will be an outpouring of God's mercy and grace to the remnant of people who will remain faithful to God, hence Shear-Jashub.

After God called Isaiah to proclaim His message, He told Isaiah that most of his work would be a ministry of judgment. Even though the prophet would speak the truth, the people would reject his words (6:10). Jesus found in these words of Isaiah's call a prediction of the rejection of His message by many of the people (Matt. 13:14–15).

Isaiah's response to this revelation from the Lord was a lament: "Lord, how long?" (Isa. 6:11). The Lord answered that Isaiah's ministry would prepare the people for judgment, but one day God's promises would be realized. Judah was to experience utter devastation, to be fulfilled with the destruction of the city of Jerusalem by the Babylonians in 586 B.C. (Is. 6:11). This destruction would be followed by the deportation of the people to Babylon (Is. 6:12). But although the tree of the house of David would be cut down, there would still be life in the stump (Is. 6:13). Out of the lineage of David would come a Messiah who would establish His eternal rule among His people.

Isaiah was a writer of considerable literary skill. The poetry of his book is magnificent in its sweep. A person of strong emotion and deep feelings, Isaiah also was a man of steadfast devotion to the Lord. His vision of God and His holiness in the temple influenced his messages during his long ministry.

Isaiah's ministry extended from about 740 B.C. until at least 701 B.C. (Is. 37–39). His 40 years of preaching doom and

promise did not turn the nation of Judah from its headlong rush toward destruction. But he faithfully preached the message God gave him until the very end.

According to a popular Jewish tradition, Isaiah met his death by being sawn in half during the reign of the evil king Manasseh of Judah. This tradition seems to be supported by the writer of Hebrews (Heb. 11:37). Certainly Isaiah is one of the heroes of the faith "of whom the world was not worthy" (Heb. 11:38).

ISHBOSHETH [ihsh BOE sheth] *(man of shame)*

A son of Saul whom Abner proclaimed king after Saul's death (2 Sam. 2:8–10). The tribe of Judah proclaimed David king after the death of Saul and Jonathan at Gilboa, but the 11 other tribes remained loyal to Saul's family. Ishbosheth reigned two turbulent years from Mahanaim, east of the Jordan River, while David ruled Judah from Hebron. Throughout the period, each side attempted unsuccessfully to gain control of the entire kingdom (2 Sam. 2:12–3:1).

Ishbosheth made a grave error in charging Abner with having relations with Saul's concubine, Rizpah. In anger, Abner changed his allegiance to David (2 Sam. 3:6–21). When Joab murdered Abner in Hebron (2 Sam. 3:27), Ishbosheth became discouraged (2 Sam. 4:1). Two captains of his guard, Baanah and Rechab, assassinated Ishbosheth as he lay napping. They carried Ishbosheth's severed head to David, who ordered it buried in the tomb of Abner in Hebron. Then David put the assassins to death (2 Sam. 4:5–12). Saul's dynasty ended with Ishbosheth's death.

ISHMAEL [IHSH may ell] *(God hears)*

The first son of Abraham, by his wife's Egyptian maidservant, Hagar. Although God had promised Abraham an heir

(Gen. 15:4), Abraham's wife, Sarah, had been unable to bear a child. When Abraham was 85, Sarah offered her maid to him in order to help fulfill God's promise (Gen. 16:1–2).

After Hagar learned that she was pregnant, she grew proud and began to despise Sarah. Sarah complained to Abraham, who allowed her to discipline Hagar. Sarah's harsh treatment of Hagar caused her to flee into the wilderness. There she met the angel of God, who told her to return to Sarah and submit to her authority. As an encouragement, the angel promised Hagar that her son, who would be named Ishmael, would have uncounted descendants. Hagar then returned to Abraham and Sarah and bore her son (Gen. 16:4–15).

When Ishmael was 13, God appeared to Abraham to tell him that Ishmael was not the promised heir. God made a covenant with Abraham that was to be passed down to the descendants of Isaac—a son who would be conceived by Sarah the following year. Because Abraham loved Ishmael, God promised to bless Ishmael and make him a great nation (Gen. 17:19–20).

At the customary feast to celebrate Isaac's weaning, Sarah saw 16-year-old Ishmael making fun of Isaac. She was furious and demanded that Abraham disown Ishmael and his mother so Ishmael could not share Isaac's inheritance. Abraham was reluctant to cast out Ishmael and Hagar, but he did so when instructed by God (Gen. 21:8–13).

Hagar and Ishmael wandered in the wilderness of Beersheba. When their water was gone and Ishmael grew weary, Hagar placed him under a shrub to await death. The angel of God again contacted Hagar and showed her a well. After drawing water, she returned to Ishmael. Ishmael grew up in the wilderness of Paran and gained fame as an archer. Hagar arranged his marriage to an Egyptian wife (Gen. 21:14–21).

When Abraham died, Ishmael returned from exile to help Isaac with the burial (Gen. 25:9). As God promised, Ishmael became the father of 12 princes (Gen. 25:16), as well as a daughter, Mahalath, who later married Esau, son of Isaac (Gen. 28:9). Ishmael died at the age of 137 (Gen. 25:17).

Ishmael was the father of the Ishmaelites, a nomadic nation which lived in northern Arabia. Modern-day Arabs claim descent from Ishmael.

ISHMAELITES [ISH may el ites]

Descendants of Ishmael, Abraham's first son. His mother was Sarah's Egyptian servant, Hagar (Gen. 16:1–16; 1 Chr. 1:28). The Ishmaelites, like the Israelites (Abraham's grandchildren through Sarah), were divided into 12 tribes (Gen. 25:16). Out of respect for Abraham, God made a great nation of the Ishmaelites, even though Ishmael was not Abraham's promised son (Gen. 21:12–13). Ishmael's 12 sons had many descendants who lived as nomads in the deserts of northern Arabia.

The Old Testament eventually used the term *Ishmaelite* in a broader sense, referring to all the Arabian merchants (Is. 13:20; Ezek. 27:20, 21). Any wild and warlike peoples of the desert could claim to be descendants of Ishmael (Gen. 16:12).

ISRAEL [IS ray ell] *(he strives with God)*

The name given to Jacob after his great struggle with God at Peniel near the brook Jabbok (Gen. 32:28; 35:10). The name Israel has been interpreted by different scholars as "prince with God," "he strives with God," "let God rule," or "God strives." The name was later applied to the descendants of Jacob. The twelve tribes were called "Israelites," "children of Israel," and "house of Israel," identifying them as the descendants of Israel through his sons and grandsons.

ISRAEL, KINGDOM OF

The northern kingdom, which existed for a number of years alongside its sister nation: the southern kingdom of Judah. The northern kingdom split from the united kingdom following the death of King Solomon. Before Solomon died, he managed to antagonize almost all his subjects. When he was succeeded by his son Rehoboam, the ten northern tribes led by Jeroboam, a former head of the forced labor units, met with him and sought relief from the burdens of work and taxation.

Rehoboam followed bad advice and refused. The northern tribes declared independence and formed a separate kingdom with Jeroboam as head. They named their kingdom "Israel." The southern section of the divided kingdom was known as Judah. This division soon attracted the attention of Shishak, pharaoh of Egypt (about 945–924 B.C.), who moved into Judah, robbed the temple of its golden objects, and destroyed a number of Judah's fortresses. This event weakened still further an already vulnerable people.

Israel's troubles had also begun. The Arameans of Damascus were becoming powerful in Syria and were beginning to put pressure on Israel's northern borders. There was internal instability in the kingdom as well, indicated by the murder of King Nadab (about 908 B.C.), two years after his father Jeroboam's death. His murderer, Baasha, fortified a site close to Jerusalem (1 Kin. 15:17). Asa, the king of Judah (about 911–870 B.C.), appealed to the Syrians for help against Baasha. Baasha's son Elah reigned for two years (about 886–884 B.C.); Elah was murdered by Zimri, who committed suicide

after seven days and plunged the nation into civil war.

Four years later the army general Omri gained control of Israel and began his own dynasty. Omri moved Israel's capital from Tirzah to Samaria, which he fortified strongly. He allied with Phoenicia, and arranged a marriage between his son Ahab and Jezebel, a princess of Tyre. When Ahab (about 874–853 B.C.) became king, he continued Omri's policy of resistance to Syria. But his support of pagan Tyrian religion in Israel drew strong criticism from the prophet Elijah (1 Kin. 18:18). The nation was punished by famine, but this did little to halt the widespread spiritual and social corruption.

About 855 B.C. the Syrian Ben-Hadad attacked Samaria (1 Kin. 20:1) but suffered heavy losses, as he also did the following year at Aphek. Israel was saved by the appearance of the powerful Assyrian forces who, under Shalmaneser III (about 859–824 B.C.), attacked allied Syrian and Israelite forces in 853 B.C. at Qarqar on the Orontes River. Ahab died while trying to recover Ramoth Gilead from Syrian control. Meanwhile Mesha, king of Moab, had refused to pay further tribute to Israel; consequently, he was attacked by Ahaziah (about 853–852 B.C.), Ahab's successor.

Jehoram (about 852–841 B.C.) of Israel enlisted Jehoshaphat of Judah (about 873–848 B.C.) in the struggle against Moab, which proved successful (2 Kin. 3) as Elisha the prophet had predicted. About 843 B.C. Ben-Hadad was murdered by Hazael (2 Kin. 8:7–13), and two years later Jehu seized the throne of Israel, carrying out a vicious purge of Ahab's house and suppressing pagan religions.

For Israel, the eighth century B.C. was marked by a period of prosperity. Jeroboam II (about 782–752 B.C.) was able to develop agriculture, trade, and commerce because the westward advance of

Assyria compelled the Syrian armies to defend their eastern territories. There was a sense that the true "golden age" had arrived.

Unfortunately, however, idolatry and the rejection of covenant spirituality were prominent in Israel. Prophets such as Amos, Hosea, Micah, and Isaiah spoke out against these abuses. They condemned the exploitation of the poor. They also rebuked the rich for accumulating land and wealth illegally, and for forsaking the simple Hebrew way of life for the luxurious living of pagan nations.

The end of all this for Israel occurred shortly after Jeroboam's death. The kingship was left to political opportunists. But they were dwarfed by the powerful Assyrian monarch Tiglath-Pileser III. About 745 B.C. he placed Menahem of Israel (752–741 B.C.) under tribute. But when Menahem died, Israel joined an alliance against Assyria.

Ahaz of Judah, alarmed by this move, appealed to Tiglath-Pileser for help. Tiglath-Pileser overthrew Damascus in 732 B.C. (Is. 8:4; 17:1; Amos 1:4). He then carried people from the territory of Naphtali captive to Assyria (2 Kin. 15:29). But he still had to reckon with the resistance from Samaria under Pekah, whose murderer, Hoshea, was later made an Assyrian vassal.

On Tiglath-Pileser's death (727 B.C.), Hoshea of Israel rebelled. This brought the Assyrians to Samaria in a siege that ended three years later with the fall of Israel and the deportation of more northern tribesmen in 722 B.C. Isaiah's prediction that God would use Assyria as the rod of His anger upon Israel (Is. 10:5–6) had been fulfilled.

ISSACHAR [IHZ ah car] *(there is hire* or *reward)*

The ninth son of Jacob; the fifth by his wife Leah (Gen. 30:17–18; 35:23). He fathered four sons: Tola, Puvah or Puah,

Job or Jashub, and Shimron. He and his sons went with their father Jacob to Egypt to escape the famine (Gen. 46:13; Ex. 1:3; Num. 26:23–24; 1 Chr. 2:1; 7:1). Before his death, Jacob described Issachar as "a strong donkey lying down between two burdens" (Gen. 49:15). In other words, Jacob saw that Issachar could be a strong fighter but that his love of comfort could also cause him to settle for the easy way out.

ISSACHAR, TRIBE OF

The tribe made up of Issachar's descendants. It consisted of four clans, the descendants of Issachar's four sons (Gen. 46:13; Num. 26:23–24; 1 Chr. 7:1). The territory allotted to this tribe was bounded on the north by Zebulun and Naphtali, on the south and west by Manasseh, and on the east by the Jordan River (Josh. 19:17–23). Most of the fertile Valley of Jezreel, or Esdraelon, fell within Issachar's territory. Its fertile, flat plains were well-suited for the raising of cattle. In spite of its reputation for seeking comfort, the tribe did fight bravely against Sisera (Judg. 5:15).

Moses prophesied a quiet and happy life for Issachar (Deut. 33:18). At the first census, the tribe numbered 54,400 fighting men (Num. 1:28–29); at the second census 64,300 (Num. 26:25). By David's time it numbered 87,000 (1 Chr. 7:5). Its leaders mentioned in the Bible were Nethaneel (Num. 1:8; 2:8; 7:18; 10:15), and Paltiel (Num. 34:26), the judge Tola (Judg. 10:1), King Baasha (1 Kin. 15:27), and Omri (1 Chr. 27:18).

In accordance with Jacob's blessing, the tribe of Issachar showed an unusual insight into political situations. The tribe switched allegiance from Saul to David (1 Chr. 12:32). Although the tribe was a member of the northern kingdom, its members attended Hezekiah of Judah's Passover feast (2 Chr. 30:18).

ITTAI [IT uh eye]

A native or inhabitant of the Philistine city of Gath who followed David during the dangerous period of Absalom's rebellion. Ittai, Abishai, and Joab each commanded a third of David's army in the battle of the woods of Ephraim, during which Absalom was killed (2 Sam. 15:18–22; 18:2, 5, 12). Joab and Abishai are mentioned after this battle, but Ittai is not. Ittai may have been killed during the battle.

IVORY

Decorative trim made from tusks of elephants. In Bible times, ivory was a rare and expensive item, found only in the palaces of kings and the homes of the very wealthy. Ornate carvings of ivory were inlaid in thrones, furniture, and the paneling used in expensive homes (1 Kin. 10:18; Ps. 45:8; Ezek. 27:6). The prophet Amos condemned the people of Samaria who lived in houses and beds decorated with ivory (Amos 3:15; 6:4) because their wealth was gained through oppression of the common people of the nation of Israel.

Excavation of the royal city of Samaria has yielded evidence of the practice to which Amos referred. About 200 ivory plaques and fragments were discovered in the palace of King Ahab.

J

JABBOK [JAB uhk]

One of the main eastern tributaries of the Jordan River (Deut. 2:37). The stream rose in Transjordan, in the hills of Bashan near Rabbah of the Ammonites (modern Amman) and entered the Jordan about 15 miles (25 kilometers) north of the Dead Sea. Near "the ford of Jabbok" Jacob "wrestled with God" and had his name changed to Israel (Gen. 32:22–32).

JABESH GILEAD [JAY besh GIL ih add]
(Jabesh of Gilead)

A town of Gilead (1 Sam. 31:11; 2 Sam. 2:4), situated about 10 miles (16 kilometers) southeast of Beth Shan and about 2 miles (3 kilometers) east of the Jordan River. It was within the territory assigned to the half-tribe of Manasseh (Num. 32:29, 40).

Jabesh Gilead refused to join in the punishment of the Benjamites (Judg. 21:8–14), an offense for which every man was put to the sword. Four hundred young virgins of Jabesh were given to the Benjamites as wives.

During King Saul's reign, the king of Ammon besieged the city of Jabesh. He promised to spare the lives of those who lived in Jabesh if each of the men would submit to having his right eye put out. A seven-day truce was called and appeal was made to Saul, who mustered an army and defeated the Ammonites (1 Sam. 11).

The people of Jabesh Gilead never forgot this act of Saul. When Saul and his sons were slain at Gilboa, the men of Jabesh Gilead rescued their bodies, cremated them, and buried the ashes near Jabesh (1 Sam. 31:1–13).

JACHIN AND BOAZ [JAY kin, BOE az]

The names of twin pillars of cast bronze on each side of the entrance to Solomon's temple in Jerusalem (2 Chr. 3:17; Jakin in NIV). The pillars stood in front of the temple and apparently had only decorative significance. When Jerusalem was defeated in 586 B.C., both pillars were destroyed and their metal was carried off to Babylon (2 Kin. 25:13).

JACKAL

The prophet Isaiah spoke of jackals—wild dogs that make their dens in desolate places (Is. 34:13). As scavengers, jackals also fed on garbage in towns and villages in Bible times.

Jackals have an unpleasant smell, and they make a yapping and howling noise at night. They are also agricultural pests. Canaanite farmers put up shelters for watchmen, who guarded their cucumber fields against jackals. Some farmers heaped up whitewashed stones to frighten the jackals, just as scarecrows are used in other places.

Bible references to jackals are confusing, since jackal, fox, dragon, and wolf may be used interchangeably, depending on the translation. The "foxes" to whose tails Samson tied torches may have been jackals which, unlike foxes, travel in packs (Judg. 15:4).

JACOB [JAY cub] (he supplants)

One of the twin sons of Isaac and Rebekah. The brother of Esau, he was known also as Israel (Gen. 32:28).

JACOB

Jacob was born in answer to his father's prayer (Gen. 25:21), but he became the favorite son of his mother (25:28). He was named Jacob because, at the birth of the twins, "his hand took hold of Esau's heel" (25:26). According to the accounts in Genesis, Jacob continued to "take hold of" the possessions of others—his brother's birthright (25:29–34), his father's blessing (27:1–29), and his father-in-law's flocks and herds (30:25–43; 31:1).

The pattern of Jacob's life is found in his journeys, much like the travels of his grandfather Abraham. Leaving his home in Beersheba, he traveled to Bethel (28:10–22); later he returned to Shechem (33:18–20), Bethel (35:6–7), and Hebron (35:27). At Shechem and Bethel he built altars, as Abraham had done (12:6–7; 12:8). Near the end of his life Jacob migrated to Egypt; he died there at an advanced age (Gen. 46–49).

The most dramatic moments in Jacob's life occurred at Bethel (Gen. 28:10–22), at the ford of the river Jabbok (32:22–32), and on his deathbed (49:1–33).

The experience at Bethel occurred when he left the family home at Beersheba to travel to Haran (a city in Mesopotamia), the residence of his uncle Laban (28:10). On the way, as he stopped for the night at Bethel, he had a dream of a staircase reaching from earth to heaven with angels upon it and the Lord above it. He was impressed by the words of the Lord, promising Jacob inheritance of the land, descendants "as the dust of the earth" in number, and His divine presence. Jacob dedicated the site as a place of worship, calling it Bethel (literally, "house of God"). More than 20 years later, Jacob returned to this spot, built an altar, called the place El Bethel (literally, "God of the house of God"), and received the divine blessing (35:6–15).

The experience at the ford of the river Jabbok occurred as Jacob returned from his long stay at Haran. While preparing for a reunion with his brother, Esau, of whom he was still afraid (32:7), he had a profound experience that left him changed in both body and spirit.

At the ford of the Jabbok, "Jacob was left alone" (32:24). It was night, and he found himself suddenly engaged in a wrestling match in the darkness. This match lasted until the breaking of the dawn. The socket of Jacob's hip was put out of joint as he struggled with this mysterious stranger, but he refused to release his grip until he was given a blessing. For the first time in the narrative of Genesis, Jacob had been unable to defeat an opponent. When asked to identify himself in the darkness, he confessed he was Jacob—the "heel-grabber."

But Jacob's struggling earned him a new name. For his struggle "with God and with men" in which he had prevailed, his name was changed to Israel (literally, "he struggles with God") [see Hos. 12:3]. In return, he gave a name to the spot that marked the change; it would be called Peniel—"For I have seen God face to face, and my life is preserved" (32:30).

In these first two instances, a deep spiritual sensitivity is evident in Jacob. He appears outwardly brash and grasping, always enriching himself and securing his future. Yet he responded readily to these night experiences—the dream and the wrestling contest—because he apparently sensed "the presence of the holy" in each of them. He also proved to be a man of his word in his dealings with Laban (Gen. 31:6), and in the fulfillment of his vow to return to Bethel (35:1–3).

At the end of his life, Jacob—now an aged man (47:28)—gathered his 12 sons about his bed to tell them what should befall them "in the last days" (49:1).

The harshest language came against Reuben, the firstborn, who was rejected by his father for his sin (49:3–4), and Simeon and Levi, who were cursed for their anger and cruelty (49:5–7). The loftiest language was applied to Judah, who would be praised by his brothers and whose tribe would be the source of royalty, even the ruler of the people (49:8–12).

Words of warning were addressed to Dan, called "a serpent" and "a viper," a life that would be marked by violence (49:16–17). The two longest speeches were addressed to Judah and to Joseph, Jacob's favorite son (49:22–26). Following this scene, Jacob died and was embalmed by the physicians (Gen. 49:33; 50:2). By his own request Jacob was carried back to the land of Canaan and was buried in the family burial ground in the cave of the field of Machpelah (Gen. 49:29–32; 50:13).

JAEL [JAY uhl] (mountain goat)

The woman who killed Sisera, Israel's mighty enemy, by driving a tent peg through his temple while he slept (Judg. 4:17–22). Sisera accepted Jael's invitation to seek refuge in her tent. She covered him with a mantle, gave him milk to quench his thirst, and promised to stand guard against intruders. Instead, Jael killed Sisera as he slept. In her famous song, the prophetess Deborah honored Jael: "Most blessed above women is Jael" (Judg. 5:24).

JAMES

1. James, the brother of Jesus. James is first mentioned as the oldest of Jesus' four younger brothers (Matt. 13:55; Mark 6:3). The Gospels reveal that Jesus' brothers adopted a skeptical attitude toward His ministry (Matt. 12:46–50; Mark 3:31–35; Luke 8:19–21; John 7:5). James apparently held the same attitude, because his name appears in no lists of the apostles, nor is he mentioned elsewhere in the Gospels.

After Jesus' crucifixion, however,

James became a believer. Paul indicated that James was a witness to the resurrection of Jesus (1 Cor. 15:7). He called James an apostle (Gal. 1:19), though like himself, not one of the original Twelve (1 Cor. 15:5, 7).

In the Book of Acts, James emerges as the leader of the church in Jerusalem. His brothers also became believers and undertook missionary travels (1 Cor. 9:5). But James considered it his calling to oversee the church in Jerusalem (Gal. 2:9). He advocated respect for the Jewish law (Acts 21:18–25), but he did not use it as a weapon against Gentiles. Paul indicated that James endorsed his ministry to the Gentiles (Gal. 2:1–10).

The decree of the Council of Jerusalem (Acts 15:12–21) cleared the way for Christianity to become a universal religion. Gentiles were asked only "to abstain from things polluted by idols, from sexual immorality, from things strangled, and from blood" (Acts 15:20). The intent of this decree was practical rather than theological. It asked the Gentiles to observe certain practices that otherwise would offend their Jewish brothers in the Lord and jeopardize Christian fellowship with them.

Both Paul and Acts portray a James who was personally devoted to Jewish tradition but flexible enough to modify it to admit non-Jews into Christian fellowship. This James is probably the author of the Epistle of James in the New Testament.

JAMES

2. James, the son of Zebedee, one of Jesus' twelve apostles. James' father was a fisherman; his mother, Salome, often cared for Jesus' daily needs (Matt. 27:56; Mark 15:40–41). In lists of the twelve apostles, James and his brother John always form a group of four with two other brothers, Peter and Andrew. The four were fishermen on the Sea of Galilee.

Their call to follow Jesus is the first recorded event after the beginning of Jesus' public ministry (Matt. 4:18–22; Mark 1:16–20).

James is never mentioned apart from his brother John in the New Testament, even at his death (Acts 12:2). When the brothers are mentioned, James is always mentioned first, probably because he was the older. After the resurrection of Jesus, however, John became the more prominent, probably because of his association with Peter (Acts 3:1; 8:14). James was killed by Herod Agrippa I, the grandson of Herod the Great, some time between A.D. 42–44. He was the first of the twelve apostles to be put to death and the only one whose martyrdom is mentioned in the New Testament (Acts 12:2).

James and John must have contributed a spirited and headstrong element to Jesus' band of followers, because Jesus nicknamed them "Sons of Thunder" (Mark 3:17). On one occasion (Luke 9:51–56), when a Samaritan village refused to accept Jesus, the two asked Jesus to call down fire in revenge, as Elijah had done (2 Kin. 1:10, 12). On another occasion, they earned the anger of their fellow disciples by asking if they could sit on Jesus' right and left hands in glory (Matt. 20:20–28; Mark 10:35–45).

James was one of three disciples—Peter, James, and John—whom Jesus took along privately on three special occasions. The three accompanied Him when He healed the daughter of Jairus (Mark 5:37; Luke 8:51); they witnessed His transfiguration (Matt. 17:1; Mark 9:2; Luke 9:28); and they were also with Him in His agony in Gethsemane (Matt. 26:37; Mark 14:33).

JAMES

3. James, the son of Alphaeus. This James was also one of the twelve apostles. In each list of the apostles he is men-

tioned in ninth position (Matt. 10:3; Mark 3:18; Luke 6:15; Acts 1:13).

JAMES THE LESS

This James is called the son of Mary (not the mother of Jesus), and the brother of Joses (Matt. 27:56; Mark 16:1; Luke 24:10). Mark 15:40 refers to him as "James the Less." The Greek word *mikros* can mean either "small" or "less." It could, therefore, mean James the smaller (in size), or younger (NIV), or James the less (well-known).

JANNES AND JAMBRES [JAN iz, jam BREZ]

Two men who, according to the apostle Paul, "resisted Moses" (2 Tim. 3:8). Although Jannes and Jambres are not named in the Old Testament, they are common figures in late Jewish tradition. According to legend, they were two Egyptian magicians who opposed Moses' demand that the Israelites be freed. They sought to duplicate the miracles of Moses in an attempt to discredit him before Pharaoh "so the magicians of Egypt, they also did in like manner with their enhancement" (Ex. 7:11–12, 22).

JAPHETH [JAY fehth]

One of the three sons of Noah, usually mentioned after his two brothers Shem and Ham (Gen. 5:32; 6:10; 1 Chr. 1:4). Japheth and his wife were two of the eight people who entered the ark and were saved from the destructive waters of the Flood (Gen. 7:7; 1 Pet. 3:20).

Japheth's descendants spread over the north and west regions of the earth: "The sons of Japheth were Gomer, Magog, Madai, Javan, Tubal, Meshech, and Tiras" (1 Chr. 1:5). The Medes, Greeks, Romans, Russians, and Gauls are often referred to as his descendants.

JASHER, BOOK OF [JAY shur]

An ancient collection of verse, now lost, which described great events in the history of Israel. The book contained Joshua's poetic address to the sun and the moon at the battle of Gibeon (Josh. 10:12–13) and the "Song of the Bow," which is David's lament over the death of Saul and Jonathan (2 Sam. 1:17–27; Jashar in NIV, NRSV, REB).

JASON [JAY suhn]

A Christian of Thessalonica who gave lodging to Paul and Silas in his home during their visit to his city (Acts 17:5–7, 9). A mob of "evil men from the marketplace," incited by "the Jews who were not persuaded," attacked the house of Jason. When they could not find Paul and Silas, they dragged Jason before the rulers of the city on charges of disturbing the peace.

JASPER

An opaque variety of chalcedony, or quartz. Jasper is usually red because of the presence of iron, but it can be brown, yellow, or green. It was the third stone in the fourth row of Aaron's breastplate (Ex. 28:20; 39:13; green jasper in REB). The Book of Revelation describes the One on the throne as "like a jasper" (Rev. 4:3). The brilliance of the New Jerusalem was "as a jasper, clear as crystal" (Rev. 21:11).

JAZER [JAY zur]

A fortified Amorite city east of the Jordan River, in or near the region of Gilead (Josh. 13:25). Israel captured Jazer from the Amorites, allotted it to the tribe of Gad, and then gave it to the Levites. Jazer was probably situated on the plain north of Heshbon. Noted for its pasture lands, Jazer and the surrounding region was a good place for livestock (Num. 32:1). It also produced luxuriant grapevines and fruit trees (Is. 16:8–9).

The Ammonites, Amorites, Israelites, and Moabites all contested the possession of Jazer and its productive lands. The KJV also spells the name as Jaazer (Num. 21:32; 32:35).

JEALOUSY OFFERING

Part of an adultery trial, also known as the "ordeal of jealousy." If a man accused his wife of adultery but had no proof of her guilt, the law provided a ritual to determine whether she was innocent or guilty (Num. 5:11–31). If she swore her innocence, the woman was forced to drink a potion made of holy water mixed with dust from the floor of the tabernacle (v. 17); and the priest burned the offering, made of barley meal, on the altar (v. 26).

If she was guilty of adultery, she would suffer; but if she was innocent, she would be spared. In this way the decision was placed in the hands of God.

JEBUSITES [JEBB you sites]

The name of the original inhabitants of the city of Jebus, their name for ancient Jerusalem (Judg. 19:10–11; 1 Chr. 11:4–6). When the Israelites invaded Palestine under the leadership of Joshua, the Jebusites were ruled by Adoni-Zedek (Josh. 10:1, 3), one of five Amorite kings who resisted the Hebrew conquest. These five kings were defeated and slain by Joshua (Josh. 10:16–27). But the Jebusites were not driven out of Jebus (Jerusalem).

After David was anointed king, he led his army against the Jebusites. His military commander, Joab, apparently entered the city through an underground water shaft and led the conquest (2 Sam. 5:6–9; 1 Chr. 11:4–8). David then made this former Jebusite stronghold, now called the "City of David," the capital of his kingdom.

The site on which Solomon's temple was built in Jerusalem was previously a threshing floor that belonged to a Jebusite by the name of Araunah (2 Sam. 24:16–24), or Ornan (1 Chr. 21:24–25). David refused to accept this property as a gift from Araunah and paid him 50 shekels of silver for the land. Apparently David treated the defeated Jebusites humanely, but his son Solomon "raised forced labor" (1 Kin. 9:21) from their ranks.

JEHOAHAZ [juh HOE uh haz] *(the Lord sustains)*

1. The son and successor of Jehu and the twelfth king of Israel (2 Kin. 10:35). His 17-year reign (815–798 B.C.) was a disaster for the nation of Israel. By not renouncing the idolatry of the golden calves set up by Jeroboam I at Dan and Bethel, Jehoahaz "did evil in the sight of the Lord." Hazael of Syria and his son Ben-Hadad severely punished Israel during Jehoahaz's reign. This drove Jehoahaz to the Lord, who heard his prayer and granted temporary deliverance from Syria (2 Kin. 13:2–5). Unfortunately, after the danger passed, Jehoahaz quickly abandoned his faith. After his death, Jehoahaz was succeeded by his son Joash (or Jehoash).

JEHOAHAZ [juh HOE uh haz] *(the Lord sustains)*

2. The youngest son of Jehoram, king of Judah (2 Chr. 21:17; 25:23). The sixth king of Judah, Jehoahaz was 42 years old at the beginning of his reign, which lasted only one year (842 or 841 B.C.). Jehoahaz is usually called Ahaziah (2 Kin. 8:24–14:13; 2 Chr. 22:1–11). Also, an inscription of the Assyrian king Tiglath-Pileser III refers to Ahaz, king of Judah, as Jehoahaz; this was evidently his full name, but the Bible always uses the abbreviated form Ahaz.

JEHOIACHIN [juh HOI uh kin] *(the Lord establishes)*

The son and successor of Jehoiakim as king of Judah, about 598 or 597 B.C. (2 Chr. 36:8–9; Ezek. 1:2). Jehoiachin did evil in the sight of the Lord, like his father. But he had little opportunity to influence affairs of state, since he reigned only three months. His brief reign ended when the armies of Nebuchadnezzar of Babylon besieged Jerusalem. When the city surrendered, Jehoiachin was exiled to Babylonia (2 Kin. 24:6–15).

Nebuchadnezzar then made Mattaniah, Jehoiachin's uncle, king in his place and changed Mattaniah's name to Zedekiah (v. 17). Zedekiah was destined to rule over a powerless land containing only poor farmers and laborers, while Jehoiachin was held a prisoner in Babylon.

In the thirty-seventh year of his captivity, Jehoiachin was finally released by a new Babylonian king, Evil-Merodach (Amel-Marduk). He must have been awarded a place of prominence in the king's court, since he ate his meals regularly in the presence of the king himself (2 Kin. 25:27–30).

Jehoiachin is also called Jeconiah (1 Chr. 3:16–17) and Coniah (Jer. 22:24). In the New Testament he is listed by Matthew as an ancestor of Jesus (Matt. 1:11–12).

JEHOIADA [juh HOI uh duh] *(the Lord knows)*

A priest during the reigns of Ahaziah, Athaliah, and Joash of Judah (2 Kin. 11:1–12:16) who helped hide the young king Joash from the wrath of Queen Athaliah (2 Chr. 22:10–12). By his courageous action, Jehoiada was instrumental in preserving the line of David, since Joash was a descendant of David and an ancestor of Jesus. Jehoiada married Jehoshabeath, daughter of King Jehoram (2 Chr. 22:11).

Even after Joash became king, Jehoiada was a powerful influence for good in his kingdom. Under his oversight, the temple of Baal was torn down and the influence of Baalism over the people was reduced. Under the prompting of the young king Joash, the temple of the Lord was restored to its former glory (2 Kin. 12; 2 Chr. 24). Jehoiada lived to be 130 years old. When he died, he was awarded the honor of burial in the royal tombs "because he had done good in Israel, both toward God and His house" (2 Chr. 24:15–16).

JEHOIAKIM [juh HOI uh kim] *(the Lord raises up)*

An evil king of Judah whose downfall was predicted by the prophet Jeremiah. A son of the good king Josiah, Jehoiakim was 25 years old when he succeeded to the throne. He reigned 11 years in Jerusalem, from 609 B.C. to 598 B.C. During his reign Pharaoh Necho of Egypt exacted heavy tribute from the people of Judah (2 Chr. 36:3, 5). Jehoiakim was forced to levy a burdensome tax upon his people to pay this tribute.

The prophet Jeremiah described the arrogance of Jehoiakim in great detail (Jer. 1:3; 24:1; 27:1, 20; 37:1; 52:2). He censured Jehoiakim for exploiting the people to build his own splendid house with expensive furnishings (Jer. 22:13–23). Unlike his father Josiah, Jehoiakim ignored justice and righteousness. Jehoiakim had no intention of obeying the Lord; he "did evil in the sight of the Lord" (2 Kin. 23:37). His 11-year reign was filled with abominable acts against God (2 Chr. 36:8). Because of this evil, Jeremiah predicted that no one would lament the death of Jehoiakim.

Jeremiah also told of Jehoiakim's execution of Urijah, a prophet of the Lord (Jer. 26:20–23). Perhaps Jehoiakim's most cynical act was his burning of Jeremiah's prophecies (Jer. 36:22–23). Jeremiah wrote a scroll of judgment against the king, but as this scroll was read, Jehoiakim cut it into pieces and threw them into the fire.

Jehoiakim could burn the Word of God, but he could not destroy its power. Neither could he avoid Jeremiah's prophecy of his approaching destruction. Recognizing the power of the Babylonians, he made an agreement with Nebuchadnezzar to serve as his vassal king on the throne of Judah. After three years of subjection, he led a foolish rebellion to regain his nation's independence. The rebellion failed and Jerusalem was destroyed by the Babylonians. Jehoiakim was bound and carried away as a captive (2 Chr. 36:6).

JEHOSHAPHAT [juh HAH shuh fat] *(the Lord is judge)*

A son of Asa who succeeded his father as king of Judah (1 Kin. 15:24). Jehoshaphat was 35 years old when he became king, and he reigned 25 years in Jerusalem (2 Chr. 20:31), from about 873 B.C. to about 848 B.C.

Jehoshaphat received an excellent heritage from his father Asa, who in the earlier years of his reign showed a reforming spirit in seeking God (2 Chr. 15:1–19). Jehoshaphat's faith in God led him to "delight in the ways of the Lord" (2 Chr. 17:6). He attacked pagan idolatry, and he sent teachers to the people to teach them more about God (2 Chr. 17:6–9). In affairs of state, Jehoshaphat also showed a willingness to rely on the Lord. In a time of danger he prayed for God's help (2 Chr. 20:6–12).

Jehoshaphat showed a high regard for justice in his dealings (2 Chr. 19:4–11). He reminded the judges whom he appointed that their ultimate loyalty was to God. His attitude toward impartial justice is reflected in these words: "Behave courageously, and the Lord will be with the good" (2 Chr. 19:11).

J

But in his dealings with Ahab, king of Israel, Jehoshaphat made some serious mistakes. Through the marriage of his son, Jehoram, to Ahab's daughter, Jehoshaphat allied himself with Ahab (2 Chr. 21:5–6). This alliance led to even further dealings with the wicked king of Israel (2 Chr. 18:1–34), which the prophet Jehu rebuked (2 Chr. 19:1–3).

Jehoshaphat and his father Asa are bright lights against the dark paganism that existed during their time. Both father and son had certain weaknesses, but their faith in the Lord brought good to themselves as well as God's people during their reigns.

JEHOSHAPHAT, VALLEY OF [juh HAH shuh fat]

A valley in which, according to Joel 3:2, 12, God will judge the nations at the end of this age. According to Jewish tradition, the Valley of Jehoshaphat was that part of the Kidron Valley between the temple and the Mount of Olives. The name Jehoshaphat means "the Lord is judge." The name may refer to a symbolic "valley of decision" (Joel 3:14) that is connected with divine judgments instead of a literal geographical place.

JEHOSHEBA [juh HAH shuh buh] (the Lord is her oath)

The courageous woman who rescued her nephew Joash from certain death at the hands of Athaliah, the wicked queen of Judah (2 Kin. 11:1–3; 2 Chr. 22:10–12). Jehosheba was the half sister of King Ahaziah. When Ahaziah was killed in battle, his mother, Athaliah, attempted to kill all her grandsons and took the throne for herself. But Jehosheba rescued the youngest of Ahaziah's sons (2 Kin. 11:2) and hid him in the temple for six years— until he was old enough to be proclaimed king.

Jehosheba's courageous act preserved "the house and lineage of David" (Luke 2:4), from which Jesus was descended.

JEHU [JEE hyoo] (the Lord is He)

The eleventh king of Israel (2 Chr. 22:7–9). Jehu was anointed by Elisha the prophet as king; he later overthrew Joram (Jehoram), King Ahab's son and successor, and reigned for 28 years (841–813 B.C.). His corrupt leadership weakened the nation. He is known for his violence against all members of the "house of Ahab" as he established his rule throughout the nation.

At Jehu's command, Jezebel, the notorious wife of Ahab, was thrown out of the window of the palace to her death, as prophesied by Elijah (1 Kin. 21:23). Ahab's murder of Naboth and the subversion of the religion of Israel had brought terrible vengeance, but more blood was to be shed by Jehu. Next to feel the new king's wrath were the 70 sons of Ahab who lived in Samaria (2 Kin. 10). Jehu ordered them killed by the elders of Samaria. Jehu's zeal extended even further, commanding the death of Ahab's advisors and close acquaintances. This excessive violence led the prophet Hosea to denounce Jehu's bloodthirstiness (Hos. 1:4).

Jehu continued his slaughter against the family of Ahaziah, king of Judah (2 Kin. 10:12–14). Then he made an alliance with Jehonadab, the chief of the Rechabites, to destroy the followers of Baal. Jehu and Jehonadab plotted to conduct a massive assembly in honor of Baal. After assuring the Baal worshipers of their sincerity and gathering them into the temple of Baal, Jehu had them all killed (2 Kin. 10:18–28). So complete was this destruction that Baalism was wiped out in Israel, and the temple of Baal was torn down and made into a garbage dump.

Although Jehu proclaimed his zeal for the Lord (2 Kin. 10:16), he failed to follow the Lord's will completely (2 Kin. 10:31). He did not completely eliminate worship of the golden calves at Dan and Bethel, and his disobedience led to the conquest of many parts of Israel by the Syrians (2 Kin. 10:32–33).

JEPHTHAH [JEF thuh]

The ninth judge of Israel, who delivered God's people from the Ammonites (Judg. 11:1–12:7). An illegitimate child, Jephthah was cast out of the family by his half brothers, to prevent him from sharing in the inheritance. He fled to "the land of Tob," where he gathered a group of "worthless men" and soon engaged in raids throughout the surrounding countryside.

When Israel was threatened by the Ammonites, the elders of Gilead asked Jephthah to free them from oppression by organizing a counterattack on Ammon. Jephthah showed shrewd foresight by insisting on a position of leadership in Gilead if he should succeed against the Ammonites. After this assurance (Judg. 11:10–11), he began his campaign.

Jephthah first tried the diplomatic approach, but Ammon wanted war. So Jephthah launched an attack through Mizpah of Gilead (Judg. 11:29) and defeated the Ammonites "with a very great slaughter" (Judg. 11:33). At this point, Jephthah made a rash vow, promising God that in exchange for victory in battle he would offer up as a sacrifice the first thing that should come out of his house to meet him on his return (Judg. 11:31).

The Lord delivered Ammon's army into Jephthah's hands. When he returned home, his daughter—his only child—came out to meet him (Judg. 11:34). Jephthah tore his clothing in distress as he realized the terrible rashness of his vow. The text seems to indicate that Jephthah followed through on his vow (Judg. 11:39), although a few scholars believe the verse means she was kept as a virgin dedicated to special service to the Lord for the rest of her life.

After this incident, Jephthah punished an arrogant group of Ephraimites at the Jordan River by using a clever strategy to confuse the enemy. He asked the soldiers to say "shibboleth." If they were Ephraimites, they would not be able to pronounce the word correctly and would say "sibboleth." Their accent would betray them as the enemy.

Jephthah was a man with remarkable abilities of leadership. In spite of rejection by his family, he exercised his many talents and rose to a position of great authority. His greatest weakness was his rash, thoughtless behavior. After his death, he was buried in a city of Gilead. The Book of Hebrews lists him as one of the heroes of faith (Heb. 11:32).

JEREMIAH [jer uh MIGH uh] *(the Lord hurls)*

The major prophet during the decline and fall of the southern kingdom of Judah and author of the Book of Jeremiah. He prophesied during the reigns of the last five kings of Judah.

Jeremiah was born in Anathoth, situated north of Jerusalem in the territory of Benjamin (Jer. 1:1–2). He was called to the prophetic ministry in the thirteenth year of Josiah's reign, about 627 B.C. He must have been a young man at the time, since his ministry lasted for about 40 years—through the very last days of the nation of Judah when the capital city of Jerusalem was destroyed in 586 B.C.

Jeremiah's call is one of the most instructive passages in his book. God declared that he had sanctioned him as a prophet even before he was born (Jer. 1:5). But the young man responded with words of inadequacy: "Ah, Lord God!"

J

(Jer. 1:6). These words actually mean "No, Lord God!" Jeremiah pleaded that he was a youth and that he lacked the ability to speak. But God replied that he was being called not because of age or ability but because God had chosen him.

Immediately Jeremiah saw the Hand of God reaching out and touching his mouth. "Behold, I have put My words in your mouth," God declared (Jer. 1:9). From that moment, the words of the prophet were to be the words of God. And his ministry was to consist of tearing down and rebuilding, uprooting and replanting: "See, I have this day set you over the kingdoms, to root out and to pull down, to destroy and to throw down, to build and to plant" (Jer. 1:10).

Because of the negative nature of Jeremiah's ministry, judgmental texts abound in his book. Jeremiah was destined from the very beginning to be a prophet of doom. He was even forbidden to marry so he could devote himself fully to the task of preaching God's judgment (Jer. 16:1–13). A prophet of doom cannot be a happy man. All of Jeremiah's life was wrapped up in the knowledge that God was about to bring an end to the Holy City and cast off His covenant people.

Jeremiah is often called "the weeping prophet" because he wept openly about the sins of his nation (Jer. 9:1). He was also depressed at times about the futility of his message. As the years passed and his words of judgment went unheeded, he lamented his unfortunate state: "O Lord, You induced me, and I was persuaded; You are stronger than I, and have prevailed. I am in derision daily; everyone mocks me" (Jer. 20:7).

At times Jeremiah tried to hold back from his prophetic proclamation. But he found that the word of the Lord was "like a burning fire shut up in my bones" (Jer. 20:9). He had no choice but to proclaim the harsh message of God's judgment.

Jeremiah did not weep and lament because of weakness, nor did he proclaim evil because of a dark and gloomy personality. He cried out because of his love for his people and his God. This characteristic of the prophet is actually a tribute to his sensitivity and deep concern. Jeremiah's laments remind us of the weeping of the Savior (Matt. 23:37–39).

As Jeremiah predicted, the nation of Judah was eventually punished by God because of its sin and disobedience. In 586 B.C. Jerusalem was destroyed and the leading citizens were deported to Babylonia. Jeremiah remained in Jerusalem with a group of his fellow citizens under the authority of a ruling governor appointed by the Babylonians. But he was forced to seek safety in Egypt after the people of Jerusalem revolted against Babylonian rule. He continued his preaching in Egypt (Jer. 43–44). This is the last we hear of Jeremiah. There is no record of what happened to the prophet during these years of his ministry.

In the New Testament (KJV), Jeremiah was referred to as Jeremy (Matt. 2:17; 27:9) and Jeremias (Matt. 16:14).

JERICHO [JEHR ih coe]

One of the oldest inhabited cities in the world. Situated in the wide plain of the Jordan valley (Deut. 34:1, 3) at the foot of the ascent to the Judean mountains, Jericho lies about 8 miles (13 kilometers) northwest of the site where the Jordan River flows into the Dead Sea, some 5 miles (8 kilometers) west of the Jordan.

Since it is approximately 800 feet (244 meters) below sea level, Jericho has a climate that is tropical and at times is very hot. Only a few inches of rainfall are recorded at Jericho each year; but the city is a wonderful oasis, known as "the city of palm trees" (Deut. 34:3) or "the city of palms" (Judg. 3:13). Jericho flourishes with date palms, banana trees, balsams, sycamores, and henna (Song 1:14; Luke 19:4).

There have been three different Jerichos throughout its long history. Old Testament Jericho is identified with the mound of Tell es Sultan, about a little more than a mile (2 kilometers) from the village of er-Riha. This village is modern Jericho, located about 17 miles (27 kilometers) northeast of Jerusalem. New Testament Jericho is identified with the mounds of Tulul Abu el-'Alayiq, about 2 kilometers west of modern Jericho and south of Old Testament Jericho.

By far the most imposing site of the three is Old Testament Jericho, a pear-shaped mound about 400 yards (366 meters) long, north to south, 200 yards (183 meters) wide at the north end, and some 70 yards (67 meters) high. It has been the site of numerous archaeological diggings and is a favorite stop for Holy Land tourists.

Old Testament Jericho first appears in the biblical record when the Israelites encamped at Shittim on the east side of the Jordan River (Num. 22:1; 26:3). Joshua sent spies to examine the city (Josh. 2:1–24) and later took the city by perhaps the most unorthodox method in the history of warfare (Josh. 6). Joshua placed a curse on anyone who would attempt to rebuild Jericho (Josh. 6:26).

As the Israelites settled into the land, Jericho was awarded to the tribe of Benjamin, although it was on the border between Ephraim and Benjamin (Josh. 16:1, 7). Jericho is only incidentally mentioned in the reign of David (2 Sam. 10:5) and does not figure prominently again in Old Testament history until the reign of King Ahab (about 850 B.C.; 1 Kin. 16:34), when Hiel the Bethelite attempted to fortify the city and Joshua's curse was realized. During the days of Elijah and Elisha, Jericho was a community of the prophets (2 Kin. 2:5) and was mentioned on other occasions as well (Ezra 2:34; Neh. 3:2; Jer. 39:5).

In the early years of Herod the Great, the Romans plundered New Testament Jericho. But Herod later beautified the city and ultimately died there. Jesus passed through Jericho on numerous occasions. Near there He was baptized in the Jordan River (Matt. 3:13–17), and on the adjacent mountain range He was tempted (Matt. 4:1–11). At Jericho Jesus healed blind Bartimaeus (Mark 10:46–52). Here too Zacchaeus was converted (Luke 19:1–10). And Jesus' parable of the Good Samaritan has the road from Jerusalem to Jericho as its setting (Luke 10:30–37).

From 1907 until 1911, the German scholars Ernst Sellin and Carl Watzinger excavated this site. But it was the British archaeologist John Garstang whose excavations from 1930 to 1936 yielded significant information. Garstang believed he found evidence of Joshua's destruction of the city. He discovered an inner wall about 12 feet (3.66 meters) thick and an outer wall about 6 feet (1.83 meters) thick. Garstang was convinced that he had found the fabled walls of Jericho.

However, archaeologist Kathleen Kenyon began seven seasons of excavation at Jericho in 1952 and found evidence that conflicted with that of Garstang. Kenyon's findings indicated that little of the city in Joshua's day remained and thus the archaeologist must turn to Hazor and other cities captured during Joshua's campaigns for information about this period. The most spectacular finds made by Kenyon were the Stone Age defenses, including a tower dating to about 7000 B.C.

JEROBOAM [jehr uh BOE ahm] (let the kinsman plead)

1. Jeroboam I, the first king of Israel (the ten northern tribes, or the northern kingdom). The son of Nebat and Zeruah, Jeroboam reigned over Israel for 22 years (1 Kin. 14:20), from about 930 to 910 B.C.

Jeroboam I first appears in the biblical record as Solomon's servant: "the officer over all the labor force of the house of Joseph" (1 Kin. 11:28). One day as Jeroboam went out of Jerusalem, the prophet Ahijah the Shilonite met him on the road and confronted him with an enacted parable. Ahijah, who was wearing a new garment, took hold of the garment and tore it into 12 pieces. He then said to Jeroboam, "Take for yourself ten pieces, for thus says the Lord, the God of Israel: 'Behold, I will tear the kingdom out of the hand of Solomon and will give ten tribes to you'" (1 Kin. 11:31).

When Solomon learned of Ahijah's words, he sought to kill Jeroboam. But Jeroboam fled to Egypt, where he was granted political asylum by Shishak I, the king of Egypt. Only after the death of Solomon did Jeroboam risk returning to his native Palestine (1 Kin. 11:40; 12:2–3).

Solomon's kingdom was outwardly rich, prosperous, and thriving. But the great building projects he undertook were accomplished by forced labor, high taxes, and other oppressive measures. Discontent and unrest existed throughout Solomon's kingdom. When the great king died, the kingdom was like a powder keg awaiting a spark.

The occasion for the explosion, the tearing of the ten northern tribes from Solomon's successor, came because of the foolish insensitivity of Solomon's son Rehoboam. Rehoboam had gone to Shechem to be anointed as the new king. A delegation led by Jeroboam, who had returned from Egypt following Solomon's death, said to Rehoboam, "Your father made our yoke heavy; now therefore, lighten the burdensome service of your father, and his heavy yoke which he put on us, and we will serve" (1 Kin. 12:4).

But Rehoboam followed the advice of his inexperienced companions and replied, "Whereas my father laid a heavy yoke on you, I will add to your yoke; my father chastised you with whips, but I will chastise you with scourges!" (1 Kin. 12:11). After this show of Rehoboam's foolishness, the ten northern tribes revolted against Rehoboam and appointed Jeroboam as their king (1 Kin. 12:16–20).

Jeroboam was concerned that the people of Israel might return to the house of David if they continued to journey to Jerusalem for the festivals and observances at the temple of Solomon. So he proposed an alternative form of idolatrous worship. He made two calves of gold that bore a close resemblance to the mounts of the Canaanite pagan god Baal. The king told his countrymen: "It is too much for you to go up to Jerusalem. Here are your gods, O Israel, which brought you up from the land of Egypt!" (1 Kin. 12:28). One calf was erected in Bethel and one in Dan.

Once committed to this sinful direction, Jeroboam's progress was downhill. He next appointed priests from tribes other than Levi. He offered sacrifices to these images and gradually polluted the worship of Israel. The Lord confronted Jeroboam by sending him an unnamed prophet who predicted God's judgment on the king and the nation.

Although outwardly he appeared to be repentant, Jeroboam would not change his disastrous idolatry. His rebellious, arrogant attitude set the pattern for rulers of Israel for generations to come. Eighteen kings sat on the throne of Israel after his death, but not one of them gave up his pagan worship.

JEROBOAM [jehr uh BOE ahm] *(let the kinsman plead)*

2. Jeroboam II, the fourteenth king of Israel, who reigned for 41 years (793–753 B.C.). Jeroboam was the son and successor of Joash (or Jehoash); he was the grandson of Jehoahaz and the great-grandson of Jehu (2 Kin. 13:1, 13; 1 Chr. 5:17). The Bible declares that Jeroboam "did evil in the sight of the Lord" (2 Kin. 14:24).

Jeroboam was successful in his military adventures. His aggressive campaigns "recaptured for Israel, from Damascus and Hamath, what had belonged to Judah" (2 Kin. 14:28). The boundaries of Israel expanded to their greatest extent since the days of David and Solomon: "He restored the territory of Israel from the entrance of Hamath to the Sea of the Arabah" (2 Kin. 14:25).

Jeroboam II was king during the prosperous interval between the economic reverses of other rulers. Hosea, Amos, and Jonah lived during his reign (Hos. 1:1; Amos 1:1–2; 2 Kin. 14:25). During this time of superficial prosperity, the prophet Amos especially spoke out against the many social abuses in Israel. A severe oppression of the poor had been instituted by the newly prosperous class. Justice was in the hands of lawless judges; dishonest merchants falsified the balances by deceit; and worship was little more than a pious smokescreen that covered the abuses of the poor. Amos prophesied that the fury of God would fall upon the house of Jeroboam (Amos 7:9).

After Jeroboam's death, his son Zechariah succeeded him on the throne of Israel (2 Kin. 14:29). Zechariah reigned in Samaria only six months before he was assassinated by Shallum (2 Kin. 15:10).

JERUSALEM [jeh ROO sah lem] *(city of peace)*

Sacred city and well-known capital of Palestine during Bible times. The earliest known name for Jerusalem was Urushalem. Salem, of which Melchizedek was king (Gen. 14:18), was a natural abbreviation for Jeru-salem. Thus, Jerusalem appears in the Bible as early as the time of Abraham, although the city had probably been inhabited for centuries before that time.

After the death of Saul, the first king of the united kingdom of the Hebrew people, David was named the new king of Israel. One of his first efforts was to unite the tribes of the north and south by capturing Jerusalem, known as Jebus, from the Jebusites, making the city the political and religious capital of the kingdom (1 Chr. 11:4–9). Because it was captured during his reign, Jerusalem also came to be known as the "City of David."

The city is often referred to by this title in the Bible.

David built a palace in the section of Jerusalem that served previously as the Jebusite stronghold. This section, situated in the highest part of the city, frequently is referred to as Mount Zion. David probably selected Jerusalem as his capital because it was centrally located between the northern and southern tribes. Thus, it was geographically convenient for the nation. The central location of the capital city tended to unite the people into one kingdom.

The topography of the city made it easy to defend. Jerusalem was situated on a hill. The eastern and western sides of the city consisted of valleys that made invasion by opposing forces difficult. The southern portion consisted of ravines that made an attack from this position unwise. The best point from which to attack Jerusalem was the north, which had the highest elevation of any portion of the city.

But the selection of Jerusalem as the capital was more than a choice by a human king. Divine providence was also involved. Jerusalem was referred to as "the place which the Lord your God shall choose out of all your tribes to put his name there" (Deut. 12:5, 11, 14, 18, 21).

The glory of Jerusalem, begun under David, reached its greatest heights under Solomon. Solomon proceeded to construct the temple about which David had dreamed (2 Chr. 3–4). He also extended the borders of the city to new limits. Because surrounding nations were engaged in internal strife, Jerusalem was spared from invasions from opposing forces during Solomon's administration.

After completing the temple, Solomon built the palace complex, a series of five structures. He also planted vineyards, orchards, and gardens that contained all types of trees and shrubs. These were watered by streams and pools that flowed through the complex. Unfortunately, this splendor came to an end with the death of Solomon about 931 B.C. The division of the kingdom into two separate nations after Solomon's reign resulted in the relapse of Jerusalem to the status of a minor city.

After the death of Solomon, the division that occurred in the kingdom resulted in the ten northern tribes establishing their own capital, first at Shechem and later at Samaria. The southern tribes, consisting of Judah and Benjamin, retained Jerusalem as the capital. Although separated politically from Jerusalem, the northern tribes continued their allegiance to the "holy city" by occasionally coming there for worship.

Although occasionally threatened and plundered by surrounding nations, Jerusalem remained intact until 586 B.C. At that time, Nebuchadnezzar, king of Babylonia, ravaged the city and carried the inhabitants into captivity. During the siege of the city, Jerusalem's beautiful temple was destroyed and the walls around the city were torn down. While a few inhabitants remained in the city, the glory of Jerusalem was gone.

For more than half a century the Jews remained captives in Babylonia, and their beloved Jerusalem lay in ruins. But this changed when Cyrus, king of Persia, defeated the Babylonians. He allowed the Jewish captives to return to Jerusalem to restore the city. During the succeeding years of domination by the Persian Empire, Jerusalem apparently enjoyed peace and prosperity.

The wise men who sought Jesus after His birth came to Jerusalem because this was considered the city of the king (Matt. 2:1–2). Although Jesus was born in Bethlehem, Jerusalem played a significant role in His life and ministry. It was to Jerusalem that He went when He was 12 years old. Here He amazed the temple leaders with His knowledge and wisdom (Luke 2:47). In Jerusalem He cleansed the temple, chasing away the money-changers who desecrated the holy place with their selfish practices. And, finally, it was outside Jerusalem where He was crucified, buried, and resurrected.

The record of the New Testament church indicates that Jerusalem continued to play a significant role in the early spread of Christianity. After the martyrdom of Stephen, the early believers scattered from Jerusalem to various parts of the Mediterranean world (Acts 8:1). But Jerusalem always was the place to which they returned for significant events. For example, Acts 15 records that when the early church leaders sought to reconcile their differences about the acceptance of Gentile believers, they met in Jerusalem. Thus, the city became a holy city for Christians as well as Jews.

The Jerusalem of New Testament times contained a temple that had been built by Herod, the Roman leader. Although the main portion of the temple was completed in 18 months, other areas of this building were still under construction during Jesus' ministry. In fact, the temple was not completed until A.D. 67—only three years before it was finally destroyed by the Roman leader, Titus, and the Roman army.

As Jesus had prophesied in Matthew 24, the city of Jerusalem was completely destroyed in A.D. 70. The temple was destroyed, and the high priesthood and the Sanhedrin were abolished. Eventually, a Roman city was erected on the site, and Jerusalem was regarded as forbidden ground for the Jews.

In 1919, under a ruling by British officials in Palestine, Jerusalem regained its status as a capital city. During the following three decades, numerous Jews, whose ancestors had been barred from the city, settled in and around Jerusalem. A new city, whose population was predominantly Jewish, was constructed west of the site of the old city. Following the Arab-Israeli War of 1948–1949, the new city was allotted to the Jews, while the old city remained in Muslim hands. Less than two decades later, as a result of what has become known as the Six-Day War, the old city and the surrounding countryside were captured by Israel. It has remained occupied by the descendants of the biblical Israelites until the present day.

See also ZION.

JERUSALEM COUNCIL, THE

A conference held in about A.D. 49 between delegates (including Paul and Barnabas) from the church at Antioch of Syria and delegates from the church at Jerusalem. This council met to settle a dispute over whether Gentile converts to Christianity first had to identify with Judaism by being circumcised (Acts 15:1–29).

According to Luke, "Certain men came down from Judea and taught the brethren, 'Unless you are circumcised according to the custom of Moses, you cannot be saved'" (Acts 15:1). They insisted that Gentiles could not be received into the church unless they were circumcised and brought under the rules of the Mosaic Law. The apostle Paul, champion of Gentile freedom, said that all people—both Jews and Gentiles—are saved by grace through faith in Jesus Christ, apart from the works of the law. To require circumcision, he argued, would destroy the Good News of God's grace.

The conclusion of the Jerusalem Council, which determined that Gentiles did not have to be circumcised, was a sweeping victory for Paul's understanding of Christianity. Speaking for the council, the apostle Peter declared, "We believe that through the grace of the Lord Jesus Christ we [Jews] shall be saved in the same manner as they [the Gentiles]" (Acts 15:11).

Why was the decision of the Jerusalem Council so important? Perhaps this question can be answered by considering another question: What would have happened to the gospel of Christ, and to Christianity, if the council had decided that circumcision is necessary for anyone to become a Christian?

Such a decision would have been disastrous. It would have forced a condition that would have been unacceptable to the Gentiles. The missionary efforts would have become more difficult, and Christianity would have become nothing but a sect within Judaism. Furthermore, the truth of the gospel would have been compromised. Instead of a gospel based on salvation by grace through faith in Jesus Christ, it would have become one based on salvation by works (the law).

The theological problem was solved, but a practical problem remained. Fellowship between the Jews and Gentiles in the early church remained on a shaky foundation. If the Gentile converts to Christianity flaunted their newfound freedom in Christ, without any concern for the sensitive feelings of the Jewish Christians, the unity of the church could be threatened. The Jerusalem Council decreed, therefore, that the Gentiles should make four reasonable concessions of their own: "We write to them to abstain from things polluted by idols, from sexual immorality, from things strangled, and from blood" (Acts 15:20; also 15:29; 21:25). In other words, Gentile converts should avoid offending the moral and religious convictions of the Jewish believers.

The Jerusalem Council was both a theological and a practical success. The concessions it called for were not "compromises"; indeed, they reaffirmed the integrity of the gospel of salvation by faith alone. They also dealt with a potentially explosive controversy by expressing concern for deeply held convictions. As the Jerusalem Council ended, the first great threat to the unity of the church brought rejoicing and encouragement instead (Acts 15:31).

JERUSALEM, NEW

The Holy City described by John in Revelation 21–22; God's perfect and eternal order of the future. This New Jerusalem is not built by human hands; it is a heavenly city—one built and provided by God Himself (Rev. 21:2).

The New Jerusalem and the new Garden of Eden (symbols of righteousness, peace, and contentment) are the dwelling place of God, Christ, and the church. John saw no temple in the New Jerusalem, "for the Lord God Almighty and the Lamb are its temple" (Rev. 21:22).

In the Book of Revelation John draws a graphic contrast between the harlot city called "Babylon the Great" (Rev. 14:8; 16:19; 17:1–18:24), the earthly and temporal city of human beings, and the "New Jerusalem" (Rev. 21:2–22:5), the heavenly and eternal city of God. John identifies "the great city, the holy Jerusalem" (Rev. 21:10), as the church, which he calls "the bride, the Lamb's wife" (Rev. 21:9).

JESSE [JES ee] (meaning unknown)

The father of King David (1 Sam. 16:18–19) and an ancestor of Jesus. Jesse was the father of eight sons and two daughters (1 Chr. 2:13–16). He is called a "Bethlehemite" (1 Sam. 16:1, 18).

On instructions from the Lord, the prophet Samuel went to Bethlehem to select a new king from among Jesse's eight sons. After the first seven were rejected, David was anointed by Samuel to replace Saul as king of Israel (1 Sam. 16:1–13). Later King Saul asked Jesse to allow David to visit his court and play soothing music on the harp. Jesse gave

his permission and sent Saul a present (1 Sam. 16:20).

The title "son of Jesse" soon became attached to David. It was sometimes used in a spirit of insult and ridicule, mocking David's humble origins (1 Sam. 20:27; 1 Kin. 12:16). But the prophet Isaiah spoke of "a Rod from the stem of Jesse" (11:1) and of "a Root of Jesse" (11:10)—prophecies of the Messiah to come. For the apostle Paul, the "root of Jesse" (Rom. 15:12) was a prophecy fulfilled in Jesus Christ.

JESUS CHRIST, LIFE OF

Jesus was born in Bethlehem, a town about 6 miles (10 kilometers) south of Jerusalem, toward the end of Herod the Great's reign as king of the Jews (37–4 B.C.). Early in His life He was taken to Nazareth, a town of Galilee. There He was brought up by His mother, Mary, and her husband, Joseph, a carpenter by trade. Hence He was known as "Jesus of Nazareth" or, more fully, "Jesus of Nazareth, the son of Joseph" (John 1:45).

Jesus was His mother's firstborn child; He had four brothers (James, Joses, Judas, and Simon) and an unspecified number of sisters (Mark 6:3). Joseph apparently died before Jesus began His public ministry. Mary, with the rest of the family, lived on and became a member of the church of Jerusalem after Jesus' death and resurrection.

The only incident preserved from Jesus' first 30 years (after his infancy) was His trip to Jerusalem with Joseph and Mary when He was 12 years old (Luke 2:41–52). Since He was known in Nazareth as "the carpenter" (Mark 6:3), He may have taken Joseph's place as the family breadwinner at an early age.

Jesus began His public ministry when He sought baptism at the hands of John the Baptist. The descent of the dove as Jesus came up out of the water was a sign that He was the One anointed by the

Spirit of God as the Servant-Messiah of His people (Is. 11:2; 42:1; 61:1). A voice from heaven declared, "You are My beloved Son; in You I am well pleased" (Luke 3:22). This indicated that He was Israel's anointed King, destined to fulfill His kingship as the Servant of the Lord described centuries earlier by the prophet Isaiah (Is. 42:1; 52:13).

Jesus ministered for a short time in southern and central Palestine, while John the Baptist was still preaching (John 3:22–4:42). But the main phase of Jesus' ministry began in Galilee after John's imprisonment by Herod Antipas. This was the signal, according to Mark 1:14–15, for Jesus to proclaim God's Good News in Galilee: "The time is fulfilled, and the kingdom of God is at hand. Repent, and believe in the gospel."

Jesus' proclamation of the kingdom of God was accompanied by works of mercy and power, including the healing of the sick, particularly those who were demon-possessed. These works also proclaimed the arrival of the kingdom of God. The demons that caused such distress to men and women were signs of the kingdom of Satan. When they were cast out, this proved the superior strength of the kingdom of God.

For a time, Jesus' healing aroused great popular enthusiasm throughout Galilee. But the religious leaders and teachers found much of Jesus' activity disturbing. He refused to be bound by their religious ideas. He befriended social outcasts. He insisted on understanding and applying the law of God in the light of its original intention, not according to the popular interpretation of the religious establishment. He insisted on healing sick people on the Sabbath day. He believed that healing people did not profane the Sabbath but honored it, because it was established by God for the rest and relief of human beings (Luke 6:6–11).

This attitude brought Jesus into conflict with the scribes, the official teachers of the law. Because of their influence, He was soon barred from preaching in the synagogues. But this was no great inconvenience. He simply gathered larger congregations to listen to Him on the hillside or by the lakeshore. He regularly illustrated the main themes of His preaching by parables. These were simple stories from daily life that would drive home some special point and make it stick in the hearer's understanding.

From among the large number of His followers, Jesus selected 12 men to remain in His company for training that would enable them to share His preaching and healing ministry. Eventually, He withdrew with them into Gentile territory to give them special training to prepare them for the crisis they would have to meet shortly in Jerusalem. He knew the time was approaching when He would present His challenging message to the people of the capital and to the Jewish leaders.

At the city of Caesarea Philippi, Jesus decided the time was ripe to encourage the Twelve to state their convictions about His identity and His mission. When Peter declared that He was the Messiah, this showed that He and the other apostles had given up most of the traditional ideas about the kind of person the Messiah would be. But the thought that Jesus would have to suffer and die was something they could not accept. Jesus recognized that He could now make a beginning with the creation of a new community. In this new community of God's people, the ideals of the kingdom He proclaimed would be realized.

At the Feast of Tabernacles in the fall of A.D. 29, Jesus went to Jerusalem with the Twelve. He apparently spent the next six months in the southern part of Palestine. Jerusalem, like Galilee, needed to hear the message of the kingdom. But

Jerusalem was more resistant to it even than Galilee. The spirit of revolt was in the air; Jesus' way of peace was not accepted. This is why He wept over the city. He realized the way that so many of its citizens preferred was bound to lead to their destruction. Even the magnificent temple, so recently rebuilt by Herod the Great, would be involved in the general overthrow.

During the week before Passover in A.D. 30, Jesus taught each day in the temple area, debating with other teachers of differing beliefs. The enthusiasm of the people when Jesus entered Jerusalem on a donkey alarmed the religious leaders. So did his show of authority when he cleared the temple of traders and moneychangers. This was a "prophetic action" in the tradition of the great prophets of Israel. Its message to the priestly establishment came through loud and clear.

The prophets' vision of the temple— "My house shall be called a house of prayer for all nations" (Is. 56:7)—was a fine ideal. But any attempt to make it measure up to reality would be a threat to the priestly privileges. Jesus' action was as disturbing as Jeremiah's speech foretelling the destruction of Solomon's temple had been to the religious leaders six centuries earlier (Jer. 26:1–6).

To block the possibility of an uprising among the people, the priestly party decided to arrest Jesus as soon as possible. The opportunity came earlier than they expected when one of the Twelve, Judas Iscariot, offered to deliver Jesus into their power without the risk of a public disturbance. Arrested on Passover Eve, Jesus was brought first before a Jewish court of inquiry, over which the high priest Caiaphas presided.

The Jewish leaders attempted first to convict Him of being a threat to the temple. Protection of the sanctity of the temple was the one area in which the Romans still allowed the Jewish authorities to exercise authority. But this attempt failed. Then Jesus accepted their charge that He claimed to be the Messiah. This gave the religious leaders an occasion to hand Him over to Pilate on a charge of treason and sedition. Death by crucifixion was the penalty for sedition by one who was not a Roman citizen.

With the death and burial of Jesus, the narrative of His earthly career came to an end. But with His resurrection on the third day, He lives and works forever as the exalted Lord. His appearances to His disciples after His resurrection assured them He was "alive after His suffering" (Acts 1:3). These appearances also enabled them to make the transition in their experience from the form in which they had known Him earlier to the new way in which they would be related to Him by the Holy Spirit.

JESUS CHRIST, TEACHINGS OF

Jesus taught several distinctive spiritual truths that set Him apart from any other religious leader who ever lived. The message Jesus began to proclaim in Galilee after John the Baptist's imprisonment was the Good News of the kingdom of God. When He appeared to His disciples after the Resurrection, He continued "speaking of the things pertaining to the kingdom of God" (Acts 1:3).

The nature of this kingdom is determined by the character of the God whose kingdom it is. The revelation of God lay at the heart of Jesus' teaching. Jesus called Him "Father" and taught His disciples to do the same. But the term that He used when He called God "Father" was *Abba* (Mark 14:36), the term of affection that children used when they addressed their father at home or spoke about him to others. It was not unusual for God to be addressed in prayer as "my Father" or "our Father." But it was most unusual for Him to be called *Abba*. By using this term, Jesus expressed His sense of nearness to God and His total trust in Him. He taught His followers to look to God with the trust that children show when they expect their earthly fathers to provide them with food, clothes, and shelter.

The ethical teaching of Jesus was part of His proclamation of the kingdom of God. Only by His death and resurrection could the divine rule be established. But even while the kingdom of God was in the process of inauguration during His ministry, its principles could be translated into action in the lives of His followers. The most familiar presentation of these principles is found in the Sermon on the Mount (Matt. 5–7), which was addressed to His disciples. These principles showed how those who were already children of the kingdom ought to live.

The people whom Jesus taught already had a large body of ethical teaching in the Old Testament law. But a further body of oral interpretation and application had grown up around the Law of Moses over the centuries. Jesus declared that He had come to fulfill the law, not to destroy it (Matt. 5:17). But He emphasized its ethical quality by summarizing it in terms of what He called the two great commandments: "You shall love the Lord your God" (Deut. 6:5) and "You shall love your neighbor as yourself" (Lev. 19:18). "On these two commandments," He said, "hang all the Law and the Prophets" (Matt. 22:40).

Jesus did not claim uniqueness or originality for His ethical teaching. One of His purposes was to explain the ancient law of God. Yet there was a distinctiveness and freshness about His teaching, as He declared His authority: "You have heard that it was said . . . But I say to you" (Matt. 5:21–22). Only in listening to His words and doing them could people build a secure foundation for their lives (Matt. 7:24–27; Luke 6:46–49).

Jesus injected new life into the ethical principles of the Law of Moses. But He did not impose a new set of laws that could be enforced by external sanctions; He prescribed a way of life for His followers. The act of murder, forbidden in the sixth commandment, was punishable by death. Conduct or language likely to provoke a breach of the peace could also bring on legal penalties. No human law can detect or punish the angry thought; yet it is here, Jesus taught, that the process that leads to murder begins. Therefore, "whoever is angry with his brother . . . shall be in danger of the judgment" (Matt. 5:22). But He was careful to point out that the judgment is God's, not man's.

Jesus' attitude and teaching also made many laws about property irrelevant for His followers. They should be known as people who give, not as people who get. If someone demands your cloak (outer garment), Jesus said, give it to him, and give him your tunic (undergarment) as well (Luke 6:29). There is more to life than abundance of possessions (Luke 12:15); in fact, He pointed out, material wealth is a hindrance to one's spiritual life.

The principle of nonviolence is deeply ingrained in Jesus' teaching. In His references to the "men of violence" who tried to bring in the kingdom of God by force, Jesus gave no sign that He approved of their ideals or methods. The course He called for was the way of peace and submission. He urged His hearers not to strike back against injustice or oppression but to turn the other cheek, to go a second mile when their services were demanded for one mile, and to take the initiative in returning good for evil.

JETHRO [JETH roe] (his excellency)

The father-in-law of Moses (Ex. 3:1), also called Reuel (Ex. 2:18), Hobab (Judg.

4:11), and Raguel (Num. 10:29; Reuel in NIV).

After Moses fled from Egypt into the region of the Sinai Peninsula, he married one of Jethro's daughters, Zipporah (Ex. 2:21). Then Moses tended Jethro's sheep for 40 years (Acts 7:30) before his experience at the burning bush (Ex. 3), when he was called to lead the Israelites from bondage in Egypt.

During the Exodus, Jethro and the rest of Moses' family joined Moses in the wilderness near Mount Sinai (Ex. 18:5). During this visit, Jethro taught Moses to delegate his responsibilities. He noted that Moses was doing all the work himself and advised Moses to decide the difficult cases and to secure able men to make decisions in lesser matters (Ex. 18:13–23).

JEWELRY

Objects of precious metals often set with gems and worn for personal adornment. Since the beginning of history, people have adorned themselves with various kinds of jewelry. To be elaborately decorated with jewelry in the ancient world was a symbol of wealth and status (2 Sam. 1:10; Dan. 5:7, 16, 29). The materials commonly used for jewelry were stone, metals, gems, ivory, shells, and carved horns.

The art of making jewelry probably developed very early in Egypt. It was known throughout the biblical world. The Hebrews learned this skill from foreign influences, probably from Egypt (Ex. 32:2–3), and obtained much of their jewelry from spoils of war.

The people of the ancient world placed great value on personal ornaments for political and religious purposes. The priestly garments of Aaron the high priest were elaborately decorated with jewels. The breastplate contained 12 engraved gems (Ex. 28:17–21). The shoulder pieces of the ephod were engraved onyx stones (Ex. 28:9–12). During Bible times, crowns were also set with gems (Zech. 9:16). Many ornaments were donated to build the tabernacle (Ex. 35:22) and to decorate the temple (1 Kin. 7:17).

Bracelets were worn by both men and women. They were made of bronze, silver, iron, and gold. Sometimes many bracelets were worn on each arm, covering the entire lower arm. Rebekah's gift from Abraham included a gold bracelet (Gen. 24:22). King Saul wore a bracelet or armlet (2 Sam. 1:10).

Ornaments for the ankles were worn by the women. These were usually made from the same material as the bracelets. Sometimes anklets were fashioned to make a tinkling sound when walking, bringing more attention to the wearer. Ankle chains were often attached to the feet to encourage smaller steps. The prophet Isaiah disapproved of this practice among the women of Jerusalem (Is. 3:18–21).

Both men and women of Bible times wore necklaces (Judg. 8:25–26). They were made of various metals, often inlaid with precious stones. Necklaces of beads made from stone or jewels were strung with cord. Sometimes crescents, bottles, or other pendants were attached to the necklaces (Is. 3:18). Gold chains were given to Joseph (Gen. 41:42) and Daniel (Dan. 5:29), indicating their high positions in government.

Earrings were worn by men, women, and children in the ancient world (Ex. 32:2–3; Num. 31:50; Judg. 8:25–26). They were loops worn alone or with pendants attached. Earrings were made from various metals and stones and were sometimes inlaid with gems. Nose rings were worn mostly by women (Gen. 24:47) and were sometimes decorated with jewels (Is. 3:21).

Most men wore signet rings for business purposes. These rings were engraved with the owner's name or symbol to show authority or ownership (Gen. 38:18; Ex. 28:11; Esth. 8:8; Dan. 6:17). The signet rings were worn on the finger or strung around the neck. They were usually made of gold and set with an engraved gem. Signet rings were given as gifts for the tabernacle (Ex. 35:22).

In the New Testament, jewels were worn much the same way as in the Old Testament. The Greeks emphasized fine, delicately worked jewelry, while the Roman jewelry was much heavier and more elaborate. In the early church the wearing of jewelry was not considered a Christian virtue by the apostle Paul, who exhorted women to modesty (1 Tim. 2:9). James apparently also had a dim view of jewelry (James 2:2).

JEWS

A name applied first to the people living in Judah (when the Israelites were divided into the two kingdoms of Israel and Judah); after the Babylonian Captivity, all the descendants of Abraham were called "Jews." The term is used in the New Testament for all Israelites as opposed to the "Gentiles," or those of non-Jewish blood.

Because the Jews were God's Chosen People, Paul could speak of the true "Jew" as being the person who pleases God, whatever his race (Rom. 2:28–29).

JEZEBEL [JEZ uh bel] (there is no prince)

The wife of Ahab, king of Israel, and mother of Ahaziah, Jehoram, and Athaliah (1 Kin. 16:31). Jezebel was a tyrant who corrupted her husband, as well as the nation, by promoting pagan worship.

She was reared in Sidon, a commercial city on the coast of the Mediterranean Sea, known for its idolatry and vice. When she married Ahab and moved to Jezreel, a city that served the Lord, she decided to turn it into a city that worshiped Baal, a Phoenician god.

The wicked, idolatrous queen soon became the power behind the throne. Obedient to her wishes, Ahab erected a sanctuary for Baal and supported hundreds of pagan prophets (1 Kin. 18:19).

When the prophets of the Lord opposed Jezebel, she had them "massacred" (1 Kin. 18:4, 13). After Elijah defeated her prophets on Mount Carmel, she swore revenge. She was such a fearsome figure that the great prophet was afraid and "ran for his life" (1 Kin. 19:3).

After her husband Ahab was killed in battle, Jezebel reigned for 10 years through her sons Ahaziah and Joram (or Jehoram). These sons were killed by Jehu, who also disposed of Jezebel by having her thrown from the palace window. In fulfillment of the prediction of the prophet Elijah, Jezebel was trampled by the horses and eaten by the dogs (1 Kin. 21:19). Only Jezebel's skull, feet, and the palms of her hands were left to bury when the dogs were finished (2 Kin. 9:30–37).

One truth that emerges from Jezebel's life is that God balances the scales of justice. Wickedness may prevail for a season, but His righteousness will eventually triumph over the forces of evil.

JEZREEL [JEZ reel] (God scatters)

The Old Testament name of the entire valley that separates Samaria from Galilee (Josh. 17:16). Some authors now refer to the western part of this valley as Esdraelon (Gr. for "Jezreel"), while the name Jezreel is restricted to the eastern part of the valley.

The entire valley is the major corridor through the rugged Palestinian hills. It was a crossroads of two major routes: one leading from the Mediterranean Sea on the west to the Jordan River valley on the east, the other leading from Syria, Phoenicia, and Galilee in the north to the hill country of Judah and to the land of Egypt on the south. Throughout history, the Valley of Jezreel has been a major battlefield of nations.

See also ARMAGEDDON.

JOAB [JO ab] *(the Lord is father)*

One of the three sons of Zeruiah (2 Sam. 2:13; 8:16; 14:1; 17:25; 23:18, 37; 1 Kin. 1:7; 2:5, 22; 1 Chr. 11:6, 39; 18:15; 26:28; 27:24) who was David's sister (or half sister). Joab was the "general" or commander-in-chief of David's army (2 Sam. 5:8; 1 Chr. 11:6; 27:34).

Joab's father is not mentioned by name, but his tomb was at Bethlehem (2 Sam. 2:32). Joab's two brothers were Abishai and Asahel. When Asahel was killed by Abner (2 Sam. 2:18–23), Joab got revenge by killing Abner (2 Sam. 3:22–27).

When David and his army went to Jerusalem, in an attempt to capture that city (then called Jebus), he said, "Whoever attacks the Jebusites first shall be chief and captain" (1 Chr. 11:6). Joab led the assault at the storming of the Jebusite stronghold on Mount Zion, apparently climbing up into the city by way of a water shaft. The city was captured, and Joab was made the general of David's army (2 Sam. 5:8).

Other military exploits by Joab were achieved against the Edomites (2 Sam. 8:13–14; 1 Kin. 11:15) and the Ammonites (2 Sam. 10:6–14; 11:1–27; 1 Chr. 19:6–15; 20:1–3). His character was deeply stained, as was David's, by his participation in the death of Uriah the Hittite (2 Sam. 11:14–25). In putting Absalom to death (2 Sam. 18:1–14), he apparently acted from a sense of duty.

When Absalom revolted against David, Joab remained loyal to David. Soon afterward, however, David gave command of his army to Amasa, Joab's cousin (2 Sam. 19:13; 20:1–13). Overcome by jealous hate, Joab killed Amasa (2 Sam. 20:8–13).

Another of David's sons, Adonijah, aspired to the throne, refusing to accept the fact that Solomon was not only David's choice but also the Lord's choice as the new king. Joab joined the cause of Adonijah against Solomon. Joab was killed by Benaiah, in accordance with Solomon's command and David's wishes. Joab fled to the tabernacle of the Lord, where he grasped the horns of the altar. Benaiah then struck him down with a sword. Joab was buried "in his own house in the wilderness" (1 Kin. 2:34).

JOANNA [joe AN uh] *(the Lord has been gracious)*

The wife of Chuza, the steward of Herod Antipas. Along with Mary Magdalene, Susanna, and others, she provided for the material needs of Jesus and His disciples from her own funds (Luke 8:3). Joanna was one of the women who witnessed the empty tomb and announced Christ's resurrection to the unbelieving apostles (Luke 24:1–10).

JOASH [JOE ash] *(the Lord supports)*

1. The eighth king of Judah; he was a son of King Ahaziah (2 Kin. 11:2) by Zibiah of Beersheba (2 Kin. 12:1). Joash was seven years old when he became king, and he reigned 40 years in Jerusalem (2 Chr. 24:1), from about 835 B.C. until 796 B.C. He is also called Jehoash (2 Kin. 11:21).

After Ahaziah died, Athaliah killed all the royal heirs to the throne. But God spared Joash through his aunt, Jehosheba, who hid him for six years in the house of the Lord (2 Kin. 11:2–3). When Joash reached the age of seven, Jehoiada the priest arranged for his coronation as king (2 Kin. 11:4–16).

Early in his reign, Joash repaired the temple and restored true religion to Judah, destroying Baal worship (2 Kin. 11:18–21). But the king who began so well faltered upon the loss of his advisor, Jehoiada. After Jehoiada died, Joash allowed idolatry to grow (2 Chr. 24:18). He even went so far as to have Zechariah, the son of Jehoiada, stoned to death for rebuking him (2 Chr. 24:20–22). God's judgment came quickly in the form of a Syrian invasion, which resulted in the wounding of Joash (2 Chr. 24:23–24). He was then killed by his own servants.

JOASH [JOE ash] (the Lord supports)

2. The thirteenth king of Israel; he was the son and successor of Jehoahaz, king of Israel, and was the grandson of Jehu, king of Israel. He is also called Jehoash (2 Kin. 13:10, 25; 14:8–17). Joash reigned in Samaria for 16 years (2 Kin. 13:9–10), from about 798 B.C. to 782/81 B.C.

Israel was revived during the reign of Joash (2 Kin. 13:7), following a long period of suffering at the hands of the Syrians. But while achieving political success, Joash suffered spiritual bankruptcy: "He did evil in the sight of the Lord; he did not depart from all the sins of Jeroboam the son of Nebat, who had made Israel sin; but he walked in them" (2 Kin. 13:11). He was succeeded by his son Jeroboam II.

JOB [jobe]

The central personality of the Book of Job. He was noted for his perseverance (James 5:11) and unwavering faith in God, in spite of his suffering and moments of frustration and doubt. All the facts known about Job are contained in the Old Testament book that bears his name. He is described as "a man in the land of Uz" (Job 1:1) and "the greatest of all the people of the East" (Job 1:3). Uz is probably a name for a region in Edom (Jer. 25:20; Lam. 4:21).

A prosperous man, Job had 7,000 sheep, 3,000 camels, 500 yoke of oxen, 500 female donkeys, and a large household, consisting of 7 sons and 3 daughters. He was also "blameless and upright, and one who feared God and shunned evil" (Job 1:1).

Satan suggested to God that Job would remain righteous as long as it was financially profitable for him to do so. Then the Lord permitted Satan to test Job's faith in God. Blow after blow fell upon Job: his children, his servants, and his livestock were taken from him and he was left penniless. Nevertheless, "In all this Job did not sin nor charge God with wrong" (Job 1:22).

Satan continued his assault by sneering, "Touch his bone and his flesh, and he will surely curse You to Your face!" (Job 2:5). The Lord allowed Satan to afflict Job with painful boils from the soles of his feet to the crown of his head, so that Job sat in the midst of ashes and scraped his sores with a piece of pottery. "Do you still hold fast to your integrity?" his wife asked him. "Curse God and die!" (Job 2:9). But Job refused to curse God. "Shall we indeed accept good from God," he replied, "and shall we not accept adversity?" (Job 2:10).

Job's faith eventually triumphed over all adversity, and he was finally restored to more than his former prosperity. He had 14,000 sheep, 6,000 camels, 1,000 yoke of oxen, and 1,000 female donkeys. He also had seven sons and three daughters. He died at a ripe old age (Job 42:12–13, 16–17).

Job is a model of spiritual integrity—a person who held fast to his faith, without understanding the reason behind his suffering. He serves as a continuing witness to the possibility of authentic faith in God in the most troubling of circumstances.

JOCHEBED [JAH kuh bed] (the Lord honors)

A daughter of Levi and the mother of Aaron, Moses, and Miriam. To protect Moses from Pharaoh's command that every male Hebrew child be killed, she placed him in an ark of bulrushes on the river. After Pharaoh's daughter discovered the baby, Jochebed became his nurse. She is noted among the heroes of the faith (Heb. 11:23).

JOEL [JOE uhl] (the Lord is God)

An Old Testament prophet and author of the Book of Joel. A citizen of Jerusalem, he spoke often of the priests and their duties (Joel 1:9, 13–14, 16). For this reason, many scholars believe he may have been a temple prophet. He also had an ear for nature (Joel 1:4–7), and included imagery from agriculture and the natural world in his messages. Some scholars believe Joel was a contemporary of the prophets Amos and Isaiah, placing his ministry at about 770 B.C.

JOHN THE APOSTLE

One of Jesus' disciples, the son of Zebedee, and the brother of James. Before his call by Jesus, John was a fisherman, along with his father and brother (Matt. 4:18–22; Mark 1:16–20). His mother was probably Salome (Matt. 27:56; Mark 15:40), who may have been a sister of Mary (John 19:25), the mother of Jesus.

Although it is not certain that Salome and Mary were sisters, if it were so it would make James and John cousins of Jesus. This would help explain Salome's forward request of Jesus on behalf of her sons (Matt. 20:20–28). The Zebedee family apparently lived in Capernaum on the north shore of the Sea of Galilee (Mark 1:21). The family must have been prosperous, because the father owned a boat and hired servants (Mark 1:19–20). Salome the mother provided for Jesus out of her substance (Mark 15:40–41; Luke 8:3). John must have been the younger of the two brothers, for he is always mentioned second to James in the Gospels of Matthew, Mark, and Luke. The brothers Zebedee were called by

Jesus after His baptism (Mark 1:19–20). This happened immediately after the call of two other brothers, Simon Peter and Andrew (Mark 1:16–18), with whom they may have been in partnership (Luke 5:10). Three of the four—Peter, James, and John—eventually became Jesus' most intimate disciples. They were present when Jesus healed the daughter of Jairus (Mark 5:37; Luke 8:51). They witnessed His Transfiguration (Matt. 17:1–2; Mark 9:2; Luke 9:28–29), as well as His agony in Gethsemane (Matt. 26:37; Mark 14:33).

James and John must have contributed a headstrong element to Jesus' band of followers, because Jesus nicknamed them "Sons of Thunder" (Mark 3:17). On one occasion (Luke 9:51–56), when a Samaritan village refused to accept Jesus, the two offered to call down fire in revenge, as the prophet Elijah had once done (2 Kin. 1:10, 12). On another occasion, they earned the anger of their fellow disciples by asking if they could sit on Jesus' right and left hands in glory (Mark 10:35–45).

Following the ascension of Jesus, John continued in a prominent position of leadership among the disciples (Acts 1:13). He was present when Peter healed the lame man in the temple. Together with Peter he bore witness before the Sanhedrin to his faith in Jesus Christ. The boldness of their testimony brought the hostility of the Sanhedrin (Acts 3–4). When the apostles in Jerusalem received word of the evangelization of Samaria, they sent Peter and John to investigate whether the conversions were genuine (Acts 8:14–25). This was a curious thing to do. The Samaritans had long been suspect in the eyes of the Jews (John 4:9). John himself had once favored the destruction of a Samaritan village (Luke 9:51–56). That he was present on this mission suggests he had experienced a remarkable change.

J

In these episodes Peter appears as the leader and spokesman for the pair, but John's presence on such errands indicates his esteem by the growing circle of disciples. After the execution of his brother James by Herod Agrippa I, between A.D. 42–44 (Acts 12:1–2), John is not heard of again in Acts. Paul's testimony to John as one of the "pillars," along with Peter and James (the Lord's brother, Gal. 2:9), however, reveals that John continued to hold a position of respect and leadership in the early church.

As might be expected of one of Jesus' three closest disciples, John became the subject of an active and varied church tradition. It was also the general opinion of the time that from Ephesus John composed the five writings that bear his name in the New Testament (Gospel of John; 1, 2, and 3 John; and Revelation).

JOHN THE BAPTIST

Forerunner of Jesus; a moral reformer and preacher of messianic hope. According to Luke 1:36, Elizabeth and Mary, the mothers of John and Jesus, were either blood relatives or close kinswomen. Luke adds that both John and Jesus were announced, set apart, and named by the angel Gabriel even before their birth.

Practically nothing is known of John's boyhood, except that he "grew and became strong in spirit" (Luke 1:80). The silence of his early years, however, was broken by his thundering call to repentance some time around A.D. 28–29, shortly before Jesus began His ministry. Matthew reports that the place where John preached was the wilderness of Judea (3:1). It is likely that he also preached in Perea, east of the Jordan River. Perea, like Galilee, lay within the jurisdiction of Herod Antipas, under whom John was later arrested.

The four gospels are unanimous in their report that John lived "in the wilderness." There he was raised (Luke 1:80) and was called by God (Luke 3:2), and there he preached (Mark 1:4) until his execution. The wilderness—a vast badland of crags, wind, and heat—was the place where God had dwelled with His people after the Exodus. Ever since, it had been the place of religious hope for Israel. John called the people away from the comforts of their homes and cities and out into the wilderness, where they might meet God.

The conviction that God was about to begin a new work among this unprepared people broke upon John with the force of a desert storm. He was called to put on the prophet's hairy mantle with the resolve and urgency of Elijah himself. Not only did he dress like Elijah, in camel's hair and leather belt (2 Kin. 1:8; Mark 1:6); he understood his ministry to be one of reform and preparation, just as Elijah did (Luke 1:17). John reminded the people of Elijah because of his dress and behavior (Matt. 11:14; Mark 9:12–13).

John's baptism was a washing, symbolizing moral regeneration, administered to each candidate only once. He criticized the people for presuming to be righteous and secure with God because they were children of Abraham (Matt. 3:9). John laid an ax to the root of this presumption. He warned that they, the Jews, would be purged and rejected unless they demonstrated fruits of repentance (Matt. 3:7–12).

John's effort at moral reform, symbolized by baptism, was his way of preparing Israel to meet God. He began his preaching with the words, "Prepare the way of the Lord, make His paths straight" (Mark 1:3). He had a burning awareness of one who was to come after him who would baptize in fire and Spirit (Mark 1:7–8). John was a forerunner of this mightier one, a herald of the messianic hope that would dawn in Jesus.

John was a forerunner of Jesus not

only in his ministry and message (Matt. 3:1; 4:17) but also in his death. Not until John's arrest did Jesus begin His ministry (Mark 1:14), and John's execution foreshadowed Jesus' similar fate. Imprisoned by Antipas in the fortress of Machaerus on the lonely hills east of the Dead Sea, John must have grown disillusioned by his own failure and the developing failure he sensed in Jesus' mission. He sent messengers to ask Jesus, "Are You the Coming One, or do we look for another?" (Matt. 11:3). John was eventually killed by a functionary of a puppet king who allowed himself to be swayed by a scheming wife, a loose daughter-in-law, and the people around him (Mark 6:14–29).

Josephus records that Herod arrested and executed John because he feared his popularity might lead to a revolt. The Gospels reveal it was because John spoke out against Herod's immoral marriage to Herodias, the wife of his brother Philip (Mark 6:17–19). The accounts are complementary, because John's moral righteousness must have fanned many a smoldering political hope to life.

Jesus said of John, "Among those born of women there has not risen one greater than John the Baptist" (Matt. 11:11). He was the last and greatest of the prophets (Matt. 11:13–14). Nevertheless, he stood, like Moses, on the threshold of the Promised Land. He did not enter the kingdom of God proclaimed by Jesus; and consequently, "he who is least in the kingdom of heaven is greater than he" (Matt. 11:11).

John's influence continued to live on after his death. When Paul went to Ephesus nearly 30 years later, he found a group of John's disciples (Acts 19:1–7). Some of his disciples must have thought of John in messianic terms. This compelled the author of the Gospel of John, writing also from Ephesus some 60 years

after the Baptist's death, to emphasize Jesus' superiority (John 1:19–27; 3:30).

JONAH [JOE nuh] *(a dove)*

The prophet who was first swallowed by a great fish before he obeyed God's command to preach repentance to the Assyrian city of Nineveh. Jonah was not always a reluctant spokesman for the Lord. He is the same prophet who predicted the remarkable expansion of Israel's territory during the reign of Jeroboam II (ruled about 793–753 B.C.; 2 Kin. 14:25). This passage indicates that Jonah, the son of Amittai, was from Gath Hepher, a town in Zebulun in the northern kingdom of Israel.

While Jonah is described as a servant of the Lord in 2 Kings 14:25, he is a sad and somewhat tragic figure in the book bearing his name. It is a mark of the integrity and reliability of the Bible that a prophet like Jonah is described in such a candid manner. The natural tendency of human writers would be to obscure and hide such a character. But the Spirit of God presents valiant heroes along with petty people to illustrate truth, no matter how weak and unpleasant these characters may have been. We know nothing of Jonah after he returned to Israel from his preaching venture in Nineveh.

JONATHAN [JAHN uh thuhn] *(the Lord has given)*

The oldest son of King Saul and a close friend of David. He made a covenant with David (1 Sam. 18:3–4) and warned David of Saul's plot against his life (1 Sam. 19:1–2). When Saul sought David's life, Jonathan interceded on behalf of David, and Saul reinstated David to his good favor (1 Sam. 19:1–7). Jonathan's loyalty to David was proven time after time as he warned David of Saul's threats of vengeance (1 Sam. 20) and encouraged David in times of danger (1 Sam. 23:16, 18).

The tragic end for Jonathan came at

Mount Gilboa when he, his father Saul, and two of his brothers were killed by the Philistines (1 Sam. 31:1–2; 1 Chr. 10:1–6). When David heard of this, he mourned and fasted (2 Sam. 1:12). He then composed a lamentation, the "Song of the Bow," in which he poured out his grief over the death of Saul and Jonathan (2 Sam. 1:17–27).

JOPPA [JAH puh] (beautiful)

An ancient seaport city on the Mediterranean Sea, about 35 miles (56 kilometers) northwest of Jerusalem. A walled city, Joppa was built about 116 feet (35 meters) high on a rocky ledge overlooking the Mediterranean. It supposedly received its name "beautiful" from the sunlight that its buildings reflected.

The first mention of Joppa in the Bible indicates it was part of the territory inherited by the tribe of Dan (Josh. 19:46; Japho, KJV). The only natural harbor on the Mediterranean between Egypt and Acco, it was the seaport for the city of Jerusalem and the site of significant shipping in both Old and New Testament times. Rafts of cedar logs from the forests of Lebanon were floated from Tyre and Sidon to Joppa and then transported overland to Jerusalem to be used in building Solomon's temple (2 Chr. 2:16).

In New Testament times, Joppa was the home of a Christian disciple, Tabitha (or Dorcas), a woman "full of good works and charitable deeds" (Acts 9:36). After she became sick and died, she was raised to life by Simon Peter. As a result, many believed on the Lord (Acts 9:36–42).

Joppa was also the home of Simon the Tanner (Acts 10:32). Simon Peter stayed many days in Joppa with Simon. On the roof of Simon's house Peter received his vision of a great sheet descending from heaven (Acts 10:9–16)—a vision that indicated that all who believe in Christ, Gentiles as well as Jews, are accepted by God.

JORAM [JOHR uhm] (the Lord is exalted)

1. The son and successor of Jehoshaphat as king of Judah (1 Chr. 3:10–11), also called Jehoram (1 Kin. 22:50). Joram reigned eight years (2 Kin. 8:17) while his brother-in-law, also named Joram, reigned in Israel. His marriage to Athaliah, Ahab's daughter, marked the beginning of Joram's downfall. Athaliah influenced Joram to promote Baal worship in Judah. This illustrates the perils of an ungodly marriage.

In addition to promoting religious atrocities (2 Chr. 21:11), Joram is remembered for murdering his six brothers and chief nobles. This mass murder assured his position as king and probably added to his wealth (2 Chr. 21:4). Little else is noted of his reign, with the exception of revolts by Edom and Libnah (2 Chr. 21:8–10).

In spite of Joram's evil ways, "The Lord would not destroy the house of David, because of the covenant that He had made with David." But through a letter from Elijah, the Lord did warn Joram of coming judgment (2 Chr. 21:7, 12–15). The king soon lost nearly all his possessions, wives, and children at the hands of Philistine and Arabian raiders as Elijah had prophesied. Joram also contracted an excruciating intestinal disease. After two years of suffering, "he died in severe pain," for "his intestines came out because of his sickness" (2 Chr. 21:19).

Because of Joram's moral and religious depravity, no one mourned his death, and he was not buried in the tombs of the kings. Thus, at the age of 40, his reign was ended prematurely. Within a year, his wife had all of his descendants executed, except one grandson, Joash (2 Kin. 11:1–3).

JORAM [JOHR uhm] (the Lord is exalted)

2. The tenth king of Israel, killed by Jehu (2 Kin. 8:16–29; 9:14–29). The son

of Ahab and Jezebel, Joram succeeded his brother, Ahaziah, as king. He was also called Jehoram (2 Kin. 1:17). His 12-year reign was characterized as an evil time, although he did manage to restrain Baal worship (2 Kin. 3:3).

One of Joram's first major projects was to enlist Jehoshaphat, king of Judah, and the king of Edom in a campaign against Moab. Joram also defended Israel against Syria. Through the aid of the prophet Elisha, Joram defeated the Syrian invaders. Later, however, Ben-Hadad of Syria besieged Samaria, leading to severe famine and even cannibalism (2 Kin. 6:8–29). In the darkest hour of the siege, however, the Lord miraculously delivered His people, just as Elisha had prophesied (2 Kin. 7:1–20).

When Hazael replaced Ben-Hadad as king of Syria, Joram made an alliance with his nephew Ahaziah, king of Judah, to occupy the city of Ramoth Gilead by force. Joram was wounded in the battle, and he went back to Jezreel to recover. Jehu, the leader of his army, came to Jezreel and assassinated Joram. Joram's body was then thrown upon the very property that Ahab and Jezebel had stolen from Naboth, thus fulfilling Elijah's prophecy that the house of Ahab would come to an end (1 Kin. 21:21–29; 2 Kin. 9:21–29).

JORDAN RIVER [JORE dun]
(descending, flowing)

The longest and most important river in Palestine. The river is part of the great rift valley that runs north to south into Africa. This rift valley is one of the lowest depressions on earth.

The headwaters of the Jordan River begin north of Lake Huleh. After the Jordan flows through Lake Huleh, it descends into the Sea of Galilee. It is possible to ford the river just below the lake where the waters are low. In the ancient world, trade caravans going from Damascus to Egypt probably crossed at this point.

At Lake Huleh the headwaters of the Jordan are about 230 feet (70 meters) above sea level. Some 10 miles (16 kilometers) south of the Sea of Galilee the river is about 700 feet (213 meters) below sea level. At the northern end of the Dead Sea (the end of the Jordan), the river has dropped to about 1,290 feet (393 meters) below sea level. This drastic drop is reflected in the name of the river, which means "the descender." The Jordan made a natural boundary as a serious obstacle in any east-to-west movement in the land of Palestine. A number of shallow spots, or fords, occur in the Jordan. Possession of these fords was an important military factor.

The distance that the Jordan covers from the southern tip of the Sea of Galilee to the northern end of the Dead Sea is only about 70 miles (113 kilometers). But the winding, zigzag pattern of the river is such that it curves for about 200 miles (323 kilometers) as it weaves its way north to south. The river varies from 90 to 100 feet (27 to 30 meters) in width and between 3 and 10 feet (1 and 3 meters) deep. The water is not really navigable. With great difficulty flat-bottom boats are able to move along parts of the waterway; they must be towed, however, through sandbars and must survive swift currents because of the descending nature of the valley. There are some 27 series of rapids in the Jordan.

When the Hebrew tribes approached the Promised Land, they did so from the eastern side of the Jordan. To some degree the Jordan River served as the boundary for the tribes (Num. 34:12). Ancient Israel occupied territory on both sides of the river. The tribes of Reuben, Gad, and half of the tribe of Manasseh settled on the eastern side of the Jordan.

Weak parties often went east of the Jordan to escape from the pressures from their opponents. For instance, Abner took Ishbosheth, the son of Saul, to the eastern side of the Jordan in opposition to David (2 Sam. 2:8). David fled to the eastern side after Absalom's initial success (2 Sam. 17:22–24; 19:15–18). However, the crossing of the Jordan from east to west was symbolic of the arrival of the Hebrews in the Promised Land. The west side of the Jordan was the area generally thought to have been promised to Abraham.

It was probably at the south end of the river, near Jericho, that ancient Israel entered the region of Canaan (Josh. 3–4). At Gilgal, near the Dead Sea, on the western side of the river about a mile from Jericho, an important shrine area was set up to commemorate the entrance of the Israelites into the land (Josh. 4:19; 1 Sam. 7:16; 10:8).

In the period between the Old Testament and the New Testament, the Jordan River formed the main eastern boundary of the Persian and Greek province of Judea. The Decapolis, a federation of ten Greek cities, was formed on the eastern side of the Jordan in the Greek period. John the Baptist carried out his ministry in the Jordan River region (Matt. 3:5–6; Mark 1:5; Luke 3:3; John 1:28; 3:26). Jesus' ministry was initiated by his baptism in the waters of the Jordan (Matt. 3:13; Mark 1:9; Luke 4:1). Jesus carried out His ministry on both sides of the Jordan (Matt. 4:15, 25; Mark 3:8; John 10:40).

JOSEPH [JOE zeph] *(may he add)*

1. The eleventh son of Jacob (Gen. 30:24). Joseph was the first child of Rachel (30:24) and his father's favorite son (37:31). This is shown by the special coat that Jacob gave to Joseph. This favoritism eventually brought serious trouble for the whole family. Joseph's ten older brothers hated him because he was Jacob's favorite and because Joseph had

dreams that he interpreted to his brothers in a conceited way. It is no surprise that Joseph's brothers hated him enough to kill him (37:4).

Joseph's brothers were shepherds in the land of Canaan. One day Jacob sent Joseph to search for his brothers, who were tending the flocks in the fields. When Joseph found them, they seized upon the chance to kill him. The only opposing voice was Reuben's, but they finally sold Joseph into slavery to passing merchants.

To hide the deed from their father Jacob, Joseph's brothers took his coat and dipped it in animal blood. When Jacob saw the coat, he was convinced that Joseph had been killed by a wild animal (37:34–35).

Joseph was taken to Egypt, where he was sold to Potiphar, an officer of the ruling pharaoh of the nation. His good conduct soon earned him the highest position in the household. Potiphar's wife became infatuated with Joseph and tempted him to commit adultery with her. When he refused, she accused him of the crime and Joseph was sent to prison.

While in prison, Joseph's behavior earned him a position of responsibility over the other prisoners. Among the prisoners Joseph met were the pharaoh's baker and his butler. When each of them had a dream, Joseph interpreted their dreams. When the butler left prison, he failed to intercede on Joseph's behalf, and Joseph spent two more years in prison.

When the pharaoh had dreams that none of his counselors could interpret, the butler remembered Joseph and mentioned him to the pharaoh. Then Joseph was called to appear before the pharaoh. He interpreted the pharaoh's dreams, predicting seven years of plentiful food, followed by seven years of famine. He also advised the pharaoh to appoint a commissioner to store up supplies during the plentiful years.

To Joseph's surprise, the pharaoh appointed him as food commissioner. This was a position of great prestige. Under Joseph's care, many supplies were stored and the land prospered (41:37–57). Joseph was given many comforts, including servants and a wife. He was called Zaphenath-Paneah. When the famine struck, Joseph was second only to the pharaoh in power. People from all surrounding lands came to buy food from him.

The famine also struck Canaan, and Joseph's brothers eventually came to Egypt to buy grain. When they met Joseph, they did not recognize him. He recognized them, however, and decided to test them to see if they had changed. He accused them of being spies. Then he sold them grain only on the condition that Simeon stay as a hostage until they brought Benjamin, the youngest brother, to Egypt with them.

Upon returning to Canaan, the brothers told Jacob of their experiences. He vowed not to send Benjamin to Egypt. But the continuing famine forced him to change his mind. On the next trip Benjamin went with his brothers to Egypt.

When they arrived, Joseph treated them royally, weeping openly at the sight of his youngest brother. Simeon was returned to them. After purchasing their grain, they started home. On their way home, however, they were stopped by one of Joseph's servants, who accused them of stealing Joseph's silver cup. The cup was found in Benjamin's bag, where Joseph had placed it. The brothers returned to face Joseph, who declared that Benjamin must stay in Egypt. At this point Judah pleaded with Joseph, saying that it would break their father Jacob's heart if Benjamin failed to return with them. Judah's offer to stay in Benjamin's place

is one of the most moving passages in the Old Testament.

Joseph was overcome with emotion. He revealed himself to them as their brother, whom they had sold into slavery years earlier. At first Joseph's brothers were afraid that Joseph would take revenge against them, but soon they were convinced that Joseph's forgiveness was genuine. Judah's plea on Benjamin's behalf was evidence of the change that Joseph had hoped to find in his brothers. He sent them back to Canaan with gifts for his father and invited the family to come live in Egypt.

JOSEPH [JOE zeph] *(may he add)*

2. The husband of Mary, mother of Jesus. Joseph took Mary as his wife after reassurance from an angel that Mary's pregnancy had occurred miraculously through the action of the Holy Spirit (Matt. 1:18–24). He is not mentioned in the biblical record after the incident when he and Mary found the boy Jesus in the temple in Jerusalem among the learned scribes and rabbis (Luke 2:41–52). Joseph may have died during Jesus' teenage or young adult years.

JOSEPH [JOE zeph] *(may he add)*

3. A Jew of Arimathea in whose tomb Jesus was laid. Joseph was probably a secret follower of Jesus. But he declared himself openly when he asked Pilate for Jesus's body so he could give it a decent burial. With help from Nicodemus, he wrapped Jesus' body and placed it in his own new tomb (see Matt. 27:57, 59; Luke 23:50–53).

JOSHUA [JAHSH oo uh] *(the Lord is salvation)*

The successor to Moses and the man who led the nation of Israel to conquer and settle the Promised Land.

Joshua was born in Egypt. He went through the great events of the Passover and the Exodus with Moses and all the Hebrew people who escaped from slavery in Egypt at the hand of God. In the Wilderness of Sinai, Moses took his assistant Joshua with him when he went into the mountains to talk with God (Ex. 24:13). Moses also gave Joshua a prominent place at the tabernacle. As Moses' servant, Joshua would remain at the tabernacle as his representative while the great leader left the camp to fellowship with the Lord (Ex. 33:11).

When Moses sent spies to scout out the land of Canaan, Joshua was selected as the representative of the tribe of Ephraim (Num. 13:8). Only Joshua and Caleb returned to the camp with a report that they could conquer the land with God's help. The other ten spies complained that they were "like grasshoppers" in comparison to the Canaanites (Num. 13:33). Because of their show of faith, Joshua and Caleb were allowed to enter the land at the end of their years of wandering in the wilderness. But all the other Israelites who lived at that time died before the nation entered the Promised Land (Num. 14:30).

At Moses' death, Joshua was chosen as his successor (Josh. 1:1–2). He led the Israelites to conquer the land (Josh. 1–2), supervised the division of the territory among the 12 tribes, and led the people to renew their covenant with God (Josh. 13–22).

When Joshua died at the age of 110, he was buried in the land of his inheritance at Timnath Serah (Josh. 24:30). As Moses' successor, Joshua completed the work that this great leader had begun. Moses led Israel out of Egypt; Joshua led Israel into Canaan. Joshua's name, an Old Testament form of Jesus, means "the Lord is salvation." By his name and by his life, he demonstrated the salvation that comes from God.

JOSIAH [joe SIGH uh]

The sixteenth king of Judah, the son of Amon, and the grandson of Manasseh (2 Kin. 21:23–23:30). The three decades of Josiah's reign were characterized by peace, prosperity, and reform. Hence, they were among the happiest years experienced by Judah. King Josiah devoted himself to pleasing God and reinstituting Israel's observance of the Mosaic Law. The Bible focuses almost exclusively on Josiah's spiritual reform, which climaxed in the eighteenth year of his reign with the discovery of the Book of the Law.

Josiah's reform actually occurred in three stages. Ascending to the throne at age eight, he apparently was blessed with God-fearing advisors who resisted the idolatrous influence of his father. More importantly, however, at the age of 16 (stage one), Josiah personally "began to seek the God of his father David" (2 Chr. 34:3).

At the age of 20 (stage two), Josiah began to cleanse Jerusalem and the land of Judah of idolatrous objects (2 Chr. 34:3–7). His reform was even more extensive than that of his predecessor, Hezekiah (2 Kin. 18:4; 2 Chr. 29:3–36). Josiah extended his cleansing of the land into the territory of fallen Israel; at the time Israel was nominally controlled by Assyria. Josiah personally supervised the destruction of the altars of the Baals, the incense altars, the wooden images, the carved images, and the molded images as far north as the cities of Naphtali. Josiah's efforts were aided by the death of the great Assyrian king, Ashurbanipal, which brought about a serious decline in Assyria's power and allowed Josiah freedom to pursue his reforms.

At the age of 26 (stage three), Josiah ordered that the temple be repaired under the supervision of Hilkiah, the high priest. In the process, a copy of the Book of the Law was discovered (2 Chr. 34:14–15). When it was read to Josiah, he was horrified to learn how far Judah had departed from the law of God. This discovery provided a new momentum for the reformation that was already in progress.

In 609 B.C. Josiah attempted to block Pharaoh Necho II of Egypt as he marched north to assist Assyria in its fight with Babylon for world supremacy. Despite the pharaoh's assurance to the contrary, Josiah saw Necho's northern campaign as a threat to Judah's security. When he engaged Necho in battle at Megiddo, Josiah was seriously injured. He was returned to Jerusalem, where he died after reigning 31 years. His death was followed by widespread lamentation (2 Chr. 35:20–27). In the New Testament, Josiah is referred to as Josias (Matt. 1:10, KJV).

JOTHAM [JOE thum] (the Lord is perfect)

A son of Uzziah (or Azariah) and the eleventh king of Judah (2 Kin. 15:32–38; 2 Chr. 26:21–23), who reigned from about 750–732 B.C. Jotham ruled as co-regent with his father when it was discovered that Uzziah had leprosy. His 18-year reign was a godly one, although the people persisted in idolatry. He was undoubtedly encouraged by the prophets Isaiah, Hosea, and Micah, who ministered during his reign (Is. 1:1; Hos. 1:1; Mic. 1:1).

Jotham built the Upper Gate of the temple and strengthened the Jerusalem wall of Ophel. He also built cities and fortified buildings throughout the countryside to further strengthen Judah. He fought and defeated the Ammonites and exacted tribute from them for three years (2 Chr. 27:3–5).

Jotham's strength and prosperity were attributed to the fact that "he prepared his ways before the Lord his God" (2 Chr.

27:6). Jotham was an ancestor of Jesus (Matt. 1:9; Joatham, KJV).

JOY

A positive attitude or pleasant emotion; delight. Joy rises above circumstances and focuses on the character of God. God's acts are the cause of rejoicing. The joy required of the righteous person (Phil. 4:4) is produced by the Spirit of God (Gal. 5:22). This kind of joy looks beyond the present to our future salvation (Rom. 5:2) and to our sovereign God, who works out all things for our ultimate good, which is Christlikeness (Rom. 8:28–30). This kind of joy is distinct from mere happiness. Joy like this is possible, even in the midst of sorrow (2 Cor. 6:10; 7:4).

JUBILEE [JOO bah lee]

The fiftieth year after seven cycles of seven years, when specific instructions about property and slavery took effect (Lev. 25:8–55). The word jubilee comes from a Hebrew word that means to be "jubilant" and to "exult." The word is related to the Hebrew word for ram's horn or trumpet. The Jubilee year was launched with a blast from a ram's horn on the Day of Atonement, signifying a call to joy, liberation, and the beginning of a year for doing justice and loving mercy.

The fiftieth year was a special year in which to "proclaim liberty throughout all the land" (Lev. 25:10). Specifically, individuals who had incurred debts and had sold themselves as slaves or servants to others were released from their debts and were set at liberty. Since all land belonged to God (Lev. 25:23), land could not be sold; but land could be lost to another for reasons of debt. In the year of Jubilee such land was returned to the families to whom it was originally given.

Like the Sabbath years, the year of Jubilee was a year for neither sowing nor reaping (Lev. 25:11). The fiftieth year became important in Israel's economic life. If anyone wished to redeem a person in debt, the price for doing so was calculated on the basis of the number of years remaining until the Jubilee.

Part of the reason why God established the Jubilee year was to prevent the Israelites from oppressing one another (Lev. 25:17). One effect of the Jubilee year was to prevent a permanent system of economic classes. The Jubilee year had a leveling effect on Israel's culture; it gave everyone a chance to start over, economically and socially. The Jubilee year reminds us that God wants people to be free (Luke 4:18–19). It also stands as a witness to God's desire for justice on earth and calls into question any social practices that lead to permanent bondage and loss of economic opportunity.

JUDAH [JOO duh] (praise)

The fourth son of Jacob and Leah and the founder of the family out of which the messianic line came (Gen. 29:35; Num. 26:19–21; Matt. 1:2). Judah saved Joseph's life by suggesting that his brothers sell Joseph to Ishmaelite merchants rather than kill him (Gen. 37:26–28). In Egypt it was Judah who begged Joseph to detain him rather than Benjamin, Jacob's beloved son. In an eloquent speech, Judah confessed what he and his brothers had done to Joseph; shortly thereafter, Joseph identified himself to his brothers (Gen. 44:14–45:1).

It appears that Judah was the leader of Jacob's sons who remained at home. Even though he was not the oldest son, Judah was sent by Jacob to precede him to Egypt (Gen. 46:28). Also Judah, rather than his older brothers, received Jacob's blessing (Gen. 49:3–10). In that blessing, Jacob foretold the rise of Judah: "Your father's children shall bow down before you. . . . The scepter shall not depart from Judah . . . until Shiloh comes" (Gen. 49:8, 10). Judah fathered twin sons, Perez

and Zerah (Gen. 38:29–30). The line of Judah ran through Perez to David and thus became the messianic line (Luke 3:30; Judas in KJV).

JUDAH, KINGDOM OF

One of the two nations into which the united kingdom of the Jews was divided following King Solomon's death in 931 B.C. Judah consisted mostly of the tribes of Judah and part of Benjamin, although Simeon apparently was included later. Judah was left suddenly independent when Rehoboam refused to lighten the heavy load of forced labor and high taxation imposed on the Israelites by his father Solomon (1 Kin. 12:1–24). Upon Rehoboam's refusal, the Ten Tribes living north of Bethel declared their independence.

Scarcely had this division occurred when another blow devastated Judah. Shishak, pharaoh of Egypt (about 945–924 B.C.), invaded the country, plundered the treasures of the temple and the royal palace, and destroyed a number of newly built fortresses (2 Chr. 12:1–12).

Rehoboam wanted to attack Israel and reunite the kingdom by force, but Shemaiah the prophet showed him how foolish the attempt would be (1 Kin. 12:21–24). Rehoboam's son Abijah (about 913–910 B.C.) regained a small area from Israel and tried to make an alliance with Syria against the northern kingdom, as did his successor Asa (about 910–869 B.C.). Asa rooted out much of the Canaanite paganism in Judah, and his reign was mostly peaceful and prosperous. He was followed (about 869 B.C.) by Jehoshaphat, who had co-ruled with Asa from about 873 B.C.

Judah prospered under the rule of Jehoshaphat, although he failed in his attempts to revive Solomon's seagoing trade. An alliance with Ahab of Israel against the Syrians at Ramoth Gilead proved to be even more disastrous

(2 Chr. 18:31–32). Jehoshaphat's son Jehoram (about 848–841 B.C.) married Athaliah, daughter of Ahab and the wicked Queen Jezebel; and their marriage led to Baal worship also being established in Jerusalem (2 Kin. 8:18). Jehoram's son Ahaziah reigned only for one year (841 B.C.) before he was killed. The pagan queen-mother Athaliah (about 841–835 B.C.) seized the throne and nearly brought the Davidic line to extinction by killing most of Ahaziah's sons. Only the infant Joash escaped; he was rescued by his aunt Jehoshabeath and her husband Jehoiada, the godly high priest (2 Chr. 22:10–12).

After six years Joash was proclaimed the lawful king, and Athaliah was executed. The new king reigned well (about 835–796 B.C.) whenever he followed Jehoiada's advice. But following the death of the high priest, idolatry crept back into the nation's life. Joash was finally assassinated by his servants following a raid on Jerusalem by the army of Syria, which pillaged the city (2 Chr. 24:23–25).

Judah enjoyed modest prosperity under Amaziah (about 796–767 B.C.), the son and successor of Joash. Amaziah regained control of Edom, which had been independent since the days of Jehoram. Thus he was able to control the trading caravans of western Arabia as Solomon had done. Amaziah was eventually murdered at Lachish as the result of a conspiracy (2 Kin. 14:19), and he was succeeded by Azariah (Uzziah) about 767 B.C.

Uzziah set about restoring Judah's military and economic strength. He suppressed Baal worship in the kingdom and promoted the traditions of the Sinai covenant. He improved agricultural productivity by constructing cisterns, which increased available water supplies. Uzziah incorporated some Philistine and Ammonite territory into his own realm; he also built new defensive positions in Jerusalem and at the outposts on the borders of Judah. Uzziah became proud of his successes, which led him to take over one of the duties of the high priest (2 Chr. 26:16–21). For this he was struck with leprosy for the rest of his life.

Jotham succeeded his father Uzziah and continued to make the southern kingdom productive. His successor, Ahaz (about 732–715 B.C.), was faced with Assyria's rise to power under Tiglath-Pileser III; but Ahaz resisted the urgings of Rezin of Syria and Pekah of Israel to join an alliance against Assyria. Instead, Ahaz sought help from Assyria, against Isaiah's advice, and received assistance in return for heavy tribute. Syria and the kingdom of Israel were destroyed, leaving Judah at the mercy of the Assyrians.

When Hezekiah (about 714–686 B.C.) succeeded Ahaz, he also disregarded Isaiah's advice and became involved in a coalition with Babylonia and Egypt against Assyria. Assyria, now ruled by Sennacherib (about 705–681 B.C.), moved against Jerusalem in 701 B.C. The Assyrians soon withdrew after suffering heavy losses, perhaps from a plague (Is. 37:36).

The rest of Hezekiah's reign was marked by a renewal of covenant faith. Hezekiah's renewal was disrupted by his son Manasseh (about 697–641 B.C.), who reacted violently against his father's religious policies. Manasseh introduced a lengthy period of paganism that brought Judah to new depths of depravity (2 Chr. 33:1–20). He was deported to Babylon by Esarhaddon (about 681–669 B.C.).

Manasseh's son Amon (about 642–640 B.C.) continued in his father's depravity, but he soon was murdered. His successor Josiah (about 640–609 B.C.) restored traditional covenant religion, which was based on the Book of the Law newly discovered in a temple storeroom (2 Chr. 34:14). Many did not follow Josiah's example, however; and the prophet Zephaniah foretold disaster for the nation.

By 610 B.C. the Assyrian Empire had collapsed under Babylonian attacks, and the victors prepared to march against Egypt, which had been helping the Assyrians. Josiah intervened and was killed at Megiddo (2 Chr. 35:20–27). Pharaoh Necho deposed Jehoahaz (Shallum) in 609 B.C. and made Jehoiakim ruler of Judah, which was now firmly under Egyptian control. The Babylonians swept down upon Jerusalem in 597 B.C. and captured it. A second attack led to Jerusalem's second defeat in 586 B.C. Captives from both campaigns were taken to Babylonia to mark the captivity of the southern kingdom.

The Babylonians appointed Gedaliah, a court official in Judah, to oversee what was left of life in the land. After three months as governor, he was assassinated. Judah's kingdom reaped the reward of its idolatry and rebellion against the Lord and disappeared from history.

JUDAH, TRIBE OF

The tribe founded by Judah. Its five tribal families sprang from Judah's three sons—Shelah, Perez, and Zerah—and two grandsons, Hezron and Hamul (Num. 26:19–21). In the first census, the tribe of Judah numbered 74,600 men (Num. 1:26–27). In the second census, the tribe numbered 76,500 (Num. 26:22).

Except for Simeon, Judah was the southernmost tribe of the Israelites. However, Simeon seems to have been absorbed into Judah at an early date. Judah's eastern border was the Dead Sea, and its western border was the Mediterranean Sea, although the Philistines usually controlled the plain along the sea. Originally, Judah's northern boundary ran from just south of Jerusalem northwest to Kirjath Jearim and Jabneel. To the south Judah's border ran south to the Ascent of Akrabbim, to the Wilderness of Zin, and south from Kadesh Barnea to the Mediterranean. During the period of the divided kingdom, its northern boundary ran north of Jerusalem.

The tribe of Judah, along with Benjamin, remained true to David's line when the tribes split after Solomon's death. Together they formed the southern kingdom of Judah, which at one time included Edom to the southeast.

JUDAIZERS [JOO dee eye zurs]

Early converts to Christianity who tried to force believers from non-Jewish backgrounds to adopt Jewish customs as a condition of salvation. Evidence of this movement within the early church first emerged about A.D. 49, when "certain men came down from Judea and taught the brethren, 'Unless you are circumcised according to the custom of Moses, you cannot be saved'" (Acts 15:1).

The apostle Paul denounced this idea, insisting that only one thing is necessary for salvation: faith in the Lord Jesus Christ (Acts 15:1–29). In the letter to the Galatians, Paul continued this same argument, insisting that the believer is justified by faith alone. To become a new person in Christ is to be set free from the requirements of the Jewish law: "For in Christ Jesus neither circumcision nor uncircumcision avails anything, but a new creation" (Gal. 6:15).

JUDAS [JOO duhs] (praise)

1. One of the twelve apostles of Jesus. John is careful to distinguish him from Judas Iscariot (John 14:22). He is called "Judas the son of James" (Luke 6:16; Acts 1:13). In the list of the Twelve given in Mark, instead of "Judas . . . of James" a Thaddaeus is mentioned (Mark 3:18). Matthew has Lebbaeus, whose surname was Thaddaeus (Matt. 10:3). He was also called Judas the Zealot. Tradition says he preached in Assyria and Persia and died a martyr in Persia.

JUDAS [JOO duhs] *(praise)*

2. One of the four brothers of Jesus (Matt. 13:55; Mark 6:3; Juda in KJV). Some scholars believe he was the author of the Epistle of Jude.

JUDAS ISCARIOT [JOO duhs iss KAR ih uht]

The disciple who betrayed Jesus. Judas was the son of Simon (John 6:71), or of Simon Iscariot (NRSV). The term Iscariot, which is used to distinguish Judas from the other disciple named Judas (Luke 6:16; John 14:22; Acts 1:13), refers to his hometown of Kerioth, in southern Judah (Josh. 15:25). Thus, Judas was a Judean, the only one of the Twelve who was not from Galilee.

The details of Judas's life are sketchy. Because of his betrayal of Jesus, Judas, however, is even more of a mystery. It must be assumed that Jesus saw promise in Judas, or He would not have called him to be a disciple.

Judas's name appears in 3 of the lists of the disciples (Matt. 10:2–4; Mark 3:16–19; Luke 6:14–16), although it always appears last. His name is missing from the list of the 11 disciples in Acts 1:13; by that time Judas had already committed suicide. Judas must have been an important disciple, because he served as their treasurer (John 12:6; 13:29).

During the week of the Passover festival, Judas went to the chief priests and offered to betray Jesus for a reward (Matt. 26:14–16; Mark 14:10–11). At the Passover supper, Jesus announced that He would be betrayed and that He knew who His betrayer was—one who dipped his hand with him in the dish (Mark 14:20), the one to whom He would give the piece of bread used in eating (John 13:26–27). Jesus was saying that a friend, one who dipped out of the same dish as He, was His betrayer. These verses in John indicate that Judas probably was reclining beside Jesus, evidence that Judas was an important disciple.

Jesus said to Judas, "What you do, do quickly" (John 13:27). Judas left immediately after he ate (John 13:30). The first observance of the Lord's Supper was probably celebrated afterward, without Judas (Matt. 26:26–29).

Judas carried out his betrayal in the Garden of Gethsemane. By a prearranged sign, he singled out Jesus for the soldiers by kissing him. The gospels do not tell us why Judas was needed to point out Jesus, who had become a well-known figure. It is possible that Judas disclosed where Jesus would be that night, so that He could be arrested secretly without the knowledge of His many supporters (Matt. 26:47–50).

Matthew reports that, realizing what he had done, Judas attempted to return the money to the priests. When the priests refused to take it, Judas threw the money on the temple floor, went out, and hanged himself. Unwilling to use "blood money" for the temple, the priests bought a potter's field, which became known as the "Field of Blood" (Matt. 27:3–10). This field is traditionally located at the point where the Kidron, Tyropoeon, and Hinnom valleys come together.

It is difficult to understand why Judas betrayed Jesus. Since he had access to the disciples' treasury, it seems unlikely that he did it for the money only; 30 pieces of silver is a relatively small amount. Some have suggested that Judas thought his betrayal would force Jesus into asserting His true power and overthrowing the Romans. Others have suggested that Judas might have become convinced that Jesus was a false messiah, and that the true Messiah was yet to come, or that he was upset over Jesus' apparent indifference to the law and His association with sinners and his violation of the Sabbath. Whatever the reason,

J

Judas's motive remains shrouded in mystery.

Acts 1:20 quotes Psalm 109:8 as the basis for electing another person to fill the place vacated by Judas: "Let another take his office." When the 11 remaining apostles cast lots for Judas's replacement, "the lot fell on Matthias. And he was numbered with the eleven apostles" (Acts 1:26).

JUDE [jood] *(praise)*

The author of the Epistle of Jude, in which he is described as "a servant of Jesus Christ, and brother of James" (Jude 1). Jude is an English form of the name Judas. Many scholars believe that the James mentioned in this passage is James the brother of Jesus. In Matthew 13:55 the people said concerning Jesus, "Is this not the carpenter's son? Is not His mother called Mary? And His brothers James, Joses, Simon, and Judas?" (Mark 6:3).

If Jude (Judas) was the brother of James and of Jesus, Jude did not believe in Him (John 7:5) until after Jesus' resurrection (Acts 1:14).

JUDEA [joo DEE uh]

The Greco-Roman name for the land of Judah. Judea is first mentioned in Ezra 5:8 (Judaea, KJV; Judah, NIV), where it is used to designate a province of the Persian Empire. The word *Judea* comes from the adjective "Jewish," a term that was used of the Babylonian captives who returned to the Promised Land, most of whom were from the tribe of Judah.

Under the rule of the Persians, Judea was a district administered by a governor; usually this governor was a Jew (Hag. 1:14; 2:2). When Herod Archelaus was banished in A.D. 6, Judea ceased to exist as a separate district and was annexed to the Roman province of Syria. The governors of Judea, called prefects or procurators, were appointed by the

emperor; their official residence was at Caesarea. However, they were supervised by the proconsul of Syria, who ruled from Antioch (Luke 3:1). It was under this political arrangement that Jesus lived and ministered.

Judea extended from the Mediterranean Sea on the west to the Dead Sea on the east, and from a few miles south of Gaza and the southern tip of the Dead Sea north to about Joppa. Thus, Judea measured about 56 miles (90 kilometers) from north to south and from east to west. The region contained four distinctive types of land: the coastal plains along the Mediterranean Sea, the lowlands in the south, the hill country, and the desert.

JUDGMENT

Discernment or separation between good and evil. God judges among people and their actions according to the standards of His Law.

In the Bible the most important judgment is the final judgment, the ultimate separation of good and evil at the end of history. The precise time of this judgment is appointed by God (Acts 17:31), but it remains unknown to us (Matt. 24:36). The return of the Lord to earth, the resurrection of the dead, and the final judgment, together with the end of the world—all these may be thought of as belonging to a single complex of events at the end of time.

God Himself is the Judge of mankind (Gen. 18:25), and He has the power and wisdom to judge with righteousness, truth, and justice (Pss. 96:13; 98:9). The final judgment is a task given specifically to God's Son (John 5:22; Acts 17:31) to conclude His work as mediator, deliver His people from sin, and destroy all God's enemies. God's people are associated with Christ in the exercise of this judgment (1 Cor. 6:2–3; Rev. 20:4).

The final judgment will be comprehensive in scope; it will include all people and nations from the beginning of the world to the end of history (Matt. 25:31–46; Rom. 14:10–12), as well as fallen angels (2 Pet. 2:4). Those who trust in the Lord, repent of sin, and walk in His ways will not be condemned but will enter into eternal life (Ps. 1). The purpose of the final judgment is the glory of God through the salvation of the elect and the condemnation of the ungodly (2 Thess. 1:3–10).

JUDGES, THE

Military heroes or deliverers who led the nation of Israel against their enemies during the period between the death of Joshua and the establishment of the kingship. The stories of their exploits are found in the Book of Judges.

During the period of the judges, from about 1380–1050 B.C., the government of Israel was a loose confederation of tribes gathered about their central shrine, the ark of the covenant. Without a human king to guide them, the people tended to rebel and fall into worship of false gods time and time again. "Everyone did what was right in his own eyes" (Judg. 17:6; 21:25) is how the Book of Judges describes these chaotic times. To punish the people, God would send foreign nations or tribes to oppress the Israelites.

These judges or charismatic leaders would rally the people to defeat the enemy. As God's agents for justice and deliverance, they would act decisively to free the nation from oppression. But the judges themselves were often weak, and their work was short-lived. The people would enter another stage of rebellion and idolatry, only to see the cycle of oppression and deliverance repeated all over again.

The judges themselves were a diverse lot. Some of them received only a brief mention in the Book of Judges. These minor judges were Shamgar (3:31), Tola (10:1–2), Jair (10:3–5), Ibzan (12:8–10), Elon (12:11–12), and Abdon (12:13–15).

The careers of other judges are explored in greater detail in the Book of Judges. Othniel, a nephew of Caleb (3:7–11), was a warrior-deliverer who led the Israelites against the king of Mesopotamia. Ehud (3:12–30) was distinguished by left-handedness and his deftness with the dagger. Jephthah (11:1–12:7) was a harlot's son whose devotion to God was matched only by his rashness. Gideon (6:11–8:35) needed many encouragements to act upon God's call. But he finally led 300 Israelites to defeat the entire army of the Midianites. The most interesting of the judges, perhaps, was Samson (13:1–16:31), whose frailties of the flesh led to his capture by the hated Philistines. The most courageous of the judges was Deborah, a woman who prevailed upon Barak to attack the mighty army of the Canaanites (4:1–5:31).

The stories of the judges make interesting reading because of their rugged personalities and the nature of the times in which they lived. The openness with which they are portrayed in all their weaknesses is one mark of the integrity of the Bible.

JUSTICE OF GOD

God's fair and impartial treatment of all people. As a God of justice (Is. 30:18), He is interested in fairness as well as in what makes for right relationships. His actions and decisions are true and right (Job 34:12; Rev. 16:7). His demands on individuals and nations to look after victims of oppression are just demands (Psalm 82).

As Lord and Judge, God brings justice to nations (Ps. 67:4) and "sets things right" in behalf of the poor, the oppressed, and the victims of injustice (Ps. 103:6; 146:6–9). For the wicked, the unjust, and the oppressor, God as supreme Judge of the earth is a dreaded force. But

J

for all who are unjustly treated, God's just action is reason for hope.

JUSTIFICATION

The process by which sinful human beings are made acceptable to a holy God. Christianity is unique because of its teaching of justification by grace (Rom. 3:24). Justification is God's declaration that the demands of His Law have been fulfilled in the righteousness of His Son. The basis for this justification is the death of Christ. Justification is based on the work of Christ, accomplished through His blood (Rom. 5:9), and brought to His people through His resurrection (Rom. 4:25).

When God justifies, He charges the sin of man to Christ and credits the righteousness of Christ to the believer (2 Cor. 5:21). Thus, "through one Man's righteous act, the free gift came to all men, resulting in justification of life" (Rom. 5:18). Because this righteousness is "the righteousness of God" which is "apart from the law" (Rom. 3:21), it is thorough; a believer is "justified from all things" (Acts 13:39). God is "just" because His holy standard of perfect righteousness has been fulfilled in Christ, and He is the "justifier," because this righteousness is freely given to the believer (Rom. 3:26; 5:16).

Although the Lord Jesus has paid the price for our justification, it is through our faith that He is received and His righteousness is experienced and enjoyed (Rom. 3:25–30). Faith is considered righteousness (Rom. 4:3, 9), not as the work of human beings (Rom. 4:5), but as the gift and work of God (Eph. 2:8; Phil. 1:29).

K

KADESH BARNEA [KAY desh bar NEE uh] *(consecrated)*

A wilderness region between Egypt and the land of Canaan where the Hebrew people camped after the Exodus. Kadesh Barnea (the modern oasis of Ain el-Qudeirat) was situated on the edge of Edom (Num. 20:16) about 70 miles (114 kilometers) from Hebron and 50 miles (61 kilometers) from Beersheba in the Wilderness of Zin. Kadesh Barnea is also said to be in the Wilderness of Paran (Num. 13:26). Paran was probably the general name for the larger wilderness area, while Zin may have been the specific name for a smaller portion of the wilderness territory.

The first mention of Kadesh Barnea occurred during the time of Abraham. Chedorlaomer, king of Elam, and his allied armies waged war against the Amalekites and Amorites from Kadesh (Gen. 14:7). When Hagar was forced by Sarah to flee from Abraham's home, she was protected by the angel of the Lord, who brought her to the well Beer Lahai Roi, between Kadesh and Bered (16:14). Later Abraham moved to Gerar, situated between Kadesh and Shur (20:1).

The most important contacts of the Israelites with Kadesh Barnea occurred during the years of the wilderness wanderings. During the second year after the Exodus from Egypt, the Israelites camped around Mt. Horeb, or Sinai. God told them to leave Sinai and take an 11-day journey to Kadesh Barnea (Num. 10:11–12; Deut. 1:2). From here the people would have direct entry into the land of Canaan. Moses selected one man from each tribe as a spy and sent them to "spy out the land" (Num. 13:2). After 40 days they returned with grapes and other fruits, proving Canaan to be a fertile, plentiful land.

Ten of these spies reported giants in the land, implying that Israel was too weak to enter Canaan (Num. 13:33). But two of the spies, Joshua and Caleb, said, "Do not fear" (Num. 14:9). The people wanted to stone the two for their report (Num. 14:10), and they went so far as to ask for another leader to take them back to Egypt.

Because of their fear and rebellion at Kadesh (Deut. 9:23), the Israelites were forced to wander in the Wilderness of Paran for 38 years. Kadesh apparently was their headquarters while they moved about during these years. In the first month of the fortieth year of the Exodus, the people again assembled at Kadesh for their final march to the Promised Land.

While they were still camped at Kadesh, a number of the leaders of the people rebelled against Moses and Aaron (Num. 16:1–3). They were killed in an earthquake (16:31, 32). Miriam, Moses' sister, also died and was buried (20:1). At Kadesh, Moses also disobeyed God by striking the rock to bring forth water (20:8–11). He had been told to speak, not strike the rock. Soon after Moses and the people began to move from Kadesh toward Canaan, Aaron died and was buried (20:23–29).

The events at Kadesh Barnea clearly demonstrate the peril of rebelling against God's appointed leaders, murmuring and complaining about God's directions, and refusing to follow God's orders.

KENEZZITES [KEE nuh zights]

An Edomite tribe of Canaan in the time of Abraham (Gen. 15:19; Kenizzites in KJV, NRSV, REB, NIV, NASB). Before the conquest of Canaan by Joshua, the Kenezzites apparently lived in the Negev, the desert of southern Judah, and in the border regions of Edom, south of the Dead Sea. Some of the Kenezzites were absorbed by the tribe of Judah and others by the Edomites.

The Kenezzites were related to the Kenites and, like the Kenites, were skilled workers in metal. Their name probably comes from Kenaz, a descendant of Esau (Gen. 36:11, 15); he is listed among the Edomite chieftains (Gen. 36:42). Jephunneh the Kenezzite apparently married a woman of the tribe of Judah; their son Caleb (the spy) was a godly man who followed the Lord God of Israel.

KENITES [KEE nights] *(metalsmiths)*

The name of a wandering tribe of people who were associated with the Midianites (Judg. 1:16) and, later, with the Amalekites (1 Sam. 15:6). The Kenites lived in the desert regions of Sinai, Midian, Edom, Amalek, and the Negev. The Bible first mentions the Kenites as one of the groups that lived in Canaan during the time of Abraham (Gen. 15:19); their territory was to be taken by the Israelites (Num. 24:21–22). The Kenites were metal craftsmen who may have traced their ancestry to Tubal-Cain (Gen. 4:22).

Around the time of Israel's exodus from Egypt, the Kenites showed kindness to Israel (1 Sam. 15:6). Moses' father-in-law, Jethro, is called a Midianite (Ex. 18:1) and a Kenite (Judg. 1:16). Some scholars suggest that the skill in smelting and casting the golden calf (Ex. 32) and the bronze serpent (Num. 21) may have been learned by Moses from the Kenites. Some Kenites were among those who entered the Promised Land along with the Israelites in the conquest led by Joshua (Judg. 1:16).

KETURAH [keh TUR uh]

A wife of Abraham (Gen. 25:1, 4), also called Abraham's concubine (1 Chr. 1:32–33). Some suggest that Keturah had been Abraham's "concubine-wife," before the death of Sarah. After Sarah died, Keturah was then elevated to the full status of Abraham's wife. Keturah bore to Abraham six sons: Zimran, Jokshan, Medan, Midian, Ishbak, and Shuah (Gen. 25:1–4). These men were the founders or ancestors of six Arabian tribes in southern and eastern Palestine. Late Arabian genealogies mention a tribe by the name of Katura dwelling near Mecca.

Keturah's sons were not on the same level as Abraham's promised son, Isaac. Through Isaac God would carry out His promise to Abraham to make of his descendants a special people. While he was still alive, therefore, Abraham gave Keturah's sons gifts and sent them to "the country of the east" (Gen. 25:6).

Abraham was already advanced in years when he married Keturah. She brought him both companionship and children in his old age. Keturah apparently outlived Abraham (Gen. 25:7).

KIDRON VALLEY [KIH drun] *(gloomy)*

A valley on the eastern slope of Jerusalem through which a seasonal brook of the same name runs. The meaning of the name is fitting, in view of the great strife that has surrounded the Kidron throughout Bible times. A torrent in the winter rains, it contains little water in the summer months.

The ravine of the Kidron valley begins north of Jerusalem, running past the temple, Calvary, the Garden of Gethsemane, and the Mount of Olives to form a well-defined limit to Jerusalem on its eastern side. From there the valley and the brook reach into the Judean wilderness, where the land is so dry that the brook takes the name of Wady en-Nar or "fire wady." Finally, its dreary course brings it to the Dead Sea.

Kidron was the brook crossed by David while fleeing from Absalom (2 Sam. 15:23, 30). While the brook is not large,

the deep ravine is a significant geographical obstacle. When David crossed the Kidron and turned east to retreat from Absalom to the safety of Hebron, he signaled his abandonment of Jerusalem (2 Sam. 15:23).

On the west side of the Kidron is the spring of Gihon which King Hezekiah tapped for city water before the Assyrians besieged Jerusalem. Hezekiah also blocked the Kidron and lesser springs in the valley to deny water to the besieging Assyrians.

Asa, Hezekiah, and Josiah, the great reforming kings of Judah, burned the idols and objects of worship of the pagan cults that they suppressed in the Kidron Valley (1 Kin. 15:13). Beside the brook King Asa destroyed and burned his mother's idol of Asherah (1 Kin. 15:13). After this, the valley became the regular receptacle for the impurities and abominations of idol worship when they were removed from the temple and destroyed (2 Kin. 23:4, 6, 12; 2 Chr. 29:16; 30:14).

From the Kidron Valley Nehemiah inspected the walls of Jerusalem at night, probably because the walls were clearly visible along that side (Neh. 2:15). In the time of Josiah, this valley was the common cemetery of Jerusalem (2 Kin. 23:6; Jer. 26:23). When Jesus left Jerusalem for the Garden of Gethsemane on the night of His arrest, He crossed the Kidron along the way.

KINGDOM OF GOD/KINGDOM OF HEAVEN

God's rule of grace in the world, a future period foretold by the prophets of the Old Testament and identified by Jesus as beginning with His public ministry. The kingdom of God is the experience of blessedness, like that of the Garden of Eden, where evil is fully overcome and where those who live in the kingdom know only happiness, peace, and joy. This was the main expectation of the Old Testament prophets about the future.

John the Baptist astonished his hearers when he announced that this expected and hoped-for kingdom was "at hand" in the person of Jesus (Matt. 3:2). Jesus repeated this message (Matt. 4:17; Mark 1:15), but He went even further by announcing clearly that the kingdom was already present in His ministry: "If I cast out demons by the Spirit of God, surely the kingdom of God has come upon you" (Matt. 12:28). Jesus was the full embodiment of the kingdom.

The entire ministry of Jesus is understood in relation to this important declaration of the presence of the kingdom. His ethical teachings, for example, cannot be understood apart from the announcement of the kingdom. They are ethics of the kingdom; the perfection to which they point makes no sense apart from the present experience of the kingdom. Participation in the new reality of the kingdom involves a follower of Jesus in a call to the highest righteousness (Matt. 5:20).

The acts and deeds of Jesus likewise make sense only in the larger context of proclaiming the kingdom. When John the Baptist asked whether Jesus was "the Coming One," or the Messiah, Jesus answered by recounting some of His deeds of healing (Matt. 11:5). The reference in these words to the expectation of a Messiah, especially of the prophet Isaiah (Is. 29:18–19; 35:5–6; 61:1), could not have been missed by John. At the synagogue in Nazareth, Jesus read a passage from Isaiah 61 about the coming messianic age and then made the astonishing announcement, "Today this Scripture is fulfilled in your hearing" (Luke 4:21).

All that Jesus did is related to this claim that the kingdom of God has dawned through His ministry. His healings were manifestations of the presence of the kingdom. In these deeds there was a direct confrontation between God and the forces of evil, or Satan and his demons. Summarizing His ministry, Jesus declared, "I saw Satan fall like lightning from heaven" (Luke 10:18). Satan and evil are in retreat now that the kingdom has made its entrance into human history. This is an anticipation of the final age of perfection that will be realized at Christ's return.

Although the gospels of Matthew, Mark, Luke, and John focus on the present aspect of the kingdom of God, it is also clear that the kingdom will be realized perfectly only at the Second Coming. The kingdom that comes through the ministry of Jesus dawns in the form of a mystery. Although it is physically present in the deeds and words of Jesus, it does not overwhelm the world. The judgment of God's enemies is postponed. The kingdom that arrived with Jesus did not include the triumphal victory so longed for by the Jews. It arrived secretly like leaven, inconspicuously like a mustard seed, or like a small pearl of great value that can be hidden in one's pocket (Matt. 13:31–46).

The Jewish people expected the kingdom of God to bring the present evil age to an end. But it arrived mysteriously without doing so. The new reality of the kingdom overlapped the present age, invading it rather than bringing it to an end. The demons reflect this oddity when they ask Jesus, "Have you come here to torment us before the time?" (Matt. 8:29). The future kingdom will bring the present age to an end and usher in the perfect age promised in the prophets. The present kingdom is both an anticipation and a guarantee of this future bliss.

The expression "kingdom of God" occurs mostly in the gospels of Matthew, Mark, and Luke. The Gospel of John and the Epistles of the New Testament refer to the same reality but in different language, using phrases such as "eternal life" or "salvation." The apostle Paul identified the kingdom of God as "righteousness and peace and joy in the Holy Spirit" (Rom. 14:17). Perhaps one reason why he described it this way is that the kingdom of God was a Jewish expression unfamiliar and possibly misleading to Gentiles.

Some interpreters of the Bible have described the phrase "kingdom of God" as a more comprehensive term referring to both heaven and earth. Likewise, they believe "kingdom of God" is a more restricted term referring to God's rule on earth, especially in relation to the nation of Israel. In this view Jesus offered the literal kingdom of heaven to Israel, but the Jews refused to accept it. Thus, it has been postponed until the Second Coming of Christ.

A careful study of the gospels, however, shows that the two phrases are used interchangeably. In parallel passages, Matthew uses "kingdom of heaven" while Mark and Luke have "kingdom of God" (Matt. 4:17; Mark 1:15). Even in Matthew the two phrases are sometimes used interchangeably, as in Matthew 19:23–24, where they are used one after the other in the same connection.

KIR HARASETH [kir HAHR uh seth]

A fortified city of Moab (2 Kin. 3:25), also spelled Kir Hareseth (Is. 16:7), Kir Heres (Is. 16:11; Jer. 48:31, 36), and Kirharesh (Is. 16:11, KJV). Kir of Moab (Is. 15:1) is also thought to be identical with Kir Haraseth.

Mesha, king of Moab, fled to Kir Haraseth after he was defeated by Jehoram, king of Israel, and Jehoshaphat, king of Judah. Accompanied by the king of Edom, these two rulers crushed the rebellion that Mesha had started (2 Kin. 3:4). Because Kir Haraseth was the only city of Moab that could not be overthrown, it was the last refuge of Mesha (2 Kin. 3:25).

The prophets foretold God's certain destruction of Kir Haraseth, a seemingly invincible city (Is. 16:7). Many commentators identify Kir Haraseth with present-day el-Kerak, about 50 miles (80 kilometers) southeast of Jerusalem.

KIRJATH JEARIM [KIR jath JEE uh rim]
(city of forests)

A fortified city that originally belonged to the Gibeonites. Kirjath Jearim is first mentioned as a member of a Gibeonite confederation of four fortress cities, which also included Gibeon, Chephirah, and Beeroth (Josh. 9:17). Kirjath Jearim was also known as Baalah (Josh. 15:9), Baale Judah (2 Sam. 6:2), and Kirjath Baal (Josh. 15:60), and Kirjath (Josh. 18:28, NKJV, KJV). These names suggest that perhaps it was an old Canaanite "high place," a place of idolatrous worship.

Originally assigned to the tribe of Judah (Josh. 15:60), and later assigned to Benjamin (Josh. 18:14–15, 28), Kirjath Jearim was on the western part of the boundary line between Judah and Benjamin (Josh. 15:9). When the ark of the covenant was returned to the Israelites by the Philistines, it was brought from Beth Shemesh to Kirjath Jearim and entrusted to a man named Eleazar (1 Sam. 7:1–2). The ark remained in Kirjath Jearim, in the house of Abinadab, the father of Eleazar, for many years. It was from here that David transported the ark to Jerusalem (2 Sam. 6:2–3).

This ancient town has been identified by some scholars with Abu Ghosh, about 8 miles (13 kilometers) northwest of Jerusalem on the Jaffa Road.

KISHON [KIGH shuhn]

A river in Palestine, which flows from sources on Mount Tabor and Mount Gilboa westward through the Plain of Esdraelon and the Valley of Jezreel, then empties into the Mediterranean Sea near the northern base of Mount Carmel. Because the Kishon falls slightly as it crosses the level plain, it often becomes swollen and floods much of the valley during the season of heavy rains.

At the river Kishon the Israelites won a celebrated victory over Sisera under the leadership of Deborah and Barak (Judg. 4:7). Fully armed with 900 chariots of iron (Judg. 4:13), the forces of Sisera became bogged down in the overflow of the Kishon (Judg. 5:21), and the Israelites defeated them. It was at the Brook Kishon, also, that the prophets of Baal were executed following their contest with Elijah on Mount Carmel (1 Kin. 18:40).

KISS

A symbolic act done to various parts of the body, especially cheeks, feet, forehead, and lips (Prov. 24:26). Ideally, a kiss shows a close relationship to another person, although the relationship and purpose may vary greatly.

Romantic kisses are mentioned infrequently in the Bible, whether genuinely loving (Song 1:2; 8:1) or seductive (Prov. 7:13). The most common type of kiss, however, was that between relatives (Gen. 29:11–13). A kiss could serve either as a greeting (Ex. 4:27) or a farewell (Ruth 1:9, 14; Acts 20:37). It could even express one's anticipation of departure by death (Gen. 48:10). The family kiss was extended in the New Testament to apply to the Christian family (1 Cor. 16:20; 1 Pet. 5:14).

Friends might kiss in greeting (1 Sam. 20:41; 2 Sam. 19:39), although occasionally such a kiss could be given insincerely (Prov. 27:6). Kissing also has figurative meaning when righteousness and peace are pictured as harmonious friends kissing each other (Ps. 85:10). A kiss can also mean betrayal. Judas's treachery is eternally symbolized by a kiss (Luke 22:47–48).

KOHATHITES [KOE hath ights]
(belonging to Kohath)

The descendants of Kohath, son of Levi (Ex. 6:16). Kohath was the father of Amram, Izhar, Hebron, and Uzziel (Ex. 6:18). Consequently, the Kohathite clan was subdivided into these four families (1 Chr. 26:23).

During Israel's journey after leaving Egypt, the Kohathites were responsible for caring for and transporting "the ark [of the covenant], the table, the lampstand, the altars, the utensils of the sanctuary with which they ministered, the screen, and [for doing] all the work related to them" (Num. 3:31).

When the Israelites camped, the Kohathites were stationed on the south side of the tabernacle (Num. 3:29, 31). At different times, the Bible specifies their numbers (Num. 3:28; 4:36). Aaron and Moses were Kohathites (Ex. 6:16, 18, 20).

KORAH

A Levite who, along with Dathan, Abiram, and On of the tribe of Reuben, led a revolt against the leadership of Moses and Aaron (Num. 16:1–49). Korah was the son of Izhar and a first cousin of Moses and Aaron (Ex. 6:21). He was equal in rank with Aaron within the tribe of Levi.

Korah apparently was jealous that Aaron held the position of high priest. The Reubenites were the descendants of Jacob's oldest son. They thought the responsibility for leading Israel should rest with their tribe rather than the Levites. The four ringleaders gathered 250 leaders of the congregation, publicly charging Moses and Aaron with abusing their power. They claimed that all members of the congregation should have equal access to the Lord.

Moses placed the dispute in the hands of the Lord, directing Korah and his company to bring containers of incense as an offering to the Lord. Korah complied with this and went with his congregation to the door of the tabernacle where the Lord appeared, threatening to "consume them in a moment" (Num. 16:21). Moses and Aaron interceded, saving the nation of Israel from destruction. The decision of leadership was again placed before the Lord as Moses instructed the congregation to "depart from the tents of these wicked men" (Num. 16:26). The decision in favor of Moses was dramatized as "the earth opened its mouth" and swallowed all the men of Korah (Num. 16:32).

Apparently some of the descendants of Korah survived to become ministers of music in the tabernacle during the time of David (1 Chr. 6:31–37).

L

LABAN [LAY bihn] (white)

Father-in-law of Jacob. Laban lived in the city of Nahor in Padan Aram, the place where Abraham sent his servant to find a wife for Isaac. Laban, brother of Rebekah, is introduced when he heard of the servant's presence, saw the golden jewelry given Rebekah, and eagerly invited Abraham's emissary into their home (Gen. 24:29–60). Laban played an important role in the marriage arrangements. His stubbornness and greed characterized his later dealings with Rebekah's son, Jacob.

Many years later, Jacob left home to escape Esau's wrath. At the well of Haran he met Rachel, Laban's daughter. Laban promised her to his nephew Jacob in return for seven years of labor from Jacob. Laban consequently dealt with Jacob with deception and greed; he gave him the wrong wife and then forced him to work seven more years for Rachel. Then he persuaded Jacob to stay longer, but the wages he promised were changed ten times in six years (Gen. 29–30).

When family situations became tense, Jacob quietly left with his wives, children, and possessions, only to be pursued by Laban (Gen. 31). Laban and Jacob eventually parted on peaceful terms, but they heaped up stones as a mutual testimony that they would have no further dealings with each other. They called upon God as their witness that they would not impose upon each other again (Gen. 31:43–55).

LACHISH [LAY kish]

An ancient walled city in the lowlands of Judah captured by Joshua and the Israelites. Lachish was situated about 30 miles (49 kilometers) southwest of Jerusalem and about 15 miles (9.5 kilometers) west of Hebron. The city covered about 18 acres and was inhabited for many years before the invasion by Joshua and the Israelites. The city is mentioned in early Egyptian sources as an important military stronghold.

After the Israelites overran the cities of Jericho and Ai, King Japhia of Lachish and four other kings formed an alliance against Israel (Josh. 10:1–4). God aided Israel against these five armies by causing the sun to stand still (Josh. 10:5–14). After a two-day siege, Lachish itself was captured (Josh. 10:31–33). It then was included in the allotment of the tribe of Judah (Josh. 15:39).

Little is known of the city until the time of Solomon when Solomon's son Rehoboam rebuilt Lachish to protect Judah from Egypt (2 Chr. 11:5–12). Many years later Amaziah, king of Judah, fled from an uprising in Jerusalem to Lachish. Because Amaziah had turned away from following God, judgment was imposed upon him; he was killed while hiding in the city (2 Kin. 14:19; 2 Chr. 25:27).

During the time of Hezekiah (701 B.C.), Sennacherib, king of Assyria, attacked Lachish (2 Kin. 18:13–17; 2 Chr. 32:9). Its capture was so important to Sennacherib that he memorialized it in a magnificent relief on the wall of his palace at Nineveh. He also sent a letter to Hezekiah, demanding his surrender (2 Kin. 18:14, 17; 19:8).

About 100 years later, Lachish was again a stronghold in the nation of Judah. Nebuchadnezzar, king of Babylon, attacked and defeated the city when he took Judah into captivity in 586 B.C. (Jer. 34:7). When the Jews returned from their years of captivity in Babylon, the city of Lachish was inhabited again (Neh. 11:30).

Archaeologists have excavated Lachish (modern Tell ed-Duweir), and it has become one of the most significant sites in the Holy Land. A small temple with an altar for burnt offerings was discovered here; and the bones of many animals also were found—perhaps representing portions of the animals that the priests ate during sacrificial observances (Lev. 7:32–34). Also discovered was a deep well that probably provided water for the city when it was under siege.

Other important finds consisted of early Hebrew writings on bowls, seals, and a stone altar. Twenty-one pottery sherds, on which were written letters about the attack on Lachish and Jerusalem by Babylon in 586 B.C., were also found. One of the letters states that signals from Azekah could no longer be seen. It was written shortly after the events noted in Jeremiah 34:7, which observe that Lachish and Azekah were the only fortified cities left in Judah.

LAMB OF GOD

A phrase used by John the Baptist to describe Jesus (John 1:29, 36). John publicly identified Jesus as "the Lamb of God who takes away the sin of the world!" Elsewhere in the New Testament Jesus is called a lamb (Acts 8:32; 1 Pet. 1:19; Rev. 5:6). The Book of Revelation speaks of Jesus as a lamb 28 times.

John's reference to Jesus as the Lamb of God calls to mind the Old Testament sacrificial system. In the sacrifice God accepted the blood of animals as the means of atonement for sin. It is likely that John had many themes from the Old Testament in mind when he called Jesus the Lamb of God. These themes probably included the sin offering (Lev. 4), the trespass offering (Lev. 5), the sacrifice on the Day of Atonement (Lev. 16), and the Passover sacrifice (Ex. 12).

But the strongest image from the Old Testament is the Suffering Servant, who "was led as a lamb to the slaughter" (Is. 53:7) and who "bore the sins of many" (Is. 53:12). Thus, this vivid description of Jesus was a pointed announcement of the Atonement He would bring about on our behalf.

LAMP

A simple oil-burning vessel used for lighting houses and public buildings in Bible times. Pottery lamps either had lips or were completely enclosed, with a hole in the middle, or a spout in the rim, for the wick. Such lamps were often decorated, and many had handles for convenient carrying. Jewish lamps were decorated with the symbol of the Menorah, the seven-branched lampstand. Christian lamps were decorated with Christian symbols such as crosses, fish, and the alpha and omega. The typical Palestinian lamp in Christ's day was plain and round, with a filling hole for oil and a spout for the wick.

Lamps could be held by hand or placed on a support, like a shelf or a lampstand. More light was provided by additional wicks. Lamps with up to seven spouts have been discovered by archaeologists. Some lamps were made of metal. They burned olive oil or fat. Lamps with a single wick would burn from two to four hours.

The lamp became a symbol of understanding (2 Sam. 22:29), guidance (Prov. 6:23), and life (Job 21:17). John the Baptist was "the burning and shining lamp" in whose light the Jews of his day rejoiced (John 5:35). In Jesus' parable of the wise and foolish virgins (Matt. 25:1–13), taking enough oil to keep the lamps burning represented good works done in obedience to Jesus' teaching. Not tak-

ing enough oil to keep the lamps burning represented disobedience to Christ.

LAODICEA [LAY ah duh SEE uh]

A city in the Lycus Valley of the province of Phrygia where one of the seven churches of Asia Minor was situated (Rev. 3:14). About 40 miles (65 kilometers) east of Ephesus and about 10 miles (16 kilometers) west of Colossae, Laodicea was built on the banks of the river Lycus, a tributary of the Maeander River.

The words of the risen Christ to Laodicea in Revelation 3:14–22 contain allusions to the economic prosperity and social prominence of the city. Founded by the Seleucids and named for Laodice, the wife of Antiochus II (261–247 B.C.), Laodicea became extremely wealthy

LAMP

during the Roman period. For example, in 62 B.C. Flaccus seized the annual contribution of the Jews of Laodicea for Jerusalem amounting to 20 pounds of gold. Moreover, when the city was destroyed by an earthquake in A.D. 60 (along with Colossae and Hierapolis), it alone refused aid from Rome for rebuilding (compare the self-sufficient attitude of the church of Laodicea in Revelation 3:17). Laodicea was known for its black wool industry; it manufactured garments from the raven-black wool produced by the sheep of the surrounding area.

The apostle Paul does not seem to have visited Laodicea at the time he wrote Colossians 2:1. Epaphras, Tychicus, Onesimus, and Mark seem to have been the early messengers of the gospel there (Col. 1:7; 4:7–15). A letter addressed to the Laodiceans by Paul (Col. 4:16) has apparently been lost; some consider it to be a copy of the Ephesian letter. A church council was supposedly held at Laodicea (A.D. 344–363), but all that has come down to us are statements from other councils.

According to the comments about the church at Laodicea in the Book of Revelation, this congregation consisted of lukewarm Christians (Rev. 3:14–22). The living Lord demands enthusiasm and total commitment from those who worship Him.

LAW

An orderly system of rules and regulations by which a society is governed. In the Bible, particularly the Old Testament, a unique law code was established by direct revelation from God to direct His people in their worship, in their relationship to Him, and in their social relationships with one another.

The biblical law code, or the Mosaic Law, was different from other ancient Near Eastern law codes in its origin.

Throughout the ancient world, the laws of most nations were believed to originate with the gods, but they were considered intensely personal and subjective in the way they were applied.

By contrast, the biblical concept was that law comes from God, issues from His nature, and is holy, righteous, and good. Furthermore, at the outset of God's ruling over Israel at Sinai, God the great King gave His laws. These laws were binding on His people, and He upheld them. God depicts His law as an expression of His love for His people (Ex. 19:5–6).

God's law, unlike those of other nations of the ancient world, also viewed all human life as especially valuable, because people are created in God's image. Thus, biblical law was more humane. It avoided mutilations and other savage punishments. Victims could not inflict more injury than they had received. Neither could criminals restore less than they had taken or stolen simply because of a class distinction. Everyone was equal before God's law.

The "eye for eye" requirement of the Mosaic Law was not a harsh statement that required cruel punishment. Instead, it was a mandate for equality before the law (Ex. 21:24). Each criminal had to pay for his own crime (Num. 35:31). Under the law codes of some pagan nations, the rich often could buy their way out of punishment. God's law especially protected the defenseless widow, fatherless child, slave, and stranger from injustice (Ex. 21:2, 20–21; 22:21–23).

Some scholars refer to Leviticus 17–26 as the "holiness code." Although it does not contain all of God's directions for ceremonial holiness, it does set forth much of what God requires. These chapters contain moral and ritual specifications regarding the tabernacle and public worship as well as the command to love one's neighbor as oneself (19:18).

The nation of Israel was to be characterized by separation from other nations. Several of these laws prohibited pagan worship. Because God is holy (21:8), Israel was to be holy and separated from other nations (20:26).

The Book of Deuteronomy is sometimes called the Deuteronomic Code. This book contains the command to love God with all one's heart, soul, and might (Deut. 6:5) as well as a second record of the Ten Commandments (Deuteronomy 5).

Biblical law is more than a record of human law. It is an expression of what God requires of people. It rests on the eternal moral principles that are consistent with the very nature of God Himself. Therefore, biblical law (the Ten Commandments) is the summary of moral law. As such it sets forth fundamental and universal moral principles.

God's people were to preserve and study the Lord's law (Deut. 4:2; 6:6–7), revere His name (Deut. 8:6; 10:12), be grateful and thankful (Deut. 8:10), and obey, love, and serve their redeemer God (Deut. 10:14–16; 6:4–5; 11:1, 13–14).

LAVER

A basin in which the priests washed their hands for purification purposes while officiating at the altar of the tabernacle or the temple. Moses was commanded to make a laver, or basin, so Aaron and the Levitical priests could wash their hands and feet before offering sacrifices (Ex. 30:18–21). The laver and its base were made from the bronze mirrors of the serving women (Ex. 38:8). It stood between the tent of meeting and the altar.

Hiram made ten bronze lavers for Solomon's temple (1 Kin. 7:27–39). Each laver rested on a bronze cart, and each cart rested on two pairs of wheels. The panels on the carts were decorated with lions, oxen, and cherubim. The lavers were divided into two groups of five and were used for washing sacrifices. The priests, however, washed in the bronze sea (2 Chr. 4:6). Later in Judah's history, King Ahaz cut the panels off the carts and removed the lavers (2 Kin. 16:17).

The ten lavers are not mentioned in the prophet Ezekiel's description of the new temple. The rebuilt temples under Zerubbabel and Herod each had a single laver.

LAZARUS [LAZ ah russ] (God has helped)

The brother of Martha and Mary of Bethany (John 11:1). One long account in the Gospel of John tells about his death and resurrection at the command of Jesus (John 11). A second account in the same gospel describes him as sitting with Jesus in the family home after the resurrection miracle (John 12:1–2). Because of the publicity surrounding this event, the chief priest plotted to kill Lazarus (John 12:9–11).

Twice John's gospel records Jesus' love for Lazarus (John 11:3, 5). Yet, upon hearing of the sickness of his friend, Jesus delayed in returning to Bethany. When He finally arrived, both Martha and Mary rebuked Jesus for not coming sooner. Jesus showed His impatience at their unbelief (11:33) as well as His personal sorrow ("Jesus wept"). Then he brought Lazarus back to life (11:43).

LEAH [LEE uh]

The older daughter of Laban, who deceitfully gave her in marriage to Jacob instead of her younger sister Rachel (Gen. 29:16–30). Although Rachel was the more beautiful of the two daughters of Laban and obviously was Jacob's favorite wife, the Lord blessed Leah and Jacob with six sons—Reuben, Simeon, Levi, Judah (Gen. 29:31–35), Issachar, and Zebulun (Gen. 30:17–20)—and a daughter, Dinah (Gen. 30:21). Leah's maid, Zilpah, added two more sons: Gad and Asher (Gen. 30:9–13).

Leah was the less-favored of the two wives of Jacob, and she must have been painfully conscious of this during all the years of her marriage. But it was Leah rather than Rachel who gave birth to Judah, through whose line Jesus the Messiah was eventually born. Apparently Leah died in the land of Canaan before the migration to Egypt (Gen. 46:6). She was buried in the Cave of Machpelah in Hebron (Gen. 49:31).

LEAVEN

A substance used to produce fermentation in dough (Ex. 12:15, 19–20; yeast, NIV). In Bible times leaven was usually a piece of fermented dough retained from a previous baking that was placed in the new dough to cause it to rise.

The use of leaven was prohibited in food offerings dedicated to the Lord by fire (Lev. 2:11). However, leavened bread was required for the peace offering (Lev. 7:13) and for the two wave loaves offered at the Feast of Weeks, or Pentecost (Lev. 23:17). During the Exodus, the Israelites had eaten unleavened bread because of their hasty departure from Egypt (Ex. 12:34, 39). The practice of this first Passover was continued in all subsequent observances of the Passover. At the beginning of the Passover season every year, all leaven was expelled from the house (Ex. 12:15) and was kept from the house for seven days (Ex. 12:19). These days, called the "Days of Unleavened Bread" (Acts 12:3), commemorated the eating of unleavened bread at the time of departure from Egypt.

Leaven is used metaphorically in the Bible of an influence that can permeate whatever it touches. Leaven is used as a symbol of either good or bad influence. In one parable, Jesus used the word *leaven* in a good sense:

"The kingdom of heaven is like leaven, which a woman took and hid in three measures of meal till it was all leavened" (Matt. 13:33). The action of the leaven in the meal—hidden, yet powerful, relentless, and pervasive—is a symbol of the growth of God's spiritual rule in the world.

On the other hand, Jesus also used the word *leaven* in an evil sense to illustrate the "fermentation" of moral and political corruption: "Take heed and beware of the leaven [doctrine] of the Pharisees and the Sadducees" (Matt. 16:6, 12).

LEBANON [LEB uh none] (white)

A nation of the Middle East that includes much of what was ancient Phoenicia in Bible times. This territory has been an important trade center linking Europe and Asia for more than 4,000 years.

In ancient times the Phoenicians used the city-states of Byblos, Sidon, and Tyre as the base of a great sea-trading empire in what is now Lebanon. Over the years, these city-states were conquered by Egyptians, Assyrians, Persians, and the Greeks under Alexander the Great. Later still, Lebanon became part of the Roman Empire, and many inhabitants became Christians. But when the Arabs conquered Lebanon in the seventh century A.D., many turned to the Muslim religion.

Early in the sixteenth century, the Arabs were overthrown by the Turks. Then in 1918 the British and French forces broke up the Turkish or Ottoman Empire and placed Lebanon under French rule. In 1943, Lebanon achieved independence. The country has continued to be the scene of strife and turmoil involving Israelis, Syrians, and Palestinian guerrillas. Civil war at times between Muslims and Christians has also added to the strife of this war-torn country.

Lebanon takes its name from the Lebanon Mountains, which run parallel to the coast of the Mediterranean Sea for almost the length of the country. The range consists of snow-capped limestone peaks that rise sharply from the shoreline, leaving just enough space for a coastal road. The 100-mile-long (160-kilometer-long) mountains are made up of two parallel ranges, the Lebanons and the Anti-Lebanons. Between the two is the fertile plain of el-Bekaa, measuring about 30 miles (48 kilometers) by 10 miles (16 kilometers), which was also called the Valley of Lebanon (Josh. 11:17).

The scenic beauty of the country has inspired many symbolic references in the Bible (Ps. 92:12; Song 4:15; 5:15). The rich vegetation of Lebanon became a symbol of fruitfulness and fertility (Ps. 72:16; Ps. 92:12).

Originally, the famed Cedars of Lebanon covered the region. But bands of marauding conquerors from Mesopotamia, Egypt, Israel, and Tyre destroyed the forests by using the wood for palaces, furniture, ships, coffins, and musical instruments. By the sixth century A.D., the beautiful groves were almost gone. Egyptian texts from many different periods refer to trade with the Phoenician cities that supplied them with lumber from Lebanon. Ugaritic and Mesopotamian texts mention that cedars from Lebanon were used in building their important temples and palaces.

In recent years a program of reforestation has been conducted in national parks. The prophets of the Old Testament used the destruction of these magnificient trees by aggressors as a symbol of Israel's destruction (Jer. 22:7; Ezek. 27:5; Zech. 11:2).

The climate of Lebanon ranges from the almost tropical heat and vegetation of the plain of Dan to heavy snow in the plain of el-Bekaa. Mainly it has a Mediterranean climate with cool, wet winters and hot, dry summers. In the spring or summer, a searing desert wind sometimes blows in from Syria.

The Lebanon Mountains formed the northwest boundary of the land of Palestine, the "Promised Land" to the Hebrew people (Deut. 1:7; 11:24). The original inhabitants of Lebanon were independent, warlike tribes of Phoenician stock. Further north were the Hivites and the Gebalites. It is occupied today by various sects of Christians and Muslims.

LEPROSY

A slowly progressing and incurable skin disease. In the Bible the word *leprosy* refers to a variety of symptoms. Modern medicine now recognizes that some of these symptoms belonged to diseases other than leprosy. There are several types of leprosy. Biblical leprosy was most likely a severe type of psoriasis, a form of the disease relatively rare in modern times.

Old Testament law was quite detailed in its instructions regarding recognition and quarantine of leprous persons. The Bible never implies that leprosy can be cured by nonmiraculous means, even though it does contain guidelines for re-admitting cured lepers into normal society. The Old Testament contains no references to treatment or remedy. Jehoram's exclamation "Am I God, to kill and make alive, that this man sends a man to me to heal him of his leprosy?" (2 Kin. 5:7) implies the belief that leprosy could be cured only by a miracle.

Leprosy is a chronic, infectious disease characterized by sores, scabs, and white shining spots beneath the skin. Modern medicine has all but eliminated the disease after learning proper methods of treatment.

The Mosaic Law was very specific about the proper methods of purification where leprosy was concerned. The priest was the central figure in the Old

Testament regulations for the care of patients and for sanitary precautions.

If the symptoms of leprosy showed up in a person, the priest was to decide if this was leprosy or some other disease. Because of the need to control the spread of a disease for which there was no cure, the law required that a leper be isolated from the rest of society (Lev. 13:45–46). While thus excluded, lepers were required to wear mourning clothes, leave their hair in disorder, and cry "Unclean! Unclean!" so everyone could avoid them.

Leprosy in a house showed up in a greenish or reddish color on the walls. When the owner of a house noticed these symptoms, he reported them to the priest. The priest purified the dwelling if the disease could be controlled, or he ordered it destroyed if the signs of leprosy lingered on (Lev. 14:33–53).

In Old Testament times, linen and woolen garments were also said to be leprous when they had patches of mildew, mold, or fungus growth (Lev. 13:47–59). Leprosy in clothes, fabrics, and leather was also indicated by greenish or reddish spots. These spots were reported to the priest, who ordered the affected article to be purified or burned (Lev. 13:47–59).

Any contact with lepers defiled the persons who touched them. Sometimes leprosy victims were miraculously cured. Moses (Ex. 4:7), Miriam, his sister (Num. 12:10), and Naaman (2 Kin. 5:1, 10) are prominent examples of such miracles. King Uzziah was a leper from middle age until death (2 Chr. 26:19–21). The leprosy inflicted upon him (2 Kin. 15:5; 2 Chr. 26:23) for his unwarranted assumption of the priesthood began in his forehead.

In the New Testament, cleansing of lepers is mentioned as a specific portion of Jesus' work of healing. On one occasion Jesus healed ten lepers, but only one returned to thank him (Luke 17:11–15).

LEVI [LEE vigh] (joined)

The third son of Jacob and Leah (Gen. 29:34). His three sons were ancestors of the three main divisions of the Levitical priesthood: the Gershonites, the Kohathites, and the Merarites (Gen. 46:11). Levi participated in the plot against Joseph (Gen. 37:4) and later took his family to Egypt with Jacob. On his deathbed Jacob cursed Simeon and Levi because of their "cruelty" and "wrath," and foretold that their descendants would be divided and scattered (Gen. 49:5–7). Levi died in Egypt at the age of 137 (Ex. 6:16).

LEVIATHAN [lih VIE uh thuhn]

A large sea creature (Job 41) that sometimes represented a cruel enemy defeated by God (Job 3:8). Some interpreters see Leviathan as a symbol of the cruel enemies of God's people, such as Egypt (Ps. 74:13–14) and the Assyro-Babylonian Empire (Is. 27:1). In "that day"—the day of the Lord's judgment—the Lord "will punish Leviathan . . . that twisted serpent; and He will slay the reptile that is in the sea" (Is. 27:1).

L

LEVIRATE MARRIAGE

A form of marriage prescribed by the Law of Moses in which a man was required to marry the widow of a brother who died with no male heir. The term *levirate* means "husband's brother." The purpose of the law was to provide an heir for the dead brother, thereby preserving his name and estate. The law also was designed to provide for the welfare of widows (Deut. 25:5–10).

The story of Ruth and Boaz, recorded in the Book of Ruth, is a good example of the levirate form of marriage. Reference to levirate marriage was also made by the Sadducees, who tested Jesus with a question about the resurrection (Matt. 22:23–33).

LEVITES [LEE vytes]

Descendants of Levi who served as assistants to the priests in the worship system of the nation of Israel. As Levites, Aaron and his sons and their descendants were charged with the responsibility of the priesthood—offering burnt offerings and leading the people in worship and confession. But all the other Levites who were not descended directly from Aaron were to serve as priestly assistants, taking care of the tabernacle and the temple and performing other menial duties (Num. 8:6).

The choice of the Levites as a people who would perform special service for God goes back to the days of the Exodus when the children of Israel were camped at Mount Sinai.

The people grew restless while they waited for Moses to return from talking with the Lord on the mountain. Breaking their covenant with God, they made a golden calf and began to worship it. The Levites were no less guilty than the other tribes. But when Moses returned and called for those on the Lord's side to come forward, the descendants of Levi were the only ones who voluntarily rallied to his side, showing zeal for God's honor (Ex. 32:26–28).

Even before this event, Aaron and his sons had been set apart for the priesthood. But many helpers were needed to attend to the needs of the tabernacle, which was built later at God's command in the wilderness of Sinai. The Levites were chosen for this honor.

The designation of a tribe for special service to God grew out of an unusual concept of the Hebrew people known as the firstfruits. According to this principle, the first part of a crop to be harvested was dedicated to God. This principle even extended to the first chil-dren to be born in a family. Just before the Exodus from Egypt, when God sent the death angel to kill the firstborn of every Egyptian family, He instructed the Israelites to put blood on their doorposts, that their firstborn might be spared the same fate. Thus, the firstborn of every Israelite family became God's special property, dedicated to Him as a memorial.

But because the Levites were the ones who voluntarily returned to their Lord after worshiping the golden image, they were chosen for service to the sanctuary, thus replacing the firstborn as God's representatives of the holiness of His people (Num. 3:12–13, 41).

A Levite's special service to God began with his consecration at about age 25. First he was sprinkled with the "water of purification" (Num. 8:7). Next, the hair was shaved from his entire body, his clothes were washed, and sacrifice was made of two young bulls, and a grain offering of fine flour mixed with oil (Num. 8:7–8). After this purification, he was brought before the door of the tabernacle and set apart for service by the laying on of the hands of the elders (Num. 8:9–15).

Young Levites began as assistants to the priests and chief Levites, then progressed through the higher duties and offices such as doorkeeper, member of the temple orchestra, or administrator. In the days before the temple was built and the people worshiped in the tabernacle, the Levites always transported the tabernacle and its furniture when the camp was moved. Then they erected and cared for the tent in its new location. They guarded it, cleaned it, and cleaned the furniture (Num. 1:50–53; 3:6–9; 4:1–33).

Since the Levites served under the priests, they were forbidden to touch any sacred furniture or the altar until it had been covered by the priests (Num. 4:15).

Temple slaves often assisted the Levites in the heavier, more menial duties such as cutting wood and carrying water (Josh. 9:21; Ezra 8:20).

The Levites also prepared the showbread and did whatever baking was needed in connection with the sacrifices. They helped the priests slaughter and skin the animals for sacrifices, examined the lepers according to the law, and led music during worship. Retiring from active service at age 50, the Levites were free to remain in the temple as overseers or to give assistance to their young successors (Num. 8:25–26).

Unlike the other tribes of Israel, the Levites received no territorial inheritance in the Promised Land of Canaan. Their portion was to be God Himself (Num. 18:20), who commanded that 48 cities be set apart for them, along with enough pasture for their cattle (Num. 35:1–8). They were to receive the tithes due God from the fruits of the fields, the flocks and herds, the fruits of the firstborn, and certain portions of the people's sacrificial offerings (Num. 18:24). Of these tithes, the Levites had to turn over a tithe (a tenth part) to the priests (Num. 18:26).

The Levites were not required to devote all their time to the sanctuary. During most of the year, they lived in their own cities. Then at fixed periods they came to the tabernacle to take their turn at work. For example, during David's reign, the Levites were divided into four classes: (1) assistants to priests in the work of the sanctuary, (2) judges and scribes, (3) gatekeepers, and (4) musicians. Each of these classes, with the possible exception of the second, was subdivided into 24 courses or families who served in rotation (1 Chr. 24–25; Ezra 6:18).

During the long period of Old Testament history, the Levites waxed hot and cold in their devotion to God, just like the rest of the nation of Israel. During the period of the judges, for example, a Levite agreed to hire his services to a man who was known as a worshiper of false gods (Judg. 17:8–13). By New Testament times, both Levites and priests presided over a form of worship that had lost its warmth and human concern (John 1:19).

In His parable of the Good Samaritan, Jesus insisted that true worship consisted of doing good to others. This is demonstrated by the lowly Samaritan traveler, who stopped to help a wounded man. His compassion is a contrast to the hands-off approach of a priest and a Levite, both of whom "passed by on the other side" (Luke 10:31–32).

See also PRIESTS.

LEVITICAL CITIES [luh VIT uh cull]

Forty-eight cities assigned to the tribe of Levi. When the land of Canaan was divided among the tribes of Israel, each tribe, except Levi, received a specific region or territory for its inheritance. The tribe of Levi, however, was made up of priests who were to serve the religious and spiritual needs of the other tribes. Thus, instead of receiving a territory of their own, they were scattered throughout the entire land.

Numbers 35:1–8 sets forth a plan whereby the tribe of Levi was to live in 48 cities scattered throughout Palestine. (This plan was fulfilled according to assignments described in Josh. 20–21 and 1 Chr. 6:54–81.) The 48 cities were apportioned in this way: the Aaronites, one of the families of the Kohathites, received 13 cities (Josh. 21:4, 9–19; 1 Chr. 6:54–60); the rest of the Kohathites received 10 cities (Josh. 21:5, 20–26; 1 Chr. 6:61). The Gershonites received 13 cities (Josh. 21:6, 27–33; 1 Chr. 6:62), and the Merarites received 12 cities (Josh. 21:7, 34–40; 1 Chr. 6:63). These 48 cities and their surrounding common lands—pastures, fields, and vineyards—were to be used exclusively by the Levites.

Six of these Levitical cities were to be cities of refuge (Num. 35:6, 9–34; Josh. 20–21). A person who caused the death of another could flee to one of these cities for protection from anyone who wanted to avenge the life of the person killed. The "refugee" thus was protected until he received a fair trial, or until the high priest of that particular city of refuge died (after which he was free to return home and claim the protection of the authorities).

Three of the cities of refuge were east of the Jordan River: Bezer (in the tribe of Reuben), Ramoth in Gilead (in Gad), and Golan (in Manasseh; Josh. 20:8). The other three cities of refuge were west of the Jordan: Kedesh (in the tribe of Naphtali), Shechem (in Ephraim), and Kirjath Arba, also known as Hebron (in Judah; Josh. 20:7). According to this plan, the Levites were situated throughout the land and could assist the other Israelites in spiritual matters. As a practical matter, since six of the Levitical cities were cities of refuge, citizens living in every part of Palestine had a refuge that was relatively near their homes.

LIBYA [LIB ih uh]

A country of northern Africa west of Egypt (Ezek. 27:10), also called Phut (Ezek. 27:10, KJV) or Put (NIV, NRSV). Some people who lived in "the parts of Libya adjoining Cyrene" (Acts 2:10) were in Jerusalem on the Day of Pentecost. Simon, the man who carried Jesus' cross, was from Cyrene, the New Testament name for Libya (Matt. 27:32).

LIME

A calcium oxide derived from limestone rock or chalk. Limestone was burned in limekilns and reduced to powder. Then it was used mainly for plastering floors and walls. The earliest mention of lime in the Bible is when God instructed Moses to whitewash stones with lime for a memorial of His covenant with Israel (Deut. 27:2, 4; plaster in KJV, REB, NIV, NRSV).

The Hebrew word for lime is also translated by various English versions as plaster, whitewash, or ash (Deut. 27:2, 4; Is. 27:9; 33:12; Dan 5:5; Amos 2:1). Lime was used by the Israelites for mortar and as plaster for floors (Dan. 5:5). The walls of cisterns were also waterproofed with plaster. Lime may have been used in dyeing to give colors a permanent set in the fabric. Archaeologists have found stone jars containing lime and potash next to dyeing vats.

LINEN

A cloth woven from fibers of the flax or hemp plant. The word *linen* is also used to describe clothes or garments made from this cloth. The Hebrew word meaning "whiteness" also is used to represent linen, because bleached linen was so white.

In Bible times, the finest linen allowed free circulation of air, keeping the wearer cool in hot weather. Because it was so expensive, it was owned by the wealthy (Luke 16:19; Ezek. 16:10), the powerful (2 Sam. 6:14), and the priests. Fine linen was used in the clothing and headdress of the priests. Ordinary linen was used for less expensive clothing and items such as sheets, curtains, and sails of ships. Linen was the material from which the tunic, or undergarment, was often made.

Fine linen garments were especially worn by kings and queens and members of their royal courts. Those who ministered in the tabernacle and temple also wore fine linen. These included the boy Samuel (1 Sam. 2:18), the temple singers (2 Chr. 5:12), and the priests (Ex. 28:39–42). They were surrounded in their places of worship by the veil and curtains, made of the finest linen (Ex. 26:1–37). At the end of time, the heavenly members of God's court will also wear fine white linen (Ezek. 9:2; Rev. 19:14), symbolizing that God provides them with the costliest and purest of garments.

After His death, the body of Jesus was wrapped in white linen (John 19:40; Luke 23:53). As a part of their burial customs, the Jews tore large linen sheets into strips and wrapped perfume inside them close to the body. Even centuries earlier, the Egyptians had wrapped their dead in the same way. Many Egyptian mummies now in museums are still wrapped in this fashion, although the linen has faded into a brownish or tan color.

The weaving of linen fabric began with the lowly flax plant. These plants were usually pulled out by the roots, dried in the sun, then pounded until the fibers separated. Then the fibers were washed and bleached. This produced a fine fiber that at times was nearly invisible. Israel had craftsmen skilled in weaving fine linen, although the craft probably was first learned in Egypt (Ex. 35:35; 38:23). Guilds of linen weavers also existed in Bible times (1 Chr. 4:21). Palestinian weavers were so skilled that their fine linen was often preferred to that produced in Egypt.

LINTEL

A horizontal beam that supports the wall above the framework of a door or window. At the time of the first Passover, the Lord told Moses to sprinkle the blood of a slain lamb on the doorposts and the lintels of the houses of the Israelites (Ex. 12:7). The blood of the lamb would be a sign of God's grace; and the Israelites would be spared as death spread throughout the land of Egypt.

LION

The lion was the most awesome and dangerous wild beast in Canaan. His tawny hide blended into the golden fields and sandy wastes. Lions hid in forests and sometimes pounced from the thickets near the Jordan River (Jer. 49:19). The Bible contains many references to lions. Daniel miraculously survived a night in a lions' den (Dan. 6). Samson and David killed lions single-handedly (Judg. 14:5–6; 1 Sam. 17:34–37). Kings hunted lions for sport. According to Ezekiel 19:1–9, lions were also captured with pits and nets.

The lion's majestic appearance and fearsome roar prompted many comparisons. The prophet Joel declared, "The Lord also will roar from Zion" (Joel 3:16). The apostle Peter wrote: "Be sober, be vigilant; because your adversary the devil walks about like a roaring lion" (1 Pet. 5:8). The prophet Hosea foretold that God would be like a protective lion for the nation of Israel (Hos. 5:14; panther in REB).

A lion looks and sounds so imposing that he symbolizes royalty and courage. The highest compliment that biblical writers could give was to indicate that a person had the face or heart of a lion. *Ari* is the most common term for lion. In Isaiah 29:1 Jerusalem is called "Ariel," perhaps implying that the capital of Israel is "the strong [lion-like] city of God." The Israelite tribes of Judah, Dan, and Gad—and also the nation of Babylon—adopted the lion as their symbol. Jesus is called "the Lion of the tribe of Judah" (Rev. 5:5). Isaiah the prophet foretold that at the end of time, the Prince of Peace would tame even the fierce heart of the lion (Is. 9:6–7; 11:1–9).

LOD [lahd]

A city about 11 miles (18 kilometers) southeast of Joppa (1 Chr. 8:12) in the fertile Plain of Sharon. Its strategic location at the intersection of two great trade routes made Lod a rich prize of war among the nations of the ancient world.

L

The prophet Nehemiah placed Lod in the "valley of craftsmen" (Neh. 11:35), referring to the various industries that produced the necessities for travel. The Greek name for the city in New Testament times was Lydda. The apostle Peter healed a paralyzed man in Lydda (Acts 9:32–35, 38).

LOIS [LOE iss]

The mother of Eunice and the grandmother of Timothy. A devout Jewess, Lois instructed both her daughter and her grandson in the Old Testament. Paul gave Lois and her daughter Eunice credit for Timothy's spiritual instruction (2 Tim. 3:15).

LORD'S DAY

The first day of the week, or Sunday; the day especially associated with the Lord Jesus Christ. A special honor was reserved for Sunday, the first day of the week. This was the day on which Jesus was raised from the dead; every Lord's Day, therefore, is a weekly memorial of Christ's resurrection. Clearly the early church assembled for worship and religious instruction on Sunday, the Lord's Day (1 Cor. 16:2).

The Lord's Day is not to be confused with the Sabbath, the Jewish day of rest. The Jewish Sabbath corresponds with our Saturday, the seventh or last day of the week. This special day to the Jews commemorated the day on which God rested after the creation of the world. The Lord's Day is our Sunday, the first day of the week; it celebrates the resurrection of Jesus from the dead.

Under the new dispensation of grace, Christians are not to be trapped by the old legalism of observing days and seasons. Some members of the early church "esteemed every day alike"; they made no distinction between days, including Jewish festivals and Sabbaths and possibly also Sunday. The apostle Paul said they were not to be judged if they were acting in good conscience out of the fear of God.

Some Jewish Christians continued to observe the Sabbath and Jewish festivals. Neither should they be judged for "esteeming one day above another," Paul declared, for their behavior was guided by conscience in the fear of God. Paul believed such observance was a matter of Christian liberty, so long as the convert did not regard the observance as necessary for salvation (Rom. 14:5–6; Gal. 4:10; Col. 2:16–17).

Paul's principle of Christian liberty about holy places and holy days comes from the Lord Jesus Christ Himself. Jesus described Himself as one who is greater than the temple (Matt. 12:6) and said, "The Son of Man is Lord even of the Sabbath" (Matt. 12:8; Luke 6:5). When accused by the Pharisees of breaking the Sabbath, Jesus replied, "The Sabbath was made for man, and not man for the Sabbath. Therefore the Son of Man is also Lord of the Sabbath" (Mark 2:27–28).

The phrase "the Lord's Day" occurs only once in the New Testament, in Revelation 1:10, where John declared, "I was in the Spirit on the Lord's Day." In Asia Minor, where the churches to which John wrote were situated, the pagans celebrated the first day of each month as the emperor's day. Some scholars also believe that a day of the week was also called by this name.

When the early Christians called the first day of the week the Lord's Day, this was a direct challenge to the emperor worship to which John refers so often in the Book of Revelation. Such a bold and fearless testimony by the early Christians proclaimed that the Lord's Day belonged to the Lord Jesus Christ and not to the emperor Caesar.

LONGSUFFERING

God's patient endurance of the wickedness of the sinful (Ex. 34:6). The purpose of God's longsuffering is to lead people to repentance (Rom. 2:4; 2 Pet. 3:9, 15). But since God is a God of justice, He cannot endure sin forever. He must ultimately punish all who do not repent and trust in Him (2 Thess. 1:5–10).

Believers are to imitate their heavenly Father in longsuffering (1 Cor. 13:4–5), because He has been patient with us (Eph. 4:31–32) and because vengeance belongs to God alone (Rom. 12:19).

LORD'S PRAYER

The model prayer that Jesus taught His disciples (Matt. 6:5–15; Luke 11:1–4). In the Gospel of Matthew, the Lord's Prayer occurs in the Sermon on the Mount. He emphasized that prayer should not be an attempt to get God's attention by repeating words. Instead, it should be a quiet, confident expression of needs to our heavenly Father.

The first part of the prayer concerns the glory of God. We call him "Father," a term that only His children by faith in Christ may rightly use. We request that God's name be "hallowed," or honored as holy. It is the mission of God's people to spread the reputation of His name throughout the world (Ezek. 36:22–23).

Next, we request that God's kingdom come. We acknowledge God as ruler of the world and obey His will. Requests relating to our own needs include food for each day, forgiveness, and help in temptation.

The conclusion of the Lord's Prayer attributes all power and glory to God forever, through all eternity. This part of the prayer should be evident in our lives each day as we seek to do God's will on earth as His disciples.

LORD'S SUPPER

The ritualistic practice, usually during a worship service, in which Christians partake of bread and wine (or grape juice) with the purpose of remembering Christ, receiving strength from Him, and rededicating themselves to His cause. It is one of two sacraments or ordinances instituted by Christ to be observed by His church until He returns.

The term "Lord's Supper" is used only in 1 Corinthians 11:20. The practice is also known as Communion (from 1 Cor. 10:16), the Lord's Table (from 1 Cor. 10:21), and the Eucharist (from the Greek word for "giving thanks"; Luke 22:17, 19; 1 Cor. 11:24). The expression "breaking of bread" (Acts 2:42, 46; 20:7, 11) probably refers to receiving the Lord's Supper with a common meal known as the love feast (2 Pet. 2:13; Jude 12).

The institution of the Lord's Supper (Matt. 26:17–30; Mark 14:12–26; Luke 22:1–23; 1 Cor. 11:23–25) took place on the night before Jesus died, at a meal commonly known as the Last Supper. Although there is considerable debate over the issue, the Last Supper probably was the Jewish Passover meal, first instituted by God in the days of Moses (Ex. 12:1–14; Num. 9:1–5).

In 1 Corinthians 10:16, the apostle Paul rebuked the Corinthians for their involvement with idolatry. He referred to the cup as "the communion of the blood of Christ" and the bread as "the communion of the body of Christ." The Greek word for "communion" has the meaning of "fellowship, participating, and sharing." From the context it appears that Paul is saying that when Christians partake of the cup and the bread, they are participating in the benefits of Christ's death (referred to as His blood) and resurrection life (His glorified body). The most important of these benefits are the assurance of sins forgiven (through

L

Christ's blood) and the assurance of Christ's presence and power (through His body).

The "one body" (the universal church) in 1 Corinthians 10:17 connects with the "body of Christ" in verse 16 in the sense that the entire church of Christ is organically related to the living, glorified human body of Christ now in heaven. The "one [loaf of] bread" (v. 17), representing Jesus the "bread of life" (John 6:35), is eaten by all believers at the Supper, symbolizing their unity and common participation in the one body of Christ. The great discourse of Jesus on the bread of life (John 6:25–68), while not intended to be a direct theological explanation of the Lord's Supper, helps to explain how receiving the Eucharist can be one way in which Christians "feed" on the Lord (John 6:55–57). Other important ways are by prayer and the hearing of God's Word through the Scriptures.

In 1 Corinthians 11:17–34 Paul rebuked the Corinthians for their pride and greed during the meal that accompanied the Eucharist (vv. 17–22). Then (vv. 23–25) he described the institution of the Lord's Supper and emphasized the need for Christians to partake in a worthy manner. Many of them who had not been doing so were weak and sick, and many had even died as a result of God's judgment (vv. 27–34).

Why does Paul use such strong language when speaking of the abuse of the Lord's Supper? The Corinthians were not properly discerning or recognizing the Lord's body. The wealthy Corinthians who shamed their poorer Christian brothers and sisters by their selfish eating practices (vv. 21–22) were not discerning the true nature of the church as Christ's body in which all distinctions of social class, race, etc. were blotted out (Gal. 3:28).

On the other hand, Christians who received the bread and the cup after be-

having disgracefully were failing to discern that Christ would not automatically bless and empower those who received the sacrament in this manner. Such persons were guilty of sin against the body and blood of Jesus (v. 27).

The Lord's Supper is a time of remembrance and Eucharist. Jesus said, "Do this in remembrance of Me" (Luke 22:19; 1 Cor. 11:24–25). This is not to be so much our dwelling on the agonies of the crucifixion as it is to be our remembering the marvelous life and ministry of our Savior. The Eucharist is to be an occasion for expressing our deepest praise and appreciation for all Jesus Christ has done for us.

Just as one step in the Jewish Passover meal was to proclaim the Hebrews' deliverance from Egyptian bondage (Ex. 12:26–27), so in the Supper Christians proclaim their deliverance from sin and misery through the death of "Christ, our Passover" (1 Cor. 5:7; 11:26).

The Supper is also a time of refreshing and communion. As we participate in the benefits of Jesus' death and resurrection life (Rom. 5:10; 1 Cor. 10:16), we are actually being nourished and empowered from the risen Christ through the Spirit. Recommitment is another dimension of the Lord's Supper. We are to examine (literally "prove" or "test") ourselves and partake in a worthy manner (1 Cor. 11:28–29). In so doing we renew our dedication to Christ and His people, in hopeful anticipation "till He comes" (1 Cor. 11:26). After Christ's return we shall partake with Him—in His physical presence—in the kingdom (Matt. 26:29).

LOT [laht]

Abraham's nephew. Lot accompanied Abraham from Mesopotamia to Canaan and to and from Egypt (Gen. 11:27–31; 12:4–5; 13:1). Both Lot and Abraham had large herds of cattle, and their herdsmen quarreled over their pasturelands. At

Abraham's suggestion, the two decided to separate.

Abraham gave Lot his choice of land; and Lot chose the more fertile, well-watered site—the Jordan River valley—as opposed to the rocky hill country. Failing to take into account the character of the inhabitants, Lot "pitched his tent toward Sodom" (Gen. 13:12, KJV).

When the Elamite king Chedorlaomer invaded Canaan with his allies, Lot was taken captive. Abraham attacked Chedorlaomer's forces by night and rescued his nephew (Gen. 13:1–14:16).

When two angels were sent to warn Lot that God intended to destroy Sodom, Lot could not control the Sodomites, who wished to abuse the two visitors carnally. The angels struck the Sodomites blind to save Lot (Gen. 19:1–11), and Lot

and his family fled the doomed city. Lot's wife, however, did not follow the angels' orders and looked back at Sodom. Because of her disobedience she was turned into a "pillar of salt" (Gen. 19:26). Our Lord Jesus warned, "Remember Lot's wife" (Luke 17:32), as a reminder of the disastrous results of disobedience.

Following his escape from Sodom, Lot lived in a cave near Zoar (Gen. 19:30–38). His two daughters served their father wine and enticed him into incest. They did this because "there is no man on the earth to come in to us as is the custom of all the earth" (Gen. 19:31). Out of that union came two sons, Moab and Ben-Ammi, the ancestors of the Moabites and the Ammonites, respectively.

Lot's character is revealed by the major decisions he made throughout his

LOTS, CASTING OF   L

WELL, LET'S SEE WHICH OF US WILL WASH THE CAMEL...

life. He chose to pitch his tent with the worldly Sodomites, seeking riches and a life of ease rather than a path of obedience to God. He prospered for a while, but this decision eventually led to his humiliation and the tragic loss of his wife and other members of his family.

LOTS, CASTING OF

A way of making decisions in Bible times, similar to drawing straws or casting a pair of dice to determine what course or direction to follow. The word *lots* occurs 70 times in the Old Testament and seven in the New Testament. Most of the occurrences were in the early period when little of the Bible was available and when God approved of this means for determining His will (Prov. 16:33).

For example, the high priest separated the scapegoat from the goat he sacrificed by casting the lot (Lev. 16:8–10). The practice occurs most often in connection with the division of the land under Joshua (Josh. 14–21), a procedure that God directed several times in the Book of Numbers (Num. 26:55; 33:54; 34:13; 36:2).

Various offices and functions in the temple were also determined by lot (1 Chr. 24:5, 31; 25:8–9; 26:13–14). The sailors on Jonah's ship (Jon. 1:7) also cast lots to determine who had brought God's wrath upon their ship. Only once in the New Testament did the casting of lots happen with God's approval. This occurred in the selection of Matthias to fill the spot vacated by Judas among the apostles (Acts 1:26).

After the Day of Pentecost (Acts 2), the casting of lots gradually fell into disfavor because more direct access became available to God's people in and through the ministry of the Holy Spirit in their lives.

In spite of the many references to casting lots in the Old Testament, nothing is known about the actual lots themselves.

They could have been sticks of various lengths, flat stones like coins, or some kind of dice.

LOVE

The high esteem that God has for His human children and the high regard which they, in turn, should have for Him and other people.

Love is not only one of God's attributes; it is also an essential part of His nature (Deut. 7:7–8). "God is love," the Bible declares (1 John 4:8, 16)—the personification of perfect love. Such love surpasses our powers of understanding (Eph. 3:19). Love like this is everlasting (Jer. 31:3), free (Hos. 14:4), sacrificial (John 3:16), and enduring to the end (John 13:1).

The warm word *agape* is the characteristic term of Christianity. This word for love is used several different ways in the Bible.

1. *Agape* love indicates the nature of the love of God toward His beloved Son (John 17:26), toward the human race generally (John 3:16; Rom. 5:8), and toward those who believe on the Lord Jesus Christ (John 14:21).

2. *Agape* love conveys God's will to His children about their attitude toward one another. Love for one another was a proof to the world of true discipleship (John 13:34–35).

3. *Agape* love also expresses the essential nature of God (1 John 4:8). Love can be known only from the actions it prompts, as seen in God's love in the gift of His Son (1 John 4:9–10). Love found its perfect expression in the Lord Jesus. Christian love is the fruit of the Spirit of Jesus in the believer (Gal. 5:22).

Love is like oil to the wheels of obedience. It enables us to run the way of God's commandments (Ps. 119:32). Without such love, we are as nothing (1 Cor.

13:3). Such Spirit-inspired love never fails (1 Cor. 13:8) but always flourishes.

LOVE FEAST

A meal shared by the early Christians when they met together for fellowship and the Lord's Supper. The purpose of the love feast was to remember Christ, to encourage His disciples, and to share God's provisions with the needy.

In the time of Christ, communal meals to express friendship and observe religious feasts were practiced in both Greek and Jewish cultures. The yearly Passover meal was the most important such event among the Jews. Jesus chose this occasion to institute the Lord's Supper, or Eucharist (Matt. 26:17–30). Thus it was natural for the early Christians, whenever they celebrated the Lord's Supper, to do it in connection with a common meal. The "breaking of bread," which the very first disciples did daily, most likely refers to this dual experience of common meal and Eucharist (Acts 2:42, 46).

Because of such abuses as those described in the New Testament (1 Cor. 11:17–34; 2 Pet. 2:13), and probably for reasons of convenience, the meal and the Eucharist became separated in some regions by the second century. The meal—known as the love feast, the agape, and even the Lord's Supper—continued for several centuries. However, at times it became merely a charity supper for the poor and at other times a lavish banquet for the wealthy. After much controversy in the church, it was finally abolished at the end of the seventh century. A few Christian groups, however, still observe the agape.

LUKE

A "fellow laborer" of the apostle Paul (Philem. 24) and the author of the Gospel of Luke and the Acts of the Apostles. By profession he was a physician (Col. 4:14). During one of Paul's imprisonments, probably in Rome, Luke's faithfulness was recorded by Paul when he declared, "Only Luke is with me" (2 Tim. 4:11). These three references are our only direct knowledge of Luke in the New Testament.

A bit more of Luke's life and personality can be pieced together with the aid of his writings (Luke and Acts) and some outside sources. Tradition records that he came from Antioch in Syria. This is possible, because Antioch played a significant role in the early Gentile mission that Luke described in Acts (Acts 11; 13; 14; 15; 18). Luke was a Gentile (Col. 4:10–17) and the only non-Jewish author of a New Testament book. A comparison of 2 Corinthians 8:18 and 12:18 has led some to suppose that Luke and Titus were brothers, but this is a guess.

Luke accompanied Paul on parts of his second, third, and final missionary journeys. At three places in Acts, the narrative changes to the first person ("we"). This probably indicates that Luke was personally present during those episodes. On the second journey (A.D. 49–53), Luke accompanied Paul on the short voyage from Troas to Philippi (Acts 16:10–17). On the third journey (A.D. 54–58), Luke was present on the voyage from Philippi to Jerusalem (Acts 20:5–21:18). Whether Luke had spent the intervening time in Philippi is uncertain, but his connection with Philippi has led some to favor it (rather than Antioch) as Luke's home.

Once in Palestine, Luke probably remained close by Paul during his two-year imprisonment in Caesarea. During this time, Luke probably drew together material, both oral and written, which he later used in the composition of his gospel (Luke 1:1–4). A third "we" passage describes in masterful suspense the shipwreck during Paul's voyage to Rome for his trial before Caesar. Each of the "we" passages involves Luke on a voyage, and the description of the journey from Jerusalem to Rome is full of observations and knowledge of nautical matters (Acts 27).

Luke apparently was a humble man, with no desire to sound his own horn. More than one-fourth of the New Testament comes from his pen, but not once does he mention himself by name. He had a greater command of the Greek language and was probably more broad-minded and urbane than any New Testament writer. He was a careful historian, both by his own admission (Luke 1:1–4) and by the judgment of later history.

Luke's gospel reveals his concern for the poor, sick, and outcast, thus offering a clue to why Paul called him "the beloved physician" (Col. 4:14). He was faithful not only to Paul, but to the greater cause he served—the publication of "good tidings of great joy" (Luke 2:10).

LYCAONIA [lik ih OE nih uh]

A Roman province in south central Asia Minor visited by the apostle Paul (Acts 14:6). In apostolic times, part of it (the part visited by Paul) was a region of the Roman province of Galatia. Lycaonia was bordered on the south by Cilicia, on the west by Phrygia and Pisidia, on the north by Galatia, and on the east by Cappadocia. Because of its remoteness, Lycaonia enjoyed political independence during much of its history. But it fell under Greek control and influence in the period following the conquests of Alexander the Great.

The apostle Paul visited the three main cities of Lycaonia—Iconium, Lystra, and Derbe—on his three journeys to Asia Minor (Acts 13:51–14:6; 2 Tim. 3:11). Timothy was from Lycaonia; apparently he was a native of Lystra (Acts 16:1).

LYCIA [LISH ih uh]

A mountainous country in southwest Asia Minor (modern Turkey). Shut in by rugged mountain ranges, Lycia made contact with the outside world mainly through its seaport cities. Lycia was united by a strong federation of cities. It enjoyed a measure of freedom and independence even under foreign rulers such as Persia, Greece, Egypt, and Rome. The apostle Paul stopped at two of Lycia's coastal cities, Patara (Acts 21:1) and Myra (Acts 27:5), during his ministry.

LYDIA [LID ih uh]

A prosperous businesswoman from the city of Thyatira who became a convert to Christianity after hearing the apostle Paul speak (Acts 16:12–15, 40). Thyatira was noted for its "purple"—its beautifully dyed cloth. Lydia, who lived in Philippi, sold dyes or dyed goods from as far away as Thyatira. Already a worshiper of God, the usual designation for a proselyte to Judaism, Lydia believed the gospel when Paul preached in Philippi. She became the first convert to Christianity in Macedonia and, in fact, in all of Europe.

Lydia is a good example for Christians in the business world today. A devout Christian and a conscientious businesswoman, she used her work to help further God's purpose.

LYE

An alkaline material used as a cleansing agent. Both Egypt and Palestine produced some form of soap for washing the body as well as clothes. This may have been natron (niter), a sodium carbonate (soda) available in its natural state in southern Egypt. This substance could have been imported into Palestine. The prophet Jeremiah's first sermon declared that the people of Judah were so full of iniquity that it could not be removed: "'For though you wash yourself with lye, and use much soap, yet your iniquity is marked before Me,' says the Lord God" (Jer. 2:22; nitre in KJV; soda in NIV).

LYSIAS, CLAUDIUS [LIS ih uhs, KLAW dih uhs]

The commander of the Roman garrison at Jerusalem who rescued the apostle Paul from an angry mob (Acts 21:31–38). Claudius Lysias sent Paul to Caesarea by night under military escort to the Roman governor, Felix (Acts 22:24–23:35). His letter to Felix (Acts 23:25–30) is an example of Roman military correspondence. The Greek noun for "commander" is *chiliarchos*, which means "ruler of a thousand." A tribune was a Roman military officer commanding a cohort, a unit of from 600 to 1,000 men.

LYSTRA [LISS truh]

A city of Lycaonia, in central Anatolia in modern Turkey, where Paul preached after being driven from Iconium. Lystra was built on a small hill about 150 feet (46 meters) above the plain that stretched northeastward to Iconium and southeastward to Derbe.

Apparently, Lystra was the home of Timothy (Acts 16:1–2). Paul wrote to Timothy, mentioning his persecutions and afflictions at Antioch (of Pisidia), Iconium, and Lystra (2 Tim. 3:11). At Lystra, when Paul healed a crippled man, the people thought they were gods, calling Barnabas Zeus and Paul Hermes (Mercury). But Jews from Antioch and Iconium later came to the city, persuading the multitudes to stone the apostle Paul (Acts 14:19).

M

MACCABEES [MACK uh bees]

The predecessors of the Hasmonean family of Jewish leaders and rulers, made up of the sons of Mattathias and their descendants, which reigned in Judea from 167 to 37 B.C. This term is especially applied to Judas Maccabeus and his brothers, who defeated the Syrians under Antiochus IV Epiphanes (the Seleucid ruler of Syria, 175–164 B.C.) in 164 B.C. and who rededicated the temple in Jerusalem.

In the spirit of an oriental tyrant, Antiochus IV Epiphanes fanatically determined to impose Hellenism—the adoption of ancient Greek language, philosophy, customs, art—on all the subjects of his empire. He prohibited the observance of the Sabbath and the traditional Jewish festivals and feast days. He also outlawed the reading of the law of Moses and gave orders that all copies should be burned. Temple sacrifices were forbidden, circumcision was outlawed, and other characteristic Jewish practices were declared illegal.

Antiochus' ultimate affront to the Jews occurred on the twenty-fifth day of the month of Kislev, in 167 B.C. He rededicated the temple to the pagan Greek god Zeus, set up a statue of Zeus in the Holy of Holies, and sacrificed pigs upon the altar. These outrages brought on the revolt of the Maccabees.

The home of Mattathias, a Jewish priest, quickly became the center of resistance against Antiochus. With Mattathias were his five sons: "John called Gaddis, Simon called Thassis, Judas called Maccabaeus, Eleazar called Avaran, and Jonathan called Apphus" (1 Macc. 2:3–5, NEB).

The title Maccabeus was first given to Judas, the third son of Mattathias, but it was soon transferred to the entire family. Some scholars believe the term is derived from a Hebrew or Aramaic word meaning "hammer," probably in allusion to the crushing blows inflicted by Judas and his successors upon their enemies.

In December 164 B.C. Judas Maccabeus and his zealous force of Jewish rebels recaptured most of Jerusalem. Then he forced the loyal priests, those who had not collaborated with Antiochus, to cleanse the Holy Place and erect a new altar. On the 25th of Kislev, 164 B.C., precisely three years after Antiochus had defiled it, Judas rededicated the temple.

Leadership of the Maccabees eventually passed from Judas to Jonathan and then to Simon. After the death of Simon, the last remaining son of Mattathias, the succession of the Maccabees was maintained by Simon's son John, known later as John Hyrcanus or Hyrcanus I.

MACEDONIA [mass uh DOH neh uh]

A mountainous country north of Greece (Achaia) in the Balkan Peninsula. This area was visited twice, and perhaps three times, by the apostle Paul. The first mention of Macedonia in the Bible is in Acts 16: the description of Paul's "Macedonian call." In a vision, a man appeared to Paul "and pleaded with him, saying, 'Come over to Macedonia and help us'" (Acts 16:9). Paul immediately set sail at Troas for Neapolis (Acts 16:11), a seaport of Philippi in the extreme eastern part of Macedonia.

Luke gives a detailed account of Paul's journey through Macedonia (Acts 16:11–17:14). At Neapolis Paul picked up the Egnatian Way—the major road of Macedonia—and came to Philippi, "the foremost city of that part of Macedonia, a colony" (Acts 16:12). At Philippi Paul made his first convert in Europe, "a cer-

tain woman named Lydia . . . [who] was a seller of purple" (Acts 16:14).

After Lydia's baptism and the healing of "a certain slave girl possessed with a spirit of divination" (Acts 16:16), and his imprisonment (Acts 16:23–24), Paul set out again on the Egnatian Way through Amphipolis and Apollonia to Thessalonica (Acts 17:1)—the capital where the proconsul (governor) resided.

The final city Paul visited before leaving Macedonia for Athens was Berea (Acts 17:10–14), where he left Silas and Timothy for a short time to assist in the work (Acts 17:15; 18:5).

At the close of this, his second missionary journey, Paul went on to Athens and Corinth and then back to Antioch of Syria (Acts 17:15–18:23). He revisited Macedonia at least once again (Acts 20:1–6), and perhaps twice (2 Cor. 2:13; 7:5; Phil. 2:24; 1 Tim. 1:3).

Several of Paul's travel companions and fellow workers were Macedonians: Gaius (Acts 19:29), Aristarchus (Acts 19:29; 27:2), Secundus (Acts 20:4), and Sopater (Acts 20:4). The Macedonian Christians' support of the needs of Paul and others is mentioned several times in Paul's letters (Rom. 15:26; 2 Cor. 8:1–5; Phil. 4:15–18).

MACHPELAH [mahk PEE luh]

A field, a cave, and the surrounding land purchased by Abraham as a burial place for his wife Sarah. The cave was to the east of Mamre, or Hebron (Gen. 23:19). At an earlier time, Abraham pitched his tent "and went and dwelt by the terebinth trees of Mamre, which are in Hebron, and built an altar there to the Lord," (Gen. 13:18). He also received three visitors who spoke of a child of promise to be born to Sarah (Gen. 18:1–15).

Abraham purchased the field of Machpelah from Ephron the Hittite. Abraham,

Sarah, Isaac, Rebekah, Jacob, and Leah were all buried here (Gen. 49:31; 50:13).

Today the modern city of el-Khalil (Hebron) is built up around the site of Machpelah. The site of the cave was once protected by a Christian church but is now marked by a Moslem mosque. The Moslems held this site so sacred that for centuries Christians were forbidden to enter the ancient shrine. It is open to the public today.

MAGDALA [MAG duh luh] *(tower)*

A place on the Sea of Galilee, perhaps on the west shore, about 3 miles (5 kilometers) northwest of Tiberias. Jesus and His disciples withdrew to this place after the feeding of the 4,000 (Matt. 15:39; Magadan, NIV, NASB, REB, NRSV). The parallel passage (Mark 8:10) has Dalmanutha. Magdala was either the birthplace or the home of Mary Magdalene.

MAGIC, SORCERY, AND DIVINATION

Occult practices, such as fortune-telling and witchcraft, which were common among the pagan nations of the ancient world. But such attempts to control evil spirits were expressly forbidden to the Hebrew people. Deuteronomy 18:10–11 mentions several specific occult practices that were forbidden by the Law of Moses.

Passing a Son or Daughter Through the Fire. This phrase refers to the practice of child sacrifice. This seems incredible to us today, but the very fact that it was outlawed by God indicates it must have been done in Bible times. Second Kings 16:3 records that King Ahaz sacrificed his son in this way: "Indeed he made his son pass through the fire." No doubt he thought that such a sacrifice would appease some pagan god. His grandson, King Manasseh, sacrificed his sons two generations later (2 Kin. 21:6; 2 Chr. 33:6). Second Kings 23:10 reveals that it was mainly the pagan god Molech who re-

quired this awful sacrifice. But other false gods apparently also demanded it (2 Kin. 17:31; Jer. 19:5).

Witchcraft. The practice of witchcraft, or divination, was a means for extracting information or guidance from a pagan god. The word describes the activity of Balaam the soothsayer, or professional prophet, who was hired to curse Israel (Num. 22:7; 23:23; Josh. 13:22). It also describes the woman at En Dor who brought up the spirit of Samuel. All the major prophets condemned divination (Is. 44:25; Jer. 27:9; 29:8; Ezek. 13:9).

The only places where information is given on the actual means people used in divination is in Genesis 44:5 and Ezekiel 21:21–23. In the case of Joseph's divining cup, the diviner apparently interpreted the shape of a puddle of oil floating on the water in the cup (Gen. 44:5). Ezekiel 21 describes the king of Babylon as he tried to decide which way to approach Jerusalem. It portrays him as throwing down a handful of arrows, hoping that a certain one will point to a route that he believes is the will of his god. It also records that "he consults the images, he looks at the liver" (Ezek. 21:21). Reading and interpreting the livers of sacrificial animals was another form of determining the will of the gods.

Soothsaying. Soothsaying is a relatively rare word in the Bible that describes some form of divination, the practitioner of which is also described by the KJV as "observer of times" (Deut. 18:10). Because it sounds like a Hebrew word for "cloud," some scholars believe it refers to cloud reading. This may have been similar to tea-leaf reading or astrology, which is a reading of the stars. God forbids the practice (Deut. 18:10, 14; Lev. 19:26). Wicked King Manasseh was also guilty of this sin (2 Kin. 21:6; 2 Chr. 33:6). The prophets of the Old Testament also condemned this occult practice (Is. 2:6; 57:3; Jer. 27:9; Mic. 5:12).

M

Conjuring Spells. This phrase, also translated as "charm," appears in Deuteronomy 18:11, once in the Psalms "Which will not heed the voice of charmers," (58:5), and twice in Isaiah (47:9, 12). Sometimes it is rendered as "enchantments." A different Hebrew word lies behind this translation in Isaiah 19:3. Because it is related to a word for "bind," it may mean "casting a spell" ("spellbinding").

Consulting Mediums. This phrase may refer to the same thing as practicing wizardry. The word describes the witch at En Dor whom Saul engaged to conduct a seance and bring up the spirit of Samuel (1 Sam. 28:3, 9; familiar spirits in KJV). The woman succeeded either by the power of God or the power of the devil. It was forbidden by the law of God, practiced by bad kings, and condemned by the prophets. In two places the prophet Isaiah hinted that consulting mediums may be a kind of ventriloquism (8:19; 29:4).

Calling Up the Dead. Necromancy is another word used for this practice. The phrase occurs only in Deuteronomy 18:11 "or one who conjures spells, or a medium, or a spiritist, or one who calls up the dead," although this is exactly what an Old Testament witch did. The Bible gives us no indication that we can expect to talk with people who have died.

MAGNIFICAT OF MARY [mag NIFF ih caht] *(it magnifies)*

Mary's song of praise when she was greeted by her cousin Elizabeth before the birth of Christ (Luke 1:46–55). In Latin the song begins with the word *magnificat.* Mary's song is modeled on the Song of Hannah (1 Sam. 2:1–10). Like Mary, Hannah was a godly woman who miraculously bore a son through the intervention of God. Hannah's son, Samuel, anointed David as king in Israel (1 Sam. 16); Mary's Son would be the final and permanent Davidic King (Luke 1:32–33).

The Magnificat has two main sections. Verses 46–49 are very personal. They celebrate God's graciousness in choosing this humble maiden to be the mother of the Messiah. Verses 50–55 connect God's activity in the coming of Jesus with God's age-long pattern of putting down the proud, the mighty, and the rich, and of raising up the lowly and the hungry.

MAGOG [MAY gog] *(land of Gog)*

The descendants of Magog (Ezek. 38:2), possibly a people who lived in northern Asia and Europe. The Jewish historian Josephus identified these people as the Scythians, known for their destructive warfare. Magog may be a comprehensive term meaning "northern barbarians." The people of Magog are described as skilled horsemen (Ezek. 38:15) and experts in the use of the bow and arrow (Ezek. 39:3, 9). The Book of Revelation uses Ezekiel's prophetic imagery to portray the final, apocalyptic encounter between good and evil at the end of this age. "Gog and Magog" (Rev. 20:8–9) symbolize the anti-Christian forces of the world.

MAHANAIM [may huh NAY im] *(two armies)*

An ancient town in Gilead, east of the Jordan River in the vicinity of the river Jabbok. Located on the border between the tribes of Manasseh and Gad (Josh. 13:26, 30), Mahanaim was later assigned to the Merarite Levites (Josh. 21:38).

On his way home after an absence of 20 years, Jacob was met by angels of God at this site "When Jacob saw them, he said, 'This is God's camp.'" He named the place Mahanaim, meaning "two armies." This was a significant moment for Jacob, who was about to meet his estranged brother Esau. The knowledge that he was being accompanied by an angelic band brought him the confidence and assurance he needed.

Following the killing of King Saul by the Philistines, Saul's son Ishbosheth reigned for two years at Mahanaim (2 Sam. 2:8, 12, 29). Later, Mahanaim became the headquarters for David during the rebellion of his son, Absalom (2 Sam. 17:24). Solomon also made Mahanaim the capital of one of his 12 districts (1 Kin. 4:14).

MALACHI [MAL ah kie] *(my messenger)*

Old Testament prophet and author of the prophetic book that bears his name. Nothing is known about Malachi's life except the few facts that may be inferred from his prophecies. He apparently prophesied after the Babylonian captivity, during the time when Nehemiah was leading the people to rebuild Jerusalem's wall and recommit themselves to following God's law. The people's negligence in paying tithes to God was condemned by both Nehemiah and Malachi (Neh. 13:10–14; Mal. 3:8–10).

MALTA [MAWL tuh]

A small island in the Mediterranean Sea between Sicily and Africa, about 90 miles (145 kilometers) southwest of Syracuse. The apostle Paul was shipwrecked on Malta (Acts 28:1). With its fine natural harbors, Malta was a convenient haven for ships. Colonized by the Phoenicians, it was captured by the Greeks (736 B.C.), the Carthaginians (528 B.C.), and the Romans (242 B.C.).

After the shipwreck, Paul stayed on Malta for three months (Acts 28:11; Melita in KJV) before he was able to board another ship to Rome. During this time he shared the gospel with the inhabitants of the island and started a church on Malta. Thus an incidental event in the life of Paul led to the expansion of the kingdom of God.

MAMRE [MAM reh]

A place in the district of Hebron, west of Machpelah, where Abraham lived. It was noted for its "terebinth trees" (Gen. 13:18; 18:1), or "oaks" (NRSV). Near Mamre was the cave of Machpelah, in which Abraham, Isaac, and Jacob—and their wives, Sarah, Rebekah, and Leah—were buried (Gen. 49:13). The site of ancient Mamre has been identified as Ramet el-Khalil, about 2 miles (3 kilometers) north of Hebron.

MANASSEH [muh NASS uh] *(causing to forget)*

1. Joseph's firstborn son who was born in Egypt to Asenath the daughter of Poti-Pherah, priest of On (Gen. 41:50–51). Like his younger brother Ephraim, Manasseh was half Hebrew and half Egyptian. Manasseh's birth caused Joseph to forget the bitterness of his past experiences. Manasseh and Ephraim were both adopted by Jacob and given status as sons just like Jacob's own sons Reuben and Simeon (Gen. 48:5).

MANASSEH [muh NASS uh] *(causing to forget)*

2. The fourteenth king of Judah, the son of Hezekiah born to Hephzibah (2 Kin. 21:1–18). Manasseh reigned longer (55 years) than any other Israelite king and had the dubious distinction of being Judah's most wicked king. He came to the throne at the age of 12, although he probably co-reigned with Hezekiah for ten years. His father's godly influence appears to have affected Manasseh only negatively, and he reverted to the ways of his evil grandfather, Ahaz.

Committed to idolatry, Manasseh restored everything Hezekiah had abolished. Manasseh erected altars to Baal; he erected an image of Asherah in the temple; he worshiped the sun, moon, and stars; he recognized the Ammonite god Molech and sacrificed his son to him (2 Kin. 21:6); he approved divination; and he killed all who protested his evil actions. It is possible that he killed the prophet Isaiah; rabbinical tradition states that Manasseh gave the command that Isaiah be sawn in two (see also Heb. 11:37). Scripture summarizes Manasseh's reign by saying that he "seduced them [Judah] to do more evil than the nations whom the Lord had destroyed before the children of Israel" (2 Kin. 21:9).

Manasseh was temporarily deported to Babylon, where he humbled himself before God in repentance (2 Chr. 33:11–13). Upon Manasseh's return to Jerusalem, he tried to reverse the trends he had set; but his reforms were quickly reversed after his death by his wicked son Amon.

MANASSEH, TRIBE OF [muh NASS uh]

The tribe descended through Manasseh's son, Machir; Machir's son, Gilead; and Gilead's six sons (Num. 26:28–34). During their first 430 years in Egypt, the tribe of Manasseh increased to 32,200 men of war (Num. 1:34–35). By the second census, 39 years later, it numbered 52,700 (Num. 26:34).

In the settlement of Canaan, land was provided for Manasseh on both sides of the Jordan River. Eastern Manasseh was able to occupy its land only after it had aided the other tribes in conquering their territories (Num. 32:1–33).

Because of the Canaanite fortresses and strong cities in the land (for example, Megiddo, Taanach, Dor, Ibleam, and Beth Shean), western Manasseh had difficulty settling its territory. When it became strong, however, it did not expel the Canaanites but subjected them to tribute (Josh. 17:11–13).

The tribe of Manasseh was known for its valor, and it claimed two famous judges: Gideon (Judg. 6:11–8:35) and Jephthah (Judg. 11:1–12:7). During Saul's reign, men from Manasseh joined David at Ziklag (1 Chr. 12:19–20). Later many people from both western and eastern Manasseh rallied to make David king at Hebron (1 Chr. 12:31, 37).

MANDRAKE

A fruit-producing plant with dark green leaves and small bluish-purple flowers. The mandrake grew abundantly throughout Palestine and the Mediterranean region. Its yellow fruit was small, sweet-tasting, and fragrant. It had narcotic qualities and may have been used medicinally. The fruit of the mandrake was also referred to as the "love apple." It was considered a love potion (Gen. 30:16).

MANGER

A feeding trough, crib, or open box in a stable designed to hold fodder for livestock (Luke 2:7, 12; 13:15). In Bible times, mangers were made of clay mixed with straw or from stones cemented with mud. In structures built by King Ahab at Megiddo, a manger cut from a limestone block was discovered. After Jesus' birth, he was placed in the humble obscurity of a manger (Luke 2:7). The baby Jesus lying in a manger was a sign to the shepherds (Luke 2:12, 16).

MANNA

The food that God provided miraculously for the Israelites in the wilderness during their Exodus (Ex. 16:15, 31, 33; Num. 11:6–9). As long as the Hebrew people wandered in the Sinai Peninsula, they were able to gather manna from the ground each morning (Ex. 16:35). They ate the manna for 40 years, "until they came to the border of the land of Canaan" (Ex. 16:35). According to Joshua 5:12, the manna did not stop until the Israelites had crossed the Jordan River, had camped at Gilgal, had kept the Passover, and "had eaten the produce of the land."

"What is it?" (Ex. 16:15). This question, asked by the astonished Israelites, led to the name "manna" being applied to the "small round substance as fine as frost" (Ex. 16:14). Manna looked "like white coriander seed." It tasted like "wafers made with honey" (Ex. 16:31) or "pastry prepared with oil" (Num. 11:8).

The manna appeared with the morning dew. The Hebrews were instructed to gather only what was needed for one day, because any surplus would breed tiny worms and be spoiled. On the sixth day, however, the Israelites were permitted to gather enough for two days; they were forbidden to gather any manna on the Sabbath. Miraculously, the two days' supply of food gathered on the sixth day did not spoil.

Manna could apparently be baked, boiled, ground, beaten, cooked in pans, and made into cakes (Ex. 16:23; Num. 11:8). Moses even commanded Aaron to put a pot of manna in the ark of the covenant (Ex. 16:32–34), so future generations might see the "bread of heaven" on which their ancestors had fed. The New Testament records that inside the Most High Place in the temple, the ark of the covenant contained, among other things, "the golden pot that had the manna" (Heb. 9:4).

Numerous attempts have been made to identify manna with substances found in the Sinai Peninsula. Insects living on the tamarisk bush produce a small, sweet substance during the early summer that has been identified as manna by some scholars. But this substance does not fulfill all the biblical requirements for manna.

Other suggestions have included resinous gums that drip from some wilderness shrubs. But such substances do not resemble the manna that the Hebrews gathered and ate. Manna certainly was

nourishing, but it cannot be identified with any known food. It was a visible reminder to the Hebrews of God's providential care for His people.

MANOAH [muh NOH uh] (quiet)

Father of Samson the judge (Judg. 13:2–23). A Danite of the city of Zorah, Manoah and his wife tried to persuade Samson not to marry a Philistine woman, but he was determined to do so. They accompanied Samson to Timnah, where the ceremonies took place. Samson was buried "between Zorah and Eshtaol in the tomb of his father Manoah" (Judg. 16:31).

MANTLE

This item of clothing was the distinctive Hebrew outer garment, made of two pieces of thick woolen material sewn together, with slits rather than sleeves for the arms. In Old Testament times the mantle was usually brightly colored. Joseph's "tunic of many colors" (Gen. 37:3) was probably a mantle of woven, bright strips.

The Lord commanded the people of Israel to add blue tassels to the corners of their outer garments, as reminders to obey His commandments (Num. 15:38). This custom degenerated into a mere outward show of piety, and it was condemned by Jesus (Matt. 23:5).

Typically, Israelites slept on the floor with their mantle used as a covering to keep them warm. This was especially true for travelers, shepherds, or poor people, so a person's mantle was not to be kept as collateral for a loan (Ex. 22:27). In times of anguish, people often tore their mantles to show their distress (Job 2:12; Ezra 9:3). A handy, one-piece garment, the mantle protected a person from the weather. Because it fitted loosely, it could also be used to conceal or carry items.

M

MARK, JOHN

An occasional associate of Peter and Paul, and the probable author of the second gospel. Mark's lasting impact on the Christian church comes from his writing rather than his life. He was the first to develop the literary form known as the "gospel" and is rightly regarded as a creative literary artist.

John Mark appears in the New Testament only in association with more prominent personalities and events. His mother, Mary, was an influential woman of Jerusalem who possessed a large house with servants. The early church gathered in this house during Peter's imprisonment under Herod Agrippa I (Acts 12:12). Barnabas and Saul (Paul) took John Mark with them when they returned from Jerusalem to Antioch after their famine-relief visit (Acts 12:25). Shortly thereafter, Mark accompanied Paul and Barnabas on their first missionary journey as far as Perga. He served in the capacity of "assistant" (Acts 13:5), which probably involved making arrangements for travel, food, and lodging; he may have done some teaching, too.

At Perga John Mark gave up the journey for an undisclosed reason (Acts 13:13); this departure later caused a rift between Paul and Barnabas when they chose their companions for the second missionary journey (Acts 15:37–41). Paul was unwilling to take Mark again and chose Silas; they returned to Asia Minor and Greece. Barnabas persisted in his choice of Mark, who was his cousin (Col. 4:10), and returned with him to his homeland of Cyprus (Acts 15:39; also Acts 4:36).

This break occurred about A.D. 49–50, and John Mark is not heard from again until a decade later. He is first mentioned again, interestingly enough, by Paul— and in favorable terms. Paul asks the Colossians to receive Mark with a welcome

(Col. 4:10), no longer as an assistant but as one of his "fellow laborers" (Philem. 24). And during his imprisonment in Rome, Paul tells Timothy to bring Mark with him to Rome, "for he is useful to me for ministry" (2 Tim. 4:11). One final reference to Mark comes also from Peter in Rome; Peter affectionately refers to him as "my son" (1 Pet. 5:13). Thus, in the later references to Mark in the New Testament, he appears to be reconciled to Paul and laboring with the two great apostles in Rome.

Information about Mark's later life is dependent on early church tradition. Writing at an early date, Papias (A.D. 60–130), whose report is followed by Clement of Alexandria (A.D. 150–215), tells us that Mark served as Peter's interpreter in Rome and wrote his gospel from Peter's remembrances. Of his physical appearance we are only told, rather oddly, that Mark was "stumpy fingered." Writing at a later date (about A.D. 325), the church historian Eusebius says that Mark was the first evangelist to Egypt, the founder of the churches of Alexandria, and the first bishop of that city. So great were his converts, both in number and sincerity of commitment, says Eusebius, that the great Jewish philosopher, Philo, was amazed.

MARKETPLACE

An open space within cities that was used for business and other public transactions and assemblies. Archaeological investigations have shown that Israelite markets were primarily used as centers of business. Like the bazaars of present-day Oriental towns, they were places for buying and selling goods.

Greek marketplaces, such as those at Philippi (Acts 16:19) and Athens (Acts 17:17), contained more open spaces and were designed to be centers of public life. They were characteristically surrounded by temples, colonnades, public buildings, and numerous statues. Often these Greek marketplaces were carefully paved with stones and shaded by trees.

MARRIAGE

The union of a man and a woman as husband and wife, which becomes the foundation for a home and family.

Marriage was instituted by God when He declared, "It is not good that man should be alone; I will make him a helper comparable to him" (Gen. 2:18). So God fashioned a woman and brought her to the man. On seeing the woman, Adam exclaimed, "This is now bone of my bones and flesh of my flesh; she shall be called Woman, because she was taken out of Man" (Gen. 2:23). This passage also emphasizes the truth that "a man shall leave his father and mother and be joined to his wife, and they shall become one flesh" (Gen. 2:24). This suggests that God's ideal is for a man to be the husband of one wife and for the marriage to be permanent.

God's desire for His people was that they marry within the body of believers. The Mosaic Law clearly stated that an Israelite was never to marry a foreigner. The Israelite would be constantly tempted to embrace the spouse's god as well (Ex. 34:10–17; Deut. 7:3–4). Likewise, the apostle Paul commanded the members of the church at Corinth, "Do not be unequally yoked together with unbelievers" (2 Cor. 6:14).

Jesus' first miracle occurred in Cana in Galilee when He and His disciples were attending a wedding (John 2:1–11). Our Lord gave His blessing and sanction to the institution of marriage.

On another occasion, when Jesus was asked about marriage and divorce, He quoted two passages from Genesis. "Have you not read that He who made them at the beginning 'made them male and female,' and said, 'For this reason a man shall leave his father and mother

and be joined to his wife, and the two shall become one flesh'? So then, they are no longer two but one flesh. Therefore what God has joined together, let not man separate" (Gen. 1:27; 2:24; Matt. 19:4–6). He taught that marriage was the joining together of two people so they become "one flesh." Not only did God acknowledge the marriage; He also joined the couple.

The church at Corinth struggled over a number of issues, including the proper view of marriage. In response to their questions, Paul gave an answer about marriage. From His answer, it seems that three faulty ideas about marriage were prominent among some believers in the church. The first was that marriage was absolutely necessary in order to be a Christian; another was that celibacy was superior to marriage; the third was that when a person became a Christian, all existing relationships such as marriage were dissolved. When chapter 7 of 1 Corinthians is read with that as background, the following teaching emerges.

First, Paul stated that celibacy is an acceptable lifestyle for a Christian; not all people need to marry. Paul declared that he himself preferred not to marry. However, the single life can be lived for God's glory only if God has given the gift of singlehood. If one does not have that gift, he should marry. And Paul expected most people would marry.

Next, Paul spoke to the problem faced by a Christian believer whose spouse does not believe. He reasoned that if the unbelieving partner is willing to live with the Christian, then the Christian should not dissolve the marriage. Remaining with the unbelieving partner could result in his or her salvation (1 Cor. 7:14).

In his letter to the Ephesians, Paul showed how a marriage relationship can best function. First, he said, "Wives, submit to your husbands, as to the Lord" (Eph. 5:22). The model for the wife's

M

submission is the church, which is subject to Christ (Eph. 5:24). Second, husbands are to love their wives. The role that the husband plays is outlined by Jesus Christ, who loved His bride, the church, so much that He died for her (Eph. 5:25).

MARTHA [MAR thuh] *(lady, mistress)*

The sister of Mary and Lazarus of Bethany (Luke 10:38–41; John 11:1–44; 12:1–3). All three were sincere followers of Jesus, but Mary and Martha expressed their love for Him in different ways. The account of the two women given by Luke reveals a clash of temperaments between Mary and Martha. Martha "was distracted with much serving" (Luke 10:40); she was an activist busy with household chores. Her sister Mary "sat at Jesus' feet and heard His word" (Luke 10:39); her instinct was to sit still, meditate, and receive spiritual instruction.

While Martha busied herself making Jesus comfortable and cooking for Him in her home, Mary listened intently to His teaching. When Martha complained that Mary was not helping her, Jesus rebuked Martha. "You are worried and troubled about many things," He declared. "But one thing is needed, and Mary has chosen that good part, which will not be taken away from her" (Luke 10:41–42). He told her, in effect, that Mary was feeding her spiritual needs. This was more important than Martha's attempt to feed Him physically.

MARY [MAIR ee]

1. Mary, the mother of Jesus (Luke 1–2). We know nothing of Mary's background other than that she was a peasant and a resident of Nazareth, a city of Galilee. She must have been of the tribe of Judah and thus in the line of David (Luke 1:32), although the genealogies in Matthew 1 and Luke 3 do not say so, because they trace Joseph's genealogy rather than Mary's. We do know that Mary's cousin, Elizabeth, was the mother of John the Baptist.

When Mary was pledged to be married to Joseph the carpenter, the angel Gabriel appeared to her. Calling her "highly favored one" and "blessed . . . among women" (Luke 1:28), the angel announced the birth of the Messiah. After Gabriel explained how such a thing could be possible, Mary said, "Let it be to me according to your word" (Luke 1:38). That Mary "found favor with God" and was allowed to give birth to His child indicates she must have been of high character and faith.

When Jesus was born in Bethlehem of Judea, Mary "wrapped him in swaddling cloths, and laid Him in a manger" (Luke 2:7). She witnessed the visits of the shepherds and the wise men and "pondered them in her heart" (Luke 2:19) and heard Simeon's prophecy of a sword that would pierce through her own soul (Luke 2:35). Joseph and Mary fled to Egypt to escape Herod's murder of all males under two years old (Matt. 2:13–18). Neither Mary nor Joseph appear again until Jesus is 12 years old, at which time He stayed behind in the temple with the teachers (Luke 2:41–52). Both Mary and Joseph accepted Jesus' explanation, realizing He was Israel's Promised One.

Mary was present at Jesus' first miracle—the turning of water into wine at the wedding feast in Cana of Galilee (John 2:1–12). Mary seemed to be asking her Son to use His power to meet the crisis. Jesus warned her that His time had not yet come; nevertheless, He turned the water into wine. At another time Mary and Jesus' brothers wished to see Jesus while He was teaching the multitudes—perhaps to warn Him of impending danger. But again Jesus mildly rebuked her, declaring that the bond between Him and His disciples was stronger than any family ties (Luke 8:19–21).

The Scriptures do not mention Mary again until she stands at the foot of the cross (John 19:25–27). Jesus' brothers were not among His followers. Of His family, only His mother held fast to her belief in His messiahship—even though it appeared to be ending in tragedy. From the cross Jesus gave Mary over to the care of the beloved disciple, John. The last mention of Mary is in the upper room in Jerusalem, awaiting the coming of the Holy Spirit (Acts 1:14).

MARY [MAIR ee]

2. Mary Magdalene, the woman from whom Jesus cast out seven demons. The

name Magdalene indicates that she came from Magdala, a city on the southwest coast of the Sea of Galilee. After Jesus cast seven demons from her, she became one of His followers.

The Scriptures do not describe her illness. Mary Magdalene has been associated with the "woman in the city who was a sinner" (Luke 7:37) who washed Jesus' feet, but there is no scriptural basis for this. According to the Talmud (the collection of rabbinic writings that make up the basis of religious authority for traditional Judaism), the city of Magdala had a reputation for prostitution. This information, coupled with the fact that Luke first mentions Mary Magdalene immediately following his account of the sinful woman (Luke 7:36–50), has led some to equate the two women.

Mary Magdalene is also often associated with the woman whom Jesus saved from stoning after she had been taken in adultery (John 8:1–11)—again an association with no evidence. We do know that Mary Magdalene was one of those women who, having "been healed of evil spirits and infirmities," provided for Jesus and His disciples "from their substance" (Luke 8:2–3).

Mary Magdalene witnessed most of the events surrounding the crucifixion. She was present at the mock trial of Jesus; she heard Pontius Pilate pronounce the death sentence; and she saw Jesus beaten and humiliated by the crowd. She was one of the women who stood near Jesus during the crucifixion to try to comfort Him. The earliest witness to the resurrection of Jesus, she was sent by Jesus to tell the others (John 20:11–18). Although this is the last mention of her in the Bible, she was probably among the women who gathered with the apostles to await the promised coming of the Holy Spirit (Acts 1:14).

MARY [MAIR ee]

3. Mary of Bethany, sister of Martha and Lazarus (Luke 10:38–42). We know nothing of Mary's family background. All we really know is that Mary, Martha, and Lazarus loved one another deeply. When Jesus visited their house in Bethany, Mary sat at Jesus' feet and listened to His teachings while Martha worked in the kitchen. When Lazarus died, Mary's grief was deep. John tells us that when Jesus came following Lazarus' death Mary stayed in the house. After she was summoned by Martha, she went to Jesus, fell at His feet weeping, and said, "Lord, if You had been here, my brother would not have died" (John 11:21, 32).

Following Lazarus' resurrection, Mary showed her gratitude by anointing Jesus' feet with "a pound of very costly oil of spikenard" (John 12:3) and wiping His feet with her hair. Judas called this anointing extravagant, but Jesus answered, "Let her alone; she has kept this for the day of My burial" (John 12:7). Jesus called Mary's unselfish act "a memorial to her" (Mark 14:9).

MARY [MAIR ee]

4. Mary, the mother of the disciple James and Joses (Matt. 27:55–61). In light of her presence at Jesus' death and resurrection, it is likely that Mary was one of the women who followed Jesus and His disciples and provided food for them (Luke 8:2–3). Since Mark 15:40 tells us that this Mary, along with Mary Magdalene, observed Jesus' burial, the "other Mary" (Matt. 27:61) must refer to this mother of James and Joses. Mary was one of the women who went to the tomb on the third day to anoint Jesus' body with spices and discovered that Jesus was no longer among the dead (Mark 16:1–8).

MATTHEW [MA thue] (gift of the Lord)

A tax collector who became one of the twelve apostles of Jesus (Matt. 9:9). Matthew's name appears seventh in two lists of apostles (Mark 3:18; Luke 6:15), and eighth in two others (Matt. 10:3; Acts 1:13).

In Hebrew, Matthew's name means "gift of the Lord," but we know from his trade that he delighted in the gifts of others as well. He was a tax collector (Matt. 9:9–11) who worked in or around Capernaum under the authority of Herod Antipas. In Jesus' day, land and poll taxes were collected directly by Roman officials, but taxes on transported goods were contracted out to local collectors. Matthew was such a person, or else he was in the service of one. These middlemen paid an agreed-upon sum in advance to the Roman officials for the right to collect taxes in an area. Their profit came from the excess they could squeeze from the people.

The Jewish people hated these tax collectors not only for their corruption, but also because they worked for and with the despised Romans. Tax collectors were ranked with murderers and robbers, and a Jew was permitted to lie to them if necessary. The attitude found in the gospels is similar. Tax collectors are lumped together with harlots (Matt. 21:31), Gentiles (Matt. 18:17), and, most often, sinners (Matt. 9:10). They were as offensive to Jews for their economic and social practices as lepers were for their uncleanness; both were excluded from the people of God.

The Matthew mentioned in Matthew 9:9–13 is probably the same person as Levi of Mark 2:13–17 and Luke 5:27–32; the stories obviously refer to the same person and event. The only problem in the identification is that Mark mentions Matthew rather than Levi in his list of apostles (Mark 3:18), thus leading one to assume two different persons. It is possible, however, that the same person was known by two names (compare "Simon" and "Peter").

MATTHIAS [muh THIGH us] (gift of the Lord)

A disciple chosen to succeed Judas Iscariot as an apostle (Acts 1:23, 26). Matthias had been a follower of Jesus from the beginning of His ministry until the day of His ascension and had been a witness of His resurrection. In this way he fulfilled the requirements of apostleship (Acts 1:21–22). Probably he was one of the "seventy" (Luke 10:1, 17). The New Testament makes no further mention of him after his election. One tradition says that Matthias preached in Judea and was stoned to death by the Jews. Another tradition holds that he worked in Ethiopia and was martyred by crucifixion.

MEAL OFFERING

Meal offerings were prepared and presented to God as a meal, symbolically presenting the best fruits of human living to God to be consumed or used as He desired (Heb. 10:5–10). A notable exception to this is that poor people could present meal offerings as sin offerings.

In the meal offering, a person presented to God a vicarious consecration of the perfect life and total property of another (Christ). There is no ground in this offering for human boasting as though the offerer were received by God on the grounds of human effort. Rather, the recognition of the person's unworthiness is emphasized by the fact that meal offerings must be accompanied by a whole burnt offering or a peace offering (Lev. 2:1; Num. 15:1–16). Both offerings were made to atone for human sin.

MEDAD [ME dad]

An Israelite who prophesied in the wilderness camp (Num. 11:26–27). When 70 elders assembled in the "tabernacle of meeting," the Spirit rested on them and they prophesied. Medad and Eldad had not gone to the tabernacle, but had remained in the camp. Nevertheless, the Spirit rested upon them also and they, too, prophesied. A young man ran and told Moses. Joshua asked Moses to forbid them; but Moses replied, "Oh, that all the Lord's people were prophets and that the Lord would put His Spirit upon them!" (Num. 11:29). This story emphasizes the truth that God's Spirit can fill any person at any place at any time.

MEDEBA [MED eh buh]

An ancient Moabite city in Transjordan, about 15 miles (24 kilometers) southeast of the place where the Jordan River runs into the Dead Sea. It is mentioned with Heshbon and Dibon (Num. 21:30).

Medeba was a source of conflict between Moab and Israel. Apparently the Ammonites controlled the city in the time of David; for the Syrian mercenaries, allies of the Ammonites, "encamped before Medeba" (1 Chr. 19:7) before their defeat by Joab, the captain of David's army. The Moabite Stone states that Omri, king of Israel, captured Medeba, probably from Moab, and the Israelites controlled the city for 40 years. Mesha, king of Moab, recaptured and rebuilt it.

Jeroboam II of Israel probably recaptured Medeba again, for "he restored the territory of Israel from the entrance of Hamath [in the north] to the Sea of the Arabah [in the south]" (2 Kin. 14:25). Jeroboam probably pushed the Moabites south of the river Arnon and regained control of the plain by Medeba. If so, it was a short-lived victory; Isaiah's oracle against Moab (Is. 15:2) indicated that in Isaiah's time Medeba was once again under Moabite control.

Medeba, now known as Madaba or Madiyabah, is on the King's Highway, the main north-south highway through Transjordan.

MEDIA [MEE dih uh]

An ancient country of Asia situated west of Parthia, north of the Persian Gulf, east of Assyria and Armenia, and south of the Caspian Sea. The country is now included in parts of Iran, Iraq, and Turkey.

A mountainous country, Media contained some fertile sections; but much of it was cold, barren, and swampy. In the southern area lush plains were used as pastureland for the large herds of horses used in the Median cavalry.

The history of the Medes is complex, because it involves many entangling alliances and the rise and fall of several nations. The Medes were an Indo-European people who invaded the rough mountain terrain south of the Caspian Sea. In the ninth and eighth centuries B.C., Assyrian kings conducted campaigns against these people, forcing them to pay tribute. The mighty Tiglath-Pileser (745–727 B.C.) invaded Media and added part of it to the Assyrian Empire. By 700 B.C., the era of the prophet Isaiah, a prosperous realm had been established.

Media is first mentioned in the Old Testament as the destination to which Shalmaneser, king of Assyria, deported the Israelites from Samaria around 721 B.C. (2 Kin. 17:6; 18:11). Medes are mentioned in Ezra in connection with Darius's search for the scroll containing the famous decree of Cyrus that allowed the Jews to return to Jerusalem (Ezra 6:2). Laws of the Medes are mentioned in the Book of Esther (1:19) and in Daniel (6:8, 15).

The prophet Daniel prophesied that King Belshazzar's Babylonian kingdom would fall to "the Medes and Persians" (Dan. 5:28). Medes were also among the people from many different nations in

Jerusalem on the Day of Pentecost (Acts 2:9).

About 710 B.C. Sargon II of Assyria defeated the Medes and forced them to pay a tribute consisting of the thoroughbred horses for which Media was famous. The Medes, however, increased in strength and joined forces with Babylon. The Medes under Cyaxares and the Babylonians under Nabopolassar captured Asshur, the ancient capital of Assyria, in 614 B.C. In 612 B.C. this alliance overthrew Nineveh, the proud capital of Assyria, causing the crash of the Assyrian Empire.

The seventh-century Hebrew prophet Nahum expressed the great relief felt by neighboring nations at Nineveh's fall (Nah. 2:3; 3:19). Nabopolassar's son, Nebuchadnezzar, married Cyaxares's daughter, strengthening the bond between the two countries. During the era of Nebuchadnezzar and the time of Jeremiah (about 605–552 B.C.), the Median kingdom reached the height of its power.

Persia was dominated by Media until the time of Cyrus II who was founder of the Persian Empire. In 549 B.C. Cyrus defeated Media. Yet under the Persians, Media remained the most important province of Persia. As a consequence, the dual name, "Medes and Persians," remained for a long time (Esth. 1:19; Dan. 5:28). The expression, "The laws of the Medes and the Persians," depicted the unchangeable nature of Median law, which even the king was powerless to change (Esth. 1:19).

The Medes and Persians were Indo-European peoples known as Aryans. Their religion was Zoroastrianism. Its adherents believed that spiritual reality was divided between Ahura Mazda, the god of light and goodness, and Angra Mainja, the god of darkness and evil.

Influenced by the moral teachings of his religion, Cyrus II of Persia was known for his humane attitude toward conquered peoples. He treated the vanquished Medes with respect. Medo-Persia, a dual nation, became a great empire that ruled Asia until it was conquered by Alexander the Great (330 B.C.). After Alexander's death, Medo-Persia became part of Syria and later a part of the Persian Empire.

MEDIATOR

One who goes between two groups or persons to help them work out their differences and come to agreement. A mediator usually is a neutral party, a go-between, intermediary, or arbitrator (Job 9:33; daysman, KJV) who brings about reconciliation in a hostile situation when divided persons are not able to work out their differences themselves.

In Jewish history the idea of mediation became associated with the office of the priest, who stands between God and human beings in spiritual matters. This term was also applied to the prophet, who serves as intermediary in giving God's word to people, and the king, who serves as mediatorial administrator between God and human beings in government. These officers discharged their duties against the background of God's covenant with his people expressed in the Law.

The central role of the covenant made Moses the supreme mediator in the Old Testament. Moses was the sole human mediator of the Sinai covenant (Ex. 20:19–22; Heb. 3:2–5). He offered sacrifice, consecrated the priestly house of Aaron, and interceded for the nation. He spoke the word of God as prophet and administered government for the nation.

From the New Testament perspective, there is ultimately only "one Mediator between God and man" (1 Tim. 2:5)— Jesus the Messiah. He alone, being fully God, can represent God to man, and at the same time, being fully man, can represent man to God. He alone can bring

M

complete reconciliation, because He alone can bring about complete payment for our sin and satisfaction of God's wrath. He alone can bring everlasting peace (Acts 15:11; Eph. 1:7).

A major theme of the Book of Hebrews is that Jesus mediated a new and better covenant, an eternal covenant (7:27–28; 9:15; 10:1; 12:24). Speaking the words of God (John 14:24), Jesus fulfills the prophetic office. As High Priest over the house of God (Heb. 3:1–6), He sacrificed Himself to secure our redemption and continues to intercede on our behalf (Heb. 7:25; 9:24; 1 John 2:1). Even our prayers are presented to God "through" His mediation (Heb. 13:15). And He is also "King of kings," having "all authority in heaven and on earth" (Phil. 2:9–11; Rev. 19:11–16).

The Christian never need worry about the certainty of His salvation. The Mediator "is able to save to the uttermost those who come to God through Him" (Heb. 7:25).

MEDITERRANEAN SEA [med ih ter RAIN ih un]

A large sea bordered by many important nations of the ancient world, including Palestine. The Hebrews referred to it by several different names. It was called "the Great Sea" (Num. 34:6), "the Western Sea" (Deut. 34:2), "the Sea of the Philistines" (Ex. 23:31), and simply "the sea" (Josh. 16:8; Jon. 1:4).

The Mediterranean Sea extends about 2,200 miles (3,550 kilometers) westward from the coast of Palestine to the Straits of Gibraltar. At its narrowest point, between Sicily and the coast of Africa, the sea is about 80 miles (130 kilometers) wide. Archaeologists believe that an open channel once existed, connecting the Mediterranean to the Red Sea, and that this channel was closed off by drifting desert sand and silt from the Nile River,

providing a land connection between Asia and Africa.

Many ancient civilizations grew up around this sea and used it for trade and commerce. The Hebrews were afraid of the Mediterranean and usually hired others, often Phoenicians (1 Kin. 9:27), to conduct their seafaring business for them. Palestine itself had few good harbors.

The apostle Paul crossed the Mediterranean Sea during his missionary journeys. He tried to avoid sailing during the winter months, but was shipwrecked on his way to Rome while sailing in late autumn (Acts 27).

MEEKNESS

An attitude of humility toward God and gentleness toward people, springing from a recognition that God is in control. Although weakness and meekness may look similar, they are not the same. Weakness is due to negative circumstances, such as lack of strength or lack of courage. But meekness is due to a person's conscious choice. It is strength and courage under control, coupled with kindness.

Meekness is a virtue practiced and commended by our Lord Jesus (Matt. 5:5; 11:29). As such it is part of the equipment that every follower of Jesus should wear (2 Cor. 10:1; Gal. 5:23; 6:1; Eph. 4:1–2).

MEGIDDO [muh GID doe]

A walled city east of the Carmel Mountain range where many important battles were fought in Old Testament times. Megiddo was situated on the main road that linked Egypt and Syria. Overlooking the Valley of Jezreel (Plain of Esdraelon), Megiddo was one of the most strategic cities in Palestine. All major traffic through northern Palestine traveled past Megiddo, making it a strategic military stronghold.

Megiddo is first mentioned in the Old Testament in the account of the 31 kings conquered by Joshua (Josh. 12:21). In the division of the land of Canaan among the tribes of the Hebrew people, Megiddo was awarded to Manasseh. But the tribe was unable to drive out the native inhabitants of the city (Josh. 17:11; Judg. 1:27; 1 Chr. 7:29).

During the period of the judges, the forces of Deborah and Barak wiped out the army of Sisera "by the waters of Megiddo" (Judg. 5:19). During the period of the united kingdom under Solomon, the Israelites established their supremacy at Megiddo. The city was included in the fifth administrative district of Solomon (1 Kin. 4:12). Along with Hazor, Gezer, Lower Beth Horon, Baalath, and Tadmor, Megiddo was fortified and established as a chariot city for the armies of King Solomon (1 Kin. 9:15–19).

The prophet Zechariah mentioned the great mourning that would take place one day "in the plain of Megiddo" (Zech. 12:11; Megiddon, KJV). The fulfillment of Zechariah's prophecy is the battle at the end of time known as the Battle of Armageddon. Armageddon is a compound word that means "mountain of Megiddo."

In the endtimes, God will destroy the armies of the Beast and the False Prophet in "the battle of that great day of God Almighty" (Rev. 16:14) when He shall gather them "together to the place called in Hebrew, Armageddon" (Rev. 16:16). Jesus Christ will ride out of heaven on a white horse (Rev. 19:11) as the "King of kings and Lord of lords" (Rev. 19:16).

MELCHIZEDEK [mel KIZ eh deck] *(king of righteousness)*

A king of Salem (Jerusalem) and priest of the Most High God (Gen. 14:18–20; Ps. 110:4; Heb. 5:6–11; 6:20–7:28). Melchizedek's appearance and disappearance in the Book of Genesis are somewhat mysterious. Melchizedek and Abraham first met after Abraham's defeat of Chedorlaomer and his three allies. Melchizedek presented bread and wine to Abraham and his weary men, demonstrating friendship and religious kinship. He bestowed a blessing on Abraham in the name of El Elyon ("God Most High"), and praised God for giving Abraham a victory in battle (Gen. 14:18–20).

Abraham presented Melchizedek with a tithe (a tenth) of all the booty he had gathered. By this act Abraham indicated that he recognized Melchizedek as a fellow-worshiper of the one true God as well as a priest who ranked higher spiritually than himself. Melchizedek's existence shows that there were people other than Abraham and his family who served the true God.

In Psalm 110, a messianic psalm written by David (Matt. 22:43), Melchizedek is seen as a type of Christ. This theme is repeated in the Book of Hebrews, where both Melchizedek and Christ are considered kings of righteousness and peace. By citing Melchizedek and his unique priesthood as a type, the writer shows that Christ's new priesthood is superior to the old Levitical order and the priesthood of Aaron (Heb. 7:1–10; Melchisedec in KJV).

Attempts have been made to identify Melchizedek as an imaginary character named Shem, an angel, the Holy Spirit, Christ, and others. All are products of speculation, not historical fact; and it is impossible to reconcile them with the theological argument of Hebrews. Melchizedek was a real, historical king-priest who served as a type for the greater King-Priest who was to come, Jesus Christ.

MEMORIAL

A monument, statue, holiday, or ritual that serves as a remembrance or reminder of a person or an event. The

Feast of the Passover was a memorial of God's sparing the firstborn of the Israelites in Egypt and of Israel's deliverance from Egyptian bondage (Ex. 12:14).

When Israel crossed the Jordan River and occupied the Promised Land, Joshua commanded that 12 stones, representing the 12 tribes of Israel, be set up in the midst of the Jordan (Josh. 4:9). "These stones," he said, "shall be for a memorial to the children of Israel forever" (Josh. 4:7).

When Jesus was in the house of Simon the leper, a woman anointed His head with oil. "Wherever this gospel is preached in the whole world," said Jesus, "what this woman has done will also be told as a memorial to her" (Matt. 26:13; Mark 14:9).

On the eve of His crucifixion Jesus instituted the Lord's Supper (Luke 22:19). The observance of the Lord's Supper is an ongoing Christian memorial that helps believers remember the sacrifice of Christ on their behalf (1 Cor. 5:7; 11:25–26).

MEMPHIS [MEM fis]

An ancient royal city during the Old Kingdom period of Egypt's history (about 3000 B.C. to 2200 B.C.). It was situated on the west bank of the Nile River about 13 miles (21 kilometers) south of Cairo. Today there is little left to mark the glorious past of the city.

In 670 B.C. Memphis was captured by the Assyrians, followed by a period of Persian dominance. After the Moslem conquest of the city, its ruins were used in the Middle Ages to build Cairo, Egypt's modern capital. The importance of Memphis is demonstrated by the multitude of pyramids and the celebrated Sphinx that are located near the site of the ancient city.

The word *Memphis* appears only once in the Bible—a translation of the Hebrew word *noph* (Hos. 9:6). In this passage the prophet Hosea condemned the Israelites for their sinfulness and predicted that some of them would be buried by Egyptians from Memphis. In seven other locations the word *noph* refers to Memphis (Is. 19:13; Jer. 2:16; 44:1; 46:14, 19; Ezek. 30:13, 16). In each passage the NIV has Memphis.

"The princes of Noph [Memphis] are deceived," wrote the prophet Isaiah (Is. 19:13). He prophesied that God would bring judgment on these deluded rulers. The prophet Jeremiah also warned the Jews to trust God and not flee to Memphis, because God was going to send destruction upon the land of Egypt (Jer. 2:16; 44:1; 46:14, 19).

MENAHEM [MEN ah him] *(comforter)*

A son of Gadi and seventeenth king of Israel (2 Kin. 15:14–23). Some scholars believe Menahem probably was the military commander of King Zechariah. When Shallum took the throne from Zechariah by killing him in front of the people, Menahem determined that Shallum himself must be killed. After Shallum had reigned as king of Israel for a month in Samaria, Menahem "went up from Tirzah, came to Samaria, and struck Shallum . . . and killed him; and he reigned in his place" (2 Kin. 15:14).

When the city of Tiphsah refused to recognize Menahem as the lawful ruler of Israel, Menahem attacked it and inflicted terrible cruelties upon its people (2 Kin. 15:16). This act apparently secured his position, because Menahem remained king for ten years (752–742 B.C.). His reign was evil, marked by cruelty, oppression, and idolatrous worship.

During his reign Menahem faced a threat from the advancing army of Pul (Tiglath-Pileser III), king of Assyria. To strengthen his own position as king and to forestall a war with Assyria, he paid tribute to the Assyrian king by exacting "from each man fifty shekels of silver"

(2 Kin. 15:20). After Menahem's death, his son Pekahiah became king of Israel (2 Kin. 15:22).

MENE, MENE, TEKEL, UPHARSIN
[MEE neh, MEE neh, TEK uhl, ue FAR sin] *(numbered, numbered, weighed, and divided)*

A puzzling inscription that appeared on the wall of the palace of Belshazzar, king of Babylon, during a drunken feast (Dan. 5:1–29). The king had just ordered that the gold and silver vessels Nebuchadnezzar had stolen from the temple in Jerusalem be used in the revelry. When the fingers of a man's hand had written the words, Belshazzar called his wise men, but they could neither read the inscription nor interpret its meaning. Daniel was then summoned. He deciphered the message and told the king what it meant.

The words of the inscription refer to three Babylonian weights of decreasing size and their equivalent monetary values. In his interpretation of this inscription, Daniel used a play on words to give the message God had for Belshazzar and Babylon.

"Mene: God has numbered your kingdom, and finished it." God had counted the days allotted to Belshazzar's rule and his time had run out. "Tekel: You have been weighed in the balances and found wanting." Belshazzar's character, his moral values and spiritual worth, had been evaluated and he was found to be deficient. "Peres: Your kingdom has been divided, and given to the Medes and Persians." Belshazzar's empire had been broken into bits and pieces, dissolved and destroyed.

Some scholars have suggested that in referring to three weights listed in declining order, Daniel may have been referring to the declining worth of various Babylonian kings. Thus, the great king Nebuchadnezzar perhaps was symbol-ized by the mina, Evil-Merodach by the shekel (in other words, only one fiftieth as great as Nebuchadnezzar), and Nabonidus and Belshazzar (father and son respectively, who reigned as co-regents) were half-shekels—implying that it took two "half-regents" to equal one Evil-Merodach.

The overall impact of Daniel's double meaning in these words was to point out that the degeneration of the rulers of Babylon cried out for God's judgment. That very night Belshazzar was killed and Babylon was conquered by the Persians.

MEPHIBOSHETH [meh FIB oh shehth]
(from the mouth of [the] *shame* [ful god Baal]*)*

a son of Jonathan and grandson of Saul. Mephibosheth was also called Merib-Baal (1 Chr. 8:34; 9:40), probably his original name, meaning "a striver against Baal." His name was changed because the word "Baal" was associated with idol worship.

Mephibosheth was only five years old when his father, Jonathan, and his grandfather, Saul, died on Mount Gilboa in the Battle of Jezreel (2 Sam. 4:4). When the child's nurse heard the outcome of the battle, she feared for Mephibosheth's life. As she fled for his protection, "he fell and became lame" (2 Sam. 4:4). For the rest of his life he was crippled.

After David consolidated his kingdom, he remembered his covenant with Jonathan to treat his family with kindness (1 Sam. 20). Through Ziba, a servant of the house of Saul, David found out about Mephibosheth. The lame prince had been staying "in the house of Machir the son of Ammiel, in Lo Debar" (2 Sam. 9:4). David then summoned Mephibosheth to his palace, restored to him the estates of Saul, appointed servants for him, and gave him a place at the royal table (2 Sam. 9:7–13).

M

When David's son Absalom rebelled, the servant Ziba falsely accused Mephibosheth of disloyalty to David (2 Sam. 16:1–4). David believed Ziba's story and took Saul's property from Mephibosheth. Upon David's return to Jerusalem, Mephibosheth cleared himself. David in turn offered Mephibosheth half of Saul's estates (2 Sam. 19:24–30), but he refused. David's return to Jerusalem as king was the only reward Mephibosheth desired.

Although Mephibosheth was often wronged and his life was filled with tragedy, he never grew angry or embittered. Even material possessions had little appeal to him—an important lesson for all followers of the Lord.

MERARITES [meh RAY ites]

The descendants of Merari (Num. 26:57). During the wilderness journey, the Merarites were stationed on the north side of the tabernacle. The Merarites had the responsibility of transporting many of the materials that made up the tabernacle (Num. 3:35–37). To enable them to transport these materials, they were assigned "four carts and eight oxen" (Num. 7:8). They were under the direction of Ithamar, Aaron's youngest son.

Twelve cities were assigned to the Merarites: four from the tribe of Zebulun (Jokneam, Kartah, Dimnah, and Nahalal), four from the tribe of Reuben (Bezer, Jahaz, Kedemoth, and Mephaath), and four from the tribe of Gad (Ramoth in Gilead, Mahanaim, Heshbon, and Jazer). One of these cities, Ramoth in Gilead, also was a city of refuge (Josh. 21:34–40).

The Merarites made up 6 of the 24 divisions of temple musicians in David's time (1 Chr. 25:3). They aided in Hezekiah's cleansing of the temple (2 Chr. 29:12). After the captivity a small number of them returned to Jerusalem (Ezra 8:18–19).

MERCY

The aspect of God's love that causes Him to help the miserable. Those who are miserable may be so either because of breaking God's law or because of circumstances beyond their control.

God shows compassion toward those who have broken His law (1 Tim. 1:13, 16), although such mercy is selective, demonstrating that it is not deserved (Rom. 9:14–18). God's mercy on the miserable extends beyond punishment that is withheld (Eph. 2:4–6). Withheld punishment keeps us from hell, but it does not get us into heaven. God's mercy is greater than this.

God also shows mercy by actively helping those who are miserable due to circumstances beyond their control. We see this aspect of mercy especially in the life of our Lord Jesus. He healed blind men (Matt. 9:27–31; 20:29–34) and lepers (Luke 17:11–19). These acts of healing grew out of his attitude of compassion and mercy. Because God is merciful, He expects His children to be merciful (Matt. 5:7; James 1:27).

MERCY SEAT

The golden lid or covering on the ark of the covenant, regarded as the resting place of God (Ex. 25:17–22; 1 Chr. 28:11; Heb. 9:5; atonement cover in NIV).

See also ARK OF THE COVENANT.

MERODACH-BALADAN [MEHR oh dack BAL ah dahn] (the god Marduk has given an heir)

The king of Babylon (721–710 and 704 B.C.) who sent emissaries to King Hezekiah of Judah (Is. 39:1; Berodach-Baladan, 2 Kin. 20:12).

To the Assyrians, Merodach-Baladan was a persistent rebel king. He appeared on the political scene during the days of Tiglath-Pileser III of Assyria. He rallied the support of the Aramean tribes in

Babylonia and arranged an alliance with Elam. In 721 B.C., when Sargon II came to power in Assyria, Merodach-Baladan entered Babylon and claimed kingship to the country.

In 710 B.C., Sargon made a determined effort to expel Merodach-Baladan and make himself king. After submitting to Sargon, Merodach-Baladan was reinstated as king of the tribe of Bit-Yakin, a district near the mouth of the Euphrates River. Merodach-Baladan remained faithful to Sargon; but when Sennacherib came to power in 705 B.C., he grew restless. In 703 B.C., Merodach-Baladan returned to Babylon, killed the ruler there, and prepared to fight Assyria. Sennacherib reacted energetically and drove Merodach-Baladan into exile once again.

Merodach-Baladan sent ambassadors to Jerusalem to visit King Hezekiah of Judah, who had just recovered miraculously from a serious illness. He sent letters and presents (2 Kin. 20:12; Is. 39:1) and inquired of the "wonder that was done in the land" (2 Chr. 32:31). This probably was a reference to the sun's shadow moving backward ten degrees on the sundial of Ahaz (2 Kin. 20:8–11). The real reason for his visit may have been to gain an ally in Hezekiah and to involve him in revolt against Assyria.

There is no indication that Hezekiah formed an alliance, but he showed the Babylonian ambassadors his wealth and arsenal—an act that brought stiff rebuke from the prophet Isaiah (2 Kin. 20:13–18). Hezekiah later revolted from Assyria, a move that resulted in Sennacherib's invasion of Judah in 701 B.C.

Merodach-Baladan was never successful in his bid for Babylonian independence. The task was left for Nabopolassar (626–605 B.C.), who was able to succeed where Merodach-Baladan had failed.

MESHA [MEE shuh]

A king of Moab who "regularly paid the king of Israel [Ahab] one hundred thousand lambs and the wool of one hundred thousand rams" (2 Kin. 3:4). After Ahab's death at Ramoth Gilead, Mesha refused to pay the tribute to Ahab's successor, Ahaziah (2 Kin. 1:1).

Mesha led the Moabites, Ammonites, and Edomites in an invasion of Judah after Jehoshaphat, Judah's king, began his religious reform. Mesha and his allies were defeated when the Lord caused them to turn on one another; Judah and Jehoshaphat won without a battle (2 Chr. 20).

When King Ahaziah died, Jehoram became king of Israel. Jehoram wanted Mesha to resume the tribute, and he asked Jehoshaphat to help him force Mesha to pay it (2 Kin. 3). The two kings, along with a king of Edom, moved around the southern end of the Dead Sea to attack Mesha. The armies nearly died of thirst, but the prophet Elisha instructed them to dig trenches to reach water.

In the glare of the early-morning sun, Mesha mistook the water for blood. He carelessly moved to attack the armies of Israel and Judah. His army was beaten, and the cities of Moab were destroyed. In a last-ditch effort to avert total defeat, Mesha offered his oldest son as a burnt offering upon the wall of Kir Haraseth as a sacrifice to the god Chemosh. The human sacrifice apparently frightened or shocked the armies of Israel and Judah, so they pulled back from the city, lifting the siege and failing to capture Kir Haraseth.

Mesha is the king of whom the famous Moabite Stone declares: "I am Mesha, son of Chemosh [Yat] . . . king of Moab, the Dibonite." Thus, he is the one who caused the Moabite Stone to be written and had it erected.

M

MESHACH [MEE shak]

The Chaldean name given to Mishael, one of Daniel's companions (Dan. 1:7). Along with Shadrach and Abed-Nego, Meshach would not bow down and worship the pagan image of gold set up by Nebuchadnezzar. They were cast into "the burning fiery furnace," but were preserved from harm by the power of God.

MESOPOTAMIA [mess oh poh TAME ih uh] (land between the rivers)

A region situated between the Tigris and Euphrates Rivers; the general area inhabited by the ancient Assyrians and Babylonians. In the New Testament the word Mesopotamia refers to the areas between and around the Tigris and Euphrates rivers, including ancient Syria, Accad, Babylonia, and Sumer. But in the Old Testament, Mesopotamia usually translates a phrase that means "Aram of the two rivers" and is restricted to northwest Mesopotamia.

Abraham sent his servant to Nahor in Mesopotamia to find a bride for Isaac (Gen. 24:10). If Nahor refers to a city, it may be the same city, Nahur, that is mentioned in the Mari texts. The Mari texts are more than 20,000 clay tablets dating from about 1750 B.C. from the city of Mari (modern Tell Hariri) on the Euphrates River near the border between modern Syria and Iraq. Many scholars believe Nahur was situated near ancient Haran.

The pagan prophet Balaam came from Pethor of Mesopotamia (Deut. 23:4). In the days of the judges, God sent "Cushan-Rishathaim king of Mesopotamia" to afflict the rebellious Hebrew people (Judg. 3:8, 10). This king's ethnic background has been much debated. He has been identified by various scholars with the Hittites, Mitanni, Horites (Hurrians), and the Habiru.

Later, when the Ammonites waged war against King David, they hired chariot and cavalry troops from Mesopotamia (1 Chr. 19:6). These troops may have been members of the warrior class that lived throughout Mesopotamia at that time.

Acts 2:9 refers to the Jews present at the Feast of Pentecost as "those dwelling in Mesopotamia." These people were probably from Jewish settlements in Babylonia such as Pumbeditha, Neherdea, Babylon, Ctesiphon, and Nippur.

Stephen spoke of Abraham's original home, Ur of the Chaldeans, as being situated in Mesopotamia (Acts 7:2). Ur lay far to the south near the Persian Gulf. Today most of Mesopotamia is in Iraq with small parts in Turkey and Syria.

MESSIAH [meh SIGH uh] (anointed one)

The one anointed by God and empowered by God's spirit to deliver His people and establish His kingdom. In Jewish thought, the Messiah would be the king of the Jews, a political leader who would defeat their enemies and bring in a golden era of peace and prosperity. In Christian thought, the term Messiah refers to Jesus' role as a spiritual deliverer, setting His people free from sin and death.

The word Messiah comes from a Hebrew term that means "anointed one." Its Greek counterpart is Christos, from which the word Christ comes. Messiah was one of the titles used by early Christians to describe who Jesus was.

In Old Testament times, part of the ritual of commissioning a person for a special task was to anoint him with oil. The phrase "anointed one" was applied to a person in such cases. In the Old Testament, Messiah is used more than 30 times to describe kings (2 Sam. 1:14, 16), priests (Lev. 4:3, 5, 16), the patriarchs (Ps. 105:15), and even the Persian king, Cyrus (Is. 45:1). The word is also used in connection with King David, who became the model of the messianic king who would come at the end of the age (2 Sam. 22:51; Ps. 2:2). But it was not until the time of Daniel (sixth century B.C.) that Messiah was used as an actual title of a king who would come in the future (Dan. 9:25–26). Still later, as the Jewish people struggled against their political enemies, the Messiah came to be thought of as a political, military ruler.

From the New Testament we learn more about the people's expectations. They thought the Messiah would come soon to perform signs (John 7:31) and to deliver His people, after which He would live and rule forever (John 12:34). Some even thought that John the Baptist was the Messiah (John 1:20). Others said that the Messiah was to come from Bethlehem (John 7:42). Most expected the Messiah to be a political leader, a king who would defeat the Romans and provide for the physical needs of the Israelites.

According to the Gospel of John, a woman of Samaria said to Jesus, "I know that Messiah is coming." Jesus replied, "I who speak to you am He" (John 4:25–26). In the Gospels of Matthew, Mark, and Luke, however, Jesus never directly referred to Himself as the Messiah, except privately to His disciples, until the crucifixion (Matt. 26:63–64; Mark 14:61–62; Luke 22:67–70). He did accept the title and function of messiahship privately (Matt. 16:16–17). Yet Jesus constantly avoided being called "Messiah" in public (Mark 8:29–30). This is known as Jesus' "messianic secret." He was the Messiah, but He did not want it known publicly.

The reason for this is that Jesus' kingdom was not political but spiritual (John 18:36). If Jesus had used the title "Messiah," people would have thought he was a political king. But Jesus understood that the Messiah, God's Anointed One, was to be the Suffering Servant (Is. 52:13–53:12). The fact that Jesus was a suffering Messiah—a crucified deliverer—was a "stumbling block" to many of the Jews (1 Cor. 1:23). They saw the Cross as a sign of Jesus' weakness, powerlessness, and failure. They rejected the concept of a crucified Messiah.

But the message of the early church centered around the fact that the crucified and risen Jesus is the Christ (Acts 5:42; 17:3; 18:5). They proclaimed the "scandalous" gospel of a crucified Messiah as the power and wisdom of God (1 Cor. 1:23–24). John wrote, "Who is a liar but he who denies that Jesus is the Christ [the Messiah]?" (1 John 2:22).

By the time of the apostle Paul, "Christ" was in the process of changing from a title to a proper name. The name is found mostly in close association with the name "Jesus," as in "Christ Jesus" (Rom. 3:24) or "Jesus Christ" (Rom. 1:1). When the church moved onto Gentile soil, the converts lacked the Jewish background for understanding the title, and it lost much of its significance. Luke wrote, "The disciples were first called Christians [those who belong to and follow the Messiah] in Antioch" (Acts 11:26).

As the Messiah, Jesus is the divinely appointed king who brought God's kingdom to earth (Matt. 12:28; Luke 11:20). His way to victory was not by physical force and violence, but through love, humility, and service.

METALSMITH

A person who worked with metal. This occupation included those who dug the ore from the ground, refined the metal, and worked the metal into useful objects. Refining metal was an ancient skill that was well developed by the time of Abraham. Long before Abraham's time, copper was mixed with tin to form bronze. Metals such as gold and silver were often hammered or forged into desired shapes by metalworkers from ancient times. The refining process became quite well developed so that ancient metalworkers produced a high quality of gold and silver.

Ancient metalsmiths were skilled in making ornamental objects of precious metals. Israel was relatively ignorant of metalworking skills before the time of David, about 1000 B.C. Recognizing the importance of metalworking, David moved to conquer Edom and its iron and copper mines (2 Sam. 8:14). Solomon brought Israel into a high stage of metalworking by importing experts from other more advanced nations (1 Kin. 7:13–14).

MICHAH

METHUSELAH [meh THUE zuh luh]

A son of Enoch and the grandfather of Noah. At the age of 187, Methuselah became the father of Lamech. After the birth of Lamech, Methuselah lived 782 years and died at the age of 969. He lived longer than any other human. He was an ancestor of Jesus (Luke 3:37; Mathusala in KJV).

MICAH [MIE kuh] *(Who is like the Lord)*

An Old Testament prophet and author of the Book of Micah. A younger contemporary of the great prophet Isaiah, Micah was from Moresheth Gath (Mic. 1:1, 14), a town in southern Judah. His prophecy reveals his country origins; he uses many images from country life (Mic. 7:1).

Micah spoke out strongly against those who claimed to be prophets of the Lord but who used this position to lead the people of Judah into false hopes and further errors: "The sun shall go down on the prophets, and the day shall be dark for them" (Mic. 3:6). Micah's love for God would not allow him to offer false hopes to those who were under His sentence of judgment.

Little else is known about this courageous spokesman for the Lord. He tells us in his book that he prophesied during the reigns of three kings in Judah: Jotham, Ahaz, and Hezekiah (Mic. 1:1). This would place the time of his ministry from about 750 to 687 B.C.

MICAIAH [mie KAY yah] *(who is like the Lord?)*

The prophet who predicted the death of King Ahab of Israel in the battle against the Syrians at Ramoth Gilead (1 Kin. 22:8–28; 2 Chr. 18:7–27). Ahab gathered about 400 prophets, apparently all in his employment. They gave their unanimous approval to Ahab's proposed attack against the Syrian king, Ben-Hadad.

King Jehoshaphat of Judah was un-convinced by this display. He asked, "Is there not still a prophet of the Lord here, that we may inquire of Him?" (1 Kin. 22:7; 2 Chr. 18:6). Ahab replied, "There is still one man, Micaiah the son of Imlah, by whom we may inquire of the Lord but I hate him, because he does not prophesy good concerning me, but evil" (1 Kin. 22:8; 2 Chr. 18:7). The prophet Micaiah was then summoned.

When Ahab asked this prophet's advice, Micaiah answered, "Go and prosper, for the Lord will deliver it into the hand of the king!" (1 Kin. 22:15; 2 Chr. 18:14).

Micaiah's answer was heavy with sarcasm, irony, and contempt. Ahab realized he was being mocked; so he commanded him to speak nothing but the truth. Micaiah then said, "I saw all Israel scattered on the mountains as sheep that have no shepherd" (1 Kin. 22:17; 2 Chr. 18:16). Ahab turned to Jehoshaphat and said, "Did I not tell you that he would not prophesy good concerning me, but evil?" (1 Kin. 22:18; 2 Chr. 18:17).

Zedekiah then struck Micaiah on the cheek and accused him of being a liar. Ahab commanded that Micaiah be put in prison until the king's victorious return from Ramoth Gilead. Then Micaiah said, "If you ever return . . . the Lord has not spoken by me" (1 Kin. 22:28; 2 Chr. 18:27). Ahab did not return; he died at Ramoth Gilead, just as Micaiah had predicted.

MICHAEL [MIE kay el] *(who is like God?)*

An archangel, or an angel of high rank, who served as prince or guardian over the destinies of the nation of Israel (Dan. 10:21; 12:1). According to the Epistle of Jude, Michael disputed with Satan over the body of Moses (Jude 9). This reference is a puzzle to scholars, because the incident to which Jude refers does not appear anywhere in the Old Testament.

M

The Book of Revelation speaks of "Michael and his angels" (Rev. 12:7), who struggled with Satan when the devil rebelled against God at the beginning of time.

MICHAL [MY kul] *(who is like God?)*

The younger daughter of King Saul who became David's wife. After David had become a hero by slaying Goliath, Saul offered to give Michal to David as his wife. But instead of a dowry, Saul requested of David "one hundred foreskins of the Philistines" (1 Sam. 18:25), hoping that David would be killed by the Philistines.

Instead, David won an impressive vic-tory. He and his warriors killed 200 Philistines and brought their foreskins to the king. Then Saul presented Michal to David to become his wife (1 Sam. 18:27–28).

After their marriage, the ark of the covenant was brought from the house of Obed-Edom to the City of David. Caught up in an inspired frenzy of religious fervor, David was filled with joy at being able to bring the ark back to Jerusalem. "Then David danced before the Lord with all his might; and David was wearing [only] a linen ephod [loincloth, kilt, or apron]" (2 Sam. 6:14). Whatever garment David was wearing, it apparently scandalized Michal, who accused him of

MICHAEL

lewd, base behavior—of "uncovering himself in the eyes of the maids" (2 Sam. 6:20).

Michal's withering sarcasm was met by David's devastating response. In effect he said, "My dance was a dance of joy, faith, and happiness in the Lord. Where is your joy in the Lord? Why do you not dance also?" By judging and condemning David, Michal had revealed a lack of love in her soul—quite a contrast to her earlier attitude (1 Sam. 18:20). Michal died barren (2 Sam. 6:21–23), one of the most terrible fates that could befall a Hebrew woman.

MICHMASH [MICK mash]

A city of Benjamin about 7 miles (11 kilometers) northeast of Jerusalem that figured prominently in the early history of Saul's reign. According to 1 Samuel 13:2, Saul gathered an army of 3,000 men in an attempt to meet the Philistine threat. Two thousand of the men were under Saul's personal command at Michmash, and 1,000 men were under the command of Jonathan at nearby Gibeah of Benjamin.

When the Philistines moved toward Michmash, Saul fled to Gilgal, where many of his soldiers deserted him. In a display of impatience and irreverence, "Saul said, 'Bring a burnt offering and peace offerings here to me.' And he offered the burnt offering." After Saul offered the sacrifice to the Lord he was severely rebuked by Samuel (1 Sam. 13:5–15). Saul then returned to Gibeah. While "Saul was sitting in the outskirts of Gibeah under a pomegranate tree" (1 Sam. 14:2), Jonathan and his armorbearer scaled the northern cliff of the gorge of Michmash. By this daring tactical maneuver, they were able to kill the enemy sentries and throw the entire Philistine camp into panic.

Several centuries later, Ezra recorded that 122 men of Michmash returned from the captivity (Ezra 2:27; Michmas in NKJV; Micmash in NIV).

MIDDLE WALL OF PARTITION

A barrier or partition that divided the inner court of the temple, open only to Jews, from the Court of the Gentiles. The Jewish historian Josephus described this partition as a stone wall, inscribed with warnings to Gentiles not to enter the holy

M

MICHMASH

WELCOME TO THE BASH AT MICHMASH!

WHILE YOU'RE IN TOWN, ENJOY OUR WORLD FAMOUS McMASH HASH!

place of the temple, under threat of death.

The "middle wall of partition" between Jews and Gentiles existed spiritually as well as physically. The Law of Moses, especially the practice of circumcision and the food laws, erected a barrier of hostility and contempt between the two peoples. The Jewish people scorned the Gentiles who were "without the law" and rejoiced in their superior religious traditions. Christ, however, "is our peace, who has made both one, and has broken down the middle wall of division between us" (Eph. 2:14).

MIDIAN [MID ee un]

The land inhabited by the descendants of Midian. Situated east of the Jordan River and the Dead Sea, the land stretched southward through the Arabian desert as far as the southern and eastern parts of the peninsula of Sinai.

MIDIANITES [MID ee un ites]

A nomadic people who were enemies of the Israelites in Old Testament times. The Midianites were distantly related to the Israelites, since they sprang from Midian, one of the sons of Abraham. But

MIDIANITES

they usually were foes rather than friends of the Hebrew people. Abraham sent the children of Midian "to the country of the east" (Gen. 25:6) which probably included the desert fringes of Moab, Edom, and perhaps parts of the Sinai Peninsula. They are known thereafter in the Old Testament as one of the "people of the East" (Judg. 6:3, 33), or inhabitants of the desert regions of southern Syria and western Arabia.

The Midianites were at least loosely associated with others of this group, including the Ishmaelites (Gen. 37:28; Judg. 8:24). Midianite travelers bought Joseph from his brothers and resold him in Egypt (Gen. 37:25–36). Moses married into a Midianite family (specifically an associated group known as the Kenites) in "the land of Midian" (Ex. 2:15). His wife Zipporah and his father-in-law Jethro were Midianites: "Then Moses was content to live with the man, and he gave Zipporah his daughter toMoses" (Ex. 2:21; 3:1). But this was the last friendly connection the Israelites had with the Midianites.

After the time of Moses, the Midianites consistently opposed the Israelites. They joined with the Moabites, in whose territory they had partly settled, in hiring the prophet-magician Balaam to curse Israel (Num. 22:4, 7). At Moab, just before the conquest of Canaan, the Midianites were among those who practiced sexual immorality as part of the ritual of their idolatrous religion. They involved some of the Israelites in this idolatry, causing God's judgment to come upon His people (Num. 25:1–9). Because of this the Midianites were singled out for destruction (Num. 25:16–18).

Perhaps the most serious Midianite threat to Israel came during the days of the judges when Midianite warriors invaded Palestine. They came on camels, an innovation in combat. The Israelites were driven into the hill country as the Midianites and other easterners raided their territory, plundering crops and cattle for seven years (Judg. 6:1–6).

Then God raised up Gideon to deliver Israel from the Midianites. He and the Ephraimites drove off the Midianites, capturing Oreb and Zeeb, two of their princes (Judg. 7:24–25), and pursuing escapees across the Jordan River to the desert fringes where their kings Zebah and Zalmunna were captured (Judg. 8:10–12). Gideon's great victory was mentioned in several later Old Testament passages as an example of God's deliverance of His people from oppression (Ps. 83:9, 11; Is. 9:4; 10:26).

MIDWIFE

A woman who helped other women give birth to their children (Gen. 35:17). Midwives were sometimes relatives or friends. Their task involved cutting the umbilical cord, bathing the baby, rubbing it down with salt, and swaddling it (Ezek. 16:4). In swaddling, the baby was wrapped snugly in cloth, binding its arms to its body. The midwife also marked which twin was the first to come forth or the firstborn (Gen. 38:28). In Egypt, Pharaoh ordered the Hebrew midwives, apparently professionals, to kill all the boy babies at birth, but the women refused to do so (Ex. 1:15–22).

MIGHTY

The brave warriors who risked their lives for David both before and after he became king of Israel. The names of David's mighty men are given in 2 Samuel 23:8–39 and 1 Chronicles 11:10–47. The term "mighty men of valor" is also used of the courageous warriors who served under Joshua (Josh. 1:14; 6:2).

MILETUS [my LEE tuhs]

An ancient seaport in Asia Minor visited by the apostle Paul (Act 20:15, 17; 2 Tim. 4:20; Miletum in KJV). Situated on the shore of the Mediterranean Sea, Miletus was about 37 miles (60 kilometers) south of Ephesus and on the south side of the Bay of Latmus. Because of silting, the site is now more than 5 miles (8 kilometers) from the coast.

Colonized by Cretans and others, Miletus became a leading harbor during the Persian and Greek periods. It prospered economically and boasted a celebrated temple of Apollo. Although Miletus was still an important trade center in Roman times, the river was already silting in the harbor.

The apostle Paul visited Miletus on his journey from Greece to Jerusalem. In Miletus Paul delivered a farewell message to the elders of the church of Ephesus (Acts 10:18–35).

MILL

Mills and millstones were tools used to grind grain. The most common household mills of Bible times were flat stones on which grain was placed and crushed as other stones rolled over the grain.

Commercial mills were of different construction and considerably larger. One type was made of two round flat stones. A wooden peg was firmly fastened in the center of the bottom stone. The upper stone, which had a funnel-shaped hole through the center, was placed over the peg. Grain was poured between the stones and around the peg through the hole. The upper stone was turned by a peg handle placed near the outside edge, crushing the grain. Some of these larger mills required two operators.

A second type of commercial mill was similar in operation but of a different shape. The lower stone was in the shape of an upside-down cone. The upper stone, with a cone-shaped hollow cut into the bottom side, was placed over the lower stone. Grain was poured through a hole in the top. The upper stone was turned either by animals hitched to wooden arms attached to the stone or by slaves or prisoners (Judg. 16:21).

A third type of mill consisted of a large circular stone set on its edge and rolled around in a trough in the lower stone. This was also operated by animals or slaves.

The sound of grinding was heard constantly in the villages and towns. Its absence was a prophetic sign of famine and death (Jer. 25:10; Rev. 18:22). The loss of a millstone could mean disaster for a family (Deut. 24:6).

MILLENNIUM, THE

The thousand-year period mentioned in connection with the description of Christ's coming to reign with His saints over the earth (Rev. 20:1–9). Many Old Testament passages are reputed to refer to the Millennium (Is. 11:4; Jer. 3:17; Zech. 14:9).

These and many other Old Testament passages are often taken to refer only to the thousand-year period itself. However, it is often difficult in these passages to see a clear dividing line between the earthly period of the Millennium and the eternal state of new heavens and earth. Therefore, it is best to let one's teaching about the Millennium be drawn specifically from the words in Revelation 20. The other great promises to Israel, while they may have a temporary fulfillment in the thousand years, still await the fulness of the new heavens and new earth and the unhindered presence of Israel's king and the church's husband—Jesus Christ our Lord.

During that thousand-year period, Satan will be bound in the bottomless pit so he will not deceive the nations until his short period of release (Rev. 20:3, 7–8). The faithful martyrs who have died for the cause of Christ will be resurrected before the Millennium. They will rule with Christ and will be priests of God and Christ (Rev. 20:4). The unbelieving dead will wait for the second resurrection (Rev. 20:5). After the thousand years, Satan will be released and will again resume his work of deceit (Rev. 20:7–8).

The most important aspect of the Millennium is the reign of Christ. Peter taught that Christ now rules from the right hand of God (Acts 2:33–36). That rule will last until His enemies are made His footstool: "The Lord said to my Lord, 'sit at My right hand, till I make Your enemies Your footstool' " (Ps. 110:1). The apostle Paul also understood Christ to be presently reigning in a period designed to bring all of God's enemies underfoot (1 Cor. 15:25–27). Thus the impact of Christ's present rule over the earth from God's right hand must not be seen as unrelated to His future reign during the Millennium.

The Millennium is viewed by interpreters in several different ways. One position holds that the Millennium only refers to Christ's spiritual rule today from heaven. This symbolic view is known as the amillennial interpretation. Another position views Christ's spiritual rule as working through preaching and teaching to bring gradual world improvement leading up to Christ's return. This is the postmillennial view.

The position that holds to an actual thousand-year period in the future is known as the premillennial view. This interpretation does not diminish the power of Christ's present rule from heaven or limit that rule to the church only. That position sees the need for a thousand-year place in history for an earthly fulfillment of Israel's promises of land and blessing. It emphasizes that the one thousand years in Revelation 20 are actual years and are not symbolic.

MILLO [MILL oh] *(fill)*

A fortification or citadel near Jerusalem. The Millo of Jerusalem was probably part of the fortification of the Jebusite city that David captured. It may have been either a solid tower full of earth or a bastion strengthening a weak point in the wall. It was already in existence when David's army captured the Jebusite city (2 Sam. 5:9).

The Millo was one of the building projects included in King Solomon's expansion program in Jerusalem in later years. He strengthened the Millo by using conscripted labor (1 Kin. 9:15). Centuries later, King Hezekiah had the Millo repaired in preparation for an invasion and siege by the Assyrians (2 Chr. 32:5). King Joash was killed "in the house of the Millo" (2 Kin. 12:20)—the victim of a conspiracy.

MINISTER, MINISTRY

M

A distinctive biblical idea that means "to serve" or "service." In reality, all believers are "ministers." The apostle Paul urged the true pastor-teacher to "equip the saints" so they can minister to one another (Eph. 4:11–12). The model, of course, is Jesus, who "did not come to be served, but to serve" (Mark 10:45). His service is revealed in the fact that He gave "His life a ransom for many" (Matt. 20:28).

Jesus' servanthood radically revised the ethics of Jew and Greek alike, because He equated service to God with service to others. When we minister to the needs of the hungry or the lonely, we actually minister to Christ (Matt. 25:31–46). And when we fail to do so, we sin against God (James 4:17). In this light, all who took part in the fellowship of service were ministers.

The concept is strengthened when the use of the Greek word *doulos* is noted. This was the term for a bondslave, one who was offered his freedom but who voluntarily surrendered that freedom in order to remain a servant. This idea typified Jesus' purpose, as described by Paul in Philippians 2:7. This passage alludes to the "servant of God" teaching of Isaiah 42–53. Truly Christ fulfilled this exalted calling, because His life was dedicated to the needs of others.

Following our Savior's example, all believers are bondslaves of God (Rom. 1:1; Gal. 1:10; Col. 4:12). We are to perform "good deeds" to all people, with a responsibility especially to fellow Christians (Gal. 6:10; Heb. 10:24).

The concepts of minister and ministry must be broadened today to include all the members of a church. The common concept of the pastor as the professional minister must be discarded, because the biblical pattern is for him to be the one who trains the congregation for ministry. All the saints are responsible for loving and ministering in various ways to one another, using the spiritual gifts distributed to each by the Holy Spirit.

MIRACLES

Historical events or natural phenomena that appear to violate natural laws but that reveal God to the eye of faith at the same time. A valuable way of understanding the meaning of miracles is to examine the various terms for miracles used in the Bible.

Both the Old Testament and the New Testament use the word *sign* (Is. 7:11, 14; John 2:11) to denote a miracle that points to a deeper revelation. *Wonder* (Joel 2:30; Mark 13:22) emphasizes the effect of the miracle, causing awe and even terror. A *work* (Matt. 11:2) points to the presence of God in history, acting for mankind. The New Testament uses the word *power* (Mark 6:7) to emphasize God's acting in strength. These terms often overlap in meaning (Acts 2:43). They are more specific than the more general term *miracle*.

Miracles in the Old Testament are connected especially with the great events in Israel's history—the call of Abraham (Gen. 12:1–3), the birth of Moses (Ex. 1:1–2:22), the Exodus from Egypt (Ex. 12:1–14:31), the giving of the law (Ex. 19:1–20:26), the entry into the Promised Land (Josh. 3:1–4:7), etc. These miracles are for salvation, but God also acts in history for judgment (Gen. 11:1–9).

The plagues of the Exodus showed God's sovereign power in judgment and salvation (Ex. 7:3–5). In parting the water, God showed His love and protection for Israel as well as His judgment on Egypt for its failure to recognize God (Ex. 15:2, 4–10). During the wilderness journey, God demonstrated His love and protection in supplying the daily Manna (Ex. 16:1–36). Another critical period in Israel's history was the time of Elijah, the champion of Israel. Elijah controlled the rain and successfully challenged the pagan priests of Baal (1 Kin. 17:1; 18:1–40). God revealed Himself as Lord, as Savior of Israel, and as punisher of the nation's enemies.

As with the Old Testament, the New Testament miracles are essentially expressions of God's salvation and glory. Why did Jesus perform miracles? Jesus answered this question Himself. When in prison, John the Baptist sent some of his disciples to Jesus to see if He was the "one to come" (Matt. 11:3). Jesus told them to inform John of what He had done: "The blind receive sight, the lame walk, those who have leprosy are cured, the deaf hear, the dead are raised, and the good news is preached to the poor" (11:5).

With these words, Jesus declared that His miracles were the fulfillment of the promises of the Messiah's kingdom as foretold by Isaiah (24:18–19; 35:5–6; 61:1). Jesus' miracles were signs of the presence of the kingdom of God (Matt. 12:39).

Jesus did not work miracles to prove

His deity or His messiahship. In fact, He clearly refused to work miracles as proofs (Matt. 12:38–42; Luke 11:29–32). His death was the proof to Israel. However, Jesus' miracles do give evidence that He was divine, that He was the Son of God, the Messiah.

The Acts of the Apostles is a book of miracles. Again, these miracles are a continuation of the miracles of Jesus, made possible through the Holy Spirit. The miracles of the apostles were done in the name of Jesus and were manifes-

tations of God's salvation (Acts 3:11). This thread of continuity is seen in Peter's miracles, which paralleled those of Jesus (Luke 7:22; 5:18–26; 8:49–56; Acts 3:1–16; 9:32–35; 36–42).

God began His church with a powerful display of miracles. At Pentecost, the Holy Spirit came on the people with great power (Acts 2:1–13), leading to conversions (Acts 2:41). When Philip went to Samaria, the Spirit of God anointed him with power (Acts 8:4–40), and the same happened with Peter and Cornelius (Acts

MIRACLES

M

10:1–48). These powerful wonders were designed to convince the apostles and the Palestinian church that other cultures were to be part of the church.

To these were added the stunning act of God through Peter when Ananias and Sapphira acted in hypocrisy (Acts 4:32–5:11), the church's power in prayer (Acts 4:23–31), and Paul's transforming vision (Acts 16:6–10).

Miraculous powers were also present in the apostles. Peter healed a lame man (Acts 3:1–6), a paralytic (Acts 9:32–35), and raised the dead (Acts 9:36–42). The apostles performed mighty miracles (Acts 5:12–16), and Peter was miraculously released from prison (Acts 12:1–11). Paul's conversion was a startling incident (Acts 9:1–19). Ability to work miracles was taken as a sign for apostleship by Paul (Rom. 15:18–19; 2 Cor. 12:12). Thus, this ability to work miracles is not only an expression of God's salvation but also God's way of authenticating His apostles.

The lists of the gifts of the Spirit in the New Testament show that miracles were one of the means by which believers ministered to others (Rom. 12:6–8; 1 Cor. 12:8–10, 28–30; Eph. 4:11–12).

MIRIAM [MER eh um]

A sister of Aaron and Moses (Num. 26:59; 1 Chr. 6:3). Called "Miriam the prophetess" (Ex. 15:20), she is described as one of the leaders sent by the Lord to guide Israel (Mic. 6:4). Although the Bible does not specifically say so, Miriam was probably the sister who watched over the infant Moses in the ark of bulrushes (Ex. 2:4–8). Miriam's song of victory after the Israelites' successful crossing of the Red Sea (Ex. 15:20–21) is one of the earliest poems.

Miriam was involved in a rebellion against Moses when he married an Ethiopian woman (Num. 12:1–2). Both she and Aaron claimed to be prophets, but

God heard their claims and rebuked them. Because of her part in the rebellion against Moses' leadership, Miriam was struck with leprosy. However, Moses interceded for her, and she was quickly healed (Num. 12:1–16). She is not mentioned again until her death and burial at Kadesh in the Wilderness of Zin (Num. 20:1).

MISHNA [MISH nah] *(repetition)*

a written collection of traditional Jewish laws handed down orally from teacher to student. It was compiled across a period of about 335 years, from 200 B.C. to A.D. 135.

The Mishna deals with all areas of Jewish life—legal, theological, social, and religious—as taught in the schools of Palestine. Soon after the Mishna was compiled, it became known as the "iron pillar of the Torah," since it preserves the way a Jew can follow the Torah, or the Law.

MIZPAH [MIZ pah] *(watchtower)*

A city of Benjamin in the region of Geba and Ramah (1 Kin. 15:22). At Mizpah Samuel assembled the Israelites for prayer after the ark of the covenant was returned to Kirjath Jearim (1 Sam. 7:5–6). Saul was first presented to Israel as king at this city (1 Sam. 10:17). Mizpah was also one of the places that Samuel visited on his annual circuit to judge Israel (1 Sam. 7:16–17). Mizpah was one of the sites fortified against the kings of the northern tribes of Israel by King Asa (1 Kin. 15:22). After the destruction of Jerusalem in 586 B.C., Gedaliah was appointed governor of the remaining people of Judah; his residence was at Mizpah (2 Kin. 25:23, 25).

After the fall of Jerusalem Mizpah became the capital of the Babylonian province of Judah. Mizpah also was reinhabited by Israelites after the Babylonian captivity (Neh. 3:7, 15, 19). The site is modern Tell en-Nasbch.

MOAB [MOE abb] *(of my father)*

A neighboring nation whose history was closely linked to the fortunes of the Hebrew people. Moab was situated along the eastern border of the southern half of the Dead Sea, on the plateau between the Dead Sea and the Arabian desert. It was about 35 miles (57 kilometers) long and 25 miles (40 kilometers) wide. Although it was primarily a high plateau, Moab also had mountainous areas and deep gorges. It was a fertile area for crops and herds.

Moab, founder of the Moabites, was a son of Lot by incest (Gen. 19:30–38). Although the Moabites were of mixed ethnic stock, the influence of Moab's descendants among them was great enough to give the country its ancient name. The story in Genesis 14 of the raid of Chedorlaomer, king of Elam, and his fellow kings records the conquest of most of Moab about 2000–1900 B.C.

Sihon's Amorite kingdom annexed much of Moab shortly before the Israelite conquest of Canaan (Num. 21:17–29). After the Israelites defeated Sihon, Balak, the king of the relatively weak Moabites, joined with the Midianites in hiring the prophet-magician Balaam to curse Israel so the Israelites could be defeated (Num. 22:1–20). Balaam's mission failed, but when the Israelites camped in Moab, the women of Moab enticed the Israelites into a form of idolatry that involved ritual sexual immorality. This resulted in God's judgment against Israel (Num. 25:1–9).

Moses saw the Promised Land from Moab's Mount Nebo (Num. 27:12–23). Here he was buried after his death (Deut. 34:6). From the region of Acacia Grove in northwest Moab, the Israelites crossed the Jordan River into the Promised Land (Josh. 3:1). The tribes of Reuben and Gad actually settled in northern Moab (Num. 32:1–37).

The nation of Israel was relatively weak during the period of the judges, after the conquest. Eglon, a king of Moab, began to oppress Israel, capturing territory east of the Jordan River as far as Jericho. Ehud the judge delivered Israel from Eglon (Judg. 3:12–30). The events of the Book of Ruth occurred during this same general period. Ruth, a Moabite woman, became an ancestor of King David and therefore of Jesus himself (Ruth 2:6; 4:13–22; Matt. 1:5–16).

The Moabites also threatened Israel in the days of Israel's first king, Saul, who was apparently successful against them (1 Sam. 14:47). Although David had some early friendships among the Moabites (1 Sam. 22:3–4), he eventually conquered Moab (2 Sam. 8:2). The Moabites remained subject to Israel until after Solomon's death.

Omri, king of Israel (885–874 B.C.), kept Moab under his control, as did his son Ahab (874–853 B.C.), until Ahab was so occupied with wars against Syria and Assyria that Moab broke free. This was described by King Mesha of Moab in his monument, the Moabite Stone. King Jehoram of Israel, King Jehoshaphat of Judah, and the king of Edom joined forces to attack Moab about 849 B.C. But they failed to conquer the Moabites because of a superstitious lack of faith when the king of Moab sacrificed his own son to show how deeply he believed in his cause (2 Kin. 3:1–27).

On another occasion, a coalition of Moabites, Ammonites, and Edomites invaded Judah, but they were destroyed by God (2 Chr. 20:1–30). The Moabites apparently raided Israelite territory during the eighth century B.C. (2 Kin. 13:20).

The Assyrians conquered Moab about 735 B.C., and invading Arabs conquered it about 650 B.C. The prophet Isaiah lamented over Moab's defeat (Is. 15–16),

M

and Jeremiah predicted Moab's destruction at the end of the seventh century B.C. (Jer. 48). When Jerusalem was destroyed by the Babylonians in 586 B.C., some of the Jews fled to Moab to escape being taken into captivity (Jer. 40:11–12).

MOABITE STONE

A black basalt memorial stone discovered in Moab by a German missionary in 1868. Nearly four feet high, it contained about 34 lines in an alphabet similar to Hebrew. The stone was probably erected about 850 B.C. by the Moabite king, Mesha.

King Mesha's story written on the stone celebrated his overthrow of the nation of Israel. This event apparently is recorded in 2 Kings 3:4–27, although the biblical account makes it clear that Israel was victorious in the battle. The passage shows that Mesha honors his god Chemosh in terms similar to the Old Testament reverence for the Lord. The inhabitants of entire cities were apparently slaughtered to appease this deity, recalling the similar practices of the Israelites, especially as described in the Book of Joshua. Besides telling of his violent conquests, Mesha boasted on the stone of the building of cities (with Israelite forced labor) and the construction of cisterns, walls, gates, towers, a king's palace, and even a highway.

The Moabite Stone has profound biblical relevance. Historically, it confirms Old Testament accounts. It has a theological parallel to Israel's worship of one god. It is also valuable geographically because it mentions no less than 15 sites listed in the Old Testament. The writing on the stone also resembles Hebrew, the language in which most of the Old Testament was originally written.

MONOTHEISM

Worship of one supreme God, an important characteristic of the worship system of the Hebrew people. Against the idolatry of surrounding nations with their many gods (polytheism), God revealed this essential aspect of His nature to Israel in the Old Testament period. The Lord is one God (Deut. 6:4).

In the New Testament God further revealed that He is One in Three and that His essential being is triune. God is the triune family of Father, Son, and Holy Spirit, united in will, purpose, holiness, and love. Accordingly, Christianity is both monotheistic and trinitarian.

Jesus' oneness with the Father is explicitly claimed in the fourth Gospel: "In the beginning was the Word, and the Word was with God, and the Word was God" (John 1:1). Jesus Himself consciously laid claim to His oneness with the Father (John 5:17–24). The absolute unity of Father, Son, and Holy Spirit is expressed throughout the New Testament (Matt. 28:19; John 14:16; 16:13–15; 2 Cor. 13:14).

MOON

The "lesser light" of the heavens (Gen. 1:16) created by God to rule over the night. The moon had a special significance for the ancient Israelites. Their festival calendar, which began each month with the rising of the new moon, was a lunar calendar. The day of the appearing of the new moon was signaled by the blowing of the ram's horn. This event was also observed with special sacrifices (Num. 10:10; 28:11–15). Since the lunar year is about 11 days shorter than the solar year, a thirteenth month was added to the Hebrew calendar every third year to keep the festival calendar on schedule with the changing seasons.

The accurate recording of the new moon as it arrived each month was important, because the moon governed the dates for other religious festivals. Clouds or fog could obscure the new moon on the night of its rising. When this happened, the Hebrew people would extend the festival days to be sure the correct day was observed. This may be why the festival of the New Moon used by David to cover his absence from Saul's court seems to have lasted for two days (1 Sam. 20:5).

Amos condemned Israel's merchants for their impatience with the interruption to business caused by the festival of the New Moon (Amos 8:4–6). Speaking through Isaiah (1:13–15), God condemned the formal observance of the New Moon festival.

Along with the sun and the planet Venus, the moon was worshiped as a cosmic god by many pagan nations of the ancient world. Ur and Haran (Gen. 11:31) were both centers of moon worship. The moon was known as Sin in Babylon and Assyria, Nanna in Sumer, and Yarih at Ugarit. This last name is related to the Hebrew word for "moon." While the worship of the moon or any other natural phenomenon was strictly forbidden among the Hebrews (Deut. 4:19; 17:3), King Manasseh established the cults of "all the host of heaven," presumably including the moon, in the court of Solomon's temple (2 Kin. 21:3–5).

MORDECAI [MAWR deh kie] (related to Marduk)

The hero of the Book of Esther. Mordecai was probably born in Babylonia during the years of the captivity of the Jewish people by this pagan nation. He was a resident of Susa (Shushan), the Persian capital during the reign of Ahasuerus (Xerxes I), the king of Persia (ruled 486–465 B.C.).

When Mordecai's uncle, Abihail, died (Esth. 2:5), Mordecai took his orphaned cousin, Hadassah (Esther), into his home as her adoptive father (Esth. 2:7). When two of the king's eunuchs, Bigthan and Teresh, conspired to assassinate King Ahasuerus, Mordecai discovered the plot and exposed it, saving the king's life (Esth. 2:21–22). Mordecai's good deed was recorded in the royal chronicles of Persia (Esth. 2:23).

Mordecai showed his loyalty to God by refusing to bow to Haman, the official second to the king (Esth. 3:2, 5). According to the Greek historian Herodotus, when the Persians bowed before their king, they paid homage as to a god. Mordecai, a Jew, would not condone such idolatry.

Haman's hatred for Mordecai sparked his plan to kill all the Jews in the Persian Empire (Esth. 3:6). Mordecai reminded his cousin, who had become Queen Esther, of her God-given opportunity to expose Haman to the king and to save her people (Esth. 3:1–4:17). The plot turned against Haman, who ironically was impaled on the same stake that he had prepared for Mordecai (Esth. 7:10).

Haman was succeeded by Mordecai, who now was second in command to the most powerful man in the kingdom. He used his new position to encourage his people to defend themselves against the scheduled massacre planned by Haman. Persian officials also assisted in protecting the Jews, an event celebrated by the annual Feast of Purim (Esth. 9:26–32).

MOREH [MOH reh] (diviner)

The site of a terebinth, or oak, tree near Shechem where Abraham built an altar (Gen. 12:6–7). The place probably was an old Canaanite sanctuary. The "terebinth tree of Moreh" was likely a sacred tree long before Abraham entered Canaan. This may have been the same tree under which Joshua set up a large memorial stone to commemorate Israel's renewed covenant with God (Josh. 24:26). The tree probably took its name from a "diviner" (a teacher or soothsayer who practiced divination) who lived here.

MORIAH [moh RYE uh]

The hill at Jerusalem where Solomon built "the house of the Lord," the temple. Originally this was the threshing floor of Ornan the Jebusite (2 Chr. 3:1), also called Araunah the Jebusite (2 Sam. 24:16–24), where God appeared to David. David purchased the threshing floor from Ornan (1 Chr. 21:15–22:1) and built an altar on the site. It was left to David's son (Solomon) to build the temple.

Some Jews believe the altar of burnt offering in the temple at Jerusalem was situated on the exact site of the altar on which Abraham intended to sacrifice Isaac. To them the two Mount Moriahs mentioned in the Bible are identical. The Muslim structure, the Dome of the Rock in Jerusalem, reputedly is situated on this site.

MORTAR

A mixture of clay, sand, lime, and water used for building material. Mortar was sometimes made of clay alone or with chopped straw, sand, or crushed stone added for strength. The Hebrews in Egypt tempered their bricks and mortar with straw (Ex. 1:14; 5:7). Lime mixed with sand or small stones was used in Palestine for mortar. This was used especially for more expensive houses. Mortar was spread on the walls, floors, and roofs of houses for more durability. The prophet Nahum suggested that the usual method of mixing mortar was treading it (Nah. 3:14).

MOSES [MOE zez]

The Hebrew prophet who delivered the Israelites from Egyptian slavery and who was their leader and lawgiver during their years of wandering in the wilderness. Moses was born into a Hebrew family in Egypt at a time when the pharaoh had given orders that no more male children among the Hebrew slaves should be allowed to live. To save the infant Moses, his mother made a little vessel of papyrus waterproofed with asphalt and pitch. She placed Moses in the vessel, floating among the reeds on the bank of the Nile River.

By God's providence, Moses was found and adopted by an Egyptian princess, the daughter of the pharaoh himself. He was reared in the royal court as a prince of the Egyptians. At the same time, the Lord determined that Moses should be taught in his earliest years by his own mother. He was founded in the faith of his fathers, although he was reared as an Egyptian (Ex. 2:1–10).

One day Moses became angry at an Egyptian taskmaster who was beating a Hebrew slave; he killed the Egyptian and buried him in the sand (Ex. 2:12). When this became known, however, he feared for his own life and fled from Egypt to the land of Midian. Moses was 40 years old when this occurred (Acts 7:23–29).

Moses' exile of about 40 years was spent in the land of Midian (mostly in northwest Arabia), in the desert between Egypt and Canaan. In Midian Moses became a shepherd and eventually the son-in-law of Jethro, a Midianite priest. Jethro gave his daughter Zipporah to Moses in marriage (Ex. 2:21); and she bore him two sons, Gershom and Eliezer (Ex. 18:3–4; Acts 7:29). During his years as a shepherd, Moses became familiar with the wilderness of the Sinai Peninsula, learning much about survival in the desert. He also learned patience and much about leading sheep. All of these skills prepared him to be the shepherd of the Israelites in later years when he led them out of Egypt and through the Wilderness of Sinai.

When the Israelites arrived at Mount Sinai, Moses went up onto the mountain for 40 days (Ex. 24:18). The Lord appeared in a terrific storm—"thunderings and lightnings, and a thick cloud" (Ex. 19:16). Out of this momentous encounter came the covenant between the Lord and Israel, including the Ten Commandments (Ex. 20:1–17).

In giving the law to the Hebrew people, Moses taught the Israelites what the Lord expected of them—that they were to be a holy people separated from the pagan immorality and idolatry of their surroundings. Besides being the lawgiver, Moses was also the one through whom God presented the tabernacle and instructions for the holy office of the priesthood. Under God's instructions, Moses issued ordinances to cover specific situations, instituted a system of judges and hearings in civil cases, and regulated the religious and ceremonial services of worship.

After leaving Mount Sinai, the Israelites continued their journey toward the land of Canaan. They arrived at Kadesh Barnea, on the border of the Promised Land. From this site, Moses sent 12 spies,

MOSES

M

one from each of the 12 tribes of Israel, into Canaan to explore the land. The spies returned with glowing reports of the fruitfulness of the land. They brought back samples of its figs and pomegranates and a cluster of grapes so large that it had to be carried between two men on a pole (Num. 13:1–25). The majority of the spies, however, voted against the invasion of the land. Ten of them spoke fearfully of the huge inhabitants of Canaan (Num. 13:31–33).

The minority report, delivered by Caleb and Joshua, urged a bold and courageous policy. By trusting the Lord, they said, the Israelites would be able to attack and overcome the land (Num. 13:30). But the people lost heart and rebelled, refusing to enter Canaan and clamoring for a new leader who would take them back to Egypt (Num. 14:1–4). To punish them for their lack of faith, God condemned all of that generation, except Caleb and Joshua, to perish in the wilderness (Num. 14:26–38).

During these years of wandering in the wilderness, Moses' patience was continually tested by the murmurings, grumblings, and complaints of the people. At one point, Moses' patience reached its breaking point and he sinned against the Lord, in anger against the people. When the people again grumbled against Moses, saying they had no water, the Lord told Moses to speak to the rock and water would flow forth. Instead, Moses lifted his hand and struck the rock twice with his rod. Apparently because he disobeyed the Lord in this act, Moses was not permitted to enter the Promised Land (Num. 20:1–13). That privilege would belong to his successor, Joshua.

After his death, Moses continued to be viewed by Israel as the servant of the Lord (Josh. 1:1–2) and as the one through whom God spoke to Israel (Josh. 1:3; 9:24; 14:2). For that reason, although it was truly the law of God, the law given

at Mount Sinai was consistently called the Law of Moses (Josh. 1:7; 4:10).

The prophets of the Old Testament remembered Moses as the leader of God's people (Is. 63:12), as the one by whom God brought Israel out of Egypt (Mic. 6:4), and as one of the greatest of the interceders for God's people (Jer. 15:1). Malachi called the people to remember Moses' Law and to continue to be guided by it, until the Lord Himself should come to redeem them (Mal. 4:4).

The writer of the Book of Hebrews spoke in glowing terms of the faith of Moses (Heb. 11:24–29). These and other passages demonstrate how highly Moses was esteemed by various writers of the Old and New Testaments.

The New Testament, however, shows that Moses' teaching was intended only to prepare humanity for the greater teaching and work of Jesus Christ (Rom. 1:16–3:31). What Moses promised, Jesus fulfilled: "For the law was given through Moses, but grace and truth came through Jesus Christ" (John 1:17).

MOUNT OF OLIVES

A north-to-south ridge of hills east of Jerusalem where Jesus was betrayed on the night before His crucifixion. This prominent feature of Jerusalem's landscape is a gently rounded hill, rising to a height of about 2,676 feet (830 meters) and overlooking the temple.

The closeness of the Mount of Olives to Jerusalem's walls made this series of hills a grave strategic danger. The Roman commander Titus had his headquarters on the northern extension of the ridge during the siege of Jerusalem in A.D. 70. He named the place Mount Scopus, or "Lookout Hill," because of the view it offered over the city walls. The whole hill must have provided a platform for the Roman catapults that hurled heavy objects over the Jewish fortifications of the city.

In ancient times the whole mount must have been heavily wooded. As its name implies, it was covered with dense olive groves. It was from this woodland that the people, under Nehemiah's command, gathered their branches of olive, oil trees, myrtle, and palm to make booths when the Feast of Tabernacles was restored after their years of captivity in Babylon (Neh. 8:15).

The trees also grew on this mountain or hill in New Testament times. When Jesus entered the city, the people who acclaimed him king must have gathered the branches with which they greeted His entry from this same wooded area.

Another summit of the Mount of Olives is the one on which the "men of Galilee" stood (Acts 1:11–12) as they watched the resurrected Christ ascend into heaven. Then there is the point to the south above the village of Silwan (or Siloam) on the slope above the spring. Defined by a sharp cleft, it faces west along the converging Valley of Hinnom. It is called the Mount of Offense, or the "Mount of Corruption" (2 Kin. 23:13), because here King Solomon built "high places" for pagan deities that were worshiped by the people during his time (1 Kin. 11:5–7).

In the New Testament, the Mount of Olives played a prominent part in the last week of our Lord's ministry. Jesus approached Jerusalem from the east, by way of Bethphage and Bethany, at the Mount of Olives (Matt. 21:1; Mark 11:1). As He drew near the descent of the Mount of Olives (Luke 19:37), the crowd spread their garments on the road, and others cut branches from the trees and spread them before Him. They began to praise God and shout, "Hosanna to the Son of David!" (Matt. 21:9). When Jesus drew near Jerusalem, perhaps as He arrived at the top of the Mount of Olives, He saw the city and wept over it (Luke 19:41).

Jesus then went into Jerusalem and cleansed the temple of the moneychangers; He delivered parables to the crowd and silenced the scribes and Pharisees with His wisdom. Later, as He sat on the Mount of Olives, the disciples came to Him privately, and He delivered what is known as "the Olivet Discourse," a long sermon that speaks of the signs of the times and the end of the age, the Great Tribulation, and the coming of the Son of Man (Matt. 24:3–25:46; Mark 13:3–37).

After Jesus had instituted the Lord's Supper on the night of His betrayal, He and His disciples sang a hymn and went out to the Mount of Olives (Matt. 26:30; Mark 14:26), to the Garden of Gethsemane (Matt. 26:36; Mark 14:32). In this garden Jesus was betrayed by Judas and delivered into the hands of His enemies.

MOURNER

A person who grieved over the dead. Paid professional mourners worked in the ancient world from very early times. They are called "mourning women" and "skilled wailing women" (Jer. 9:17), "singing men" and "singing women" (2 Chr. 35:25). These mourners sang or chanted funeral songs or dirges: "There shall be wailing in all streets, and they shall say in all the highways, 'Alas! Alas!' They shall call the farmer to mourning and skillful lamenters to wailing" (Amos 5:16). They were often accompanied by musical instruments (Matt. 9:23).

MUSIC

Vocal or instrumental sounds with rhythm, melody, and harmony. Music was part of everyday life for the ancient Hebrew people. Music was a part of family merrymaking, such as the homecoming party for the prodigal son (Luke 15:25). Music welcomed heroes and celebrated victories. Miriam and other women sang, danced, and played timbrels when the Israelites miraculously escaped the Egyptians (Ex. 15:20), and the

Song of Moses in Exodus 15 is the earliest recorded song in the Bible. Jephthah's daughter greeted him with timbrels to celebrate his victory over the Ammonites (Judg. 11:34). David's triumph brought music (1 Sam. 18:6).

Music was used in making war and crowning kings (Judg. 7:18–20; 1 Kin. 1:39–40; 2 Chr. 20:28). Wartime music-making was apparently little more than making noise, as in the fall of Jericho (Josh. 6). There was music for banquets and feasts (Is. 5:12; 24:8–9) and royal courts and harems (Eccl. 2:8). The Bible gives examples of occupational songs (Jer. 31:4–5), dirges and laments (Matt.

9:23), and cultic chants (Ex. 28:34–35; Josh. 6:4–20).

The Israelites were apparently a very musical people. The Assyrian king, Sennacherib, demanded as tribute from King Hezekiah of Judah male and female musicians—a most unusual ransom. Psalm 137 relates that the Babylonians demanded ''songs of Zion'' from the Jews while they were in captivity (v. 3). During the period between the Testaments, Strabo, a Greek geographer, called the female singers of Palestine the most musical in the world.

Our greatest clue to Hebrew music lies in the Book of Psalms, the earliest existing hymnbook. As hymns, these indi-

MUSIC

I GOT SAND IN MY HOOVES, FLEAS IN MY GROOVES, SORE HUMP WHEN IT MOVES, I GOT THOSE WILDERNESS BLUES . . .

vidual psalms were suitable for chanting and singing in the worship of God.

The New Testament contains little information about music. But it does give some additional hymns to add to the Old Testament hymns—those of Mary (Luke 1:46–55) and Zacharias (Luke 1:68–79), the Magnificat and the Benedictus. Early Christians sang Hebrew songs accompanied by music (2 Chr. 29:27–28). The apostle Paul refers to "psalms and hymns and spiritual songs" (Eph. 5:19; Col. 3:16). Matthew 26:30 records that Christ and His disciples sang a hymn after the Passover supper, probably the second half of the Hallel, or Psalms 115–118.

The New Testament also contains accounts of the early Christians singing hymns for worship and comfort (Acts 16:25; Eph. 5:19; Col. 3:16). Some fragments of early Christian hymns also appear in the New Testament (Eph. 5:14; 1 Tim. 3:16). Pliny the Younger, at the beginning of the second century A.D., reported that Christians sang songs about Christ and their faith in Him.

MUSTARD

A plant that grew wild along roadsides and in fields, reaching a height of about 15 feet (4.6 meters). The black mustard of Palestine seems to be the species to which Jesus referred (Matt. 13:31–32; Mark 4:31–32; Luke 13:19). It was cultivated for its seeds, which were used as a condiment and for oil.

The mustard seed was the smallest seed known in Jesus' day (Matt. 13:32). Nevertheless, Jesus said that if one has faith like a mustard seed, he can move mountains (Matt. 17:20) or transplant a mulberry tree in the sea (Luke 17:6).

MUTE SPIRIT

The NKJV uses this phrase for a disorder that was probably epilepsy. It is marked by erratic electrical discharges of the central nervous system and manifested by convulsive attacks. A certain man brought his epileptic son to Jesus for help (Mark 9:17–29). The KJV says the boy had a "dumb spirit." Jesus healed him. Among the scores of people brought to Jesus for healing were epileptics (Matt. 4:24; lunaticks in KJV).

An ancient theory held that epilepsy was caused by the moon; people referred to epileptics as being "lunatic" or "moonstruck." Psalm 121:6 may reflect this idea when it says, "The sun shall not strike you by day, nor the moon by night."

MYRRH

An extract from a stiff-branched tree with white flowers and plum-like fruit. After myrrh was extracted from the wood, it soon hardened and was valued as an article of trade. It was an ingredient used in anointing oil (Ex. 30:23), and was used as perfume (Ps. 45:8; Prov. 7:17; Song 3:6), in purification rites for women (Esth. 2:12), as a gift for the infant Jesus (Matt. 2:11), and in embalming (John 19:39). According to the Gospel of Mark (15:23), the drink offered to Jesus before His crucifixion was "wine mingled with myrrh."

The reference to myrrh in Genesis 37:25 and 43:11 is thought to be ladanum, sometimes called onycha, from a species of rockrose and not the true myrrh.

MYSIA [MISS ee uh]

A province in northwestern Asia Minor (present-day Turkey). Paul and Silas passed through Mysia on their way to Troas, one of its main cities, during Paul's first missionary journey (Acts 16:7–8). Three other cities of Mysia are mentioned in the New Testament: Assos (Acts 20:13), Adramyttium (Acts 27:2), and Pergamos (Rev. 1:11).

M

MYSTERY

The hidden, eternal plan of God that is being revealed to God's people in accordance with His plan.

In the Old Testament, "mystery" occurs only in the Aramaic sections of Daniel (Dan. 2:18, 27–30, 47; 4:9). Some of God's mysteries were revealed to Daniel and King Nebuchadnezzar. In the New Testament, "mystery" refers to a secret that is revealed by God to His servants through His Spirit. As such, it is an "open secret." Jesus told His disciples, "To you it has been given to know the mystery of the kingdom of God" (Luke 8:10). Jesus explained the mystery of God's kingdom to His disciples. But to others He declared, "All things come in parables" (Mark 4:11).

"Mystery" refers to the revelation of God's plan of salvation as that plan focuses in Christ. The gospel itself is a "mystery which was kept secret since the world began" (Rom. 16:25). This mystery was revealed by God through the prophetic Scriptures to Paul and the church (1 Cor. 2:7; Eph. 6:19; Col. 4:3).

MYSTERY RELIGIONS

Secret religions that flourished in Syria, Persia, Anatolia, Egypt, Greece, Rome, and other nations several centuries before and after the time of Christ. The mystery religions were quite popular in the first century A.D. and thus provided strong religious competition for Christianity. They were called mysteries because their initiation and other rituals were kept secret.

By means of the secret rituals of these religions—which might involve ceremonial washings, blood-sprinkling, drunkenness, sacra-mental meals, passion plays, or even sexual relations with a priest or priestess—their followers became one with their god and believed that they participated in the life of that god.

N

NAAMAN [NAY a man] *(pleasant)*

A commander of the Syrian army who was cured of leprosy by the Lord through the prophet Elisha. Naaman was a "great and honorable man in the eyes of his master [Ben-Hadad, king of Syria] . . . but he was a leper" (2 Kin. 5:1–27). Although leprosy was a despised disease in Syria, as in Israel, those who suffered from the disease were not outcasts.

On one of Syria's frequent raids of Israel, a young Israelite girl was captured and became a servant to Naaman's wife. The girl told her mistress about the prophet Elisha, who could heal Naaman of his leprosy. Ben-Hadad sent a letter about Naaman to the king of Israel. Fearing a Syrian trick to start a war, the king of Israel had to be assured by Elisha that Naaman should indeed be sent to the prophet. To demonstrate to Naaman that it was God, not human beings, who healed, Elisha refused to appear to Naaman. Instead, he sent the commander a message, telling him to dip himself in the Jordan River seven times.

Naaman considered such treatment an affront and angrily asked if the Syrian rivers, the Abana and the Pharpar, would not do just as well. His servants, however, persuaded him to follow Elisha's instructions. Naaman did so and was healed. In gratitude, Naaman became a worshiper of God and carried two mule-loads of Israelite earth back to Syria in order to worship the Lord "on Israelite soil," even though he lived in a heathen land.

Before he departed for Damascus, however, Naaman asked Elisha's understanding and pardon for bowing down in the temple of Rimmon when he went there with Ben-Hadad (2 Kin. 5:18). Elisha said to him, "Go in peace" (v. 19), thus allowing Naaman to serve his master, the king.

NABAL [NAY bal]

A wealthy sheepmaster of Maon and a member of the house of Caleb (1 Sam. 25:2–39). Nabal pastured his sheep near the Judahite town of Carmel on the edge of the wilderness. Nabal was "harsh and evil in his doings" and was "such a scoundrel" that no one could reason with him (1 Sam. 25:3, 17).

While David was hiding from Saul, he sent ten men to Nabal to ask for food for himself and his followers. Nabal refused. David, who had protected people in the area from bands of marauding Bedouin, was so angered by Nabal's refusal that he determined to kill Nabal and every male in his household (1 Sam. 25:4–22).

Nabal's wife Abigail was "a woman of good understanding and beautiful appearance" (v. 3). She realized the danger threatening her family because of her husband's stupidity. "Then Abigail made haste and took two hundred loaves of bread, two skins of wine, five sheep already dressed, five seahs of roasted grain, one hundred clusters of raisins, and two hundred cakes of figs, and loaded them on donkeys" (1 Sam. 25:18). She took these gifts of food to David, fell to the ground, and apologized for her husband's behavior. Her quick action soothed David's anger.

When Abigail returned home, she found a great feast in progress. Oblivious to his narrow brush with death, "Nabal's heart was merry within him, for he was very drunk" (1 Sam. 25:36). Abigail waited until the next morning to tell him of the destruction and death that he almost brought upon his household. Immediately, Nabal's "heart died within

him, and he became like a stone" (1 Sam. 25:37). He died about ten days later.

When David heard that Nabal was dead, he proposed to Abigail; and she later became one of his wives. She is referred to as "Abigail the Carmelitess, Nabal's widow" (1 Sam. 27:3).

NABATEA [nab uh TEE ah]

An Arabic territory between the Dead Sea and the Gulf of Aqaba. Nebajoth, son of Ishmael and brother-in-law of Edom (Gen. 25:13; 28:9), may have been the ancestor of the Nabateans. Some time during the sixth century B.C. these peoples invaded the territory of the Edomites and Moabites. Their name first occurred in 646 B.C. when a people called the Nabaiate revolted against Ashurbanipal, king of Assyria. It took the Assyrians seven years to subdue these people.

In 312 B.C. Antigonus, one of the successors of Alexander the Great, sent an expedition against the Nabatean capital of Petra. This rose-red city was situated more than 50 miles (80 kilometers) south of the Dead Sea in the wilderness and surrounded by mountains. Petra had only one entrance, a narrow passageway sometimes as little as eight feet wide, between cliffs rising 200 to 300 feet (60 to 90 meters) above the road. The Greek army was unable to take the city.

At a later time the Nabateans took advantage of the turmoil of the Seleucid kingdom and extended their territory all the way to Damascus. During the first century B.C. they engaged in a war with the Maccabean King Alexander Jannaeus. An officer of the Nabatean King Aretas IV attempted to detain the apostle Paul at Damascus (2 Cor. 11:32). Eventually the Romans, under Trajan, annexed Nabatea, and it became the province of Arabia in A.D. 106.

The Nabateans controlled the desert highways south of the Dead Sea, demanding outrageous fees from caravans before they allowed them to pass. They developed an advanced civilization in the middle of the desert wilderness. Out of the red sandstone cliffs they carved beautiful obelisks, facades, and altars at which they worshiped pagan gods. They also developed a beautiful, thin pottery that was decorated with floral designs. With the rise of Palmyra, the trade that formerly passed through Petra was diverted; and the Nabateans were absorbed into the surrounding Arab population.

NABOPOLASSAR [nay boh puh LASS ur] *(may the god Nabu protect the son)*

A king of Babylon (626–605 B.C.) who founded the Chaldean dynasty. He was the father of Nebuchadnezzar II, the Babylonian king who defeated Jerusalem and carried the Jewish people into captivity (2 Kin. 25:1–7). Nabopolassar brought Babylon to greatness by defeating the Assyrians. Nebuchadnezzar continued his father's policies by capturing other surrounding nations.

NABOTH [NAY bahth]

An Israelite of Jezreel who owned a vineyard next to the summer palace of Ahab, king of Samaria (1 Kin. 21:1). Ahab coveted this property. He wanted to turn it into a vegetable garden to furnish delicacies for his table. He offered Naboth its worth in money or a better vineyard. But Naboth refused to part with his property, explaining that it was a family inheritance to be passed on to his descendants.

Jezebel obtained the property for Ahab by bribing two men to bear false witness against Naboth and testify that he blasphemed God and the king. Because of their lies, Naboth was found guilty; and both he and his sons (2 Kin. 9:26) were stoned to death. Elijah the prophet pronounced doom upon Ahab

and his house for this disgusting act of false witness (1 Kin. 21:1–29; 2 Kin. 9:21–26).

NADAB [NAY dab] *(liberal or willing)*

1. A son of Aaron and Elisheba (Ex. 6:23). Nadab is always mentioned in association with Abihu, Aaron's second son. Nadab was privileged to accompany Moses, Aaron, Abihu, and 70 elders of Israel as they ascended Mount Sinai to be near the Lord (Ex. 24:1–10). Along with his father and brothers—Abihu, Eleazar, and Ithamar—he was consecrated a priest to minister at the tabernacle (Ex. 28:1).

Later, Nadab and Abihu were guilty of offering "profane fire before the Lord" in the Wilderness of Sinai; and both died when "fire went out from the Lord and devoured them" (Lev. 10:1–2).

NADAB [NAY dab] *(liberal or willing)*

2. A king of Israel (about 910–909 B.C.). Nadab was the son and successor of Jeroboam I (1 Kin. 14:20; 15:25). About the only noteworthy event that happened during Nadab's reign was the siege of Gibbethon by the Israelites. During the siege, Nadab was assassinated by his successor, Baasha (1 Kin. 15:27–28).

NAHASH [NAY hash] *(serpent)*

A king of the Ammonites who besieged Jabesh Gilead and was defeated by Saul (1 Sam. 12:12). When Nahash's men surrounded the city, the inhabitants of Jabesh Gilead sought peace (1 Sam. 11:1). Nahash refused to accept the tribute tax and threatened to put out all their right eyes. He allowed the people of Jabesh Gilead one week to appeal for help from the rest of Israel; after that they were to surrender to him. When Saul, the newly proclaimed king of Israel, heard about this, he was enraged. He quickly assembled an army and defeated the Ammonites (1 Sam. 11:4–11).

NAHUM [NAY hum] *(compassionate)*

An Old Testament prophet and author of the Book of Nahum whose prophecy pronounced God's judgment against the mighty nation of Assyria. Very little is known about Nahum. His hometown, Elkosh in the nation of Israel (Nah. 1:1), has not been located. But he must have lived some time shortly before 612 B.C., the year when Assyria's capital city, Nineveh, was destroyed by the Babylonians. Nahum announced that the judgment of God would soon be visited upon this pagan city.

The Book of Nahum is similar to the Book of Obadiah, since both these prophecies were addressed against neighboring nations. Obadiah spoke the word of the Lord against Edom, while Nahum prophesied against Assyria. Both messages contained a word of hope for God's covenant people, since they announced that Israel's enemies would soon be overthrown.

While little is known about Nahum the man, his prophetic writing is one of the most colorful in the Old Testament. The Book of Nahum is marked by strong imagery, a sense of suspense, and vivid language, with biting puns and deadly satire. Nahum was a man who understood God's goodness, but he could also describe the terror of the Lord against His enemies.

NAIN [nane] *(delightful)*

A town in southwestern Galilee where Jesus raised a widow's son from the dead (Luke 7:11–17). Nain was about 5 miles (8 kilometers) southeast of Nazareth on the northern edge of the Plain of Esdraelon. The present-day Arab village of Nein covers ruins of a much larger town.

NAOMI [nay OH mee] *(my joy)*

The mother-in-law of Ruth. After her husband and two sons died, Naomi returned to her home in Bethlehem, accompanied by Ruth. Naomi advised Ruth to work for a near kinsman, Boaz (Ruth 2:1), and to seek his favor. When Boaz and Ruth eventually married, they had a son, whom they named Obed. This child became the father of Jesse, the grandfather of David, and an ancestor of Jesus Christ (Ruth 4:21–22; Matt. 1:5).

NAPHTALI [NAF tuh lie] *(my wrestling)*

The sixth son of Jacob (Gen. 35:25). Because Jacob's wife Rachel was barren and her sister Leah had borne four sons to Jacob, Rachel was distraught. She gave her maidservant Bilhah to Jacob. Any offspring of this union were regarded as Rachel's. When Bilhah gave birth to Dan and Naphtali, Rachel was joyous. "With great wrestlings I have wrestled with my sister," she said, "and indeed I have prevailed" (Gen. 30:8). So she called his name Naphtali, which means "my wrestling."

NAPHTALI, TRIBE OF [NAF tuh lie]

The tribe that sprang from Naphtali and the territory it inhabited (Num. 1:15, 42–43). The tribe's four great families were descendants of Naphtali's four sons: Jahzeel, Guni, Jezer, and Shillem or Shallum (Num. 26:48–49). The first wilderness census numbered the tribe of Naphtali at 53,000 fighting men (Num. 2:29–30); the second census put it at 45,400 (Num. 26:50).

Along with Asher, Naphtali was the northernmost tribe of Israel, occupying a long, narrow piece of land—about 50 miles (80 kilometers) north to south and 10 to 15 miles (16 to 24 kilometers) from east to west. Naphtali was mountainous (Josh. 20:7) and very fertile. Fortified cities within the tribe's boundaries included Ramah, Hazor, Kedesh, Iron, and Beth Anath (Josh. 19:36–38). The three cities given to the Levites in Naphtali were Kedesh (a city of refuge), Hammoth Dor, and Kartan (Josh. 21:32).

The tribe of Naphtali did not drive out all the Canaanites, but it did receive tribute from them. Members of the tribe of Naphtali fought bravely under Deborah and Barak (Judg. 4:6, 10; 5:18) and responded to Gideon's call (Judg. 6:35; 7:23). When Saul's son Ishbosheth challenged David for the throne, 37,000 fighting men of Naphtali, led by 1,000 captains, joined David (1 Chr. 12:34).

A part of the northern kingdom after the Israelites divided into two kingdoms, Naphtali was ravaged by the Syrian king Ben-Hadad (1 Kin. 15:20). The Assyrian king Tiglath-Pileser III carried many from Naphtali into captivity (2 Kin. 15:29). Isaiah prophesied that one day the land of Naphtali, "in Galilee of the Gentiles," would see a great light (Is. 9:1–7).

Indeed, Jesus made the cities of Chorazin, Capernaum, and Tiberias—all situated within the former territory of Naphtali—a focal point of His ministry: "And leaving Nazareth, He came and dwelt in Capernaum, which is by the sea, in the regions of Zebulun and Naphtali" (Matt. 4:12–16).

NATHAN [NAY thun] *(he gave)*

A prophet during the reign of David and Solomon. Nathan told David that he would not be the one to build the temple (1 Chr. 17:1–15). Using the parable of the "one little ewe lamb," Nathan confronted David ("You are the man!") with his double sin, the murder of Uriah the Hittite and his adultery with Bathsheba, Uriah's wife (2 Sam. 12:1–15). Nathan, as the Lord's official prophet, named Solomon Jedidiah, which means "Beloved of the Lord" (2 Sam. 12:25). Nathan was also involved in David's arrangement of the musical services of the sanctuary (2 Chr. 29:25).

When David was near death, Nathan advised Bathsheba to tell David of the plans of David's son Adonijah to take the throne. Bathsheba related the news to David, who ordered that Solomon be proclaimed king (1 Kin. 1:8–45). Nathan apparently wrote a history of David's reign (1 Chr. 29:29) and a history of Solomon's reign (2 Chr. 9:29).

NATHANAEL [nuh THAN ih el] *(God has given)*

A native of Cana in Galilee (John 21:2) who became a disciple of Jesus (John 1:45–49). Nathanael was introduced to Jesus by his friend Philip, who claimed Jesus was the Messiah. This claim troubled Nathanael. He knew that Nazareth, the town where Jesus grew up, was not mentioned in the Old Testament prophecies. He considered Nazareth an insignificant town, hardly the place where one would look to find the Redeemer of Israel. "Can anything good come out of Nazareth?" he asked. Philip did not argue with him, but simply said, "Come and see." After Nathanael met Jesus, he acknowledged Him to be the Messiah, calling Him "the Son of God" and "the King of Israel" (John 1:46, 49).

Nathanael was one of those privileged to speak face to face with Jesus after His resurrection (John 21:1–14). Some scholars see Nathanael as a type, or symbol, of a true Israelite—"an Israelite indeed" (John 1:47)—who accepts Jesus as Lord and Savior by faith. Nathanael is probably the same person as Bartholomew (Matt. 10:3), one of the twelve apostles of Christ.

NAZARETH [NAZ ah reth] *(watchtower)*

A town of lower Galilee where Jesus spent His boyhood years (Matt. 2:23). For centuries Nazareth has been a beautifully secluded town nestled in the southernmost hills of the Lebanon Mountain range. Situated in the territory belonging to Zebulun, the city must have been of late origin or of minor importance. It is never mentioned in the Old Testament.

Nazareth lay close to the important trade routes of Palestine. It overlooked the Plain of Esdraelon through which caravans passed as they traveled from Gilead to the south and west. North of the city was the main road from Ptolemais to the Decapolis, a road over which the Roman legions frequently traveled. This fact may account for the possible source of the name Nazareth in the Aramaic word meaning "watchtower."

However, Nazareth itself was situated in something of a basin, a high valley about 1,200 feet (366 meters) above sea level overlooking the Esdraelon valley. To the north and east were steep hills, while on the west the hills rose to an impressive 1,600 feet (488 meters). Nazareth, therefore, was somewhat secluded and isolated from nearby traffic.

This apparent isolation of Nazareth as a frontier town on the southern border of Zebulun contributed to the reputation that Nazareth was not an important part of the national and religious life of Israel. This, coupled with a rather bad reputation in morals and religion and a certain crudeness in the Galilean dialect, prompted Nathanael, when he first learned of Jesus of Nazareth, to ask, "Can anything good come out of Nazareth?" (John 1:46).

Although it was not an important town before the New Testament era, Nazareth became immortal as the hometown of Jesus the Messiah. It was here that the angel appeared to Mary and informed her of the forthcoming birth of Christ (Luke 1:26–38). Jesus was born in Bethlehem (Luke 2). But after their sojourn in Egypt (Matt. 2:19–22) to escape the ruthless murders of Herod the Great (Matt. 2:13–18), Joseph and Mary brought the baby Jesus to Nazareth, where they had

NATHANAEL

lived (Matt. 2:23). Here Jesus was brought up as a boy (Luke 4:16) and spent the greater part of His life (Mark 1:9; Luke 3:23). Apparently Jesus was well received as a young man in Nazareth (Luke 2:42; 4:16). But this changed after He began His ministry. His own townspeople twice rejected Him (Mark 6:1–6; Luke 4:28–30).

Because of His close association with this city, Christ became known as "Jesus of Nazareth" (Luke 18:37; 24:19; John 1:45). There is prophetic significance as well to His being known as a "Nazarene." Matthew records that Joseph and Mary returned to their city during the reign of Herod Archelaus (ethnarch of Judea, Idumea, and Samaria, 4 B.C.-A.D. 6) "that it might be fulfilled which was spoken by the prophets, 'He shall be called a Nazarene'" (Matt. 2:23).

NAZIRITE [NAZZ uh right] *(separated, consecrated)*

A person who took a vow to separate from certain worldly things and to consecrate himself to God (Num. 6:1–8). Among the Hebrew people anyone could take this vow; there were no tribal restrictions as in the case of the priest. Rich or poor, man or woman, master or slave—all were free to become Nazirites.

Nazirites did not withdraw from society and live as hermits; however, they did agree to follow certain regulations for a specified period of time. While no number of days for the vow is given in the Old Testament, Jewish tradition prescribed 30 days or a double period of 60 or even triple time of 90 to 100 days.

Samson, Samuel, and John the Baptist were the only "Nazirites for life" recorded in the Bible. Before they were born, their vows were taken for them by their parents.

Once a person decided to make himself "holy to the Lord" (Num. 6:8) for some special service, he then agreed to abstain from wine. This prohibition was so strict that it included grapes, grape juice, and raisins. Perhaps this was to guard the Nazirite from being controlled by any spirit other than God's (Prov. 20:1; Eph. 5:17–18).

While under the Nazirite vow, a person also refused to cut his hair, including shaving (Num. 6:5). The purpose of this long hair was to serve as a visible sign of the Nazirite's consecration to the Lord (Num. 6:7).

A Nazirite also refused to touch or go near a dead body because this would make him ceremonially unclean. The Nazirite could not even help to bury his own relatives.

If a person accidentally broke his Nazirite vow, he had to undergo a ceremony of restoration for cleansing (Num. 6:9–12). He shaved his head, brought two turtledoves or two pigeons to the priest for offerings, and the priest made atonement for him. In addition, a Nazirite had to present a lamb for a trespass offering. It was as if he were starting all over again and the days already served under the vow did not count.

When the specified period of time was completed, the Nazirite could appear before the priest for the ceremony of release (Num. 6:13–21). After offering a male lamb for a burnt offering, he would then offer a ewe lamb for a sin offering. This was followed by a ram to be used as the peace offering. Next came the usual items for peace offerings (Num. 6:15). The prescribed sacrifices were completed with a meal offering and a drink offering. When the person cut off his hair and burned it on the altar, he was fully released from the vow.

The strong man of the Bible, Samson, was a Nazirite (Judg. 13:7; 16:17). His parents were told by an angel before his birth that he would "be a Nazirite to God from the womb to the day of his death" (Judg. 13:7).

While Samuel is not specifically called

a Nazirite, 1 Samuel 1:11, 28 hints that he probably was. His mother, Hannah, made a vow before his birth: "No razor shall come upon his head" (1 Sam. 1:11). Samuel was probably a "Nazirite for life" like Samson and John the Baptist. John's refusal to drink wine (Matt. 11:18–19) is an indication that he was a Nazirite. His manner of living also indicates this probability (Luke 1:15).

The presence of many Nazirites was considered a sign of God's blessings on Israel. There were many Nazirites during the time of the prophet Amos. Amos strongly condemned the people for tempting the Nazirites to break their vows by offering them wine to drink (Amos 2:11–12).

The Nazirite vow was a part of the old law and is not imposed on modern Christians. But because it was personal and voluntary, we do have much to learn from this Old Testament practice. God wants us to live a separated, holy life and to abstain from things of the world. Christians must be dedicated to God's service not just for 30 days or one year but for a lifetime.

NEAPOLIS [nee AP oh lus] (new city)

A seaport in northeastern Macedonia near the border of Thrace that served as the port city of Philippi. On his second missionary journey, the apostle Paul landed at Neapolis as he traveled from Troas and Samothrace to Philippi (Acts 16:11). Paul may have visited this city again on his second tour of Macedonia (Acts 20:1–2).

NEBO, MOUNT [NEE boe]

A mountain of the Abarim range in Moab opposite Jericho (Num. 33:47). From Nebo Moses was permitted to view the Promised Land. He was buried in a nearby valley (Deut. 32:49, 50; 34:6).

NEBUCHADNEZZAR [neb you kad NEZ ur] (O god Nabu, protect my son)

The king of the Neo-Babylonian Empire (ruled 605–562 B.C.) who captured Jerusalem, destroyed the temple, and carried the people of Judah into captivity in Babylonia. He plays a prominent role in the books of Jeremiah (21-52) and Daniel (1:1–5:18) and also appears in 2 Kings (24:1–25:22), Ezra (1:7–6:5), and Ezekiel (26:7–30:10).

Nebuchadnezzar II was the oldest son of Nabopolassar, the founder of the Neo-Babylonian, or Chaldean, dynasty of Babylon. Nabopolassar apparently was a general appointed by the Assyrian king. But in the later years of Assyria he rebelled and established himself as king of Babylon in 626 B.C. Nebuchadnezzar succeeded his father as king in 605 B.C., continuing his policies of conquest of surrounding nations.

In about 602 B.C., after being Nebuchadnezzar's vassal for three years, King Jehoiakim of the nation of Judah rebelled against the Babylonians. Nebuchadnezzar then "came up against him and bound him in bronze fetters to carry him off to Babylon" (2 Chr. 36:6). Apparently, however, Nebuchadnezzar's intention of carrying him to Babylon was abandoned; according to Jeremiah, Jehoiakim was "dragged and cast out beyond the gates of Jerusalem" and "buried with the burial of a donkey" (Jer. 22:19). After reigning for 11 years, Jehoiakim was succeeded by his son Jehoiachin.

Jehoiachin was only eight years old when he became king, and he reigned in Jerusalem about three months (2 Chr. 36:9). At that time Nebuchadnezzar took Jehoiachin captive to Babylon along with the prophet Ezekiel and "costly articles from the house of the Lord" (2 Chr. 36:10). He made Mattaniah, Jehoiachin's uncle (2 Kin. 24:17), king over Judah and Jerusalem, changing his name to Zedekiah.

For about eight years Zedekiah endured the Babylonian yoke and paid tribute to Nebuchadnezzar. In 589 B.C., however, in the ninth year of his reign, Zedekiah rebelled against the king of Babylon, perhaps trusting in the Egyptian promises of military aid. Nebuchadnezzar and his army came against Jerusalem and besieged the city for about two years (2 Kin. 25:2). The siege may have been temporarily lifted with the approach of the Egyptian army (Jer. 37:5).

In 586 B.C. Jerusalem fell to the army of Nebuchadnezzar. Under cover of darkness, Zedekiah and many of his men fled through a break in the city wall. But they were overtaken by the Chaldeans in the plains of Jericho and brought captive to Riblah, a city in the land of Hamath where Nebuchadnezzar was camped. Nebuchadnezzar ordered that the sons of Zedekiah be killed before his eyes. Then Zedekiah was bound and taken captive to Babylon, along with the leading citizens of Jerusalem (2 Kin. 25:1–7).

Nebuchadnezzar's policy of resettling conquered peoples and transporting them to other provinces of his empire provided him with slave labor for conducting his extensive building projects. He rebuilt many sanctuaries, including the temple of Nebo at Borsippa and the great temple of Marduk at Babylon. He accomplished an immense fortification of Babylon, including the building of its great wall.

Although the famous "hanging gardens" cannot be identified among the impressive ruins of Babylon, this fabulous construction project—one of the "seven wonders of the ancient world"— was built by Nebuchadnezzar on the plains of Babylon to cheer his wife, who was homesick for her native Median hills. Nebuchadnezzar also built a huge reservoir near Sippar, providing interconnecting canals in an elaborate irrigation system.

Nebuchadnezzar made an arrogant boast about all that he achieved (Dan. 4:30). But he was stricken at the height of his power and pride by God's judgment. Nebuchadnezzar was temporarily driven out of office, living with the beasts of the field and eating grass like an ox (Dan. 4:32). Later, he was succeeded as king by his son, Evil-Merodach.

NEBUZARADAN [neb you zar AY dan]
(the god Nabu has given offspring)

The captain of Nebuchadnezzar's bodyguard who played an important part in the destruction of Jerusalem in 586 B.C. An important Babylonian official, Nebuzaradan may have been second in command to Nebuchadnezzar himself. When Jerusalem fell to the Babylonians, Nebuzaradan came to the city (2 Kin. 25:1, 8) and took charge of destroying it. He commanded the troops who burned the temple, the palace, and all the houses of Jerusalem and tore down the walls of the city. He also was in charge of deporting the Israelites to Babylonia (2 Kin. 25:9–11).

After the fall of Jerusalem, Nebuchadnezzar told Nebuzaradan to take good care of the prophet Jeremiah (Jer. 39:11). Nebuzaradan showed kindness to Jeremiah and gave him the choice of remaining in Jerusalem or going to Babylon (Jer. 40:1–4).

NECHO [NEE koe]

A pharaoh of Egypt who defeated Josiah in the Valley of Megiddo (609 B.C.). Pharaoh Necho II was himself defeated by Nebuchadnezzar, king of Babylon, in the battle of Carchemish (605 B.C.; 2 Chr. 35:20, 22). Variant spellings of this name in different passages and translations of the Bible include Neco, Necoh, and Nechoh.

NECKLACE

An ornament worn around the neck in Bible times. Necklaces were very popular throughout the ancient world. They frequently appear on monuments and paintings and many have been discovered by archaeologists. Moon-shaped or crescent-shaped pendants were worn around camels' necks, perhaps as amulets of the goddess Astarte. Many necklaces worn by people were probably amulets or charms as well. Necklaces were made of precious metals and strings of jewels (Song 1:10; Ezek. 16:11). Gold chains were worn by people of high rank (Gen. 41:42; Dan. 5:17; 5:29).

NEEDLE

The Old Testament has many references to needlework or embroidery, particularly the woven linen used in the tabernacle hangings (Ex. 26:1–13) and the fine clothes of wealthy Israelites (Ezek. 16:10–18; 27:7, 16, 24). Needles must have been used also for sewing and repairing family clothing (Gen. 3:7; Job 16:15; Eccl. 3:7; Ezek. 13:18). Needles found in numerous archaeological excavations are made of bone, bronze, or iron. They are of various sizes, from very fine to the size of large darning needles. Their shape is similar to the common needles of today.

Jesus' words in Matthew 19:24 (also Mark 10:25; Luke 18:25), that it is easier for a rich man to enter heaven than "for a camel to go through the eye of a needle," reflect an idea found in early rabbinic writing. There is no archaeological or historical support for the common idea that the "needle's eye" was a small pedestrian gate through the city wall. The statement simply means that humanly speaking, this is an impossible thing. Only a divine miracle can make it possible.

NEGEV, THE [NEG ev] (dry, parched)

A term used by some English translations of the Bible for the southern desert or wilderness area of Judah, including about 4,500 square miles. Abraham journeyed in the Negev (Gen. 12:9; 13:1, 3; the South, NKJV). When the 12 spies explored the land of Canaan, they went up by way of the Negev (Num. 13:17, 22) and saw the Amalekites who lived there (Num. 13:29). The Canaanite king of Arad also lived in the Negev (Num. 21:1).

The prophet Isaiah described the Negev as a land of trouble and anguish, hardship and distress—a badland populated by lions and poisonous snakes (Is. 30:6). Through its arid wastes donkey and camel caravans made their way to and from the land of Egypt. Negev is also spelled Negeb.

The Negev contained important copper deposits, and it connected Israel to trade centers in Arabia and Egypt. King Solomon built fortresses in the Negev to guard the trade routes. He also established at Ezion Geber, on the Gulf of Aqaba, a port from which he shipped goods to foreign lands. King Uzziah made great efforts to develop the region, building fortresses and expanding agriculture (2 Chr. 26:10).

In modern times, the desert is being made to "blossom as the rose" (Is. 35:1); the Israelis have built an impressive irrigation system that channels life-giving water from northern Galilee to the dry, parched region of the Negev.

NEHEMIAH [knee uh MY ah] (the Lord is consolation)

The governor of Jerusalem who helped rebuild the wall of the city (Neh. 1:1; 8:9; 10:1; 12:26, 47). Nehemiah was a descendant of the Jewish population that had been taken captive to Babylon in 586 B.C. In 539 B.C. Cyrus the Persian gained control over all of Mesopotamia. He permitted the Jewish exiles to return to the city of Jerusalem. Nearly a century later, in Nehemiah's time, the Persian ruler was Artaxerxes I Longimanus (ruled 465–424 B.C.). Nehemiah was his personal cupbearer (Neh. 1:11).

In 445 B.C. Nehemiah learned of the deplorable condition of the returned exiles in Jerusalem (Neh. 1:2–3). The wall of the city was broken down, the gates were burned, and the people were in distress. Upon hearing this, Nehemiah mourned for many days, fasting and praying to God. His prayer is one of the most moving in the Old Testament (Neh. 1:5–11).

Nehemiah then received permission from Artaxerxes to go to Judah to restore the fortunes of his people. He was appointed governor of the province with authority to rebuild the city walls.

Once in Jerusalem, Nehemiah surveyed the walls at night (Neh. 2:12–15). He gave his assessment of the city's condition to the leaders and officials and then organized a labor force to begin the work.

Nehemiah and his work crew were harassed by three enemies: Sanballat the Horonite (a Samaritan), Tobiah the Ammonite official, and Geshem the Arab (Neh. 2:10, 19; 6:1–14). But neither their ridicule (Neh. 4:3) nor their conspiracy to harm Nehemiah (Neh. 6:2) could stop the project. The builders worked with construction tools in one hand and weapons in the other (Neh. 4:17). To the taunts of his enemies, Nehemiah replied: "I am doing a great work, so that I cannot come down" (Neh. 6:3). Jerusalem's wall was finished in 52 days (Neh. 6:14)—a marvelous accomplishment for such a great task. Nehemiah's success stems from the fact that he kept praying, "O God, strengthen my hands" (Neh. 6:9).

Nehemiah's activities did not stop with the completion of the wall. He also led

many social and political reforms among the people, including a return to pure worship and a renewed emphasis on true religion.

NEPHILIM [NEFF ih lem] *(fallen ones)*

The offspring of marriages between the "sons of God" and the "daughters of men" (Gen. 6:4). The word "Nephilim" is translated as "giants" by the KJV and NKJV (Gen. 6:4; Num. 13:33; Nephilim in NIV, REB, NASB, NRSV). Some scholars believe the Nephilim were descended from famous rulers, outstanding leaders, and mighty warriors who lived before the Flood. These men, so the theory goes, gathered great harems and were guilty of the sin of polygamy. The Nephilim were the product of these marriages.

NERO [NEE row]

The fifth emperor of Rome (ruled A.D. 54–68), known for his persecution of Christians. Nero began his reign with the promise that he would return to the policies of the great emperor Augustus. For several years he succeeded, thanks mainly to the guidance of Burrus and Seneca, two of his advisors. Under his reign Rome extended its borders, solidified certain territories of the Roman Empire, and incorporated some good qualities of Greek culture.

Nero had considerable artistic interests. He wanted to change the image of Rome from a violent society to one that was more humane. The Romans, however, despised his love for the Greek way of life. His extravagance, coupled with poor management, brought on heavy taxation, depreciation of the Roman currency, and the confiscation of large landholdings by the state.

Nero's personal life was filled with tragedy. His mother, Agrippina, and Octavia, his legal wife, were murdered. Many of his advisors and officials were either killed or exiled. Tension became so great that by A.D. 68, after several attempted conspiracies, the Praetorian guard revolted and Nero was forced to flee Rome. In that same year, at the age of 30, he took his own life.

Many of Nero's cruelties are linked to the time of the great fire in Rome (A.D. 64). Nero was accused of setting fire to the city in order to divert attention from himself, but this has never been proven with certainty. The Christians, however, were made the scapegoats for this arson. Many of them, possibly even Peter and Paul, lost their lives.

Nero became a kind of apocalyptic figure, a person associated with the end times. Rumors persisted that he was alive and would some day return and reign again. Some interpreters of Scripture believe that Nero is the beast from the sea whose "deadly wound was healed" (Rev. 13:3, 12). Some Bible students have found in the mysterious number 666 (Rev. 13:18), when decoded, the name Nero Caesar. Possible references to Nero in the New Testament include Acts 25:11–12; 26:32; and Philippians 4:22.

NETHINIM [NEHTH uh neam]

A group of people of non-Jewish background who served as temple servants in Old Testament times. As assistants to the Levites, they performed such menial chores as cleaning the temple, carrying water and wood to the altar, and scrubbing utensils used in the sacrificial ceremonies. Some of the Nethinim returned to Jerusalem with Ezra after the captivity (Ezra 7:7).

NEW BIRTH

Inner spiritual renewal as a result of the power of God in a person's life. The phrase "new birth" comes from John 3:3, 7, where Jesus told Nicodemus, "Unless one is born again, he cannot see the kingdom of God." Jesus meant that all people are so sinful in God's eyes that

they need to be regenerated—recreated and renewed—by the sovereign activity of God's Spirit (John 3:5–8).

The activity of God's Spirit that regenerates sinful people comes about through faith in Jesus Christ (John 3:10–21). Without faith there is no regeneration, and without regeneration a person does not have eternal life. Regeneration occurs at the moment a person exercises faith in Christ. At that point, his sins are forgiven and he is born again by the power of the Holy Spirit working on behalf of Christ. The new birth is a decisive, unrepeatable, and irrevocable act of God.

NEW YEAR

A solemn occasion that occurred in the month of Tishri or Ethanim (1 Kin. 8:2), the first month in the Hebrew year. The Law of Moses directed that this holiday should be observed by "blowing the trumpets" (Num. 29:1). Thus, this festival is also known as the Feast of Trumpets. Today this event is known as Rosh Hashanah (literally, beginning of the year), a Jewish high holy day that marks the beginning of the Jewish new year.

NICODEMUS [nick oh DEE mus]
(conqueror of the people)

A Pharisee and a member of the Sanhedrin who probably became a disciple of Jesus (John 3:1, 4, 9; 7:50). He was described by Jesus as "the teacher of Israel," implying he was well trained in Old Testament law and tradition.

Nicodemus was a wealthy, educated, and powerful man—well respected by his people and a descendant of the patriarch Abraham. Yet Jesus said to him, "You must be born again" (John 3:7). The Greek adverb translated "again" can also mean "from the beginning" (suggesting a new creation) and "from above" (that is, from God). In other words, Jesus told Nicodemus that physical generation was not enough, nor could his descent from the line of Abraham enable him to be saved. Only as a person has a spiritual generation—a birth from above—will he be able to see the kingdom of God.

The next time Nicodemus appears in the Gospel of John, he shows a cautious, guarded sympathy with Jesus. When the Sanhedrin began to denounce Jesus as a false prophet, Nicodemus counseled the court by saying, "Does our law judge a man before it hears him and knows what he is doing?" (John 7:51).

Nicodemus appears a third and final time in the Gospel of John. Obviously a wealthy man, he purchased about a hundred pounds of spices to be placed between the folds of the cloth in which Jesus was buried (John 19:39). Nothing else is known of Nicodemus from the Bible. But there is reason to believe that he became a follower of Jesus.

Christian tradition has it that Nicodemus was baptized by Peter and John, suffered persecution from hostile Jews, lost his membership in the Sanhedrin, and was forced to leave Jerusalem because of his Christian faith. Further mention is made of him in The Gospel of Nicodemus, an apocryphal narrative of the crucifixion and resurrection of Christ.

NICOLAITANS [nick oh LAY ih tuns]

An early Christian heretical sect made up of followers of Nicolas, who was possibly the deacon of Acts 6:5. The group is mentioned explicitly only in Revelation 2:6, 14–15, where it is equated with a group holding "the doctrine of Balaam," who taught Israel "to eat things sacrificed to idols, and to commit sexual immorality."

Balaam probably was responsible for the cohabitation of the men of Israel with the women of Moab (Num. 25:1–2; 31:16). Therefore, the error of this group was moral rather than doctrinal. If the "Jeze-

bel" of Revelation 2:20–23 was a teacher of this sect, as many believe, their sexual laxity was indeed strong. Most likely, they were a group of anti-law practitioners who supported a freedom that became self-indulgence. It may have been the same heresy condemned in 2 Peter 2:15 and Jude 11. Some early church leaders believed the Nicolaitans later became a Gnostic sect.

NICOPOLIS [nih COP oh liss] *(city of victory)*

A city in which the apostle Paul decided to spend the winter (Titus 3:12). Many cities in the first-century world were named Nicopolis. Most scholars believe the city of which Paul spoke was the Nicopolis in Epirus, a province in northwestern Greece. It was on the Adriatic Sea, about 4 miles (6 kilometers) north of Actium.

NILE RIVER [nile]

The great river of Egypt that flows more than 3,500 miles (5,700 kilometers) from central Africa north through the desert to a rich delta area on the Mediterranean Sea. The source of the Nile is derived from two rivers: the Blue Nile from Ethiopia and the White Nile from Lake Victoria in central Africa.

The Blue Nile provides about twice as much water as the White Nile during the rainy season. This flood water, with the soil that it eroded, provided fertile topsoil for the agriculture of northern Egypt. Low flood levels usually meant a famine year, while a high flood level would result in a year of plenty. The Aswan Dam and the High Dam now enable the modern nation of Egypt to control these floods and provide a more constant flow of water.

Because the Nile was so essential to the life and prosperity of Egypt, it was personified as a god called Hapi. Egyptians had religious celebrations at the beginning of the annual flooding of the Nile. One text discovered by archaeologists contains praises in adoration of the Nile for the blessings that it provides.

The river was also one of the chief methods of transportation for the Egyptians. The Nile delta produced papyrus, which the Egyptians wove together to make household mats, baskets, sails for their boats, and paper. The Nile supported a fishing industry as well, and ancient drawings show the pharaohs hunting wild game in the thick undergrowth of the Nile Valley.

The river in Pharaoh's dream (Gen. 41:1–36) was the Nile. The seven fat cows that pastured in the lush grass by the Nile represented seven years when the Nile would flood and there would be plenty of food. The seven thin cows represented years when there would be little grass because of low flood waters.

Later when the Israelites were slaves under persecution by a pharaoh who did not know Joseph, the king ordered that all male children born to the Israelites must be thrown into the Nile (Ex. 1:22). In an attempt to save her child, Moses' mother put him in a waterproofed papyrus basket and placed him among the papyrus reeds near where Pharaoh's daughter came to bathe (Ex. 2:1–5). When she saw the child, she had compassion on him; thus Moses was not killed.

Eighty years later Moses returned to Egypt to deliver the Israelites from

NILE RIVER

slavery. In order that the children of Israel might believe that God had sent Moses, God gave him three signs to perform; the last was to pour water from the Nile on dry ground and have it turn to blood (Ex. 4:9). After hearing God's word and seeing these signs, the people believed God and worshiped Him (Ex. 4:29–31).

Because Pharaoh refused to let the Israelites leave Egypt, God sent ten plagues. Moses met Pharaoh at the Nile (Ex. 7:15) and turned the Nile to blood to prove to him that the Nile was not a god, but that Moses' God was the true God (Ex. 7:17–21; Ps. 78:44). Some believe the water was turned to a reddish-brown color from the eroded red soil in the flood water and that bacteria from the polluted water may have killed the fish. This naturalistic interpretation does not explain the intensity of the plague or the ability of Moses to start and conclude the plague on command. Since Pharaoh's magicians were able to reproduce a somewhat similar phenomenon, Pharaoh's heart was not moved to release the Israelites (Ex. 7:22–25).

The prosperity that the river provided and the annual flooding of the Nile were spoken of symbolically in the prophetic writings (Is. 23:10; Jer. 46:7–8). The judgment on Egypt was often described in terms of the drying up of the Nile (Ezek. 29:10; 30:12; Zech. 10:11), because the Nile will fail, the papyrus will wither, the grain will wilt, and the fishermen will mourn (Is. 19:5–8). Yet in spite of this judgment, the day will come when some from Egypt will turn to God and become His people (Is. 19:18–25).

NIMROD [NIM rahd]

A son of Cush and grandson of Ham, the youngest son of Noah (Gen. 10:8–12; 1 Chr. 1:10). Nimrod was a "mighty one on the earth"—a skilled hunter-warrior who became a powerful king. He is the first mighty hero mentioned in the Bible.

The principal cities of Nimrod's Mesopotamian kingdom were "Babel, Erech, Accad, and Calneh, in the land of Shinar" (Gen. 10:10). From the land of Babylon he went to Assyria, where he built Nineveh and other cities (Gen. 10:11). In Micah 5:6 Assyria is called "the land of Nimrod."

The origin and meaning of the name Nimrod is uncertain, but it is doubtful that it is Hebrew. It may be Mesopotamian, originating from the Akkadian (northern Babylonian) god of war and hunting, Ninurta, who was called "the Arrow, the mighty hero."

Some scholars believe Nimrod was Sargon the Great, a powerful ruler over Accad who lived about 2400 B.C. Others think he was the Assyrian king Tukulti-Ninurta I (about 1246–1206 B.C.), who conquered Babylonia. However, if Nimrod was indeed a Cushite, he may have been the Egyptian monarch Amenophis III (1411–1375 B.C.).

Nimrod was more likely Assyrian. His fierce aggressiveness, seen in the combination of warlike prowess and the passion for the chase, makes him a perfect example of the warrior-kings of Assyria.

NINEVEH [NIN eh vuh]

Ancient capital city of the Assyrian Empire, a place associated with the ministry of the prophet Jonah. The residents of this pagan city repented and turned to God after Jonah's preaching of a clear message of God's judgment (Jon. 3:5–10).

Founded by Nimrod (Gen. 10:8–10), Nineveh was the capital of the great Assyrian Empire for many years. Its fortunes rose and fell as Babylonia and Assyria struggled with each other for the dominant position in the ancient world. During some periods Babylonia was stronger, while the Assyrians gained the upper hand at other times.

In 612 B.C. Nineveh was destroyed, as prophesied by the Hebrew prophets, especially Nahum. Many scholars questioned the existence of Nineveh until its discovery by A. H. Layard and H. Rassam in 1845–1854. The site has now been excavated thoroughly. Occupational levels on the site go back to prehistoric times, before 3100 B.C. Some of the pottery indicates the city may have originated with the Sumerians.

One of the exciting discoveries in this excavation was the great palace of the Assyrian King Sargon. Along with this find was a library of Cuneiform documents and many striking wall ornamentations. This clear evidence of Sargon's existence verifies the accuracy of the Book of Isaiah in the prophet's mention of this pagan king (Is. 20:1).

The wall around the city indicated that Nineveh was about 3 miles (2 kilometers) long and less than half that distance wide. The Hebrews, however, perhaps like other foreigners, included other cities under the name of Nineveh.

An example from today would be our reference to New York, which is actually made up of a complex of many cities. Cities included in references to Nineveh were Calah, Resen, and Rehoboth-Ir.

At the time of the greatest prosperity of Nineveh as described by Jonah, the city was surrounded by a circuit wall almost 8 miles (13 kilometers) long. This "great city" (Jon. 1:2) would have had an area sufficient to contain a population of 120,000, as indicated by Jonah 4:11 and 3:2. Evidence for this is provided by Calah to the south, where 69,754 persons lived in a city half the size of Nineveh. As a result, it would have required a "three day's journey" to go around the city, and a "day's journey" would have been needed to reach the city center from the outlying suburbs, just as the Book of Jonah reports (Jon. 3:4).

Several centuries before Jonah's preaching mission to the city, Nineveh became one of the royal residences of Assyrian kings. Sennacherib (705–681 B.C.) made it the capital of the Assyrian Empire to offset the rival capital of Dur-Sharrukin (Khorsabad), built by his father Sargon II (722–705 B.C.). He greatly beautified and adorned Nineveh. The splendid temples, palaces, and fortifications made it the chief city of the empire (2 Kin. 19:36).

In Sennacherib's day the wall around Nineveh was 40 to 50 feet high. It extended for 2.5 miles (4 kilometers) along the Tigris River and for 8 miles (13 kilometers) around the inner city. The city wall had 15 main gates, 5 of which have been excavated. Each of the gates was guarded by stone bull statues. Both inside and outside the walls, Sennacherib created parks, a botanical garden, and a zoo. He built a water system containing the oldest aqueduct in history at Jerwan, across the Gomel River. To bring new water supplies to the city, he cut channels for 30 miles (20 kilometers) from the Gomel River at Bavian and built a dam at Ajeila to control the flooding of the Khosr river.

In the years 1849–1851 archaeologist A. Layard unearthed the 71-room palace of Sennacherib. The mound also yielded the royal palace and library of Ashurbanipal, which housed 22,000 inscribed clay tablets. These tablets included Assyrian creation and flood accounts that furnished Old Testament scholars with valuable information for background studies on the Book of Genesis.

It was to Nineveh that Sennacherib brought the tribute he exacted from King Hezekiah of Judah (2 Kin. 18:15). He also returned here after his campaign against

Jerusalem and Judah in 701 B.C. In 681 B.C. he was assassinated in the temple of Nisroch, which must have been situated within the city walls.

Esarhaddon, the younger son and successor to Sennacherib, recaptured Nineveh from rebels in 680 B.C. Here he built a palace for himself, although he spent much time in his other residence in Calah. One of his twin sons, Ashurbanipal, returned to live mainly at Nineveh where he had been crown prince during his school days. It was during his last days and the years of his sons Ahsur-etil-ilani and Sin-shar-ishkun that Assyria's vassals revolted.

At the same time the Medes, with the help of the Babylonians, sacked Ashur and Calah in 614 B.C. Two years later Nineveh fell to these combined forces. Nineveh was left in ruins (Nah. 2:10, 13) and grazed by sheep (Zeph. 2:13–15), just as the Hebrew prophets of the Old Testament had predicted.

Nineveh is such a large site that it will probably never be fully excavated. A modern village covers one of its larger palaces. A nearby mound, named "Mound of the Prophet Jonah," contains the palace of Esarhaddon. The popular tradition is that Jonah is buried beneath the mosque at Nebi Yunas.

NO/NO AMON [noe, NO a mahn]

The royal city of southern Egypt at modern Luxor, about 350 miles (565 kilometers) south of Cairo. Some modern versions translate Thebes (NASB, NIV, NRSV).

Thebes (or No) was of major importance from the time of Abraham about 2000 B.C. until it was sacked by the Assyrians in 663 B.C. Thebes not only was the capital of Egypt; it also served as the center of worship of the great Egyptian god Amon (Jer. 46:25) and as the place where many kings and queens were buried.

On the east bank of the Nile River the huge temple complexes at Karnak and Luxor where the Egyptians worshiped their gods can still be seen. On the west bank are temples that contain the tombs of pharaohs, queens, and noblemen. The most magnificent of all discoveries in this Valley of the Kings was the tomb of Tutankhamun (King Tut), a pharaoh who flourished about 1358 B.C.

Nahum prophesied that Nineveh, the capital of Assyria, would be destroyed by God, just as No Amon was pillaged by the Assyrians in 663 B.C. (Nah. 3:8). Later Jeremiah (46:25) and Ezekiel (30:14–16) predicted that Nebuchadnezzar, king of Babylon, would punish the king of Egypt, destroy the gods of Egypt, and bring further desolation to Thebes. This was proof that God had power over all nations and that their gods were powerless.

NOAH [NOE uh] (rest, relief)

A son of Lamech and the father of Shem, Ham, and Japheth. He was a hero of faith who obeyed God by building an ark (a giant boat), thus becoming God's instrument in saving mankind from total destruction by the Flood (Gen. 5:28–9:29). The line of descent from Adam to Noah was as follows: Adam, Seth, Enosh, Cainan, Mahalaleel, Jared, Enoch, Methuselah, Lamech, and Noah (Gen. 5:1–32). If this genealogy does not allow for any gaps, Noah was only nine generations removed from Adam; and his father, Lamech, was 56 years old at the time of Adam's death.

Noah lived at a time when the whole earth was filled with violence and corruption. Yet Noah did not allow the evil standards of his day to rob him of fellowship with God. He stood out as the only one who "walked with God" (Gen. 6:9), as was true of his great-grandfather Enoch (Gen. 5:22). Noah was a just or righteous man (Gen. 6:9). The Lord singled out Noah from among all his contemporaries and chose him as the man to accomplish a great work.

When God saw the wickedness that prevailed in the world (Gen. 6:5), He disclosed to Noah His intention to destroy the world by a flood. He instructed Noah to build an ark in which he and his family would survive the catastrophe. Noah believed God and obeyed Him and "according to all that God commanded him, so he did" (Gen. 6:22). He is therefore listed among the heroes of faith (Heb. 11:7).

With unswerving confidence in the word of God, Noah started building the ark. For 120 years the construction continued. During this time of grace, Noah continued to preach God's judgment and mercy, warning the ungodly of their approaching doom (2 Pet. 2:5). He preached for 120 years, however, without any converts (1 Pet. 3:20). People continued in their evil ways and turned deaf ears to his pleadings and warnings until they were overtaken by the Flood.

When the ark was ready, Noah entered in with all kinds of animals "and the Lord shut him in" (Gen. 7:16), cut off completely from the rest of mankind.

Noah was grateful to the Lord who had delivered him from the Flood. After the Flood he built an altar to God (Gen. 8:20) and made a sacrifice, which was accepted graciously (Gen. 8:21). The Lord promised Noah and his descendants that He would never destroy the world again with a flood (Gen. 9:15). The Lord made an everlasting covenant with Noah and his descendants, establishing the rainbow as the sign of His promise (Gen. 9:12–17). The Lord also blessed Noah and restored the creation command, "Be fruitful and multiply, and fill the earth" (Gen. 9:1). These were the same words He had spoken earlier to Adam (Gen. 1:28).

Noah became the first tiller of the soil and keeper of vineyards after the Flood. His drunkenness is a prelude to the curse that was soon to be invoked on Canaan and his descendants, the Canaanites (Gen. 9:18–27). The Bible is silent about the rest of Noah's life after the Flood, except to say that he died at the age of 950 years (Gen. 9:28–29).

In the gospels of the New Testament, the account of Noah and the Flood is used as a symbol of the end times. Warning His hearers about the suddenness of His return, Jesus referred to the sudden catastrophe that fell upon unbelievers at the time of the Flood: "As the days of Noah were, so also will the coming of the Son of Man be" (Matt. 24:37).

NOB [knob]

A town allotted to the priests (1 Sam. 22:19) in the territory of Benjamin (Neh. 11:32), about 2 miles (3 kilometers) northeast of Jerusalem, and apparently within sight of the Holy City (Is. 10:32). When David fled from King Saul, he went to Nob and obtained from Ahimelech the priest some showbread, or "holy bread," as provisions for his men (1 Sam. 21:1–9).

This incident was mentioned by Jesus when the Pharisees criticized His disciples for gathering grain to eat on the Sabbath (Matt. 12:1–8; Mark 2:23–28). It was not wrong, Jesus implied, for David and his men to eat the showbread, for they were hungry and in need.

A likely location of Nob is Mount Scopus, on the northern part of the Mount of Olives. The site is northeast of Jerusalem, overlooking the city. Three centuries after the time of David, the Assyrian army made its camp at Nob in preparation for an assault on Jerusalem. "As yet he will remain at Nob that day; he will shake his fist at the mount of the daughter of Zion" (Is. 10:32).

OAK

A large tree with a massive trunk that grew abundantly in Palestine and the surrounding countries. Many Hebrew words refer to the oak. Some scholars think these words could have referred to any large tree such as the terebinth or elm. The oak tree was an important historical landmark to the Hebrews. Some specific oak trees are mentioned in the Bible. These include the oaks of Bashan (Is. 2:13; Zech. 11:2), the oak of Bethel (Gen. 35:8, KJV; terebinth tree in NKJV), and the oaks of Mamre (Gen. 13:18, NRSV; terebinth trees in NKJV).

OATH

A solemn statement or claim used to validate a promise. In Bible times, oaths were sometimes accompanied by protective curses to make sure the oaths were kept (1 Sam. 14:24; Gen. 24:41). Such curses were also used to protect property rights from thieves (Judg. 17:2) or from those who found a stolen object or knew of a theft (Lev. 5:1).

An oath was used to seal treaties, insuring that neither party broke their promise (Gen. 26:28). Oaths were also used in Israel's treaty with God at Sinai (Deut. 27:11–28:68; 29:11–20). In the Bible oaths were sometimes taken lightly, as if all parties expected them to be broken (Hos. 10:4). In legal cases oaths were sometimes used to make a person admit guilt (1 Kin. 8:31–32). However, oaths were not to be used in wrongful accusations of people (Ex. 20:7; Job 31:30; Ps. 10:7; Hos. 4:2).

Sometimes people pronounced a curse upon themselves in connection with an oath which they had taken. David vowed not to eat until evening with these words: "God do so to me, and more also, if I taste bread or anything else till the sun goes down" (2 Sam. 3:35). This was a strong pledge on his part that he expected to keep his promise.

Oaths could be taken with symbolic gestures such as raising the hand (Gen. 14:22; Dan. 12:7; Rev. 10:5–6) or touching the sex organs (Gen. 24:2; 47:29), possibly symbolizing a person's life and power. Oaths were taken very seriously (Ex. 20:7; Lev. 19:12). Lying about an oath could result in death (Ezek. 17:16–18). Jesus himself was bound by an oath (Matt. 26:63–64), as was Paul (2 Cor. 1:23; Gal. 1:20). Even God bound Himself by oath to keep His promises to Abraham (Heb. 6:13–18).

OBADIAH [oh bah DIE ah] (servant of the Lord)

A prophet of Judah (Obad. 1). The fourth of the "minor" prophets, Obadiah's message was directed against Edom. Some scholars believe Obadiah was a contemporary of Jehoram, during whose reign (about 844 B.C.) Jerusalem was invaded by Philistines and Arabians (2 Chr. 21:16–17). Other scholars suggest a date following 586 B.C., the time of the destruction of Jerusalem by the Babylonians. Still others suggest an earlier Babylonian assault on Jerusalem, in 605 B.C.

Whatever date is assigned to Obadiah, he lived during a time of trouble for Jerusalem. His prophecy against Edom condemned the Edomites for taking sides against Jerusalem in its distress (Obad. 15). The strongest mountain fortresses would be no defense for the Edomites against the Day—the time when God would bring His final judgment upon the world.

OBED-EDOM [OH bed EE dum] (servant of Edom)

A Gittite, possibly a Levite from Gath Rimmon, a Levitical city in Dan (2 Sam. 6:10–12; 1 Chr. 13:13–14; 15:25). Some scholars believe, however, that the word

Gittite indicates he was a native of the Philistine city of Gath. If so, Obed-Edom was probably a member of David's bodyguard. David stored the ark of the covenant in the house of Obed-Edom for three months before moving it on to Jerusalem. During this time, Obed-Edom and all his household were blessed.

OBEDIENCE

Carrying out the word and will of another person, especially the will of God. In both the Old and New Testaments, the word *obey* is related to the idea of hearing. Obedience is a positive, active response to what a person hears. God summons people to active obedience to His revelation. In the Old Testament covenant between God and human beings, obedience was the basis for knowing God's blessing and favor (Ex. 24:1–8).

In the New Testament, the obedience of Christ stands in contrast to the disobedience of Adam. The disobedience of Adam brought death, but the perfect obedience of Christ brought grace, righteousness, and life (Rom. 5:12–21).

ODED [OH dead]

A prophet of Samaria during the reign of Pekah, king of Israel (2 Chr. 28:9). Pekah invaded Judah and defeated the army of Ahaz. Pekah then carried 200,000 captives to Samaria, the capital of the northern kingdom of Israel. As the victorious army drew near the city, Oded the prophet met them, urging a policy of mercy and forgiveness toward the Judahite captives. His request had a transforming effect on the Israelites, who fed and clothed the captives, brought them to Jericho, and gave them their freedom.

OG [ahg]

A king of the Amorites of the land of Bashan, a territory east of the Jordan River and north of the river Jabbok (Num. 21:33; 32:33). Og was king over 60 fortified cities, including Ashtaroth and Edrei. He was defeated by Moses and the Israelites (Deut. 3:6). Then his kingdom was given to the tribes of Reuben, Gad, and the half-tribe of Manasseh.

Og was the last survivor of the race of giants (Deut. 3:11). His huge iron bedstead was kept on display in Rabbah long after his death (Deut. 3:11).

OINTMENT

A perfumed oil, sometimes used in Bible times to anoint people as well as bodies for burial. The term *ointment* frequently means oil, particularly olive oil mixed with aromatic ingredients such as spices, myrrh, and extracts of the nard plant. Many of these ingredients were expensive, leading the prophet Amos to associate those who used "the best ointment" with a life of self-indulgence (Amos 6:6). The use of ointment originated with the Egyptians, and it eventually spread to neighboring nations, including Israel. Ointment was often imported from Phoenicia in small alabaster boxes that best preserved its aroma. Some of the better ointments were known to keep their distinctive scents for centuries.

Perfumed ointments were widely used in warm climates of the ancient world to combat perspiration odor. Ointment had a cosmetic use among the Greeks, Romans, Egyptians, and probably the Jews. It was customary to anoint the head and clothing on festive occasions; and ointment containing myrrh was used to anoint the dead before burial (Luke 23:56). In ancient times, as today, ointment was also used to soothe wounds and bruises.

Ointments, or perfumed oil, are often mentioned in the Bible for both their practical and ceremonial uses. God instructed Moses to compound a "holy anointing oil" composed of pure myrrh, sweet cinnamon, sweet calamus, cassia, and olive oil (Ex. 30:25). The vessels in the tabernacle were anointed with this holy ointment. It was also used to consecrate Aaron and his sons to the priesthood (Ex. 26–30). Ointments were also used by the Hebrew prophets to anoint new kings (2 Kin. 9:3). It was also used in anointing the sick (James 5:14) and in preparing bodies for burial (Mark 14:8; Luke 23:56).

Jesus was deeply touched by people who anointed Him with perfumed ointment. He seemed to accept these deeds as acts of worship (Matt. 26:6–13; Luke 7:36–50; John 12:1–8). At the home of Simon the leper in Bethany, Mary poured ointment of costly nard on Jesus' head. This spontaneous expression of love moved the Master to silence her critics with His beautiful tribute: "Let her alone . . . She has done a good work for me . . . She has come beforehand to anoint my body for burial" (Mark 14:6, 8).

OLIVE

A fruit-bearing tree about 20 feet (6 meters) tall with a gnarled, twisted trunk, white flowers, and berries that ripen to a black color. The olive tree grew slowly and continued to bear fruit after reaching a great age. Before it died, new branches sprouted from its roots. The fruit was harvested by beating the boughs of the olive tree with a stick (Deut. 24:20), or by shaking the tree (Is. 17:6). The ripe fruit was enjoyed fresh, and the green fruit was often pickled or made into a relish.

The best oil was obtained from the green olive fruit. It was used as fuel for lamps (Ex. 27:20), as anointing oil (Lev. 2:1), as an article of commerce (1 Kin. 5:11), and for dressing wounds (Luke 10:34). Olive trees were cultivated in groves or orchards (Ex. 23:11; Josh. 24:13). The most famous olive garden

mentioned in the Bible is Gethsemane, meaning "oil press" (Matt. 26:36).

OLIVET DISCOURSE

Jesus' discussion on the Mount of Olives about the destruction of Jerusalem and the end of the world (Matt. 24:1–25:46; Mark 13:1–37; Luke 21:5–36).

In response to Jesus' prophecy that the temple would be destroyed, the disciples asked when this would occur and how they would know it was about to happen. The disciples believed that the temple would be destroyed at the end of the world when, among other things, Jesus would return. That is why Matthew records the two questions, "When will these things [the destruction of the temple] be? And what will be the sign of Your coming, and of the end of the age?" (Matt. 24:3). What makes the Olivet discourse difficult to understand is that Jesus intermingles His answers to these two questions.

The key to unraveling His answers is the repetition of the key phrase "take heed" (Mark 13:5, 23, 33). The disciples' first question was, "When will these things be? And what will be the sign when all these things will be fulfilled?" (Mark 13:4). Jesus began by saying, "Take heed that no one deceives you" (Mark 13:5); then He described the events leading up to the temple's destruction (vv. 6–22). He then said, "But take heed; see, I have told you all [these] things beforehand" (Mark 13:23). By repeating the phrase "these things" He provides a conclusion to the first answer.

The key note in this first answer is the warning "take heed": there will be persecutions (Mark 13:9–13), wars and famines (13:7–8), false prophets, and false messiahs (13:6), all of which will lead up to the destruction of Jerusalem (13:14–23). But despite all these woes, the disciples must "take heed" because "the end [of the world] is not yet" (13:7). Mark

13:6–23 is therefore the answer to the question of when the temple will be destroyed. Furthermore, it is an accurate picture of the havoc that existed in Jerusalem during the Roman siege of A.D. 70 when the city and the temple were finally destroyed. Jesus' prophecy was therefore fulfilled in the years leading up to the temple's destruction (although some would say it is also a picture of what will be fulfilled again at the end of time).

The disciples had assumed that the temple would be destroyed only at the end of the world. They were mistaken, and Jesus said that despite all the woes leading up to the temple's destruction, when it happens the end of the world still will not be in sight. Therefore in Mark 13:24–27 He answered the next logical question: what signs will precede the end of the world? The phrase "in those days" is a common Old Testament expression used when speaking of the end times. In those days there will be signs in the heavens; and then Jesus, the Son of Man, will come.

We must be prepared for His coming and must not be taken by surprise. In Mark's Gospel, Jesus remarked that no one except the Father knows exactly when "that day"—Christ's return at the end of time—will be (Mark 13:32). Therefore we must be on our guard. Matthew and Luke close with further warnings to wait carefully in anticipation.

OMNIPOTENCE [om NIP oh tunce]

A theological term that refers to the all-encompassing power of God. The almighty God expects human beings to obey Him, and He holds them responsible for their thoughts and actions. He is the all-powerful Lord who has created all things and sustains them by the Word of His power (Gen. 1:1–3; Heb. 1:3).

OMNIPRESENCE [om nih PRES ence]

A theological term that refers to the unlimited nature of God or His ability to be everywhere at all times. God is not like the manufactured idols of ancient cultures that were limited to one altar or temple area. God reveals Himself in the Bible as the Lord who is everywhere. God was present as Lord in all creation (Ps. 139:7–12), and there is no escaping Him.

OMNISCIENCE [om NISH unce]

A theological term that refers to God's superior knowledge and wisdom, His power to know all things. God is the Lord who knows our thoughts from afar. He is acquainted with all our ways, knowing our words even before they are on our tongues (Ps. 139:1–6, 13–16). He needs to consult no one for knowledge or understanding (Is. 40:13–14). He is the all-knowing Lord who prophesies the events of the future, including the death and resurrection of His Son (Isaiah 53) and the return of Christ at the end of this age when death will be finally overcome (Rom. 8:18–39; 1 Cor. 15:51–57).

OMRI [UM rih]

The sixth king of the northern kingdom of Israel (885–874 B.C.). Omri is first mentioned as the commander of the army of Israel under King Elah. While Omri besieged the Philistine city of Gibbethon, another military figure, Zimri, conspired against Elah, killed him, and established himself as king. Zimri, however, had little support in Israel, and the army promptly made Omri its king. Omri returned to the capital with his army, besieged the city, and Zimri committed suicide. Tibni, the son of Ginath, continued to challenge Omri's reign; but after four years Tibni died and Omri became the sole ruler of Israel (1 Kin. 16:21–28).

Omri was a king of vision and wisdom.

From Shemer he purchased a hill on which he built a new city, Samaria, making it the new capital of Israel. Samaria was more defensible than Tirzah had been. Because it was strategically located, Omri was able to control the north-south trade routes in the region. Archaeological excavations at Samaria revealed buildings of excellent workmanship—an indication of the prosperity the city enjoyed during his reign.

The Moabite Stone tells of Omri's success against King Mesha of Moab (2 Kin. 3:4). But Omri's conflict with Syria proved to be less successful, and he was forced to grant a number of cities to the Syrians (1 Kin. 20:34).

ONESIMUS [oh NESS ih muss] (useful)

A slave of Philemon and an inhabitant of Colosse (Col. 4:9; Philem. 10). When Onesimus fled from his master to Rome, he met the apostle Paul. Paul witnessed to him, and Onesimus became a Christian. In his letter to Philemon, Paul spoke of Onesimus as "my own heart" (Philem. 12), indicating that Onesimus had become like a son to him.

Paul convinced Onesimus to return to his master, Philemon. He also sent a letter with Onesimus, encouraging Philemon to treat Onesimus as a brother rather than a slave. Paul implied that freeing Onesimus was Philemon's Christian duty, but he stopped short of commanding him to do so. Onesimus accompanied Tychicus, who delivered the Epistle to the Colossians as well as the Epistle to Philemon.

Some scholars believe this Onesimus is Onesimus the bishop, praised in a letter to the second-century church at Ephesus from Ignatius of Antioch.

ONESIPHORUS [on ee SIF oh rus] (profitable)

A Christian from Ephesus who befriended the apostle Paul (2 Tim. 1:16–18; 4:18). Not only did Onesiphorus minister to Paul while the apostle was in Ephesus; he also ministered to Paul during his imprisonment in Rome (2 Tim. 1:17). Onesiphorus overcame any fears he had for his own safety to visit and minister to Paul in prison. Unable to repay Onesiphorus for his "mercy," Paul prayed that he might "find mercy from the Lord in that Day" (2 Tim. 1:18), referring to the Judgment Day.

ONYX

A form of chalcedony with contrasting layers of colors in parallel lines. The colors are usually black and white or brown and white. The onyx was used for engraving seals and for various ornaments. It was included in the treasures from Havilah, in Arabia (Gen. 2:12).

The shoulder stones of Aaron's ephod were onyx with the names of six tribes of Israel engraved on each stone (Ex. 28:9). It was also the second stone in the fourth row of Aaron's breastplate (Ex. 28:20; 39:6). David included the onyx in the material he gathered for the temple (1 Chr. 29:2). Job considered the wisdom from God a greater possession than even the precious onyx (Job 28:16).

OPHEL [OH fell] (knoll)

The northeast part of the triangular hill in ancient Jerusalem on which the City of David stood. Situated south of the temple area, the hill was the site of the original city of the Jebusites. Surrounded on three sides by deep valleys, the ancient city was so strongly fortified that it was considered unconquerable. But David captured this center of Canaanite power and made it his new capital city (2 Sam. 5:6–9).

Usually the name Ophel is given to the entire hill. But it is more accurate to identify the hill of Ophel with the fortifications built on the eastern ridge of the hill that overlooks the Kidron Valley.

Jotham, king of Judah (750–732 B.C.), built extensively on the wall of Ophel (2 Chr. 27:3). Manasseh, king of Judah (696–642 B.C.), built a high wall outside the City of David; and it enclosed Ophel (2 Chr. 33:14). The Nethinim, or temple servants, lived in Ophel after the captivity (Neh. 3:26–27; 11:21).

OPHIR [OH fur]

A region from which David and Solomon obtained gold (1 Kin. 9:28; 1 Chr. 29:4). Although Ophir is mentioned several times in the Old Testament, its exact location remains a mystery. Some believe Ophir was an island situated in the Red Sea; others think it was in India; still others believe it was in Africa, perhaps Somaliland, or on the southwest corner of the Arabian peninsula, perhaps in the land of Sheba.

Ophir is consistently associated in the Old Testament with gold, probably its most noteworthy product. The gold may have come from Ophir itself, or it may have simply passed through Ophir from its place of origin. King Solomon sent ships to Ophir for gold (2 Chr. 8:17–18). In addition, they brought a great abundance of algum trees (sandalwood) and precious stones from Ophir (2 Chr. 9:10). Near the end of his life, David announced that he had collected 3,000 talents of gold of Ophir and 7,000 thousand talents of refined silver for the building of the temple (1 Chr. 29:4). Later, Jehoshaphat unsuccessfully attempted to send ships to Ophir for gold (1 Kin. 22:48).

The air of mystery about Ophir adds to its significance when spoken of in a symbolic way in the Bible. Psalm 45:9 speaks of "the queen in gold from Ophir." Job 28:16 says that wisdom "cannot be valued in the gold of Ophir," suggesting its incomparable worth.

ORACLE [OR uh cull]

A prophetic speech, utterance, or declaration. In Greek religion, an oracle was a response given by a pagan god to a human question. Oracles were uttered by persons entranced, by those who interpreted dreams, and by those who saw or heard patterns in nature. The most famous oracle, in this sense, was the Oracle at Delphi. Delphi was the shrine of Apollo—the Greek god of the sun, prophecy, music, medicine, and poetry.

The word *oracle* is used in several ways in the Bible. In the Book of Numbers, it is used to describe the prophecies of Balaam the son of Beor, the soothsayer (Num. 23–24; Josh. 13:22). The Hebrew word translated "oracle" means a "similitude, parable, or proverb." In 2 Samuel 16:23 the word *oracle* is a translation of a Hebrew word that means "word" or "utterance." It refers to a communication from God given for man's guidance.

A different Hebrew word is translated "oracle" in Jeremiah 23:33–38 (burden, KJV). This word means "a thing lifted up"; it can refer to a prophetic utterance as well as a physical burden. Jeremiah plays upon this double meaning and speaks of the prophetic oracle as a burden that is difficult to bear.

When the New Testament speaks of oracles, it sometimes refers to the Old Testament or some portion of it (Acts 7:38; Rom. 3:2). Hebrews 5:12 uses the term to speak of both the Old Testament revelation and the Word made flesh, Jesus Christ. First Peter 4:11 warns that the teacher of Christian truths must speak as one who utters oracles of God— a message from God and not his own opinions.

ORION [oh RYE un]

The name of a constellation, consisting of thousands of stars, which is mentioned in the Old Testament (Job 9:9; 38:31; Amos 5:8). The constellation is near Gemini and Taurus, and contains the giant red star Betelgeuse and Rigel, a blue-white star of first magnitude. Most of the stars of Orion cannot be seen without the aid of a telescope.

ORPAH [AWR pah]

A Moabite woman who married Chilion, one of the two sons of Elimelech and Naomi (Ruth 1:4). When Elimelech and his sons died in Moab, Orpah accompanied Naomi, her mother-in-law, part of the way to Bethlehem and then returned "to her people and to her gods" (Ruth 1:14) in Moab.

OSTRICH

Several Scripture passages that refer to owls in the KJV are rendered ostrich

ORACLE

ORACLE OR NOT, YOU'VE GOT A CASE OF TONSILITIS!

JONNY HAWKINS

in the NRSV. This strange bird was a common sight in the deserts of Israel and Sinai in Bible times. Earth's largest living bird, the ostrich may stand about 8 feet (2.5 meters) tall. While it cannot fly, this unusual animal with its long steps, which can cover 15 feet per stride at top speed, can outrun a horse. Sometimes an ostrich will use its wings as a sail to achieve even greater speed. An adult ostrich fears only people and lions, and it may live as long as 70 years.

The popular belief that ostriches hide their heads in the sand is not true. However, when a young ostrich senses danger, it will crouch near the ground and stretch out its long neck to lessen the possibility of being seen.

This enormous bird has only a walnut-sized brain. But God has given it certain helpful instincts, along with its great physical stamina. Like a camel, the ostrich is fitted for desert life. It eats coarse food and can go for a long time without water. Its head, neck, and powerful legs have no feathers. This helps to keep the bird cool in the hot desert climate. Its huge eyes enable it to spot danger from a great distance, and its long eyelashes protect its eyes from dust and sand. The male ostrich has a cry that is similar to a lion's roar.

Unlike most other birds, the ostrich does not build a nest to protect its young. The female ostrich deposits her eggs on the desert floor and covers them with sand. These eggs are generally left unattended during the day, since the desert sun serves as a natural incubator. Job compared these habits unfavorably with the more traditional nesting instincts of the stork (Job 39:13–18).

OTHNIEL [OATH nih el]

The first judge of Israel (Judg. 1:13; 3:9, 11). Othniel was a son of Kenaz and probably was a nephew of Caleb. When the Israelites forgot the Lord and served the pagan gods of Canaan, the king of Mesopotamia oppressed them for eight years. When the Israelites repented of their evil and cried out to the Lord for deliverance, Othniel was raised up by the Lord to deliver His people. Othniel was one of four judges (the other three were Gideon, Jephthah, and Samson) of whom the Scripture says, "The Spirit of the Lord came upon him" (Judg. 3:10).

OVEN

Cooking was usually done in small clay or stone ovens (Lev. 2:4; 26:26; Hos. 7:4). Ovens were either rectangular or circular, about two feet (60 centimeters) in diameter and about one foot (30 centimeters) high, with the top flattened and slightly hollow. The food was cooked on the flat top, with the fire inside the oven or stove. The usual fuel was animal dung or wood, but straw was used to make a quick fire and to rekindle the embers.

Malachi 4:1 describes the Day of Judgment when the evildoers will be destroyed in a day "burning like an oven." Nehemiah 3:11 and 12:28 mention the "Tower of the Ovens" on the city wall. This may have been a section of the city where commercial baking was carried on, but more likely it is a reference to either potter's or brickmaker's kilns or to metal smelters.

OVERSEER

A person responsible for controlling and managing a group of people or a task. In the Old Testament, "overseer" refers to those responsible for getting a job done (2 Chr. 2:8) and to those who helped rule a people (Neh. 11:9). A captain in Pharaoh's guard made Joseph the overseer of his house (Gen. 39:4–5). When an overseer was responsible for slaves, he was sometimes called a taskmaster. The taskmasters over the Israelite slaves in Egypt were particularly cruel (Ex. 1:11–14). Overseers were also sometimes called drivers, foremen, and slavemasters. In the New Testament, an overseer is an officer in the church. Some scholars equate this officer with the "elder," while others see it as a distinct office.

P

PADAN ARAM [PAD uhn AH rem] (the plain of Aram)

The area of Upper Mesopotamia around Haran and the home of Abraham after he moved from Ur of the Chaldeans (Gen. 25:20; Paddan Aran in NIV; Paddan-aram in NRSV). Abraham later sent his servant to Padan Aram to find a bride for his son Isaac (Gen. 25:20). Much later, Isaac's son Jacob fled to Padan Aram to avoid the wrath of his brother Esau and dwelt there with Laban (Gen. 28:2, 5–7). The region was also referred to as Padan (Gen. 48:7; Paddan in NIV, NRSV).

PALESTINE [PAL ess tyne]

The land promised by God to Abraham and his descendants and eventually the region where the Hebrew people lived.

Palestine (or Palestina) is a tiny land bridge between the continents of Asia, Africa, and Europe. The word itself originally identified the region as "the land of the Philistines," a warlike tribe that inhabited much of the region alongside the Hebrew people. But the older name for Palestine was Canaan, the term most frequently used in the Old Testament. The Amarna Letters of the fourteenth century B.C. referred to "the land of Canaan," applying the term to the coastal region inhabited by the Phoenicians. After the Israelites took the land from the Canaanites, the entire country became known as the "land of Israel" (1 Sam. 13:19; Matt. 2:20) and the "land of promise" (Heb. 11:9).

The term Palestine as a name for the entire land of Canaan, beyond the coastal plains of the Phoenicians, was first used by the fifth-century B.C. historian Herodotus. After the Jewish revolt of A.D. 135, the Romans replaced the Latin name Judea with the Latin Palaestina as their name for this province. Although the prophet Zechariah referred to this region as the "Holy Land" (Zech. 2:12), it was not until the Middle Ages that this land became popularly known as the Holy Land.

The medieval concept that Palestine was the center of the earth (see Ezek. 5:5) is not as farfetched as one might expect. This tiny strip of land not only unites the peoples and lands of Asia, Africa, and Europe but also the five seas known as the Mediterranean Sea, the Black Sea, the Caspian Sea, the Red Sea, and the Persian Gulf. Palestine was sandwiched in between two dominant cultures of the ancient world—Egypt to the south and Babylon-Assyria-Persia between the Tigris and Euphrates rivers to the northeast.

Palestine is also the focal point of the three great world religions: Judaism, Christianity, and Islam. It has been the land corridor for most of the world's armies and, according to the Book of Revelation, will be the scene of the final great conflict of history, the Battle of Armageddon (Rev. 16:16).

To the jet-age traveler Palestine seems quite small. The expression "from Dan to Beersheba" (1 Sam. 3:20) refers to a north-south distance of only about 150 miles (240 kilometers). The width of the region is even less impressive. In the north, from Acco on the coast to the Sea of Galilee is a distance of only 28 miles (45 kilometers). In the broader south, from Gaza on the coast to the Dead Sea is a distance of only 54 miles (88 kilometers). The distance between Jaffa and Jericho is only 45 miles (72 kilometers); Nazareth to Jerusalem is only 60 miles (98 kilometers).

The land area from Dan to Beersheba in Cisjordan (the region west of the Jordan River) is approximately 6,000 square miles—a region smaller than Hawaii. If the area east of the Jordan River (Transjordan) is included, the maximum total area of Palestine amounts to only 10,000 square miles—an area smaller than the state of Maryland.

PAMPHYLIA [pam FIL ih uh] *(a region of every tribe)*

A Roman province on the southern coast of central Asia Minor (modern Turkey). The province consisted mainly of a plain about 80 miles (130 kilometers) long and up to about 20 miles (32 kilometers) wide. The capital city of Pamphylia, its largest city, was Perga (Acts 13:13–14).

Pamphylia is first mentioned in the New Testament in Acts 2:10. People from Pamphylia were among those present in Jerusalem on the Day of Pentecost. In Pamphylia Paul first entered Asia Minor (Acts 13:13) during his first missionary journey. It was at Pamphylia that John Mark left Paul and Barnabas (Acts 15:38). On his voyage to Rome, Paul sailed off the coast of Pamphylia (Acts 27:5).

PAPHOS [PAY fuhs]

A city on the southwestern extremity of the island of Cyprus. Paul, Barnabas, and John Mark visited Paphos during Paul's first missionary journey, about A.D. 47 or 48 (Acts 13:6–13). Two settlements in the same general area of Cyprus are known as Old Paphos (modern Konklia), and New Paphos, about 10 miles (16 kilometers) to the northwest. New Paphos is the Paphos mentioned in the Book of Acts (modern Baffa). At Paphos, Paul met the Roman proconsul Sergius Paulus, who believed the gospel (Acts 13:12) when he witnessed Paul's rebuke of Elymas the sorcerer.

PAPYRUS [puh PIE russ]

A tall aquatic plant of southern Europe and northern Africa, especially of the Nile River valley. This plant is now unknown in its wild state in Egypt; but it still grows plentifully in the Sudan. Extensive growths of papyrus may also be found in the marshes at the northern end of Lake Huleh in Palestine.

The Hebrew word translated as "papyrus" in Job 8:11 is also used in Exodus 2:3. Apparently the "ark of bulrushes" in which Moses was hidden by his mother was woven from papyrus plants. The Egyptians made blankets, boats, shoes, and other articles from papyrus.

A paper made from the pith, or the stems, of the papyrus was used in ancient times as a writing material. The story of the cutting and burning of Jeremiah's scroll by King Jehoiakim (Jer. 36:20–23) suggests papyrus rather than leather; indeed, the Septuagint assumes it was a papyrus scroll. Scholars believe that John's reference to "paper and ink" (2 John 12) is to papyrus writing material because the Greek noun used in this verse refers to the papyrus roll or sheet used in writing a letter.

The ancient Egyptians did not burn their paper rubbish; they simply piled it in the sand and let the blowing sand cover it layer upon layer. Thousands of pages of papyrus documents were found in rubbish heaps by the British archaeologists Grenfell and Hunt, who explored ancient Egyptian tombs in search of documents. They knew that the Egyptians believed that since people lived on in another world, all of their comforts should be buried with them for further use,

P

including books. Whenever these books were discovered, they were an archaeologist's treasure.

In the year 1891 the great era of papyrus discoveries was born, when Sir Flinders Petrie and E. Wallis Budge discovered some leaves or rolls of outstanding literary merit. Most of these documents were dated in the third century B.C. Perhaps the most important discovery of the period was by Adolf Deissmann, who realized that the language written on the papyri he found was identical to that of his Greek New Testament. Clearly New Testament Greek was not a special biblical language created by the Holy Spirit as many had claimed.

The oldest manuscripts of the New Testament, the majority of the Dead Sea Scrolls, and the large collection of Gnostic documents at the Nag Hammadi library were written on papyrus. The English word *paper* comes from the word *papyrus*.

PARABLE

A short, simple story designed to communicate a spiritual truth, religious principle, or moral lesson; a figure of speech in which truth is illustrated by a comparison or example drawn from everyday experiences.

A parable is often no more than an extended metaphor or simile, using figurative language in the form of a story to

PAPYRUS

illustrate a particular truth. The Greek word for "parable" literally means "a laying by the side of" or "a casting alongside," thus "a comparison or likeness." In a parable something is placed alongside something else, in order that one may throw light on the other. A familiar custom or incident is used to illustrate some less familiar truth.

Jesus' characteristic method of teaching was through parables. His two most famous parables are the parable of the lost son (Luke 15:11–32) and the parable of the Good Samaritan (Luke 10:25–37). Both parables illustrate God's love for sinners and God's command that we show compassion to all people. Actually, the parable of the lost son (sometimes called the parable of the Prodigal Son or the parable of the loving father) is the story of two lost sons: the younger son (typical of tax collectors and prostitutes) who wasted possessions with indulgent living, and the older son (typical of the self-righteous scribes and Pharisees) who remained at home but was a stranger to his father's heart.

Although parables are often memorable stories, impressing the listener with a clear picture of the truth, even the disciples were sometimes confused as to the meaning of parables. For instance, after Jesus told the parable of the wheat and the tares (Matt. 13:24–30), the disciples needed interpretation in order to understand its meaning (Matt. 13:36–43). Jesus sometimes used the parabolic form of teaching to reveal the truth to those who followed Him and to conceal the truth from those who did not (Matt. 13:10–17; Mark 4:10–12; Luke 8:9–10). His parables thus fulfilled the prophecy of Isaiah 6:9–10. Like a double-edged sword, they cut two ways—enlightening those who sought the truth and blinding those who were disobedient.

PARACLETE [pair uh KLEET]

A transliteration of the Greek word *parakletos,* which means "one who speaks in favor of," as an intercessor, advocate, or legal assistant. The word, translated as "Comforter" or "Counselor," appears only in the Gospel of John. Jesus applied the term to the Holy Spirit, who would be an advocate on behalf of Jesus' followers after His ascension; the Spirit would plead their cause before God (John 14:16, 26; 15:26; 16:7).

PARAN [PAH ruhn]

A wilderness region in the central part of the Sinai Peninsula. Although the boundaries of this desert region are somewhat obscure, it probably bordered the Arabah and the Gulf of Aqaba on the east. The modern Wadi Feiran in central Sinai preserves the ancient name.

Paran is frequently mentioned in the Old Testament. Chedorlaomer, one of the four kings who attacked Sodom, conquered as far as "El Paran, which is by the wilderness" (Gen. 14:6). After Hagar was driven from Abraham's household (Gen. 21:21), she fled to this wilderness with her son Ishmael. The Israelites crossed Paran during their Exodus from Egypt (Num. 10:12; 12:16), and Moses dispatched spies from Paran to explore the land of Canaan (Num. 13:3). After their mission, these spies returned "unto the wilderness of Paran, to Kadesh" (Num. 13:26).

Much later, after the death of Samuel, David fled to Paran (1 Sam. 25:1). After revolting from King Solomon, Hadad went through Paran on his flight to Egypt (1 Kin. 11:18).

PARTHIANS [PAHR thih uhns]

A tribal group from Parthia, a region southeast of the Caspian Sea in ancient Persia (Iran). Parthians are mentioned in Acts 2:9 as one of the many national and language groups gathered in Jerusalem for the Feast of Pentecost.

Parthia was one of the original Persian administrative districts established by Darius I (Dan. 6:1). Late in the fourth century B.C., the Persian Empire fell to Alexander the Great and his successors, the Macedonian emperors known as the Seleucids. In the middle of the third century B.C., the Parthians revolted from the Seleucids under the leadership of King Arsaces. The kings who followed Arsaces gradually built a great empire; it extended from the Euphrates River in Mesopotamia to the Indus River in (modern) Pakistan. Fierce warriors, the Parthians were formidable in battle; their archers fought while mounted on horseback. Even the Roman armies were largely unsuccessful against the Parthians.

The Babylonians settled some citizens of the nation of Judah in Parthia after their deportation from Judah in 586 B.C. (2 Chr. 36:20). The Jewish historian Josephus reported that some of the Jews who settled in Parthia continued to practice the Israelite faith, apparently without harassment from the natives. Thus the "Parthians" in Jerusalem on Pentecost (Acts 2:9) may have included remnants of these deported Jewish people as well as converts to Judaism from among native Parthians.

PARTRIDGE

From early times, the partridge has been a game bird. They were among the birds that could be eaten as clean food by the Hebrew people. Two species, the sand-partridge (Is. 34:15, REB) and the chukar, are common in Israel.

Partridges live in fields, feeding on grain and insects. They usually travel in coveys of 12 to 30 birds. Their meat is tasty, and the bird is clever enough to give the hunter a fine chase. It takes sharp eyes to spot the mottled feathers of a partridge. When alarmed, the bird

will hide in a hole, crouch among loose stones, or fly from tree to tree with loudly whirring wings. David compared himself to a partridge when he was fleeing from Saul (1 Sam. 26:20).

The prophet Jeremiah compared the person who gathered riches by unrighteous means to a partridge that gathers a brood of young birds that she has not hatched (Jer. 17:11).

PASSOVER, FEAST OF

The Passover was the first of the three great festivals of the Israelite people. It referred to the sacrifice of a lamb in Egypt when the people of Israel were slaves. They smeared the blood of the lamb on their doorposts as a signal to God that He should "pass over" their houses when He destroyed all the firstborn of Egypt (Ex. 12:13).

Passover was observed on the fourteenth day of the first month, Abib, with the service beginning in the evening (Lev. 23:6). It was on the evening of this day that Israel left Egypt. Passover commemorated this departure from Egypt in haste. Unleavened bread was used in the celebration because this showed that the people had no time to put leaven in their bread as they ate their final meal as slaves in Egypt.

Several regulations were given concerning the observance of Passover. Passover was to be observed "in the place which the Lord your God will choose." This implied the sanctuary of the tabernacle or the temple in Jerusalem.

Joshua 5:10–12 refers to the observing of Passover in the plains of Jericho near Gilgal. Second Chronicles 30:1, 3, 13, 15 describes a Passover during the reign of Hezekiah. Messengers were sent throughout the land to invite the people to come to Jerusalem to observe the Passover. Many refused; some even scorned the one who carried the invitation. Because the people were not ready to observe the Passover, a delay of one month was recommended. That year the Passover was on the fourteenth day of the second month. Even after the delay many still were not ready to observe the Passover.

In New Testament times, large numbers gathered in Jerusalem to observe the annual Passover. Jesus was crucified in the city during one of these Passover celebrations. He and His disciples ate a Passover meal together on the eve of His death. Like the blood of the lamb that saved the Hebrew people from destruction in Egypt, His blood, as the ultimate Passover sacrifice, redeems us from the power of sin and death (1 Cor. 5:7).

PATHROS [PATH rahs] *(the southern land)*

The Hebrew name for Upper Egypt, roughly the southern region of the Nile River Valley between Cairo and Aswan (Is. 11:11). After the siege of Jerusalem (597 B.C.), the idolatrous Jews who offered incense to other gods fled to Pathros and formed a Jewish colony in Egypt. The prophet Jeremiah predicted that their disobedience would be judged by the king of Babylon (Jer. 44:1, 15). Ezekiel also prophesied that Pathros would be humiliated by Nebuchadnezzar (Ezek. 30:10–14), but that the Jews would recognize their sins and turn to God (Ezek. 29:14).

PATMOS [PAT muhs]

A small rocky island to which the apostle John was banished and where he wrote the Book of Revelation (Rev. 1:9). The island, about 10 miles (16 kilometers) long and 6 miles (10 kilometers) wide, lies off the southwest coast of Asia Minor (modern Turkey). Because of its desolate and barren nature, Patmos was used by the Romans as a place to banish criminals, who were forced to work at hard labor in the mines and quarries of the island. Because Christians were regarded as criminals by the Roman emperor Domitian (ruled A.D. 81–96), the apostle John probably suffered from harsh treatment during his exile on Patmos. An early Christian tradition said John was in exile for 18 months.

PATRIARCH [PAY trih ark] *(head of a father's house)*

The founder or ruler of a tribe, family, or clan; the forefathers of the Israelite nation. The phrase "the patriarchs" usually refers to the tribal leaders of Israel who lived before the time of Moses. Specifically, it is used of Abraham, Isaac, Jacob, and the 12 sons of Jacob. Therefore, the patriarchs were the ancestors of the Israelites from Abraham to Joseph (Acts 7:8–9; Heb. 7:4).

PAUL, THE APOSTLE

The earliest and most influential interpreter of Christ's message and teaching; an early Christian missionary; correspondent with several early Christian churches. Paul was born at Tarsus, the chief city of Cilicia (southeast Asia Minor). He was a citizen of Tarsus, "no mean city," as he called it (Acts 21:39). He was also born a Roman citizen (Acts 22:28), a privilege that worked to his advantage on several occasions during his apostolic ministry.

The first martyr of the Christian church was Stephen, one of the most outspoken leaders of the new Christian movement. Paul publicly associated himself with Stephen's executioners and then embarked on a campaign designed to suppress the church. Paul himself related how he "persecuted the church of God beyond measure and tried to destroy it" (Gal. 1:13).

At the height of Paul's campaign of repression, he was confronted on the road to Damascus by the risen Christ. In an instant his life was reoriented. The Jewish law was replaced as the central theme of Paul's life by Jesus Christ. He became the leading champion of the cause he had tried to overthrow.

After leaving Damascus, Paul paid a short visit to Jerusalem to make the acquaintance of Peter. During his two weeks' stay there, he also met James, the Lord's brother (Gal. 1:18–19). Paul could not stay in Jerusalem because the animosity of his former associates was too strong. He had to be taken down to Caesarea on the Mediterranean coast and put on a ship for Tarsus.

Paul spent the next ten years in and around Tarsus, actively engaged in the evangelizing of Gentiles. At the end of that time Barnabas came to Tarsus from Antioch and invited Paul to join him in caring for a young church there. A spontaneous campaign of Gentile evangelization had recently occurred at Antioch, resulting in the formation of a vigorous church. Barnabas himself had been commissioned by the apostles in Jerusalem to lead the Gentile evangelization in the city of Antioch.

About a year after Paul joined Barnabas in Antioch, the two men visited Jerusalem and conferred with the three "pillars" of the church there—the apostles Peter and John, and James the Lord's brother (Gal. 2:1–10). The result of this conference was an agreement that the Jerusalem leaders would concentrate on the evangelization of their fellow Jews, while Barnabas and Paul would continue to take the gospel to Gentiles.

Barnabas and Paul were released by the church of Antioch to pursue a missionary campaign that took them to Barnabas's native island of Cyprus and then into the highlands of central Asia Minor (modern Turkey), to the province of Galatia. There they preached the gospel and planted churches in the cities of Pisidian Antioch, Iconium, Lystra, and Derbe.

The missionaries then returned to Antioch in Syria.

The great increase of Gentile converts caused alarm among many of the Jewish Christians in Judea. They feared that too many Gentiles would hurt the character of the church. Militant Jewish nationalists were already attacking them. A movement began that required Gentile converts to become circumcised and follow the Jewish law. The leaders of the Jerusalem church, with Paul and Barnabas in attendance, met in A.D. 48 to discuss the problem. It was finally decided that circumcision was not necessary, but that Gentile converts should conform to the Jewish code of laws in order to make fellowship between Jewish and Gentile Christians less strained (Acts 15:1–29).

With other missionary associates, Paul made other far-ranging tours throughout Gentile territory, preaching the gospel, instructing converts, and founding churches. He conducted some of his most influential work in the cities of Ephesus and Corinth.

Paul had organized a relief fund among the Gentile churches to help poorer members of the Jerusalem church. He insisted on returning to Jerusalem with some of these Gentile Christians to give the Jerusalem Christians an opportunity to see some of their Gentile brethren face to face in addition to receiving their gifts.

A few days after his arrival in Jerusalem, Paul was attacked by a mob in the area of the temple. He was rescued by a detachment of Roman soldiers and kept in custody at the Roman governor's headquarters in Caesarea for the next two years. At the end of that period he exercised his privilege as a Roman citizen and appealed to Caesar in order to have his case transferred from the provincial governor's court in Judea to the emperor's tribunal in Rome. He was sent to Rome in the fall of A.D. 59. The great apostle spent a further two years in Rome under house arrest, waiting for his case to come up for hearing before the supreme tribunal.

The restrictions under which Paul lived in Rome should have held back his efforts to proclaim the gospel, but just the opposite actually happened. These restrictions, by his own testimony, "actually turned out for the furtherance of the gospel" (Phil. 1:12). Although he was confined to his lodgings, shackled to one of the soldiers who guarded him in four-hour shifts, he was free to receive visitors and talk to them about the gospel. The soldiers who guarded him and the officials in charge of presenting his case before the emperor were left in no doubt about the reason for his being in Rome. The gospel actually became a topic of discussion. This encouraged the Christians in Rome to bear more open witness to their faith, allowing the saving message to be proclaimed more fearlessly in Rome than ever before "and in this," said Paul, "I rejoice" (Phil. 1:18).

From Rome, Paul was able to correspond with friends in other parts of the Roman Empire. Visitors from those parts came to see him, bringing news of their churches. These visitors included Epaphroditus from Philippi and Epaphras from Colosse. From Colosse, too, Paul received an unexpected visitor, Onesimus, the slave of his friend Philemon. He sent Onesimus back to his master with a letter commending him "no longer as a slave but . . . as a beloved brother" (Philem. 16).

The letters of Philippi and Colosse were sent in response to the news brought by Epaphroditus and Epaphras, respectively. At the same time as the letter to Colosse, Paul sent a letter to Laodicea and a more general letter that we now know as Ephesians. The Roman captivity became a very fruitful period for Paul and his ministry.

We have very little information about the rest of Paul's career. We do not know the outcome of his trial before Caesar. He was probably discharged and enjoyed a further period of liberty. It is traditionally believed that Paul's condemnation and execution occurred during the persecution of Christians under the Roman Emperor Nero. The probable site of his execution may still be seen at Tre Fontane on the Ostian Road. There is no reason to doubt the place of his burial marked near the Basilica of St. Paul in Rome. There, beneath the high altar, is a stone inscription going back to at least the fourth century: "To Paul, Apostle and Martyr."

The relevance of Paul's teaching for human life today may be brought out in a summary of four of his leading themes:

1. True religion is not a matter of rules and regulations. God does not deal with men and women like an accountant, but He accepts them freely when they respond to His love. He implants the Spirit of Christ in their hearts so they may extend His love to others.

2. In Christ, men and women have come of age. God does not keep His people on puppet strings but liberates them to live as His responsible sons and daughters.

3. People matter more than things, principles, and causes. The highest of principles and the best of causes exist only for the sake of people. Personal liberty itself is abused if it is exercised against the personal well-being of others.

4. Discrimination on the grounds of race, religion, class, or sex is an offense against God and humanity alike.

PEACE OFFERING

This sacrificial offering was also called a heave offering and a wave offering. This was a bloody offering presented to God (Lev. 3:1; fellowship offering in NIV). Part of the offering was eaten by the priest (representing God's acceptance) and part was eaten by worshipers and their guests (nonofficiating priests or Levites and the poor, Deut. 12:18; 16:11). Thus, God hosted the meal, communing with the worshiper and other participants. This sacrifice celebrated covering of sin, forgiveness by God, and the restoration of a right and meaningful relationship with God and with life itself (Judg. 20:26; 21:4).

There were three kinds of peace offerings: (1) thank offerings in response to an unsolicited special divine blessing; (2) votive (vowed) offerings in pursuit of making a request or pledge to God; and (3) freewill offerings spontaneously presented in worship and praise.

PEKAH [PEE kuh] ([God] *has opened the eyes*)

The son of Remaliah and eighteenth king of Israel (2 Kin. 15:25–31; 2 Chr. 28:5–15). Pekah became king after he assassinated King Pekahiah. Pekah continued to lead Israel in the idolatrous ways of Jeroboam I (2 Kin. 15:28).

Pekah took the throne at the time when Tiglath-Pileser III, king of Assyria, was advancing toward Israel. To resist this threat, Pekah formed an alliance with Rezin, king of Syria. He also hoped to enlist the sister Israelite nation of Judah in the alliance. Under the counsel of the prophet Isaiah, however, Judah's kings, Jotham and later Ahaz, refused. Pekah and Rezin attempted to enlist Judah by force, marching first against Jerusalem. They were unsuccessful, and so they divided their armies.

Rezin successfully captured Elath, and

Pekah killed thousands in the districts near Jericho, taking many prisoners into Samaria. Later, these prisoners were returned to Jericho upon the advice of the prophet Oded. Pekah probably was unaware that he was God's instrument to punish Judah (2 Chr. 28:5–6).

As Tiglath-Pileser III of Assyria advanced, King Ahaz of Judah met him to pay tribute and ask his help against Syria and Israel (2 Kin. 16:10). Assyria planned to march against Syria, and so Damascus was taken and Rezin was killed. The Assyrians also invaded northern Israel, with city after city taken and their inhabitants deported to Assyria. Through the Assyrian army God brought His judgment on Israel and Syria, even as the prophet Isaiah had warned (Is. 7:8–9).

Pekah was left with a stricken nation, over half of which had been plundered and stripped of its inhabitants. Soon Hoshea, son of Elah, conspired against Pekah and assassinated him. However, in his own writings Tiglath-Pileser III claimed that he was the power who placed Hoshea on the throne of Israel, possibly indicating he was a force behind the conspiracy. Pekah's dates as king of Israel are usually given as 740–732 B.C.

PEKAHIAH [pek uh HIGH uh] *(the Lord has opened the eyes)*

A son of Menahem and the seventeenth king of Israel (2 Kin. 15:22–26). Pekahiah assumed the throne after his father's death. He was an evil king who continued the idolatrous worship first introduced by King Jeroboam I. After reigning only two years (about 742–740 B.C.), Pekahiah was killed by his military captain, Pekah, and 50 Gileadites. Pekah then became king.

PENTATEUCH [PEN tuh tuke]

A Greek term meaning "five-volumed" which refers to the first five books of the

Old Testament. The Jews traditionally refer to this collection as "the Book of the Law," or simply "the Law." Another word for this collection, "Torah," means "instruction, teaching, or doctrine." It describes such basic sections of the Pentateuch as parts of Exodus, Leviticus, and Deuteronomy.

This ancient division of the Law into five sections is supported by the Septuagint, a third-century B.C. translation of the Hebrew Old Testament into Greek, and also by the Samaritan Pentateuch, which is even earlier.

The five books together present a history of humanity from creation to the death of Moses, with particular attention to the development of the Hebrew people. The activity of God receives special emphasis throughout, and the Pentateuch reveals a great deal about God's nature and His purposes for mankind.

The Pentateuch is generally divided into six major sections: (1) the creation of the world and its inhabitants (Gen. 1–11); (2) the period from Abraham to Joseph (Gen. 12–50); (3) Moses and the departure of the Israelites from Egypt (Ex. 1–18); (4) God's revelation at Sinai (Ex. 19-Num. 10); (5) the wilderness wanderings (Num. 11–36); and (6) the addresses of Moses (Deut. 1–34).

From the time it was written, the Pentateuch was consistently accepted as the work of Moses. His specific writing or compiling activity is mentioned in the Pentateuch (Ex. 17:14; 24:4; 34:27), while in the postexilic writings the Law, or Torah, was often attributed directly to Moses (Neh. 8:1; 2 Chr. 25:4; 35:12). This tradition was supported by Christ in New Testament times (Mark 12:26; John 7:23).

The Pentateuch was also called the Law of the Lord (2 Chr. 31:3; Luke 2:23–24) and "the Book of the Law of God" (Neh. 8:18). The word "book" should not be understood in its modern sense, for several different writing materials were used by Old Testament scribes, including papyrus and leather scrolls or sheets, pieces of broken pottery, clay tablets, and stone. The word "book" has two important usages in connection with the Law. First, it indicates that the material referred to was in written form at an early period. Second, it shows the combination of divine authorship and human transmission that gave the Law its supreme authority and made it "The Book" for the ancient Hebrews.

PENTECOST, FEAST OF

This feast was observed early in the third month on the fiftieth day after the offering of the barley sheaf at the Feast of Unleavened Bread. It included a holy convocation with the usual restriction on manual labor. Numbers 28:26–31 describes the number and nature of offerings and Deuteronomy 16:9–12 describes those who were to be invited to this feast. They include servants, sons and daughters, Levites, the fatherless, the widow, and the stranger.

This feast was also known as the Feast of Harvest as well as the Feast of Weeks. The early Christian believers, who were gathered in Jerusalem for observance of this feast, experienced the outpouring of God's Holy Spirit in a miraculous way (Acts 2:1–4).

PENUEL [pih NOO uhl] (face of God)

A place north of the river Jabbok where Jacob wrestled with "a Man" until daybreak. Hosea 12:4 calls the "man" an "angel." Jacob called the place Penuel, "For I have seen God face to face" (Gen. 32:30). A city was built there later, not far to the east of Succoth. When Gideon and his band of 300 men pursued the Midianites, the people of Succoth and Penuel insulted Gideon, refusing to give supplies to his army. Gideon later killed the men of the city (Judg. 8:17). Penuel is about 40 miles (65 kilometers) northeast of Jerusalem. It is also called Peniel (Gen. 32:30).

PEREA [peh REE ah] *(the land beyond)*

The Greek term for Transjordan. The name Perea does not occur in the New Testament (except in a variant reading of Luke 6:17), but it is used regularly by the Jewish historian Josephus to describe the area east of the Jordan River. The New Testament refers to this area by using the phrase "beyond the Jordan" (Matt. 4:25; Mark 3:8). Josephus described Perea as the region between the Jabbok and the Arnon rivers, east of the Jordan.

PERGA [PUR guh]

The capital city of Pamphylia, a province on the southern coast of Asia Minor, twice visited by the apostle Paul. During Paul's first missionary journey, he sailed to Perga from Paphos, on the island of Cyprus (Acts 13:13–14). Some time later, Paul and Barnabas stopped a second time at Perga (Acts 14:25).

PERGAMOS [PURR guh mos]

The chief city of Mysia, near the Caicus River in northwest Asia Minor (modern Turkey) and the site of one of the seven churches of Asia (Rev. 1:11; 2:12–17; Pergamum in NRSV, NIV, REB, NASB). The city, situated opposite the island of Lesbos, was about 15 miles (24 kilometers) from the Aegean Sea.

In its early history Pergamos became a city-state, then a powerful nation after Attalus I (241–197 B.C.) defeated the Gauls (Galatians). It stood as a symbol of Greek superiority over the barbarians. Great buildings were erected and a library containing over 200,000 items was estab-

lished. The Egyptians, concerned with this library, which rivaled their own at Alexandria, refused to ship papyrus to Pergamos. As a result, a new form of writing material, Pergamena charta, or parchment, was developed.

In the days of Roman dominance throughout Asia Minor, Pergamos became the capital of the Roman province of Asia. In a gesture of friendship, Mark Antony gave the library of Pergamos to Cleopatra; its volumes were moved to Alexandria.

Not only was Pergamos a government center with three imperial temples, but it was also the site of the temple of Asklepios (the Greco-Roman god of medicine and healing), and the medical center where the physician Galen worked (about A.D. 160). Here also was a temple to Athena and a temple to Zeus with an altar showing Zeus defeating snake-like giants. In the Book of Revelation, John spoke of Pergamos as the place "where Satan's throne is" (Rev. 2:13). This could be a reference to the cult of emperor worship, because Pergamos was a center where this form of loyalty was pledged to the emperor of the Roman Empire.

PERIZZITES [PER uh zights] *(villagers)*

Inhabitants of the "forest country" (Josh. 17:15) in the territory of the tribes of Ephraim, Manasseh, and Judah (Judg. 1:4–5). The Perizzites, who lived in Canaan as early as the time of Abraham and Lot (Gen. 13:7), were subdued by the Israelites. After the conquest of the land of Canaan under Joshua, the Perizzites were allowed to live. They entered into marriages with their conquerors and seduced the Israelites into idolatry (Judg. 3:5–6). In the time of the judges, Bezek was their stronghold and Adoni-Bezek was their leader (Judg. 1:4–5). In the days of King Solomon the Perizzites were recruited for the king's forced-labor force (1 Kin. 9:20).

PERSEPOLIS [purr SEP oh liss] *(Persian city)*

The ceremonial capital of the Persian Empire under Darius the Great (522–486 B.C.), his son Xerxes (486–465 B.C.), and their successors. The city was second in importance to Shushan (or Susa), the administrative capital. Persepolis was destroyed in 330 B.C. by Alexander the Great. Its ruins are situated about 30 miles (49 kilometers) northeast of the modern city of Shiraz in southwestern Iran. Although Persepolis is not mentioned in the Bible, it appears in 2 Maccabees (2 Macc. 9:1–2).

PERSIA [PURR zyah]

An ancient world empire that flourished from 539–331 B.C. The Babylonian Empire fell to the Persians, setting the stage for the return of the Jews to Jerusalem in 538 B.C., following their long period of captivity by the Babylonians.

The Old Testament contains many references to the nation of Persia and its representatives. Ezra 9:9 refers to the "kings of Persia." Ezra 6:14 cites "Cyrus, Darius, and Artaxerxes king of Persia." Daniel 8:20 speaks of the "kings of Media and Persia." Daniel 10:13 mentions the "prince of the kingdom of Persia." The Book of Esther refers to the "powers of Persia and Media" (1:3), the "seven princes of Persia and Media" (1:14), and the "ladies of Persia and Media" (1:18). Daniel 5:28 prophesied that Belshazzar's kingdom would be "given to the Medes and Persians."

The Persians apparently sprang from a people from the hills of Russia known as Indo-Aryans. As early as 2000 B.C., they began to settle in Iran and along the Black Sea coast. Two of these Indo-European tribes settled on the Elamite border and to the east of the Zagros mountain range. The first references to them are made in the inscriptions of Shalmaneser III (858–824 B.C.). They are noted as the Parsua (Persians) and Madai (Medes).

The first mention of a Persian chieftain refers to his role as an ally aligned against Sennacherib of Assyria. His son was called "King, Great King, King of the City of Anshan." His grandson fathered Cyrus II, also known as Cyrus the Great, who was one of the most celebrated kings of history. He is called by the prophet Isaiah "My shepherd" (Is. 44:28). In another passage he is referred to as "His [the Lord's] Anointed" (Is. 45:1), a term used in the Old Testament of the Messiah. He is the only pagan king to be so designated in the Old Testament.

Cyrus II, founder of the mighty Persian Empire, ascended the throne in Anshan in 559 B.C. He conquered the Median King Astyages. Then he defeated Lydia (about 546 B.C.) and Babylon (539 B.C.), finally establishing the Persian Empire. This last conquest is referred to in Daniel 5. Cyrus's rule was a result of the sovereignty of God. Cyrus was the Persian king who issued the decree restoring the Jews to their homeland, following their long period of captivity by the Babylonians (2 Chr. 36:22–23; Ezra 1:1–4).

Cyrus was the founder of the system under which each province, or satrapy, was governed by an official who answered to the great king. However, he allowed a remarkable degree of freedom of religion and customs for the vassal states, including Palestine. He developed roads, cities, postal systems, and legal codes, and treated the subject nations kindly and humanely. The Bible refers to Cyrus in favorable terms (Is. 44:28–45:3).

Cambyses II (530–522 B.C.), the son of Cyrus, reigned after his father. During his reign, Egypt was added to the list of nations conquered by Persia. According to the Greek historian Herodotus, Cambyses accidentally wounded himself with his own sword in 522 B.C..

P

The next Persian king, Darius I (521–486 B.C.), was not a direct descendant of Cyrus but was of royal, Achaemenid blood. He defeated nine kings to claim all 23 Persian satrapies. This was recorded on the famous Behistun Inscription, which was written in the Akkadian, Elamite, and Old Persian languages.

Darius I further unified the Persian Empire by using an efficient gold coinage, state highways, and a more efficient postal system. He was defeated by the Greeks at the Battle of Marathon in 490 B.C. This is the same Darius who, in his second year, ordered the Jewish temple at Jerusalem to be rebuilt after work on it had been discontinued for 16 years (Ezra 4:24; 6:1). He also gave a generous subsidy that made it possible to complete the temple. The extent of the Persian Empire under Darius is reflected in Esther 1:1 and 10:1. The vast territory was nearly 3,000 miles (4,900 kilometers) long and 500 to 1,500 miles (800 to 2,400 kilometers) wide.

Xerxes ruled Persia from 486 to 465 B.C. He was the Ahasuerus of the Book of Esther. Esther did not become queen until the seventh year of his reign, which would be about 479 B.C. This was shortly after his devastating defeat at Salamis (480 B.C.), which ended Persia's last hope for conquering Greece.

Among the kingdoms of the ancient world, Persia is remembered because it built many important cities. Persepolis was a showpiece of Persian power. Pasargadae was the ancestral capital rapidly supplanted in importance. Ecbatana served as the capital of the Median Empire and became a resort area for the Persians. Susa (the Shushan of Esther) was the former capital of the Elamite Empire.

The religion of the Persians centered around a reformation of the old Iranian religions developed by Zoroaster. He believed in a dualism in which Ahura Mazda (or Ormazd) headed the gods of goodness (Amesha Spentas) and Angra Mainyu (or Ahriman) headed the gods of evil (daevas). Some of this is revealed in the Jewish apocryphal literature, which developed from the fifth century B.C. to the time of Christ.

PERSEVERANCE

The steadfast effort to follow God's commands and to do His work. The New Testament makes it clear that faith alone can save. But it makes it equally clear that perseverance in doing good works is the greatest indication that an individual's faith is genuine (James 2:14–26). Through persevering in God's work, Christians prove their deep appreciation for God's saving grace (1 Cor. 15:57–58). As a result of perseverance, the Christian can expect not only to enhance the strength of the church, but also to build up strength of character (Rom. 5:3–4).

PETER, SIMON

The most prominent of Jesus' twelve apostles. The New Testament gives a more complete picture of Peter than of any other disciple, with the exception of Paul. Peter is often considered to be a big, blundering fisherman. But this is a shallow portrayal. The picture of his personality portrayed in the New Testament is rich and many-sided. A more fitting appraisal of Peter is that he was a pioneer among the twelve apostles and the early church, breaking ground that the church would later follow.

Peter's given name was Simeon or Simon. His father's name was Jonah (Matt. 16:17; John 1:42). Simon's brother, Andrew, also joined Jesus as a disciple (Mark 1:16). The family probably lived at Capernaum on the north shore of the Sea of Galilee (Mark 1:21, 29), although it is possible they lived in Bethsaida (John 1:44).

The Gospel of John reports that Andrew and Peter were disciples of John the Baptist before they joined Jesus. John also reports that Peter was introduced to Jesus by his brother Andrew, who had already recognized Jesus to be the Messiah (John 1:35–42). Whether Andrew and Peter knew Jesus because they were disciples of John is uncertain. But it is clear that they followed Jesus because of His distinctive authority.

Peter was the first disciple to be called (Mark 1:16–18) and the first to be named an apostle (Mark 3:14–16). His name heads every list of the Twelve in the New Testament. He was apparently the strongest individual in the band. He frequently served as a spokesman for the disciples, and he was their recognized leader (Mark 1:36; Luke 22:32).

An inner circle of three apostles existed among the Twelve. Peter was also the leader of this small group. The trio— Peter, James, and John—was present with Jesus on a number of occasions. They witnessed the raising of a young girl from the dead (Mark 5:37; Luke 8:51); they were present at Jesus' transfiguration (Matt. 17:1–2); and they were present during Jesus' agony in Gethsemane (Matt. 26:37; Mark 14:33).

The purpose of Jesus' existence in the flesh was that people would come to a true picture of who God is and what He has done for our salvation. The first apostle to recognize that was Peter. He confessed Jesus as Lord in the region of Caesarea Philippi (Matt. 16:13–17).

How ironic that the one who denied Jesus most vehemently in His hour of suffering should be the first person to witness His resurrection from the dead. Yet according to Luke (Luke 24:34) and Paul (1 Cor. 15:5), Peter was the first apostle to see the risen Lord. We can only marvel at the grace of God in granting such a blessing to one who did not seem to deserve it. Peter's witnessing of the Resurrection was a sign of his personal restoration to fellowship with Christ. It also confirmed His appointment by God to serve as a leader in the emerging church.

Peter exercised a key leadership role in the church for a number of years. Indeed, the first 11 chapters of Acts are built around the activity of the apostle Peter. When the Holy Spirit visited the church in Samaria, the apostles sent Peter and John to verify its authenticity (Acts 8:14–25). But this event was only a prelude to the one event that concluded Peter's story in the New Testament: the preaching of the gospel to the Gentiles (Acts 10–11).

The chain of events that happened before the bestowal of the Holy Spirit on Gentile believers—beginning with Peter's staying in the house of a man of "unclean" profession (Acts 9:43), continuing with his vision of "unclean" foods (Acts 10:9–16), and climaxing in his realization that no human being, Gentile included, ought to be considered "unclean" (Acts 10:34–48)—is a masterpiece of storytelling. It demonstrates the triumph of God's grace to bring about change in stubborn hearts and the hardened social customs of Jewish believers.

According to early Christian tradition, Peter went to Rome, where he died. Only once in the New Testament do we hear of Peter's being in Rome. Even in this case, Rome is referred to as "Babylon" (1 Pet. 5:13). Little is known of Peter's activities in Rome, although Papias, writing about A.D. 125, stated that Peter's preaching inspired the writing of the first gospel, drafted by Mark, who was Peter's interpreter in Rome. Peter was also the author of the two New Testament epistles that bear his name.

PETRA [PET ruh] *(rock)*

The capital of Nabatea, situated about 170 miles (275 kilometers) southwest of modern Amman and about 50 miles (80 kilometers) south of the Dead Sea. Petra is not mentioned by name in the Bible, but many scholars believe it was the same place as Sela (Judg. 1:36; 2 Kin. 14:7).

Petra is one of the most spectacular archaeological ruins in the Near East and is a popular attraction on Holy Land tours. Most of the buildings and tombs of Petra are cut into the rose-red rock cliffs of the area.

Petra's ruins consist of about 750 monuments, most of them dating from the second half of the first century B.C. to the second century after Christ. In A.D. 131 the Roman emperor Hadrian (ruled A.D. 117–38) visited the city and ordered construction to begin on the so-called treasury, which has been called "Petra's gem"—a temple to Isis.

PHARAOH [PHAY row]

The title of the kings of Egypt until 323 B.C. In the Egyptian language the word *pharaoh* means "great house." This word was originally used to describe the

PETRA

palace of the king. Around 1500 B.C. this term was applied to the Egyptian kings. It meant something like "his honor, his majesty." In addition to this title, the kings also had a personal name (Amunhotep, Rameses) and other descriptive titles (King of Upper and Lower Egypt).

The pharaoh was probably the most important person in Egyptian society. The Egyptians believed he was a god and the key to the nation's relationship to the cosmic gods of the universe. While the pharaoh ruled, he was the son of Ra, the sun god, and the incarnation of the god Horus. He came from the gods with the divine responsibility to rule the land for them. His word was law, and he owned everything. Thus there were no law codes, because the king upheld order and justice and insured the stability of society.

When the pharaoh died, Egyptians believed that he became the god Osiris, the ruler of the underworld and those who live after death. The pharaoh was the head of the army as well as a central figure in the nation's religious life. As an intermediator between gods and people, the pharaoh functioned as a high priest in the many temples in Egypt. Because the Egyptian people believed their fate was dependent on that of the pharaoh, they seldom attempted to overthrow the government, although some pharaohs were very cruel.

In several instances the Israelites came into contact with a pharaoh. Abram (Abraham) went to Egypt around 2000 B.C. because of a famine in the land of Canaan. Because Abram lied about Sarai (Sarah) being his sister, Pharaoh wanted to take her into his harem; but God stopped him by sending a plague (Gen. 12:10–20). About 200 years later Joseph was thrown into prison in Egypt because the wife of Potiphar, the captain of Pharaoh's guard, lied about Joseph's behavior (Gen. 39).

While in prison Joseph met two of Pharaoh's servants, the butler and the baker, who had been put in prison because they displeased the powerful pharaoh (Gen. 40). Joseph correctly interpreted the dreams of the butler and baker and later was brought from prison to interpret the dream of the pharaoh (Gen. 41). The Egyptian priestly magicians could not interpret Pharaoh's dream. But because God told Joseph the meaning of the dream, Joseph was appointed as second in command to collect one-fifth of the nation's crops during the seven years of plenty.

Because of the severity of the seven years of famine, the Egyptians had to sell their cattle, their property, and themselves to the pharaoh for grain; thus the pharaoh owned everything (Gen. 47:13–20). The pharaoh sent carts to bring Joseph's brothers to Egypt (Gen. 45:16–20) and settled them in the fertile land of Goshen (Gen. 47:1–6).

After about 300 more years in Egypt, a new dynasty came to power. Its kings did not acknowledge Joseph and his deeds to save Egypt (Ex. 1:8). Therefore all the Israelites but Moses were enslaved. He was raised in the pharaoh's own court (Ex. 1:11–2:10; Acts 7:21–22). At 80 years of age, Moses returned to Pharaoh to ask permission to lead the Israelites out of Egypt. Pharaoh did not know or accept the God of the Israelites and refused to obey Him (Ex. 5:1–2).

On a second visit Moses functioned as God to Pharaoh by delivering a divine message (Ex. 7:1), but the miracles and initial plagues only hardened Pharaoh's heart (Ex. 7:8–13, 22; 8:15, 32). Each plague was carried out so the Israelites, the Egyptians, and the pharaoh would know that Israel's God was the only true God and that the Egyptian gods and their "divine pharaoh" were powerless before Him (Ex. 7:5, 17; 8:10, 22; 9:14, 29–30; 10:2).

Eventually Pharaoh admitted his sin, but before long he again hardened his heart (Ex. 9:27, 34; 10:16, 20). When Pharaoh's own "divine" first-born son was killed in the last plague, he finally submitted to God's power and let the people go (Ex. 12:29–33). Pharaoh later chased the Israelites to bring them back, but he and his army were drowned in the Red Sea (Ex. 14:5–31).

Solomon formed an alliance with an Egyptian pharaoh through marriage with his daughter (1 Kin. 3:1; 7:8; 9:24), thus demonstrating that Israel was a more powerful nation than Egypt. This pharaoh later gave the city of Gezer to his daughter (1 Kin. 9:16). The next pharaoh had less friendly relationships with Solomon and gave refuge to Solomon's enemy, Hadad the Edomite (1 Kin. 11:14–22). This may have been the Pharaoh Shishak who protected Jeroboam (1 Kin. 11:40) and captured Jerusalem in the fifth year of Rehoboam (1 Kin. 14:25–28). Hoshea, the king of Israel, had a treaty with So, the king of Egypt (2 Kin. 17:4). The Pharaoh Tirhakah may have had a similar relationship with Hezekiah (2 Kin. 19:9).

In 609 B.C. the Pharaoh Necho marched north through Palestine to save the Assyrians. King Josiah opposed this move, so Necho killed him (2 Kin. 23:29). Nebuchadnezzar later defeated Necho and took control of Judah (Jer. 46:2). It was possibly Pharaoh Hophra who challenged the Babylonians during the siege of Jerusalem in 587 B.C. (Jer. 37:5–10; 44:30; Ezek. 17:17).

The prophets Isaiah, Jeremiah, and Hosea condemned Pharaoh and the Israelites who trusted in him and his army (Is. 30:1–5; 31:1; Jer. 42:18; Hos. 7:11). But the prophecies of Ezekiel are by far the most extensive (Ezek. 29–32). Pharaoh is quoted as saying, "My River is my own; I have made it for myself" (Ezek. 29:3). Because Pharaoh claimed the power and authority of God, Ezekiel declared, God will destroy Pharaoh and Egypt (Ezek. 29:19; 30:21; 31:2; 32:2, 12).

The "king of the South" in (Dan. 11:5, 9, 11, 14, 25, 40) probably refers to one or more of the Greek kings, called Ptolemy, who ruled Egypt after the line of pharaohs ended in 323 B.C.

PHARISEES [FARE uh sees] *(separated ones)*

A religious and political party in Palestine in New Testament times. The Pharisees were known for insisting that the law of God be observed as the scribes interpreted it and for their special commitment to keeping the laws of tithing and ritual purity.

The Pharisees had their roots in the group of faithful Jews known as the Hasidim (or Chasidim). The Hasidim arose in the second century B.C. when the influence of Hellenism on the Jews was particularly strong and many Jews lived little differently than their Gentile neighbors. But the Hasidim insisted on strict observance of Jewish ritual laws.

When the Syrian King Antiochus IV tried to do away with the Jewish religion, the Hasidim took part in the revolt of the Maccabees against him. Apparently from this movement of faithful Hasidim came both the Essenes—who later broke off from other Jews and formed their own communities—and the Pharisees, who remained an active part of Jewish life. Indeed, during the period of independence that followed the revolt, some of the Greek rulers who controlled Palestine favored the Pharisaic party.

As a result of this favoritism, Pharisees came to be represented on the Sanhedrin, the supreme court and legislative body of the Jews. At times, the Pharisees even dominated the assembly. In New Testament times, Pharisees, though probably in the minority, were still an effective part of the Sanhedrin.

One distinctive feature of the Pharisees was their strong commitment to observing the law of God as it was interpreted and applied by the scribes. Although the priests had been responsible for teaching and interpreting the law (Lev. 10:8–11; Deut. 33:8–10) in Old Testament times, many people had lost all respect for the priests because of the corruption in the Jerusalem priesthood. They looked to the scribes instead to interpret the law for them. Some scribes were priests; many were not. Still, they lived pious, disciplined lives; and they had been trained to become experts in the law. It was natural, then, for people to follow their leading rather than that of the priests.

The way in which the Pharisees spelled out the meaning of the Mosaic Law, the ways in which they adapted that law to suit the needs of their day, the time-honored customs they endorsed—all these became a part of the "tradition of the elders" (Mark 7:3). Although these traditions were not put into writing, they were passed on from one scribe to another and from the scribes to the people. From this tradition, they claimed, the Jewish people could know the way God's law should be observed. The Pharisees agreed, and they were known for supporting and keeping the "tradition of the elders."

The Pharisees also believed it was important to observe all the laws of God, which they taught were 613 in all. But they were especially known for their commitment to keep the laws of tithing and ritual purity.

According to the New Testament, the Pharisees were concerned about strictly interpreting and keeping the law on all matters (Acts 26:5), including the Sabbath (Mark 2:24), divorce (Mark 10:2), oaths (Matt. 23:16–22), the wearing of phylacteries and fringes (Matt. 23:5), and so on. But they showed special zeal in insisting that laws of tithing and ritual purity be kept (Matt. 23:23–26; Mark 7:1–13; Luke 11:37–42; 18:12).

Since Pharisees found that other Jews were not careful enough about keeping those laws, they felt it was necessary to place limits on their contacts with other Jews as well as with Gentiles. For example, they could not eat in the home of a non-Pharisee, since they could not be sure that the food had been properly tithed and kept ritually pure.

Unlike the Sadducees, the Pharisees did believe in the resurrection of the dead. On this point, they were on common ground with the early Christians (Acts 23:6–9). The scribe in Mark 12:28 who thought that Jesus had answered the Sadducees well concerning the resurrection was probably a Pharisee.

In the New Testament, the Pharisees appear frequently in the accounts of Jesus' ministry and the history of the early church. In these passages a number of the typical failings of the Pharisees are evident. Pharisees observed the law carefully as far as appearances went, but their hearts were far from God. Their motives were wrong because they wanted human praise (Matt. 6:2, 5, 16; 23:5–7). They also had evil desires that were hidden by their pious show (Matt. 23:25–28). That is why Pharisees are often called hypocrites: their hearts did not match their outward appearance.

PHILADELPHIA [fill ah DELL fih uh]
(brotherly love)

A city of the province of Lydia in western Asia Minor (modern Turkey) and the site of one of the seven churches of Asia to which John wrote in the Book of Revelation (Rev. 1:11).

Philadelphia was situated on the Cogamus River, a tributary of the Hermus (modern Gediz) and was about 28 miles (45 kilometers) southeast of Sardis. It was founded by Attalus II (Philadelphus), who reigned as king of Pergamos from 159 B.C. until 138 B.C. Philadelphia was a center of the wine industry. Its chief deity was Dionysus, in Greek mythology the god of wine (the Roman Bacchus).

In the Book of Revelation, John describes the church in Philadelphia as the faithful church and the church that stood at the gateway of a great opportunity (Rev. 3:7–13). Christ said to this church, "See, I have set before you an open door and no one can shut it" (v. 8). The "open door" means primarily access to God, but it also refers to opportunity for spreading the gospel of Jesus Christ. Still a city of considerable size, Philadelphia is known today as Alashehir.

PHILEMON [fie LEE mun]

A wealthy Christian of Colossae who hosted a house church. Philemon was converted under the apostle Paul (Philem. 19), perhaps when Paul ministered in Ephesus (Acts 19:10). He is remembered because of his runaway slave, Onesimus, who, after damaging or stealing his master's property (Philem. 11, 18), made his way to Rome, where he was converted under Paul's ministry (Philem. 10).

Accompanied by Tychicus (Col. 4:7), Onesimus later returned to his master, Philemon. He carried with him the Epistle to the Colossians, plus the shorter Epistle to Philemon. In the latter, Paul asked Philemon to receive Onesimus, not as a slave but as a "beloved brother" (Philem. 16).

PHILIP [FILL ihp] *(lover of horses)*

1. One of the twelve apostles of Christ (Matt. 10:3; Mark 3:18; Luke 6:14) and a native of Bethsaida in Galilee (John 1:44; 12:21). According to the Gospel of John, Philip met Jesus beyond the Jordan River during John the Baptist's ministry. Jesus called Philip to become His disciple.

Philip responded and brought to Jesus another disciple, named Nathanael (John 1:43–51) or Bartholomew (Mark 3:18). Philip is usually mentioned with Nathanael.

Before Jesus fed the five thousand, He tested Philip by asking him how so many people could possibly be fed. Instead of responding in faith, Philip began to calculate the amount of food it would take to feed them and the cost (John 6:5–7).

When certain Greeks, who had come to Jerusalem to worship at the Feast of Passover, said to Philip, "Sir, we wish to see Jesus" (John 12:21), Philip seemed unsure of what he should do. He first told Andrew, and then they told Jesus of the request. Philip was one of the apostles who was present in the Upper Room following the resurrection of Jesus (Acts 1:13).

PHILIP [FILL ihp] *(lover of horses)*

2. Philip the evangelist, one of the seven men chosen to serve the early church because they were reported to be "full of faith and the Holy Spirit" (Acts 6:5). Their task was to look after the Greek-speaking widows and probably all of the poor in the Jerusalem church. Following the stoning of Stephen, the first Christian martyr, many Christians scattered from Jerusalem (Acts 8:1). Philip became an evangelist and, in Samaria, preached the gospel, worked miracles, and brought many to faith in Christ (Acts 8:5–8).

Probably the most noted conversion as a result of Philip's ministry was the Ethiopian eunuch, an official under Candace, the queen of the Ethiopians. Philip met the eunuch on the road from Jerusalem to Gaza. The eunuch was reading from Isaiah 53, the passage about the Suffering Servant. Philip used this great opportunity to preach Jesus to him. The eunuch said, "I believe that Jesus Christ is the Son of God" (Acts 8:37). Then Philip baptized him.

After this event, Philip preached in Azotus (the Old Testament Ashdod) and Caesarea (Acts 8:40). He was still in Caesarea many years later when the apostle Paul passed through the city on his last journey to Jerusalem (Acts 21:8). Luke adds that Philip had "four virgin daughters who prophesied" (Acts 21:9).

PHILIPPI [FIL uh pie] *(city of Philip)*

A city in eastern Macedonia (modern Greece) visited by the apostle Paul. Situated on a plain surrounded by mountains, Philippi lay about 10 miles (16 kilometers) inland from the Aegean Sea. The Egnatian Way, the main overland route between Asia and the West, ran through the city. Philippi was named for Philip II of Macedonia, the father of Alexander the Great. In 356 B.C. Philip enlarged and renamed the city, which was formerly known as Krenides. Philip resettled people from the countryside in Philippi and built a wall around the city and an acropolis atop the surrounding mountain. Although they date from later periods, other points of interest in Philippi include a forum the size of a football field, an open-air theater, two large temples, public buildings, a library, and Roman baths.

In 42 B.C. Mark Antony and Octavian (later Augustus Caesar) combined forces to defeat the armies of Brutus and Cassius, assassins of Julius Caesar, at Philippi. In celebration of the victory, Philippi was made into a Roman colony; this entitled its inhabitants to the rights and privileges usually granted those who lived in cities in Italy. Eleven years later, Octavian defeated the forces of Antony and Cleopatra in a naval battle at Actium, on the west coast of Greece. Octavian punished the supporters of Antony by evicting them from Italy and resettling them in Philippi. The vacated sites in It-

aly were then granted to Octavian's own soldiers as a reward for their victory over Antony.

The apostle Paul visited Philippi on his second missionary journey in A.D. 49 (Acts 16:12; 20:6). Evidently the city did not have the necessary number of Jewish males (ten) to form a synagogue, because Paul met with a group of women for prayer outside the city gate (Acts 16:13).

French excavations at Philippi between 1914 and 1938 unearthed a Roman arch that lay about one mile west of the city. This arch may have served as a zoning marker to restrict undesirable religious sects from meeting in the city. Lydia, one of the women of Philippi who befriended Paul, was a dealer in purple cloth (Acts 16:14). A Latin inscription uncovered in excavations mentions this trade, thus indicating its economic importance for Philippi. Philippi also is mentioned or implied in Acts 20:16; Philippians 1:1; and 1 Thessalonians 2:2.

PHILISTINES [fih LIS teens]

An aggressive nation that occupied part of southwest Palestine from about 1200 to 600 B.C. The name *Philistine* was used first among the Egyptians to describe the sea people defeated by Rameses III in a naval battle about 1188 B.C. Among the Assyrians the group was known as Pilisti or Palastu. The Hebrew word *pelishti* is the basis of the name Palestine, a later name for Canaan, the country occupied by God's covenant people.

Little is known about the origins of the Philistines except what is contained in the Bible—that they came from Caphtor (Gen. 10:14), generally identified with the island of Crete in the Mediterranean Sea. Crete also was supposed to be the home of the Cherethites, who were sometimes associated with the Philistines (Ezek.

25:16). Philistine territory was considered Cherethite in 1 Samuel 30:14, suggesting that both peoples were part of the invading group defeated earlier by Rameses III of Egypt.

Liberal scholars have assumed that references to the Philistines during Abraham's time are incorrect historically and that the Philistine occupation actually occurred in the twelfth century B.C. More careful examination indicates there were two Philistine settlements in Canaan, one early and another later. Both these settlements were marked by significant cultural differences.

The Philistines of Gerar, with whom Abraham dealt (Gen. 20–21), evidently were a colony of the early settlement located southeast of Gaza in southern Canaan. This colony was situated outside the area occupied by the five Philistine cities after 1188 B.C. Gerar was also a separate city-state governed by a king who bore the name or title of Abimelech.

That Abimelech's colony was the chief one in the area seems probable from his title, "king of the Philistines" (Gen. 26:1, 8). This is different from a later period when the Philistines were governed by five lords. Unlike the later Philistines who were Israel's chief foes in the settlement and monarchy periods, the Gerar Philistines were peaceful. They encouraged the friendship of Abraham and Isaac. Finally, Gerar was not included among the chief cities of Philistia (Josh. 13:3). It was not mentioned as one of the places conquered by the Israelites. It is best, therefore, to regard the Genesis traditions as genuine historical records.

The early Philistine settlements in Canaan took on a new appearance when five cities—Ashkelon, Ashdod, Ekron, Gath, and Gaza—and the areas around them were occupied by the Philistines in the twelfth century B.C. Probably all of these except Ekron were already in existence when the sea peoples con-

quered them. These five Philistine cities formed a united political unit. Archaeological discoveries in the area have illustrated how they expanded to the south and east. Broken bits of Philistine pottery were found at archaeological sites in those areas.

The Philistines possessed superior weapons of iron when they began to attack the Israelites in the eleventh century B.C. The tribe of Dan moved northward to escape these Philistine attacks, and Judah also came under increasing pressure (Judg. 14–18). In Samuel's time the Philistines captured the ark of the covenant in battle. Although the ark was recovered later, the Philistines continued to occupy Israelite settlements (1 Sam. 10:5).

The threat of the Philistines prompted Israel's demands for a king. But even under Saul the united nation was still menaced by the Philistines—a threat that ultimately resulted in Saul's death (1 Sam. 31). David's slaying of Goliath, a giant from Gath, was a key factor in his rise to fame. By this time the Philistines had moved deep into Israelite territory. Archaeological evidence shows they had occupied Tell Beit Mirsim, Beth Zur, Gibeah, Megiddo, and Beth Shean. Yet by the end of David's reign their power had begun to decline significantly. By the time Jehoshaphat was made king of Judah (873–848 B.C.), the Philistines were paying tribute (2 Chr. 17:11), although they tried to become independent under Jehoshaphat's son, Jehoram (2 Chr. 21:16–17).

When the Assyrians began to raid Palestine in later years, the Philistines faced additional opposition. The Assyrian Adad-Nirari III (about 810–783 B.C.) placed the Philistine cities under heavy tribute early in his reign, while Uzziah of Judah (791–740 B.C.) demolished the defenses of several Philistine strongholds, including Gath. When he became king, Ahaz of Judah (732–715 B.C.) was attacked by Philistine forces, and cities in the Negev and the Judean lowlands were occupied. The Assyrian king Tiglath-Pileser III responded by conquering the chief Philistine cities.

In 713 B.C. Sargon II, king of Assyria, invaded Philistia and conquered Ashdod. The following year he launched another campaign against other Philistine cities. Hezekiah of Judah (716–686 B.C.) attacked Gaza (2 Kin. 18:8), supported by the people of Ekron and Ashkelon; but in 701 B.C. Sennacherib brought Philistine territory under his control to prevent any Egyptian interference. When Nebuchadnezzar came to power in Babylon, the Philistines formed an alliance with Egypt; but when the Jews were exiled to Babylonia between 597 and 586 B.C., the Philistines, too, were deported.

The Philistines worshiped three gods—Ashtoreth, Dagon, and Baal-Zebub—each of which had shrines in various cities (Judg. 16:23; 1 Sam. 5:1–7; 2 Kin. 1:2). Philistine soldiers apparently carried images of their gods into battle, perhaps as standards (2 Sam. 5:21). Like other Near Eastern peoples, the Philistines were superstitious. They respected the power of Israel's ark of the covenant (1 Sam. 5:1–12).

The Philistines were important culturally because they adopted the manufacture and distribution of iron implements and weapons from the Hittites. Goliath's equipment was obviously of Philistine manufacture. The golden objects that were offered to Israel's God (1 Sam. 6:4–5) show that the Philistines were skilled goldsmiths as well.

Some Philistine burial places discovered at Tell Far'ah reveal bodies encased in clay coffins shaped to match the human body. The coffin lid was decorated with crude figures of the head and clasped arms of the deceased.

PHINEHAS [FIN ih uhs] *(the Nubian)*

1. A son of Eleazar and grandson of Aaron (Ex. 6:25). During the wilderness wandering, Phinehas killed Zimri, a man of Israel, and Cozri, a Midianite woman whom Zimri had brought into the camp (Num. 25). This action ended a plague by which God had judged Israel for allowing Midianite women to corrupt Israel with idolatry and harlotry. For such zeal, Phinehas and his descendants were promised a permanent priesthood (Num. 25:11–13). Phinehas became the third high priest of Israel, serving for 19 years. His descendants held the high priesthood until the Romans destroyed the temple in A.D. 70, except for a short period when the house of Eli served as high priests.

PHINEHAS [FIN ih uhs] *(the Nubian)*

2. The younger of the two sons of Eli the priest (1 Sam. 1:3). Phinehas and his brother, Hophni, were priests also; but they disgraced their priestly office by greed, irreverence, and immorality (1 Sam. 2:12–17, 22–25). The Lord told Eli his two sons would die (1 Sam. 2:34). They were killed in a battle with the Philistines. When Phinehas's wife heard the news, she went into premature labor and died in childbirth. The child was named Ichabod, which means "The glory has departed from Israel!" (1 Sam. 4:22). Because of the evil actions of Phinehas and Hophni, the high priesthood later passed from Eli's family.

PHOEBE [FEE bih]

A servant of the church in Cenchrea, the eastern port of Corinth (Rom. 16:1; Phebe in KJV). The apostle Paul tells us little about Phoebe, other than "she has been a helper of many and of myself also" (Rom. 16:2). The Greek words he used to describe her suggest that Phoebe was a wealthy businesswoman. Many scholars believe she delivered Paul's letter to the Romans.

PHOENICIA [foe KNEE shih uh]

The land north of Palestine on the eastern shore of the Mediterranean Sea, between the Litani and Arvad rivers. Phoenicia is a Greek word, that means "land of purple." The area was famous from early times for its purple dyes, produced from shellfish. In the KJV, Phoenicia is spelled Phenicia.

Phoenicia was a long, narrow country on the seacoast covering much of the territory that today is called Lebanon and southern Latakia (coastal Syria). Like Israel, much of it is mountainous, with only a narrow coastal plain. The low hills and plains are very fertile. Phoenicia was famous in biblical times for its lush plant life, which included fruit, flowers, and trees (Hos. 14:5–7): "They shall be revived like grain, and grow like the vine. Their scent shall be like the wine of Lebanon" (v. 7).

The cedars of Phoenicia were cut and shipped as far away as Egypt and eastern Mesopotamia, because most other nations in this part of the world had very few trees suitable for timber. Many direct land and sea routes connected Phoenicia to northern Israel. The Phoenicians had many contacts with the Israelites. During their long history, the Hebrew people often fell into paganism and idolatry because of the influence of Phoenician religion.

PHRYGIA [FRIJ ih uh]

A large province of the mountainous region of Asia Minor (modern Turkey), visited by the apostle Paul (Acts 2:10; 16:6; 18:23). Because of its size, Phrygia was made a part of other provinces. In Roman times the region was split between two provinces. The cities of Colosse, Laodicea, and Hierapolis belonged to Asia, while Iconium and Antioch belonged to Galatia.

The apostle Paul visited Phrygia on two journeys (Acts 13:14–14:5, 21; 16:6). He apparently also passed through Phrygia on his third journey (Acts 18:22–24), although his letter to the Colossians suggests he did not found a church there (Col. 2:1). Jews who were at Jerusalem on the Day of Pentecost may have been the first Phrygian converts (Acts 2:10). Jews settled in Phrygia during the Seleucid period. Some of them apparently adopted non-Jewish practices. Consequently, strict Jews became hostile to new ideas (Acts 13:44–14:6).

PHYLACTERIES [fie LACK tuh rees]

Small square leather boxes or cases, each containing four strips of parchment inscribed with quotations from the Pentateuch, the first five books of the Old Testament (Ex. 13:1–10; 13:11–16; Deut. 6:4–9; 11:13–21). Phylacteries were worn by every male Israelite above 13 years of age during morning prayer, except on the Sabbath and holidays. Although orthodox Jews still observe this practice, reformed Judaism has discontinued it.

Phylacteries consisted of two small hollow cubes made of the skin of clean animals. These boxes were attached to leather straps that were used to fasten them to the left hand and to the forehead during morning worship. The custom of wearing phylacteries can be traced to Deuteronomy 6:8: "You shall bind them as a sign upon your hand, and they shall be as frontlets between your eyes."

The discovery of portions of phylacteries in the Dead Sea caves reveals they were not standardized before the time of Christ. Certainly not all the people wore them, but the Pharisees possibly wore them constantly during the time of Jesus.

The word *phylacteries* occurs only once in the New Testament: "They [the scribes and Pharisees] make their phylacteries broad and enlarge the borders of their garments" (Matt. 23:5). In this passage Jesus criticized the display of some religious leaders who wanted to impress people with their piety.

PILATE, PONTIUS [PIE lat, PON chus]

The fifth Roman prefect of Judea (ruled A.D. 26–36), who issued the official order sentencing Jesus to death by crucifixion (Matt. 27; Mark 15; Luke 23; John 18–19).

The Jewish historian Josephus provides what little information is known about Pilate's life before A.D. 26, when Tiberius appointed him procurator of Judea. The sketchy data suggests that Pilate was probably an Italian-born Roman citizen whose family was wealthy enough for him to qualify for the middle class. Probably he held certain military posts before his appointment in Judea. He was married (Matt. 27:19), bringing his wife, Claudia Procula, to live with him at Caesarea, the headquarters of the province. Pilate governed the areas of Judea, Samaria, and the area south as far as the Dead Sea to Gaza. As prefect he had absolute authority over the non-Roman citizens of the province. He was responsible to the Roman governor who lived in Syria to the north (Luke 2:2).

Pilate never became popular with the Jews. He seemed to be insensitive to their religious convictions and stubborn in the pursuit of his policies. But when the Jews responded to his rule with enraged opposition, he often backed down, demonstrating his weakness. He angered the Jews when he took funds from the temple treasury to build an aqueduct to supply water to Jerusalem. Many Jews reacted violently to this act, and Pilate's soldiers killed many of them in this rebellion. It may be this or another incident to which Luke refers in Luke 13:1–2. In spite of this, Pilate continued in office

for ten years, showing that Tiberius considered Pilate an effective administrator.

Pilate's later history is also shrouded in mystery. Josephus tells of a bloody encounter with the Samaritans, who filed a complaint with Pilate's superior, Vitellius, the governor of Syria. Vitellius deposed Pilate and ordered him to stand before the emperor in Rome and answer for his conduct. Legends are confused as to how Pilate died. Eusebius reports that he was exiled to the city of Vienne on the Rhone in Gaul (France) where he eventually committed suicide.

Since the Jews could not execute a person without approval from the Roman authorities (John 18:31), the Jewish leaders brought Jesus to Pilate to pronounce the death sentence (Mark 14:64). Pilate seemed convinced that Jesus was not guilty of anything deserving death, and he sought to release Jesus (Matt. 27:24; Mark 15:9–11; Luke 23:14; John 18:38–40; 19:12). Neither did he want to antagonize the Jews and run the risk of damaging his own reputation and career. Thus, when they insisted on Jesus' crucifixion, Pilate turned Jesus over to be executed (Matt. 27:26; Mark 15:12–15; Luke 23:20–25; John 19:15–16).

Pilate is a good example of the unprincipled achiever who will sacrifice what is right to accomplish his own selfish goals. Although he recognized Jesus' innocence and had the authority to uphold justice and acquit Jesus, he gave in to the demands of the crowd rather than risk a personal setback in his career. This is a real temptation to all people who hold positions of power and authority.

PILLAR OF FIRE AND CLOUD

The phenomenon by which God guided the Israelites during their travels through the wilderness after leaving Egypt (Ex. 14:24). The pillar of fire and cloud is first mentioned in Exodus 13:21–22, where some of its characteristics are described. In the form of cloud by day and fire by night, the pillar was constantly visible to the Israelites. By this phenomenon, God led the people on their journey from the border of Egypt as they marched toward the Promised Land. As a pillar of fire, it gave enough light for the people to travel by night.

The pillar of fire and cloud was also a visible sign or representation of God's presence with His people. In a sense God could be said to be "in" the pillar (Ex. 14:24); in it He "came down" to the tabernacle of meeting (Num. 12:5), and "appeared" at the tabernacle (Deut. 31:15).

After the tabernacle was built in the wilderness, it was covered by a cloud that had the appearance of fire by night. Although this cloud was not described as a pillar, it must have been the same phenomenon. While the cloud remained over the tabernacle, the people did not break camp. But they set out when the cloud was taken up. Wherever it settled down again was to be the next stopping place.

PISGAH [PIZ guh]

A word that refers to the rugged ridge that crowns a mountain. As a proper noun, the word *Pisgah* was sometimes identified with Mount Nebo. But the word more likely refers to the entire ridge of the Abarim Mountains, which extends from the Moabite plateau toward the Dead Sea.

Nebo is the highest peak of this "pisgah." From the top of Pisgah, Moses was permitted to survey the Promised Land. The particular peak upon which he stood was on or near Mount Nebo (Num. 21:20; 23:14; Deut. 3:27; 34:1).

Balaam offered sacrifices upon seven altars at the field of Zophim on the top of Pisgah (Num. 23:14). From the Pisgah ridge, steep slopes drop about 2,600 feet (792 meters) into the Jordan valley below (Deut. 3:17). Ashdoth-Pisgah, "the slopes

of Pisgah" (translated "the springs of Pisgah" in Deut. 4:49, KJV), was allotted to the tribe of Reuben (Josh. 13:20, KJV). This ridge originally marked the southern limits of the territory of Sihon, king of the Amorites (Josh. 12:3).

PISIDIA [pih SID ih uh]

A mountainous province in central Asia Minor (modern Turkey), twice visited by the apostle Paul (Acts 13:14; 14:24). Pisidia was a wild, mountainous country infested with bandits. When Paul wrote that he had been "in perils of robbers" (2 Cor. 11:26), he may have been referring to his dangerous journey through the mountains of Pisidia. While in Perga, Paul intended to travel north through this rugged and dangerous mountain terrain to Antioch of Pisidia. The synagogue in Antioch of Pisidia was the scene of one of Paul's most impressive sermons (Acts 13:16–41).

PITHOM [PIE thuhm]

One of the supply cities, or store cities, in Lower Egypt built by the Israelites while they were slaves in Egypt (Ex. 1:11). Pithom was in the general area of Raamses. Some archaeologists suggest that the temple, fortress, and storage chambers discovered at Tell el-Maskhutah, in the valley connecting the Nile River and Lake Timsah, are the remains of biblical Pithom. Others believe that Pithom should be identified with Tell er-Ratabah, about 10 miles (16 kilometers) to the west and closer to the land of Goshen. The site of Pithom remains a subject of doubt and debate.

It is possible that Pithom and Raamses (Ex. 1:11) were built during the reign of Pharaoh Rameses II (who ruled from about 1292–1225 B.C.). Rameses II, however, often made claims to "build" a city, when actually he "rebuilt" it, or strengthened its fortifications. Pithom is supposed by some scholars to be identical with Succoth (Ex. 12:37)—Pithom being the sacred, or religious name and Succoth being the secular or civil name.

PLAGUE

An affliction sent by God as punishment for sin and disobedience. In most cases in the Bible the affliction is an epidemic or disease. The Hebrew word for "plague" literally means a blow or a lash, implying punishment or chastisement.

Plagues appear throughout the biblical record. The first mention of a plague in Scripture was that sent on Pharaoh for the protection of Sarah, Abraham's wife (Gen. 12:17). The next plagues were the ten afflictions experienced by the Egyptians when the pharaoh refused to release the Hebrew people from bondage. While these plagues were phenomena with which the Egyptians were familiar, they exhibited miraculous features that were characteristic of God's judgment.

Later, during the years of the Exodus, a plague was sent upon the Hebrews for making and worshiping a golden calf (Ex. 32:35). Another occurred because of their murmuring against the food that God provided for them (Num. 11:33–34). The spies who brought faithless reports about the Promised Land were inflicted with a plague (Num. 14:37).

When the Hebrews complained about the righteous punishment of the rebels Korah, Dathan, and Abiram, 14,700 people died of a plague (Num. 16:46–50). In another plague sent upon the Hebrews because of idolatry at Baal-peor, 24,000 people died (Num. 25:9; Josh. 22:17; Ps. 106:29–30).

The plagues were sometimes miraculous events. At other times they appeared as natural phenomena. But always they represented God's aggressive acts to punish sin and disobedience among His people.

PLAGUES OF EGYPT

The series of ten afflictions used by God to break the will of Pharaoh and to bring about the release of the Hebrew people from slavery in Egypt.

After the Hebrews had been in Egypt for about 400 years, "there arose a new king over Egypt, who did not know Joseph" (Ex. 1:8). This new king enslaved the Hebrews and forced them to labor in his extensive building projects. When the Hebrews cried out for deliverance, God sent Moses to lead them from bondage. The pharaoh resisted the release of the Hebrew people. The plagues of Egypt occurred as God's action to change the mind of the pharaoh, thus bringing the Hebrews' freedom.

Scholars generally agree that the first nine plagues were regular, natural occurrences in Egypt. They were remarkable only in their intensity and in the timing with which they happened. But this does not mean that they were purely natural phenomena. They were miraculous in that God used natural forces to achieve His purpose. The method does not diminish the miraculous nature of the occurrence.

The tenth plague, the death of the firstborn of Egypt, was altogether supernatural. There is no known natural phenomenon closely related to this highly selective plague.

The sequence of the plagues has been studied and compared with the observations of travelers to Egypt. Many scholars point out that the first nine plagues are logical consequences of an unusually high flooding of the Nile River. Such flooding usually occurred in July, August, and September. Based on the best estimates that can be made from the biblical account, the plagues probably occurred over a period of about seven to nine months, beginning in July or August and continuing until around April or May.

The plagues may be viewed as God's intervention to seek the release of the Hebrew people. They also represented God's challenge to the Egyptian religious system. To the Egyptians, the Nile River was a god. From it came the power and life of the Egyptian culture. They worshiped the Nile and the abundance of resources that it provided. Since the first nine plagues seem to be a natural progression of God's attack on the Nile River, all of these plagues relate to God's challenge to the Egyptian religious system.

Following are the ten plagues, as recorded in Exodus 7:14–12:30:

1. *The Water of the Nile Turned into Blood* (Ex. 7:14–25). This first plague probably was the pollution of the Nile River by large quantities of fine, red earth, brought down from the Sudan and Ethiopia by abnormal flooding. The pollution of the water provided a favorable environment for the growth of micro-organisms and parasitic bacteria. Their presence could have led to the death of the fish in the river (Ex. 7:21).

2. *Frogs Cover the Land* (Ex. 8:1–15). Seven days after the first plague, frogs came out of the river and infested the land. The frogs would have been driven from the Nile and its canals and pools by the polluted water. When Moses prayed to God, the frogs died in the houses, courtyards, and fields. The frogs were symbols of the Egyptian goddess, Heqt, who was supposed to help women in childbirth. This plague was another demonstration of the superior power of God over the gods of Egypt.

3. *Lice Throughout the Land* (Ex. 8:16–19). Insects of various kinds are common in Egypt. It is not easy to identify the exact pests involved in the third plague. Various translations have lice (KJV, NKJV), gnats (NASB, NRSV, NIV), and maggots (REB).

4. *Swarms of Flies* (Ex. 8:20–32). Many kinds of flies are common in Egypt. The mounds of decaying frogs would have provided an ideal breeding ground for these pests. Some scholars suggest that the swarms mentioned here were a species known as the stable fly, a blood feeder that bites people as well as cattle. This fly is a carrier of skin anthrax, which is probably the disease brought on by the sixth plague.

5. *Pestilence of Livestock* (Ex. 9:1–7). Either the frogs or the insects may have been the carriers of this infection. The livestock of the Israelites were miraculously protected (Ex. 9:6–7).

6. *Boils on Man and Beast* (Ex. 9:8–12). This infection was probably skin anthrax, carried by the flies of the fourth plague. The festering boils broke into blisters and running sores.

7. *Heavy Hail, with Thunder and Lightning* (Ex. 9:13–35). Egypt was essentially an agricultural country. By destroying the crops, this plague and the next struck at the heart of Egypt's economy.

8. *Swarms of Locusts* (Ex. 10:1–20). This plague must have followed the hail very closely. Heavy rainfall in July-September would have produced conditions favorable for locusts in March. These locusts, swarms of foliage-eating grasshoppers, probably were driven into the Egyptian delta by strong winds. They wiped out the vegetation that had survived the earlier destruction.

9. *Three Days of Darkness* (Ex. 10:21–29). This darkness could have been caused by a severe dust storm. For three days darkness covered the land (Ex. 10:23). This storm would have been intensified by fine earth deposited over the land by previous flooding. By showing God's power over the light of the sun—represented by one of Egypt's chief deities, the sun-god Ra—this plague was a further judgment on the idolatry of the Egyptians.

10. *Death of Egyptian Firstborn* (Ex.

11:1–12:30). The tenth plague was the most devastating of all—the death of the firstborn males in Egyptian families. The Hebrews were spared because they followed God's command to sprinkle the blood of a lamb on the doorposts of their houses. The death angel "passed over" the houses where the blood was sprinkled—hence, the name Passover for this religious observance among the Jewish people. Only a supernatural explanation can account for the selective slaughter of the tenth plague.

PLEIADES [PLEE uh deez]

A brilliant cluster of stars seen in the shoulder of Taurus (the Bull). The name Pleiades comes from the seven daughters of Atlas and Pleione in Greek mythology. This constellation consists of several hundred stars, although the naked eye can usually see only six or seven. Job declared that God made the Pleiades (Job 9:9) and bound them in a cluster (Job 38:31).

PLOW

The earliest plows were probably simple wooden sticks used to scratch furrows in the ground for planting seeds. Eventually, larger forked branches drawn by animals were used. These "single-handed" plows were light enough for one man to lift around obstructions. They had the advantage of leaving one hand free for the farmer to guide the animals.

By the time of Saul (about 1050 B.C.), iron tips were commonly fastened to the wooden plows. This made it easier to cultivate the stony soil of Israel. The Philistines were concerned that the Israelites not learn the secrets of iron smelting (1 Sam. 13:19–22). They apparently recognized it would be easy to make "plowshares into swords" for warfare (Joel 3:10). On the other hand, the age of the Messiah, the "Prince of Peace," was to be a time when "they shall beat their swords into plowshares" (Is. 2:4; Mic. 4:3).

POLYGAMY

The practice of having several spouses, especially wives, at one time. Polygamy includes polygyny (marriage to more than one woman) and polyandry (marriage to more than one man). The term *polygamy* is more often used, however, as a synonym for polygyny, which was common throughout the ancient world.

According to the custom of the times, Abraham took Hagar, the Egyptian maidservant of his wife Sarah, to be his wife when Sarah was unable to bear a child (Gen. 16:1–4). Abraham's son, Isaac, had only one wife; but Abraham's grandson, Jacob, took two wives (Leah and Rachel) and two concubines, Zilpah and Bilhah (Gen. 29:15–30:13).

The Bible presents monogamy as the divine ideal. The Creator made marriage as a union between one man and one woman (Gen. 2:18–24; Matt. 19:4–6; 1 Cor. 6:16). Apparently polygamy, like divorce, was tolerated because of the hardness of people's hearts (Matt. 19:8).

After the time of Moses, polygamy continued to be practiced, especially by wealthy individuals, such as Gideon, Elkanah, Saul, and David (Judg. 8:28–30; 1 Sam. 1:2; 2 Sam. 5:13; 1 Kin. 11:3). But the most famous polygamist in the Bible was King Solomon: "And he had seven hundred wives, princesses, and three hundred concubines; and his wives turned away his heart" (1 Kin. 11:3). The criticism of polygamy expressed in Deuteronomy 17:17 is not surprising: the ideal king to whom Israel's obedience can be rightly given shall not "multiply wives for himself, lest his heart turn away."

P

POMEGRANATE

A round, sweet fruit about four inches (ten centimeters) across with a hard rind. It is green when young and turns red when ripe. There are numerous edible seeds inside the pomegranate. The pomegranate tree has been cultivated in Palestine and Egypt since ancient times (Num. 13:23; Deut. 8:8). It grew as a bush or small tree, sometimes reaching a height of about 30 feet (9 meters) with small, lance-shaped leaves. The blossoms were bright red. The fruit usually ripened in August or September.

The hem of Aaron's robe was decorated with images of pomegranates (Ex. 28:33–34; 39:24–26). It was listed among the pleasant fruits of Egypt (Num. 20:5). Solomon decorated the temple with the likeness of the pomegranate (1 Kin. 7:18, 20). A spiced wine was made from the juice (Song 8:2).

PONTUS [PONN tus]

A province in northern Asia Minor (modern Turkey) mentioned in the Book of Acts. Pontus was situated on the southern shore of the Pontus Euxinus, or the Black Sea. A mountainous area broken by fertile plains, Pontus produced olives, grain, and timber.

Pontus was made part of the Galatian-Cappadocian province of the Roman Empire by Nero in A.D. 64. It is mentioned twice in the Book of Acts. People from Pontus were in Jerusalem on the Day of Pentecost (Acts 2:9) and it was the birthplace of Aquila, the husband of Priscilla (Acts 18:2). The First Epistle of Peter is addressed to "the pilgrims of the Dispersion in Pontus, Galatia, Cappadocia, Asia, and Bithynia" (1 Pet. 1:1). From this we may assume that Christians were living in Pontus.

PORTER

A keeper of the door. This person guarded the entrance to a city, public building (John 18:17), temple, rich man's house (Mark 13:34), or sheepfold (John 10:3). A guard was stationed at any entrance through which someone unwanted might enter, especially at night. This must have been a lowly job because of the contrast implied in Psalm 84:10, where "doorkeeper" is the opposite of the most luxurious and favorable position. Porters were also called gatekeepers. The duties of the gatekeepers are listed in 1 Chronicles 9:17, 21; 15:17–18, 23–24.

POTIPHAR [PAHT uh fur] (dedicated to Ra)

The Egyptian to whom the Ishmaelites (Gen. 39:1) sold Joseph when he was brought to Egypt as a slave. Potiphar was a high officer of Pharaoh and a wealthy man (Gen. 37:36). In time, he put Joseph in charge of his household. But Potiphar's wife became attracted to Joseph and attempted to seduce him. When he rejected her advances, she falsely accused him and had him imprisoned (Gen. 39:6–19).

POTTERY

Vessels or other objects manufactured from clay and hardened by fire. In modern usage, the term *pottery* generally refers only to vessels (bowls, plates, jars, etc.). But the products of the potter's craft were very diverse in Bible times.

Clay is the basic material from which pottery is produced. The clay was mixed with water, then sifted to remove stones and larger particles. This was accomplished with the use of settling basins, a series of refining pits that produced gradually finer grades of clay. Straw, sand, shell, or pulverized potsherds were often added to the clay. These ingredients minimized shrinkage and helped to prevent cracking of the vessel during the drying or firing process.

Pottery-making was revolutionized

with the invention of the potter's wheel. A primitive wheel, called a turntable or tournette, is datable in Palestine to about 2500 B.C. This device consisted of a single horizontal disk that was turned by hand. The slow rotation created the centrifugal force that allowed the potter to "throw" the vessel. The true potter's wheel added a second disk or kick wheel, operated by foot, that increased the speed of rotation.

Pottery is the most common artifact from the ancient world. It was found in the poorest houses and in the most luxurious palaces, on the surfaces of ancient streets and in building foundations. Burials, from the simplest to the most

elaborate, yield quantities of pottery, usually whole vessels.

An archaeological excavation will produce thousands of sherds (fragments of pottery) and many intact vessels. The fact that pottery finds far outnumber any type of archaeological artifact is due mainly to its indestructibility. Fired clay will not disintegrate even if buried for thousands of years.

Pottery has changed through the centuries. These changes are reflected in form, decoration, clay composition, manufacturing technique, and quality of firing. Pottery is, therefore, one of the indicators of the technical and artistic

POTTERY

P

achievements of a culture. The presence of imported pottery, clearly distinguishable from the styles and wares of local pottery, enables the archaeologist to identify and study foreign influence, such as trade relations, population movements, and conquest. The most important contribution of pottery to the study of ancient cultures is its value as a dating tool.

Jeremiah 18:1–6 is the most vivid passage about pottery-making in the Bible. It contains a realistic description of the potter's workshop (18:1–4), and it uses figurative language for the potter's craft. The image of God as the Master Potter also appears in Genesis 2:7; Isaiah 29:16; 64:8; Job 10:8–9, and Romans 9:20–24.

PRAETORIAN GUARD

A special group of Roman soldiers in New Testament times, established to guard the emperor of the Roman Empire. Originally, they were restricted to the city of Rome, but later they were sent to the Roman provinces as well. This guard was an elite corps of soldiers whose salaries, privileges, and terms of service were better than the other soldiers of the Roman Empire.

In the NKJV, Praetorium is mentioned with reference to a place (Matt. 27:27; Mark 15:16; John 18:28, 33; 19:9). The implication from the Gospels is that the Praetorium was part of Herod's palace or the governor's residence in Jerusalem. Paul, when he was in prison in Caesarea, was "kept in Herod's Praetorium" (Acts 23:35).

Philippians 1:13 refers to the "imperial guard" (NRSV) or to the "whole palace guard" (NKJV). Commentators are not sure whether this reference is limited to the guard or whether it may refer to the imperial high court as well.

The Praetorium guard was discontinued in the third century A.D. because they had become too powerful, threatening the authority of the Roman emperor himself.

PRAISE

An act of worship or acknowledgment by which the virtues or deeds of another are recognized and extolled. The praise of God toward people is the highest commendation they can receive. Such an act of praise reflects a true servant's heart (Matt. 25:21; Eph. 1:3–14).

Our praise toward God is the means by which we express our joy to the Lord. We are to praise God both for who He is and for what He does (Ps. 150:2). Praising God for who He is is called adoration; praising Him for what He does is known as thanksgiving. The godly person will echo David's words, "My praise shall be continually of You . . . And [I] will praise You yet more and more" (Ps. 71:6, 14).

PRAYER

Communication with God. Christians recognize their dependence upon their Creator. They have every reason to express gratitude for God's blessings. But they have far more reason to respond to God than this. They respond to the love of God for them. God's love is revealed through the incarnation and life of Christ, His atoning provision at the Cross, His resurrection, and His continuing presence through the Holy Spirit.

Prayer cannot be replaced by devout good works in a needy world. Important as service to others is, at times we must turn away from it to God, who is distinct from all things and over all things. Neither should prayer be thought of as a mystical experience in which people lose their identity in the infinite reality. Effective prayer must be a scripturally informed response of persons saved by grace to the living God who can hear and answer on the basis of Christ's payment of the penalty that sinners deserved.

The most meaningful prayer comes

from a heart that places its trust in the God who has acted and spoken in the Jesus of history and the teachings of the Bible. God speaks to us through the Bible, and we in turn speak to Him in trustful, believing prayer. A confident prayer life is built on the cornerstone of Christ's work and words as shown by the prophets and apostles in the Bible.

In worship we recognize what is of highest worth—not ourselves, others, or our work, but God. Only the highest divine being deserves our highest respect. Guided by Scripture, we set our values in accord with God's will and perfect standards.

Awareness of God's holiness leads to consciousness of our own sinfulness. By sinning we hurt ourselves and those closest to us; but first of all, and worst of all, sin is against God (Ps. 51:4). We need not confess our sins to another being. But we should confess them directly to God, who promises to forgive us of all our unrighteousness (1 John 1:9).

Christ does not require us to withdraw from society, but to render service to the needy in a spirit of prayer. He wept over Jerusalem in compassionate prayer, and then He went into the city to give His life a ransom for many. Authentic prayer will be the source of courage and productivity, as it was for the prophets and apostles.

For good reasons God's holy and wise purpose does not permit Him to grant every petition just as it is asked. Prayer is request to a personal Lord who answers as He knows best. We should not think that we will always have success in obtaining the things for which we ask. In His wisdom, God hears and answers in the way that is best.

PREDESTINATION

The biblical teaching that declares the sovereignty of God over human beings in such a way that the freedom of the human will is also preserved.

Two major concepts are involved in the biblical meaning of predestination. First, God, who is all-powerful in the universe, has foreknown and predestined the course of human history and the lives of individuals. If He were not in complete control of human events, He would not be sovereign and, thus, would not be God.

Second, God's predestination of human events does not eliminate human choice. A thorough understanding of how God can maintain His sovereignty and still allow human freedom seems to be reserved for His infinite mind alone. Great minds have struggled with this problem for centuries.

Two views of predestination are prominent today. One view, known as Calvinism, holds that God offers irresistible grace to those whom he elects to save. The other view, known as Arminianism, insists that God's grace is the source of redemption but that it can be resisted by people through free choice. In Calvinism, God chooses the believer; in Arminianism, the believer chooses God.

All Christians agree that creation is moving within the purpose of God. This purpose is to bring the world into complete conformity to His will (Rom. 8:28). From the very beginning of time, God predestined to save humankind by sending His Son to accomplish salvation. Thus, "God would have all men to be saved and come to the knowledge of the truth" (1 Tim. 2:4).

The doctrine of predestination does not mean that God is unjust, deciding that some people will be saved and that others will be lost. Mankind, because of Adam's fall in the Garden of Eden, sinned by free choice.

Thus, no person deserves salvation.

But God's grace is universal. His salvation is for "everyone who believes" (Rom. 1:16).

See also ELECTION.

PREPARATION DAY

The day immediately before the Sabbath and other Jewish festivals. Preparation Day always fell on Friday among the Jewish people, because all religious festivals began on the Sabbath, or Saturday (Matt. 27:62; John 19:14, 31).

With a week of holidays ahead, the Preparation Day for the Passover was especially busy. The details for preparing the Passover supper had to be completed by afternoon. Preparations included baking the unleavened bread, gathering festive garments to wear for the occasion, and taking a ceremonial bath.

But above all, the paschal lamb had to be slain. Slaughtering began an hour or more earlier than for the usual daily evening sacrifice. At the temple, the priests slaughtered thousands of lambs brought in by the people. Their blood was poured at the foot of the altar. Then the lambs were roasted whole in preparation for the Passover meal in each home that evening.

PRESS

A device used to crush fruits in order to make oil or juice. The cultivation of olives was an important part of the agricultural activity in Israel, since olive oil was a major item of trade and export. To extract the oil from the fruit, olives were placed in large shallow presses hewn out of rock and crushed with a large stone roller operated by two people. The oil was collected in a container, then strained to remove impurities before being bottled in clay pottery jars.

The New Testament name Gethsemane (Matt. 26:36; Mark 14:32) is a compound word meaning "oil press." Gethsemane was the place where the ol-

ives from the groves on the Mount of Olives were processed.

Wine presses were deep pits dug out of the rock. The grapes were put in and trampled by the workers with their bare feet (Amos 9:13). If the harvest was good, this was a joyous occasion and a time of singing and celebration (Is. 16:10; Jer. 25:30). The juice was channeled to another pit where it was allowed to settle before being put into skin bags or pottery jars for fermentation.

The description of Gideon threshing wheat in a winepress illustrates how carefully he had to hide the crop from the invading Midianites. Threshing such as this was normally done on the high ground to take advantage of the wind. But he was threshing in a pit in the valley (Judg. 6:11).

PRIESTS

Official ministers or worship leaders in the nation of Israel who represented the people before God and conducted various rituals to atone for their sins. This function was carried out by the father of a family (Job 1:5) or the head of a tribe in the days before Moses and his brother Aaron. But with the appointment of Aaron by God as the first high priest, the priesthood was formally established. Aaron's descendants were established as the priestly line in Israel. They carried out their important duties from generation to generation as a special class devoted to God's service.

The Bible often speaks of priests and Levites as if these two offices were practically the same (1 Chr. 23:2; 24:6, 31). They were closely related, in that both priests and Levites sprang from a common ancestor. They traced their lineage back to Levi, head of one of the original twelve tribes of Israel. But these two offices were different, in that priests (a specific branch of Levites descended through Aaron) and Levites (all descendants of

Levi in general) performed different duties.

Priests officiated at worship by offering various offerings and by leading the people to confess their sins. The Levites were assistants to the priests. They took care of the tabernacle and the temple and performed other menial tasks, such as providing music, serving as doorkeepers, and preparing sacrifices for offering by the priests.

In their function of offering sacrifices at the altar, the priests acted as mediators between people and God, offering sacrifices so that sin might be forgiven (Lev. 4:20, 26, 31). Each sacrifice was a demonstration that the penalty of sin is death (Ezek. 18:4, 20), and that there can be no forgiveness of sin without the shedding of blood (Heb. 9:22).

When God established Israel as His chosen people at Mount Sinai after their deliverance from slavery in Egypt (Ex. 6:7; 19:5–6), He established a formal priesthood through Aaron and his descendants. As descendants of Levi, they were to represent the nation of Israel in service to God at the tabernacle and altar (Num. 8:9–18).

The priesthood was given to Aaron and his descendants "as a gift for service" (Num. 18:7) and as "an everlasting priesthood throughout their generations" (Ex. 40:15). Since the office was hereditary, the descendants of Aaron were obligated to accept the responsibility and meet the qualifications. No person with a physical defect or disqualifying disease could serve as a priest (Lev. 21:16–21). Bodily perfection was to symbolize the priest's spiritual wholeness and holiness of heart. Even the priest's home life and relationship with his wife were to show his consecration to God (Lev. 21:7).

The clothes the priests wore carried great significance. Their white linen garments symbolized holiness and glory.

They also wore a coat woven in one piece without a seam to indicate their spiritual integrity, wholeness, and righteousness. The four-cornered cloth of the coat signified that the priest belonged to the kingdom of God. The cap, resembling an opening flower, symbolized the fresh, vigorous life of the one who wore it. The girdle, or sash, a belt that encircled the priest's body, was the priestly sign of service. It showed that the wearer was an office-bearer and administrator in the kingdom of God (Ex. 39).

The priests had several responsibilities as mediators between the sinful people and their holy God. They lit the incense and cleaned, trimmed, and lit the lamps. Ministering before God at the altar, the priests had to make sure the offerings of the people were correct and that the sacrificial rituals were carried out correctly. Otherwise, the people could not be cleansed of their sin until the priests had made atonement for the error (Num. 18:1).

By their example, the priests also taught the people how to "distinguish between holy and unholy, and between unclean and clean" (Lev. 10:10). Living in cities scattered throughout the nation of Israel, the priests were in a good position to fulfill this function (Josh. 21). In addition, the priests served as judges, acting as a kind of supreme court for Israel (Deut. 17:8–13). In special cases, the high priests declared the will or judgment of God through the Urim and Thummim, the medium through which God sometimes communicated His divine will (Ex. 28:30; Lev. 8:8; Deut. 33:8).

When the land of Canaan was conquered and divided among the tribes of Israel, 48 cities with their surrounding land were allotted to the priests and Levites as residences for their families and pasturelands for their flocks (Josh. 21:41). Across the centuries, the priests increased to a numerous body. King

P

David divided them into 24 groups (1 Chr. 24:1–19). Except for the great festivals when all the divisions served at the tabernacle at the same time, each division officiated for a week at a time on a rotating basis.

As long as the king and the people of Israel remained loyal to God and His law, the priests were highly respected and exercised a healthy influence in the land. But the priests eventually sank to immorality, departed from God, and worshiped idols, along with the rest of the people (Ezek. 22:26).

In the final book of the Old Testament, the prophet Malachi pointed to the neglect, corruption, and false teaching of the priests. According to Malachi, this was the reason why the people began to neglect the offerings and festivals of the temple. They lost their respect for the persons who held the office, and finally the office itself (Mal. 1:6; 2:7–9). Thus, the Old Testament closes with the announcement that God in His judgment "will suddenly come to His temple . . . like a refiner's fire" to purify the priests (Mal. 3:1–3). God was determined to preserve His human priests until the appearance of His true Priest, Jesus Christ.

By the New Testament period, the position of priests in the nation of Israel had changed considerably. The temple functions were taken over by the "chief priests." Rank-and-file priests were also overshadowed by the scribes and Pharisees, two special groups that arose to present the law and interpret its meaning for the people. But in spite of the diminished role of priests, Jesus respected the office and called upon the priests to witness His healing of lepers in keeping with the Law of Moses (Mark 1:44; Luke 17:12–14).

But the priests themselves were some of the most zealous opponents of Jesus. As leaders of the Sanhedrin, the Jewish high court, they bore much of the responsibility for His crucifixion. They also led the opposition to the apostles and the early church.

The office of priest was fulfilled in Jesus Christ. The Son of God became a man (Heb. 2:9–14) so that He might offer Himself as a sacrifice "once to bear the sins of many" (Heb. 9:28). Hence, there is no longer a need for priests to offer a sacrifice to atone for man's sin. A permanent sacrifice has been made by Jesus Christ through His death on the cross.

See also LEVITES.

PRISCILLA [prih SIL uh]

The wife of Aquila and a zealous advocate of the Christian cause (Rom. 16:3; 1 Cor. 16:19). Her name is also given as Prisca (2 Tim. 4:19). Aquila and Priscilla left their home in Rome for Corinth when the emperor Claudius commanded all Jews to depart from the city (Acts 18:2). Thus, they were fellow passengers of the apostle Paul from Corinth to Ephesus (Acts 18:18), where they met Apollos and instructed him further in the Christian faith (Acts 18:26).

PRISON

A place of forcible restraint or confinement. Most prisons of the ancient world were crude and dehumanizing. Persons guilty of violating the laws of a community were detained in several different types of prisons.

Most common were natural pits or cavelike dungeons, where prisoners survived on the bread and water "of affliction" (1 Kin. 22:27). Prison pits provided places in which to conceal the slain (Jer. 41:7). The prophet Jeremiah may have been cast into a dungeon because this was a convenient way to kill him without bloodshed (Jer. 38:6).

Another example of a natural pit used for holding prisoners is the one on the plain of Dothan, into which Joseph's jealous brothers threw him (Gen. 37:20–28).

Less common were man-made structures or prison houses like the one in which Samson was held at Gaza (Judg. 16:21, 25) and the one provided by King Ahab at Samaria (1 Kin. 22:26–27).

Old Testament kings were usually held in prison by conquering armies (Jer. 52:11). Hebrew prophets who were at odds with the policies of their kings were often thrown into prison, notably Hanani the seer under King Asa of Judah (2 Chr. 16:10).

During the wandering of the Hebrews in the desert after their escape from Egypt, some of the people were held "in custody" or "under guard" (Lev. 24:12; Num. 15:34). Since imprisonment was not specifically called for by Mosaic Law, it was not practiced in Israel until the time of the monarchy, when the prison is mentioned as a special part of the king's house (Neh. 3:25; Jer. 32:2; 37:21).

The New Testament uses four related terms that are translated as "prison." The cell of John the Baptist was a "place of bonds" (Matt. 11:2). The apostles were arrested in Jerusalem and placed in the common prison ("place of custody or public watching") by the Sadducees (Acts 5:18). The apostle Peter was imprisoned in a "house" (Acts 12:7). Paul and Silas were thrown into a prison ("place of guarding") at Philippi (Acts 16:23–40).

Jewish prisons mentioned in the New Testament were used to detain persons awaiting trial or execution (Acts 5:21, 23; Acts 4:3; 5:18). Imprisonment as a form of punishment was also known (Acts 22:19).

Roman prisons are more fully described in the New Testament than the prisons of other nations. Roman authorities used imprisonment to control behavior (Matt. 18:30) and as punishment for minor lawbreakers (Matt. 11:2; Acts 16:26). Prisons were usually part of the government headquarters: examples are the Praetorium at Jerusalem (Mark 15:16) and the Caes-area prison in Herod's judgment hall, where Paul was detained for two years (Acts 23:35; 24:27).

Paul had so many prison experiences that he called himself a "prisoner of the Lord" (Eph. 4:1). When Paul and Silas were cast into the Roman prison at Philippi, the jailer fastened their feet in stocks (Acts 16:23–24). Under Roman military rule, the soldier who guarded the prison was responsible for the safety of the prisoners. After Paul and Silas were miraculously released by God (Acts 16:25–34), their jailer would have killed himself if Paul had not prevented it. Paul was bound with chains at the Jerusalem Tower of Antonia (Acts 21:33, 37), from which his declaration of Roman citizenship freed him. He was also imprisoned in Rome, but under lenient surveillance in his own dwelling.

Christ showed concern for prisoners (Matt. 25:36). He made several references to prisons (Matt. 5:25; 18:30; 25:36). His parable of the unmerciful debtor reveals the custom of casting men and their families into prison for their debts (Matt. 18:24–35). Jesus himself became Jerusalem's most notable prisoner, detained at first by the Sanhedrin and later at the Praetorium.

PROCONSUL [pro CON suhl]

A title given to the governor of a senatorial province in the Roman Empire. Under the Roman system of government, the empire was divided into senatorial provinces and imperial provinces. Imperial provinces were administered by representatives of the emperor. The senatorial provinces were presided over by proconsuls appointed by the Roman senate. Two proconsuls are mentioned in the New Testament: Sergius Paulus (Acts 13:7–8, 12), and Gallio (Acts 18:12; deputy in KJV; governor in REB).

PROPHECY

Predictions about the future and the end-time; special messages from God, often uttered through human spokesmen, which indicate the divine will for mankind on earth and in heaven.

Prophecy was technically the task of the prophet. But all truth or revelation is prophetic, pointing to some future person, event, or thing. The full panorama of God's will takes many forms; it may be expressed through people, events, and objects. Historical events such as the Passover anticipated Jesus Christ (1 Cor. 5:7), as did various objects in the tabernacle, including Manna (John 6:31–35) and the inner veil (Matt. 27:51; Heb. 10:20).

Prophecy may also be expressed in many different forms through the prophet himself, whether by his mouth or some bodily action. The prophets received God's messages from the voice of an angel (Gen. 22:15–19), the voice of God, a dream (Dan. 2), or a vision (Ezek. 40). The prophetic speech might range from the somber reading of a father's last will (Gen. 49) to an exultant anthem to be sung in the temple (Ps. 96:1, 13).

Sometimes a prophet acted out his message symbolically. Isaiah's nakedness (Is. 20) foretold the exile of the Egyptians and the Cushites. Hosea's marriage symbolized God's patience with an unfaithful wife, the nation of Israel. Ahijah divided his garment to foretell the division of the monarchy (1 Kin. 11:30–31).

Prophecy declared God's word for all time, so the time of fulfillment of a prophecy is rarely indicated in the Bible. Exceptions to this rule include the timetable assigned to Daniel's seventy weeks' prophecy (Dan. 9:24–27), the prophecy of Peter's denial (Matt. 26:34), and predictions of someone's death (Jer. 28:16–17). The common problem of knowing the time for the fulfillment of a prophecy is acknowledged by Peter (2 Pet. 1:11).

Several questions are raised when there appear to be more than one possible fulfillment for a prophecy. Does a primary fulfillment in one passage rule out a secondary application to another passage? Not necessarily. Did the author intend both fulfillments with one as an analogy or illustration for the other? Did the author intend a dual fulfillment for two different audiences at two different times? Joel 2:30, speaking about signs on the earth, was applied by the apostle Peter to the tongues of fire at Pentecost (Acts 2:3–4, 18–19). But Jesus seemed to apply this prophecy to His Second Coming (Mark 13:24; Luke 11:25).

Over 300 prophecies in the Bible speak of Jesus Christ. Specific details given by these prophecies include His tribe (Gen. 49:10), His birthplace (Mic. 5:2), dates of His birth and death (Dan. 9:25–26), His forerunner John the Baptist (Mal. 3:1; 4:5; Matt. 11:10), His career and ministry (Is. 52:13–53:12), His crucifixion (Ps. 22:1–18), His resurrection (Ps. 16:8–11; Acts 2:25–28), His ascension (Ps. 2; Acts 13:33), and His exaltation as a priest-king (Ps. 110; Acts 2:34). The kingly magnificence of His Second Coming is also graphically portrayed. Psalms 2, 45, and 110 picture His conquest and dominion over the nations.

PROPHET

A person who spoke for God and who communicated God's message courageously to God's chosen people—the nation of Israel.

Prophets received their call or appointment directly from God. Some prophets, like Jeremiah or John the Baptist, were called before birth (Jer. 1:5; Luke 1:13–16), but their privilege was not a birthright. Their authority came from God alone whose message they bore (Ex. 7:1). A prophetic call was a call to liberty and freedom to be oneself (John 8:31–32). It enabled the prophet to be unaffected by human bias and criticism. The call of the prophets required that they not be intimidated or threatened by their audience (Jer. 1:7–8; Ezek. 2:6).

Prophets sometimes became quite dramatic and acted out their messages. Isaiah went naked and barefoot for three years (Is. 20:2–3). Ezekiel lay on his left side for 390 days and on his right side for 40 more (Ezek. 4:1–8). Zechariah broke 2 staffs (Zech. 11:7–14). Making themselves a spectacle, prophets not only aroused curiosity but also invited the scorn of their peers (Jer. 11:21).

Except for God's call, prophets had no special qualifications. They appeared from all walks of life. They included sheepbreeders and farmers like Amos (Amos 7:14) and Elisha (1 Kin. 19:19) but also princes like Abraham (Gen. 23:6) and priests like Ezekiel (Ezek. 1:3). Even women and children became prophets (1 Sam. 3:19–20; 2 Kin. 22:14). In rare circumstances, God used the hesitant or unruly to bear His message. Balaam prophesied (Num. 22:6–24:24) the Lord's message but was actually an enemy of God (2 Pet. 2:15–16; Rev. 2:14). Saul certainly was not in fellowship with God when he prophesied (1 Sam. 10:23–24).

Some prophets were called for a lifetime. But sometimes prophets spoke briefly and no more (Num. 11:25–26). In either case, a prophet spoke with the authority of the Holy Spirit (Num. 11:29; 24:4). One trait characterized them all: a faithful proclamation of God's word and not their own (Jer. 23:16; Ezek. 13:2). Jesus' reference to Himself as a prophet in John 12:49–50 rests upon this standard of faithfully repeating God's word to people.

Many scholars deny that prophecy includes the prediction of future events. But fulfillment was, in fact, the test of a prophet's genuineness (Deut. 18:20–22).

Whether prophets' words were fulfilled within their lifetime or centuries later, they were filfilled to the letter (1 Kin. 13:3; 2 Kin. 23:15–16). But regardless of the time of fulfillment, the prophets' messages applied to their generation as well as to ours.

PROPITIATION [pro pish ih AY shun]

The atoning death of Jesus on the cross, through which He paid the penalty demanded by God because of people's sin, thus setting them free from sin and death. The word means "appeasement." Thus, propitiation expresses the idea that Jesus died on the cross to pay the price for sin that a holy God demanded.

PROSELYTE [PROS eh lite]

A convert from one religious belief or party to another. In the New Testament (Matt. 23:15; Acts 2:10), the term is used in a specific sense to designate Gentile converts who had committed themselves to the teachings of the Jewish faith or who were attracted to the teachings of Judaism. A full-fledged proselyte, or convert, to Judaism underwent circumcision and worshiped in the Jewish temple or synagogue. They also observed all rituals and regulations concerning the sabbath, clean and unclean foods, and all other matters of Jewish custom.

By New Testament times proselytes were a significant part of Judaism, as the references to them in the Book of Acts (2:10; 6:5; 13:43) make clear. They proved to be a rich mission field for the early church. Unable to accept the binding requirements of the Jewish law, many of them turned to Christianity. This new faith welcomed all people, regardless of their background, culture, or religious tradition.

PROSTITUTION

The act or practice of promiscuous sexual relations, especially for money.

Several words are used for a woman who engages in illicit sexual activity for pay, including harlot, whore, and prostitute.

One type of harlot was the temple prostitute, who performed sexual acts at a heathen temple (Hos. 4:12–14). Both male and female cult prostitutes presided at these temples. Whenever Judah was ruled by a righteous king, this king sought to remove the temple prostitutes from the land (2 Kin. 23:4–14).

Jerusalem is pictured as playing the part of a harlot. But instead of being paid for her services, she paid others (Ezek. 16:15–59)! Those who worshiped idols were also referred to in a symbolic way as harlots (Judg. 2:17).

PROVIDENCE

The continuous activity of God in His creation by which He preserves and governs. The doctrine of providence affirms God's absolute lordship over His creation and confirms the dependence of all creation on the Creator. It is the denial of the idea that the universe is governed by chance or fate.

Divine government is the continued activity of God by which He directs all things to the ends He has chosen in His eternal plan. God is King of the universe who has given Christ all power and authority to reign (Matt. 28:18–20; Eph. 1:20–23). He governs insignificant things (Matt. 10:29–31), apparent accidents (Prov. 16:33), and good (Phil. 2:13) and evil deeds (Acts 14:16).

God acts in accordance with the laws and principles that He has established in the world. The laws of nature are nothing more than our description of how we perceive God at work in the world. They neither have inherent power nor work by themselves.

We are not free to choose and act independently of God's will and plan; we choose and act in accordance with them. In His sovereignty, God controls people's choices and actions (Gen. 45:5; Prov. 21:1). God's actions, however, do not violate the reality of human choice or negate our responsibility as moral beings.

PROVINCE

An administrative district of the government or civil ruling authority. The word *province* is used only four times of rulers in Israel. All these occurrences come from the time of King Ahab (1 Kin. 20:14–15, 17, 19). The other occurrences of the word refer to the administrative districts during the Babylonian and Persian rules (Ezra 2:1; 4:15; Neh. 1:3). The term occurs only twice in the New Testament (Acts 23:34; 25:1).

During New Testament times the government of the Roman Empire had senatorial and imperial provinces. The senatorial provinces were the ten older provinces of the empire, which had no need of a large military force. These were ruled by proconsuls like Sergius Paulus of Cyprus (Acts 13:7) and Gallio of Achaia (Acts 18:12). The proconsuls were appointed for one year.

The imperial provinces of the Roman Empire consisted of frontier provinces that had large installations of Roman troops under the leadership of the emperor. Each of these provinces was governed by a military leader.

The second kind of imperial provinces were those consisting of special cases such as rugged terrain (alpine districts) or difficult people to rule (Judea and Egypt). They were ruled by an imperial governor appointed by the emperor.

These regional governors were responsible to both the emperor and the local provincial military ruler. In Jesus' day, Judea was governed by the governor or prefect Pilate (Luke 3:1). In Paul's day, it was ruled by the governors Felix (Acts 23:24) and Festus (Acts 25:1).

PSALMS

Prayers, poems, and hymns that focus the worshiper's thoughts on God in praise and adoration. The Book of Psalms in the Old Testament contains 150 of these psalms. Parts of this book were used as a hymnal in the worship services of ancient Israel.

We may think of the psalms as a description of our human response to God. At times God is presented in all His majesty and glory. Our response is wonder, awe, and fear: "Sing to God, you kingdoms of the earth" (68:32). But other psalms portray God as a loving Lord who is involved in our lives. Our response in these cases is to draw close to His comfort and security: "I will fear no evil; for You are with me" (23:4).

God is the same Lord in both these psalms. But we respond to Him in different ways, according to the specific needs of our lives. What a marvelous God we worship, the psalmist declares—One who is high and lifted up beyond our human experiences but also one who is close enough to touch and who walks beside us along life's way.

Other psalms might be described as outcries against God and the circumstances of life rather than responses to God because of His glory and His presence in our lives. The psalmist admits he sometimes feels abandoned by God as well as his human friends (Ps. 88). He agonizes over the lies directed against him by his false accusers (Ps. 109). He calls upon God to deliver him from his enemies and to wipe them out with His wrath (Ps. 59). The writers of these psalms were realistic about human feelings and the way we sometimes respond to the problems and inequities of life.

But even in these strong psalms of lament, the psalmist is never totally engulfed by a feeling of despair. The fact that he uttered his protest to the Lord is a sign of hope in God and His sense of justice. This has a significant message for all believers. We can bring all our feelings to God, no matter how negative or complaining they may be. And we can rest assured that He will hear and understand. The psalmist teaches us that the most profound prayer of all is a cry for help as we find ourselves overwhelmed by the problems of life.

The psalms also have a great deal to say about the person and work of Christ. Psalm 22 contains a remarkable prophecy of the crucifixion of the Savior. Jesus quoted from this psalm as He was dying on the cross (Ps. 22:1; Matt. 27:46; Mark 15:34). Other statements about the Messiah from the psalms that were fulfilled in the life of Jesus include these predictions: He would be a priest like Melchizedek (Ps. 110:4; Heb. 5:6); He would pray for His enemies (Ps. 109:4; Luke 23:34); and His throne would be established forever (Ps. 45:6; Heb. 1:8).

PTOLEMAIS [tahl uh MAY iss]

A seaport in northern Palestine between Tyre and Caesarea. The apostle Paul visited Ptolemais for one day on his return to Jerusalem during his third missionary journey (Acts 21:7). In the Old Testament the city is known as Acco (Judg. 1:31; Accho in KJV). Today the city is about 9 miles (15 kilometers) north of Haifa and about 12 miles (19 kilometers) south of Lebanon.

PTOLEMY [TOL eh mih]

A general title (similar to pharaoh) of the 14 Greek kings who ruled Egypt between the conquest of Alexander the Great and the Roman conquest of Egypt in 30 B.C.

After the death of Alexander the Great in 323 B.C., his empire eventually fell into the hands of two of his generals, Seleucus I and Ptolemy I Soter. Seleucus established a dynasty in Syria, Asia, and the east, while Ptolemy I Soter and his descendants ruled in Egypt. During this period the Ptolemies engaged in many wars with the Seleucid rulers in Syria over the control of Palestine. Daniel 11 contains a prediction of many of these events.

Ptolemy I Soter (323–285 B.C.) conducted three campaigns in Palestine against the Seleucids (Dan. 11:5), and by 301 B.C. he controlled Phoenicia and Palestine, which his successors retained for a century. His capital, Alexandria, situated on the northern coast of Egypt, became the center of intellectual life for the eastern Mediterranean. Ptolemy settled many Jewish prisoners of war in Alexandria.

Ptolemy's son, Ptolemy II Philadelphus (285–246 B.C.), continued to battle the Seleucids (Dan. 11:6). At Alexandria he established a famous library and museum that comprised a university promoting the spread of Greek culture throughout the ancient world.

Along with prisoners of war, many Jews chose to migrate to Alexandria and elsewhere in Egypt. In Alexandria they eventually adapted to the prevailing culture, producing learned Jewish writings in the fields of philosophy, history, and biblical interpretation.

Ptolemy II Philadelphus commissioned 70 Jewish students of the Bible to

PTOLEMY

translate the Old Testament from He- brew to Greek (this is called the Septua- gint). This translation was the Bible for many Greeks and Greek-speaking Jews for years to come.

Judea, a state ruled by a high priest and his council, the Sanhedrin, was con- tent under Ptolemaic rule; it was allowed a certain measure of self-rule as long as it paid taxes to the Ptolemy and abided under his ultimate rule. There was an influx of Greeks and Hellenistic culture into Palestine during this era.

During the reign of Ptolemy III Euer- getes (246–222 B.C.), the fighting between the Ptolemies and the Seleucids contin- ued (Dan. 11:7–9). During this time syna- gogues were established for the Jews who lived in Egypt.

Ptolemy IV Philopater (222–205 B.C.) defeated Antiochus III (Dan. 11:11–12), but his successor, Ptolemy V Epiphanes (205–180 B.C.), brought about a measure of peace by forming an alliance through intermarriage (Dan. 11:14–16). It was this Ptolemy who wrote the Rosetta Stone that led to the decipherment of the mys- terious Egyptian hieroglyphics.

Judea passed into Seleucid control in 200 B.C. From that time on, Egypt began to decline in power.

During the reign of Ptolemy VI Phi- lometor (180–146 B.C.), the Jewish priest Onias III from Jerusalem was allowed to build a Jewish temple in Egypt at Leonto- polis. The Egyptian and Seleucid wars continued (Dan. 11:25–29). Some of these events are described in the apocryphal books of Maccabees, and by Josephus and Aristobulus. Murder, revolt, bribery, and trickery characterized the last group of Ptolemies.

During the reign of Ptolemy VI Phi- lometor, Egypt was attacked by Anti- ochus IV. Only Roman intervention forced his withdrawal. This was the be- ginning of the end for the Ptolemies. Ex- ternally, Egypt was doomed to be incorporated into Rome's spreading sphere of influence and power. Inter- nally, native revolts grew more frequent in response to crippling taxation and in- justice in bureaucratic, nationalized Egypt.

The line of Ptolemies came to an end with Cleopatra VII (51–30 B.C.)—the daughter of Ptolemy XI—and her son by Julius Caesar, Ptolemy XIV Caesarion (36–30 B.C.), when Cleopatra committed suicide. Egypt then passed into Roman hands (30 B.C.) and became a lucrative province of the Roman Empire. The Ptol- emies had ruled Egypt with selfish mo- tives without gaining much support from the native population.

The clashes between Seleucid Syria and Ptolemaic Egypt are mentioned in Daniel 11 to illustrate God's control over His people. "The king of the South" is the representative Ptolemy, as the references to Egypt in verses 8, 42, and 43 indicate: Ptolemy I (v. 5), Ptolemy II (v. 6), Ptolemy III (vv. 7–9), Ptolemy IV (v. 11), Ptolemy V (vv. 14–15), and Ptolemy VI (vv. 25, 27). Daniel's descriptions of these events long before they took place is proof of God's sovereign control over nations.

PUBLIUS [PUHB lih uhs] *(pertaining to the people)*

The leading citizen of the island of Malta (Melita, KJV) who showed hospital- ity to the apostle Paul and his compan- ions when they were shipwrecked (Acts 28:1–10). Publius may have been a native official or perhaps the chief Roman offi- cial on Malta, which at that time was part of the province of Sicily. Paul healed Pub- lius's father, who suffered from a fever and dysentery (Acts 28:8).

PUL [pool]

An Assyrian king who invaded Israel during the reign of King Menahem. When Menahem paid tribute to Pul, giv- ing him 1,000 talents of silver (2 Kin.

15:19), Pul withdrew his army from Israel (v. 20). Pul did, however, carry the tribes east of the Jordan River into captivity (1 Chr. 5:26). Pul is the same person as Tiglath-Pileser III. Tiglath-Pileser was the throne-name he bore as king of Assyria; Pul was the throne-name he bore in Babylonia as king of Babylon.

PURIFICATION

The act of making clean and pure before God and people. The Mosaic Law provided instructions for both physical and spiritual purification. These laws and regulations were much more than sanitary instructions. The act of purification also involved religious and spiritual cleansing.

The Mosaic Law recognized and detailed purification rituals for three distinct categories of uncleanness. These were skin diseases (Lev. 13–14), sexual discharges (Lev. 15), and contact with a dead body (Num. 19:11–19).

By the time of Jesus, much had been added to the laws of purification, making them a burden to the people. Jesus denounced such rituals, teaching that defilement and uncleanness came from the inner motives of the mind and heart (Mark 7:14–23). He taught that genuine purification is possible only by following Him and giving heed to His message of love and redemption (John 15:3).

PURIM [POOR im] *(lots)*

This feast commemorates the deliverance of the Jewish people from destruction by an evil schemer named Haman during the days of their captivity by the Persians. It took its name from the Babylonian word *put,* meaning "lot," because Haman cast lots to determine when he would carry out his plot against the Jews. The Feast of Purim took place on the fourteenth and fifteenth of Adar, and during its celebration the Book of

Esther is read as a reminder of their deliverance. A happy ceremony, Purim is accompanied with the giving of gifts and much celebration.

PUT [put]

A son of Ham and the land where his descendants lived. This nation is mentioned in the Bible in connection with Egypt and Ethiopia (Cush). Some scholars identify this land with Punt, an area on the eastern shore of Africa (possibly Somaliland), famous for its incense. Since Put and Punt are not identical in spelling and because Put was known for its warriors rather than its incense, other scholars believe Put refers to certain Libyan tribes west of Egypt.

Men from Put and Lubim (Libya) were used as mercenary soldiers by the King of Tyre (Ezek. 27:10) and Magog (Ezek. 38:5). But most references in the Bible picture them as allies with Egypt (Jer. 46:9; Ezek. 30:5; Nah. 3:9). Although the warriors of Put were hired to help these different nations secure their borders and win their wars, the prophets point to the futility of such forces in the face of God's mighty power and judgment.

PUTEOLI [poo TEE uh lih]

A seaport on the western shore of southern Italy visited by the apostle Paul (Acts 28:13). Puteoli was one of the most important harbors in Italy. At Puteoli the great grain ships from Alexandria were unloaded. Paul stayed with the Christians at Puteoli for a week before he traveled overland toward Rome (Acts 28:14).

Puteoli is now called Pozzuoli, across the Bay of Naples from Pompeii and Mount Vesuvius. The city boasts an ancient Roman amphitheater, built like the Colosseum of Rome. With a capacity of 40,000 to 60,000 people, it was overshadowed in size only by the Colosseum and the amphitheater at nearby Capua.

QUAIL

In Israel, the quail is a migrating bird that arrives in droves along the shores of the Mediterranean Sea. With their strong flying muscles, these birds can fly rapidly for a short time. When migrating, however, they stretch their wings and allow the wind to bear them along. Sometimes they reach land so exhausted after their long flight that they can be caught by hand.

Most of the time quail remain on the ground, scratching for food and helping farmers by eating insects. Their brown-speckled bodies are inconspicuous, but they often give away their presence by a shrill whistle.

The Hebrew people probably ate dried, salted quail while they were enslaved by the Egyptians. When they longed for meat in the Sinai desert, God promised He would provide enough meat for a month. Then He directed thousands of quail to their camp, where the birds dropped in exhaustion (Num. 11:31–34; Ex. 16:13; Ps. 105:40).

QUEEN OF HEAVEN

A fertility goddess to whom the Israelites, especially the women, offered sacrifice and worship in the days before the fall of the southern kingdom of Judah (Jer. 7:18; 44:17–19, 25). In the time of Jeremiah, many people in Jerusalem and other cities of Judah worshiped the queen of heaven. Their worship included burning incense and pouring out drink offerings to her (Jer. 44:17). This was obviously a form of idolatry, but it is not clear exactly which pagan god was worshiped.

The phrase "queen of heaven" may be a title for the goddess Ishtar (perhaps the same goddess as the biblical Ashtoreth). Cakes were also baked in honor of the "queen of heaven" (Jer. 7:18). These cakes may have been in the shape of stars, crescent moons, or the female figure. The worship of this goddess was one of the evils that brought God's judgment upon Judah: "Behold, My anger and My fury will be poured out on this place" (Jer. 7:20).

QUIRINIUS [kwy REN ih us]

Roman governor of Syria at the time of Jesus' birth (Luke 2:1–5; Cyrenius, KJV). Quirinius is mentioned in connection with a census taken for tax purposes. The census was not a local affair; the Roman emperor Augustus (ruled 31 B.C.-A.D. 14) had decreed that all the world, or the Roman Empire, should be taxed. For this purpose, Joseph and Mary made their pilgrimage to Bethlehem. While they were there, Jesus was born.

The Gospel of Luke reports that Quirinius was governor of Syria at a time when Herod was still alive. According to historians, the governor of Syria at this time was Quintilius Varus. Quirinius may have been a military commander who shared civil duties with Varus.

QUMRAN, KHIRBET [KOOM rahn, KIR beht]

An ancient ruin on the northwestern shore of the Dead Sea. In 1947 a wandering goatherder looking for his goats in caves above the dry river bed, or wadi, of Qumran found several large jars. These jars contained ancient scrolls that have since become known as the Dead Sea Scrolls.

Khirbet Qumran was a Jewish community that was active from 130 B.C. to A.D. 135. Scholars have suggested that the people who lived here were a small group of Jews who were disgusted with the corruption and lawlessness of the priests and leaders responsible for worship at the temple in Jerusalem. The Qumran community sought to purify itself from the sin of those who distorted the law. Large baths or pools were found in Khirbet Qumran and were probably used for daily ritual baths.

R

RAAMSES [RAM seez] (the god Ra has fathered a son)

The royal city of the Egyptian kings of the nineteenth and twentieth dynasties (about 1300–1100 B.C.) situated in the northeastern section of the Nile Delta. While the people of Israel were slaves in Egypt, they were forced to work on at least two of Pharaoh's vast construction projects—building the supply cities of Pithom and Raamses (Ex. 1:11, KJV, NASB, NKJV; Rameses in NIV, NRSV, REB).

The reference to "the land of Rameses" (Gen. 47:11) in the story of Joseph, well before Pharaoh Ramses II lived, suggests that the author of Genesis used the "modern" name (Rameses)—the name that was common in his day and not the earlier name of the city, which was used during the time of Joseph. This may also be true of the use of Rameses in the account of the Exodus, because the Hebrews apparently left Egypt around 1446 B.C., well before the time of King Ramses.

"The land of Rameses" (Gen. 47:11) was "the best of the land"—the most fertile district of Egypt. This almost certainly refers to the Land of Goshen, in the northeastern Nile Delta.

RABBAH [RAB uh] (great)

The chief city of the Ammonites. Known as Rabbah of the people of Ammon (Deut. 3:11; 2 Sam. 12:26), Rabbah was at the headwaters of the Jabbok River, 23 miles (37 kilometers) east of the Jordan.

Rabbah is first mentioned as the place where the giant King Og had his massive iron bedstead (Deut. 3:11; Rabbath in KJV). Rabbah remained the capital of Ammon during David's reign, when the Ammonites and Arameans joined forces to fight against Israel. While Joab and the Israelites camped before the gate of Rabbah, the Arameans marched to Medeba (1 Chr. 19:7). In the decisive battle, the Israelite armies defeated both the Arameans and the Ammonites, also subjecting the Ammonites to forced labor (2 Sam. 12:27–31; 1 Chr. 20:1–3). During this conflict, Uriah the Hittite was killed at David's orders (2 Sam. 11:1, 15). Later the Ammonites recovered the city. Throughout its history Israel's prophets denounced Rabbah (Jer. 49:2–6; Ezek. 21:20; Amos 1:14).

Sitting astride the King's Highway, Rabbah's strategic location put it in the middle of most of the conflicts and wars of the biblical period. Consequently, it repeatedly was destroyed and rebuilt. Under Ptolemy Philadelphus (285–246 B.C.) the city became an important trading center renamed Philadelphia. It was the southernmost of the ten cities of the Decapolis. During the Byzantine period of the fourth century A.D., Rabbah ranked in importance with Gerasa (Jerash). Destroyed during the Muslim conquest, Rabbah has once again gained its ancient splendor. Today it is one of the most important Arab cities of the Middle East—Amman, Jordan.

RABBI [RAB eye] (my teacher)

A title of honor and respect given by the Jews to a doctor (teacher) of the law. The ordained spiritual leader of a Jewish congregation, the rabbi is an official formally authorized to interpret Jewish law.

In Jesus' day, however, the term had not yet become a formal title. Instead, it was a term of dignity given by the Jews to their distinguished teachers (see Matt. 23:7–8). Jesus was often addressed by this title (John 3:26).

RACHEL [RAY chuhl] *(lamb)*

The younger daughter of Laban; the second wife of Jacob; and the mother of Joseph and Benjamin. Jacob met Rachel, the beautiful younger daughter of his uncle Laban, at a well near Haran in Mesopotamia as he fled from his brother Esau (Gen. 29:6, 11). Jacob soon asked Laban for Rachel as his wife (Gen. 29:15–18).

However, it was customary in those days for the groom or his family to pay the bride's family a price for their daughter. Having no property of his own, Jacob served Laban seven years for Rachel, only to be tricked on the wedding day into marrying Rachel's older sister, Leah (Gen. 29:21–25). Jacob then had to serve another seven years for Rachel (Gen. 29:26–30).

Although Rachel was Jacob's favorite wife, she envied Leah, who had given birth to four sons—Reuben, Simeon, Levi, and Judah—while she herself had remained childless (Gen. 29:31–35). Rachel's response was to give her handmaid Bilhah to Jacob. According to this ancient custom, the child of Bilhah and Jacob would have been regarded as Rachel's. Bilhah bore Dan and Naphtali (Gen. 30:1–8), but Rachel named them, indicating they were her children. Rachel's desperate desire to become fruitful is illustrated by her asking for Reuben's mandrakes, which she believed would bring fertility (Gen. 30:14–16). Mandrakes were considered love potions or magic charms by people of the ancient world.

Only after Zilpah, Leah's handmaid, produced two sons—Gad and Asher (Gen. 30:9–13)—and after Leah had borne two more sons and a daughter—Issachar, Zebulun, and Dinah (Gen. 30:17–21)—did Rachel finally conceive. She bore to Jacob a son named Joseph (Gen. 30:22–24), who became his father's favorite and who was sold into Egypt by his jealous brothers. Rachel died following the birth of her second son, whom she named Ben-Oni (son of my sorrow). But Jacob later renamed him Benjamin (son of the right hand).

Jacob buried Rachel near Ephrath (or Bethlehem) and set a pillar on her grave (Gen. 35:16–20). Jews still regard Rachel's tomb with great respect. The traditional site is about a mile north of Bethlehem and about four miles south of Jerusalem.

Although Rachel was Jacob's favorite wife, the line of David and ultimately the messianic line passed through Leah and her son Judah, not Rachel. "Rachel weeping for her children" (Jer. 31:15; Rahel in KJV; Matt. 2:18) became symbolic of the sorrow and tragedy suffered by the Israelites. Matthew points out that the murder of all the male children in Bethlehem, from two years old and under, by Herod the Great, was the fulfillment of Jeremiah's prophecy (Matt. 2:16–18).

RAHAB [RAY hab]

A harlot of Jericho who hid two Hebrew spies, helping them to escape, and who became an ancestor of David and Jesus (Josh. 2:1–21; 6:17–25; Matt. 1:5). Rahab's house was on the city wall of Jericho. Rahab, who manufactured and dyed linen, secretly housed the two spies whom Joshua sent to explore Jericho and helped them escape by hiding them in stalks of flax on her roof (Josh. 2:6).

Rahab sent the king's messengers on a false trail, and then let the two spies down the outside wall by a rope through the window of her house (Josh. 2:15). When the Israelites captured Jericho, they spared the house with the scarlet

R

cord in the window—a sign that a friend of God's people lived within. Rahab, therefore, along with her father, her mother, her brothers, and all her father's household, was spared. Apparently she and her family were later brought into the nation of Israel.

Matthew refers to Rahab as the wife of Salmon (Ruth 4:20–21; Matt. 1:4–5; Luke 3:32; Salma, 1 Chr. 2:11). Their son Boaz married Ruth and became the father of Obed, the grandfather of Jesse, and the great-grandfather of David. Thus, a Canaanite harlot became part of the lineage of King David out of which the Messiah came (Matt. 1:5; Rachab, KJV)—perhaps an early sign that God's grace and forgiveness is extended to all, that it is not limited by nationality or the nature of a person's sins.

The Scriptures do not tell us how Rahab, who came out of a culture where harlotry and idolatry were acceptable, recognized the Lord as the one true God. But her insights recorded in Joshua 2:9–11 leave no doubt that she did so. This Canaanite woman's declaration of faith led the writer of the Epistle to the Hebrews to cite Rahab as one of the heroes of faith (Heb. 11:31), while James commended her as an example of one who has been justified by works (James 2:25).

According to rabbinic tradition, Rahab was one of the four most beautiful women in the world and was the ancestor of eight prophets, including Jeremiah and the prophetess Huldah.

RAHAB THE DRAGON [RAY hab]

A mythological sea monster or dragon representing the evil forces of chaos that God subdued by His creative power. The name Rahab as it occurs in Job 9:13 (NIV), Job 26:12 (NIV), Psalm 87:4 and 89:10, Isaiah 30:7 (NIV), and Isaiah 51:9 has no connection with the personal name of Rahab, the harlot of Jericho, in Joshua 2:1–21. The references to Rahab in the

books of Job, Psalms, and Isaiah speak of an evil power overcome by God.

God's smiting of Rahab is described in Job 26:12 (NIV) to signify God's power over the chaos of primeval waters at the creation. The NKJV translates as the storm for Rahab. Because the Rahab-dragon imagery was used in describing the deliverance from Egypt, the name Rahab also became a synonym for Egypt itself (Ps. 87:4; Is. 30:7; Rahab-Hem-Shebeth, NKJV). In its widest sense, the dragon can represent any force that opposes God's will. It is a fitting symbol for Satan (Rev. 20:2).

RAINBOW

An arch of colors in the sky, caused by light passing through moisture in the air. The most important reference to the rainbow in the Bible occurs in Genesis 9:13–17, where the rainbow serves as a sign of God's covenant with Noah. This covenant was a promise by God to the world that it would never again be destroyed by a flood. The rain clouds and the rainbow were never again to be regarded by people as a threat of ultimate judgment, but as an unchanging indicator of God's mercy. This passage does not state that this was the first rainbow, but that it gained this new significance after the Flood.

The remaining references to the rainbow in the Bible develop this symbolism. They all occur in passages where judgment is to be announced, notably in Revelation 4:3 and 10:1 in connection with God's judgment of the world (Ezek. 1:28). In all these cases, however, the rainbow is a sign of the glorious presence of God. It is a reminder that His mercy and grace will finally triumph.

RAMAH [RAY mah] (height)

Ramah of Benjamin, one of the cities allotted to the tribe of Benjamin (Josh. 18:25) in the vicinity of Bethel (Judg. 4:5) and Gibeah (Judg. 19:13). According to Judges 4:5, Deborah lived between Ramah and Bethel.

Shortly after the division of the nation of Israel into two kingdoms, King Baasha of Israel fortified Ramah against King Asa of Judah (1 Kin. 15:16–17). Ramah lay on the border between the two kingdoms. The fortification was done to guard the road to Jerusalem so no one from the northern kingdom would attempt to go to Jerusalem to worship. Baasha was also afraid these people would want to live in the southern kingdom.

When Asa learned that Baasha was fortifying the city, he bribed the Syrians to invade the north (1 Kin. 15:18–21) so Baasha's attention would be turned away from Ramah. Meanwhile, Asa dismantled Ramah and used the stones to build two forts of his own nearby at Geba and Mizpah (1 Kin. 15:22; 2 Chr. 16:6).

When Nebuchadnezzar invaded Judah, he detained the Jewish captives,

RAHAB THE DRAGON

including Jeremiah, at Ramah (Jer. 40:1). The captives who were too old or weak to make the trip to Babylonia were slaughtered here. This was the primary fulfillment of the prophecy, "A voice was heard in Ramah, lamentation and bitter weeping, Rachel weeping for her children" (Jer. 31:15), although Matthew also applies it to Herod's slaughter of children after the birth of Christ (Matt. 2:18). This city also figures in the prophecies of Isaiah (10:29) and Hosea (5:8).

RAMESES [RAM uh seez] (the god Ra has fathered a son)

The royal city of the Egyptian kings of the nineteenth and twentieth dynasties (about 1300–1100 B.C.) situated in the northeastern section of the Nile Delta. While the people of Israel were slaves in Egypt, they were forced to work on at least two of Pharaoh's vast construction projects—building the supply cities of Pithom and Raamses (Ex. 1:11, KJV, NASB, NKJV; Rameses, NIV, NRSV, REB).

"The land of Rameses" (Gen. 47:11) was "the best of the land"—the most fertile district of Egypt. This almost certainly refers to the Land of Goshen, in the northeastern Nile Delta.

RAMOTH GILEAD [RAY muhth GIL ee uhd] (heights of Gilead)

An important fortified city in the territory of Gad near the border of Israel and Syria. It was approximately 25 miles (40 kilometers) east of the Jordan River. Ramoth Gilead was designated by Moses as one of the cities of refuge (Deut. 4:43; Josh. 20:8). In the time of Solomon, one of the king's 12 district officers was stationed at Ramoth Gilead to secure food for the king's household, since it was a commercial center.

Because of its strategic location near the border of Israel and Syria, Ramoth Gilead was frequently the scene of battles between the two nations. The Jewish historian Josephus says that the city was captured by King Omri from Ben-Hadad I. It then changed hands several times. King Ahab enlisted the aid of King Jehoshaphat to retake the city, but he was mortally wounded in the attempt (2 Chr. 28–34). Ahab's son Joram was likewise wounded while attacking Ramoth Gilead (2 Kin. 8:28). While Jehu was maintaining possession of Ramoth Gilead, Elisha sent his servant to anoint Jehu king of Israel (2 Kin. 9:1–13).

RAMPART

A fortification consisting of an elevation or embankment, often provided with a wall to protect soldiers. A rampart was used as a protective barrier against an attacking army. The Hebrew word translated as rampart (Lam. 2:8; Nah. 3:8) means encirclement; it is variously translated by the KJV as army, bulwark, host, rampart, trench, and wall. The general sense of the word is that of the outer fortification, or the front line of defense, encircling a city (2 Sam. 20:15; Hab. 2:1). This fortification included moats and towers as well as walls and earthworks.

See also FORTIFICATION.

REAPING

The practice of harvesting grain. A sickle, with a short handle and a curved blade, was normally used for reaping. These tools were made of flint, bone, bronze, and iron. A supervisor organized the reapers (Ruth 2:5), who were often hired for daily wages (Deut. 24:15; Matt. 20:1–16) and were provided with food (Job 24:10–11). The workers were followed by the poor and the foreigners such as Ruth, who gathered the leftover grain from the harvest (Deut. 24:19; Ruth 2:23).

See also GLEANING.

REBEKAH [ruh BEK uh]

The wife of Isaac and the mother of Esau and Jacob. The story of Rebekah (Gen. 24) begins when Abraham, advanced in age, instructs his chief servant to go to Mesopotamia and seek a bride for Isaac. Abraham insisted that Isaac marry a young woman from his own country and kindred, not a Canaanite.

When Abraham's servant arrived at Padan Aram, he brought his caravan to a well outside the city. At the well he asked the Lord for a sign that would let him know which young woman was to be Isaac's bride. When Rebekah came to the well carrying her water pitcher, she not only gave the servant a drink of water from her pitcher but she also offered to draw water for his camels. These actions were the signs for which the servant had prayed, and he knew that Rebekah was the young woman whom the Lord had chosen for Isaac.

When the servant asked Rebekah her name and the name of her family, he learned that she was the granddaughter of Nahor (Abraham's brother) and, therefore, was the grand-niece of Abraham. The servant then told Rebekah and her father the nature of his mission, and she chose to go to Canaan and become Isaac's wife.

When a famine struck the land of Canaan, Isaac took Rebekah to Gerar, a city of the Philistines (Gen. 26:1–11). Fearful that Rebekah's beauty would lead the Philistines to kill him and seize his wife, he told them she was his sister. Abimelech, king of the Philistines, criticized Isaac for this deception. A similar story is told of Abraham and Sarah, who were scolded for their deception by Abimelech, king of Gerar (Gen. 20:1–18).

Nor was Rebekah above deception. When the time came for Isaac to give his birthright to Esau, she conspired with Jacob and tricked Isaac into giving it to Jacob instead. Jacob was forced to flee to Padan Aram to escape Esau's wrath.

As a result of her scheming, Rebekah never again saw her son. Apparently she died while Jacob was in Mesopotamia. She was buried in the cave of Machpelah (Gen. 49:30–31), where Abraham, Isaac, Jacob, Sarah, and Leah were also buried. Rebekah's name is spelled Rebecca in the New Testament (Rom. 9:10).

RECHABITES [REE kab ights]

A Kenite tribe founded by Jonadab, the son of Rechab (Jer. 35:1–9; Recabites in NIV). The Rechabites were convinced it was easier to live a godly life as nomads than in the settled life of the cities, where they would be tempted with idolatry and immorality. They did not drink wine or other intoxicating drink; they chose to live in tents rather than houses; and they refused to plant crops or own vineyards. This strict lifestyle was similar to the law of the Nazirite (Num. 6:1–21).

The only biblical description of the Rechabites occurs in Jeremiah 35. When Nebuchadnezzar's army attacked Judah and besieged Jerusalem, the Rechabites sought refuge in the city (Jer. 35:11). At God's command, Jeremiah tested them to see if they would live up to their vows. He set wine before them and encouraged them to drink, but they refused. Jeremiah praised them and held them up as an object lesson to the people of Judah who had disobeyed the laws of God.

Because of their faithfulness, Jeremiah promised that the Rechabites would never cease to exist (Jer. 35:18–19). A rabbinic tradition says that the daughters of the Rechabites were married to the sons of the Levites and that their children ministered in the temple. Followers of this group still live in the Middle East— in Iraq and Yemen.

R

RECONCILIATION

The process by which God and people are brought together again. The Bible teaches that they are alienated from one another because of God's holiness and human sinfulness. Although God loves the sinner (Rom. 5:8), it is impossible for Him not to judge sin (Heb. 10:27). Therefore, in biblical reconciliation, both parties are affected. Through the sacrifice of Christ, people's sins are atoned for and God's wrath is appeased. Thus, a relationship of hostility and alienation is changed into one of peace and fellowship.

The initiative in reconciliation was taken by God—while we were still sinners and "enemies," Christ died for us (Rom. 5:8, 10). Reconciliation is thus God's own completed act, something that takes place before human actions such as confession, repentance, and restitution. God Himself "has reconciled us to Himself through Jesus Christ" (2 Cor. 5:18).

RED SEA

A narrow body of water that stretches in a southeasterly direction from Suez to the Gulf of Aden for about 1,300 miles (2,100 kilometers). It is an important section of a large volcanic split in the earth that goes southward into east Africa and continues north along the Jordan valley to the Lebanon mountain range.

The Red Sea separates two large portions of land. On the east are Yemen and Saudi Arabia. On the west are Egypt, the Sudan, and Ethiopia. From ancient times the Red Sea has been an impressive sea covering some 169,000 square miles. It measures about 190 miles (310 kilometers) at its widest part and about 9,500 feet (almost 2,900 meters) at its greatest depth. The Red Sea branches at its northern end into two distinct channels, the northeasterly one being the Gulf of Aqaba and the northwesterly one named the Gulf of Suez. The Suez branch is fairly shallow and has broad plains on either side. By contrast, the Gulf of Aqaba is deep and clear, with a narrow shoreline.

The Red Sea is usually bright turquoise, but periodically algae grow in the water. When they die, the sea becomes reddish-brown, thus giving it the name, the Red Sea. This body of water has the reputation of being one of the hottest and saltiest on earth. The reason for this is the presence of volcanic slits in the ocean floor that have become filled with salt deposits and other minerals. The sea is heavily traveled because the Suez Canal links it with the Mediterranean. But navigation is difficult at the southern end because of outcroppings of coral reefs that force ships into a narrow channel of water. No large rivers flow into the Red Sea, and there is little rainfall in the area it crosses.

The name "Red Sea" has found its way into the Bible as a translation of the Hebrew *yam suph*, which means "sea of reeds" and not "Red Sea." The term *suph* comes from the Egyptian *twf*, meaning "papyrus." This confusion is unfortunate because papyrus reeds and similar vegetation do not grow in the Red Sea or in the Gulf of Suez. This fact excludes them as the area that witnessed the deliverance of the Hebrew captives at the time of the Exodus.

The term *yam suph*, however, seems to have been applied from the time of Solomon onwards to some area near to, or identical with, the Gulf of Aqaba. In 1 Kings 9:26 Ezion Geber, Sol-omon's port in the Gulf, is described as being on the shore of the *yam suph* in the land of Edom. A further possible reference to the Gulf of Aqaba is in Jeremiah 49:21. In this prophecy dealing with Edom, Jeremiah spoke of their desolation being heard as far as the *yam suph*.

Perhaps the place-name Suph in Deuteronomy 1:1, where Moses spoke God's words to the Israelites, was either a shortened form of *yam suph,* indicating the Gulf of Aqaba, or some settlement in that area. Just before Korah, Dathan, and Abiram met their end as the result of an earthquake, the Israelites had been instructed to go into the wilderness by way of the *yam suph* (Deut. 1:40). At a later stage, after the death of Aaron, the Hebrews left Mount Hor by a route near the *yam suph* to go around hostile Edomite territory (Num. 21:4). Such a journey would have brought them to the northeast of the Gulf of Aqaba, which might suggest that this body of water was being described by the term *yam suph.*

There is a strong argument against identifying the Gulf of Aqaba with the *yam suph,* or "Red Sea," that the fleeing Israelites crossed under the leadership of Moses. A crossing of the Gulf of Aqaba would have taken the Israelites much too far from the Goshen area. To reach the gulf they would have had to skirt the western edge of the Wilderness of Shur and make a direct southeast journey through the rugged central Sinai region and the Wilderness of Paran. Having crossed this *yam suph,* the Israelites would then have had to go north and then return to the Sinai Peninsula to meet with God at Mount Horeb.

An alternative suggestion is to regard the term *yam suph* not merely as describing a specific body of water, but as a general title that could be applied to any marshy area where reeds and papyri grew. The Egyptians used such terms in a wide sense. In the fifteenth century B.C., they spoke of both the Mediterranean and the Red Sea as the "Great Green Sea." Since there were several marshes in the Nile Delta, *yam suph* could apply to any one of them. It is even possible that the *yam suph* of Numbers 33:10–11 referred to the Gulf of Suez but

that the Israelite visit there occurred after the Exodus. The view that the Gulf of Suez extended much further northward into the area of the Bitter Lakes during the time of the Exodus cannot be supported by archaeological evidence or other studies.

The best understanding of *yam suph* is that it does not refer to the Red Sea or any of its branches. Instead, it probably refers to water bordered by papyrus reeds and located somewhere between the southern edge of Lake Menzaleh and the lakes close to the head of the Gulf of Suez that were drained when the Suez Canal was constructed. Such a location for the Exodus would be directly opposite the Wilderness of Shur, which was the first encampment of the Israelites after crossing the *yam suph* (Ex. 15:22).

REDEMPTION

Deliverance by payment of a price; salvation from sin, death, and the wrath of God by Christ's sacrifice.

In the Old Testament, redemption was applied to property, animals, persons, and the nation of Israel as a whole. In nearly every instance, freedom from obligation, bondage, or danger was secured by the payment of a price, a ransom, bribe, satisfaction, or sum of money paid to obtain freedom, favor, or reconciliation.

The New Testament emphasizes the tremendous cost of redemption: "the precious blood of Christ" (Eph. 1:7), which is also called an atoning sacrifice, "a propitiation by His blood" (Rom. 3:25). Believers are exhorted to remember the "price" of their redemption as a motivation to personal holiness (1 Pet. 1:13–19). The Bible also emphasizes the result of redemption: freedom from sin and freedom to serve God through Jesus Christ our Lord.

R

REGENERATION

The spiritual change brought about in a person's life by an act of God. In regeneration a person's sinful nature is changed, and he or she is enabled to respond to God in faith. The literal meaning of regeneration is "being born again." There is a first birth and a second birth. The first, as Jesus told Nicodemus (John 3:1–12) is "of the flesh"; the second birth is "of the Spirit." Being born of the Spirit is essential before a person can enter the kingdom of God.

Regeneration involves an enlightening of the mind, a change of the will, and a renewed nature. It extends to the total nature of people, changing their desires and restoring them to a right relationship with God in Christ. The need for regeneration grows out of humanity's sinfulness. It is brought about through God's initiative. God works in the human heart, and the person responds to God through faith. Thus, regeneration is an act of God through the Holy Spirit, resulting in resurrection from sin to a new life in Jesus Christ (2 Cor. 5:17).

REHOBOAM [ree uh BOE uhm] *(the people is enlarged)*

The son and successor of Solomon and the last king of the united monarchy and first king of the southern kingdom, Judah (reigned about 931–913 B.C.). His mother was Naamah, a woman of Ammon (1 Kin. 14:31).

Rehoboam became king at age 41 (1 Kin. 14:21) at a time when the northern tribes were discontented with the monarchy. They were weary of Solomon's heavy taxation and labor conscription. To promote unity, Rehoboam went to Shechem—center of much of the discontent among the northern tribes—to be made king officially and to meet with their leaders. They in turn demanded relief from the taxes and conscription.

Rehoboam first sought advice from older men who were of mature judgment and who had lived through Solomon's harsh years. They assured him that if he would be the people's servant, he would enjoy popular support.

When he also sought the counsel of younger men, his arrogant contemporaries, he received foolish advice that he should rule by sternness rather than kindness. Misjudging the situation, he followed this foolish advice. The northern tribes immediately seceded from the kingdom and made Jeroboam king.

When Rehoboam attempted to continue his control over the northern tribes by sending Adoram to collect a tax from the people (1 Kin. 12:18), Adoram was stoned to death. Rehoboam fled in his chariot to Jerusalem. The prophet Shemaiah prevented Rehoboam from retaliating and engaging in civil war (1 Kin. 12:22–24).

To strengthen Judah, Rehoboam fortified 15 cities (2 Chr. 11:5–12) to the west and south of Jerusalem, undoubtedly as a defensive measure against Egypt. The spiritual life of Judah was strengthened, too, by the immigration of northern priests and Levites to Judah and Jerusalem because of the idolatrous worship instituted at Bethel and Dan by Jeroboam (2 Chr. 11:13–17).

Rehoboam's military encounters were primarily with Jeroboam and Egypt. No specific battles with Jeroboam are described in the Bible, but "there was war between Rehoboam and Jeroboam all their days" (1 Kin. 14:30). This warring probably involved border disputes over the territory of Benjamin, the buffer zone between the two kingdoms.

In Rehoboam's fifth year Judah was invaded by Shishak (Sheshonk I), king of Egypt, who came against Jerusalem and carried away treasures from the temple and from Solomon's house. When Shemaiah told him that this invasion was

God's judgment for Judah's sin, Rehoboam humbled himself before God and was granted deliverance from further troubles (2 Chr. 12:1–12).

Rehoboam did not follow the pattern of David. Instead, he was an evil king (2 Chr. 12:14). During his 17-year reign, the people of Judah built "high places, sacred pillars, and wooden images" (1 Kin. 1:23) and permitted "perverted persons" to prosper in the land (1 Kin. 14:24). When he died, he was buried in the City of David (1 Kin. 14:31)

REMNANT

The part of a community or nation that remains after a dreadful judgment or devastating calamity, especially those who have escaped and remain to form the nucleus of a new community (Is. 10:20–23). The survival of a righteous remnant rests solely on God's providential care for His chosen people and His faithfulness to keep His covenant promises.

The concept of the remnant has its roots in the Book of Deuteronomy (4:27–31; 28:62–68; 30:1–10), where Moses warned the people of Israel that they would be scattered among the nations. But God also promised that He would bring the people back from captivity and establish them again in the land of their fathers. This concept was picked up by the prophets, who spoke of the Assyrian and Babylonian captivities. The concept was extended to apply also to the gathering of a righteous remnant at the time when the Messiah came to establish His kingdom.

In Amos and Isaiah, the remnant consisted of those chosen by God who were rescued from the impending doom of the nation (Is. 1:9; Amos 5:14–15). As such, they were labeled "the poor," those who suffer for God (Is. 29:19; 41:17). At the same time, they serve God and stand before the nation as witnesses, calling the people to repent of their rebellion.

In the New Testament, the apostle Paul picked up the teaching of Isaiah and other prophets about the remnant and applied it to the church (Rom. 11:5). Paul showed that God's purpose is seen in the "remnant" out of Israel who have joined the Gentiles to form the church, the new people of God. Further, Jesus' choice of twelve apostles built upon remnant themes. Symbolizing the Twelve Tribes, the apostles became the remnant who erected a new structure, the church, upon the foundation of Israel. In the church, both Jews and Gentiles, circumcised and uncircumcised, find their true spiritual home when they believe in Christ.

REPENTANCE

A turning away from sin, disobedience, or rebellion and a turning back to God (Matt. 9:13; Luke 5:32). In a more general sense, repentance means a change of mind (Gen. 6:6–7) or a feeling of remorse or regret for past conduct (Matt. 27:3). True repentance is a "godly sorrow" for sin, an act of turning around and going in the opposite direction. This type of repentance leads to a fundamental change in a person's relationship to God.

In the New Testament the keynote of John the Baptist's preaching was, "Repent, for the kingdom of heaven is at hand" (Matt. 3:2). When Jesus began His ministry, He took up John's preaching of the message of repentance, expanding the message to include the good news of salvation: "The time is fulfilled, and the kingdom of God is at hand. Repent and believe in the gospel" (Matt. 4:17).

Repentance and faith are two sides of the same coin: by repentance, one turns away from sin; by faith, one turns toward God in accepting the Lord Jesus Christ. Such a twofold turning, or conversion, is necessary for entrance into the kingdom (Matt. 18:3). "Unless you repent," said Jesus, "you will all likewise perish" (Luke 13:3, 5). This is the negative, or judgmental, side of Jesus' message. The positive, or merciful, side is seen in these words: "There is joy in the presence of the angels of God over one sinner who repents" (Luke 15:10).

After Jesus' crucifixion and resurrection, His disciples continued His message of repentance and faith (Acts 2:38; 3:19; 26:20). Repentance is a turning from wickedness and dead works (Heb. 6:1) toward God and His glory (Acts 20:21), eternal life (Acts 11:18), and a knowledge of the truth (2 Tim. 2:25).

REPHAIM [REF ih yuhm]

A race of giants who lived in Palestine before the time of Abraham (Gen. 14:5; 15:20). The last survivor of the Rephaim was Og, king of Bashan (Deut. 3:11). The kingdom of Og—Gilead, Bashan, and Argob—was called "the land of the giants [Rephaim]" (Deut. 3:13).

RESTITUTION

The act of restoring to the rightful owner something that has been taken away, stolen, lost, or surrendered. Leviticus 6:1–7 gives the Mosaic law of restitution; this law establishes the procedure to be followed in restoring stolen property.

Full restitution of the property had to be made and an added 20 percent (one-fifth of its value) must be paid as compensation (Lev. 5:16). If a man stole an ox or donkey or sheep, and the animal was recovered alive, the thief had to make restitution of double the value stolen (Ex. 22:4). If the thief had killed or sold the animal, however, he had to make a fourfold (for a sheep) or a fivefold (for an ox) restitution (Ex. 22:1; 2 Sam. 12:6).

Zacchaeus, a chief tax collector, said to Jesus, "If I have taken anything from anyone by false accusation, I restore fourfold" (Luke 19:8).

RESURRECTION OF JESUS CHRIST

A central doctrine of Christianity that affirms that God raised Jesus from the dead on the third day. Without the Resurrection, the apostle Paul declared, Christian preaching and belief are meaningless (1 Cor. 15:14). The Resurrection is the point at which God's intention for Jesus becomes clear (Rom. 1:4) and believers are assured that Jesus is the Christ.

So significant is the resurrection of Jesus that without it there would be no church or Christianity, and we would still be in our sins (1 Cor. 15:17). In spite of the centrality of the Resurrection, however, scholars have frequently debated a number of the elements in the resurrection accounts in the New Testament.

Some critics argue that because Paul does not speak of an empty tomb, the idea of the resurrection of Jesus must have developed years after His earthly life and ministry was over. But Paul refers to the burial (1 Cor. 15:4), which argues both for a proper tomb and against the body being dumped into a pit or a common criminal's grave.

Critics have also pointed to variations in the accounts of Jesus' resurrection in the gospels, such as how many women came to the tomb and who they were. Why did they come: to anoint the body (Mark and Matthew) or to see the tomb (Matthew)? Was there one angel (Mark and Matthew) or were there two (Luke and John) at the tomb? Did the angel say, "He is going before you into Galilee" (Mark and Matthew) or "Remember how He spoke . . . when He was still in Galilee" (Luke)? Did the women say "nothing to anyone" (Mark) or did they report the message to the disciples (Matthew)?

It is well to remember that these variations were recognized by early Christians and were not discovered by recent critics. As early as the second century, Tatian wrote his *Diatessaron*, or harmony of the Gospels, expecting that Christians would gladly accept his work as a substitute for the four Gospels. But while Christians read Tatian, they refused to substitute his harmony for the witnesses of the four Gospel writers. The faithfulness of these writers in transmitting to us the Gospel texts is a testimony to Christian integrity. It is also a witness to their early understanding that the Gospels were Holy Scripture, inspired by God.

Furthermore, these writers knew the tomb was empty; because if it had not been empty, the body would soon have been supplied. The only other alternative is that the disciples stole the body as the Jews (Matt. 28:13) and some modern critics have suggested. But such a view is self-defeating because the Gospel accounts themselves witness to the surprise of both the women and the disciples about the empty tomb.

Moreover, while it may seem incredible to us, the Gospel writers generally refrain from using the empty tomb as a basis for faith. Furthermore, the stone was not rolled away to let Jesus out; he did not need open doors to move about (Luke 24:31, 36; John 20:19, 26). The stone was removed to begin communicating the Resurrection to the followers of Jesus. But the empty tomb did not

RESURRECTION OF JESUS CHRIST

R

convince them that Jesus was alive. It was at first frustrating to the disciples and "seemed to them like idle tales" (Luke 24:11). Would anyone constructing a story and trying to prove the Resurrection use such an approach? These testimonies have an element of authenticity that inventors of stories seldom duplicate.

While the above testimonies about the empty tomb seem to have little to do with the faith of these early Christians, the appearances of Jesus are clearly at the heart of early Christian belief. The consistent witness of the New Testament is that in the appearances of Jesus something incredible happened. The two followers in Emmaus, upon realizing it was the risen Jesus, forgot their concern with the lateness of the hour and rushed back to Jerusalem to tell the others (Luke 24:29–33). The doubting Thomas uttered Christianity's greatest confession when he realized that the risen Christ was actually addressing him (John 20:27). Peter left his fishing nets for good when the risen Savior asked him, "Do you love Me?" (John 21:15). And at a later time (1 Cor. 15:8), the persecutor Paul was transformed into a zealous missionary as the result of a special appearance by the risen Lord (Acts 9:1–22).

But what was the nature of these appearances? Some have suggested that the appearance of Jesus to Paul seemed to be of a spiritual nature, similar to the revelation of Jesus to Christians today. Since Paul lumps all of the appearances together in 1 Corinthians 15:5–8, these critics argue that all the appearances must be spiritual in nature. They reject the idea that the risen Jesus could be touched (Matt. 28:9; Luke 24:39; John 20:27) or that He could eat (Luke 24:41–42).

Such a line of argument not only judges the witnesses on the basis of rationalistic assumptions, but it flies in the face of Paul's own admission that his experience was somewhat irregular. Another approach is that advocated by the German theologian Rudolph Bultmann, who speaks of an "Easter faith" of the disciples rather than an actual bodily resurrection of Jesus. Accordingly, he splits the Jesus of history from the spiritual experience of the Christ of faith.

But when the New Testament writers speak of the resurrection of Jesus, they are bearing witness not to what God did for them but what God did to Jesus. Certainly, as a result of the resurrection of Jesus human lives were transformed. For Paul this transformation of Christians is not termed resurrection but salvation. "In Christ" is the expression Paul uses for the spiritual experience of the living Christ.

Finally, the resurrection of Jesus, His exaltation to the right hand of the Father (Acts 2:33), and the giving of the Spirit (John 20:22) are all to be seen as a single complex of events. Although the elements may be viewed as separate happenings, the New Testament writers see them as closely integrated theologically. Together they represent the firstfruits of the new age.

REUBEN [ROO ben] (behold a son)

The firstborn son of Jacob, born to Leah in Padan Aram (Gen. 29:31–32; 35:23). Leah named her first son Reuben because the Lord had looked upon her sorrow at being unloved by her husband. By presenting a son to Jacob, she hoped he would respond to her in love.

The only reference to Reuben's early childhood is his gathering of mandrakes for his mother (Gen. 30:14). Years later, as the hatred of Jacob's sons for Joseph grew, it was Reuben who advised his brothers not to kill their younger brother. He suggested that they merely bind him, which would have allowed him to return later to release Joseph to his father (Gen. 37:20–22). It also was Reuben who reminded his brothers that all their troubles and fears in Egypt were their just reward for mistreating Joseph (Gen. 42:22).

When Jacob's sons returned from Egypt, Reuben offered his own two sons as a guarantee that he would personally tend to the safety of Benjamin on the next trip to Egypt (Gen. 42:37). In view of these admirable qualities, it is tragic that he became involved in incest with Bilhah, his father's concubine (Gen. 35:22).

As the firstborn, Reuben should have been a leader to his brothers and should have received the birthright—the double portion of the inheritance (Deut. 21:17). His act of incest, however, cost him dearly. He never lost his legal standing as firstborn, but he forfeited his right to the birthright.

REUBEN, TRIBE OF

The tribe whose ancestor was Reuben (Num. 1:5). During 430 years in Egypt, the descendants of Reuben increased from four sons to 46,500 men of war (Num. 1:20–21). In the wilderness the tribe of Reuben was represented in a conspiracy against Moses. As representatives of the tribe, Dathan and Abiram tried to assert their legal rights as descendants of Jacob's oldest son to a role of leadership in Israel (Num. 16:1–3), but their efforts failed.

The Reubenites were a pastoral people. The tribe requested an early inheritance east of the Jordan River where the land was suitable for cattle (Num. 32:1–33). They helped the other tribes claim their land, however, and Joshua commended them for their efforts (Josh. 22:9–10). The tribe also built an altar—along with the tribe of Gad and the half-tribe of Manasseh—in the Jordan valley as a witness to their unity with the tribes west of the Jordan (Josh. 22:11–34).

Later, members of the tribe of Reuben refused to assist Deborah and Barak in fighting the Canaanite Sisera (Judg. 5:16), although the tribe apparently assisted the other tribes in their war against Benjamin (Judg. 20:11). During Saul's reign, Reuben joined Gad and Manasseh in fighting the Hagrites (1 Chr. 5:18–22). When the kingdom divided under Rehoboam, Reuben joined the northern kingdom under Jeroboam.

While never prominent, the tribe of Reuben was never forgotten. Ezekiel remembered Reuben in his description of Israel (Ezek. 48:6). The tribe is also represented in the 144,000 sealed—12,000 from each of the twelve tribes of Israel (Rev. 7:5).

REVELATION

God's communication to people concerning Himself, His moral standards, and His plan of salvation. God is a personal Spirit distinct from the world; He is absolutely holy and is invisible to the view of physical, finite, sinful minds. Although people, on their own, can never create truth about God, God has graciously unveiled and manifested Himself to mankind. Other religions and philosophies result from the endless human quest for God; Christianity results from God's quest for lost mankind.

God has made Himself known to all people everywhere in the marvels of nature and in the human conscience, which is able to distinguish right from wrong. Because this knowledge is universal and continuous, by it God has displayed His glory to everyone (Ps. 19:1–6).

Some Christians think that only believers can see God's revelation in nature, but the apostle Paul said that unbelievers know truth about God: The unrighteous must have the truth to "suppress" it (Rom. 1:18); they "clearly see" it (Rom. 1:20); knowing God, they fail to worship Him as God (Rom. 1:21); they alter the truth (Rom. 1:25); they do not retain God in their knowledge (Rom. 1:28); and knowing the righteous judgment (moral law) of God, they disobey it (Rom. 1:32). The reason the ungodly are "inexcusable" (Rom. 2:1) before God's righteous judgment is that they possessed but rejected the truth God gave them.

What can be known of God from nature? God's universal revelation makes it clear that God exists (Rom. 1:20), and that God, the Creator of the mountains, oceans, vegetation, animals, and mankind, is wise (Ps. 104:24) and powerful (Pss. 29; 93; Rom. 1:20). People aware of their own moral responsibility, who know the difference between right and wrong conduct and who have a sense of guilt when they do wrong, reflect the requirements of God's moral law (the Ten Commandments) that is written on their hearts (Rom. 2:14–15).

What is the result of divine revelation in nature? If people lived up to that knowledge by loving and obeying God every day of their lives, they would be right with God and would not need salvation. However, people do not love God with all that is in them. Nor do they love their neighbors as themselves. People worship and serve things in creation rather than the Creator (Rom. 1:25). The problem does not lie with the revelation, which like the law is holy, just, and good (Rom. 7:12); the problem is with the sinfulness of human lives (Rom. 8:3). The best human being (other than Jesus Christ) comes short of the uprightness God requires.

Because of God's universal revelation in nature, the philosopher Immanuel Kant could say, "Two things fill the mind with ever new and increasing admiration and awe . . . the starry heavens above me and the moral law within me."

When Christians defend justice, honesty, and decency in schools, homes, neighborhoods, businesses, and governments, they do not impose their special beliefs upon others. They merely point to universal principles that all sinners know but suppress in their unrighteousness (Rom. 1:18).

As valuable as general revelation is for justice, honesty, and decency in the world today, it is not enough. It must be completed by the Good News of God's mercy and His gracious gift of perfect righteousness. Nature does not show God's plan for saving those who do wrong: that Jesus was the Son of God, that He died for our sins, and that He rose again from the dead. The message of salvation was seen dimly through Old Testament sacrifices and ceremonies. It was seen more clearly as God redeemed the Israelites from enslavement in Egypt and as God disclosed to prophets the redemptive significance of His mighty acts of deliverance.

The full and final revelation of God has occurred in Jesus Christ: "God, who at various times and in different ways spoke in time past to the fathers by the prophets, has in these last days spoken to us by His Son, whom He has appointed heir of all things, through whom also He made the worlds" (Heb. 1:1–2). Christ has "declared" God to us personally (John 1:18). To see Christ is to see the Father (John 14:9). Christ gave us the words the Father gave Him (John 17:8). At the cross Jesus revealed supremely God's self-giving love. There He died, "the just for the unjust, that He might bring us to God" (1 Pet. 3:18). And the Good News is not complete until we hear that He rose again triumphantly over sin, Satan, and the grave, and is alive forevermore.

Christ chose apostles and trained them to teach the meaning of His death and resurrection, to build the church, and to write the New Testament Scriptures. We are to remember the words of these eyewitnesses to Christ's resurrection. The content of God's special revelation concerning salvation, given to specially gifted spokesmen and supremely revealed in Christ, is found in "the words which were spoken before by the holy prophets, and of the commandment of . . . the apostles of the Lord and Savior" (2 Pet. 3:2). "The Holy Scriptures . . . are able to make you wise for salvation through faith which is in Christ Jesus" (2 Tim. 3:15).

REZIN [REE zin]

The last king of Syria. Rezin was killed by Tiglath-Pileser III, king of Assyria, in 732 B.C. Rezin allied himself with Pekah, king of Israel, to try to take away Judah's throne from Ahaz and the line of David (2 Kin. 15:37; 16:5–9). Together Rezin and Pekah besieged Jerusalem, but they were unable to capture Ahaz's stronghold. The prophet Isaiah counseled Ahaz not to fear Rezin and Pekah (Is. 7:4).

Instead of trusting the Lord, however, Ahaz panicked. He appealed for help to Tiglath-Pileser III, king of Assyria, by sending him silver and gold from the temple and Ahaz's palace. The Assyrian king marched against Damascus and besieged it in 734 B.C. After a two-year siege, Damascus fell to the Assyrians, Rezin was killed by Tiglath-Pileser, and the Syrians were carried away as captives to Kir (2 Kin. 16:9).

RHODA [ROE duh] *(rose)*

A servant girl in the home of Mary, the mother of John Mark (Acts 12:13). According to tradition, this house in Jerusalem was the site of the Last Supper; it may also have been the headquarters of the early church in Jerusalem. Following his miraculous release from prison, the apostle Peter went to Mary's house. Rhoda answered his knock and was filled with such surprise and joy that she forgot to let him in and ran back to tell the others. Peter had to continue knocking until someone let him in (Acts 12:16).

RHODES [roedz] *(a rose)*

A large island in the Aegean Sea off the southwest coast of Asia Minor visited by the apostle Paul (Acts 21:1). The island is about 42 miles (68 kilometers) long and about 15 miles (24 kilometers) wide; it lies about 12 miles (19 kilometers) off the coast of the province of Caria.

On the northeast corner of the island was the city of Rhodes, an important commercial, cultural, and tourist center for the Greeks as well as the Romans. At the entrance to the harbor of Rhodes stood the famous Colossus of Rhodes, a huge bronze statue of the sun-god Apollo built by the Greek sculptor Chares between 292 and 280 B.C. This towering statue was one of the seven wonders of the ancient world.

Because the island of Rhodes was on the natural shipping route from Greece to Syria and Palestine, the ship on which Paul traveled during his third missionary journey stopped at Rhodes (Acts 21:1). There is no evidence that Paul conducted any missionary activity on the island during his brief visit; he was in a hurry to get to Jerusalem for the Day of Pentecost: "For Paul had decided to sail past Ephesus" (Acts 20:16).

RIBLAH [RIB luh]

A Syrian city in the land of Hamath (2 Kin. 23:33; 25:21). Situated at the headwaters of the Orontes River in the broad plain between the Lebanon and the Anti-Lebanon Mountains, Riblah was approximately 65 miles (105 kilometers) north of Damascus and about 35 miles (57 kilometers) northeast of Baalbek. This area was blessed with abundant water, fertile lands, and the famous cedar forests of the nearby Lebanon Mountains. Consequently, it was an ideal campsite for the armies that regularly invaded the land of Israel. Riblah was easy to defend, and it

R

commanded a main route from Egypt to the Euphrates.

Following Josiah's defeat at Megiddo and the sack of Kadesh-on-the-Orontes in 609 B.C., Pharaoh Necho made Riblah his headquarters. Here he deposed King Jehoahaz, appointed Eliakim (Jehoiakim) as king in his place, and forced Judah to pay him tribute (2 Kin. 23:31–34). A few years later (605 B.C.), Nebuchadnezzar, king of Babylon, defeated the Egyptians at Carchemish (2 Chr. 35:20). He, too, chose Riblah as his command post. He directed the capture of Jerusalem in 586 B.C. from Riblah. Once he had subdued the city, he brought King Zedekiah to Riblah in captivity. There he forced Zedekiah to watch his sons killed, after which he was blinded (2 Kin. 25:6–21; Jer. 52:9–11).

RIDDLE

A puzzling question posed as a problem to be solved or guessed; an enigma. "Riddle" is a translation of a Hebrew word that means "something twisted, bent, or tied in a knot." While the word *riddle* appears in the Old Testament occasionally, other words are also used to translate the Hebrew word (for instance, dark sayings, Ps. 49:4; hard questions, 1 Kin. 10:1; and sinister schemes, Dan. 8:23; intrigue, NIV).

The classic use of riddle in the Old Testament occurs in the story of Samson. Samson posed it to the Philistines at Timnah: "Out of the eater came something to eat/and out of the strong came something sweet" (Judg. 14:14). This riddle was suggested to Samson by a swarm of bees and honey that he saw in the carcass of a lion (v. 8).

When the queen of Sheba heard of the fame of Solomon, she came to Jerusalem "to test him with hard questions" (1 Kin. 10:1; 2 Chr. 9:1). Literally, she tested his wisdom with riddles. According to the Jewish historian Josephus, King Solomon was particularly fond of riddles; he and Hiram, king of Tyre, engaged in a contest of riddles.

The "riddle" or "parable" of the eagles and the vine posed by Ezekiel (Ezek. 17:1–21) actually is an allegory. Ezekiel's parable may have been a riddle to some, had he not chosen to give its interpretation.

In the New Testament there is one instance where the Greek word often translated "riddle" is used: "For now we see in a mirror, dimly [*ainigma*], but then face to face" (1 Cor. 13:12). Our present life, and even God's revelation to us, contains riddles; but one day the riddles will be solved.

RIGHTEOUSNESS

Holy and upright living, in accordance with God's standard. The word *righteousness* comes from a root word that means "straightness." It refers to a state that conforms to an authoritative standard. Righteousness is a moral concept. God's character is the definition and source of all righteousness (Gen. 18:25; Rom. 9:14). Therefore, the righteousness of human beings is defined in terms of God's.

In the Old Testament, the term *righteousness* is used to define our relationship with God (Ps. 50:6; Jer. 9:24) and with other people (Jer. 22:3). In the context of relationships, righteous action is action that promotes the peace and well-being of human beings in their relationships to one another.

Sin is disobedience to the terms that define our relationship with God and with other people. Since the fall in the Garden of Eden, people have been inherently unrighteous. We cannot be righteous in the sight of God on our own merits. Therefore, people must have God's righteousness imputed, or transferred, to them.

The cross of Jesus is a public demonstration of God's righteousness. God accounts or transfers the righteousness of Christ to those who trust in Him (Rom. 4:3–22; Phil. 3:9). We do not become righteous because of our inherent goodness; God sees us as righteous because of our identification by faith with His Son.

RIZPAH [RIZ puh]

A daughter of Aiah who became a concubine of King Saul (2 Sam. 3:7; 21:8, 10–11). She bore two sons, Armoni and Mephibosheth. After Saul's death, Abner had sexual relations with Rizpah (2 Sam. 3:7)—an act that amounted to claiming the throne of Israel. Ishbosheth (also called Esh-Baal), one of Saul's sons by another woman, accused Abner of immorality and, by implication, of disloyalty to Ishbosheth's authority. This accusation so enraged Abner that he transferred his loyalty from Saul to David.

Rizpah is a good example of the undying devotion of a mother. After the death of her sons, she kept vigil over their bodies for several months. When David heard of this, he ordered that Saul and Jonathan's bones, still unburied, be mingled with those of Saul's sons and grandsons and that they be buried "in the country of Benjamin in Zelah, in the tomb of Kish his [Saul's] father" (2 Sam. 21:14).

ROCK BADGER

The rock badger or rock hyrax is a rabbit-sized furry animal. With short ears, sharp teeth, and black-button eyes, it resembles an overgrown guinea pig (Lev. 11:5; coney in KJV, NIV).

"The rock badgers are a feeble folk, yet they make their homes in the crags," says Proverbs 30:26, holding them up as little things that are "exceedingly wise." Feeble or defenseless they may be, but they find safety in steep, rocky terrain. Their feet have a suction-like grip that enables them to scamper among rocky

out-croppings. Their enemies easily overlook a rock badger stretched out motionless on a sun-warmed rock.

ROMAN EMPIRE

The powerful pagan empire that controlled most of the known world during New Testament times. In 63 B.C., Judea became formally subject to Rome and this was the case during the entire New Testament period. The emperor Octavian, who was also known as Augustus, became emperor in 27 B.C. He was still reigning at the time of Jesus' birth.

Jesus' crucifixion occurred during the reign of the emperor Tiberius. The martyrdom of James, the brother of John, took place in the reign of Claudius (Acts 11:28; 12:1–2). It was to Nero that Paul appealed (Acts 25:11). The destruction of Jerusalem prophesied by Jesus (Matt. 24; Mark 13; Luke 19:41–44) was accomplished in the year A.D. 70 by Titus, who later became emperor. Thus, all of the New Testament story unfolded under the reign of Roman emperors.

The Roman Empire reached the height of its power from about A.D. 100 to 175. By the end of the second century, however, the Romans and their power had begun to decline. Because of the vast expanse of its territory, the empire grew increasingly difficult to administer. High taxation and political in-fighting also took their toll.

Morally, Rome was also a sick society; its life of sin and debauchery served to hasten its collapse from within, even as barbaric tribes moved in to challenge the Romans' military rule. By A.D. 450 the Roman Empire was only a skeleton of its former self, reduced to a third-rate power among the nations of the ancient world.

Under Roman rule the Jews were given a special status with certain legal rights. They were permitted to practice their own religion and to build their

R

synagogues. They also were exempt from military service and were not required to appear in court on the Sabbath.

Relationships between the Jews and the Romans were mostly positive. But a few major disturbances did occur. The emperor Caligula alienated the Jews by opposing their belief in one God and forcibly erecting a statue of himself in their synagogues. Also, in A.D. 19, the emperor Tiberius expelled some Jews from Italy. This edict was renewed under Claudius in A.D. 49 (Acts 18:2). Apparently this edict did not last long, because Jews were living in Rome when Paul arrived there about A.D. 62.

The situation of the Jews varied considerably under the different Roman rulers. Basically, the Romans treated the Jews fairly. Herod the Great began to rebuild the temple in 20 B.C., and Herod Agrippa sought Jewish favor by persecuting the Christians (Acts 12:1–3). Archelaus, on the other hand, was a cruel and tyrannical ruler who massacred many Jews (Matt. 2:22).

Resentful of the presence of these foreign oppressors, the Jews refused to recognize anyone but God as sovereign. Revolutionary activities of Jewish nationalists such as the Zealots increased and threatened the peace in Palestine. By A.D. 66, Rome was forced to subdue a Jewish revolt in Judea. And in A.D. 70, Titus, a Roman general who later became emperor, marched on the city of Jerusalem to destroy Jewish resistance. Many Jews lost their lives by crucifixion and other violent means. A small group of freedom fighters held out at Masada, but they took their own lives just before the Roman soldiers broke into their fortress.

The destruction of Jerusalem did not wipe out the Jewish state or religion. In some ways, it made the Jews more determined to resist. During the next 60 years Rome and the Jews clashed on a number of occasions. From A.D. 132–135 a second

rebellion was led by a self-proclaimed messiah, Simon Bar Koseba. Hadrian, emperor at the time, issued an edict that virtually destroyed Judaism. Jerusalem was rebuilt as a Roman colony, complete with a pagan Roman temple, erected on the site of the Jewish temple. The province of Judea was replaced by Syria Palestine. In this rebellion, some 500,000 Jews were killed and many others were sold into slavery. Those who survived were scattered beyond this new province.

The Book of Acts shows how Christianity spread throughout the Roman Empire. Under Paul, the great missionary to the Gentiles, the gospel may have been preached as far west as Spain (Rom. 15:28). A Christian church existed in Rome as early as A.D. 50 (Acts 18:2–3). By the time Paul wrote his Epistle to the Romans (A.D. 58), a large Christian community existed in the imperial city.

Paul's appearance in Rome was ironic, because he came as a prisoner and not as a missionary (Acts 25:12; 27:1; 28:19–31). Here he was held in confinement awaiting a trial that apparently never took place. According to tradition, Paul lost his life under Nero's persecution about A.D. 64.

In its early stages, Christianity was regarded by Rome as a sect of Judaism. This is why it was ignored during its early years. On several occasions, Roman authorities viewed conflicts between Jews and Christians as an internal matter, not worthy of their attention (Acts 18:12–17). When Christians were accused by the Jews of breaking the law, they were acquitted (Acts 16:35–39). Rome even protected Christians from Jewish fanatics (Acts 19:28–41; 22:22–30; 23:23–24) and assured Paul the right of a proper trial (Acts 23:26; 28:31).

The first known persecution of Christians by the Roman authorities took place under Nero. But this was an isolated case and not a general policy. Many Christians, including Paul, lost their lives at this time. Tacitus, a Roman historian, refers to vast multitudes of Christians who were arrested, tortured, crucified, and burned.

Hardships came to Christians in parts of Asia while Domitian was emperor. Later, under Trajan, there were further problems, especially in Bithynia, where Pliny was governor (A.D. 112). Ignatius, bishop of Antioch, was martyred during this persecution. Rome may have feared that Christians could become a political threat because they would not acknowledge Caesar as lord.

Marcus Aurelius took official action against Christianity. As emperor, he was responsible for the death of Justin Martyr (A.D. 165). Celsius (A.D. 249–251) launched attacks against Christians and, like Nero, used them as scapegoats for his own failures.

Under Diocletian intense persecution of the church took place for three years (A.D. 303–305). Many churches were destroyed. Bibles were burned, and Christians were martyred. With the coming of Constantine, however, this policy of persecution was reversed. His Edict of Milan in A.D. 313 made Christianity the official religion of the Roman Empire.

ROME, CITY OF

Capital city of the ancient Roman Empire and present capital of modern Italy. Founded in 753 B.C., Rome was situated 15 miles (24 kilometers) from where the Tiber River flows into the Mediterranean Sea. From its initial settlement on the Palatine Hill near the river, the city gradually grew and embraced the surrounding area. Ultimately, the city was situated on seven hills.

The Book of Acts describes the thrilling story of the early church as it shared the gospel, beginning at Jerusalem and finally reaching Rome. The apostle Paul's first known connection with Rome was when he met Aquila and Priscilla at Corinth (Acts 18:2). They had left Rome when Claudius expelled all the Jews from the city. Some few years after meeting Aquila and Priscilla, Paul decided that he "must also see Rome" (Acts 19:21). When he wrote his letter to the Christians at Rome, his plan was to visit friends in the city on his way to Spain (Rom. 15:24).

However, Paul actually went to Rome under very different conditions than he had originally planned. To keep from being killed by hostile Jews in Jerusalem, Paul appealed to Caesar. The binding effect of that appeal ultimately brought him to the capital city as a prisoner. Here he waited for his trial. The Book of Acts closes at this point, and one must rely on secular history and references in the Pastoral Epistles for the rest of the story. Tradition holds that Paul was ultimately martyred by Nero during the emperor's persecution of Christians.

The city to which Paul came was very similar to a modern city. The public buildings and other structures were lavishly constructed. A new senate house and a temple to honor Caesar had been constructed in A.D. 29. In A.D. 28 the senate had authorized Augustus to rebuild or restore some 82 temples in need of repair. In the process, he built a great temple to Apollo near his palace on the Palatine Hill. Other buildings included the Colosseum, where Roman games occurred.

The houses of the wealthy people of Rome were elaborately constructed and situated on the various hills, but most of the people lived in tenements. These crowded apartment dwellings were multistoried buildings that engulfed the city. Over a million people lived in these tenements, which were surrounded by narrow and noisy streets with a steady flow of traffic day and night.

The people of Rome were provided

with food and entertainment by the state. Wine was also plentiful and cheap. Admission to the games was free. Large crowds attended these games, which included chariot racing, gladiatorial contests, and theatrical performances.

Like Babylon, the city of Rome became a symbol of paganism and idolatry in the New Testament. The Book of Revelation contains several disguised references to the pagan city. Most scholars agree that Revelation 17–18 should be interpreted as predictions of the fall of Rome.

RUBY

A variety of corundum, the hardest of all minerals next to the diamond. The ruby has a deep red color because of traces of chromium. Rubies are the rarest and most precious of all jewels. Thus, they serve in the Bible as an appropriate standard for comparing other things that are even more precious (wisdom, knowledge, a good wife, etc). The Hebrew word translated as "rubies" in the NKJV and KJV may have been pink pearl or red coral (Job 28:18; Prov. 3:15; 8:11; 20:15; 31:10; Lam. 4:7).

RULER OF THE SYNAGOGUE

The leader or president of a synagogue. As an administrator, he was charged with supervision of all matters pertaining to the synagogue. Elected by the board of elders, he chose the men to read the Scriptures, to offer prayer, and to preach or explain the Scripture for each meeting in the synagogue. Rulers of the synagogue mentioned by name in the New Testament are Jairus (Mark 5:22; Luke 8:41), Crispus (Acts 18:8), and Sosthenes (Acts 18:17).

RUTH [rooth] *(friendship)*

The mother of Obed and great-grandmother of David. A woman of the country of Moab, Ruth married Mahlon, one of the two sons of Elimelech and Naomi. With his wife and sons, Elimelech had migrated to Moab to escape a famine in the land of Israel. When Elimelech and both of his sons died, they left three widows: Naomi, Ruth, and Orpah (Ruth's sister-in-law). When Naomi decided to return home to Bethlehem, Ruth chose to accompany her, saying, "Wherever you go, I will go" (Ruth 1:16).

In Bethlehem, Ruth was permitted to glean in the field of Boaz, a wealthy kinsman of Elimelech (Ruth 2:1). At Naomi's urging, Ruth asked protection of Boaz as next of kin—a reflection of the Hebrew law of levirate marriage (Deut. 25:5–10). After a nearer kinsman waived his right to buy the family property and provide Elimelech an heir, Boaz married Ruth. Their son, Obed, was considered one of Naomi's family, according to the custom of the day.

Ruth's firm decision—"Your people shall be my people, and your God, my God" (Ruth 1:16)—brought a rich reward. She became an ancestor of David and Jesus (Matt. 1:5).

S

SABBATH [SAB bahth]

The practice of observing one day in seven as a time for rest and worship. This practice apparently originated in creation, because God created the universe in six days and rested on the seventh (Gen. 1). By this act, God ordained a pattern for living—that people should work six days each week at subduing and ruling the creation and should rest one day a week. This is the understanding of the creation set forth by Moses in Exodus 20:3–11, when he wrote the Ten Commandments at God's direction.

The Old Testament prophets recounted God's blessings upon those who properly observed the Sabbath (Is. 58:13). They called upon the people to observe the Sabbath (Neh. 10:31; 13:15–22), while soundly condemning those who made much of external observance and ignored the heart and moral issues to which the Sabbath bound them (Is. 1:13; Hos. 2:11; Amos 8:5).

During the period between the Old and New Testaments, Jewish religious leaders added greatly to the details of Sabbath legislation. They sought to insure proper and careful observance by making certain that people did not even come close to violating it. This substituted human law for divine law (Matt. 15:9), made the law a burden rather than a rest and delight (Luke 11:46), and reduced the Sabbath to little more than an external observance (Matt. 12:8). Jesus, like the Old Testament prophets, kept the Sabbath Himself (Luke 4:16) and urged others to observe the day (Mark 2:28). But He condemned the pharisaical attitude that missed the deep spiritual truth behind Sabbath observance (Matt 12:14; Mark 2:23; Luke 6:1–11; John 5:1–18).

Many Christians feel that God still expects His people to set aside one day in seven to Him. They argue that such an observance is a creation ordinance that is binding until this creation comes to an end and our ultimate rest as Christians is realized in heaven (Heb. 4). They also believe that as part of the moral system known as the Ten Commandments, the Sabbath is morally binding upon all people for all time.

Historically, Christians of this persuasion usually observe Sunday, the first day of the week, as the Christian Sabbath. They note that Christ arose on the first day of the week (Matt. 28:1) and, thereafter, the New Testament church regularly worshiped on Sunday (Acts 20:7; 1 Cor. 16:2; Rev. 1:10). This day on which

Jesus arose was called the Lord's Day (Rev. 1:10). A few Christian groups, however, deny that observance of the seventh day as the Sabbath was ever abolished. Among them are Seventh-Day Adventists and Seventh-Day Baptists.

The Sabbath is a means by which our living pattern imitates God's (Ex. 20:3–11). Work is followed by rest. This idea is expressed by the Hebrew word for Sabbath, which means "cessation."

Sabbath rest is also a time for God's people to think about and enjoy what God has accomplished. Another Hebrew word meaning "rest" embodies this idea, "But the seventh day is the Sabbath of the Lord your God. In it you shall not do any work," (Deut. 5:14). God's people are directed to keep the Sabbath because God delivered and redeemed His people from the bondage in Egypt. Thus, the Sabbath is an ordinance that relates redemption directly to history.

Sabbath rest also holds promise of the ultimate salvation that God will accomplish for His people. As certainly as He delivered them from Egypt through Moses, so will He deliver His people from sin at the end of the age through the Great Redeemer (Gen. 3:15; Hebrews 4).

SABBATH DAY'S JOURNEY

The distance a Jew could travel on the Sabbath without breaking the law. This phrase occurs in the Bible in Acts 1:12, where Mount Olivet is described as being "near Jerusalem, a Sabbath day's journey." This distance is usually reckoned to be about a thousand yards (Josh. 3:4, NIV; two thousand cubits, REB, NRSV, NKJV), because of the distance between the ark of the covenant and the rest of the Israelite camp in the wilderness.

The idea behind the Jewish law (see Ex. 16:29) was that every person within the camp or city would be close enough to the center of worship to take part in the services without having to travel such a great distance that the Sabbath became a harried and busy day. This law, although noble in intent, was soon abused by a strict legalism. In the New Testament, Jesus often clashed with the Pharisees because of their blind legalism over observance of the Sabbath (Matt. 12:1–9).

SABBATICAL YEAR

A year of rest and redemption that occurred every seven years in the Hebrew nation. By God's prescription, Israel was to set apart every seventh year by letting the land go uncultivated (Lev. 25:4–5). The crops and harvest that were reaped during this year were considered the common possession of all people and animals (Ex. 23:11; Deut. 15:1–18). None of this harvest was to be stored for future use.

During a Sabbath year, Israelites were to cancel all debts owed to them by their fellow Israelites (Deut. 15:1–5). At the least, a period of grace was to be set aside in which payment was not required. The people of Israel were also to free their Hebrew slaves, remembering that they were also slaves in the land of Egypt at one time and that God had redeemed them by His goodness.

God's anger fell on Israel because the Sabbath year was not observed from the time of Solomon (Jer. 34:14–22). This was one reason why Israel spent 70 years in bondage at the hands of the Babylonians.

SACKCLOTH

A rough, coarse cloth, or a bag-like garment made of this cloth and worn as a symbol of mourning or repentance. In the Bible sackcloth was often used to symbolize certain actions. In the case of mourning, either over a death (Gen. 37:34; Joel 1:8) or another calamity (Esth. 4:1–4; Job 16:15), the Israelites showed their grief by wearing sackcloth and ashes. This was done also in instances of confession and grief over sin (1 Kin. 21:27).

Sackcloth was often worn by prophets, perhaps to show their own brokenness in the face of their terrible message of judgment and doom (Is. 20:2; Rev. 11:3). The word for sackcloth in the Bible can also mean sack. Joseph ordered that the sacks of his brothers be filled with grain (Gen. 42:25). Rizpah spread sackcloth on a rock, using it as bedding material (2 Sam. 21:10). But sackcloth was most commonly used as an article of clothing.

SACRIFICE

The ritual through which the Hebrew people offered the blood or the flesh of an animal to God as a substitute payment for their sin. Sacrifice and sacrificing originated in the Garden of Eden soon after the Fall of mankind. Various principles of sacrifice are confirmed in the account of Cain and Abel (Gen. 4:3–5). Abel offered a better sacrifice than Cain for two reasons. First, he gave the best that he had, whereas Cain simply offered whatever happened to be available. Second, Abel's offering demonstrated that he was motivated by faith in God and that his attitude was pleasing to God (Gen. 4:4–5; Heb. 11:4). Cain, by contrast, would soon demonstrate that his attitude was displeasing to God. He would become selfish, angry, and deceitful. He would then murder his brother, lie to God, and refuse to confess his sin or show remorse.

When Noah came out of the ark, his first act was to build an altar upon which he sacrificed animals to God. This pleased God because Noah's act was a recognition that God understood his sinfulness, its penalty, and the necessity of blood sacrifice as a divine provision (Heb. 11:39–40). Noah represented all mankind who now recognized God's gracious provision and promise. God pledged never again to curse the ground

(Gen. 8:20–22), and He blessed Noah because of his faith.

The fullest explanation of the concept of sacrifice is found in the Mosaic Law. In this code sacrifice has three central ideas: consecration, expiation (covering of sin), and propitiation (satisfaction of divine anger). Only consecration had a kind of sacrifice which spoke of it alone. This was the vegetable or grain offerings. These could not be brought to God, however, unless they were preceded by an expiatory offering, or an animal or bloody sacrifice. There was no consecration (commitment) to God apart from expiation (dealing with the penalty and guilt of sin). People could not approach God and be right with Him without the shedding of blood.

The Old Testament also referred to sacrifices as food for the Lord (Lev. 3:11, 16; 22:7) and an offering made by the fire for the satisfaction of the Lord (Lev. 2:2, 9). As a spiritual being, God did not need physical food. Nevertheless, He did insist that these sacrifices be given to Him. Sacrifice as worship is people giving back to God what God has previously given them as a means of grace. Ultimately, these sacrifices speak of the one final and perfect sacrifice of Jesus Christ (Heb. 10:11–18).

Both the Old Testament and the New Testament confirm that sacrifices were presented as a symbolic gesture. People were obligated, because of their sins, to present offerings by which they gave another life in place of their own. These substitutes pointed forward to the ultimate substitute, Jesus Christ (Heb. 10:1–18).

According to God's command, the animal sacrificed had to be physically perfect in age and condition. Through the perfection of this animal, perfection was presented to God. Ultimately, this symbolized the necessity for people to present themselves perfect before God

by presenting the perfect one in their place (1 Pet. 1:18–19). The true Lamb of God, innocent of all sin, took away sin (John 1:29).

After the animal was selected and presented at the altar, the first act was the laying on of hands by the person presenting the offering. By this act the worshipers symbolically transferred their sin and guilt to the sacrificial animal that stood in their place. The sacrifice symbolically pointed to the Savior, who would do for the believers what they could not do for themselves. He would take upon Himself sin and guilt and accomplish redemption for His people (Is. 53:4–12; Matt. 1:21).

In the festival of the Day of Atonement, two goats depicted this redemptive act. One goat died, its death symbolizing how the ultimate sacrifice in the future would pay the penalty for the believer's sin. Its blood was applied to the mercy seat in the Most High Place, symbolizing how the great sacrifice would cover people's sin, bring them into God's presence, and make full restitution to God. To the head of the second goat the priest symbolically transferred the sin of God's people. Then this goat, known as the scapegoat, was sent into the wilderness to symbolize the removal of the people's sin (Lev. 16).

SADDUCEES [SAJ uh seez]

Members of a Jewish faction that opposed Jesus during His ministry. Known for their denial of the bodily resurrection, the Sadducees came from the leading families of the nation—the priests, merchants, and aristocrats. The high priests and the most powerful members of the priesthood were mainly Sadducees (Acts 5:17).

The Sadducees rejected "the tradition of the elders," that body of oral and written commentary that interpreted the Law of Moses. This placed them in direct conflict with another Jewish group, the

Pharisees, who had made the traditions surrounding the law almost as important as the law itself. The Sadducees insisted that only the laws that were written in the Law of Moses (the Pentateuch, the first five books of the Old Testament) were really binding. The Sadducees thought this way because of religious practices that had taken place for several centuries.

The Sadducees rejected this approach to authority in favor of the written Law of Moses. They felt the original law alone could be trusted. Naturally, they felt Sadducean priests should be the ones to serve as the law's interpreters.

The Sadducees did not believe in the resurrection of the dead or the immortality of the soul, since these doctrines are not mentioned in the Law of Moses. Neither did they believe in rewards or punishments handed out after death, as in the doctrines of heaven and hell. Acts 23:8 indicates that they did not believe in angels or spirits, either. They believed in free will—that people are responsible for their own prosperity or misfortune. They interpreted the law literally and tended to support strict justice as opposed to mercy toward the offender.

Only a few references are made to the Sadducees in the New Testament. They opposed the early church (Acts 4:1–3; 5:17–18), much more so than even the Pharisees (Acts 5:34–39; 15:5; 23:6–9). Since the chief priests usually came from among the Sadducees, it is clear that they played a major role in the arrest of Jesus and the preliminary hearing against Him (Mark 14:60–64), and that they urged Pilate to crucify Him (Mark 15:1, 3, 10–11). Jesus warned His disciples about the "leaven"—the "doctrine" or teaching—of the Sadducees (Matt. 16:1–12). John the Baptist was suspicious of their supposed "repentance" (Matt. 3:7–12).

One incident when Jesus clashed with the Sadducees is recorded in all three of the synoptic Gospels (Matt. 22:23–33; Mark 12:18–27; Luke 20:27–40). Apparently one of the favorite sports of the Sadducees was to make fun of their opponents by showing how their beliefs led to ridiculous conclusions. They approached Jesus with a "what if" question, designed to show the absurd consequences that can arise from believing in the resurrection of the dead. "Suppose," they asked, "a woman had seven husbands in this life, and each of them died without leaving children? Whose wife would she be in the world to come?"

Jesus replied with a two-part answer. First, He said that they were wrong to suggest that earthly relationships, such as marriage, will continue after the resurrection. Second, Jesus pointed out that they were wrong in not believing in the resurrection at all: "Have you not read what was spoken to you by God, saying, 'I am the God of Abraham, the God of Isaac, and the God of Jacob'? God is not the God of the dead, but of the living" (Matt. 22:31–32; also Ex. 3:6, 15–16).

Jesus' argument was that God told Moses that He was the God of Abraham, Isaac, and Jacob. Of course, these three men had died long before the time of Moses. Yet, if they were not "alive" at the time of Moses (that is, if they did not live on after their deaths), then God would not have called Himself their God, for "God is not the God of the dead, but of the living." Abraham, Isaac, and Jacob must live on if God is still their God; therefore, it is wrong to deny life after death and the resurrection of the dead.

After posing His reasons, Jesus stated that the Sadducees were "greatly mistaken" in their beliefs (Mark 12:27). The multitude who heard Jesus' argument were "astonished at His teaching" (Matt. 22:33) and the Sadducees were "silenced" (Matt. 22:34).

SALAMIS [SAL uh mis]

A port city on the east coast of the island of Cyprus visited by Paul and Barnabas during Paul's first missionary journey. These two missionaries preached in several Jewish synagogues at Salamis, assisted by John Mark (Acts 13:5). The city has traditionally been recognized as the birthplace of Barnabas. According to tradition, Barnabas was stoned to death here by a Jewish mob. Salamis was famous for its copper mines, flax, wine, fruit, and honey.

SALEM [SAY luhm] *(peaceful)*

A city ruled by Melchizedek, the king to whom Abraham gave a tithe (Gen. 14:18). Salem is usually identified with ancient Jerusalem, or Jebus, the Jebusite city captured by David and turned into the capital city of the nation of Judah (1 Chron. 11:4–9).

SALOME [suh LOE mee] *(peace)*

1. The daughter of Herodias by her first husband Herod Philip, a son of

SADDUCES

Herod the Great. The New Testament identifies her only as Herodias' daughter (Matt. 14:6–11; Mark 6:22–28). At the birthday celebration of Herod Antipas, who was now living with Herodias, Salome danced before the king and pleased him greatly. He offered to give her anything she wanted. At her mother's urging, Salome asked for John the Baptist's head on a platter. Salome later married her uncle Philip, tetrarch of Trachonitis (Luke 3:1), and then her cousin Aristobulus.

SALOME [suh LOE mee] *(peace)*

2. One of the women who witnessed the crucifixion of Jesus and who later brought spices to the tomb to anoint His body (Mark 15:40; 16:1). Salome apparently was the mother of James and John, two of the disciples of Jesus. She is pictured in the Gospel of Matthew as asking special favors for her sons (Matt. 20:20–24). Jesus replied that Salome did not understand what kind of sacrifice would be required of her sons.

SALT

This mineral is sodium chloride, a white crystalline substance used mainly for seasoning and as a preservative (Job 6:6). Salt is not only one of the most important substances mentioned in the Bible, but it is a necessity of life. The Hebrew people were well aware of the importance of salt to health (Job 6:6). High concentrations of salt exist in the Dead Sea, a body of water that is nine times saltier than the ocean and is sometimes called the Salt Sea (Gen. 14:3). The ancient cities of Sodom and Gomorrah may have been located near the south end of the Dead Sea. Here Lot's wife was turned into a pillar of salt (Gen. 19:26).

An ancient method of extracting salt from sea water was to collect salt water in saltpits—holes dug in the sand; the water evaporated, leaving the salt behind

(Zeph. 2:9). Saltpans were later used for this purpose.

Salt had a significant place in Hebrew worship. It was included in the grain offering (Lev. 2:13), the burnt offering (Ezek. 43:24), and the incense (Ex. 30:35). Part of the temple offering included salt (Ezra 6:9). It was also used to ratify covenants (Num. 18:19; 2 Chr. 13:5). Newborn babies were rubbed with salt in the belief that this promoted good health (Ezek. 16:4).

During times of war, the enemies' lands were sown with salt to render them barren (Judg. 9:45). In Roman times salt was an important item of trade and was even used for money. Roman soldiers received part of their salary in salt. Jesus described His disciples as the salt of the earth, urging them to imitate the usefulness of salt (Matt. 5:13; Col. 4:6).

SALVATION

Deliverance from the power of sin; redemption. The need for salvation goes back to the removal of Adam and Eve from the Garden of Eden (Gen. 3). After the Fall, the lives of people were marked by strife and difficulty. Increasingly, corruption and violence dominated their world (Gen. 6:11–13). When God destroyed the world with the Flood, He also performed the first act of salvation by saving Noah and his family. These eight people became the basis of another chance for mankind. The salvation of Noah and his family was viewed by the apostle Peter as a pattern of the full salvation that we receive in Christ (1 Pet. 3:18–22).

The doctrine of salvation in the Bible reached its fulfillment in the death of Christ on our behalf. Jesus' mission was to save the world from sin and the wrath of God (Matt. 1:21; Rom. 5:9). During His earthly ministry, salvation was brought to us by His presence and the power of faith (Luke 19:9–10). Now, our salvation is based on His death and resurrection (Mark 10:25).

The salvation that comes through Christ may be described in three tenses: past, present, and future. When people believe in Christ, they are saved (Acts 16:31). But we are also in the process of being saved from the power of sin (Rom. 8:13). Finally, we shall be saved from the very presence of sin (Titus 2:12–13). God releases into our lives today the power of Christ's resurrection (Rom. 6:4) and allows us a foretaste of our future life as His children (2 Cor. 1:22). Our experience of salvation will be complete when Christ returns (Heb. 9:28) and the kingdom of God is fully revealed (Matt. 13:41–43).

SANCTIFICATION

The process of God's grace by which the believer is separated from sin and becomes dedicated to God's righteousness. Accomplished by the Word of God (John 17:7) and the Holy Spirit (Rom. 8:3–4), sanctification results in holiness, or purification from the guilt and power of sin.

Sanctification as separation from the world and setting apart for God's service is a concept found throughout the Bible. Spoken of as "holy" or "set apart" in the Old Testament were the land of Canaan, the city of Jerusalem, the tabernacle, the Temple, the Sabbath, the feasts, the prophets, the priests, and the garments of the priests. God is sanctified by the witness of believers (1 Pet. 3:15) and by His judgments upon sin (Ezek. 38:16). Jesus also was "sanctified and sent into the world" (John 10:36).

As the process by which God purifies the believer, sanctification is based on the sacrificial death of Christ. In his letters to the churches, the apostle Paul noted that God has "chosen" and "reconciled" us to Himself in Christ for the purpose of sanctification (Eph. 1:4; Titus 2:14). Because our cleansing from sin is made possible only by Christ's death and resurrection, we are "sanctified in Christ Jesus" (1 Cor. 1:2; 1 Cor. 1:30; 6:11).

Numerous commands in the Bible imply that believers also have a responsibility in the process of sanctification. We are commanded to "be holy" (Lev. 11:44; 1 Pet. 1:15–16); to "be perfect" (Matt. 5:48); and to "present your members as slaves of righteousness for holiness" (Rom. 6:19).

These commands imply effort on our part. We must believe in Jesus, since we are "sanctified by faith in Him" (Acts 26:18). Through the Holy Spirit we must also "put to death the evil deeds of the body" (Rom. 8:13). Paul itemized the many "works of the flesh" from which we must separate ourselves (Gal. 5:19–21). Finally, we must walk in the Spirit in order to display the fruit of the Spirit (Gal. 5:22–24).

SAMARIA, CITY OF [suh MAR ih uh]
(lookout)

The capital city of the northern kingdom of Israel. Built about 880 B.C. by Omri, the sixth king of Israel (1 Kin. 16:24), Samaria occupied a 300-foot (91-meter) high hill about 42 miles (68 kilometers) north of Jerusalem and 25 miles (40 kilometers) east of the Mediterranean Sea. This hill was situated on the major north-south road through Palestine. It also commanded the east-west route to the Plain of Sharon and the Mediterranean Sea. Because of its hilltop location, Samaria could be defended easily. Its only weakness was that the nearest spring was a mile distant, but this difficulty was overcome by the use of cisterns.

Samaria withstood an attack by Ben-Hadad, king of Syria (2 Kin. 6:24–25), but it finally fell to the Assyrians, in 722 B.C., and its inhabitants were carried into captivity. The city was repopulated by "people from Babylon, Cuthah, Ava, Hamath, and from Sepharvaim" (2 Kin. 17:24), all bringing their pagan idolatries with them. Intermarriage of native Jews with these foreigners led to the mixed race of Samaritans so despised by full-blooded Jews during the time of Jesus (John 4:1–10).

In excavations of Samaria, archaeologists have uncovered several different levels of occupation by the Israelites. The first two levels, from the reigns of Omri and Ahab, show careful construction, apparently by Phoenician craftsmen. At this time, the city may have been 20 acres in extent, enclosed by an outer wall 20 to 30 feet (6 to 8 meters) thick, with a more narrow inner stone wall about 5 feet (2 meters) thick. A two-story palace was constructed at the higher western end of the hill around some courtyards. In one of these courtyards a pool about 17 by 33 feet (5 by 9 meters) was discovered. This may have been the pool where the blood of Ahab was washed from his chariot after he was killed in a battle against the Syrians (1 Kin. 22:38).

The palace was described as an "ivory house" (1 Kin. 22:39; Amos 3:15). Excavations near the pool uncovered a storeroom housing 500 plaques or fragments of ivory used for inlay work in walls and furniture.

The third level of the city, from the period of Jehu (about 841–813 B.C.), gave evidence of additions and reconstruction. Levels four to six covered the period of Jereboam II and showed that repairs had been made to Samaria before the Assyrians captured it in 722 B.C. From this period came several pieces of pottery inscribed with administrative records describing shipments of wine and oil to Samaria. One potsherd recorded the name of the treasury official who received the shipment, the place of origin, and the names of the peasants who had paid their taxes. Structures from the Greek period can still be seen in ruined

form. A round tower is a magnificent monument of the Hellenistic age in Palestine. Roman remains include a colonnaded street leading from the west gate, an aqueduct, a stadium, and an impressive theater.

The small village of Sebastiyeh—an Arabic corruption of the Greco-Roman name Sebaste—now occupies part of the ancient site of this historic city. Even after the Israelite residents of Samaria were deported, the city continued to be inhabited by several different groups under the successive authority of Assyria, Babylonia, Persia, Greece and Rome. Herod the Great, ruler in Palestine (ruled 37 B.C.—A.D. 4) when Jesus was born, made many improvements to Samaria and renamed it Sebaste—the Greek term for Augustus—in honor of the emperor of Rome. This Herodian city is probably the "city of Samaria" mentioned in the Book of Acts (8:5).

SAMARIA, REGION OF [suh MAR ih uh]
(lookout)

A territory in the uplands of central Canaan that corresponded roughly with the lands allotted to the tribe of Ephraim and the western portion of Manasseh. Samaria consisted of about 1,400 square miles of attractive, fertile land, bounded by Bethel on the south and Mount Carmel on the north. Its rich alluvial soil produced valuable grain crops, olives, and grapes. This productivity was made all the more important by the presence of two north-south and three east-west roads. Samaria was able to engage in commerce with neighboring Phoenicia as well as the more distant nations of Syria and Egypt.

Because Samaritan soil was considerably more fertile than the soil in Judah, the northern kingdom was always more prosperous. But the very attractiveness of the territory brought invaders, while trade with such pagan nations exposed the people to corrupt foreign religions. The prophets strongly condemned the wickedness of Samaria—its idolatry, immorality, idle luxury, and oppression of the poor (Hos. 7:1; 8:5–7).

In the time of Jesus, Palestine west of the Jordan River was divided into the three provinces of Galilee, Samaria, and Judea. Because of their intermarriage with foreigners, the people of Samaria were shunned by orthodox Jews. Situated between Galilee and Judea, Samaria was the natural route for traveling between those two provinces. But the pure-blooded Jews had no dealings with the Samaritans (John 4:9). They would travel east, cross the Jordan River, and detour around Samaria.

SAMARITANS [suh MAR ih tuhns]

Natives or inhabitants of Samaria, a distinct territory or region in central Canaan. Until the rise of Assyrian power in the ancient Near East, Samaria was occupied by the tribes of Ephraim and the western portion of the tribe of Manasseh. Many of the sites in Samaria held important places in Israelite history. Mount Gerizim and Mount Ebal were the scene of the covenant-renewal ceremony in Joshua's time (Josh. 8:30–35). Shechem, situated near Mount Gerizim, was an ancient Canaanite town that regained its earlier prosperity during the monarchy. It became capital of the northern kingdom of Israel briefly under Jeroboam I (about 931–910 B.C.; 1 Kin. 12:25), but it was replaced by Penuel and then Tirzah.

Construction on the city of Samaria was begun by Omri about 880 B.C. and completed by his son Ahab (about 874–853 B.C.). Samaria became the new capital of Israel, and successive kings added to it and rebuilt sections to make it a well-fortified capital. But the city fell to the Assyrians in 722–721 B.C. Most of the leading citizens of the northern kingdom were deported to places in Syria, Assyria, and Babylonia.

Sargon replaced the deported Israelites with foreign colonists (2 Kin. 17:24). These new-comers intermarried among the Israelites who remained in Samaria. Later their numbers were increased when Esarhaddon and Ashurbanipal (the biblical Osnapper; Ezra 4:10) sent more Assyrian colonists to the district of Samaria. These people took the name "Samaritans" from the territory and attempted to settle the land. However, "they did not fear the Lord, and the Lord sent lions among them, which killed some of them" (2 Kin. 17:25). In despair they sent to Assyria for "one of the priests" who would "teach them the rituals of the God of the land" (2 Kin. 17:27). Thereafter the Samaritans worshiped the God of Israel. But they also continued their idolatry, worshiping the pagan gods imported from foreign lands (2 Kin. 17:29).

So the Samaritans were a "mixed race" contaminated by foreign blood and false worship. The Jewish historian Josephus indicates that the Samaritans were also opportunists. When the Jews enjoyed prosperity, the Samaritans were quick to acknowledge their blood relationship. But when the Jews suffered hard times, the Samaritans disowned any such kinship, declaring that they were descendants of Assyrian immigrants.

When a group of Jews, led by Zerubbabel, returned from the Babylonian captivity, the Samaritans offered to help Zerubbabel rebuild the temple. When their offer was rejected, they tried to prevent the Jews from finishing their project (Ezra 4:1–10). When Nehemiah attempted to rebuild the wall of Jerusalem, he was opposed by Arab and Samaritan groups (Neh. 2:10–6:14). The breach between the Samaritans and the Jews widened even further when Ezra, in his zeal

S

for racial purity, pressured all Israelite men who married during the captivity to divorce their pagan wives (Ezra 10:18–44).

The final break between the two groups occurred when the Samaritans built a rival temple on Mount Gerizim, claiming Shechem rather than Zion (Jerusalem) as the true "Bethel" (house of God), the site traditionally chosen and blessed by the Lord.

Present-day Samaritans trace their beginnings to the time of Eli, who established the sanctuary for worship of God in Shiloh. They also believe their religion is distinctive because they base their beliefs and practices on the Torah, or the Law—the first five books of the Old Testament. They recognize no other Hebrew Scriptures as authoritative.

At what stage the pagan elements of Mesopotamian religion were removed from Samaritan belief is impossible to determine. But probably by the time of Nehemiah (about 450 B.C.), the Samaritans considered themselves orthodox. The Samaritans also claimed that Ezra changed the Hebrew text to favor Jerusalem over Mount Gerizim as the site for the second temple. But the Samaritans themselves may also be guilty of changing the wording of the law to reflect favorably on their traditions.

In the Roman period the Samaritans appeared to prosper. Their religion was made legal in the empire, being practiced in synagogues in Italy and Africa. Suffering persecution from Christians, they finally revolted in the fifth and sixth centuries. The Roman emperor Justinian (ruled A.D. 527–565) suppressed the Samaritans and brought them almost to extinction, a condition from which they never recovered. But two small units of Samaritans survive until the present time—one group in Nablus (ancient Shechem) and a second group near Tel Aviv.

The pride of the modern Samaritan community at Nablus is a large scroll of the Books of the Law, inscribed in an angular script much as Hebrew was written long before the time of Christ.

The Samaritans retained their belief in God as the unique creator and sustainer of all things. They also worshiped Him in the three feasts prescribed in the Books of the Law—Passover, Pentecost, and Booths (or Tabernacles)—and the solemn Day of Atonement. But their faith was influenced in later periods by Islamic and other beliefs, unlike the orthodox Jewish community. To this day they sacrifice lambs on Mount Gerizim during the Feast of Passover.

SAMSON [SAM suhn] *(sunny)*

A hero of Israel known for his great physical strength as well as his moral weakness. The last of the "judges," or military leaders, mentioned in the Book of Judges, Samson led his country in this capacity for about 20 years.

Samson lived in a dark period of Israelite history. After the generation of Joshua died out, the people of Israel fell into a lawless and faithless life. The author of the Book of Judges summarized these times by declaring, "There was no king in Israel; everyone did what was right in his own eyes" (Judg. 17:6; 21:25). The standard of God's Word, His law as handed down by Moses, was ignored.

Samson was a product of that age, but his parents gave evidence of faith in the Lord. During a time when the Philistines were oppressing the Israelites (Judg. 13:1), the Lord announced to Manoah and his wife that they would bear a son who would be raised as a Nazirite (Judg. 13:5, 7). This meant that Samson should serve as an example to Israel of commitment to God. Through most of his life, however, Samson fell far short of this mark.

Samson's mighty physical feats are well-known. With his bare hands he killed a young lion that attacked him (Judg. 14:5–6). He gathered 300 foxes (jackals in Judg. 15:4, REB) and tied them together, then sent them through the grain fields with torches in their tails to destroy the crops of the Philistines.

On one occasion, he broke the ropes with which the enemy had bound him (Judg. 15:14). He killed a thousand Philistine soldiers with the jawbone of a donkey (Judg. 15:15). And, finally, he carried away the massive gate of Gaza, a city of the Philistines, when they thought they had him trapped behind the city walls (Judg. 16:3).

But in spite of his great physical strength Samson was a foolish man. He took vengeance on those who used devious means to discover the answer to one of his riddles (Judg. 14). When deceived by his enemies, his only thought was for revenge, as when his father-in-law gave away his wife to another man (Judg. 15:6–7). He had not learned the word of the Lord, "Vengeance is mine" (Deut. 32:35).

Samson's life was marred by his weakness for pagan women. As soon as he became of age, he fell in love with one of the daughters of the Philistines. He insisted on marrying her, in spite of his parents' objection (Judg. 14:1–4).

This was against God's law, which forbade intermarriage of the Israelites among the women of Canaan. On another occasion he was almost captured by the Philistines while he was visiting a prostitute in the city of Gaza.

Samson eventually became involved with Delilah, a woman from the Valley of Sorek (Judg. 16:4), who proved to be his undoing (Judg. 16). The Philistines bribed her to find out the key to his strength. She teased him until he finally revealed that the secret was his uncut hair, allowed to grow long in accord with the Nazirite law. While Samson slept, she called the Philistines to cut his hair and

turned him over to his enemies. Samson became weak, not only because his hair had been cut but also because the Lord had departed from him (Judg. 16:20).

After his enslavement by the Philistines, Samson was blinded and forced to work at grinding grain. Eventually he came to his senses and realized that God had given him his great strength to serve the Lord and his people. After a prayer to God for strength, he killed thousands of the enemy by pulling down the pillars of the temple of Dagon (Judg. 16:28–31). That one great act of faith cost Samson his life, but it won for him a place among the heroes of faith (Heb. 11:32). Out of weakness he was made strong by the power of the Lord (Heb. 11:34).

Samson was a person with great potential who fell short because of his sin and disobedience. Mighty in physical strength, he was weak in resisting temptation. His life is a clear warning against the dangers of self-indulgence and lack of discipline.

SAMUEL [SAM yoo uhl] *(name of God)*

The earliest of the great Hebrew prophets (after Moses) and the last judge of Israel. Samuel led his people against their Philistine oppressors. When he was an old man, Samuel anointed Saul as the first king of Israel and later anointed David as Saul's successor. Samuel is recognized as one of the greatest leaders of Israel (Jer. 15:1; Heb. 11:32).

Samuel's birth reveals the great faith of his mother, Hannah (1 Sam. 1:2–22; 2:1). Unable to bear children, she prayed earnestly for the Lord to give her a child. She vowed that if the Lord would give her a son, she would raise him as a Nazirite (1 Sam. 1:11) and dedicate him to the Lord's service. Eventually, Samuel was born as an answer to Hannah's prayer.

Hannah made good on her promise to dedicate her son to the Lord's service. At a very early age, Samuel went to live with Eli the priest, who taught the boy the various duties of the priesthood. Here Samuel heard the voice of God, calling him to special service as a priest and prophet in Israel (1 Sam. 3:1–20). After Eli's death, Samuel became the judge of Israel in a ceremony at Mizpah (1 Sam. 7). This event was almost turned to disaster by an attack from the Philistines, but the Lord intervened with a storm that routed the enemies and established Samuel as God's man. The godly Samuel erected a memorial stone, which he called "Ebenezer," meaning "Stone of Help." "Thus far the Lord has helped us," he declared (1 Sam. 7:12).

In the early part of his ministry, Samuel served as a traveling judge. With his home in Ramah, he made a yearly circuit to Bethel, Gilgal, and Mizpah. In the person of Samuel, judges became more than military leaders called upon for dramatic leadership in times of national crises. Samuel became a judge with a permanent leadership office, an office approaching that of a king.

When the people clamored for a king like those of the surrounding nations (1 Sam. 8:5), Samuel was reluctant to grant their request. He took this as a rejection of his long years of godly service on behalf of the people. He also was aware of the evils that went along with the establishment of a royal house. But the Lord helped Samuel to see the real issue: "Heed the voice of the people in all that they say to you; for they have not rejected you, but they have rejected Me, that I should not reign over them" (1 Sam. 8:7).

The person whom Samuel anointed as first king of Israel turned out to be a poor choice. Saul was handsome, likeable, and tall. But he had a tragic flaw that led ultimately to his own ruin. He disobeyed God by taking spoils in a battle rather than wiping out all living things, as God had commanded (1 Sam. 15:18–26).

Saul's false pride and extreme jealousy toward David also led him into some serious errors of judgment.

When God rejected Saul as king, He used Samuel to announce the prophetic words (1 Sam. 15:10–35). Samuel was faithful in presenting the stern words of rejection. Although he had no further dealings with Saul, Samuel mourned for him and for the death of the dream (1 Sam. 15:35). Samuel was then sent by the Lord to Bethlehem, to the house of Jesse, where he anointed the young man David as the rightful king over His people (1 Sam. 16:1–13).

In addition to his work as judge, prophet, and priest, Samuel is also known as the traditional author of the Books of First and Second Samuel. He may have written much of the material contained in 1 Samuel during the early years of Saul's reign. After Samuel's death (1 Sam. 25:1), these books were completed by an unknown writer, perhaps Abiathar, the priest who served during David's administration.

When Samuel died, he was buried in his hometown of Ramah and was mourned by the nation (1 Sam. 25:1; 28:3). But he had one more message to give. After Samuel's death, Saul visited a fortune teller at En dor (1 Sam. 28). This fortune teller gave Saul a message that came from the spirit of Samuel: "The Lord has departed from you and has become your enemy" (1 Sam. 28:16). Even from the grave Samuel still spoke the word of God.

In many ways Samuel points forward to the person of the Savior, the Lord Jesus Christ. In the story of Samuel's birth, the direct hand of the Lord can be seen. In his ministry as judge, prophet, and priest, Samuel anticipates the ministry of the Lord as well as the work of his forerunner, John the Baptist. As Samuel marked out David as God's man, so John the Baptist pointed out Jesus as the Savior.

SANBALLAT [san BAL uht] *(the god Sin has given life)*

A leading opponent of the Jews after their return from the Babylonian captivity; he tried to hinder Nehemiah in his work of rebuilding the walls of Jerusalem (Neh. 2:10, 19–20; 4:1–23; 6:1–19; 13:28).

Sanballat's designation as the Horonite probably indicates the town of his origin, possibly Horonaim of Moab (Is. 15:5; Jer. 48:3, 5, 34) or Beth Horon in Ephraim near Jerusalem (2 Chr. 8:5). In papyri found at the Jewish settlement in Elephantine, Egypt, Sanballat is called the governor of Samaria. His daughter married "one of the sons of Joiada, the son of Eliashib the high priest" (Neh. 13:28). Nehemiah viewed such a "mixed marriage" as a defilement of the priesthood, so he drove Joiada away.

Sanballat's opposition to Nehemiah's work may have stemmed from jealousy. He may have felt that his authority was threatened by the reawakening of the land of Judah. After mocking Nehemiah and his crew, he tried to slip through the broken wall of Jerusalem with people from other enemy nations to kill the Jews. Nehemiah thwarted this plot, setting up guards from half the people while the other half worked (Neh. 4:7–23). Neither did he fall for Sanballat's ploy to come outside the wall for a "friendly" discussion (Neh. 6:3).

In spite of Sanballat's open opposition and trickery, Nehemiah carried out the task he felt called by God to accomplish. After the wall was completed, he reported that even the enemies of the project realized "this work was done by our God" (Neh. 6:16).

SANDALS

The sandals worn by the Israelites were of cloth, wood, or dried grass, held on the foot by a thong or strap (Is. 5:27; Mark 1:7). Sandals were worn by all classes in Canaan, unlike Egypt where some people went barefoot. Women wore them too, as in the Song of Solomon (7:1). A certain kind of sandal for females had two straps, one between the big toe and the second toe, and another circling the instep and heel.

During mealtimes, people apparently removed their sandals, as when Jesus washed His disciples' feet (John 13:5–6). However, the Israelites kept their sandals on their feet while eating the Passover meal, preparing to leave Egypt (Ex. 12:11). Sandals were to be taken off as a sign of reverence, as God said to Moses: "Take your sandals off your feet, for the place where you stand is holy ground" (Ex. 3:5).

SANHEDRIN [SAN hee drun] *(a council or assembly)*

The highest ruling body and court of justice among the Jewish people in the time of Jesus. Headed by the high priest of Israel, the Sanhedrin was granted limited authority over certain religious, civil, and criminal matters by the foreign nations that dominated the land of Israel at various times in its history. The Sanhedrin was exercising this limited power when it charged Jesus with the crime of blasphemy but then sent him to Pilate, the Roman official, for a formal trial and sentencing.

The word *Sanhedrin* is not found in the NKJV; instead the word *council* is used. Usually the assembly itself is meant, although the word may also refer to the assembly meeting (John 11:47) or to the place where the assembly met (Luke 22:66; Acts 4:15). The same word is also used for smaller, local courts of

S

justice (Matt. 10:17; Mark 13:9). The Sanhedrin is also implied in Bible passages that mention a meeting of the various groups that made up the council: the chief priests, the elders, and the scribes (Mark 14:53–55). Sometimes some of the members of the Sanhedrin are simply called rulers (Luke 24:20; Acts 4:5).

The Sanhedrin had 71 members. The New Testament mentions some of them by name: Joseph of Arimathea (Mark 15:43), Gamaliel (Acts 5:34), Nicodemus (John 3:1; 7:50), the high priests Annas and Caiaphas (Luke 3:2), and Ananias (Acts 23:2). The high priest was always president of the Sanhedrin. Some scholars suggest that the apostle Paul was a member of the Sanhedrin before his conversion to Christianity, but this is not known for sure.

The Sanhedrin grew out of the council of advisors for the high priest when the Jewish people lived under the domination of the Persian and Greek empires. In the beginning, the council was made up of the leading priests and the most distinguished aristocrats among the laypeople. Later, however, as the influence of the scribes grew, they were also given some positions on the Sanhedrin.

In this way, the Sanhedrin came to include both Sadducees—or "chief priests" and "elders"—and Pharisees or scribes. These were the two main groups within Judaism, and the Sanhedrin usually tried to maintain a balance of power between them. But Acts 23:1–10 shows that the Sanhedrin would sometimes divide along party lines. As he stood before the Sanhedrin, the apostle Paul was shrewd enough to pit the Pharisees against the Sadducees to his own advantage.

After A.D. 6 the official authority of the Sanhedrin extended only to the province of Judea in southern Palestine. Still, Jews living elsewhere respected the Sanhedrin highly and would often be guided by its decisions. Within the province of Judea, which included the city of Jerusalem, the Romans left most of the business of governing the Jews to the Sanhedrin. The Sanhedrin even had its own police force, or temple police, so it could make arrests on its own. This is the force that arrested Jesus in the Garden of Gethsemane (Mark 14:43; Acts 4:1–3).

The Sanhedrin also served as the supreme court of the Jews. This does not mean that people who were dissatisfied with the verdict of the lower court could appeal to the Sanhedrin for a different decision. But matters of special importance and other matters that lower courts were unable to resolve were brought to the Sanhedrin. The Roman rulers did, however, reserve the right to interfere with what the Sanhedrin was doing, as happened in the case of Paul (Acts 23:10; 24:7), but this probably happened very seldom. The Romans denied the power of capital punishment to the Sanhedrin. This is why the Jews said to Pilate after they had tried Jesus, "It is not lawful for us to put anyone to death" (John 18:31).

In the New Testament, the Sanhedrin was involved in hearings against Jesus (Matt. 26:59; Mark 14:55), Peter and John and the other apostles (Acts 4:1–23; 5:17–41), Stephen (Acts 6–7), and Paul (Acts 22–24). Jesus probably was not officially tried by the Sanhedrin. It is more likely that He was given a preliminary hearing to establish the charges against Him and then taken to Pilate. It is also not clear whether Stephen was officially condemned and executed by the Sanhedrin or simply was stoned by an angry mob without due process of law (Acts 7:54–60).

SAPPHIRA [suh FIGH ruh]

A dishonest woman who, along with her husband Ananias, held back goods from the early Christian community after they had agreed to share everything. Because of their hypocrisy and deceit, they were struck dead by God (Acts 5:1–11). This may seem like a severe punishment for such an offense. But it points out the need for absolute honesty in all our dealings with God.

SAPPHIRE

The modern sapphire, a blue variety of corundum, was probably not used until the third century B.C. The Hebrew word for sapphire refers to lapis lazuli—a silicate of alumina, calcium, and sodium. It was highly regarded as an ornamental stone (Song 5:14; Lam. 4:7; Ezek. 28:13). Rich beds of sapphire deposited in limestone rock were found in the mountainous regions of ancient Persia.

Sapphire was the second jewel in the second row of Aaron's breastplate (Ex. 28:18; 39:11). It was also the second stone in the foundation of the New Jerusalem (Rev. 21:19).

SARAH [SAR uh] *(noble lady)*

The wife of Abraham, and the mother of Isaac. Sarah's name was originally Sarai, but it was changed to Sarah by God, much as her husband's name was changed from Abram to Abraham. Ten years younger than Abraham, Sarah was his half sister; they had the same father but different mothers (Gen. 20:12).

Sarah was about 65 years old when she and Abraham left Haran (Gen. 12:5; 17:7). Passing through Egypt, Abraham introduced Sarah as his sister, apparently to keep himself from being killed by those who would be attracted by Sarah's beauty (Gen. 12:10–20; also see 20:1–18).

In spite of God's promise to Abraham that he would become the father of a chosen nation, Sarah remained barren. When she was 75, she decided that the only way to realize God's promise was to present to Abraham her Egyptian maidservant, Hagar, by whom he could father

a child. Hagar bore a son named Ishmael (Gen. 16:1–16).

When Sarah was 90 years old, far beyond her childbearing years, she gave birth to a son, Isaac—the child of promise (Gen. 21:1–7). After Isaac was born, Sarah caught Ishmael mocking the young child and, with God's approval, sent both Ishmael and Hagar into the wilderness.

At the age of 127, Sarah died at Kirjath Arba (Hebron) and was buried by Abraham in the cave of Machpelah (Gen. 23:1–20). Sarah is the only woman in the Bible whose age was recorded at death—a sign of her great importance to the early Hebrews. The prophet Isaiah declared Abraham and Sarah as the father and mother of the Hebrew people: "Look to Abraham your father, and to Sarah who bore you" (Is. 51:2).

In the New Testament, the apostle Paul pointed out that "the deadness of Sarah's womb" (Rom. 4:19) did not cause Abraham to waver in his faith; he believed the promise of God (Rom. 9:9). The apostle Peter cited Sarah as an example of the holy women who trusted in God, possessed inward spiritual beauty, and were submissive to their husbands (1 Pet. 3:5–6). The writer of the Epistle to the Hebrews also includes Sarah as one of the spiritual heroines in his roll call of the faithful (Heb. 11:11).

SARDIS [SARR dis]

The capital city of Lydia in the province of Asia, in western Asia Minor (modern Turkey). The church at Sardis was one of the seven churches mentioned by John in the Book of Revelation (Rev. 3:1–6).

Sardis was situated on the east bank of the Pactolus River about 50 miles (80 kilometers) east of Smyrna; it occupied a rocky spur of Mount Tmolus and a valley at the foot of this mountain. In ancient times Sardis was well fortified and

S

easily defended. It became the capital of the ancient Lydian empire, then passed successively to the Persians, the Greeks, and the Romans during their respective dominance of the ancient world.

During its days as a Roman city, Sardis became an important Christian center. However, the church at Sardis was evidently affected by the complacency of the city and its reliance on past glory: "You have a name that you are alive, but you are dead" (Rev. 3:1). Sardis, the dead church, was like "whitewashed tombs which . . . appear beautiful outwardly, but inside are full of dead men's bones" (Matt. 23:27). Its thriving, healthy appearance masked an inner decay.

The most impressive building of ancient Sardis must have been its magnificent temple of Artemis, built in the fourth century B.C. The temple was 327 feet (100 meters) long and 163 feet (50 meters) wide and had 78 Ionic columns, each 58 feet (17.7 meters) high. Some of these columns remain standing until this day.

SARGON II [SAHR gahn] *(the king is legitimate)*

A king of Assyria and Babylonia (722–705 B.C.) whose military campaigns are important for understanding the prophecies of Isaiah. Sargon's predecessor Shalmaneser besieged Samaria for three years (2 Kin. 17:3–6; 18:9–12) and apparently died shortly before its fall in 722 B.C. Nevertheless, Sargon claimed credit for the victory. On an inscription found in his palace he says: "The city of Samaria I besieged, I took; 27,290 of its inhabitants I carried away; fifty chariots that were among them I collected."

The people of Samaria were deported to Mesopotamia, where they were resettled; and people from the east were brought to Samaria (2 Kin. 17:6, 24). In 720 B.C. the kingdom of Judah, under King Ahaz, paid tribute to Sargon II, along with Edom, Moab, and Philistia.

At about this same time (720 B.C.) Sargon II also defeated the Egyptian king So (2 Kin. 17:4). So had come to the aid of the people of Gaza, who also were defying the Assyrians. In 717 B.C. Sargon put down a rebellion by Carchemish in Syria and destroyed that ancient center of Hittite culture.

The city of Ashdod rebelled in 713 B.C. under the promise of Egyptian aid (Is. 20). Egyptian ambassadors tried to enlist the aid of Hezekiah, king of Judah (Is. 18). But Isaiah the prophet opposed such action, symbolizing the folly of trusting in Egypt by walking about Jerusalem "naked and barefoot" (Is. 20:1–6). Apparently Judah listened to Isaiah's wise counsel, because the nation escaped harm during the time of Ashdod's rebellion. In 1963, several fragments of an Assyrian monument containing Sargon's name were found during archaeological excavations at Ashdod.

Merodach-Baladan, a king of Babylon, convinced the nations subject to Sargon to revolt against Assyrian rule. In 712 B.C., Sargon sent troops against Ashdod, capturing it the following year (Is. 20:1—the only verse in the Bible in which Sargon's name appears). In 710 B.C. Sargon captured Merodach-Baladan's capital and took the title "king of Babylon."

After a reign of 17 years, Sargon apparently was murdered by one of his own soldiers.

SATAN [SAY tuhn] *(adversary)*

The great opposer, or adversary, of God and humankind; the personal name of the devil. Genesis 3 describes a serpent who tempted the first human couple. That serpent was none other than Satan himself (Rev. 12:9; 20:2).

Two Old Testament passages (Is. 14:12–15; Ezek. 28:11–19) have been held to furnish a picture of Satan's original condition and the reasons for his loss of that position. These passages were addressed originally to the kings of Babylon and Tyre. But in their long-range implications, some scholars believe, they refer to Satan himself.

Revelation 12 sketches the further stages in Satan's work of evil. In his fall from God's favor, Satan persuaded one-third of the angels to join him in his rebellion (Rev. 12:3–4). Throughout the Old Testament period he sought to destroy the messianic line. When the Messiah became a man, Satan tried to eliminate Him (Rev. 12:4–5). During the future period of tribulation before the Messiah's Second Coming, Satan will be cast out of the heavenly sphere (Rev. 12:7–12). Then he will direct his animosity toward the Messiah's people (Rev. 12:13–17). Revelation 20 notes the final phases of Satan's work. He will be bound for a thousand years and then finally cast into the lake of fire (Rev. 20:2, 10).

As a result of his original status and authority, Satan has great power and dignity. So great is his strength that Michael the archangel viewed him as a foe too powerful to oppose (Jude 9). Satan's influence in worldly affairs is also clearly revealed. His various titles reflect his control of the world system: "the ruler of this world" (John 12:31), "the god of this age" (2 Cor. 4:4), and "the prince of the power of the air" (Eph. 2:2). The Bible declares, "The whole world lies under the sway of the wicked one" (1 John 5:19).

Satan exercises his evil power through demons (Matt. 12:24; 25:41; Rev. 12:7, 9). An outburst of demonic activity occurred when Jesus came to earth the first time because of the Savior's attack against Satan's kingdom (Matt. 12:28–29; Acts 10:38). Another such outburst is expected just before the Second Coming of Christ, because this will bring about the downfall of Satan and his angels (Rev. 9:3–17; 12:12; 18:2).

Satan also has high intelligence. Through it he deceived Adam and Eve and took over their rule of the world for himself (Gen. 1:26; 3:1–7; 2 Cor. 11:3). His cleverness enables him to carry out his deceptive work almost at will.

Yet Satan's attributes, impressive as they are, are not limitless. His power is subject to God's restrictions (Job 1:12; Luke 4:6; 2 Thess. 2:7–8). The reins of God on his activities are illustrated by Satan's request to God for permission to afflict Job (Job 1:7–12). Satan is permitted to afflict God's people (Luke 13:16; 1 Thess. 2:18; Heb. 2:14). But he is never permitted to win an ultimate victory over them (John 14:30–31; 16:33).

Satan's nature is malicious. His efforts in opposing God, His people, and His truth are tireless (Job 1:7; 2:2; Matt. 13:28). He is always opposed to our best interests (1 Chr. 21:1; Zech. 3:1–2). Through his role in introducing sin into the human family (Gen. 3), Satan has gained the power of death—a power that Christ has broken through His crucifixion and resurrection (Heb. 2:14–15).

Of the various methods used by Satan in carrying out his evil work, none is more characteristic than temptation (Matt. 4:3; 1 Thess. 3:5). Satan leads people into sin by various means. Sometimes he does it by direct suggestion, as in the case of Judas Iscariot (John 13:2, 27); sometimes through his agents who disguise themselves as messengers of God (2 Thess. 2:9; 1 John 4:1); and sometimes through a person's own weaknesses (1 Cor. 7:5). He tempted Christ directly, trying to lead Him into compromise by promising Him worldly authority and power (Luke 4:5–8).

Along with his work of tempting mankind, Satan also delights in deception (1 Tim. 3:6–7; 2 Tim. 2:26). His lying nature stands in bold contrast to the truth

S

for which Christ stands (John 8:32, 44). The great falsehood he uses so frequently is that good can be attained by doing wrong. This lie is apparent in practically all his temptations (Gen. 3:4–5). As the great deceiver, Satan is an expert at falsifying truth (2 Cor. 11:13–15).

Satan's methods are designed ultimately to silence the gospel. He seeks to stop the spread of God's Word (Matt. 13:19; 1 Thess. 2:17–18). When the gospel is preached, Satan tries to blind people's understanding so they cannot grasp the meaning of the message (2 Cor. 4:3–4; 2 Thess 2:9–10). At times he opposes the work of God by violent means (John 13:2, 27; 1 Pet. 5:8; Rev. 12:13–17). He brings disorder into the physical world by afflicting human beings (Job 1–2; 2 Cor. 12:7; Heb. 2:14). Sometimes God allows him to afflict His people for purposes of correction (1 Tim. 1:20).

Satan is destined to fail in his continuing rebellion against God. His final defeat is predicted in the New Testament (Luke 10:18; John 12:31; Rev. 12:9; 20:10). The death of Christ on the cross is the basis for Satan's final defeat (Heb. 2:14–15; 1 Pet. 3:18, 22). This event was the grand climax to a sinless life during which Jesus triumphed over the enemy repeatedly (Matt. 4:1–11; Luke 4:1–13). The final victory will come when Jesus returns and Satan is cast into the lake of fire (Rev. 20:1–15).

Strength for a Christian's victory over sin has also been provided through the death of Christ. We have assurance that "the God of peace will crush Satan under your feet" (Rom. 16:20). But such personal victory depends on our will to offer resistance to Satan's temptations (Eph. 4:25–27; 1 Pet. 5:8–9). To help Christians win this battle against Satan, God has provided the power of Christ's blood (Rev. 12:11), the continuing prayer of Christ in heaven for believers (Heb. 7:25), the leading of the Holy Spirit (Gal. 5:16), and various weapons for spiritual warfare (Eph. 6:13–18).

See also DEVIL.

SAUL [sawl] (asked [of God])

The first king of Israel (1 Sam. 9:2–31:12; 1 Chr. 5:10–26:28). Saul lived in turbulent times. For many years, Israel had consisted of a loose organization of tribes without a single leader. In times of crisis, leaders had arisen; but there was no formal government. Samuel was Saul's predecessor as Israel's leader; but he was a religious leader, not a king. Threatened by the warlike Philistines, the people of Israel pressured Samuel to appoint a king to lead them in their battles against the enemy. Samuel gave in to their demands and anointed Saul as the first king of the nation of Israel.

Saul had several admirable qualities that made him fit to be king of Israel during this period in its history. He was a large man of attractive appearance, which led to his quick acceptance by the people. In addition, he was from the tribe of Benjamin, situated on the border between Ephraim and Judah. Thus, he appealed to both the northern and southern sections of Israel. Furthermore, he was a capable military leader, as shown by his victories early in his career.

One of the most important episodes of Saul's career was his first encounter with the Philistines. Saul took charge of 2,000 men at Michmash, leaving his son Jonathan with 1,000 men at Gibeah. After Jonathan made a successful, but unplanned, attack on a company of Philistines at Geba, the reaction of the Philistine forces drove the Israelites back to Gilgal. The Philistines gained control of central Canaan, and Saul's defeat seemed imminent.

But Jonathan burst in unexpectedly upon the Philistines at Michmash, succeeding in starting a panic in their camp.

Saul took advantage of this and routed the Philistines. This victory strengthened Saul's position as king.

Saul's first sin was his failure to wait for Samuel at Gilgal (1 Sam. 13:8–9). There he assumed the role of a priest by making a sacrifice to ask for God's blessing. His second sin followed soon afterward. After defeating Moab, Ammon, and Edom, Saul was told by Samuel to go to war against the Amalekites and to "kill both man and woman, infant and nursing child, ox and sheep, camel and donkey" (1 Sam. 15:3). Saul carried out his instructions well except that he spared the life of Agag, the king, and saved the best of the animals. When he returned, he lied and told Samuel that he had followed instructions exactly.

Saul's disobedience in this case showed that he could not be trusted as an instrument of God's will. He desired to assert his own will instead. Although he was allowed to remain king for the rest of his life, the Spirit of the Lord departed from Saul. He was troubled by an evil spirit that brought bouts of madness. Meanwhile, Samuel went to Bethlehem to anoint David as the new king.

Saul's last years were tragic, clouded by periods of depression and gloom. David was brought into Saul's court to play soothing music to restore him to sanity. Saul was friendly toward David at first, but this changed as David's leadership abilities emerged. Enraged by jealousy, Saul tried to kill David several times. But David succeeded in eluding these attempts on his life for many years, often with the aid of Saul's son Jonathan and his daughter Michal.

The closing years of Saul's life brought a decline in his service to his people and in his personal fortunes. Rather than consolidating his gains after his early victories, Saul wasted his time trying to kill David. Meanwhile, the Philistines sensed Israel's plight and came with a large army to attack the Hebrew nation. Saul's army was crushed, and three of his sons, including Jonathan, were killed. Wounded in the battle, Saul committed suicide by falling on his own sword.

Saul is one of the most tragic figures in the Old Testament. He began his reign with great promise but ended it in shame. As Israel's first king, he had the opportunity to set the pattern for all future leaders. His weakness was his rebellious nature and his inability to adapt to the necessity of sharing power and popularity.

Saul also used his power to pursue unworthy purposes and wasted much time and energy in fruitless attempts on David's life. Commercial enterprises were not encouraged during his reign. As a result, the economic condition of the nation was not good. Saul also failed to unite the various tribes into one nation.

Saul allowed the religious life of his people to deteriorate as well. However, he did provide distinct services to his people through his military actions. His victories paved the way for the brilliant career of his successor David.

SCAPEGOAT

A live goat over whose head Aaron confessed all the sins of the people of Israel. The goat was then sent into the wilderness on the Day of Atonement, symbolically taking away their sins (Lev. 16:8, 10, 26; Azazel in NRSV).

The derivation of "scapegoat" is not clear. Scholars suggest it communicates such ideas as "passing away in his strength," "strength of God," "loneliness," or "desert." The most probable meaning is the idea of "far removed" or "going far away."

The scapegoat was one of two goats that served as a sin offering on the Day of Atonement (Lev. 16:5). One of the goats was sacrificed as a part of the sin offering

(Lev. 16:9). The other was kept alive so it could be taken into the wilderness by an escort (Lev. 16:10, 21). The person who released the goat was to wash his clothes and bathe afterwards (Lev. 16:26). The goat symbolized the removal of the sins of the people into an uninhabited land (Lev. 16:21–22). The process represented the transfer of guilt from the people of Israel, the complete removal of guilt from their midst.

SCEVA [SEE vuh]

A Jewish chief priest at Ephesus during Paul's time (Acts 19:14). Sceva's seven sons attempted to cast out an evil spirit in the name of Jesus. But they were wounded instead by the demon-possessed man and had to flee naked and humiliated.

SCORPION

The scorpion is a small crawling animal that looks like a flat lobster. A member of the spider family, it has eight legs, two sets of pincers, and a tail with a poisonous stinger. A scorpion feeds on spiders and insects, which it rips apart with its claws. It uses its poisonous sting only when threatened or when it attacks large prey. This sting is seldom fatal, but it can be very painful (Rev. 9:5).

During the day scorpions escape the desert heat by hiding under rocks. They come out at night to hunt and eat. Inhabitants of Bible lands feared scorpions. These animals were an ever-present danger when Moses led the children of Israel through the hot, rocky wilderness (Deut. 8:15).

Jesus' words in Luke 11:12 about giv-

SCAPE GOAT

YOUR FATHER WAS A SCAPEGOAT... HE HAD TO GO ON A GUILT TRIP.

JONNY HAWKINS

ing a person a scorpion instead of an egg may refer to a light-colored scorpion that could be mistaken for an egg when in a coiled position. The prophet Ezekiel was told by God not to be afraid of his enemies, who were referred to symbolically as scorpions (Ezek. 2:6). King Rehoboam's threat did not mean he would use scorpions as whips (1 Kin. 12:14). In those days a barbed whip or scourge was called a "scorpion."

SCOURGE

A whip used as a means of punishment. In the Old Testament, "scourge" is generally a word that describes punishment, either by people (1 Kin. 12:11) or by God (Is. 10:26). The Mosaic Law prescribed that a wicked person could be beaten with forty blows (Deut. 25:2–3).

In the New Testament, to be "examined under scourging" (Acts 22:24) referred to an investigation that began with the beating of the prisoner. Another word describes the "whip of cords" with which Jesus cleansed the temple (John 2:15). It also graphically describes the beating Jesus received before His crucifixion (Matt. 27:26).

The whip used for this type of punishment consisted of a handle to which one or more leather cords or thongs were attached. Sometimes these cords were knotted or weighted with pieces of metal or bone to make the whip more effective as a flesh-cutting instrument. In his prediction of the coming of the Messiah, the prophet Isaiah declared, "He was wounded for our transgressions; He was bruised for our iniquities" (Is. 53:5), referring to the scourging of Jesus.

SCRIBES

Members of a learned class in ancient Israel through New Testament times who studied the Scriptures and served as copyists, editors, and teachers. After the Jews returned from the captivity in Babylon, the era of the scribes began. The reading of the law before the nation of Israel by Ezra (Neh. 8–10) signaled the nation's return to exact observance of all the laws and rites that had been given. Following the law and the traditions that had grown up around it became the measure of devotion and spirituality.

At first the priests were responsible for the scientific study and professional communication of this legal code. But this function eventually passed to the scribes. Their official interpretation of the meaning of the law eventually became more important than the law itself. This position of strength allowed these early scribes to enforce their rules and practices with a binding authority. To speak of the scribes as interpreters of Scripture means that they provided rules for human conduct out of their study.

By the time of Jesus, the scribes were a new upper class among the Jewish people. Large numbers of priests in Jerusalem before A.D. 70 served as scribes. One of these was Josephus, the Jewish historian. Some scribes came from among the Sadducees. Others came from the ordinary priestly ranks. But the largest group of scribes came from among every other class of people, including merchants, carpenters, flax combers, tentmakers, and even day laborers, like Hillel, who became a famous Jewish teacher.

The young Israelite who devoted his life to become a scribe went through a set course of study for several years. Josephus began his preparation when he was 14. Students were in continual contact with the teacher, listening to his instruction. The disciple-scribe first had to master all the traditional material and the unique method of interpretation of the Jewish Halakah. The aim was to give the apprentice competence in making decisions on questions of religious legislation and penal justice.

According to the tradition of the scribes, there were "secrets" of interpretation, forbidden degrees of knowledge, that were not to be expounded before three or more persons. Some chapters in the Bible were to be explained only to sages (2 Esdras 14:1–5).

Sometimes the Gospels refer to the scribes as lawyers (Matt. 22:35; Luke 7:30)—a title that identifies them as experts in the Mosaic Law. This law was regarded as the sole civil and religious authority governing Jewish life. In Jesus' day, the scribes were usually associated with the Pharisees (Matt. 12:38; Mark 7:5; Luke 6:7; teachers of the law in NIV). In the Gospels, they are sometimes called "the scribes of the Pharisees" (Mark 2:16, NRSV, NASB; the teachers of the law who were Pharisees, NIV). This phrase identifies scribes who were members of the Pharisaic party.

Many of the scribes were members of the Sanhedrin, the highest legal and administrative body in the Jewish state in Roman times. Gamaliel was one of these (Acts 5:34), as was Nicodemus (John 3:1). They sat as administrators of the law "in Moses' seat" (Matt. 23:2). This administration intensified after the destruction of Jerusalem by the Romans.

Since a scribe was not paid for his services, he had to earn a livelihood in another way. This rule may have been enforced to keep down the problem of bribery among the scribes in their application of the law. The scribes often developed attitudes based on their professional privileges, and this often resulted in pride (Matt. 23:5–7). Jesus warned against these excesses, and He boldly attacked the religious hypocrisy of the scribes (Matt. 23).

SCROLL

A roll of papyrus, leather, or parchment on which an ancient document—particularly a text of the Bible—was writ-ten (Ezra 6:2). Rolled up on a stick, a scroll was usually about 35 feet (11 meters) long—the size required, for instance, for the Gospel of Luke or the Book of Acts. Longer books of the Bible required two or more scrolls.

One of the scrolls written by the prophet Jeremiah was read in the temple and in the king's palace, then destroyed by King Jehoiakim. The king cut it into pieces and threw it into the fire to show his contempt for God's prophet. But Jeremiah promptly rewrote the scroll through his scribe, Baruch (Jer. 36:1–32).

Books did not exist until the second or third century A.D., when the codex was introduced. The codex had a page arrangement much like our modern books.

SCYTHIANS [SITH ee uhns]

A barbaric race who lived in Scythia, an ancient region of southeastern Europe and southwestern Asia, now generally identified as Russia. In biblical times, the Scythians were a tribe of nomadic raiders notorious for their cruelty and barbarism.

Originally from western Siberia, the Scythians migrated to southern Russia about 2000 B.C. Several centuries later they moved into northern Persia. Eventually they became allies of the Assyrians and oppressed western Persia for almost three decades. After the Medes became a world power, they finally drove the Scythians back to southern Russia.

Famous as raiders, the Scythians carried out a major campaign of plunder against Syria and Palestine in the late seventh century B.C. The prophets Zephaniah and Jeremiah may have referred to this raid. Jeremiah spoke of waters that would rise out of the north and eventually become "an overflowing flood" of God's judgment against the nations of that region of the world (Jer. 47:2).

SEAL

A device such as a signet ring or cylinder, engraved with the owner's name, a design, or both (Ex. 28:11; Esth. 8:8). It was used by an official much like a personal signature to give authority to a document. A medallion or ring used as a seal featured a raised or recessed signature or symbol so it could be impressed on wax, moist clay, or ink to leave its mark (Job 38:14).

The seal was strung on a cord and hung around the neck or worn on one's finger (Gen. 38:18, NRSV; signet ring in Jer. 22:24). The seal was an emblem of royal authority (Gen. 41:42). Zerubbabel, who had been chosen by God to lead the returned captives in Jerusalem (Hag. 2:23), was compared to a signet ring, signifying that God had invested him with the highest honor.

SECOND COMING

Christ's future return to the earth at the end of the present age. Although the Bible explicitly speaks of Christ's appearance as a "second time," the phrase "second coming" occurs nowhere in the New Testament. Many passages, however, speak of His return. In fact, in the New Testament alone it is referred to over 300 times.

The night before His crucifixion, Jesus told His apostles that He would return (John 14:3). When Jesus ascended into heaven, two angels appeared to His followers, saying that He would return in the same manner as they had seen Him go (Acts 1:11). The New Testament is filled with expectancy of His coming, even as Christians should be today.

The time of the Second Coming is unknown. In fact, Jesus stated that only the Father knew the time. Therefore, the return of the Lord should be a matter of constant expectancy. As He came the first time, in the "fullness of time" (Gal. 4:4),

so will the Second Coming be. The believer's task is not to try to determine the time of the Second Coming. We should share the gospel message diligently until He returns (Acts 1:8–11).

SEIR [SEE ur] (hairy, rough)

The mountainous country stretching from the Dead Sea to the Red Sea, east of the gorge called the Arabah (Gen. 14:6). The elevations of Seir range from 600 feet (183 meters) to 6,000 feet (1,830 meters). Two of Seir's outstanding features are Mount Hor, where Aaron died (Num. 20:27–28), and the ancient city of rock, Petra or Sela (Is. 16:1). The region was named after a Horite (Hurrian) patriarch whose descendants settled in this area.

God gave this land to Esau and his descendants, who drove out the Horites, or Hurrians (Deut. 2:12). Esau and his descendants, the Edomites, lived in Seir (Deut. 2:29). This explains why God directed the people of Israel not to invade this territory when they moved from Egypt toward the Promised Land (Deut. 2:4–5).

Although Seir was originally the name of the mountain range in Edom, the name came to signify the entire territory of Edom south of the Dead Sea (2 Chr. 20:10). King David made these people his servants (2 Sam. 8:14).

Later, in the days of King Jehoshaphat of Judah, the people of Mount Seir (the Edomites) joined the Ammonites and the Moabites in an invasion against Judah (2 Chr. 20:10, 22–23). Later, the prophet Ezekiel predicted God's destruction of "Mount Seir" because of their strong hatred of Israel and their desire to possess the lands of Israel and Judah (Ezek. 35:1–15).

SELEUCIA [sih LOO shuh]

A seaport near Antioch of Syria from which Paul and Barnabas began their first missionary journey. Apparently they also landed at Seleucia when they returned to Antioch (Acts 14:26). Seleucia was an important Roman city because of its strategic location on the trade routes of the Mediterranean Sea.

SENNACHERIB [suh NAK uh rib] *(Sin [the moon-god] has compensated me with brothers)*

An Assyrian king (705–681 B.C.) noted for his military campaigns against the southern kingdom of Judah. He was the son and successor of Sargon II and was succeeded by his son Esarhaddon in 681 B.C. after a reign of 24 years.

Upon taking the throne, Sennacherib led his armies south, removing Merodach-Baladan (Is. 39:1), also called Berodach-Baladan (2 Kin. 20:12), from the throne of Babylon and reducing the city to ruins in 689 B.C. Sennacherib then marched his army east against the Kassites in the Zagros mountain range.

Sennacherib's military campaigns in the west have caused a great deal of controversy because his account and the Bible's (2 Kin. 18:13–19:37; 2 Chr. 32:1–22; Is. 36:1–37:38) describe the events so differently. Earlier, during the military campaign of Sargon II in 711 B.C., King Hezekiah of Judah (reigned 716–687 B.C.) had been asked to join the rebellion against the Assyrians, but he refused. During the reign of Sennacherib, Hezekiah went against the wise counsel of the prophet Isaiah and joined a coalition against Assyria led by Tyre and Egypt.

Sennacherib began his western military campaign in 701 B.C., when Tyre and Sidon refused to pay tribute to Assyria. He marched down the Phoenician coast and captured Sidon and many other cities. The cities that refused to submit were destroyed. After the Assyrians defeated the Egyptians, they laid siege to Lachish, which, along with Jerusalem, was one of the bestfortified cities in

Judah. The account of his campaign in Judah is found in 2 Kings 18:13–19:37 and Isaiah 36–37.

After a cruel siege, Lachish fell. Sennacherib sacked 46 towns and villages in Judah, taking away thousands of prisoners and much spoil. Hezekiah refused Sennacherib's demand to surrender Jerusalem (2 Kin. 18:17; Is. 36:1–21), but he did agree to pay 300 talents of silver and 30 talents of gold in tribute.

The siege of Jerusalem proved unsuccessful for two reasons: (1) Hezekiah protected his water supplies (2 Kin. 20:20) and (2) Hezekiah steadfastly trusted in God rather than in material and military support from his allies (2 Kin. 19:32–34).

Although Sennacherib, in his description of the siege of Jerusalem, boasts of shutting up Hezekiah "like a bird in a cage," he makes no reference to the outcome of the siege—evidence that his campaign failed. The Bible narrates what happened in dramatic words: "And it came to pass on a certain night that the angel of the Lord went out, and killed in the camp of the Assyrians one hundred and eighty-five thousand; and when people arose early in the morning, there were the corpses—all dead" (2 Kin. 19:35).

The ancient Greek historian Herodotus tells of a similar incident, although he sets the scene in Egypt: "Thousands of field mice swarmed over them during the night, and ate their quivers, their bowstrings, and the leather handles of their shields, so that on the following day, having no arms to fight with, they abandoned their position and suffered severe losses during their retreat."

The "field mice" mentioned by Herodotus may have been plague-carrying rodents, instruments of the Lord's judgment. An army of mice bearing the "Black Death" (the bubonic plague) would have been more than a match for the mighty Assyrian army.

After the destruction of his army, Sennacherib returned to Nineveh. While worshiping in the temple of his god Nisroch, he was assassinated by his sons Adrammelech and Sharezer. He was succeeded by Esarhaddon, another son (2 Kin. 19:36–37; Is. 37:37–38).

SERAPHIM [SER uh fim] *(fiery, burning ones)*

Angelic or heavenly beings associated with Isaiah's vision of God in the temple when he was called to his ministry (Is. 6:1–7). This is the only place in the Bible that mentions these mysterious creatures. Each seraph had six wings. They used two to fly, two to cover their feet, and two to cover their faces (Is. 6:2). The seraphim flew about the throne on which God was seated, singing His praises as they called special attention to His glory and majesty.

These beings apparently also served as agents of purification for Isaiah as he began his prophetic ministry. One placed a hot coal against Isaiah's lips with the words, "Your iniquity is taken away and your sin is purged" (Is. 6:7).

SERGIUS PAULUS [SUR jee uhs PAW luhs]

The Roman proconsul, or governor, of Cyprus who was converted to Christianity when the apostle Paul visited that island on his first missionary journey, about A.D. 46 (Acts 13:7). He may have been the same man as L. Sergius Paulus, a Roman official in charge of the Tiber during the reign of the emperor Claudius (ruled A.D. 41–54).

SERMON ON THE MOUNT

The title given to Jesus' moral and ethical teachings as recorded in Matthew 5 through 7. The Sermon on the Mount was brought on by Jesus' growing popularity (Matt. 4:25). At first, the people were attracted to Him because of His healing ministry. When Jesus began to teach, the people remained to hear what He said. They also were impressed with the authority with which He taught. Although many people heard the Sermon on the Mount, it was primarily directed to Jesus' followers or disciples.

The central theme of the Sermon is summarized in Matthew 5:48, "You shall be perfect just as your Father in heaven is perfect." The word *perfect* does not refer to sinless or moral perfection. It means completeness, wholeness, maturity—being all that God wants a person to be. It is a goal that is never attained in our earthly life, but it continuously challenges us to greater achievements for the Lord.

The Beatitudes (5:2–12). Jesus began His teachings by stating the way to happiness. The word *blessed* is appropriately translated as "happy." The poor in spirit, those who recognize their spiritual poverty, will attain the kingdom of heaven. Those who mourn, who are truly sorry for their sins, will receive comfort. The meek, those who have disciplined strength, will inherit the earth. The quest for righteousness will be satisfied. The merciful will receive mercy; the pure in heart will see and understand the heart of God; the peacemakers shall be called God's children. And those who endure persecution for doing God's commands will inherit the kingdom of God.

Influence (5:13–16). Jesus used two symbols, salt and light, to describe the influence that His followers should have on the world. Salt has a preserving quality, and light clears away the darkness. Salt and light bring about noticeable changes, but they are seldom noticed themselves.

Righteousness (5:17–48). Jesus did not come to give a new law. He came to uncover the intentions of the law and the prophets and to bring them to their fullest expression. He gave five illustrations of what it means to fulfill the law: (1) Murder is wrong, but so is the hateful attitude that leads to it. (2) The act of adultery is wrong, but so is the lustful look. (3) The marriage relationship should be permanent. (4) We should be honest in our words and deeds. (5) We should love our enemies. Each of these righteous admonitions was contrasted with the legalistic teachings of the Pharisees.

Giving, Praying, and Fasting (6:1–18). Good religious practices may be done for the wrong reasons. Jesus called attention to three: (1) Almsgiving, kind deeds to help the needy, should be done, but not for the personal recognition the giver might receive; (2) prayer should be offered, but not in a way to seek the recognition of others; (3) fasting should be a sincere spiritual experience and not an attempt to impress others with our goodness and spirituality.

Material Resources (6:19–24). Jesus used three concepts—treasures, light, and slavery—to remind us that we cannot serve two masters. We must have single-minded devotion to the values of God's kingdom if we are to be His loyal followers.

Anxiety (6:25–34). Worldly people are those who live only for material things: food, drink, clothes. Jesus' disciples are to place God's kingdom first and to live with faith that God will provide for their needs.

Judgment: Right and Wrong (7:1–6). Disciples should not be judgmental in their attitude toward others. They should continuously judge themselves in terms of God's expectations.

Persistence (7:7–12). Jesus challenged His followers to maintain persistence in their commitment to God, to ask God to empower them to persevere, and to take the initiative to treat other people as they would like to be treated.

Choosing (7:13–14). Jesus stated that there are two lifestyles, or roads, that a person can take. The broad road leads to destruction; the narrow road leads to life. Every person is on one or the other of these two roads.

Performance (7:15–23). As Jesus neared the end of His teachings, He began to focus on the need to put His teachings into action. He warned against following false teachers and instructed His followers to put truth into action.

Life's Foundation (7:24–27). Although much attention has been focused on the two houses in this story, Jesus emphasized the builders. The difference between the two builders is the obedience of one and the other's failure to obey God's command.

SERVANT OF THE LORD

A theological concept in the Book of Isaiah that points forward to Jesus the Messiah. Passages in the book that express this idea are Isaiah 42:1–4; 49:1–6; 50:4–9; and 52:13–53:12.

But even before Isaiah's time, the concept of God's servant was deeply rooted in the history of the nation of Israel. The term *servant* was frequently applied to those who performed some service, task, or mission for the Lord. It was applied to Abraham (Gen. 26:24), Isaac (Gen. 24:14), Jacob (Ezek. 28:25), and Moses (Deut. 34:5), as well as many of the prophets of the Old Testament.

But in the "Servant Songs" of his book, the prophet Isaiah used the phrase "Servant of the Lord" in a specialized or messianic sense. The Servant of the Lord not only would encounter and accept suffering in the course of His work, but He also would realize that His vicarious suffering would become the means by which He would give His life as a ransom for others.

The New Testament writers are unanimous in stating that the Servant of the Lord is a messianic figure and that Jesus is that Servant. The first of Isaiah's "Servant Songs" (Is. 42:1–4) was quoted by Matthew as being fulfilled in Jesus (Matt. 12:18–21). The Book of Acts emphasized the suffering and hostility the Messiah underwent to accomplish redemption (Acts 3:13, 26; 4:27, 30). In these passages Jesus is referred to as "His Servant Jesus" (Acts 3:13, 26) and "Your holy Servant Jesus" (Acts 4:27, 30).

The violent treatment suffered by Jesus was precisely what the "Servant Songs" of Isaiah prophesied about God's Servant. Jesus saw His role as that of a servant (Mark 10:45, in fulfillment of Isaiah 53:10–11). He taught His followers to view His mission, and theirs as well, in terms of servanthood. Thus the Servant of the Lord, spoken of by Isaiah the prophet, is preeminently Jesus Himself.

According to Isaiah, the Servant of the Lord would "bring forth justice to the Gentiles" (Is. 42:1) and establish "justice in the earth" (Is. 42:4). He would bring Jacob back to the Lord (Is. 49:5) and would be "a light to the Gentiles" (Is. 49:6). He would not hide His face from shame and spitting (Is. 50:6). He would be the sin-bearing Servant, giving His life for the redemption of His people (Is. 52:13–53:12).

Through Jesus the ancient mission given by God to Abraham—to be a blessing to all the families of the earth (Gen. 12:1–3)—is now entrusted to the church. The church's responsibility is to preach the gospel to Jew and Gentile, bondslave and freeman, male and female, rich and poor. To be a servant of God is to serve Him continually (Dan. 6:20). As His mission was that of a servant, so must ours be (Mark 10:42–45).

SEVEN CHURCHES OF ASIA

The seven Christian congregations to which John addressed special messages in the Book of Revelation. From the Isle of Patmos, John wrote seven messages to "the seven churches which are in Asia" (Rev. 1:4, 11). These seven messages, found in Revelation 2–3, were to Ephesus, the Loveless Church (2:1–7); Smyrna, the Persecuted Church (2:8–11); Pergamos, the Compromising Church (2:12–17); Thyatira, the Corrupt Church (2:18–29); Sardis, the Dead Church (3:1–6); Philadelphia, the Faithful Church (3:7–13); and Laodicea, the Lukewarm Church (3:14–22).

The Roman province of Asia included more churches than these seven. Why did John single them out?

One theory is that these seven cities may have been centers of seven postal districts. These seven churches all stand on the great circular road that formed a rough circle around the west central part of the Roman province of Asia. As such, these seven sites served as good centers of communication for the surrounding districts. Letters in the first century had to be handwritten, and a letter sent to one church would be passed on to be read by Christians in other congregations.

The letters to the seven churches called for the Christians to repent of sin and return to faithfulness and good works; encouraged them to stand firm for Christ against the temptations, trials, and persecutions of the Roman Empire; and promised specific rewards to the martyrs who faced death without denying Christ.

SEVENTY WEEKS

A term that the prophet Daniel used in his prophecy of the future (Dan. 9:24–27). In Daniel's vision, God revealed that the captivity of His people in Babylon would come to an end and they would be restored to glory as a nation within a period of 70 weeks of seven years each—or a total of 490 years.

Scholars interpret this seventy weeks prophecy in different ways. Some insist that Daniel is not a book of prophecy at all but that he was writing about events that had already happened. Others believe the 490-year period came to a grand climax with Jesus' death on the cross. Still others believe this prophecy is yet to be fulfilled in the future.

SHADRACH [SHAD rak] (command of [the god] Aku)

The name that Ashpenaz, the chief of Nebuchadnezzar's eunuchs, gave to Hananiah, one of the Jewish princes who was carried away to Babylon in 605 B.C. (Dan. 1:7; 3:12–30).

Shadrach was one of the three faithful Jews who refused to worship the golden image that King Nebuchadnezzar of Babylon set up (Dan. 3:1). Along with his two companions, Meshach and Abed-Nego, Shadrach was "cast into the midst of a burning fiery furnace" (Dan. 3:11, 21). But they were protected by a fourth "man" in the fire (Dan. 3:25), and they emerged without even the smell of fire upon them (Dan. 3:27).

SHALLUM [SHAL uhm] (the requited one)

A son of Jabesh (2 Kin. 15:10), Shallum became the sixteenth king of Israel by assassinating Zechariah and claiming the throne, thus bringing the dynasty of Jehu to a close. He reigned only one month before being assassainated and replaced by Menahem (2 Kin. 15:10–15).

SHALMANESER V [shal muh NEE zur] (reigned 727–722 B.C.).

The son and successor of Tiglath-Pileser III (745–727 B.C.; called "Pul" in 2 Kin. 15:19). He is the only Assyrian king named Shalmaneser mentioned in the Bible (unless Shalman of Hosea 10:14 is a contraction of the name). Shalmaneser received tribute from Hoshea, king of Israel. Then he imprisoned Hoshea and besieged Samaria for three years (2 Kin.

17:3–6; 18:9–10), until it fell in 722 B.C. This marked the end of the northern kingdom of Israel.

SHAMGAR [SHAM gahr]

The third judge of Israel (Judg. 3:31) who delivered the nation from oppression by the Philistines. Using an ox goad as a weapon, Shamgar killed 600 Philistines who were terrorizing the main travel routes. Shamgar was a "son of Anath"—which may mean he was a resident of Beth Anath (Judg. 1:33), a fortified city in the territory of Naphtali.

SHARON [SHAR uhn]

The chief coastal plain of Palestine, running approximately 50 miles (80 kilometers) from south of the Carmel Mountain range to the vicinity of Joppa (1 Chr. 27:29). This lowland region was extremely fertile and was known for its agriculture (Is. 33:9). In ancient times, an important caravan route ran along the Plain of Sharon, connecting Egypt, Mesopotamia, and Asia Minor. The flowers of Sharon (Is. 35:2), particularly the rose of Sharon (Song 2:1), were beautiful. Sharon is also called Lasharon (Josh. 12:18).

SHEBA [SHEE buh] (oath)

A mountainous country in southwest Arabia (1 Kin. 10:1–13), identified as the land of "the queen of the South" (Luke 11:31) who came to investigate Solomon's fame and wisdom. By means of its international trade and control of trade routes through its land, Sheba developed into a strong commercial power. Its trade specialties were perfumes and incense. Camel caravans followed routes northward across its dry regions, bearing their precious commodities for the royal courts of the countries bordering the Mediterranean Sea. Thus the Queen of Sheba's visit to Solomon may have been motivated also by her interest in trade and in the unhindered movement of her caravans into the large territory under Solomon's control.

SHEBA, QUEEN OF

A queen who came to visit King Solomon. She tested him with "hard questions" and found that Solomon's wisdom and prosperity exceeded his fame (1 Kin. 10:1–13). Some scholars believe she represented the region of Ethiopia, south of Egypt. But others insist she ruled among the tribes of southwestern Arabia. In the New Testament, Jesus referred to her as "the queen of the South," who "came from the ends of the earth to hear the wisdom of Solomon" (Matt. 12:42).

SHECHEM [SHEK uhm] *(shoulder)*

An ancient fortified city in central Canaan and the first capital of the northern kingdom of Israel. Its name means "shoulder," probably because the city was built mainly on the slope, or shoulder, of Mount Ebal. Situated where main highways and ancient trade routes converged, Shechem was an important city long before the Israelites occupied Canaan. The city has been destroyed and rebuilt several times through the centuries.

Shechem is first mentioned in connection with Abraham's journey into the land of Canaan. When Abraham eventually came to Shechem, the Lord appeared to him and announced that this was the land He would give to Abraham's descendants (Gen. 12:6; Sichem, KJV). This fulfilled God's promise to Abraham at the time of his call (Gen. 12:1–3). In response, Abraham built his first altar to the Lord in Canaan at Shechem (Gen. 12:7). Because of this incident, Shechem is an important place in the religious history of the Hebrew people.

Upon his return from Padan Aram, Jacob, a grandson of Abraham, also built an altar to the Lord at Shechem (Gen.

33:18–20). This marked Jacob's safe return to the Promised Land from the land of self-imposed exile. According to Jewish tradition, Jacob dug a deep well here (John 4:12). Jacob's Well is one of the few sites visited by Jesus that is identifiable today.

After the Israelites conquered Canaan under the leadership of Joshua, an altar was built at Shechem. Its building was accompanied by a covenant ceremony in which offerings were given and the blessings and curses of the law were recited (Josh. 8:30–35). This was done in obedience to the command of Moses, given earlier in Deuteronomy 27:12–13. Because Shechem was situated between Mount Ebal and Mount Gerizim, this covenant ceremony took on a symbolic meaning. To this day Mount Gerizim is forested while Mount Ebal is barren. Thus the blessings of faithfully keeping the covenant were proclaimed from Mount Gerizim, while the curses of breaking the covenant were proclaimed from Mount Ebal.

At the close of his life, Joshua gathered the tribes of Israel at Shechem. Here he reviewed God's gracious dealings with Israel and performed a covenant-renewing ceremony on behalf of the nation. He closed his speech with his famous statement, "Choose for yourselves this day whom you will serve . . . but as for me and my house, we will serve the Lord" (Josh. 24:15).

The significance of Shechem in Israel's history continued into the period of the divided kingdom. Rehoboam, successor to King Solomon, went to Shechem to be crowned king over all Israel (1 Kin. 12:1). Later, when the nation divided into two kingdoms, Shechem became the first capital of the northern kingdom of Israel (1 Kin. 12:25). Samaria eventually became the permanent political capital of the northern kingdom, but

S

Shechem retained its religious importance. It apparently was a sanctuary for worship of God in Hosea's time in the eighth century B.C. (Hos. 6:9).

At Shechem (sometimes identified with Sychar) Jesus visited with the Samaritan woman at Jacob's Well (John 4). The Samaritans had built their temple on Mount Gerizim, where they practiced their form of religion. To this outcast woman of a despised sect Jesus offered salvation. This is a vivid example of the truth that the gospel of Christ is meant for all people.

SHEEP

Sheep are mentioned more frequently than any other animal in the Bible—about 750 times. This is only natural, since the Hebrew people were known early in their history as a race of wandering herdsmen. Even in the days of the kings, the simple shepherd's life seemed the ideal calling. The Bible makes many comparisons between the ways of sheep and human beings. In the New Testament, the church is often compared to a sheepfold.

Well-suited for Canaan's dry plains, sheep fed on grass, woods, and shrubs. They could get along for long periods without water. Sheep in clusters are easily led, so a single shepherd could watch over a large flock.

Sheep today are bred for white wool. But the sheep of Bible times were probably brown or a mixture of black and white. Modern farmers clip off the tails of sheep for sanitary reasons, but fat tails were prized on biblical sheep. The Hebrews called this "the whole fat tail." When they offered this prized part of the sheep as a burnt offering to God, they burned the "entire fat-tail cut off close by the spine" (Lev. 3:9, REB).

Sheep were also valuable because they provided meat for the Hebrew diet. Mutton was a nutritious food, and it could be packed away and preserved for winter. And before people learned to spin and weave wool, shepherds wore warm sheepskin jackets.

By nature, sheep are helpless creatures. They depend on shepherds to lead them to water and pasture, to fight off wild beasts, and to anoint their faces with oil when a snake nips them from the grass. Sheep are social animals that gather in flocks, but they tend to wander off and fall into a crevice or get caught in a thorn bush. Then the shepherd must leave the rest of his flock to search for the stray. Jesus used this familiar picture when He described a shepherd who left 99 sheep in the fold to search for one that had wandered off. The God of Israel revealed His nurturing nature by speaking of himself as a shepherd (Ps. 23). Jesus also described Himself as the Good Shepherd who takes care of His sheep (John 10:1–18).

A unique relationship existed between shepherd and sheep. He knew them by name, and they in turn recognized his voice. Sheep were models of submissiveness. Because he demonstrated purity and trustful obedience to the Father, Jesus was also called "the Lamb of God" (John 1:29, 36).

Wild sheep, high-spirited and independent, lived among the tall peaks of Canaan's mountains. Like their domesticated cousins, they flocked together, but their disposition more nearly resembled goats. They are referred to as mountain sheep (Deut. 14:5, NKJV, NRSV, NIV, NASB), chamois (KJV), and rock goats (REB).

SHEKINAH [shuh KIGH nuh] (dwelling)

A visible manifestation of the presence of God (also spelled Shechinah and Shekhinah). Although the word is not found in the Bible, it occurs frequently in later Jewish writings. It refers to the instances when God showed Himself visibly, as, for example, on Mount Sinai (Ex. 24:9–18) and in the Most High Place of the tabernacle and in Solomon's temple. The Shekinah was a luminous cloud that rested above the altar in the place of worship and lit up the room. When the Babylonians destroyed the temple, the Shekinah glory vanished. There was no Shekinah in the temples rebuilt later under Zerubbabel and Herod.

SHEM [shem] *(renown)*

The son of Noah and brother of Ham and Japheth. Shem was born after Noah became 500 years old (Gen. 5:32). He was one of eight people who entered Noah's ark and survived the Flood (Gen. 7:7, 13). Shem was married at the time of the Flood but had no children. After the Flood he became the father of Elam, Asshur, Arphaxad, Lud, and Aram (usually identified by scholars as Persia, Assyria, Chaldea, Lydia, and Syria, respectively). Thus Shem was the ancestor of the people of the ancient Near East generally, and the Hebrews specifically.

Shem died at the age of 600 (Gen. 11:10–11). He is listed by Luke as an ancestor of Jesus Christ (Luke 3:36; Sem in KJV).

SHEMA, THE [shuh MAH] *(hear thou)*

The Jewish confession of faith that begins, "Hear, O Israel: The Lord our God, the Lord is one!" (Deut. 6:4). The complete Shema is found in three passages from the Old Testament: Numbers 15:37–41, Deuteronomy 6:4–9 and 11:13–21.

The first of these passages stresses the unity of God and the importance of loving Him and valuing His commands. The second passage promises blessing or punishment according to a person's obedience of God's will. The third passage commands that a fringe be worn on the edge of one's garments as a continual reminder of God's laws. These verses make up one of the most ancient features of worship among the Jewish people. Jesus quoted from the Shema during a dispute with the scribes (Mark 12:28–30).

SHEOL [SHE ole]

In Old Testament thought, the abode of the dead. Sheol is the Hebrew equivalent of the Greek *Hades,* which means "the unseen world." Sheol was regarded as an underground region (Num. 16:30, 33; Amos 9:2), shadowy and gloomy, where disembodied souls had a conscious but dull and inactive existence (2 Sam. 22:6; Eccl. 9:10). The Hebrew people regarded sheol as a place to which both the righteous and unrighteous go at death (Gen. 37:35; Ps. 9:17; Is. 38:10; death in NIV; Deut. 32:22; the realm of death in NIV), a place where punishment is received and rewards are enjoyed. Sheol is pictured as having an insatiable appetite (Is. 5:14; Hab. 2:5; the grave, NIV.

However, God is present in sheol (Ps. 139:8; hell in NKJV; the depths in NIV). It is open and known to Him (Job 26:6; Prov. 15:11; death in NIV). This suggests that in death God's people remain under His care, and the wicked never escape His judgment. Sheol gives meaning to Psalm 16:10. Peter saw the fulfillment of this messianic psalm in Jesus' resurrection (Acts 2:27).

See also HELL.

SHEPHERD

A person who takes care of sheep. Figuratively, the Old Testament pictures God as Israel's Shepherd-Leader (Ps. 80:1; Ezek. 34:14). The New Testament reveals Jesus as the Good Shepherd who gave His life for His sheep. When He said, "I am the good shepherd" (John 10:11), Jesus linked His own divine nature with one of the most ordinary occupations in Israel.

Abel is the first shepherd mentioned

in the Bible (Gen. 4:2). Kings who led Israel (Jer. 6:3; 49:19) and certain ministers (Jer. 23:4) are also called shepherds.

The sons of Abraham, Isaac, and Jacob herded sheep (Gen. 13:7; 26:20; 30:36). Rachel was a shepherdess (Gen. 29:3). David (2 Sam. 5:2; Ps. 78:70–72), Moses (Ex. 3:1), and Amos (Amos 1:1) found herding to be excellent preparation for future leadership roles.

Jesus' life exemplifies these leadership traits. Jesus knows each of His sheep intimately (John 10:3–5). Sometimes several shepherds will pen their sheep together in a cave or a sheepfold at night. The next morning the shepherds call out to their own sheep. Each sheep knows its shepherd's voice and responds immediately. Even in a large flock, one individual sheep will run to its shepherd when its own pet name is called. "My sheep hear My voice, and I know them, and they follow Me," (John 10:27).

Sheep are curious but dumb animals, often unable to find their way home even if the sheepfold is within sight. Knowing this fault, shepherds never take their eyes off their wandering sheep (Ps. 32:8). Often sheep will wander into a briar patch or fall over a cliff in the rugged Palestinian hills. The shepherds tenderly search for their sheep and carry them to safety (Luke 15:6).

In water-hungry Syria and Palestine, shepherds have always had to search diligently for water, sometimes for hours every day. Sheep must be watered daily. The shepherd might find a bubbling stream for the sheep that are always on the move and needing fresh pastures every day (Ps. 23:2). An old well with a quiet pool or trough close by might provide the water (Gen. 29:7; 30:38; Ex. 2:16). Often the shepherd carries a small pail, patiently filling it many times for the thirsty sheep who cannot reach the available water.

A trusted shepherd also provides loving protection for the flock. Shepherds on the Bethlehem hillsides still use a sling, made of goat's hair or leather and immortalized by David against Goliath (1 Sam. 17:49). At times shepherds will throw their rods at stubborn, straying sheep that refuse to hear their voice. At other times shepherds gently nudge the strays with the end of a six-foot staff, crooked at one end. Both the rod and the staff work together to protect the sheep (Ps. 23:4).

The presence of the shepherd also offers comfort to the flock. David recognized this in Psalm 23. Sheep are content merely to be in the same field with their shepherd; Christians are comforted by the very presence of the Lord. This thought is especially comforting when darkness overshadows the believer. Jesus is our Door; nothing can touch our lives without touching Him first. This is a perfect picture of shepherds, who literally become the living door of the sheepfold. They curl up in the door or in the entrance of a cave. They put their bodies between the sleeping sheep and ravenous animals or thieves.

One day Jesus the Chief Shepherd will return, gather His flock into one fold, and divide the sheep from the goats (Matt. 25:31–33). Until that time, Jesus continues His search for every lost sheep (Matt. 18:12–14). His sheep are to yield themselves to Him for His useful service until, at last, they "will dwell in the house of the Lord forever" (Ps. 23:6).

SHIBBOLETH [SHIBB oh lehht]

The password used by the Gileadites at the fords of the Jordan River to detect the fleeing Ephraimites (Judg. 12:6). In a conflict between the people of Ephraim, who lived west of the Jordan, and the people of Gilead, who lived east of the Jordan, the Gileadites were victorious. Led by the judge Jephthah, the Gileadites seized the fords of the Jordan, where they met the fleeing invaders and asked them to say "Shibboleth."

Because of a difference in dialect, an Ephraimite "could not pronounce it right" (v. 6), saying "Sibboleth" instead. Betrayed by his own speech, the unlucky Ephraimite was then killed at the fords of the Jordan by Jephthah and his men.

SHILOH [SHIGH loe]

A city in the territory of Ephraim which served as an Israelite religious center during the days before the establishment of the united kingdom. Shiloh was "north of Bethel, on the east side of the highway that goes up from Bethel to Shechem, and south of Lebonah" (Judg. 21:19). This pinpoints Khirbet Seilun, about 10 miles (16 kilometers) northeast of Bethel.

At Shiloh the tabernacle received its first permanent home, soon after the initial conquest of Canaan by the children of Israel (Josh. 18:1). This established Shiloh as the main sanctuary of worship for the Israelites during the period of the judges (Judg. 18:31). Here the last seven tribes received their allotments of land (Josh. 18:8–10).

Hannah prayed for a son at Shiloh (1 Sam. 1:3, 11). God granted her request by giving her Samuel. The tabernacle, with the ark of the covenant, was still located in Shiloh during Samuel's early years as priest and prophet (1 Sam. 1:9; 4:3–4). However, the ark was captured by the Philistines because God had forsaken Shiloh as the center of worship (Ps. 78:60).

When the ark was returned to the Israelites by the Philistines, it was not returned to Shiloh (2 Sam. 6:2–17). Archaeologists have determined that Khirbet Seilun (Shiloh) was destroyed about 1050 B.C.

After the ark was moved to another city, Shiloh gradually lost its importance. This loss was made complete when Jeru-salem was established as capital of the kingdom. After the division of the kingdom, Jeroboam established worship centers at Dan and Bethel; but Ahijah, the prophet of the Lord, still remained at Shiloh (1 Kin. 14:2, 4). From here, Ahijah pronounced the doom of Jeroboam's rule (1 Kin. 14:7–16).

In the days of the prophet Jeremiah, Shiloh was in ruins (Jer. 7:12, 14), although some people continued to live on the site of this former city (Jer. 41:5). Shiloh became an inhabited town again in the days of the Greeks and Romans several centuries later.

SHIMEI [SHIM ih uh]

A son of Gera of Saul's family and the tribe of Benjamin (2 Sam. 16:5–13; 1 Kin. 2:8). Shimei grew bitter because David had taken the throne from the family of Saul. He insulted David when the king was fleeing from his own son, Absalom. When David finally won the struggle for the throne, Shimei repented. David accepted Shimei's apology and promised to let him live. After David's death, his son and successor, Solomon, would not allow Shimei to go beyond Jerusalem's walls. Shimei obeyed Solomon's command at first, but eventually he left the city and was promptly executed at Solomon's command.

SHINAR [SHIGH nahr]

The land of southern Mesopotamia, later known as Babylonia or Chaldea, through which the Tigris and Euphrates rivers flow (Gen. 10:10; 11:2). Secular historians sometimes refer to the area as Sumer. Nimrod's kingdom in Shinar consisted of the cities of Babel (Babylon), Erech (Uruk), Accad (Akkad or Agade), and Calneh (Gen. 10:10). It was here that the Tower of Babel was situated (Gen. 11:2).

In the days of Abraham, Amraphel, a king of Shinar, was involved in the attack

S

and defeat of five kings of Canaan, including the kings of Sodom and Gomorrah (Gen. 14:1, 9).

In about 605 B.C. Nebuchadnezzar, king of Babylon, took the temple vessels from Jerusalem to Shinar (Dan. 1:2), from where Isaiah had predicted God's people would return to Israel (Is. 11:11). After the return from the Babylonian captivity, the prophet Zechariah saw a vision of the removal of a woman from Israel to Shinar (Zech. 5:11). Some scholars associate this woman with the great harlot, "Babylon the great" (Rev. 17:5), a symbol of imperial Rome.

SHISHAK [SHIGH shak]

A Libyan war chieftain who became pharaoh of Egypt (reigned from about 940 B.C. to about 915 B.C.). Shishak (Sheshonk in Egyptian) is known for his expedition against the southern kingdom of Judah after the united kingdom split into two nations following Solomon's death about 920 B.C.

In about 926 B.C., in the fifth year of the reign of King Rehoboam (reigned about 931–913 B.C.), Shishak invaded Judah and captured many of its fortified cities (1 Kin. 14:25). He then marched against Jerusalem, Rehoboam's capital city, forcing Rehoboam to pay tribute and plundering the treasures of the temple and Rehoboam's palace (1 Kin. 14:25–26).

The Egyptian account of Shishak's invasion of Judah was recorded on the wall of the temple of the Egyptian god Amon at Karnak (ancient Thebes), in southern Egypt. More than 100 cities captured or destroyed by Shishak are listed, including Adoraim, Aijalon, and Socoh. Cities from the northern kingdom of Israel, such as Shechem, Beth Shean, and Megiddo, are also listed on this monument as being captured by Shishak.

SHOWBREAD

Holy or consecrated bread placed in the sanctuary of the tabernacle or temple every Sabbath to symbolize God's presence and His provision for His people. The ritual always involved 12 loaves of bread, representing the 12 tribes of the nation of Israel. It was called show-

SHOWBREAD

bread (shewbread in KJV; bread of the Presence in NIV) because it was kept continually before God's presence in the tabernacle.

The Levites descended through the family of Kohath were in charge of preparing the showbread each week. On each Sabbath, they placed fresh bread on the table of showbread and removed the week-old bread from the sanctuary (1 Chr. 9:32). The older bread was eaten by the priests; whatever was left was burned with incense as an offering to the Lord (Lev. 24:5–9).

When David fled from King Saul, he and his men came to Nob, where the tabernacle was located. David and his men were hungry, but Ahimelech, the high priest, had no ordinary food. So David asked for the "holy bread," the showbread that had been taken from the Holy Place (1 Sam. 21:1–6).

When the Pharisees criticized Jesus' disciples for picking and rubbing heads of grain to eat as they walked through the fields on the Sabbath, Jesus reminded them of what David had done (Mark 2:25–26). In this situation, Jesus and His disciples were also hungry and in need of nourishment. This illustrated His teaching that human need often was more important than a legalistic keeping of the law. Or, as He declared to the Pharisees, "The Sabbath was made for man, and not man for the Sabbath" (Mark 2:27).

The showbread symbolized the continual presence of the Lord and the people's dependence on God for their spiritual and physical needs.

SHUR [shoor] (enclosure)

A desert in the northwest part of the Sinai Peninsula where the angel of the Lord found Hagar by a spring in the wilderness (Gen. 16:7). Shur was probably a caravan route from Beersheba to Egypt known as Darb esh-Shur.

The Wilderness of Shur must have been immediately east of the Red Sea. As soon as Moses brought the people of Israel from the Red Sea, they went out into the Wilderness of Shur (Ex. 15:22). Some scholars believe the name Shur comes from a series of fortifications built by the Egyptians on their northeastern frontier as a defense against invaders.

SHUSHAN [SHOO shan]

The ancient capital of Elam, in southwestern Iran; later a royal residence and capital of the Persian Empire (Neh. 1:1; Susa in NASB, NIV, NRSV). The site is present-day Shush, about 150 miles (240 kilometers) north of the Persian Gulf.

Long before the time of Abraham in the Old Testament, Shushan was the center of Elamite civilization. Some scholars believe it was a cult city centering around worship of one of the chief Elamite gods. The city had frequent contacts with Mesopotamia.

The Assyrian King Ashurbanipal (the biblical Osnapper, Ezra 4:10) led a military campaign against Shushan about 642–639 B.C. In about 640 B.C. he sacked the city and carried some of its inhabitants (Susanchites, Ezra 4:9, KJV) into exile in Samaria (v. 10).

When Cyrus the Great (reigned 550–529 B.C.) established the Persian Empire, he made Shushan its capital. At Shushan Darius the Great (ruled about 521–486 B.C.) built his magnificent royal palace. This palace, when occupied by Ahasuerus (Xerxes, 486–465 B.C.), figured prominently in the story of Esther.

In fact, most of the events recorded in the Book of Esther took place in Shushan (Esth. 1:2–5; 2:3–8; 3:15; 4:8–16; 8:14–15; 9:6–18). It was in Shushan also that the prophet Daniel had his vision of the ram and the goat (Dan. 8:2) and where Nehemiah lived in exile (Neh. 1:1).

According to a tradition of the Shiite Muslims, the present-day village of

S

Shush (ancient Shushan) is the site of the tomb of the prophet Daniel.

SICKLE

A small hand tool used for cutting stalks of grain. The oldest known examples have flint teeth set in wood or bone handles. Later, metal blades were used. The grain was held in one hand and cut off near the ground by the sickle. The final judgment is sometimes pictured in terms of reaping with a sickle (Joel 3:13; Rev. 14:14–19).

SIDON [SIGH dun]

An ancient Phoenician city on the Mediterranean coast in northern Palestine. Sidon dominated the coastal plain in the area of the Lebanon Mountains. Built on a hill across several small islands, it was connected by bridges.

Sidon was the oldest of the Phoenician cities. Founded by the son of Canaan (Gen. 10:15), it became a principal Canaanite stronghold (Gen. 10:19; 1 Chr. 1:13; Zidon in KJV). So dominant was Sidon originally that Sidonian and Phoenician became interchangeable terms. Even after the city of Tyre on the coast to the south assumed a position of dominance, Ethbaal, king of Tyre, was called king of the Sidonians (1 Kin. 16:31).

After the Israelites settled the land of Canaan, Sidon was near the territory of Zebulun (Gen. 49:13) and Asher (Josh. 19:28). But the tribe of Asher failed to drive out the inhabitants of Sidon (Judg. 1:31). This indicates something of the strength of the city. Sidon, however, frequently was destroyed by foreign invaders during the next several centuries. But it was rebuilt following each defeat and restored to a position of prominence.

By the time of Alexander the Great in the fourth century B.C., Sidon was still a major Phoenician city. Alexander was received by the Sidonians as a deliverer, and they assisted Alexander as he be-

sieged their neighboring city of Tyre. Later, under Roman rule Sidon was given the privilege of self-government, which it enjoyed during New Testament times.

Not only did the city of Sidon resist the efforts of the tribe of Asher to inhabit that region, but it also oppressed Israel during the period of the judges (Judg. 10:12). Once they were settled in the land, the Israelites began to worship the gods of Sidon, including their chief god Baal (1 Kin. 16:31) but especially Ashtoreth, the goddess of fertility (2 Kin. 23:13). Ethbaal, the king of Sidon, was the father of Jezebel (1 Kin. 16:31), who was mainly responsible for introducing the worship of pagan gods into Israel.

The people of Sidon came to Galilee to hear the preaching of Christ and to be healed by His touch (Mark 3:8; Luke 6:17). Jesus even went to the borders of Tyre and Sidon (Matt. 15:21–28; Mark 7:24–31), where He healed the Syro-Phoenician woman's daughter. Herod Agrippa I was displeased by the people of Tyre and Sidon, but they won over his servant Blastus and begged for peace "because their country was supplied with food by the king's country" (Acts 12:20).

The apostle Paul stopped briefly at Sidon on his way to Rome, meeting with Christian friends there (Acts 27:3). In early Christian history, the city became an important Christian center, sending a bishop to the Council of Nicea in A.D. 325.

Frequently Sidon was the subject of prophecies of judgment. Isaiah predicted that Sidon would pass into the control of Cyprus (Is. 23:12). Jeremiah predicted its defeat by Nebuchadnezzar, king of Babylon (Jer. 27:3, 6). Ezekiel denounced Sidon (Ezek. 28:20–24) because her inhabitants had been "a pricking brier [and] a painful thorn for the house of Israel" (Ezek. 28:24). Joel denounced

Sidon for helping to plunder Jerusalem (Joel 3:4–6).

In the eighth century B.C. Sidon was noted for its artistic metalwork and skilled tradesmen who made objects of silver and gold. Like the citizens of Tyre, the Sidonians were also known for their purple dye. The art of glass blowing was in evidence in the first century B.C. at Sidon. In the first century, learned Sidonians were also noted for their study in the sciences of astronomy and arithmetic. Sidon also had a law school that was famed throughout the ancient world.

SIEGE

A prolonged military blockade of a city or fortress to force it to surrender. The purpose of a siege was to take away the advantage of the city's massive defensive walls by cutting off its supplies and contacts from the outside. Without supplies, the defending city would be forced to surrender or to attack the besieging army.

The attacking army would sometimes press the siege by trying to scale the walls with ladders or ramps. Other techniques included battering down the walls or tunneling under them. But attack was dangerous because the city's defenders were well protected and could carry on the battle from a superior position.

A siege might continue for several months. To shorten a siege, the attacking army usually tried to capture a city's water supplies. These were usually situated outside the city walls.

Much of the warfare described in the Old Testament is siege warfare. For instance, Joab laid siege to Rabbah (2 Sam. 12:26–31) and Sennacherib besieged Jerusalem and all the fortified cities of Judah (Is. 36:1). In the New Testament, Jesus predicted the Roman siege of Jerusalem (Luke 19:43–44).

SIHON [SIGH hun]

A king of the Amorites defeated by the Israelites during their journey toward the land of Canaan. Moses asked Sihon to let the Israelites pass peacefully through his kingdom, located east of the Jordan River. Sihon refused and later attacked the Israelites at Jahaz. In the battle that followed Sihon and his army were killed (Num. 21:21–32), and his territory was given to the tribes of Gad and Reuben (Num. 32:33). Sihon's defeat is mentioned often in the Old Testament (Deut. 1:4; Josh. 2:10; Ps. 135:11; Jer. 48:45).

SILAS [SIGH lus] (person of the woods)

A prominent member of the early church at Jerusalem and companion of the apostle Paul. Silas accompanied Paul to Antioch of Syria to report the decision of the Jerusalem Council to accept Gentile Christians into the church (Acts 15:22, 27, 32).

Paul chose Silas as his companion on his second missionary journey. During their travels, Paul and Silas were imprisoned at Philippi (Acts 16:19, 25, 29). Silas and Paul were also together during the riot at Thessalonica (Acts 17:4). Later they were sent to Berea, where Silas remained with Timothy; both Silas and Timothy soon followed Paul to Athens (Acts 17:14–15), although they may not have caught up with him until reaching Corinth (Acts 18:5). Silas played an important role in the early Christian work in Corinth.

In his letters, Paul referred to Silas as Silvanus (1 Thess. 1:1, 2 Thess. 1:1). The time, place, and manner of his death are unknown.

SILK

Cloth woven from thread that was made from the Chinese silkworm. Although the word *silk* occurs a few times

S

in the KJV and the NKJV, many scholars think the Hebrew word for silk should be rendered "fine linen" or "costly fabric" (Ezek. 16:10, 13; Prov. 31:22).

The use of silk among the Egyptians is unknown, but it did appear among the Chinese and other people of ancient Asia. From the earliest times, trade existed between India and China on the one hand and India and the Mesopotamian valley on the other. So it is possible that Solomon's extensive trade could have brought silk to Israel. Certainly after the campaigns of Alexander the Great, silk reached the Near East.

As one of the finest and most vividly colored fabrics, silk was highly prized. The rich and powerful people called the Babylonians wore it, according to Revelation 18:12. At one time people of the ancient world bought silk for its weight in gold (around A.D. 275).

SILOAM [sigh LOW um] (sent)

A storage pool and water tunnel that provided a water supply for early residents of the city of Jerusalem. The pool and tunnel drew water from the Gihon spring outside the city wall.

Under the peril of an impending invasion by the armies of Sennacherib, king of Assyria (reigned about 705–681 B.C.), King Hezekiah of Judah "made a pool and a tunnel [or conduit] and brought water into the city" (2 Kin. 20:20). The parallel account in 2 Chronicles says he "stopped the water outlet of Upper Gihon, and brought the water by tunnel to the west side of the City of David" (2 Chr. 32:30).

Hezekiah's tunnel was discovered accidentally in 1838 and was explored by the American traveler, Edward Robinson, and his missionary friend, Eli Smith. They found the Siloam tunnel to be about 1,750 feet (518 meters) long, although the straight line distance between the storage pool and the Gihon

spring is only 1,090 feet (332 meters). The course has numerous twists and turns. Some scholars have suggested that by following such a crooked course, the tunnel builders were trying to avoid the royal tombs cut into the same area through which the conduit was cut. But it is just as possible that more accurate surveying methods were unavailable to Hezekiah's technicians. By any standards, however, Hezekiah's tunnel was a notable achievement.

The tunnel was explored in 1867, but it was not until 1880 that an important Hebrew inscription was discovered near the entrance to the reservoir. It gave a graphic description of how the tunnel was built. Two work crews cut the tunnel through solid rock, working from opposite ends until they met in the middle.

It may have been through another tunnel or gap such as this that David's warriors entered the ancient city of Jerusalem about 1000 B.C. The city was known as Jebus at that time. David captured it and turned it into the capital city of his kingdom.

The Bible does contain some puzzling references to a more ancient pool. The prophet Isaiah, for instance, speaks of Hezekiah's "reservoir between the two walls for the water of the old pool" (Is. 22:11). Perhaps Hezekiah and his craftsmen used an existing reservoir and linked it to his tunnel and pool.

SILVER

This mineral is actually a silvery-white metal capable of a high polish. In ancient times it was valued next to gold. Silver was harder than gold, but not as hard as copper. It was usually extracted from lead ore, although it was also found in its native state. Silver never tarnishes when exposed to air, unless sulphur is present.

The main sources of silver were Asia Minor, Arabia, Mesopotamia, Armenia, and Persia. Palestine imported most of its silver from these countries, especially during Solomon's time (about 970–931 B.C.), when "the king made silver as common in Jerusalem as stones" (1 Kin. 10:27; 2 Chr. 9:27). Silver was refined and then cast into molds (Judg. 17:4; Ps. 12:6) by silversmiths (Jer. 10:9; Acts 19:24). Abraham's wealth included silver (Gen. 13:2), which he used as a medium of exchange (Gen. 23:15).

SIMEON [SIM ih un] *([God] hears)*

1. The second son of Jacob and Leah (Gen. 29:33). Simeon's descendants became one of the twelve tribes of Israel. He and his brother Levi tricked the Hivites of Shechem and massacred all the males because one of them had raped Dinah, their sister (Gen. 34:2, 25, 30). Simeon was the brother whom Joseph kept as security when he allowed his brothers to leave Egypt and return to their father Jacob in the land of Canaan (Gen. 42:24).

SIMEON [SIM ih un] *([God] hears)*

2. A devout Jew who blessed the infant Jesus in the temple (Luke 2:25, 34). The Holy Spirit had promised Simeon that he would not die until he had seen the long-awaited Messiah. Simeon recognized the child as the Messiah when Mary and Joseph brought him to the temple to present Him to the Lord.

SIMEON, TRIBE OF

One of the twelve tribes of Israel, descended from the son of Jacob (Rev. 7:7). Simeon had six sons—Jemuel (Nemuel), Jamin, Ohad, Jachin (Jerib), Zohar (Zerah), and Shaul—and all but Ohad founded tribal families (Ex. 6:15).

The tribe of Simeon numbered 59,300 fighting men at the first census in the wilderness (Num. 1:23; 2:13) and 22,200 at the second (Num. 26:12–14). This tribe was omitted in Moses' blessing of the nation of Israel (Deut. 33). A comparison of the cities assigned to Simeon with those assigned to Judah (Josh. 15:20–63; 19:1–9; 1 Chr. 4:28–33) makes it appear that the tribe of Simeon had been assimilated into the tribe of Judah, thus fulfilling Jacob's prophecy (Gen. 49:5–7).

When the land of Canaan was divided, the second lot fell to Simeon. The tribe received land in the extreme southern part of Canaan, in the middle of Judah's territory (Josh. 19:1–9). Simeon united with Judah in fighting the Canaanites (Judg. 1:1, 3, 17). Among the Simeonite cities were Beersheba, Hormah, and Ziklag (Josh. 19:1–9). Although the descendants of Simeon disappeared as a tribe, Ezekiel mentions it in his prophecies about a future land of Canaan (Ezek. 48:24–25, 33). The Book of Revelation mentions 12,000 of the tribe of Simeon who were sealed (Rev. 7:7).

SIMON [SIME un] *([God] hears)*

1. A disciple of Jesus, called the Canaanite to distinguish him from Simon Peter. The name may also indicate he was a member of a fanatical Jewish sect, the Zealots (Matt. 10:4; Mark 3:18; Luke 6:15; Acts 1:13). Members of this group were fanatical opponents of Roman rule in Palestine. As a Zealot, Simon would have hated any foreign domination or interference.

SIMON [SIME un] *([God] hears)*

2. A man of Cyrene who was forced to carry Jesus' cross (Matt. 27:32; Mark 15:21; Luke 23:26). Simon was the father of Alexander and Rufus, men who were known to the early Christians in Rome (Rom. 16:13).

SIMON [SIME un] *([God] hears)*

3. A Pharisee in whose house Jesus ate (Luke 7:36–50). On that occasion a woman who was a sinner anointed Jesus' feet. Simon felt that Jesus should not have allowed her to come near

S

Him. But Jesus explained that sinners like her were the very ones who needed forgiveness.

SIMON [SIME un] ([God] hears)

4. A sorcerer known as Simon Magus, or Simon the magician, who tried to buy spiritual powers from the apostle Peter (Acts 8:9–24). Simon's feats were so impressive that the people of Samaria declared, "This man is the great power of God" (Acts 8:10), and followed him. But when Philip the evangelist preached, the Samaritans believed and were baptized. Simon also believed and was baptized.

Later the apostles Peter and John visited Samaria to make sure these believers received the power of the Holy Spirit. When Simon saw that the Holy Spirit was bestowed by the laying on of hands, he attempted to buy this power. Peter rebuked him, "Your money perish with you, because you thought that the gift of God could be purchased with money! You have neither part nor portion in this matter, for your heart is not right in the sight of God" (Acts 8:20–21).

SIN

Lawlessness (1 John 3:4) or transgression of God's will, either by omitting to do what God's law requires or by doing what it forbids.

Mankind was created without sin, morally upright and inclined to do good (Eccl. 7:29). But sin entered into human experience when Adam and Eve violated the direct command of God by eating the forbidden fruit in the Garden of Eden (Gen. 3:6). Because Adam was the head and representative of the whole human race, his sin affected all future generations (Rom. 5:12–21). Associated with this guilt is a corrupted nature passed from Adam to all his descendants. Out of this perverted nature arise all the sins that people commit (Matt. 15:19); no person is free from involvement in sin (Rom. 3:23).

Satan continues to lure people into sin (1 Pet. 5:8); nevertheless, people remain fully responsible for what they do. God is not the author of sin, but His plan for world redemption does include His dealing with the reality of sin (2 Sam. 24:1; 1 Chr. 21:1). This truth is dramatically witnessed in the death of Jesus Christ. The crucifixion happened according to God's will; but at the same time, it was the worst crime of human history (Acts 2:23).

Sin is not represented in the Bible as the absence of good, or as an illusion that stems from our human limitations. Sin is portrayed as a real and positive evil. Sin is more than unwise, inexpedient, calamitous behavior that produces sorrow and distress. It is rebellion against God's law—the standard of righteousness (Ps. 119:160).

Since God demands righteousness, sin must be defined in terms of mankind's relation to God. Sin is thus the faithless rebellion of creatures against the just authority of their Creator. For this reason, breaking God's law at any point involves transgression at every point (James 2:10).

Violation of the law of God in thought, word, and deed shows the sinfulness of the human heart. Sin is actually a contradiction to the holiness of God, whose image mankind bears. This depraved condition is called "original sin" because it comes from Adam and characterizes all persons from the moment of their birth.

Sin involves the denial of the living God from whom human beings draw their life and existence (Acts 17:28); the consequence of this revolt is death and the torment of hell. Death is the ultimate penalty imposed by God for sin (Rom. 6:23).

Against this dark background of sin and its reality, the gospel comes as the good news of the deliverance that God has provided through His Son. Jesus bears the penalty of sin in place of His people (Mark 10:45). He also redeems us from lawlessness and makes us long for good works in service to God and others (Titus 2:14).

SIN OFFERING

This bloody offering, also known as a guilt offering, was presented for unintentional or intentional sins for which there was no possible restitution (Lev. 4:5–13; 6:24–30). If the offering was not accompanied by repentance, divine forgiveness was withheld (Num. 15:30). Expiation or covering (forgiveness) of sin was represented by the blood smeared on the horns of the altar of incense or burnt offering and poured out at the base of the altar.

The size and sex of the animal offered as a sacrifice depended on the rank of the offerers. The higher their post, the more responsibility they bore. The penalty for all sin, death, was vicariously inflicted on the animal. Guilt for the worshiper's sin was transferred symbolically through the laying on of the offerer's hands.

SINAI, MOUNTAIN OF [SIGH nih eye]

The mountain where God met Moses and gave him the law (Ex. 19:3, 20). This mountain is to be identified with Mount Horeb (Ex. 3:1), or perhaps Horeb refers to a mountain range or ridge and Sinai to an individual summit on that ridge. The name *Sinai* is used at the time when the Israelites were actually at the foot of the mountain (Ex. 19:11), whereas *Horeb* is used upon reflection about the events that happened here.

Although several mountains have been identified as possibilities, there are only two serious contenders for the title— Jebel Serbal (6,791 feet or 2,070 meters) in central Sinai and Jebel Musa (about 7,500 feet or 2,286 meters) in southern Sinai. One of a cluster of three peaks,

Jebel Musa, Arabic for "Mount Moses," has a broad plain at its base, where the Israelites may have camped.

During their years of wandering in the Sinai wilderness, the census was taken (Num. 1:1–46), the firstborn were redeemed (Num. 3:40–51), the office and duties of the Levites were established (Num. 4:1–49), and the first tabernacle was built (Num. 9:15).

SINAI, PENINSULA OF [SIGH nih eye]

The peninsula of Sinai is an area of great contrasts. It appears to hang from the southeast corner of the Mediterranean Sea with its base serving as the land bridge between Egypt and Israel. The peninsula is bounded on the west by the Gulf of Suez and on the east by the Gulf of Aqaba.

The Sinai peninsula is about 150 miles (240 kilometers) wide at the northern end and about 250 miles (400 kilometers) long. Its land area is desert and a tableland rising to about 2,500 feet (762 meters). On the north the Sinai plateau slopes away to the Mediterranean Sea. Near the south end of the peninsula a series of granite mountains rise 4,000 to 9,000 feet (1,209 to 2,743 meters) high, in striking contrast to the surrounding wastelands.

SINAI, WILDERNESS OF [SIGH nih eye]

Exodus 19:1 indicates that "in the third month after the children of Israel had gone out of the land of Egypt, on the same day, they came to the Wilderness of Sinai." This phrase may refer only to the particular desert that lies at the foot of Mount Sinai and in which the Israelites pitched their camp. But the phrase may also refer in a broader sense to the entire desert area of the Sinai Peninsula. If this is the case, it would include the Wilderness of Sin, through which the Israelites passed between Elim and Mount

Sinai (Ex. 16:1); the Wilderness of Paran, in the central Sinaitic Peninsula (Num. 10:12); the Wilderness of Shur, east of Egypt in the northern Sinai (Gen. 16:7); and the Wilderness of Zin, close to the border of Canaan (Num. 13:21).

SLAVERY

An ancient practice (Gen. 9:25), slavery existed in several different forms in biblical times. Household or domestic slavery was its most common form; this is illustrated by Hagar, who lived in the home of Abram and Sarai (Gen. 16:1) and by Jesus in His parables (Matt. 13:24–30; 21:33–44). State slavery, another common form, is illustrated by the Israelites' experience under their Egyptian taskmasters (Ex. 5:6–19; 13:3), and later by Solomon, who enslaved some of the Canaanite peoples (1 Kin. 9:20–21). Temple slavery is illustrated by the practice of Moses and Joshua, who assigned certain people as slaves to the Levites for temple service (Num. 31:25–47; Josh. 9:21–27).

One could purchase slaves, as in the case of Joseph. He was sold into slavery by his brothers for 20 shekels of silver (Gen. 37:28). Israelites could also buy foreign slaves (Lev. 25:44). People captured in war frequently became slaves (Gen. 14:21; Num. 31:9). Occasionally those who wanted slaves might kidnap them, but this practice was forbidden by Israelite law (Ex. 21:16; 1 Tim. 1:10).

People could become slaves in several ways. The poor who were unable to pay their debts could offer themselves as slaves (Ex. 21:2–6; Neh. 5:1–5). A thief who could not repay what he had stolen could also be sold as a slave. Children born of slave parents became "house-born slaves" (Gen. 15:3; 17:12–13). Sometimes children would be taken as slaves in payment for debts (2 Kin. 4:1–7).

Treatment of slaves generally depended on the character of the master (Gen. 24; 39:1–6). But a set of regulations governed the treatment of domestic slaves (Ex. 21; Deut. 15). Repeatedly, Israel was instructed by the law not to rule over a fellow Israelite harshly (Lev. 25:39; Deut. 15:14). If a master beat a slave or harmed him, the law provided that the slave could go free (Ex. 21:26–27); and the killing of a slave called for a penalty (Ex. 21:20).

Slaves were allowed to secure their freedom. Under the law, no Hebrew was to be the permanent slave of another Hebrew. After six years of service, a slave was to be released (Ex. 21:2; Deut. 15:12). In the year of Jubilee, no matter how long a slave had served, he was to be released (Lev. 25:37–43). If a slave desired to continue with his master, he would have a mark made in the ear; this mark would signify that he had chosen to remain a slave (Ex. 21:5–6). A slave could also buy his freedom, or another person could buy his freedom for him (Lev. 25:47–49).

Among the Romans in New Testament times, freedom for a slave could be arranged if ownership was transferred to a god. The slave could then receive his freedom in return for contracting his services. He would continue with his master, but now as a free man.

The Bible contains warnings about the practice of slavery. The prophet Amos spoke woe to Gaza and Tyre for their practices of slave-trading entire populations (Amos 1:6–9). The Book of Revelation declares that disaster awaits those who sell slaves (Rev. 18:13). As for Christians, the apostle Paul advised slaves to obey their masters (Eph. 6:5; Col. 3:22; Titus 2:9). Paul appealed to Philemon to receive back Onesimus, a runaway slave who was now a Christian and therefore a brother (Philem. 1:16). Elsewhere Paul counseled believing slaves to seek freedom if they could (1 Cor. 7:21). Since slave practices were part of the culture in biblical times, the Bible contains no direct call to abolish slavery. But the implications of the gospel, especially the ethic of love, stand in opposition to slavery.

Both slave and free are called upon to receive the gospel of Jesus Christ. In Christ, social distinctions such as slavery no longer apply (Gal. 3:28; Col. 3:11); in Christ all are brothers and sisters. The excitement of such new relationships is expressed by Paul: "Therefore you are no longer a slave but a son, and if a son, then an heir of God through Christ" (Gal. 4:7).

In a spiritual sense, people apart from Christ are slaves to sin. To commit sin is to demonstrate that sin has control of one's life (John 8:34). Christ can set us free from this kind of slavery (John 8:36)—to be obedient to Christ and to do righteousness (Rom. 6:16–18).

Paul spoke of himself as a "servant," a word sometimes rendered as "bond-servant" but frequently also as "slave" (Rom. 1:1; Titus 1:1). Christians, especially ministers, are not hired servants but slaves committed to service to Jesus. Slaves do not manage their own lives. People who call themselves slaves of Christ acknowledge that the Savior has power over them.

SLING

The sling was first developed and used by shepherds for protecting their livestock against wild animals. This was a simple weapon, composed generally of a small piece of leather or animal hide. Small stones or pebbles were generally used as ammunition in a sling. While the sling is a simple weapon in terms of construction, it is difficult to fire with accuracy. Only trained and experienced soldiers were equipped with slings.

Next to archers, the slingmen were the most effective long-range warriors in Old Testament times. The advantage of such a long-range weapon is illustrated by the

most famous sling story of all—David's victory over Goliath. The young, inexperienced David killed the giant because of his trust in God. David also had a decided advantage in the contest because Goliath was armed with a spear and a sword, both of which were short-range weapons.

Slingers were important elements in the Israelite army. The Benjamites also had a unit of 700 left-handed slingers who could "sling a stone at a hair's breadth and not miss" (Judg. 20:16).

SMYRNA [SMER nuh] *(myrrh)*

A city in western Asia Minor (modern Turkey) where one of the seven churches in the Book of Revelation was situated (Rev. 1:11; 2:8–11). Smyrna's superb natural harbor made the city an important commercial center. In spite of keen competition from the neighboring cities of Ephesus and Pergamum, Smyrna called itself "the first city of Asia."

As early as 195 B.C., Symrna foresaw the rising power of Rome and built a temple for pagan Roman worship. In 23 B.C., Smyrna was given the honor of building a temple to the Emperor Tiberius because of its years of faithfulness to Rome. Thus, the city became a center for the cult of emperor worship—a fanatical "religion" that later, under such emperors as Nero (ruled A.D. 54–68) and Domitian (ruled A.D. 81–96), brought on severe persecution for the early church. The apostle John encouraged the persecuted Christians of Smyrna to be "faithful unto death" and they would receive a "crown of life" (Rev. 2:10).

Smyrna, known today as Izmir, is the chief city of Anatolia and one of the strongest cities in modern Turkey. Excavations in the central part of Izmir have uncovered a Roman marketplace from the second century A.D.

S

SO [soh]

A king of Egypt whom Hoshea, the last king of Israel (ruled about 732–723 B.C.), tried to enlist as an ally against Assyria (2 Kin. 17:4). Some scholars identify So with Sib'e. In 720 B.C. this Egyptian king allied himself with Hanunu, the king of Gaza, against Sargon of Assyria. Sargon soundly defeated this coalition at the Battle of Raphia, about 20 miles (32 kilometers) south of Gaza. Other scholars regard So as the name of a city, Sais, in the western delta of Egypt. This was the residence of Tefnakhte, an Egyptian ruler during the days of King Hoshea. If this theory is correct, then 2 Kings 17:4 would read: "He had sent messengers to So [Sais], to the king of Egypt."

SODOM [SOD um]

A city at the southern end of the Dead Sea destroyed because of its wickedness (Gen. 10:19; Rom. 9:29). Together with her sister cities—Gomorrah, Admah, Zeboiim, and Zoar—Sodom formed the famous pentapolis of the plain or circle of the Jordan (Gen. 10:19; 13:10; 14:2) in the valley that surrounded the Dead Sea (Gen. 14:3).

Although Sodom was a notoriously wicked city, when Lot separated himself and his herdsmen from Abraham, he chose to pitch his tent toward Sodom (Gen. 13:5–13). This was because the fertile plain that surrounded the city "was well watered everywhere" (Gen. 13:10).

When Sodom was plundered by Chedorlaomer, the goods and captives he carried away had to be rescued by Abraham (Gen. 14:11, 21–24). However, the wickedness of the people of the city continued, and God finally had to destroy Sodom.

Fire and brimstone fell from heaven and consumed Sodom and Gomorrah and the other cities of the plain. When Lot's wife looked back at Sodom, she was changed instantly into a pillar of salt (Gen. 19:26).

Early tradition held that the northern end of the Dead Sea was the Valley of Sodom. But the geological conditions of the southern end of the Dead Sea matched those of the area around Sodom. Salt formations, asphalt, and sulfur are found in large quantities here. Many scholars believe the cities of the plain may be located beneath the shallow end of the Dead Sea.

The basin surrounding the shallow southern end of the Dead Sea is fed by five streams, including the Wadi Zered (Num. 21:12), which would have provided for a fertile, well-watered plain. In addition, Zoar, one of the cities of the plain (Gen. 13:10), is reported by the Jewish historian Josephus to have been visible during his time at the southern end of the sea. Other scholars have recently claimed that the most likely site for the cities of the plain is on the eastern shore of the Dead Sea opposite Masada.

The sin, vice, and infamy of Sodom and the judgment of God on this city is referred to often throughout the Bible (Is. 1:9–10; Ezek. 16:46–49; Amos 4:11; Rom. 9:29).

SODOMY [SAHD uh me]

Unnatural sexual intercourse, especially that between two males. These English words are derived from Sodom, an ancient city in the land of Canaan noted for such depraved activities. The men of Sodom came to Lot's house, demanding that he allow them to have sexual relations with two men inside (Gen. 19:5). But Lot refused. The next day Lot escaped from Sodom and God destroyed the city because of its great sin (Gen. 19).

SOLDIER

A member of a military force. Before Saul, Israel had no professional soldiers, although each tribe specialized in training its adult males in the use of a particular weapon (1 Chr. 12). With a few exceptions (Deut. 20:5–8), all men over the age of 20 were liable to be called to arms in emergencies (Num. 1:3). In addition to the militia, Saul chose certain capable fighters to serve him permanently (2 Sam. 13:15). David followed Saul's example in this (1 Sam. 22:2). Solomon boasted a large professional soldiery including cavalrymen, or troops on horseback—the first in Israel's history (1 Kin. 10:26).

These professional soldiers were sometimes referred to in more specific terms. A guard was a soldier assigned to protect a particular person or thing. A charioteer was a soldier who fought from a chariot. As warfare became more developed, chariots were made to hold a driver and one or more fighting soldiers (1 Kin. 22:34; 2 Chr. 18:33). A commander was a soldier who led other soldiers.

During New Testament times, the Romans had a very elaborate and complex army. Specific Roman soldiers are sometimes mentioned in the Bible. A centurion was a noncommissioned officer commanding at least 100 men. A sergeant was often the local policeman, enforcing the law, with punishment pronounced by the magistrate.

SOLOMON [SAHL uh mun] (peaceful)

The builder of the temple in Jerusalem and the first king of Israel to trade commercial goods profitably to other nations; author of much of the Book of Proverbs and perhaps also the author of the Song of Solomon and Ecclesiastes.

Solomon succeeded David his father as king of Israel. According to the chronology in 1 Kings 11:42, Solomon was about 20 years old when he was crowned. He assumed leadership of Israel at a time of great material and spiritual prosperity. During his 40-year reign (970–931 B.C.), he expanded his kingdom until it covered about 50,000 square miles—from Egypt in the south to Syria in the north to the borders of Mesopotamia in the east.

Solomon is usually remembered as a wise man. His Proverbs and his "Song of Songs" demonstrate his deep knowledge of the natural world (plants, animals, etc.). He also had a profound knowledge of human nature, as demonstrated by the two women who claimed the same child. His suggestion that the child be physically divided between the two was a masterful strategy for finding out who was the real mother (1 Kin. 3:16–28). Solomon's concern with the ethics of everyday life is evident in his Proverbs. They show that Solomon loved wisdom and was always trying to teach it to others. They also indicate he was a keen observer who could learn from the mistakes of others.

During his lifetime, Solomon's fame as a man of wisdom spread to surrounding lands, and leaders came from afar to hear him speak. When the queen of Sheba came to test his wisdom, he answered all her questions with ease. After she saw the extent of his empire and the vastness of his knowledge, she confessed that she had underestimated him (2 Chr. 9:1–12).

One of Solomon's first major feats was the construction of the temple in Jerusalem as a place for worship of the God of Israel. The task was enormous, involving much planning and many workers. A work force of 30,000 was employed in cutting timber from the cedars of Lebanon. Also working on this massive project were 80,000 cutters of stone in the quarries of Jerusalem, 70,000 ordinary workers, and many superintendents. Gold, silver, and other precious metals were imported from other lands. Hiram, king of Tyre, sent architects and other craftsmen to assist with the project.

The building was completed after

seven years. The temple was famous not for its size—since it was relatively small—but for the quality of its elaborate workmanship (1 Kin. 6–7). After completing the temple, Solomon built the palace complex, a series of five structures that took 13 years to complete. He also built many cities to assist the development of his trade empire. Among these were Tadmor (also called Palmyra) and Baalath (also called Baalbek) in Syria. To protect his kingdom, he built fortresses and lodgings for his army. These fortifications, especially the ones at Jerusalem, Gezer, Megiddo, and Hazor, had strong double walls and massive gateways.

Trade with other nations was another of Solomon's contributions to the nation of Israel. The international situation was favorable for a strong leader to emerge in Israel; traditional centers of strength in Egypt and Syria were at an all-time low. Solomon entered into trade agreements with a number of nations, increasing Israel's wealth and prestige.

Although Solomon had a strong army, he relied upon a system of treaties with his neighbors to keep the peace. Egypt was allied with Israel through the marriage of Solomon to the daughter of the pharaoh. The seafaring cities of Tyre and Sidon were also united to Israel by trade agreements.

Some of Israel's trade was conducted overland by way of camel caravans. But the most significant trade was by sea across the Mediterranean Sea through an alliance with Tyre. Solomon's ships apparently went as far west as Spain to bring back silver.

Solomon's reign brought changes not only to Israel but also to his own life. Near the end of his life, the king lost the ideals of his youth, becoming restless and unsatisfied. The Book of Ecclesiastes, proclaiming that "all is vanity" ("meaningless," NIV), supports the view that the world's wisest man had become a pathetic figure in his old age.

Solomon's greatest sin was his loss of devotion to the God of the Hebrew people. In this, he fell victim to his own trade agreements. By custom, beautiful women were awarded to the most powerful member of a treaty to seal the covenant. The constant influx of wives and concubines in Solomon's court led eventually to his downfall. Thus, Solomon broke the Mosaic Law and violated the warning not to stray from the path of his father David.

The large number of foreign women in Solomon's court made many demands upon the king. He allowed these "outsiders" to practice their pagan religions. The result was that Jerusalem, and even its holy temple, was the scene of pagan practices and idol worship (1 Kin. 11:1–13).

Solomon's own faith was weakened. Eventually he approved of, and even participated in, these idolatrous acts. The example he set for the rest of the nation must have been demoralizing. This unfortunate error was a severe blow to the security of Solomon's throne and to the nation he had built.

Years before Solomon's death, his heavy taxation of the people brought unrest and rebellion. Surrounding nations began to marshal their forces to free themselves of Israel's tyranny, but the most serious uprising came from within the nation itself. When Solomon's son Rehoboam ascended the throne after his father, Jeroboam, a young leader who had been exiled to Egypt, returned to lead a successful civil war against him. The result was a division of Solomon's united kingdom into two separate nations—the southern kingdom of Judah and the northern kingdom of Israel.

SOSTHENES [SOS thuh knees]

The ruler of the synagogue at Corinth during the apostle Paul's first visit to this city (Acts 18:17). When the Roman ruler of the area refused to deal with the angry mob's charges against Paul, they beat Sosthenes. This may be the same Sosthenes as the one greeted by Paul in one of his Corinthian letters (1 Cor. 1:1). If so, he must have become a Christian some time after the mob scene in his city.

SOUL

The inner life of a person, the seat of emotions, and the center of human personality. The first use of the word *soul* in the Old Testament expresses this meaning: "And the LORD God formed man of the dust of the ground, and breathed into his nostrils the breath of life; and man became a living being (soul)" (Gen. 2:7). This means more than being given physical life; the biblical writer declares that man became a "living soul," or a person, a human being, one distinct from all other animals.

SPARROW

Sparrow is the name given to several different species of birds in the Bible. They ate grain and insects and gathered in noisy flocks. The psalmist wrote, "I . . . am like a sparrow alone on the housetop" (Ps. 102:7). These tiny birds were such social creatures that a lone sparrow was the symbol of deep loneliness.

In Jesus' time sparrows sold for a very low price—two for a copper coin, five for two copper coins (Matt. 10:29; Luke 12:6). Perhaps this was the temple price, because they were considered a poor man's sacrifice. Those who could not afford to sacrifice a sheep or a goat might bring a sparrow. Moses once directed healed lepers to bring two sparrows to the temple for a cleansing ceremony (Lev. 14:1–7).

Sometimes it seems that only God cares for sparrows. Cats, hawks, and naughty boys prey upon them. People complain about how they multiply, considering them pests. Yet, Jesus declared, "Not one of them falls to the ground apart from your Father's will" (Matt. 10:29). We may not esteem the little sparrow, but the Son of God used it to illustrate our heavenly Father's watchful care: "You are of more value than many sparrows" (Matt. 10:31; Luke 12:7).

SPICES

Sweet-smelling plant substances used as incense, holy anointing oil, cosmetics, and perfume. Such spices were also used to prepare bodies for burial. Myrrh, cinnamon, calamus (or aromatic cane), and cassia were mixed with pure olive oil to make a holy anointing oil (Ex. 30:23–33). This was used to anoint items of worship in the temple or tabernacle sanctuary. Holy anointing oil was also used to consecrate Aaron, the high priest, and his sons for their service in the priesthood.

Stacte, onycha, and galbanum were mixed with pure frankincense to make incense or perfume. This was placed in the tabernacle of the congregation where God would meet with Moses (Ex. 30:34–36). Spices were also used to prepare bodies for burial (2 Chr. 16:14). Nicodemus brought "a mixture of myrrh and aloes, about a hundred pounds" (John 19:39), with which he prepared the body of Jesus for burial after His death on the cross.

Most spices used in Canaan came from southern Arabia (Ezek. 27:22), but some came from Syria (Gen. 37:25). Spices were valuable and expensive, and they were considered a luxury among the Jewish people. The disciples rebuked a woman for her indulgence when she anointed Jesus with a costly oil. But Jesus replied, "Let her alone. . . . She has done

S

what she could. She has come beforehand to anoint my body for burial" (Mark 14:6, 8).

SPIKENARD

A costly oil derived from the dried roots and stems of the nard, an herb of Asia. This oil was used as a liquid or made into an ointment. Solomon praised the fragrance of spikenard (Song 1:12; 4:13–14). Spikenard was imported from India in alabaster boxes. These were stored and used only for special occasions. When household guests arrived, they were usually anointed with this oil. Jesus was anointed on two occasions as an honored guest (Mark 14:3; John 12:3).

Many spikes grew from a single nard

SPIRITUAL GIFTS

root that produced clusters of pink flowers. The stems were covered with hair, giving them a woolly appearance. Some translations of the Bible refer to spikenard as nard.

SPIRITUAL GIFTS

Special gifts bestowed by the Holy Spirit upon Christians for the purpose of building up the church. The list of spiritual gifts in 1 Corinthians 12:8–10 includes wisdom, knowledge, faith, healing, miracles, prophecy, discerning of spirits, speaking in tongues, and interpretation of tongues. Similar lists appear in Ephesians 4:7–13 and Romans 12:3–8.

The apostle Paul indicated that these gifts are equally valid but not equally valuable. Their value is determined by their worth to the church. In dealing with this matter, he used the analogy of the human body. All members of the body have functions, Paul declared, but some are more important than others. The service of each Christian should be in proportion to the gifts that person possesses (1 Cor. 12–14).

Since these gifts are gifts of grace, according to Paul, their use must be controlled by the principle of love—the greatest of all spiritual gifts (1 Cor. 13).

STAR OF BETHLEHEM

The heavenly sign by which God announced the birth of Christ. The star is mentioned only in the Gospel of Matthew in connection with the visit of the wise men (Matt. 2:2, 7, 9–10). "Where is He who has been born King of the Jews? For we have seen His star in the East and have come to worship Him" (v. 2). This star, observed by wise men from the East (probably Mesopotamia), may be what the Mesopotamian prophet Balaam refers to in Numbers 24:17: "A Star shall come out of Jacob."

Various attempts have been made to explain the star in scientific terms. Since the wise men were Babylonian astrologers, it is reasonable to assume they were people who had seen the star during their regular observations of the heavens. Those who were familiar with the night sky would readily identify any new object.

Some scholars suggest that a supernova, or exploding star, recorded by Chinese astronomers at about the time of Christ, might have led the wise men to Bethlehem. Others argue that a rare alignment of planets in the sky signaled a highly unusual event to the astrologers. The appearance of a meteor or an unidentified comet has also been suggested.

The event as recorded in Matthew indicates the star was a supernatural phenomenon. The Bible clearly declares that the star "went before them, till it came and stood over where the young Child was" (Matt. 2:9). None of the proposed natural explanations fits this description adequately. Matthew obviously understood the star as an occurrence beyond the reach of rationalistic explanations. At the same time, our attention should be focused not on the star of Bethlehem, but on the Messiah, Jesus Christ, whose birth the star proclaimed.

STEPHEN

One of the first seven deacons of the early church and the first Christian martyr. In the period following Pentecost, the number of Christians in the New Testament church grew steadily. Followers were eventually recruited not only from among the Jews in Palestine but also from among the Jews in Greek settlements. The church had to appoint several men to handle the work of providing aid to these needy Christians.

Stephen was one of the first seven "good and worthy men" chosen to provide relief to these needy Christians from Greek backgrounds. Since Stephen is

S

mentioned first in the list of the seven administrators, he was probably the most important leader in this group. Although they are not specifically named as deacons, these seven men are considered to be the forerunners of the office of deacon that developed later in the early church. Stephen assumed a place of prominence among these seven leaders as the church grew (Acts 6:7).

Stephen was probably critical of the system of Old Testament laws, claiming they had already lost their effectiveness because they had reached fulfillment in Christ. This viewpoint, which Stephen argued very skillfully, brought him into conflict with powerful leaders among the Jewish people. Stephen became well-known as a preacher and a miracle-worker (Acts 6:8). His work was so effective that renewed persecution of the Christians broke out.

Members of certain Jewish synagogues felt that Stephen had blasphemed Moses and God. They accused him of being disloyal to the temple and rejecting Moses. He was also accused of hostility toward Judaism—a charge that had never been made before against other disciples. In debates the Jews were no match for Stephen; even Saul was outwitted by him. Thus, they resorted to force.

Stephen was arrested and brought before the Sanhedrin, the Jewish council, where charges were placed against him. False witnesses testified against him. The high priest then asked Stephen if these things were true. Stephen was not dismayed. When he stood before them his face was "as the face of an angel" (Acts 6:15).

The lengthy speech Stephen made in his own defense is reported in detail in Acts 7:2–53. Stephen summarized Old Testament teachings, showing how God had guided Israel toward a specific goal. He reviewed Israel's history in such a

way that he replied to all the charges made against him without actually denying anything. This amounted to a criticism of the Sanhedrin itself. Stephen denounced the council as "stiff-necked and uncircumcised in heart and ears" and accused them of resisting the Holy Spirit. Then he charged that they had killed Christ, just as their ancestors had killed the prophets. He accused them of failing to keep their own law (Acts 7:51–53).

Stephen's speech enraged the Sanhedrin so that they were "cut to the heart, and they gnashed at him with their teeth" (Acts 7:54). At this moment Stephen had a vision of God in heaven, with Jesus on His right hand. Stephen's fate was sealed when he reported this vision to his enemies. The crowd rushed upon him, dragged him out of the city, and stoned him to death (Acts 7:55–58).

Among the people consenting to Stephen's death that day was Saul, who later became the apostle Paul—great Christian missionary to the Gentiles. As he was being stoned, Stephen asked God not to charge his executioners with the sin of his death (Acts 7:59–60).

Stephen's martyrdom was followed by a general persecution that forced the disciples to flee from Jerusalem into the outlying areas. This scattering led to the preaching of the gospel first to the Samaritans and then to the Gentiles in the nations surrounding Palestine.

STEWARD

A person entrusted with caring for a superior's goods. In the Old Testament, a steward was over an entire household. He was responsible for managing the householder's material goods (Gen. 43:19). In the New Testament the word *steward* refers to a guardian or curator (Matt. 20:8; Gal. 4:2) in addition to its Old Testament meaning as a manager or superintendent of a household (Luke 8:2–3; 1 Cor. 4:1–2).

The apostle Paul called himself a steward of Christ's household, responsible to Christ the Master for carrying out an assigned task—to preach the gospel to the Gentiles. All Christians are stewards under Christ (1 Pet. 4:10).

STOICISM [STOW uh siz em]

The doctrine of the Stoics, a Greek school of philosophy that taught that human beings should be free from passion, unmoved by joy or grief, and submissive to natural law, calmly accepting all things as the result of divine will. Stoicism was one of the most influential Greek schools of philosophy in the New Testament period. It took its name from the Stoa Poikile, the portico or lecture place in Athens where its founder, Zeno, taught.

The Stoics believed that people are part of the universe, which itself is dominated by reason. God is identified with the world-soul and so inhabits everything. Therefore, one's goal is to identify oneself with this universal reason that determines destiny, to find one's proper place in the natural order of things. Since people cannot change this grand design, it is best for them to cooperate and to take their part in the world order. Moreover, they must live above any emotional involvement with life, exemplifying a detached virtue in serving others. Above all, they must be self-sufficient, living life with dignity and pride.

The apostle Paul used the word *self-sufficient* in a radically different sense in Philippians 4:11. Here Paul spoke of the believer's self-sufficiency in God. Paul's speech on the Areopagus, or Mars' Hill (Acts 17:16–34), interacts with Stoic ideas, arguing that the highest good is not internal (in our union with nature) but external (in a right relationship with God).

In his address Paul quoted one of the Stoic poets (Aratus), who said, "For we are also His offspring" (Acts 17:28). Some of these philosophers ridiculed Paul, but others invited him to address them again about the Christ in whom he believed so strongly (Acts 17:32).

STONE

A hardened, granite-like mass formed from soil, clay, and minerals. The soil of Palestine was rough and rocky. The most common stones were limestone (Is. 27:9) and flint. Because wood was scarce, city walls, houses (Lev. 14:45; Amos 5:11), palaces (1 Kin. 7:1, 9), temples (1 Kin. 6:7), courtyards, columns, and streets were built of hewn stone.

The abundance of stones cleared from fields (Is. 5:2) provided the people with excellent weapons against their enemies. Stones were thrown on an enemy's field to ruin it and were used to stop up his wells (2 Kin. 3:19, 25; Eccl. 3:5). Knives were made from flint stones. Larger weapons of war, such as slings (1 Sam. 17:40, 49), catapults (2 Chr. 26:15), and bows also made use of stones. Stoning was a common form of capital punishment. Stones served also as boundary and treaty markers (Gen. 31:46; Deut. 19:14; 27:17; Job 24:2) for individuals and nations.

In addition to their practical uses, stones were also used for sacred, spiritual purposes. Memorials were built from large stones to mark an unusual event (Gen. 28:18; 31:45; Josh. 4:9; 1 Sam. 7:12). Stone mounds also marked graves (2 Sam. 18:17). Small, smooth stones occasionally became a part of the Israelites' idol worship (Is. 57:6). The Hebrew people were apparently influenced by surrounding pagan cultures and believed that meteorites were sacred. While the Gentiles believed that meteorites talked and served as protection from evil, the Israelites often dedicated them to God

(Gen. 28:18–22; Is. 19:19) but did not worship them as pagan nations did.

In a figurative way, stones imply firmness and strength (Gen. 49:24) as well as insensibility and hardness (1 Sam. 25:37; Ezek. 11:19). "Jesus Christ Himself being the chief cornerstone" (Eph. 2:20) describes best the stone's symbolism for Christ as the strength and foundation of Christianity. The references to the cut stone from the mountainside in Daniel 2:34–35, 45 have been interpreted to represent Christ and the church.

STONING

The usual method of capital punishment in ancient Israel. People who broke specific statutes of the Law of Moses were put to death by stoning. Stoning was usually carried out by the men of the community (Deut. 21:21), upon the testimony of at least two witnesses, who would then cast the first stones (Deut. 17:5–7; John 8:7; Acts 7:58). Stoning usually took place outside the settlement or camp (Lev. 24:14, 23; 1 Kin. 21:10, 13).

Acts punishable by stoning were certain cases of disobedience (Josh. 7:25), child sacrifice (Lev. 20:2), consultation with magicians (Lev. 20:27), blasphemy (John 10:31–32), Sabbath-breaking (Num. 15:32–36), the worship of false gods (Deut. 13:10), rebellion against parents (Deut. 21:21), and adultery (Ezek. 16:40).

Jesus once encountered a woman who was about to be stoned because she had been found guilty of adultery. Her accusers walked away when He declared, "He who is without sin among you, let him throw a stone at her first" (John 8:7).

STORAGE CITY, STOREHOUSE

A supply depot or warehouse for the storage of government supplies, such as food, treasures, and military equipment (1 Chr. 26:15; 27:25; 2 Chr. 11:11). The difference between a storehouse and a storage city may be only one of size or complexity.

The Hebrew slaves in Egypt were forced to build Pithom and Raamses, "supply cities" for Pharaoh (Ex. 1:11; store cities in REB, NIV; treasure cities in KJV; storage cities in NASB). Various kings of the Israelites also built storage cities. These included Solomon (1 Kin. 9:19; 2 Chr. 8:4, 6), who built facilities to house his chariots, horses, and cavalry; Baasha (2 Chr. 16:5–6); Jehoshaphat (2 Chr. 17:12); and Hezekiah (2 Chr. 32:27–29).

The concept of the storage city or storehouse is at least as old as the time of Joseph. He established a food reserve that saved Egypt from famine (Gen. 41). During seven years of plenty, Joseph had the Egyptian farmers store one-fifth of their produce. Then, when seven years of famine struck, the grain in the storehouses kept starvation from the land.

In the ancient world, storehouses were sometimes situated underground. Oil and wine were often kept in cellars. At Megiddo, archaeologists discovered a large underground silo pit for grain storage. This pit, with a capacity of almost 13,000 bushels of grain, apparently dates back to the time of King Solomon.

The prophet Malachi accused the people of his day of robbing God by withholding from Him their tithes and offerings (Mal. 3:8–9). Then he said, "Bring all the tithes into the storehouse" (Mal. 3:10). "Storehouse" apparently refers to a special treasury-chamber, probably within the temple precincts and administered by Levites.

SUICIDE

The act of taking one's own life. The word *suicide* does not occur in the Bible. Neither are there any laws relating to it. But the Bible does give several examples of suicide, including Saul and his armorbearer (1 Sam. 31:4–5); and Zimri, king of Israel, who "burned the king's house down upon himself with fire" (1 Kin. 16:18), when Tirzah was besieged. In the New Testament, Judas killed himself because of his shame and grief at betraying Jesus (Matt. 27:5).

Human life is sacred, since we are created in God's image (Gen. 1:27). God as the Creator has power over all existence. He alone should control life, whether it continues or stops (Job 1:21; 1 Cor. 6:19).

SUMER [SOO mehr]

The southern division of ancient Babylonia, consisting primarily of the fertile plain between the Tigris and Euphrates rivers. This area is now the southern part of modern Iraq.

In the Old Testament, Sumer is the territory referred to as "Shinar" (Gen. 10:10; Is. 11:11; Zech. 5:11) or Chaldea (Jer. 50:10; Ezek. 16:29). The term *Shinar* is also used to describe the land of the great tyrant and empire builder Nimrod, who founded his kingdom in Babel, Erech (Sumerian Uruk), Accad (Akkad or Agade), and Calneh, "in the land of Shinar" (Gen. 10:10). The Tower of Babel was also built "in the land of Shinar" (Gen. 11:2), or Sumer.

Archaeologists believe the inhabitants of ancient Sumer, or the Sumerians, developed the first high civilization in the history of mankind, before 3000 B.C. The Sumerians were the first people to develop writing, consisting of a form of Cuneiform script. Major cities of ancient Sumer included the biblical Ur (Gen. 11:28, 31; 15:7), the city from which Abraham migrated.

Before 2100 B.C. Sumer was conquered by invading tribesmen from the west and north. A mighty warrior named Sargon (later known as Sargon I, Sargon the Great, and Sargon of Akkad) conquered this area and extended his empire from the Persian Gulf to the Mediterranean Sea. He founded a new capital city,

Agade, which was, for more than half a century, the richest and most powerful capital in the world. This magnificent capital was destroyed during the reign of Naram-Sin, Sargon's grandson, by the Guti, semibarbaric mountain tribes.

Sumer enjoyed a brief revival at Ur (about 2050 B.C.), only to decline before the rise of the Elamites, a people to their east. Finally, in about 1720 B.C., Hammurapi of Babylon united Sumer (the southern division of ancient Babylon) and Akkad (the northern division of ancient Babylon) into one empire. This conquest by Hammurapi marked the end of ancient Sumer. But the cultural and intellectual impact of the Sumerians continued until after the Persians became the dominant force in this part of the ancient world.

SUN, WORSHIP OF

A form of pagan idolatry commonly practiced in the ancient world, especially by the Assyrians, Chaldeans (Babylonians), Egyptians, and Phoenicians. Worship of the sun and other heavenly bodies was specifically forbidden among the Hebrew people (Deut. 4:19). But a few cases of this form of idolatry did occur among the nation of Israel during their long history.

King Manasseh of Judah built altars for worship of "all the host of heaven" during his administration (2 Kin. 21:5). The prophet Ezekiel also portrayed the abomination of men who had rejected the temple of the Lord and had turned their faces toward the east to worship the rising sun (Ezek. 8:15–16).

SUNDIAL OF AHAZ

A time-keeping device by which God gave Hezekiah the sign that he would be healed (2 Kin. 20:1–11; Is. 38:4–8). Hezekiah asked that the sun's shadow go backward ten degrees or steps as a sign of his healing. This "dial" was probably not a small disk, as modern readers might suppose, but an escalating stairway on which the sun cast its shadow higher and higher during the day. The biblical writers identified this stairway with Ahaz, probably because it was constructed during his reign.

SURETY

A pledge made to secure against default; one who contracts to assume the debts of another in the event of default. The practice of one man standing as surety for another apparently was prevalent in Old Testament times, judging from the frequency with which the Book of Proverbs warns against its dangers (Prov. 17:18; 22:26). And certainly as financial advice, the proverbial warnings are sound.

But there is a surety more significant than a financial pledge. Judah, for example, pledged to be surety for Benjamin (Gen. 43:9), thus taking responsibility for the life of his brother. This is the kind of far-reaching responsibility the psalmist had in mind when he asked God

SUN, WORSHIP OF

to stand as surety for him in the face of his oppressors (Ps. 119:122). This is the kind of responsibility Christ took by dying and becoming for all people "a surety of a better covenant" (Heb. 7:22; guarantee in NIV, NASB; guarantees in REB).

SWADDLING BAND

A long, narrow strip of cloth used to wrap a newborn baby. To swaddle a child was to wrap an infant in strips of cloth, much like narrow bandages. This was believed to ensure the correct early development of the limbs. Thus, swaddling was a mark of parental love and care, while the need for swaddling symbolized the humble, dependent position of the newborn child (Ezek. 16:4).

Although she could offer Jesus no better crib than an animal's manger, Mary showed her mother's love by wrapping her baby in swaddling clothes (Luke 2:7, 12). The baby Jesus in swaddling bands reminds us of the great humility of our Lord in becoming a human being for our sakes.

SWINE

The Hebrew people had nothing to do with pigs, but these animals still received much attention in the Bible. In Psalm 80:13, Israel's enemies were likened to a "boar out of the woods." Vicious wild pigs (boars) ranged throughout Canaan. Owners of vineyards hated them, because they devoured grapes and trampled their vines. Dogs and men alike feared their razor-sharp tusks. In modern times, the boar is the largest game animal in Israel.

Domesticated pigs (swine) were also raised in Canaan—by Gentiles or unorthodox Jews. Pigs were ceremonially unclean, supposedly because they did not "chew the cud." The symbol of greed and filth, pigs symbolized a person's unredeemed nature (2 Pet. 2:22). Jesus told

a story of a prodigal son who really hit bottom when he had to take care of hogs and even eat food intended for them (Luke 15:15–16).

SYCHAR [SIGH car]

A city of Samaria mentioned in connection with Jesus' visit to Jacob's Well (John 4:5). The reference indicates it was not a well-known spot—"a city of Samaria which is called Sychar." The fame of Sychar is associated with Jesus' conversation with the woman who came there to draw water, her conversion, and the conversion of many of the Samaritans during His two days in the area. Many scholars identify Sychar with ancient Shechem (Gen. 33:18). Jacob's Well, one of the best attested sites in Palestine, is situated on the eastern edge of the valley that separates Mount Gerizim from Mount Ebal.

SYNAGOGUE

A congregation of Jews for worship or religious study. The word *synagogue* comes from the Greek *synagoge* (literally, "a leading or bringing together"), which refers to any assembly or gathering of people for secular or religious purposes. Eventually the term came to refer exclusively to an assembly of Jewish people.

The synagogue was a place where local groups of Jews in cities and villages anywhere could gather for the reading and explanation of the Jewish sacred Scriptures and for prayer. The original emphasis was not on preaching but instruction in the Law of Moses.

A distinction must be made between synagogue worship and tabernacle or temple worship. The tabernacle of Moses' day was enclosed by a fence of curtains. None but the priests dared enter this area. The people brought their animals for sacrifice to the gate of the court but could go no further. The later temples of Solomon, Zerubbabel, and Herod

S

(the temple of Jesus' day) did have courts or porches where the people could pray or have discussions (Matt. 26:55; Luke 2:46; Acts 2:46), but the temple precincts proper were for the priests only.

In synagogues, on the other hand, the people took part in worship, reading of the Scriptures, and prayer. By New Testament times, synagogues were very numerous and popular. They became centers of community activity, playing a number of roles.

Sometimes they were local courts of justice that could sentence the offender as well as inflict the punishment of scourging (Matt. 10:17; 23:34). The synagogue was also an elementary school for teaching children to read. It was, no doubt, a center of social life for the Jewish community.

In Jesus' day synagogues were common even in the villages. They must have been well established with the customary officials and order of worship (Luke 4:14–30; 8:41). Paul found synagogues in cities throughout the Roman Empire (Acts 9:2, Damascus; 13:5, Salamis; 13:14, Antioch in Pisidia; 14:1, Iconium; 17:1, Thessalonica; 17:10, Berea; 17:16–17, Athens; 19:1, 8, Ephesus). This shows that the synagogue had existed for a long time.

A synagogue could not be formed unless there were at least ten Jewish men in the community. Some synagogues paid ten unemployed men a small sum to be present at every service to be sure this rule was met. A board of elders made up of devout and respected men of the community regulated the policies of the synagogue. There could be one or more rulers. They were appointed by the elders. Their duty was to attend to matters concerning the building and the planning of the services.

The minister (chazzan) of the synagogue had several duties. He had charge of the sacred scrolls; he attended to the lamps; and he kept the building clean. If an offender was found guilty by the council of elders, the chazzan administered the number of lashes prescribed for the scourging. During the week, the chazzan taught elementary children how to read.

Before each service the ruler chose a capable person to read the Scripture lesson, to lead in prayer, and to preach or comment on the Scripture. Jesus was selected for this office in the synagogue in Nazareth (Luke 4:16–20). The Scriptures were written in ancient Hebrew. By Jesus' day the people spoke Aramaic, a language related to Hebrew but different enough to call for an interpreter.

Synagogue worship has influenced both Christian and Moslem worship. The earliest Christians were Jews. Therefore, church worship followed the synagogue pattern with Scripture reading, prayer, and a sermon. In the seventh century A.D., Muhammad learned much from Jewish customs and also spent some time at Bosora or Bostra in the desert east of Gilead where a Christian bishopric was located. Hence, the mosques of Islam reflect worship patterns from both Jewish and Christian services.

SYRACUSE [SEAR ih coos]

A Greek city on the southeast coast of the island of Sicily (Acts 28:12). The apostle Paul spent three days in Syracuse before he proceeded on to Rome as a prisoner.

SYRIA [SIHR ih uh]

A major nation northeast of Palestine that served as a political threat to the nations of Judah and Israel during much of their history. The name *Syria* comes from the Greek language. The Hebrew language of the Old Testament uses the word *Aram* for the region. Almost 2 percent of the Old Testament was originally written in the Aramaic language.

The boundaries of Syria changed often in biblical times. Often a particular group of Syrians such as those of Damascus or Zobah or else some combination of cities or regions are referred to as "Syria" or "the Syrians" in the Old Testament. Most of these references designate the region that makes up the southeastern part of the modern nation of Syria.

The Syrians (Arameans) were part of the massive migrations of population groups that occurred from about 3000 to 2100 B.C. They eventually settled in several parts of the ancient world, including much of northern Mesopotamia. One group, probably seminomads from the Arabian desert fringes, settled in force in the area north and east of Canaan. It is this group that the Israelites had most contact with during the time of the Israelite kings.

Gradually, these settlements produced the Aramean states known as Hamath, Zobah, and Damascus, each of which was an independent city-state. At times all of these states were allied together against a common threat, such as that posed by the Assyrians. One or another of these "states" was often at war with Israel, until the Assyrians, under one of their kings, Tiglath-Pileser III (745–727 B.C.), defeated Syria and annexed it to the Assyrian Empire.

After this conquest, many Syrians were exiled to various parts of the Assyrian Empire, just as many citizens of the northern kingdom of Israel were carried away (2 Kin. 17:23). Some Syrians were even forced to settle in Samaria (2 Kin. 17:24). Thereafter Syria was ruled as a province by Babylonia, Persia, the Seleucids, and Rome in successive conquests by these ancient world powers.

In New Testament times, Syria was a Roman province, linked with Cilicia. Syrians were among those who first responded to Jesus' preaching and healing ministry (Matt. 4:23–24). The gospel spread rapidly in Syria. Many of the places mentioned in the Book of Acts (Damascus, Antioch, Seleucia, Caesarea Philippi) were located in Syria.

Saul of Tarsus (the apostle Paul) was converted in Syria, while he was on the road to Damascus (Acts 9:3). His first missionary journey began from the great church at Antioch of Syria (Acts 13:1–3), and he traveled through Syria on several occasions (Acts 15:41; 18:18; Gal. 1:21).

SYRO-PHOENICIAN [sigh row feh KNEE shun]

A Gentile woman whose daughter was healed by Jesus (Mark 7:26). She was from Phoenicia, a nation northeast of Palestine that had been incorporated into the Roman province of Syria—thus the term, Syro-Phoenician. Although she was not a citizen of the Jewish nation, she believed Jesus could heal her daughter. Jesus commended her because of her great faith.

S

TAANACH [TAY uh nak]

An ancient royal city of the Canaanites whose king was conquered and slain by Joshua, but whose inhabitants were not driven out of the land (Josh. 12:21; Judg. 1:27). Tanaach was occupied by the tribe of Manasseh and was assigned to the Levites of the family of Kohath (Josh. 17:11–13; 21:25, Tanach in KJV). According to the Song of Deborah, the kings of Canaan fought against Deborah and Barak at Taanach, but they were defeated (Judg. 5:19).

The ruins of Taanach, Tell Taannek, are on the southwestern edge of the Valley of Jezreel about 5 miles (8 kilometers) southeast of Megiddo.

TABERNACLE [TAB ur nack el]

The tent that served as a place of worship for the nation of Israel during their early history. On Mount Sinai, after the Lord had given the commandments to Moses, He instructed Moses to construct the tabernacle. This was to be a center for worship and a place where the people could focus upon the presence of the Lord.

This tabernacle was to replace the temporary tent that had been pitched outside the camp (Ex. 33:7–11). God began the description of this building by giving His people the opportunity to participate in its construction. They did this by giving an offering of the needed materials, including a combination of rare and beautiful fabrics and precious metals, along with supplies easily available in the wilderness.

After describing the offering (Ex. 25:1–9), the Lord proceeded to specify in minute detail the pattern for the tabernacle. He began by giving a description of the holiest item in the entire structure: the ark of the covenant (Ex. 25:10–22). Other items in the tabernacle for which the Lord gave minute construction details included the seven-branched lampstand (Ex. 25:31–39); the intricate curtains of the tabernacle (Ex. 26:1–25); the veils, and the screen (Ex. 26:1–37); the large bronze altar of burnt offering (Ex. 27:1–8); and the hangings for the courtyard (Ex. 27:9–19).

The description of the actual building of the tabernacle is recorded in Exodus 35–40. The workers were first enlisted. Then the building of each item of the tabernacle is described in Exodus 36–39. The record of the tabernacle's construction occurs in Exodus 40. Up to this time, the nation of Israel had used a temporary tent called the tabernacle of the congregation; it is mentioned in Exodus 33:7–11. The tabernacle continued to be called the tabernacle of the congregation, among other names, after its construction. When the Israelites pitched camp in the wilderness, the tabernacle was to be placed in the center, with the Levites camping next to it (Num. 1:53). Then the tribes were to be arrayed in specific order on the four sides of the tabernacle (Num. 2).

Responsibilities for the care and moving of the tabernacle were delegated to various families of the tribe of Levi (Num. 1:50–52; Numbers 3–4). The Levitical family of Kohath was to disassemble the structure and cover the tabernacle furnishings with the badger skins. The tapestries were the responsibility of the family of Gershon. Merari's family had charge of the boards, pillars, foundations, pins, and cords. All these Levitical families were commissioned to care for the sanctuary.

During the conquest of the land of Canaan by the Israelites the tabernacle remained at Gilgal, while the ark of the covenant was evidently carried from place to place with the armies of Israel. The ark was reported at the crossing of the Jordan (Josh. 3:6), at Gilgal (Josh.

4:11), at the conquest of Jericho (Josh. 6:4), at the campaigns against Ai (Josh. 7:6), and at Mount Ebal (Josh. 8:33).

The tabernacle was finally placed on the site it was to occupy during the duration of the period of conquest and judges, at Shiloh (Josh. 18:1). Here the tribes were assigned their territorial allotments.

As the years passed, certain other structures were added to the tabernacle while it remained at Shiloh. These included living quarters for the priests and Levites who served at the tabernacle. By the end of the period of the judges, during the administration of Eli, at least some of the attendants lived on the premises (1 Sam. 3:3).

The New Testament uses some terminology and concepts drawn directly from the tabernacle. The supreme event of all the ages is the existence of God's Son in human form. The Bible declares that the Word became flesh and "tabernacled" (Greek word rendered as "dwelt" in the NKJV) among us (John 1:14). In his final speech, Stephen accepted the Old Testament account of the tabernacle as historical (Acts 7:44). In Revelation 13:6 and 15:5, reference is made to the heavenly tabernacle. Practically every feature of the tabernacle is found in the Book of Hebrews.

TABERNACLES, FEAST OF

A festival observed on the fifteenth day of the seventh month to celebrate the completion of the autumn harvest. Features of the celebration included a holy convocation on the first and eighth days, and the offering of many animal sacrifices. The Israelites were also commanded to live in booths made of palm and willow trees during the festival to commemorate their period of wilderness wandering when they lived in temporary shelters. This feast is also known as the Feast of Booths.

References to the Feast of Tabernacles in the Bible include Exodus 23:16; 34:22; Leviticus 23:33–36; 39–43; Numbers 29:12–32; Deuteronomy 16:13–16; Ezra 3:4; and Zechariah 14:16, 18–19.

TABOR, MOUNT [TAY buhr]

A mountain of limestone in the northeastern part of the Valley of Jezreel (Josh. 19:22). Now called Jebel et-Tur, Tabor is 5.5 miles (8.8 kilometers) southeast of Nazareth and about 10 miles (16 kilometers) southwest of the Sea of Galilee. Mount Tabor rises some 1,350 feet (411 meters) above the plain. It rises steeply to form a dome-shaped summit. No other mountains are adjacent to Mount Tabor.

Because of its strategic location and commanding height, Mount Tabor frequently was fortified with protective walls. In 218 B.C. Antiochus III captured a town on the summit and fortified it. As a Jewish general, Josephus added a defensive rampart to the fortress in A.D. 66. The remains of this structure can still be seen today.

Situated where the borders of Issachar, Zebulun, and Naphtali meet (Josh. 19:22), Mount Tabor played an important role in Israel's history. Here Barak gathered 10,000 men of Naphtali and Zebulun and attacked the Canaanite armies of Sisera at Megiddo (Judg. 4:6, 12, 14; 5:18). Also at Tabor the Midianite kings Zebah and Zalmunna killed the brothers of Gideon (Judg. 8:18–19). During the time of the prophets, the top of the mountain was a sanctuary for idolatry (Hos. 5:1). In fact, the mountain may have been the site of a pagan sanctuary from ancient times (Deut. 33:19).

TADMOR [TAD mohr]

A city known to the Greeks and Romans as Palmyra, about 120 miles (193 kilometers) northeast of Damascus (1 Kin. 9:18). The city was built on an oasis in the Syrian desert, astride the main east-west trade route that ran from Mesopotamia to Canaan. The city was also situated on the main north-south trade route. Because of its strategic location, Tadmor became an important commercial center and military outpost.

According to 2 Chronicles 8:4, Solomon "built Tadmor in the wilderness." This city, which marked the northeastern boundary of his empire, helped Solomon control the entire region. After Solomon's death, Tadmor came under the control of the Arameans.

In its subsequent history, Tadmor became the center of the kingdom ruled by Septimius Odaenathus and his wife, the legendary Queen Zenobia. The armies of the Roman Empire brought an end to Tadmor, laying siege to the city in A.D. 272.

Tadmor is one of the most impressive ruins of the ancient Near Eastern world. Here archaeologists have excavated an outer wall that enclosed the city—a wall dating from the time of Zenobia. The ruins of a great colonnade, an agora (marketplace), a theater, a senate building, and a huge sanctuary of Bel have been unearthed.

TAHPANHES [TAH puh neez]

A city on the eastern frontier of lower Egypt, in the area of the Nile delta (Jer. 2:16; Tahapanes in KJV; Ezek. 30:18, Tehaphnehes). This city was probably named for a powerful general who brought the surrounding area under firm Egyptian control in the eleventh century B.C.

Tahpanhes became a place of refuge for Jews who fled their homeland after the assassination of Gedaliah, the governor of Judah placed in power by the Babylonians. Jeremiah warned the Jews against this move (Jer. 42:16). He dramatically visualized this for them by hiding stones at Tahpanhes for the foundation

of the throne of Nebuchadnezzar, the king of Babylon (Jer. 43:9–10).

Tahpanhes is identified with the modern Tell Defneh, a small mound bordering Lake Menzaleh in northern Egypt.

TALMUD

A collection of books and commentary compiled by Jewish rabbis from A.D. 250–500. The Hebrew word *talmud* means "study" or "learning." This is a fitting title for a work that is a library of Jewish wisdom, philosophy, history, legend, astronomy, dietary laws, scientific debates, medicine, and mathematics.

The Talmud is made up of interpretation and commentary of the Mosaic and rabbinic law contained in the Mishna, an exhaustive collection of laws and guidelines for observing the law of Moses. As a guide to following the law, the Talmud also serves as a basis for spiritual formation. More than 2,000 scholars or rabbis worked across a period of 250 years to understand the meaning of God's word for their particular situation. Out of these efforts they produced the Talmud.

The Pharisees were the first to give greater attention to the laws of Moses. The Roman historian Josephus reported that their oral tradition included regulations that were not recorded in the Mosaic Law at all. The Mishna collected all of these oral regulations into one permanent record. In response to the Mishna, wide discussions concerning its content and meaning began, resulting in the Talmud.

At some points during Jewish history, traditions and the Talmud have been considered equal to or better than the Scripture itself. Jesus encountered such an attitude among the Pharisees even before the existence of the Talmud (Matt. 15:3). Christians must be careful not to make the same mistake in regard to our own traditions.

TAMAR [TAY mur] *(palm)*

1. The lovely daughter of David by Maacah and sister of Absalom (2 Sam. 13:1–22, 32; 1 Chr. 3:9). Tamar was raped by her half brother Amnon. She fled to Absalom, who plotted revenge. Two years later Absalom got his revenge for Tamar by arranging Amnon's murder.

TAMAR [TAY mur] *(palm)*

2. The widow of Er and Onan, sons of Judah (Gen. 38:6–30; Matt. 1:3; Thamar in KJV). According to the law of levirate marriage, Judah's third son, Shelah, should have married Tamar; their first child would have been regarded as his brother's and would have carried on his name. However, Judah withheld his third son from marrying Tamar. Undaunted, Tamar disguised herself as a harlot and offered herself to Judah. Twin sons, Perez and Zerah, were born of their union. Judah and Tamar became ancestors of Jesus through Perez (Matt. 1:3).

TANNER

A person who converted animal skins into leather and made useful or ornamental items from it. Tanning was widespread in the ancient world. Early Israelite families tanned their own hides. But with the growth of cities, leather craftsmen arose. Peter once stayed with a tanner named Simon (Acts 10:6). Tanning animal skins was an involved process requiring much skill. The hides were soaked until all fat, blood, and hair was removed. After the leather was tanned, it was used for many purposes, including tents (Ex. 26:14), sandals (Ezek. 16:10), hats, skirts, and aprons.

TARSHISH [TAR shish] *(jasper)*

A city or territory in the western portion of the Mediterranean Sea with which the Phoenicians traded (2 Chr. 9:21; Ps. 72:10). Tarshish is believed by some to be Tartessus, in southern Spain, near Gibraltar. When Jonah fled from God's instruction to go to Nineveh, he boarded a ship bound for Tarshish, in the opposite direction from Nineveh (Jon. 1:3; 4:2). Tarshish was famous for its ships (Ps. 48:7; Is. 2:16), which carried gold, silver, iron, tin, lead, ivory, apes, and monkeys (1 Kin. 10:22; Jer. 10:9).

Because the ships of Tarshish carried such great riches, they became symbols of wealth, power, and pride. When God judged the nations for their sinful ways, He destroyed their ''ships of Tarshish'' to humble them and to demonstrate His great power (2 Chr. 20:35–37; Is. 2:16–17).

TARSUS [TAHR suss]

The birthplace of the apostle Paul (Acts 21:39; 22:3), formerly known as Saul of Tarsus (Acts 9:11). Tarsus was the chief city of Cilicia, a province of southeast Asia Minor (modern Turkey). This important city was situated on the banks of the Cydnus River about 10 miles (16 kilometers) north of the shore of the Mediterranean Sea.

Because of its strategic location, protected on the north by the Taurus Mountains and open to navigation from the Mediterranean, the city of Tarsus was a prize location for the Hittites, Mycenean Greeks, Assyrians, Persians, Seleucids, and Romans. In the post-Roman period it dwindled to a small city in the wake of battles between various Christian and Muslim powers.

During the Seleucid period, however, Tarsus became a free city (about 170 B.C.), and was open to Greek culture and education. By the time of the Romans, Tarsus competed with Athens and Alexandria as the learning center of the world. ''I am a Jew from Tarsus, in Cilicia,'' wrote the apostle Paul, ''a citizen of no mean city'' (Acts 21:39).

North of Tarsus were the famous

Cilician Gates, a narrow gorge in the Taurus Mountains through which ran the only good trade route between Asia Minor and Syria. The location of Tarsus in a fertile valley brought great wealth to the city.

The apostle Paul spent his early years at Tarsus (Acts 9:11; 21:39; 22:3) and revisited it after his conversion to Christianity (Acts 9:30; 11:25).

TAX COLLECTOR

An agent or contract worker who collected taxes for the government during Bible times. The Greek word translated "tax collector" (tax gatherer in NASB) is incorrectly rendered "publican" by the KJV. Publicans were wealthy men, usually non-Jewish, who contracted with the Roman government to be responsible for the taxes of a particular district of the imperial Roman state. These publicans would often be backed by military force.

By contrast, the tax collectors to which the New Testament refers (with the possible exception of Zacchaeus) were employed by publicans to do the actual collecting of monies in the restricted areas where they lived. These men were Jews, usually not very wealthy, who could be seen in the temple (Luke 18:13). They were probably familiar to the people from whom they collected taxes.

These tax collectors gathered several different types of taxes. Rome levied upon the Jews a land tax, a poll tax, even a tax for the operation of the temple. The distinctions between the kind of rule a given province received dictated the kinds of taxes its people had to pay. For example, since some provinces, like Galilee, were not under an imperial governor, taxes remained in the province rather than going to the imperial treasury at Rome. These differences within the taxation system prompted the Pharisees in Judea (an imperial province) to ask Jesus, "Is it lawful to pay taxes to Caesar, or not?" (Matt. 22:17).

As a class, the tax collectors were despised by their fellow Jews. They were classified generally as "sinners" (Matt. 9:10–11; Mark 2:15), probably because they were allowed to gather more than the government required and then to pocket the excess amount. John the Baptist addressed this when he urged tax collectors to gather no more money than they should (Luke 3:12–13). But even further, the tax collectors were hated because their fellow countrymen viewed them as mercenaries who worked for a foreign oppressor of the Jewish people.

Jesus, however, set a new precedent among the Jews by accepting and associating with the tax collectors. He ate with them (Mark 2:16), He bestowed His saving grace upon them (Luke 19:9), and He even chose a tax collector (Matthew) as one of His twelve disciples (Matt. 9:9). The message of Jesus was that God would welcome the repentant and humble tax collector, while He would spurn the arrogant Pharisee (Luke 18:9–14). His mission was to bring sinners—people like the tax collectors of His day—into God's presence (Matt. 9:11–13).

TEKOA [tuh KOE uh] *(trumpet blast)*

The birthplace of the prophet Amos. Situated in Judah (1 Chr. 2:24; 4:5), Tekoa is identified today with Khirbet Taqu'a, about 6 miles (10 kilometers) southeast of Bethlehem and about 10 miles (16 kilometers) south of Jerusalem. It was built on a hill in the wilderness of Tekoa toward En Gedi (2 Chr. 11:6; 20:20).

Tekoa is first mentioned in the Bible in connection with Joab employing a "wise woman" (2 Sam. 14:2) to bring reconciliation between David and Absalom (2 Sam. 14:2, 4, 9; Tekoah, KJV). Later Rehoboam, king of Judah (ruled 931–913 B.C.), fortified the site in order to prevent an invasion of Jerusalem from the south (2 Chr. 11:6).

Because of its elevation—about 2,790 feet (850 meters) above sea level—Tekoa became a station for warning Jerusalem of the approach of its enemies (Jer. 6:1). From Tekoa a person can see the Mount of Olives in Jerusalem and Mount Nebo beyond the Dead Sea. About two miles from Tekoa, Herod the Great (ruled 37–4 B.C.) built a fortress, the Herodium, in the Judean wilderness.

TELL

A mound of rubble that marks the site of an ancient city. When a city was destroyed, a new city would often be built on the rubble. Thus, these mounds grew higher and higher across the centuries. The ultimate prophetic judgment on a city was that it would become a "desolate mound" (Jer. 49:2).

TEMPLE IN JERUSALEM

Because they were wandering herdsmen, the patriarchs such as Abraham and Jacob did not build temples. However, they did have shrines and altars in places where God had revealed Himself to them, such as by the oak of Moreh (Gen. 12:6–7; 33:20), at Bethel (Gen. 12:8; 28:18–22), and at Beersheba (Gen. 21:33; 26:23–25).

Once the land of Canaan was fully conquered and all the tribes of Israel were properly settled, it was important that the worship of God be centralized. David was not allowed to build the temple, but he was allowed to gather the materials for it and to organize the project (1 Chr. 22:1–19). The actual work on the temple began during Solomon's reign. The temple was completed about 959 B.C. (1 Kin. 6:37–38).

In biblical times three temples were built on the same site: Solomon's, Zerubbabel's, and Herod's. Solomon built the temple on the east side of Jerusalem on Mount Moriah, "where the Lord had appeared to his father David, at the place that David had prepared on the threshing floor of Ornan the Jebusite" (1 Chr. 21:28; 2 Chr. 3:1).

Shishak, king of Egypt, took away the treasures of the temple built by Solomon during the reign of Rehoboam, Solomon's son (1 Kin. 14:26). Asa used the temple treasure to buy an ally (1 Kin. 15:18) and to buy off an invader (2 Kin. 16:8). Manasseh placed Canaanite altars and a carved image of Asherah, a Canaanite goddess, in the temple (2 Kin. 21:4, 7). Ahaz introduced an altar patterned after one he saw in Damascus (2 Kin. 16:10–16). By about 630 B.C., Josiah had to repair the temple (2 Kin. 22:3–7). After robbing the temple of its treasures and gold during his first attack (2 Kin. 24:13), in 586 B.C. the Babylonian King Nebuchadnezzar looted, sacked and burned the temple (2 Kin. 25:9, 13–17).

Cyrus, king of Persia, authorized the return of the Jewish captives, the return of the temple vessels Nebuchadnezzar had looted, and the reconstruction of the temple (about 538 B.C.), which was finished about 515 B.C. The completed temple was smaller than and inferior to Solomon's (Ezra 3:12).

King Herod, an Idumean, sought to appease his Jewish subjects by constructing an enormous, ornate, cream-colored temple of stone and gold that began in 19 B.C. The main building was finished by 9 B.C., but the entire structure was not completed until A.D. 64. The Romans destroyed it in A.D. 70.

Jesus related to the temple in four distinct ways. First, as a pious Jew who was zealous for the Lord, Jesus showed respect for the temple. He referred to it as "the house of God" (Matt. 12:4) and "My Father's house" (John 2:16). He taught that everything in it was holy because of the sanctifying presence of God (Matt. 23:17, 21).

Second, Jesus' zeal led Him to purge the temple of the moneychangers (Mark 11:15–17; John 2:16) and to weep over it as He reflected on its coming destruction (Mark 13:1; Luke 19:41–44). Because Malachi 3:1 prophesied the cleansing of the temple as something the Lord and His Messenger would do, Jesus' act implied His deity and messiahship. Consequently, the hard-hearted scribes and chief priests "sought how they might destroy Him" (Mark 11:18; Luke 19:47).

Third, because He was the Son of God incarnate, Jesus taught that He was greater than the temple (Matt. 12:6). Jesus' teaching that if the temple of His body was destroyed, in three days He would raise it up (John 2:19), likewise affirms His superiority to the temple building. That saying of Jesus may have provided the basis for the claim of the two false witnesses at His trial who stated that Jesus said, "I am able to destroy the temple of God and to build it in three days" (Matt. 26:60–61; 27:40; Mark 14:57–58; 15:29).

Finally, Jesus taught that the church (Matt. 16:18) is the new, eschatological temple (Matt. 18:19–20; John 14:23).

At Jesus' death, the curtain of the temple was torn from top to bottom (Matt. 27:51; Mark 15:38; Luke 23:45). By His death, Jesus opened a new way into the presence of God. A new order replaced the old. No longer was the temple in Jerusalem to be the place where people worshiped God. From now on they would worship Him "in spirit and truth" (John 4:21–24).

TEMPTATION

An enticement or invitation to sin. The supreme tempter is Satan (Matt. 4:3; 1 Thess. 3:5), who is able to play upon the weakness of corrupted human nature (James 1:14) and so to lead people to destruction.

The gospel of Jesus Christ directs us to resist temptation, promising blessedness to those who do (James 1:12). The gospel also directs us to pray for deliverance from exposure to temptation and from surrender to it (Matt. 6:13). The Lord will not allow His people to encounter temptation beyond their Spirit-given ability to resist (1 Cor. 10:13).

In the temptation of Jesus (Matt. 4:1–11), Satan enticed the Son of God to forsake His messianic commitment. Jesus, however, did not prove to be a disloyal Son. He did not put the Lord to the test, or tempt God, like Israel of old. He lives "by every word that proceeds from the mouth of God" (Matt. 4:4). Having resisted satanic temptation Himself, Christ is able to comfort and aid His followers who are tempted in similar fashion (Heb. 4:15).

TEMPTATION OF CHRIST

The 40-day period in the wilderness when Jesus was tempted by the devil (Matt. 4:1–13; Mark 1:12–13). Jesus' first temptation (to turn stones to bread) was to use His divine power to satisfy His own physical needs. The second (to jump off the temple) was to perform a spectacular feat so the people would follow Him. The third was to gain possession of the world by worshiping Satan.

One motive lay behind all these temptations: Satan wanted to destroy Jesus' mission. Because Jesus' death would destroy Satan's power, Satan wanted Jesus to pollute His life and ministry. The ultimate issue behind these temptations was idolatry. The real purpose of Satan's temptation was that he might be worshiped instead of God.

TEN COMMANDMENTS

The ten "words" (a technical term meaning "stipulations") of the covenant that God made with His people (Ex. 34:28; Deut. 4:13; 10:4). These laws are often called the *Decalogue,* from the Greek word that means "ten words." All ten were inscribed on each of two stone tablets (Ex. 31:18), one for the Sovereign (God) and the other for the subjects (Israel).

Although God gave the Ten Commandments to His people through Moses at Mount Sinai more than 3,000 years ago, they are still relevant today. They have an abiding significance, because God's character is unchangeable. These laws originate from God and from His eternal character; therefore, their moral value cannot change.

Almost 1,500 years after God gave the laws, Jesus upheld them, calling them the "commandments" and listing five of them for the rich young ruler (Matt. 19:16–19). And in the Sermon on the Mount, Jesus showed that His coming had not canceled the commandments. He specifically mentioned the laws against killing (Matt. 5:21) and committing adultery (Matt. 5:27).

Jesus actually placed these laws on a higher plane by demanding that the spirit as well as the legal aspects of the law be kept (Matt. 5:17–28). Jesus placed His eternal stamp of approval on the law by declaring, "Do not think that I came to destroy the Law or the Prophets. I did not come to destroy but to fulfill" (Matt. 5:17–19).

The holy God uttered His commandments from the top of Mount Sinai amid smoke and fire—visible expressions of His power, majesty, and authority (Ex. 19:16–20:17). Later the commandments were engraved on two tablets of stone, "written with the finger of God" (Ex. 31:18). The awesome nature of the events surrounding the giving of the law is mentioned a number of times in the Bible, perhaps to emphasize the solemnity of the occasion (Ex. 19:16–19; Deut. 4:11–12).

God never intended for the Ten Commandments to be a set of regulations by which the people of Israel would earn salvation. God's favor had already been freely granted (Ex. 20:1–2). This was overwhelmingly demonstrated by His deliverance of Israel from Egyptian bondage (Deut. 4:37). Therefore, at the heart of the covenant relationship lay an act of divine grace. God even prefaced the Ten Commandments with a reminder of His deliverance (Ex. 20:2).

The Ten Commandments (Ex. 20:3–17; Deut. 5:7–21) are still relevant today. The world desperately needs to see the name and character of God displayed in the lives of Christians who still take His Word seriously. These commandments, particularly coupled with the teachings of Christ, are still the best guidelines for practical daily living known to humankind.

The first four commandments deal with our relationship to God, while the last six focus on our relationship to each other.

1. "You shall have no other gods before Me" (Ex. 20:3). God is one (Deut. 6:4) and unique (Deut. 4:38, 39), and therefore belief in and worship of other so-called gods is out of the question. Since God's character forms the basis of the covenant with His people, He demands absolute loyalty.

2. "You shall not make for yourself a carved image" (Ex. 20:4). The second commandment is necessary because people do not always keep the first. The Israelites made a golden calf to worship even as the Lord gave the laws to Moses. And since Israel had so many contacts with people who did worship images, including replicas of their earthly rulers, God gave them this law. God has never been a tangible, visible Being (Deut. 4:12), but always a Spirit (John 4:24). Idolatry therefore always misrepresents Him.

3. "You shall not take the name of the Lord your God in vain" (Ex. 20:7). God's name and His character are inseparable.

Using His holy name lightly in a vain, empty manner is insulting and degrading. This could be done by perjuring oneself in a court of law (Lev. 19:12) or by cursing. However, this commandment also applies to hypocritical worship, using God's name in meaningless prayer and praise (Is. 29:13).

4. "Remember the Sabbath day, to keep it holy" (Ex. 20:8). Sabbath means "rest," but God intended for this day to stand for more than an absence of work. It was to be a day of worship as well—a day for setting aside all thoughts of materialistic gain and thinking about Him. God Himself set the pattern by ceasing from His labors after creating the world.

5. "Honor your father and your mother, that your days may be long upon the land" (Ex. 20:12). God established parents as the authority figures in the family unit. Children often get their first impressions about God from their parents. Parents who walk in the Spirit, honestly desiring to follow the guidelines of the Scriptures, will set better examples for their children. And children who want to please God will respect their parents.

6. "You shall not murder" (Ex. 20:13). This law reveals God's attitude toward people who are created in His image. No one has the right to take that life from another (Gen. 9:6).

7. "You shall not commit adultery" (Ex. 20:14). Technically, this commandment refers to being sexually involved with a married person; but it is traditionally used by extension to prohibit all sexual relationships outside of marriage. Again, this commandment involves a right relationship with God and with others. Adultery is possible only if people are prepared to hurt others, to enjoy themselves at the expense of other people.

8. "You shall not steal" (Ex. 20:15). Stealing involves taking something that does not belong to you. This could be another's property, marriage partner, or reputation. This law also emphasizes the importance of getting all you own through lawful channels.

9. "You shall not bear false witness against your neighbor" (Ex. 20:16). A good relationship demands truthfulness and honesty in speaking of another. God's people ought to cherish their own reputations and that of others. If people are unwilling to speak ill of someone, they are less likely to steal from that person or to commit murder.

10. "You shall not covet" (Ex. 20:17). Jesus elaborated on this commandment by stating, "You shall love your neighbor as yourself" (Matt. 22:39). The negative and the positive work together. You do not harm people you care about.

TENTMAKER

An ancient craft, tentmaking consisted of cutting and sewing together cloth, frequently of goat's hair, and attaching ropes and loops. Paul, Aquila, and Priscilla were tentmakers (Acts 18:2–3).

TERAH [TEE ruh]

The father of Abraham and an ancestor of Christ (Gen. 11:26–27; Luke 3:34; Thara in KJV). Descended from Shem, Terah also was the father of Nahor and Haran. He lived at Ur of the Chaldeans most of his life; at Ur he worshiped the moon-god (Josh. 24:2). From Ur, Terah migrated with his son Abraham, his grandson Lot (Haran's son), and his daughter-in-law Sarah (Abraham's wife) to Haran, a city about 500 miles (800 kilometers) north of Ur and about 275 miles (445 kilometers) northeast of Damascus. Terah died in Haran, another city where the moon-god was worshiped, at the age of 205 (Gen. 11:24–32).

TERAPHIM [TEHR uh fim]

Figurines or images in human form used in the ancient world as household gods. Teraphim were probably of Mesopotamian origin, but apparently they were widespread in Hebrew households. Possibly made of clay, these objects may have been similar to the objects in Rome that were connected with superstition, idolatry, and magic.

The term *teraphim*, translated as "household idols" (NKJV), occurs in Judges 17:5 and 18:14, 17–18, 20, where it is linked with an ephod and with carved images and molded images. All of these items formed part of the equipment of Micah's idolatrous shrine. In Hosea 3:4 teraphim is again linked with ephod in a reference to the absence of all forms of religion from Israel during her time of punishment.

The household gods (teraphim) of Genesis 31:19, 34–35 were probably idolatrous images that Rachel wanted to bring with her to Palestine, perhaps for the safety they might provide on the perilous journey and in a strange land.

In other contexts teraphim are directly related to idolatry. Both the idols that speak delusion (Zech. 10:2) and the idolatry that is linked with iniquity (1 Sam. 15:23) are translations of the word *teraphim*. In his reformation of religion, King Josiah of Judah sought to restore true worship by abolishing the practices of consulting mediums and spiritists and using household gods (teraphim) and images (2 Kin. 23:24).

TERTULLUS [tur TUHL uhs] *(third)*

A professional orator hired to prosecute the Jews' case against the apostle Paul (Acts 24:1–2). Tertullus accompanied Ananias the high priest and the elders from Jerusalem to Caesarea to accuse Paul before Felix, the Roman governor of Judea.

Tertullus's speech followed the common Roman pattern of his day. He began by flattering the judge, the "most noble Felix," for the peace and prosperity he had brought to the nation. He then charged Paul with crimes the apostle had not committed (Acts 21:26–40; 23:26–30; 24:10–21).

THADDAEUS [tha DEE uhs]

One of the twelve apostles of Jesus (Matt. 10:3; Mark 3:18; Thaddeus in KJV), also called Lebbaeus (Matt. 10:3) and Judas the son of James (Luke 6:16; Acts 1:13). He is carefully distinguished from Judas Iscariot (John 14:22). Nothing else is known about this most obscure of the apostles, but some scholars attribute the Epistle of Jude to him.

THEOPHILUS [thih AHF uh luhs] *(lover of God)*

A Christian to whom Luke dedicated the Gospel of Luke and the Book of Acts (Luke 1:3; Acts 1:1). The fact that Luke spoke of Theophilus as "most excellent" indicates that he was a prominent man of high rank and possibly a Roman. He may have chosen the name when he was converted to Christianity. According to tradition, both Luke and Theophilus were natives of Antioch in Syria. Much speculation surrounds Theophilus, but little is known for certain about him.

THESSALONICA [thes uh luh NIGH kuh]

A city in Macedonia visited by the apostle Paul (Acts 17:1, 11, 13; 27:2; Phil. 4:16). Situated on the Thermaic Gulf, Thessalonica was the chief seaport of Macedonia. The city was founded in about 315 B.C. by Cassander, who resettled the site with inhabitants from 26 villages that he had destroyed. He named the city after his wife, the sister of Alexander the Great and daughter of Philip II of Macedonia. The Egnatian Way, the main overland route from Rome to the East, ran directly through the city and can still be traced today.

Under Roman rule, Thessalonica achieved prominence. In 167 B.C. the Romans divided Macedonia into four districts, Thessalonica becoming capital of the second district. Some 20 years later Macedonia became a Roman province with Thessalonica as its capital. After the battle of Philippi in 42 B.C., when Octavian and Mark Antony defeated Brutus and Cassius, the assassins of Julius Caesar, Thessalonica became a free city. It was the most populous city of Macedonia.

In the third century A.D., Thessalonica was selected to oversee a Roman temple, and under Decius (ruled A.D. 249–251), infamous for his persecution of Christians, the city achieved the status of a Roman colony, which entitled it to the rights and privileges of the Roman Empire. The city was surrounded by a wall, stretches of which still stand. Archaeolo-

THESSALONICA

gists have uncovered a paved Roman forum some 70 by 110 yards (63 by 99 meters) in size, dating from the first or second centuries A.D.

The apostle Paul visited Thessalonica in A.D. 49 or 50 during his second missionary journey (Acts 17:1–9). Paul's evangelistic efforts met with success. Within a short time a vigorous Christian congregation had blossomed, consisting of some members of the Jewish synagogue, as well as former pagans.

The Book of Acts leads some to assume that Paul stayed in Thessalonica only a few weeks before being forced to leave because of Jewish opposition. But in reality he probably stayed at least two or three months. A shorter stay would scarcely account for Paul's receiving two gifts of aid from the Philippians (Phil. 4:16), or for the depth of affection that developed between Paul and the Thessalonians (1 Thess. 2:1–12). Thessalonica was also the home of two of Paul's co-workers, Aristarchus and Secundus (Acts 20:4; 27:2).

THEUDAS [THOO duhs]

A false leader of whom Gamaliel spoke before the Sanhedrin, about A.D. 32. According to Gamaliel's account, about 400 men joined Theudas, but "he was slain, and all who obeyed him were scattered and came to nothing" (Acts 5:36).

Scholars are uncertain of the identity of Theudas. Luke records that Judas the Galilean rose up in the days of the census. It is certain that this Judas was Judas the Gaulanite who, according to the Jewish historian Josephus, incited a riot over the census in the time of Quirinius, about A.D. 6. Then Josephus mentions a magician named Theudas who, acting as a false prophet, persuaded many people to cross the Jordan River and was beheaded for his efforts by the Romans. But this Theudas lived about 4 B.C., after Judas.

Josephus has rarely been found in error, but Luke has also been established as a reliable historian. It is not unlikely then that there were two insurrectionists named Theudas who lived many years apart. Perhaps Luke's Theudas was one of the revolutionaries who arose during the turbulent last year of Herod the Great's rule. Or Theudas may have been the Greek name for one of the three revolutionaries named by Josephus: Judas, Simon, or Matthias.

THOMAS [TAHM uhs] *(twin)*

One of the twelve apostles of Jesus; also called *Didymus,* the Greek word for "twin" (Matt. 10:3; Mark 3:18; Luke 6:15). Thomas is best known for his inability to believe that Jesus had risen from the dead. For that inability to believe, he forever earned the name "doubting Thomas."

Thomas was not present when Jesus first appeared to His disciples after His resurrection. Upon hearing of the appearance, Thomas said, "Unless I see in His hands the print of the nails, and put my finger into the print of the nails, and put my hand into His side, I will not believe" (John 20:25). Eight days later, Jesus appeared again to the disciples, including Thomas. When Jesus invited him to touch the nail prints and put his hand into His side, Thomas' response was, "My Lord and my God!" (John 20:28). Of that incident the great church father Augustine remarked, "He doubted so that we might believe."

Thomas appears three other times in the Gospel of John. (Except for the listing of the disciples, Thomas does not appear in the other three gospels.) When Jesus made known his intention to go into Judea, Thomas urged his fellow disciples, "Let us also go, that we may die with Him" (John 11:16). Knowing that His earthly life would soon end, Jesus said He was going to prepare a place for His followers and that they knew the way. Thomas asked, "Lord, we do not know where You are going, and how can we know the way?" (John 14:5). To that Jesus gave his well-known answer: "I am the way, the truth, and the life" (John 14:6).

After the resurrection of Jesus, Thomas was on the Sea of Galilee with six other disciples when Jesus signaled to them from the shore and told them where to cast their net (John 21:2). Thomas was also with the other disciples in the Jerusalem upper room after the ascension of Jesus.

According to tradition, Thomas spread the gospel in Parthia and Persia, where he died. Later tradition places Thomas in India, where he was martyred. The Mar Thoma Church in India traces its origins to Thomas.

THORN IN THE FLESH

A reference to some extreme difficulty "in the flesh" that the apostle Paul encountered in his ministry (2 Cor. 12:7). The context of this reference is Paul's experiences of visions and revelations that came to him from the Lord (2 Cor. 12:1–6). The purpose of this difficulty was to prevent Paul from being "exalted above measure." The thorn was designated as a "messenger of Satan," perhaps to indicate that Satan, as an adversary, resisted Paul's ministry. The Greek word for "thorn" may be used to refer to a stake on which a person could be impaled.

Many explanations have been offered about the identity of Paul's "thorn in the flesh." If the best translation is "in the flesh," referring to the physical flesh, the thorn may refer to some physical infirmity such as epilepsy, malaria, or bad eyesight. An eye ailment seems to be supported by Galatians 4:13–15. If the translation is "for the flesh," referring to our lower nature, the thorn may refer to some painful experience that was spiri-

tual in nature, such as temptation or the opposition of the Jews.

The purpose of the thorn, however, was to eliminate spiritual arrogance in Paul. Although Paul prayed for its removal, the Lord said to him, "My grace is sufficient for you, for My strength is made perfect in weakness" (2 Cor. 12:9). Thus Paul could boast in his "infirmities," because of the victorious power of Christ in his life (2 Cor. 12:9).

THRESHING SLEDGE

The purpose of threshing was to separate usable grain from the waste straw or chaff. This was usually done by spreading the stalks of grain several inches deep on a smooth flat area that was on a high piece of ground open to the wind. Specially shod animals walked around on the stalks until the grain separated from the hulls.

Frequently, threshing sledges (Is. 28:27) made of wood (2 Sam. 24:22) with stone or metal teeth embedded in the bottom side were dragged over the grain by these animals.

The city of Damascus was called under judgment because that nation "threshed Gilead with implements of iron" (Amos 1:3–5) or behaved with unnecessary cruelty against a conquered people. God promised to make His people into a "new threshing sledge" with sharp teeth and use them to bring judgment on those who oppress the godly (Is. 41:15).

THYATIRA [thigh uh TIE ruh]

A city of the province of Lydia in western Asia Minor (modern Turkey) situated on the road from Pergamos to Sardis. The city was on the southern bank of the Lycus River, a branch of the Hermus River.

Although never a large city, Thyatira was a thriving manufacturing and commercial center during New Testament times. Archaeologists have uncovered evidence of many trade guilds and unions here. Membership in these trade guilds, necessary for financial and social success, often involved pagan customs and practices such as superstitious worship, union feasts using food sacrificed to pagan gods, and loose sexual morality.

The Book of Revelation refers to a certain woman known as "Jezebel" who taught and beguiled the Christians at Thyatira to conform to the paganism and sexual immorality of their surroundings (Rev. 1:11; 2:18–29). In the church at Thyatira, one of the "seven churches which are in Asia" (Rev. 1:4), Jezebel's followers seem to have been a minority because the majority of Christians in this church are commended.

The apostle Paul's first convert in Europe was "a certain woman named Lydia . . . a seller of purple from the city of Thyatira" (Acts 16:14). The modern name of Thyatira is Akhisar, which means "white castle."

TIBERIAS [tigh BEER ee uhs]

A city on the western shore of the Sea of Galilee. Tiberias stands on a rocky cliff about 12 miles (19 kilometers) south of where the Jordan River flows into the Sea of Galilee. Still, Tiberias is 682 feet (208 meters) below the level of the nearby Mediterranean Sea, and it has a semi-tropical climate that is mild in winter but humid in summer.

The city was founded by Herod Antipas (about A.D. 20) and named after the Roman emperor, Tiberius Caesar. It was said to have occupied the site of Rakkath, an old town of Naphtali (Josh. 19:35), and to have been built over a graveyard. Because of this, it was declared unclean by the Jews, who would not enter the city. Although Tiberias was an important city in the days of Christ, there is no record that He ever visited it. In fact, it is only mentioned once in the New Testament (John 6:23).

The city enjoyed a commanding view of Lake Galilee. Because of the numerous hot springs just south of the city, it was a popular resort for the Romans. Pliny the Elder mentions the healthful nature of the springs. Today the city contains a number of health spas.

Although the Jews would not enter the ancient Roman town, after the fall of Jerusalem in A.D. 135, Tiberias ironically became the center of rabbinic learning. Here the Mishna was completed about A.D. 200 and the Jerusalem (or Palestinian) Talmud was finished about A.D. 400. The pointing system later used by the Masoretes to add vowels to the Hebrew text was first developed in Tiberias.

TIBERIUS [tie BEER ih us] (son of the Tiber)

Tiberius Claudius Nero Caesar (42 B.C.-A.D. 37), the second emperor of Rome (A.D. 14–37). The adopted son and son-in-law of Octavian (Augustus Caesar), Tiberius succeeded Augustus as emperor.

Tiberius is mentioned by name only once in the Bible. Luke 3:1 states that John the Baptist began his ministry "in the fifteenth year of the reign of Tiberius Caesar," or A.D. 28. Luke 3:1 is very important in helping to establish the chronology of the life and ministry of Jesus. Tiberius is also frequently referred to simply as "Caesar" (Luke 23:2; John 19:12, 15). The Pharisees and Herodians sought to entrap Jesus by asking him a question concerning tribute to Caesar: "Tell us . . . is it lawful to pay taxes to Caesar, or not?" The "Caesar" in question is Tiberius, and the coin they brought to Jesus bore Tiberius's image (Matt. 22:15–22; Mark 12:13–17; Luke 20:20–26). Jesus began his ministry and was crucified during the reign of Tiberius.

Born in Rome on November 16, 42 B.C., Tiberius became emperor in his fifty-fifth year and reigned for twenty-three years, until his death in March, A.D. 37, at the age of seventy-eight. Some historians believe that Caligula, the mad successor to Tiberius, hastened Tiberius' death.

The city of Tiberias, on the Sea of Galilee, was built in the emperor's honor, about 20 B.C., by Herod, Roman governor of Galilee and Perea.

TIGLATH-PILESER [TIG lath puh LEE zur] *(the firstborn of* [the god] *Esharra is my confidence)*

A king of Assyria (ruled 745–727 B.C.) and, under the name Pul (2 Kin. 15:19), king of Babylonia (729–727 B.C.). He is also called Tilgath-Pilneser (1 Chr. 5:6, 26; 2 Chr. 28:20).

The accession of Tiglath-Pileser to the throne ended a period of political and military weakness in Assyrian history. He moved first to reestablish Assyrian dominance in Babylon and also attacked his powerful opponent to the north, Urartu. In 740 B.C. he conquered Arpad in northern Syria. The effect of this victory was far-reaching (2 Kin. 19:13; Is. 37:13). Tribute came in from Tyre, Damascus, Cilicia, and Carchemish.

During this period, Tiglath-Pileser penetrated all the way to Israel, where he received tribute from Menahem. The fabulous sum of 1,000 talents of silver "from all the very wealthy" probably resulted in the unpopularity of Menahem (2 Kin. 15:17–22). When Pekahiah, Menahem's son, succeeded to the throne, he ruled for only two years before he was assassinated. In all likelihood, the murder was a result of his father's unpopular policy of submission to Assyria (2 Kin. 15:23–26).

While serving as king of Israel, Pekah adopted a strong anti-Assyrian policy by aligning himself with Rezin, king of Syria. Both Pekah and Rezin sought to force Ahaz, king of Judah, to join the revolt.

But Ahaz appealed to Tiglath-Pileser for help. In 734 B.C. Tiglath-Pileser moved south along the coast to cut off possible Egyptian aid to the revolt. In 733 B.C. he marched into Israel, devastating much of Galilee and deporting many Israelites (2 Kin. 15:29). Finally, he moved against the real power of the region, Damascus, which fell in 732 B.C.

After devastating the countryside, Tiglath-Pileser captured the city of Damascus, executed Rezin, and sent much of the Syrian population into exile. Meanwhile, Hoshea had assassinated Pekah to become the new king of Israel (2 Kin. 15:30). Hoshea paid tribute to Tiglath-Pileser, as did the kings of Ashkelon and Tyre. When Tiglath-Pileser died in 727 B.C., the borders of his country had been dramatically enlarged and every enemy of Assyria had been severely weakened.

TIGRIS [TIE gris]

A major river of southwest Asia. Flowing about 1,150 miles (1,850 kilometers) from the Taurus Mountains of eastern Turkey, the Tigris joins the Euphrates River north of Basra. The Tigris and Euphrates flow roughly parallel to each other for hundreds of miles in the "Land of the Two Rivers," or Mesopotamia. The Tigris is identical with Hiddekel (Gen. 2:14, KJV, NKJV), one of the four branches of the river that flowed from the Garden of Eden.

TIMBREL

A percussion instrument that was carried and beaten by hand. Considered inappropriate for the temple, it was probably played primarily by women (Ps. 68:25). The timbrel may have been excluded from the temple instruments because of its great popularity with the Canaanite fertility cults. Among the Hebrew people, it was associated with merrymaking and processions (Gen. 31:27). Remnants of timbrels with pieces of bronze inserted in the rim have been uncovered by archaeologists. Thus, the instrument could be shaken as well as beaten.

The Hebrew word for "timbrel" is rendered by other English translations as "tabret" and "tambourine."

TIMOTHY [TIM uh thih] (honored by God)

Paul's friend and chief associate, who is mentioned as joint sender in six of Paul's epistles (2 Cor. 1:1; Phil. 1:1; Col. 1:1; 1 Thess. 1:1; 2 Thess. 1:1; Philem. 1).

Timothy first appears in the second missionary journey when Paul revisited Lystra (Acts 16:1–3). Timothy was the son of a Gentile father and a Jewish-Christian mother named Eunice, and the grandson of Lois (Acts 16:1; 2 Tim. 1:5). Timothy may have been converted under Paul's ministry, because the apostle refers to him as his "beloved and faithful son in the Lord" (1 Cor. 4:17) and as his "true son in the faith" (1 Tim. 1:2). Timothy was held in high regard in Lystra and Iconium, and Paul desired to take him along as a traveling companion (Acts 16:3).

Timothy played a prominent role in the remainder of the second missionary journey. When Paul was forced to leave Berea because of an uproar started by Jews from Thessalonica, Silas and Timothy were left behind to strengthen the work in Macedonia (Acts 17:14). After they rejoined Paul in Athens (Acts 18:5), Paul sent Timothy back to the believers in Thessalonica to establish them and to encourage them to maintain the faith (1 Thess. 3:1–9). Timothy's report of the faith and love of the Thessalonians greatly encouraged Paul.

During Paul's third missionary journey, Timothy was active in the evangelizing of Corinth, although he had little success. When news of disturbances at Corinth reached Paul at Ephesus, he sent Timothy, perhaps along with Erastus (Acts 19:22), to resolve the difficulties. The mission failed, perhaps because of fear on Timothy's part (1 Cor. 16:10–11). Paul then sent the more forceful Titus, who was able to calm the situation at Corinth (2 Cor. 7). Later in the third journey, Timothy is listed as one of the group that accompanied Paul along the coast of Asia Minor on his way to Jerusalem (Acts 20:4–5).

Timothy also appears as a companion of Paul during his imprisonment in Rome (Col. 1:1; Phil. 1:1; Philem. 1). From Rome, Paul sent Timothy to Philippi to bring back word of the congregation that had supported the apostle so faithfully over the years.

Timothy's strongest traits were his sensitivity, affection, and loyalty. Paul commends him to the Philippians, for example, as one of proven character, faithful to Paul like a son to a father, and without rival in his concern for the Philippians (Phil. 2:19–23; also 2 Tim. 1:4; 3:10). Paul's warnings, however, to "be strong" (2 Tim. 2:1) suggest that Timothy suffered from fearfulness (1 Cor. 16:10–11; 2 Tim. 1:7) and perhaps youthful lusts (2 Tim. 2:22). But in spite of his weaknesses, Paul was closer to Timothy than to any other associate.

Writing about A.D. 325, Eusebius reported that Timothy was the first bishop of Ephesus. In 356 Constantius transferred what was thought to be Timothy's remains from Ephesus to Constantinople (modern Istanbul) and buried them in the Church of the Apostles, which had been built by his father, Constantine.

TITHE

The practice of giving a tenth of one's income or property as an offering to God. The custom of paying a tithe was an ancient practice found among many nations of the ancient world.

The practice of giving a tenth of income or property extends into Hebrew history before the time of the Mosaic Law. The first recorded instance of tithing in the Bible occurs in Genesis 14:17–20. After returning from rescuing Lot and defeating his enemies, Abraham met Melchizedek, the "king of Salem" and "priest of God Most High." The text states simply that Abraham gave Melchizedek a tithe of all the goods he had obtained in battle. The author of the Book of Hebrews, in recounting this episode, considered the Levitical priests who descended from Abraham and who appeared centuries later as having paid tithes to Melchizedek through Abraham (Heb. 7:1–10). There is no recorded demand of Abraham for a tenth. Neither is an explanation given about why Abraham gave a tithe to Melchizedek. Jacob also, long before the Law of Moses, promised that he would give to the Lord a tenth of all he received (Gen. 28:22).

The Law of Moses prescribed tithing in some detail. Leviticus 27:30–32 stated that the tithe of the land would include the seed of the land and the fruit of the tree. In addition, the Hebrew people were required to set apart every tenth animal of their herds and flocks to the Lord.

Mosaic legislation on tithing is also found in two other passages. Numbers 18:21–32 stated that the tithes in Israel would be given to the Levites, because the Levites did not receive a land inheritance like the other tribes of Israel. The Levites, in turn, were to offer a heave offering to the Lord. This would constitute a tithe on their part of the goods which they received. The rest of the goods which the Levites received would provide their living as the reward for their work in the tabernacle.

The third passage dealing with the tithe is Deuteronomy 12:5–7, 11–12, 17–18. This passage instructed Israel to take their tithes to the place the Lord prescribes, eventually the city of Jerusalem. In Deuteronomy, only a vegetable tithe is mentioned. In 2 Chronicles 31:6, however, the tithe of cattle is mentioned.

In Deuteronomy 26:12–15 the third year is called the year of tithing. This may indicate that the tithes were not collected annually. Apparently in this year only the goods that were given as tithes could be offered and stored locally. The offering of the tithe also took the form of a ritual meal (Deut. 12:7, 12). Some suggest that there were three tithes, but this seems unlikely. There is no mention of a tithe in Exodus but only the giving of the firstfruits (Ezek. 44:29–30). Finally, the prophet Malachi indicated that Israel had robbed God in withholding tithes and offerings. Thus the Israelites were exhorted to bring their tithes into the storehouse in order to enjoy the Lord's blessing (Mal. 3:8–12).

In the Old Testament, the purpose of the giving of a tenth was to meet the material need of the Levite, the stranger, the fatherless (the orphan), and the widow (Deut. 26:12–13). The tithe was an expression of gratitude to God by His people. Basic to tithing was the acknowledgment of God's ownership of everything in the earth.

In the New Testament, the words *tithe* and *tithing* appear only eight times (Matt. 23:23; Luke 11:42; 18:12; Heb. 7:5–6, 8–9). All of these passages refer to Old Testament usage and to current Jewish practice. Nowhere does the New Testament expressly command Christians to tithe. However, as believers we are to be generous in sharing our material possessions with the poor and for the support of Christian ministry. Christ Himself is our model in giving. Giving is to be voluntary, willing, cheerful, and given in the light of our accountability to God. Giving should be systematic and by no means limited to a tithe of our incomes. We recognize that all we have is from God. We are called to be faithful stewards of all our possessions (Rom. 14:12; 1 Cor. 9:3–14; 16:1–3; 2 Cor. 8–9).

TITUS [TIGH tuhs]

A "partner and fellow worker" (2 Cor. 8:23) of the apostle Paul. Although Titus is not mentioned in the Book of Acts, Paul's letters reveal that he was the man of the hour at a number of key points in Paul's life.

Paul first mentions Titus in Galatians 2:1–3. As an uncircumcised Gentile, Titus accompanied Paul and Barnabas to Jerusalem as a living example of a great theological truth: Gentiles need not be circumcised in order to be saved.

Titus next appears in connection with Paul's mission to Corinth. While Paul was in Ephesus during his third missionary journey, he received disturbing news from the church at Corinth. After writing two letters and paying one visit to Corinth, Paul sent Titus to Corinth with a third letter (2 Cor. 7:6–9). When Titus failed to return with news of the situation, Paul left Ephesus and, with a troubled spirit (2 Cor. 7:5), traveled north to Troas (2 Cor. 2:12–13).

Finally, in Macedonia, Titus met the anxious apostle with the good news that the church at Corinth had repented. In relief and joy, Paul wrote yet another letter to Corinth (2 Corinthians), perhaps from Philippi, sending it again through Titus (2 Cor. 7:5–16). In addition, Titus was given responsibility for completing the collection for the poor of Jerusalem (2 Cor. 8:6, 16–24; 12:18).

Titus appears in another important role on the island of Crete (Titus 1:4). Beset by a rise in false teaching and declining morality, Titus was told by Paul to strengthen the churches by teaching sound doctrine and good works, and by appointing elders in every city (Titus 1:5). Paul then urged Titus to join him in Ni-copolis (on the west coast of Greece) for winter (Titus 3:12). Not surprisingly, Titus was remembered in church tradition as the first bishop of Crete.

A final reference to Titus comes from 2 Timothy 4:10, where Paul remarks in passing that Titus has departed for mission work in Dalmatia (modern Yugoslavia).

Titus was a man for the tough tasks. According to Paul, he was dependable (2 Cor. 8:17), reliable (2 Cor. 7:6), and diligent (2 Cor. 8:17); and he had a great capacity for human affection (2 Cor. 7:13–15). Possessing both strength and tact, Titus calmed a desperate situation on more than one occasion. He is a good model for Christians who are called to live out their witness in trying circumstances.

TOMB

An elaborate burial place for the dead. In Palestine ordinary people were buried in shallow graves covered by stones or a stone slab. People of importance and wealth were placed in tombs.

The most elaborate examples of tombs are the pyramids of Egypt, which served as burial places for the pharaohs. Other and more conventional tombs are found in the Valley of the Kings near Luxor, Egypt. Placed in the tomb with the body were items needed in the afterlife—treasures often later taken by grave robbers. Such treasures were found in the tomb of Tutankhamun. His tomb escaped the robbers because he died as a teenager and was therefore thought to have been buried with relatively little wealth. Its location was unknown until Howard Carter discovered it in 1922.

Josephus, the Jewish historian, tells of the riches placed in David's tomb (1 Kin. 2:10) in Jerusalem. The traditional site of the tomb of Herod the Great is the Herodium, about 4 miles (6 kilometers) southeast of Bethlehem. At his request he was buried there in 4 B.C. Although the Herodium has been partially excavated, Herod's tomb has not yet been found there.

Tombs were of two types—natural caves and those hewn out of rock. The most famous natural tomb is the cave of Machpelah, which Abraham purchased from Ephron the Hittite as a burial place for Sarah (Gen. 23). Abraham himself was later buried there (Gen. 25:9–10). Isaac, Rebekah, Leah, and Jacob were also buried in this cave (Gen. 49:29–33; 50:12–13). Rachel, Jacob's other wife, died in childbirth near Bethlehem. She was buried in a grave upon which Jacob set a pillar (Gen. 35:16–20). Today a building stands over the site.

Tombs were usually at a distance from the places where the living dwelt. In special cases, such as David and other kings, they might be situated within the city walls (1 Kin. 2:10) or in a garden near a person's house (2 Kin. 21:18). Usually they were outside a city or town (Luke 8:27), but they might be in a garden (John 19:41).

If burial caves were not large enough to accommodate the number of bodies, they were enlarged by excavation (Gen. 50:5). In smaller families, places for the bodies were hewn out of the cave or tomb floor. For instance, to the right of the entrance to the Garden Tomb in Jerusalem are places for two bodies side by side. To the left of the entrance beyond a dividing wall, the tomb is unfinished.

TONGUES, GIFT OF

The Spirit-given ability to speak in languages not known to the speaker or in an ecstatic language that could not normally be understood by the speaker or the hearers.

In an appearance to His disciples after His resurrection, Jesus declared, "And these signs will follow those who believe: In My name they will cast out demons; they will speak with new tongues" (Mark 16:17).

On the Day of Pentecost, the followers of Christ "were all filled with the Holy Spirit and began to speak with other tongues, as the Spirit gave them utterance" (Acts 2:4). The people assembled in Jerusalem for this feast came from various Roman provinces representing a variety of languages. They were astonished to hear the disciples speaking of God's works in their own languages. Some have suggested that the miracle was in the hearing rather than in the speaking. This explanation, however, would transfer the miraculous from the believing disciples to the multitude who may not have been believers.

Tongues, as a gift of the Spirit, is especially prominent in 1 Corinthians 12 and 14. In 1 Corinthians 12 the phenomenon of tongues is listed with other gifts of the Spirit. As one of the several gifts given to believers as a manifestation of the Holy Spirit, tongues is intended, with the other gifts, to be exercised for the building up of the church and the mutual profit of its members. In 1 Corinthians 13 the apostle Paul puts the gift of tongues in perspective by affirming that though we "speak with the tongues of men and of angels" (v. 1), if we do not have love, the gift of tongues has no value.

In 1 Corinthians 14, Paul deals more specifically with the gift of tongues and its exercise in the church. In this chapter the tongue is not an intelligible language, because it cannot be understood by the listeners. Therefore, a parallel to the gift of tongues is the gift of interpretation. The gift of tongues was used as a means of worship, thanksgiving, and prayer. While exercising this gift, individuals address God, not people; and the result is to edify themselves and not the church (1 Cor. 14:2, 4). This gift is never intended for self-exaltation but for the praise and glorification of God.

Paul does not prohibit speaking in tongues in a public service (14:39). But he seems to assign it to a lesser place than the gift of prophecy. Paul claims for himself the gift of tongues-speaking, but apparently he exercised this gift in private and not in public (14:18–19).

The gift of tongues is to be exercised with restraint and in an orderly way. The regulations for its public use are simple and straightforward. People who speak in an unknown tongue are to pray that they may interpret (1 Cor. 14:13). Or, someone else is to interpret what is said. Only two or three persons are to speak, with each having an interpretation of what is said. Each is also to speak in turn. If these criteria are not met, they are to remain silent (1 Cor. 14:27–28). The gifts of speaking in tongues and their interpretation are to be Spirit-inspired.

The phenomenon of speaking in tongues in the New Testament is not some psychological arousal of human emotions that results in strange sounds. This is a genuine work of the Holy Spirit.

TOPHET [TOE fet]

A place southeast of Jerusalem, in the Valley of Hinnom, where child sacrifices were offered and the dead bodies were buried or consumed (Is. 30:33; Jer. 7:31–32; 19:6, 11–14; Topheth, 2 Kin. 23:10). Chemosh, a Moabite god (1 Kin. 11:7, 33; 2 Kin. 23:13), and Molech, an Ammonite god (1 Kin. 11:7; 2 Kin. 23:10), were worshiped at Tophet through a practice despised by God—infant sacrifice (2 Kin. 16:3; Jer. 7:31; 19:5; 32:35).

Two kings of Judah—Ahaz, or Jehoahaz (2 Kin. 16:3), and Manasseh (2 Kin. 21:6)—made their own sons "pass through the fire." Godly King Josiah stopped this horrible practice (2 Kin. 23:10), possibly by dumping the garbage of Jerusalem at Tophet.

The prophet Isaiah used Tophet as a symbol of the death and destruction God would use as judgment against the king of Assyria (Is. 30:33). Jeremiah proclaimed that God's judgment would fall upon the people of Judah for sacrificing their infants to Baal (Jer. 19:5–6). The burial of slaughtered Judahites at this place would be so great, said Jeremiah, that the name *Tophet* would be changed to "Valley of Slaughter" (Jer. 7:31–32; 19:6). Jeremiah also announced that God would make Jerusalem itself a defiled place like Tophet because of the idolatry of the city (Jer. 19:6, 11–14).

See also HINNOM, VALLEY OF.

TORAH [toe RAH]

Guidance or direction from God to His people. In earlier times, the term *Torah* referred directly to the five books of Moses, or the Pentateuch. Both the hearing and the doing of the law made the Torah. It was a manner of life, a way to live based upon the covenant that God made with His people.

TRANSFIGURATION

A display of God's glory in the person of His Son, Jesus Christ (Matt. 17:1–8; Mark 9:2–8; Luke 9:28–36). Peter cites the transfiguration as historical proof of the true gospel of Christ (2 Pet. 1:16–18).

It is hard to imagine what Jesus looked like when He was transfigured, or changed in form. The gospel writers speak of His face becoming bright like the sun, and of His clothes being dazzling white. Peter explains that God gave Him honor and glory (2 Pet. 1:17).

Moses and Elijah appeared also. Both of these were Old Testament figures who did not have a normal death and burial. Luke indicates they discussed Jesus' approaching death, which He was going to accomplish at Jerusalem (Luke 9:31). Throughout his Gospel, Luke emphasizes that Jerusalem was the city of

T

destiny for Jesus, who carefully accomplished all that the Old Testament prophesied and all that God wanted him to do. Jesus was destined for the Cross.

Peter offered to make three tabernacles—one for Jesus, one for Moses, and one for Elijah. He may have been thinking that the Jews would have a final great celebration of the Feast of Tabernacles when the Messiah came. However, this was not the time for that, because Jesus still had to endure the Cross.

A cloud overshadowed Jesus during His transfiguration. This has symbolic as well as historical significance. It is a subtle reminder of the Exodus and the appearance of God to Moses on Mount Sinai (Ex. 24), when God also spoke from a cloud. The transfiguration occurred about a week after Peter's confession of Jesus as the Messiah at Caesarea Philippi; Moses had to wait on the mountain about that long. Both Moses and Jesus were accompanied by three companions on their respective experiences. The word *decease* (Luke 9:31; exodus in KJV; departure in NIV) occurs in the conversation of Moses and Elijah. Thus the Old Testament Exodus points forward to Christ and His redeeming work.

At the same time, symbols of the Second Coming of Christ are also present in the transfiguration account. Jesus will come with clouds and be revealed as God's chosen one. He will stand on a mountain, the Mount of Olives. The Feast of Tabernacles was associated in Jewish thinking with the return of the Messiah as well as with the journey in the wilderness after the Exodus. Moses gave the law, yet also symbolized Jesus, the great prophet of the last days (Deut. 18:15). Elijah, too, was expected by the Jews to come in the last days (Mal. 4:5–6). The transfiguration calls to mind both God's redemption through the Exodus and the future return and glory of Christ, His Son.

The transfiguration concludes with God's voice speaking from the cloud, which marked God's presence (Ex. 40:34–38). When the disciples heard that Jesus was God's beloved Son, the chosen one with whom He was well pleased, they probably remembered Psalm 2:7, Isaiah 42:1, and possibly Genesis 22:2. All Scripture focuses on the person of the Lord Jesus Christ.

In the transfiguration God showed clearly that Jesus is His one and only Son, superior even to the two great Old Testament figures, Moses and Elijah. His disciples are to listen to Him. At the conclusion of the transfiguration, no one is seen but Jesus. He alone is worthy.

TRANSGRESSION

The violation of a law, command, or duty. The Hebrew word most often translated as "transgression" in the Old Testament means "revolt" or "rebellion." The psalmist wrote, "Blessed is he whose transgression is forgiven, whose sin is covered" (Ps. 32:1).

See also SIN.

TRANSJORDAN [trans JORE dahn]

A large plateau east of the Jordan River, the Dead Sea, and the Arabah. The term Transjordan is not used in the NKJV, KJV, or NRSV, but the general area is often called "beyond the Jordan" (Gen. 50:10–11; Deut. 3:20; Judg. 5:17; Is. 9:1; Matt. 4:15; Mark 3:8). The King's Highway (Num. 20:17; 21:22) crossed the entire length of Transjordan from north to south.

Before the time of Joshua, Transjordan was made up of the kingdoms of Ammon, Bashan, Gilead, Moab, and Edom. After the conquest, this area was occupied by the tribes of Reuben and Gad and the half-tribe of Manasseh.

TREE OF KNOWLEDGE

One of two special trees planted by God in the Garden of Eden. The other was the Tree of Life (Gen. 2:9). Since "the tree of the knowledge of good and evil" symbolized all moral knowledge, knowledge that only God could have, its fruit was forbidden to Adam and Eve (Gen. 2:17). But the tempter suggested to them that, by adding to their knowledge, the tree's fruit would make them "like God" (Gen. 3:5). So they chose to disobey God. This act of rebellion marked the entrance of sin into the world.

The result was quite different than Adam and Eve expected. Instead of gaining superior knowledge that made them equal with God, they gained awareness or knowledge of their guilt, shame, and condemnation.

TREE OF LIFE

The tree in the Garden of Eden that bestowed continuing life (Gen. 2:9, 17; 3:1–24). Before Adam and Eve sinned, they had free access to the Tree of Life; after their act of rebellion, two cherubim guarded the way to its fruit.

TREE OF KNOWLEDGE AND TREE OF LIFE

Adam and Eve's inability to eat from this tree after their sin showed that they failed to gain immortality, or eternal life. Because of their sin, they were subject to death and dying. This condition lasted until the coming of Jesus Christ, the Second Adam, who offers eternal life to all who believe in Him (John 3:16; 1 John 5:11–12).

TRESPASS OFFERING

This was a bloody offering presented for unintentional or intentional sins of a lesser degree and for which the violater could make restitution (Lev. 5:15). The sprinkling of the blood on the sides of the altar rather than on its horns gave further evidence that this offering addressed sins of a lesser degree. Special provisions were made for the poor by allowing less valuable offerings to be substituted in this kind of sacrifice.

The amount of restitution (money paid) was determined by the officiating priest. Restitution declared that the debt incurred was paid. Significantly, Christ was declared a trespass offering in Isaiah 53:10 (guilt offering in NIV). He not only bore the sinner's penalty and guilt but made restitution, restoring the sinner to right standing with God.

TRIBE

A social group composed of many clans and families, together with their dependents, outside the ties of blood kinship, who had become associated with the group through covenant, marriage, adoption, or slavery. The nation of ancient Israel, especially at the time of the events recorded in the Book of Judges, was a tribal society (Num. 1; 2; 26; Josh. 13–21; Judg. 19–21). Several neighboring nations also were organized along tribal lines (Gen. 25:13–16).

Israel was an association of twelve tribes, designated by the names of the ancestors from whom they were descended (Deut. 27:12–13; Ezek. 48:1–35). The historical origins of the tribal units may be traced to the Book of Genesis. Jacob, whose name was later changed to Israel (Gen. 32:28), was the father of 12 sons (Gen. 29:31–30:24; 35:18, 22–26). The sons of Jacob, excluding Levi and Joseph but including Joseph's sons, Manasseh and Ephraim, were the ancestors of the later tribal units in the nation's history. The development of the tribes begins with the events described in the Book of Exodus.

The sons of Jacob, together with their father and families, migrated to Egypt to join their brother Joseph and to escape the famine in Canaan (Gen. 46:1–27; Ex. 1:16). They grew significantly in number for the next 400 years (Gen. 15:13; Ex. 12:40). Then the descendants of Jacob's sons left Egypt in the Exodus under the leadership of Moses. They were joined by many who were not descendants of Jacob. The Exodus people are thus characterized as a "mixed multitude" (Ex. 12:38; Num. 11:4).

The number of dependents, those not of blood kinship, continued to increase as the tribal units developed. Moses' father-in-law, whose clan joined Israel in the wilderness, was a Midianite (Num. 10:29). Caleb, who figured prominently in the conquest of the land of Canaan, was called a Kenizzite (Josh. 14:13–14). Later the Calebites were given an inheritance among the tribe of Judah (Josh. 15:13).

The tribal confederation with its institutions reached its highest form during the period recorded in the books of Joshua and Judges. The rigidity of Israel's tribal structure did weaken somewhat with the establishment of the united kingdom under David and Solomon. But tribal organization and association was maintained throughout later biblical history (Luke 2:36; Acts 4:36; Rom. 11:1; Heb. 7:14).

TRIBUTE

A compulsory fee or financial contribution levied on an inferior by a superior ruler or nation. Before the establishment of the united kingdom under David and Solomon, the judge Ehud brought tribute money to Eglon, the king of Moab (Judg. 3:15–18). During the time of the united kingdom, Israel was strong and received tribute. David received tribute from Moab and Syria (2 Sam. 8:2, 6; 1 Chr. 18:2, 6), and Solomon accepted tribute from "all kingdoms from the River [Euphrates] to the land of the Philistines, as far as the border of Egypt" (1 Kin. 4:21).

After the division of the kingdom in 931 B.C., King Ahab of the northern kingdom of Israel received tribute from the king of Moab (2 Kin. 3:4–5). In the southern kingdom of Judah, Jehoshaphat received tribute from the Philistines and the Arabians (2 Chr. 17:11). Uzziah also forced the Ammonites to pay tribute to Judah (2 Chr. 26:8).

Even more is reported in the Bible about Israel and Judah paying tribute to foreign nations. Israel's king Jehoash paid tribute to Hazael of Syria to prevent attack (2 Kin. 12:17–18). Hoshea paid tribute to Shalmaneser V of Assyria (2 Kin. 17:3). Judah's King Ahaz sent tribute to Tiglath-Pileser III of Assyria (2 Kin. 16:7–8). King Hezekiah paid tribute to Sennacherib of Assyria (2 Kin. 18:13–16). Jehoiakim paid tribute to Pharaoh Necho II of Egypt just before Judah was captured by Babylon (2 Kin. 23:33–35). Although Israel was supposed to depend only on God for protection, the nation occasionally depended on foreign kings, paying heavily in tribute.

TRINITY

The coexistence of the Father, the Son, and the Holy Spirit in the unity of the Godhead (divine nature or essence). The doctrine of the Trinity means that within the being and activity of the one God there are three distinct persons: Father, Son, and Holy Spirit.

God revealed Himself as one to the Israelites: "Hear, O Israel: The Lord our God, the Lord is one!" (Deut. 6:4). This was a significant religious truth because the surrounding nations worshiped many gods and had fallen into idolatry, worshiping the creation rather than the true Creator (Rom. 1:18–25). In the New Testament, God revealed that He is not only one but a family of persons—an eternal, inexhaustible, and dynamic triune family of Father, Son, and Holy Spirit, who are one in will and purpose, love and righteousness.

The relationship of Father and Son is prominent in the Gospels because Jesus, the eternal Son who takes on human flesh, is most visible to us as He strikes a responsive chord through the Father-Son relationship. All the while the Holy Spirit is in the background, serving as our eyes of faith. The unity of Father, Son, and Holy Spirit is portrayed by Jesus' trinitarian teaching (John 14–16). This truth is expressed in the total ministry of Jesus as recorded in all four Gospels as well as in the rest of the New Testament. The triune family cooperates as one in bringing the lost person home again into a redeemed family of believers.

The most distinctive characteristic of the persons of the triune family is their selfless love for one another. Each esteems and defers to the other in a way that makes the original family of the trinity a model for the Christian family of believers in the church.

The Father gives all authority to the Son and bears witness to Him, as does Jesus to Himself (John 8:18). Yet the Son claims nothing for Himself; He gives all glory to the Father who has sent Him (John 12:49–50). The key to unlocking the mystery of the trinity is to observe how

T

the persons of the triune family give themselves to one another in selfless love. They are always at one another's disposal.

The Trinity was at work in the incarnation of Jesus, the Son of the Most High, as He was conceived in the womb of Mary by the power of the Holy Spirit (Luke 1:30–35). At His baptism Jesus the Son received approval from the Father in the presence of the Holy Spirit (Luke 3:21–22), fulfilling two Old Testament prophetic passages (Is. 42:1). The Trinity was also present in the temptation, as Jesus, full of the Holy Spirit, was led by the Spirit for 40 days in the wilderness.

In His preaching in the synagogue at Nazareth Jesus fulfilled Isaiah 61:1–2, claiming that "the Spirit of the Lord is upon Me" (Luke 4:18) and indicating that the triune family was at work in Him as the servant Son. At the transfiguration, the voice of the Father spoke again in approval of Jesus the Son to the innermost circle of disciples (Luke 9:35).

Jesus rejoiced in the Holy Spirit and in the Father who had delivered all things to the Son (Luke 10:21–22). He claimed to be acting in the place of God and through the Holy Spirit's power, which is the "finger" of God (Matt. 12:28). Jesus' cleansing of the Temple was a claim of identification with the house of God His Father (Luke 19:45–46) that paralleled His concern for being in His Father's house at a much younger age (Luke 2:41–51).

Following His resurrection, Jesus sent the disciples to baptize "in the name of the Father and of the Son and of the Holy Spirit" (Matt. 28:19). The fulfillment of Jesus' prophecy as spokesman for the Father and the Holy Spirit (Acts 1:4–8) occurred at Pentecost. This continued throughout the Book of Acts when the Holy Spirit inspired Peter and the apostles to preach a trinitarian gospel of Father, Son, and Holy Spirit (Acts 2:32–33; 10:38).

TROAS [TROW as]

An important city on the coast of Mysia, in northwest Asia Minor (modern Turkey), visited at least three times by the apostle Paul (Acts 16:8, 11; 20:5–6; 2 Cor. 2:12; 2 Tim. 4:13). Troas was situated about ten miles (16 kilometers) southwest of Hissarlik, the ruins of ancient Troy.

At Troas, on his second missionary journey, the apostle Paul saw a vision of a "man of Macedonia" inviting him to preach the gospel of Christ in Europe (Acts 16:8–9). After ministering in Greece (Acts 20:2), Paul returned to Troas. Here he restored to life a young man named Eutychus, who had fallen from a third-story window while Paul preached late into the night (Acts 20:5–12).

TROPHIMUS [TROF ih muss]

A Gentile Christian who lived in Ephesus and who accompanied Paul to Jerusalem at the end of Paul's third missionary journey (Acts 20:4). When certain Jews from Asia saw Trophimus the Ephesian with Paul in Jerusalem, they supposed that Paul had brought "Greeks" (uncircumcised Gentiles) into the Court of Israel (an inner court beyond the Court of the Gentiles), defiling the temple (Acts 21:28–29).

The people seized Paul, dragged him out of the temple, and tried to kill him. But Paul was rescued by the commander of the Roman garrison and sent to Rome for trial.

Apparently Trophimus accompanied Paul on the trip toward Rome. In his Second Epistle to Timothy, Paul revealed, "Trophimus I have left in Miletus sick" (2 Tim. 4:20).

TRUMPET

A wind instrument was used by the priests during services of sacrifice, especially to signal the Day of Atonement. The trumpet was also used to rally troops on the battlefield (Josh. 6:4).

Made of metal or bones, the trumpet featured a sounding air column not quite two feet long. This short length gave this instrument a high, shrill sound. The tone of the trumpet apparently could be regulated (2 Chr. 5:12). Some trumpets were probably made from the horn of an animal; the word "horn" is used for this instrument in some English translations (1 Chr. 25:5, KJV). Other words used for trumpet include cornet (Ps. 98:6, KJV), and bugle (1 Cor. 14:8, NASB, NRSV).

One distinctive type of trumpet or horn used by the Hebrew people was the ram's horn, also known by its Hebrew name, the shophar (Hos. 5:8). The shophar was the greatest of the Jewish ritual instruments. Eventually the horn of a mountain goat was used for this instrument, rather than the horn of a ram. The shophar was basically a signaling instrument, used to assemble the army (Judg. 3:27; 1 Sam. 13:3), to sound an attack (Job 39:24–25), and to sound an alarm (Jer. 6:1; Amos 3:6).

TRUTH

Conformity to fact or actuality; faithfulness to an original or to a standard.

In the Old and New Testaments, truth is a fundamental moral and personal quality of God. God proclaimed that He is "merciful and gracious, longsuffering, and abounding in goodness and truth" (Ex. 34:6). He is a "God of truth . . . without injustice" (Deut. 32:4). Furthermore, all of His paths are "mercy and truth" (Ps. 25:10). All of God's works, precepts, and judgments are done in righteousness and truth (Pss. 111:8). Because of His perfect nature and will, God has to speak and act in truth; He cannot lie (1 Sam. 15:29; James 1:17–18).

Jesus is the Word of God who became flesh, "the only begotten of the Father, full of grace and truth" (John 1:14). All Jesus said was true, because He told the truth He heard from God (John 8:40). He promised His disciples that He would send "the Spirit of truth" (John 14:17; 16:13)—a Helper who would abide in Christians forever (John 14:16), testify about Jesus (John 15:26), guide Christians into all truth (John 16:13), and glorify Jesus (John 16:14).

TWELVE, THE

A term for the band of Jesus' closest disciples (Mark 4:10). Early in His ministry Jesus selected 12 of His followers and named them "apostles" (Luke 6:12–16). They are also referred to as the "twelve disciples" (Matt. 10:1). Jesus appointed them to travel with Him, preach, heal, and cast out demons (Mark 3:14–15). There was a symbolic significance to the Twelve, similar to that of the twelve sons of Israel (1 Cor. 15:5; Rev. 21:14), whose descendants became the twelve tribes of the Hebrew nation.

TYCHICUS [TIKE ih kuhs]

A Christian of the province of Asia (Acts 20:4). Tychicus was a faithful friend, fellow worker, and messenger of the apostle Paul (Eph. 6:21–22; Col. 4:7–8). Along with other disciples, Tychicus traveled ahead of Paul from Macedonia to Troas, where he waited for the apostle's arrival (Acts 20:4).

Paul also sent Tychicus to Ephesus to deliver and perhaps to read his epistle to the Christians in that city (Eph. 6:21). He did the same with the Epistle to the Colossians (Col. 4:7). Paul sent him as a messenger to Titus in Crete (Titus 3:12) and afterward to Ephesus (2 Tim. 4:12).

T

TYRE [tire] *(rock)*

An ancient seaport city of the Phoenicians situated north of Israel. Tyre was the principal seaport of the Phoenician coast, about 25 miles (40 kilometers) south of Sidon and 35 miles (56 kilometers) north of Carmel. It consisted of two cities: a rocky coastal city on the mainland and a small island city. The island city was just off the shore. The mainland city was on a coastal plain, a strip only 15 miles (24 kilometers) long and 2 miles (3 kilometers) wide.

Behind the plain of Tyre stood the rocky mountains of Lebanon. Tyre was easily defended because it had the sea on the west, the mountains on the east, and several other rocky cliffs (one the famous "Ladder of Tyre") around it, making it difficult to invade.

Tyre was an ancient city. According to one tradition, it was founded about 2750 B.C. However, Sidon—Tyre's sister city—was probably older (Gen. 10:15), perhaps even the mother city (Is. 23:2, 12). The Greek poet Homer mentioned "Sidonian wares," without reference to Tyre. This seems to confirm that Sidon was older. About 1400 B.C. Sidon successfully besieged the city of Tyre and maintained supremacy over it. However, when sea raiders left Sidon in ruins about 1200 B.C., many people migrated to Tyre. The increasing greatness of Tyre over Sidon, and its closer location to Israel, caused the order of mentioning Tyre first and then Sidon to be established by biblical writers (Jer. 47:4; Mark 3:8).

The most celebrated product of Tyrian commerce was the famous purple dye made from mollusks found in the waters near Tyre. This dye became a source of great wealth for Tyrians. In addition they produced metal work and glassware, shipping their products to and buying wares from peoples in remote parts of the earth (1 Kin. 9:28).

Friendly relations existed between the Hebrews and the Tyrians. Hiram was on excellent terms with both David and Solomon, aiding them with materials for the building of David's palace (1 Kin. 5:1; 1 Chr. 14:1), Solomon's temple, and other buildings (1 Kin. 4:1; 9:10–14; 2 Chr. 2:3, 11). Hiram and Solomon engaged in joint commercial ventures (1 Kin. 9:26–28).

The dynasty of Hiram came to an end early in the ninth century B.C. when a priest named Ethbaal revolted and assumed the throne. Still, cordial relations between the Tyrians and Israelites continued. Ethbaal's daughter Jezebel married Ahab of Israel (1 Kin. 16:31). From this union, Baal worship and other idolatrous practices were introduced into Israel.

While the people of Tyre were mostly interested in sea voyages, colonization, manufacturing, and commerce, they were frequently forced into war. Phoenician independence ended with the reign of Ashurnasirpal II (883–859 B.C.) of Assyria. More than a century later Shalmaneser V laid siege to Tyre and it fell to his successor, Sargon II. With the decline of Assyria after the middle of the seventh century B.C., Tyre again prospered.

Several prophets of the Old Testament prophesied against Tyre. They condemned the Tyrians for delivering Israelites to the Edomites (Amos 1:9) and for selling them as slaves to the Greeks (Joel 3:5–6). Jeremiah prophesied Tyre's defeat (Jer. 27:1–11). But the classic prophecy against Tyre was given by Ezekiel.

Ezekiel prophesied the destruction of Tyre (Ezek. 26:3–21). The first stage of this prophecy came true when Nebuchadnezzar, king of Babylon, besieged the mainland city of Tyre for 13 years (585–572 B.C.) and apparently destroyed it. However, Nebuchadnezzar had no navy; so he could not flatten the island city. But losing the mainland city was devastating to Tyre. This destroyed Tyre's influence in the world and reduced its commercial activities severely.

The second stage of Ezekiel's prophecy was fulfilled in 332 B.C., when Alexander the Great besieged the island city of Tyre for seven months. He finally captured it when he built a causeway from the mainland to the island. Hauling cedars from the mountains of Lebanon, he drove them as piles into the floor of the sea between the mainland and the island. Then he used the debris and timber of the ruined mainland city as solid material for the causeway. Hence, the remarkable prophecy of Ezekiel was completely fulfilled.

During the Roman period Tyre again was rebuilt, eventually achieving a degree of prosperity. A Roman colony was established at the city. Herod I rebuilt the main temple, which would have been standing when Jesus visited the coasts of Tyre and Sidon (Matt. 15:21–28; Mark 7:24–31). People of Tyre listened to Jesus as He taught (Mark 3:8; Luke 6:17). The Lord Jesus even cited Tyre as a heathen city that would bear less judgment than the Galilaean towns in which He had invested so much of His ministry (Matt. 11:21–22; Luke 10:13–14).

In the New Testament period, a Christian community flourished at Tyre. At the close of Paul's third missionary journey he stopped at Tyre and stayed with the believers there for a week (Acts 21:1–7).

U

UGARIT [YOU guh rit]

An ancient Canaanite city (modern Ras Shamra) in western Syria. Ugarit was situated about 25 miles (40 kilometers) southwest of Antioch, about one-half mile from the Mediterranean Sea and directly east of the island of Cyprus. Although Ugarit is not mentioned in the Bible, it is important to Bible students because of the archaeological discoveries made at this site.

The excavation of Ugarit began in 1929 under the direction of Claude F. A. Schaeffer. Although interrupted by World War II, the excavation resumed in 1948. These excavations reveal that the city of Ugarit reached the height of its importance between the time of Abraham and David (2000 to 1000 B.C.).

The discoveries at Ugarit have had a great impact on the understanding of the Old Testament. The language of Ugarit is similar to biblical Hebrew. The Ugaritic myths describe the false religion of Baal that the prophets of Israel condemned. Several of the religious institutions in Ugarit are similar to those found in the Bible.

These details are known because the archaeologists discovered a library containing a large number of clay tablets written in several ancient Near Eastern languages. The texts in the Ugaritic language contain many words, grammatical forms, and idioms that are common to the Hebrew language. The poetic texts are especially similar to the style and imagery of the Book of Psalms.

One of the Ugaritic texts is a myth about the struggles of the gods to gain control of the earth. Mot, the god of death and the dry season, struggles with Baal, the god of life and the wet season. Baal worshipers hoped to encourage Baal to bless their crops with rain and fertility by offering sacrifices to Baal and by their involvement with the sacred prostitutes at the Baal temples and high places. The drought that God sent during the time of Elijah (1 Kin. 17:1, 7) proved that the God of Israel, not Baal, was in charge of fertility and rain. Later Elijah prayed and God sent the rain (1 Kin. 18:41–45). Baal worship was especially encouraged by Ahab and Jezebel, who built an altar and temple for Baal in Samaria (1 Kin. 16:29–33), and Athaliah and Manasseh, who built altars to Baal in Jerusalem (2 Kin. 11:13–20; 21:1–4).

The prophets condemned the Israelites for their worship of Baal, but the Israelites did not listen. God destroyed both Israel (2 Kin. 17:1–20) and Judah (2 Chr. 36:9–21) because of their sinful worship of this false god.

UNCLEAN, UNCLEANNESS

To be unclean refers to foods that are unfit, to defilement of a moral or religious character, and to spiritual impurity. The Old Testament distinguishes between what is clean and helpful and what is unclean and unacceptable (Lev. 10:10; 11:47).

There were different kinds of uncleanness. One type was unclean food. Several kinds of birds and certain animals were labeled unclean (Lev. 11:1–19). Besides foods, persons were designated unclean under certain conditions. Through a discharge or because of menstruation, men and women were considered unclean (Lev. 15:2–13, 19–24). Body emissions from open sores also rendered the person unclean. A leprous person was unclean (Lev. 13:11).

The land could be defiled through idolatry (Ezek. 36:18) or through the sacrifice of innocent children (Ps. 106:38). God's Temple was defiled because of the entry of pagans (Ps. 79:1). The prophet Haggai used the notion of uncleanness of things to speak of immoral behavior of people (Hag. 2:13–14).

In the Gospels, the word "unclean" describes those who are possessed by undesirable or even demonic spirits. Jesus exercised command over these unclean spirits (Luke 4:36) and effectively rebuked them (Luke 9:42). The disciples were also given power over unclean spirits (Mark 6:7; Acts 5:16). Jesus often cast out unclean spirits (Mark 1:23, 26–27; 5:2).

The laws about uncleanness are a powerful statement of the living God of the universe. Those made clean through His provision, however, will enjoy eternal life.

UNLEAVENED BREAD

Bread baked from unfermented dough, or dough without yeast or "leaven" (Gen. 19:3; Josh. 5:11; 1 Sam. 28:24). Unleavened bread was the flat bread used in the Passover celebration and the priestly rituals (Lev. 23:4–8). The tradition of eating unleavened bread goes back to the time of the Exodus, when the Hebrews left Egypt in such haste that they had no time to bake their bread (Ex. 12:8, 15–20, 34, 39; 13:6–7). Leaven was produced by the souring of bread dough. Its exclusion from ceremonial breads probably symbolized purity.

UR

Abraham's native city in southern Mesopotamia; an important metropolis of the ancient world situated on the Euphrates River. Strategically situated about halfway between the head of the Persian Gulf and Baghdad, in present-day Iraq, Ur was the capital of Sumer for two centuries until the Elamites captured the city. The city came to be known as "Ur of the Chaldeans" after the Chaldeans entered southern Babylonia after 1000 B.C.

Abraham lived in the city of Ur (Gen. 11:28, 31) at the height of its splendor. The city was a prosperous center of religion and industry. Thousands of recovered clay documents attest to thriving business activity. Excavations of the royal cemetery, which dates from about 2900 to 2500 B.C., have revealed a surprisingly advanced culture. Uncovered were beautiful jewelry and art treasures, including headwear, personal jewelry, and exquisite dishes and cups.

The Babylonians worshiped many gods, but the moon god Sin was supreme. Accordingly, the city of Ur was a kind of theocracy centered in the moon deity. Ur-Nammu, the founder of the strong Third Dynasty of Ur (around 2070–1960 B.C.), built the famous ziggurats, a system of terraced platforms on which temples were erected. The Tower of Babel (Gen. 11:3–4) was probably a ziggurat made of brick. It is a miracle of God's providence that Abraham resisted Ur's polluted atmosphere and set out on a journey of faith to Canaan that would bless all mankind.

Ur's glory was suddenly destroyed about 1900 B.C. Foreigners stormed down from the surrounding hills and captured the reigning king, reducing the city to ruins. So complete was the destruction that the city was buried in oblivion until it was excavated centuries later by archaeologists.

URIAH [you RYE uh] *(the Lord is my light)*

A Hittite married to Bathsheba. Uriah was one of David's mighty men (2 Sam. 11:3–26; 12:9–10, 15; 1 Kin. 15:5; Matt. 1:6; Urias, KJV). Judging from the usual interpretation of his name and good conduct, Uriah was a worshiper of God. David's adultery with Uriah's wife, Bathsheba, occurred while Uriah was engaged in war at Rabbah, the Ammonite capital. Uriah was immediately recalled to Jerusalem to hide what had happened, but his sense of duty and loyalty only frustrated the king.

Failing to use Uriah as a shield to cover his sin with Bathsheba, David ordered this valiant soldier to the front line of battle, where he was killed.

URIM AND THUMMIM [YOU rim, THUME em]

Gems or stones carried by the high priest and used by him to determine God's will in certain matters. Many scholars believe these gems were lots that were cast, much as dice are thrown, to aid the high priest in making important decisions.

The Urim and Thummim were either on, by, or in the high priest's breastplate. For this reason the breastplate is often called the breastplate of judgment, or decision. In the instructions for making the breastplate, the linen was to be doubled to form a square (Ex. 28:16). If the top edge was not stitched together, the breastplate would be an envelope or pouch. Many scholars believe the Urim and Thummim were kept in this pouch and were stones or gems with engraved symbols that signified yes-no or true-false. By these the high priest reached a decision, according to this theory.

The Jewish historian Josephus (about A.D. 37–100), a contemporary of the apostle John, believed that the Urim and Thummim had to do with the flashing of the precious stones in the breastplate. Later Jewish writers believed that the letters in the names of the twelve tribes of Israel engraved on the stones stood out or flashed in succession to spell out God's answer. This theory does imply that the Urim and Thummim could produce answers to questions that called for more than a mere yes or no reply. Another theory is that by staring at the Urim and Thummim, the high priest went into a state of ecstasy or trance during which God spoke to him.

The student or Bible teacher should bear in mind that all of these theories are pure guesswork. No one knows the

U

exact nature of the Urim and Thummim or precisely how they were used.

There are few allusions to the Urim and Thummim in the Bible. They are first mentioned in the description of the breastplate of judgment (Ex. 28:30; Lev. 8:8). When Joshua succeeded Moses, he was to have answers from the Urim through Eleazar the priest (Num. 27:21). They are next mentioned in Moses' dying blessing upon Levi (Deut. 33:8). There are places in the Bible where Urim and Thummim may be implied but are not named (Josh. 7:14–18; 1 Sam. 14:37–45; 2 Sam. 21:1).

Saul sought direction from the witch of Endor when he could receive no answer from the Lord, "either by dreams or by Urim or by the prophets" (1 Sam. 28:6). Another interesting reference to the Urim and Thummim occurred during the period after the return of the Jewish people from their years in captivity by the Babylonians. The Persian governor of Jerusalem denied the people permission to observe some of their ancient Jewish food laws until "a priest could consult with the Urim and Thummim" (Ezra 2:63).

USURY [YOU zhu ree]

Interest paid on borrowed money. In the Bible the word *usury* does not necessarily have the negative connotations of our modern meaning of lending money at an excessive interest rate. Instead, it usually means the charging of interest on money that has been loaned.

The Old Testament prohibited charging usury to fellow Israelites; their need was not to become an opportunity for profit (Ex. 22:25; Deut. 23:19–20; Neh. 5:1–13). However, foreigners were often traders and merchants, and usury was a part of their everyday lives. Thus they could be charged usury (Deut. 23:20).

By the time of the New Testament, Is-rael's economy had changed so much from Old Testament days that usury was common practice, even among God's people. Therefore, Jesus did not condemn receiving usury. But He did insist that the rates be fair and justly applied (Matt. 25:27; Luke 19:23). Usury, as all other aspects of life, was to be handled in a spirit of love and genuine concern for the welfare of others (Luke 6:31).

UZZIAH [you ZIE uh] *(the Lord is my strength)*

The son of Amaziah and Jecholiah; ninth king of Judah and father of Jotham (2 Kin. 15:1–7; 2 Chr. 26). Uzziah is also called Azariah (2 Kin. 14:21; 15:1–7).

Uzziah ascended the throne at age 16 and reigned longer than any previous king of Judah or Israel—52 years. He probably co-reigned with his father and had his son Jotham as his co-regent during his final years as a leper. A wise, pious, and powerful king, he extended Judah's territory and brought the nation to a time of great prosperity. In the south he maintained control over Edom and rebuilt port facilities at Elath on the Gulf of Aqaba. To the west he warred against the Philistines, seizing several cities. He also apparently defeated and subdued the Ammonites.

The foolishness of Uzziah's father Amaziah in fighting Joash, the king of Israel, had left the city of Jerusalem in a vulnerable position (2 Chr. 25:23). So Uzziah focused his attention on securing the defenses of both his capital and his country. He reinforced the towers of the city gates. On these towers and walls he placed huge catapults capable of shooting arrows and hurling stones at the enemy (2 Chr. 26:15). He also maintained a well-equipped army and fortified strategic places in the desert.

Uzziah's successes were directly related to his spiritual sensitivity, because he sought the Lord through a prophet who encouraged him to honor and obey God (2 Chr. 26:5).

However, Uzziah's heart was lifted up in pride. No longer satisfied to be a mortal king, he desired to be like some of his contemporaries—a divine king. He entered the temple to burn incense. When Azariah the high priest and 80 associates confronted him, he responded in anger instead of repentance. God judged him by striking him with leprosy. Uzziah was forced to live the rest of his life in a separate place, with his son Jotham probably acting as king. At Uzziah's death, the prophet Isaiah had a transforming vision of the Lord, high and lifted up on a throne (Is. 1:1; 6:1–13; 7:1).

V

VIRGIN BIRTH OF JESUS

The theological doctrine that Jesus was miraculously begotten by God and born of Mary, who was a virgin. The term "virgin birth" explains the way in which the Son of God entered human existence; it means that Mary had not had sexual relations with any man when she conceived Jesus.

This unparalleled act of God is described beautifully in Luke 1:26–38. The angel of God appeared to a virgin who was engaged to Joseph. In those days engagement was a legal arrangement in which a woman was betrothed, or pledged, to a man. But engagement did not permit sexual relations.

Since Mary had not "known" Joseph sexually, she wondered how she could bear a child. The angel explained that this would be encouraged by "the power of the Highest" as the Holy Spirit would "overshadow her." There was nothing physical about this divine act; this is emphasized by the statement that the child would be the "Holy One" (Luke 1:35).

The angel also declared that the child would be called "the Son of God." This clearly teaches that it was only through the virgin birth that Jesus, a human being, could also be properly identified as the Son of God. The one person, Jesus, has two natures—divine and human.

The eternal, divine nature of the Son of God was joined, in Mary's womb, with a human nature by the direct act of God.

The parallel account in Matthew 1:18–25 views the virgin birth from Joseph's perspective. Because of the legal nature of engagement, a man who found his fiancée pregnant would normally divorce her. Because Joseph was a fair and just man, he did not want to shame Mary by divorcing her publicly; so he decided to do so privately. But the angel prevented this by assuring him that Mary was still a virgin. Her child was conceived by the Holy Spirit, as predicted in Isaiah 7:14.

After this revelation, Joseph took Mary as his wife but did not unite with her sexually until Jesus was born. This implies (but does not prove) that Joseph and Mary later united sexually and had other children.

Some scholars claim that the reference in Luke 2:27, 33, and 41 to Jesus' parents (Joseph and Mary) implies that the virgin birth was not a part of early Christian tradition. But these words were written by the same writer who described the annunciation of the virgin birth in Luke 1:26–38. Some Bible students also express concern over the lack of reference to the virgin birth elsewhere in the New Testament. However, the other Gospels say nothing about Jesus' birth, so it is not strange that they do not speak of the virgin birth.

Since the gospel message concerns the death, burial, and resurrection of Christ (1 Cor. 15:1–3), the virgin birth is not a natural part of its proclamation. But the virgin birth is a wonderful and personal truth that clearly belongs to Christian doctrine.

VISIONS

Experiences similar to dreams through which supernatural insight or awareness is given by revelation. The most noteworthy examples in the Old Testament of recipients of visions are Ezekiel and Daniel. Visions in the New Testament are most prominent in the Gospel of Luke, the Book of Acts, and the Book of Revelation.

The purpose of visions was to give guidance and direction to God's servants and to foretell the future. Daniel's vision, for example, told of the coming of the Messiah (Dan. 8:1, 17).

VOCATION

The invitation God has given to all people to become His children through Christ's work. This vocation, or calling, does not come to people because they deserve it; it comes strictly as a result of God's grace (2 Tim. 1:9). God requires that Christians labor to be worthy of their divine vocation (Eph. 4:1). If people accept the Christian vocation and labor in it, they can expect—just as they might expect from their professional vocations—a great reward (Eph. 1:18).

VOW

A solemn promise or pledge that binds a person to perform a specified act or to behave in a certain manner. The first mention of a vow in the Bible is of Jacob at Bethel (Gen. 28:20–22; 31:13). Other people who made a vow are Jephthah (Judg. 11:30–31, 39), Hannah (1 Sam. 1:11), David (Ps. 132:2–5), and Absalom (2 Sam. 15:7–8).

In the New Testament, the apostle Paul, probably at the end of a 30-day period of abstinence from meat and wine, had his hair cut off at Cenchrea, "for he had taken a vow" (Acts 18:18). The vow that Paul had taken may have been the Nazirite vow (Num. 6:1–21). Samson was an Old Testament hero for whom the Nazirite vow was taken before his birth (Judg. 13:5, 7; 16:17).

All vows were made to God as a promise in expectation of His favor (Gen. 28:20) or in thanksgiving for His blessings (Ps. 116:12–14). Vowing might be a part of everyday devotion (Ps. 61:8) or the annual festivals (1 Sam. 1:21). Vows had to be paid to God in the congregation at the tabernacle or temple (Deut. 12:6, 11; Ps. 22:25).

Vowing was voluntary. But after a vow was made, it had to be performed (Deut. 23:21–23; Eccl. 5:4–6). Vows, therefore, were to be made only after careful consideration (Prov. 20:25) and in keeping with what pleased God (Lev. 27:9–27). Sinful people do not know what will please God; they need God's direction in making vows.

Vowing is joyful worship in faith and love (Ps. 61:4–5, 8), often associated with the proclamation of God's salvation (Ps. 22:22–27; 66:13–20). For this reason, deception in vowing is an affront to God and brings His curse (Mal. 1:14).

VULTURE

Vultures are large, loathsome members of the hawk family. The largest species have a wingspread of nine to ten feet. Most vultures have bare heads and necks. However, the lammergeier (bearded vulture) has dirty-white neck feathers and a tassel of dark feathers hanging from its beak. The Egyptian vulture likewise has neck feathers. A griffon's long neck is covered with fine white down.

Vultures feed on dead bodies. For this reason they were considered unclean animals by the Hebrew people (Lev. 11:13; Deut. 14:12–13). Other versions of the Bible translate the word as buzzard, falcon, bustard, or carrion vulture.

W

WANDERINGS OF ISRAEL

The activities of the Israelite tribes during the period between their departure from Egypt under Moses and the time when they were encamped by the Jordan River, ready to be led into Canaan by Joshua. The period of time covered by these events is traditionally 40 years, much of which was spent in the area of Kadesh-barnea.

The wanderings of the Hebrew people began with the crossing of the Red Sea, a papyrus-reed marsh probably situated in the region of the Bitter Lakes. Immediately thereafter they entered the Wilderness of Shur, an area in northwest Sinai lying south of the coastal road from Egypt to Philistia and bounded on the east by the Wadi el-Arish. This was the first stage of the journey to Mount Sinai (Ex. 15:22), which was probably followed in a southeasterly direction along the east coast of the Gulf of Suez. In this region the water table is high and many springs and wells are available. In spite of this, the Israelites experienced many difficulties (Ex. 15:23–25). They were relieved when they arrived at the oasis of Elim.

It is extremely difficult to identify most of the encampments of the wilderness period. This is partly because many of the names may have been given to the locations by the Israelites themselves as a result of specific happenings (for example, Marah, Ex. 15:23; Taberah, Num. 11:3), and not because those were the local names. Even if they had been named before the Hebrews arrived, only the most important of them would have survived in modern Arabic.

An example of one place name that has survived is Jebel Musa ("Mountain of Moses") as one possible location of Mount Sinai. This imposing peak in the Sinai range is the traditional site of the covenant with Israel, although two other locations, Jebel Serbal and Ras es-Safsafeh, have also been suggested.

The Israelites encamped in the Wilderness of Sin at Rephidim, possibly the Wadi Refayid in southwest Sinai, and drove off an Amalekite attack (Ex. 17:8–16) before reaching Mount Sinai. There they received God's law and settled for nearly a year (Num. 1:1; 10:11) while Moses worked at organizing the new nation. At this stage of the wanderings the construction of the tabernacle and the regulations governing its use were given careful attention because of their importance for the future life of the Israelites.

Even these precautions, however, were not enough to stop dissatisfaction among the wandering Israelites as they traveled toward Kadesh. The people complained about the lack of food in the wilderness. Even when God provided manna, they soon began to dislike it. To punish them, God sent a flock of quail for food, which made the people ill and caused many deaths (Num. 11:32–33).

From the Wilderness of Paran Moses sent spies into Canaan, but they returned with discouraging reports about the inhabitants (Num. 13:32–33). The people

W

then refused to enter Canaan and rebelled against their leaders. God was angry with them. With the exception of Joshua and Caleb, all the people alive at that time were condemned to spend the rest of their lives in the wilderness. Korah, Dathan, and Abiram accused Moses and Aaron of assuming too much priestly authority. They were punished by being swallowed up in a spectacular earthquake (Num. 16:32–33). The Israelites became angry at this, and God would have killed them all if Moses had not interceded on their behalf.

Because of an act of disobedience at Kadesh (Num. 20:8–12), Moses and Aaron were forbidden to enter the Promised Land. Nevertheless, they and the Israelites attempted to go to Canaan along the King's Highway which passed through Edomite territory. But they were refused permission. The people then journeyed to Mount Hor on the border of Edom, where Aaron died (Num. 20:28). A skirmish with the Canaanite king of Arad took place before the Hebrews moved toward the wilderness area east of Moab (Num. 21:1–3). When the Amorite King Sihon refused them access to the King's Highway, he was defeated in battle (Num. 21:21–32). Shortly afterwards Og, king of Bashan, suffered the same fate (Num. 21:33–35).

The Israelites now occupied a large area of territory in Transjordan. This alarmed Balak, king of Moab. He hired Balaam, a Mesopotamian soothsayer, to curse the Israelites, but by divine intervention he blessed them instead (Num. 22–24). Unfortunately, the Israelites committed sin with the Moabite women, and this was to prove an indication of what lay ahead in Canaan.

While the people were in the plains of Moab, across the Jordan River from Jericho, a second census of the people was taken, apparently in preparation for the crossing into Canaan, for which

Joshua was appointed leader (Num. 27:18–23). Perhaps because of the immorality with the Moabite women, Moses proclaimed a series of regulations involving offerings and festivals that would be observed once the Israelites were in Canaan (Num. 28–29).

The hold of the Israelites on Transjordanian territory was consolidated by a successful attack upon the Midianites. This resulted in a great deal of plunder. The conquered lands were ideal for raising herds and flocks, so the tribes of Gad and Reuben and half of the tribe of Manasseh were given that territory as their own. Moses then issued instructions for the conquest of Canaan and appointed leaders who would divide the land among the tribes.

After reviewing Israel's wilderness wanderings (Num. 33:1–49) and composing a victory song (Deut. 32:1–43), Moses climbed Mount Nebo to see the land that he had been forbidden to enter. With a final blessing upon Israel, Moses died on Mount Nebo. With his death the wilderness wanderings ended and the occupation of Canaan began.

WATCHMAN

A person who guarded or watched over a city or harvest field. Because of the danger of being raided, every Palestinian city or village had a watchman, especially at night. These watchmen were stationed on the city walls (2 Sam. 18:24), a watchtower (2 Kin. 9:17), or a hilltop (Jer. 31:6). Watchmen were responsible for reporting any hostile action or approaching suspicious person. These watchmen sometimes patrolled the city, called out the hours of the night, and especially looked forward to dawn (Is. 21:11–12).

At harvest times watchmen guarded the crops at night. Israel's prophets were responsible for watching for impending divine judgment or blessing (Is. 21:6;

52:8; Jer. 6:17) and bringing the news to the people. Watchmen are sometimes referred to as sentries and lookouts.

WATER OF BITTERNESS

Part of a ceremonial test, or trial by ordeal, of a woman accused of adultery (Num. 5:11–31). When a Hebrew man suspected his wife of infidelity but he had no proof, he would bring her before the priest with the charge. The priest would mix "holy water"—probably water from a sacred spring—with dust from the tabernacle floor and curses scraped from a book. This potion, known as the water of bitterness, would be drunk by the woman after she had sworn her innocence under oath.

If the woman had lied to the priest and to God, this potion would turn bitter in her mouth and cause her belly to swell and her thigh to rot. If she was not guilty, the mixture would not harm her.

WAVE OFFERING

A bloody offering presented to God (Lev. 3:1; fellowship offering, NIV) and signifying the covering of sin, forgiveness by God, and the restoration of a right and meaningful relationship with God and with life itself (Judg. 20:26; 21:4). Part of the offering was eaten by the priest (representing God's acceptance) and part was eaten by worshipers and their guests (nonofficiating priests or Levites and the poor, Deut. 12:18; 16:11). Thus, God hosted the meal, communing with the worshiper and other participants.

WEAVER

A person who fashioned threads into cloth. Weaving was known in the ancient world from about 2000 B.C. Almost every household had a loom, and women spent much time at this task (Prov. 31:13, 19, 22, 24). A woman sat before her loom and passed the shuttle back and forth through the warp thread while manipulating the loom. She also made her own yarn or thread from animal hair or plant fibers. For instance, flax was made into linen. In other countries, such as Egypt and Assyria, weaving was done by men. Such professional weavers worked in urban areas. Even urban areas in Israel boasted professional weavers.

WEDDING

A marriage ceremony with its accompanying festivities (Luke 12:36; 14:8). Among the Israelites a wedding was a festive occasion in which the whole community participated.

When the day for the wedding arrived, the bride put on white robes, decked herself with jewels, covered herself with a veil, and placed a garland on her head. The bridegroom set out for the house of the bride's parents, accompanied by his friends, by musicians and singers, and by persons bearing torches if the procession moved at night.

The groom received his bride from her parents with their blessings and the good wishes of friends. Then he conducted the whole party back to his own house or his father's house with song, music, and dancing. On the way back they were joined by additional friends of the bride and groom. A feast was served and celebrated with great joy and merrymaking. In the evening the bride was escorted to the nuptial chamber by her parents, and the groom by his companions or the bride's parents. On the next day the festivities were resumed, continuing for seven days.

See also MARRIAGE.

WELL

A pit or hole sunk into the earth to provide water. References in English versions of the Bible sometimes confuse wells, natural springs, and cisterns. Many different types of wells are mentioned in the Bible. These include a cistern dug in the ground (Gen. 16:14; 2 Sam. 17:18); a spring (Ps. 84:6); a fountain, also called a living spring (Neh. 2:13); and a pit or hole (John 4:11–12).

Wells in Palestine were dug from solid limestone rock. Sometimes they were furnished with descending steps that allowed a person to dip directly from the pool of water (Gen. 24:16). The brims of still other wells had a curb or low wall of stone that often bore the marks of the furrows worn over the years by ropes in drawing water. Jesus sat on a curb of this sort when he talked to the woman of Samaria (John 4:6).

There is no information on how biblical wells were dug. But the process must have been very difficult, because only crude tools were available. Isaac (Gen. 26:18–22) and Uzziah (2 Chr. 26:10) are the most active well-diggers mentioned in the Bible. Many ancient wells descended to a great depth. Jacob's Well is still 75 feet deep and at one time it may have been twice as deep. These deep wells were necessary because of the problem of shallow wells running dry in the summer.

Even in very favorable locations, the water in Palestine almost vanishes during the summer drought. Some wells are not covered because the soil in the area is not likely to drift and fill them up, but desert wells are always covered. They taper to a point so that the opening is easily closed.

Wells were often situated outside towns, where they became local landmarks and meeting places (Gen. 24:11, 20; John 4:6–8). Sometimes they were in

isolated locations, enabling livestock to be grazed nearby (Gen. 29:3, 8–10; Ex. 2:15–18). Both the ownership and the use of wells could become matters of dispute (Gen. 21:25; Ex. 2:17–19). Occasionally, old dry wells were used as prisons (Gen. 27:24; Jer. 38:6).

The Bible's most famous wells were at Bethlehem, for whose water David longed (2 Sam. 23:15–16), and at Sychar in Samaria, where Jesus spoke about His free gift of unfailing living water.

WHEAT

The most important cereal grass mentioned in the Bible. It was cultivated in Bible lands from early times: "Now Reuben went in the days of wheat harvest" (Gen. 30:14). Egyptian wheat was the many-eared variety called "mummy wheat." This was the wheat of Pharaoh's dream (Gen. 41:5–57). It was also depicted on Egyptian monuments.

Wheat was sown after barley in November or December. It was usually broadcast and then either plowed or trodden into the soil by oxen or other animals (Is. 32:20). This grain was used for bread (Ex. 29:32), and was also eaten parched (Lev. 23:14; Ruth 2:14). It was used in ceremonial offerings (Lev. 2:1; 24:5–7) and as an article of commerce (Ezek. 27:17; Acts 27:38).

When corn is mentioned in the Bible, it refers to wheat, as corn was not known in Bible times (Ps. 72:16; Matt. 12:1; Mark 4:28). Jesus compared His death to a grain of wheat that must die to produce fruit (John 12:24).

WHEEL

The potter's wheel was a device used by potters to make their pottery even and symmetrical. Before its invention, pots and jars were built up of coils of clay smoothed and shaped by hand. The "slow wheel" was a small flat disk on a spindle, with a larger stone disk on the other end. It was spun by hand as the potter alternated between keeping the wheel in motion and shaping the clay.

The "fast wheel" was really two wheels, one above the other, with an axle joining them. The potter sat on a bench and turned the lower wheel with his feet. This way, he could keep it going rapidly, yet still have both hands free to shape the clay on the upper wheel.

The most symbolic and descriptive use of a potter's wheel in the Bible appears in the Book of Jeremiah. Jeremiah visited a potter at his wheel. He compared the potter who molds his clay to God who has the power to mold the nation of Israel (Jer. 18:2–8).

WINE

The fermented juice of grapes. Wine is first mentioned in the Bible when Noah became intoxicated after the Flood (Gen. 9:20–21). Wine was a common commodity in Hebrew life and was regularly included in summaries of agricultural products (Gen. 27:28; 2 Kin. 18:32; Jer. 31:12).

In Palestine, grape harvesting occurred in September and was accompanied by great celebration. The ripe fruit was gathered in baskets (Jer. 6:9) and carried to winepresses. The grapes were placed in the upper one of two vats that formed the winepress. Then the grapes were trampled or "treaded." The treading was done by one or more people, according to the size of the vat. These grape treaders encouraged one another with shouts (Is. 16:9–10; Jer. 25:30; 48:33).

Sometimes the juice from the grapes was served in an unfermented state, but generally it was bottled after fermentation. If the wine was to be kept for some time, a substance was added to give it body (Is. 25:6). Consequently, the wine was always strained before it was served (Is. 25:6).

Wine was stored in either clay jars or

W

wineskins, which were made by tying up the holes of skins taken from goats. Old wineskins could not be used a second time because the fermentation process would cause the old skins to burst and the wine would be lost (Matt. 9:17; Mark 2:22; Luke 5:36–38).

Wine was a significant trade item in Palestine. Solomon offered Hiram 20,000 baths of wine in exchange for timber (2 Chr. 2:10, 15). Damascus was a market for the "wine of Helbon" (Ezek. 27:18). Fines were sometimes paid with wine (Amos 2:8).

Wine was also used in worship. Libations to false gods were condemned (Deut. 32:27–38; Is. 57:6; 65:11; Jer. 7:18; 19:13), but the drink offering prescribed by the Law of Moses was a libation of wine offered to the Lord. The daily offering (Ex. 29:40; Num. 28:7), the offering of the firstfruits (Lev. 23:13), the burnt offering, and the freewill offering (Num. 15:4) required one-fourth of a hin of wine. The sacrifice of a ram was accompanied by a hin of wine (Num. 15:6–7). In the temple organization set up by David, Levites were appointed to supervise these wine offerings (1 Chr. 9:29).

Wine was also used as a common beverage, or drink, in Palestine. A part of the daily fare of the Hebrew people, wine was a creation of the Lord to cheer the heart (Ps. 104:15), a gift given by Him and not by Baal (Hos. 2:8), as the idol worshiper thought.

Wisdom is said to have mixed her wine (Prov. 9:2) in furnishing her table. Melchizedek brought wine and bread to Abraham when Abraham returned from battle (Gen. 14:18). Jesse sent David with bread, a skin of wine, and a young goat as a present when Saul was fighting the Philistines (1 Sam. 16:20). Job's children were drinking wine at their brother's house when disaster struck (Job 1:13, 18).

Wine was also used as medicine. It was said to revive the faint (2 Sam. 16:2) and was suitable as a sedative for people in distress (Prov. 31:6). Mixed with a drug, it was used to ease suffering (Matt. 27:34; Mark 15:23). The Samaritan poured oil and wine on the wounds of the injured traveler (Luke 10:34). The apostle Paul charged Timothy, "No longer drink only water, but use a little wine for your stomach's sake" (1 Tim. 5:23).

The dangers of drunkenness are abundantly recognized in the Bible (Prov. 20:1; 23:29–35). Wine often enslaved the heart (Hos. 4:11). The prophets accused Israel of being overcome with wine (Is. 28:1), of drinking wine by bowlfuls (Amos 6:6), and of wanting prophets who spoke of wine (Mic. 2:11). While the use of wine continued in New Testament times, Paul admonished his readers to be filled with the Holy Spirit rather than with wine (Eph. 5:18).

WINESKIN

A bag for holding and dispensing wine, made from the skin of a goat or another animal (Job 32:19). Jesus used the analogy of wineskins to show that the Jewish legalism of the Old Testament was inflexible and outdated and could not contain the dynamic new faith of Christianity (Matt. 9:17).

WISDOM LITERATURE

A type of literature, common to the peoples of the ancient world, that included ethical and philosophical works. The wisdom literature of the Old Testament consists of the books of Job, Proverbs, and Ecclesiastes, and certain of the psalms (Pss. 1; 19; 37; 49; 104; 107; 112; 119; 127; 128; 133; 147; 148).

In general, two principal types of wisdom are found in the wisdom literature of the Old Testament—practical and speculative.

Practical wisdom consists mainly of wise sayings that offer guidelines for a successful and happy life. These are maxims of commonsense insight and observation about how intelligent people should conduct themselves. The Book of Proverbs is a good example of practical wisdom; it encourages the pursuit of wisdom and the practice of strict discipline, hard work, and high moral standards as the way to happiness and success.

Speculative wisdom, such as that found in the books of Job and Ecclesiastes, goes beyond practical maxims about daily conduct. It reflects upon the deeper issues of the meaning of life, the worth and value of life, and the existence of evil in the world.

A good example of this type of wisdom is the Book of Job, which seeks to explain the ways of God to humankind. One of the themes of the book is the suffering of the righteous and the apparent prosperity of the wicked. The answer to such questions is that the prosperity of the wicked is brief and illusory (Job 15:21–29; 24:24) while the righteous, although presently suffering, will eventually receive God's reward.

WISE MEN

The men from the East who were led by a star to come to Palestine to worship the infant Christ (Matt. 2:1, 7, 16). The Greek word for wise men in this account (*magoi*) is rendered as "astrologers" where it occurs in the Septuagint, the Greek translation of the Old Testament (Dan. 1:20; 2:2) and as "sorcerer" in its other occurrences in the New Testament (Acts 13:6, 8).

The Greek historian Herodotus, writing in the fifth century B.C., identified the Magi as a caste of Medes who had a priestly function in the Persian Empire. In the Book of Daniel the "astrologers" (magoi) are grouped with magicians, sorcerers, and Chaldeans as advisers to the court of Babylon with responsibility for interpreting dreams.

The role of the star in Matthew 2 suggests a connection with astrology. These astrologers, pursuing their observations of the stars in the heavens, encountered a sign of God (Matt. 24:29–30). God broke through their misguided system to make the great event known.

WITNESS

A person who gives testimony; testimony given for or against someone, often in a law-court setting, where there is considerable concern for the truth of the testimony.

The Old Testament prophets often pictured God either as bearing witness against Israel (Mic. 1:2) or as challenging Israel to bear witness against Him (Mic. 6:3). God is also seen in the Old Testament as witnessing covenants between individuals (Gen. 31:50) as well as covenants between Himself and the nation of Israel or individuals (Deut. 31:19–26).

The believer's life and word serve as a witness to the world. Sometimes this witness to the world is represented in the witness of the apostles, who are Christ's special witnesses—witnesses of His resurrection (Acts 1:22; 2:32; 10:41; 13:31). The believer's model in witness is none other than Christ Himself (1 Tim. 6:13; Rev. 1:5).

WORD OF GOD

The means by which God makes Himself known, declares His will, and brings about His purposes.

God acts in the world by means of His word, and He becomes personally known through His word (1 Sam. 3:21). His word is powerfully creative (Ezek. 37:4) and its purposes are irresistible (Is. 55:11; Jer. 23:29). God's word is totally dependable; it represents His permanent commitment (Is. 40:8). When heard and responded to, His word meets deep

W

needs in the human heart and provides joy, satisfaction, and confident direction that can be achieved in no other manner (Deut. 8:3; Ps. 119:162; Jer. 15:16). God's word has the power to penetrate all pretense and discern "the thoughts and intents of the heart" (Heb. 4:12).

God's speaking of His word reaches a culmination in the sending of His Son (John 1:1, 14; Heb. 1:1–2). All that is true of God's earlier word is supremely true of Jesus. The gospel of Jesus Christ is, in a special way, the word of God as it makes known and brings into operation the reconciliation with God that is His purpose for mankind (2 Cor. 5:18–19).

WORSHIP

Reverent devotion and allegiance pledged to God; the rituals or ceremonies by which this reverence is expressed. The English word *worship* comes from the Old English word *worthship*, a word that denotes the worthiness of the one receiving the special honor or devotion.

In Old Testament times, Abraham built altars to the Lord and called on His name (Gen. 12:8; 13:18). This worship of God required no elaborate priesthood or ritual. After God's appearance to Moses and the deliverance of the Israelites from slavery in Egypt, the foundations of Israelite ritual were laid. This worship took place in the light of history, especially the Exodus of the Hebrew people from Egypt. Through Moses, God established the form and principles of Israelite worship (Ex. 25–31; 35–40).

After the occupation of the Promised Land, Israel's exposure to Canaanite worship affected the nation's own worship. The Old Testament reveals clearly that Israel adopted some of the practices of the pagan people around them. At various times God's people lapsed into idolatry. Some idols were placed on pedestals, and sometimes they were adorned or fastened with silver chains (Is. 40:19) or fastened with pegs lest they totter and fall (Is. 41:7). Shrines and altars were sometimes erected to these pagan gods. But such idolatry was condemned by God and His special spokesmen, the prophets of the Old Testament.

New Testament worship was characterized by joy and thanksgiving because of God's gracious redemption in Christ. This early Christian worship focused on God's saving work in Jesus Christ. True worship was that which occurred under the inspiration of God's Spirit (John 4:23–24; Phil. 3:3).

The Jewish Sabbath was quickly replaced among Christians by the first day of the week as the time for weekly public worship (Acts 20:7; 1 Cor. 16:2); it was called the Lord's Day (Rev. 1:10). This was the occasion for celebration of the resurrection of Jesus, since He arose on the first day of the week (Mark 16:2).

At first, worship services were conducted in private houses. Possibly for a time, the first Christians worshiped in the synagogues as well as private homes. Some scholars believe the Jewish Christians would go to the synagogues on Saturday and to their own meeting on Sunday.

Many early Christians of Jewish background continued to follow the law and customs of their people. They observed the Sabbath and the Jewish holy days, such as the great annual festivals. However, the apostle Paul held himself free from any obligation to these and never laid an obligation to observe them on his converts (Col. 2:16). The New Testament itself contains no references to any yearly Christian festivals.

Although the New Testament does not instruct worshipers in a specific procedure to follow in their services, several elements appear regularly in the worship practices of the early church.

Prayer apparently had a leading place

in Christian worship. The letters of Paul regularly open with references to prayer for fellow Christians who are instructed to "pray without ceasing" (1 Thess. 5:17). Praise, either by individuals or in hymns sung in common, reflects the frequent use of psalms in the synagogue. Also, possible fragments of Christian hymns appear scattered through the New Testament (Acts 4:24–30; Eph. 5:14; 1 Tim. 3:16; Rev. 4:8, 11; 5:9–10, 12–13).

Lessons from the Bible to be read and studied were another part of the worship procedure of the New Testament church. Emphasis was probably given to the messianic prophecies that had been fulfilled in Jesus Christ. His teachings also received a primary place.

Prophecy, inspired preaching by one filled with the Holy Spirit, helped build up the church, the body of Christ (Ro. 12:6). Contributions were also collected on the first day of each week (1 Cor. 16:2).

Other details about the worship procedures of the early Christians in New Testament times are spotty. But these elements must have been regularly included in the weekly worship service.

WRATH

The personal manifestation of God's holy, moral character in judgment against sin. God's wrath is an expression of His holy love. The Bible declares that all people are "by nature children of wrath" (Eph. 2:3) and that "the wrath of God is revealed from heaven against all ungodliness and unrighteousness of men, who suppress the truth in unrighteousness" (Rom. 1:18). Since Christians have been "justified by His blood, we shall be saved from wrath through Him" (Rom. 5:9). The magnitude of God's love is manifested in the Cross, where God's only Son experienced wrath on our behalf.

Y

YHWH

The Hebrew name of the God of Israel, probably originally pronounced Yahweh. Eventually the Jews gave up pronouncing it, considering the name too holy for human lips. Instead they said *Adonai* or "Lord." This oral tradition came to be reflected in the written Greek translation of the Old Testament as *kurios* or "Lord," and it is often so quoted in the New Testament (Mark 1:3; Rom. 4:8). English versions of the Old Testament also tend to translate this word as "Lord."

YOKE

A type of harness that connected a pair of animals to a plow or similar tool. Oxen were the most common animals used in working the land. A yoke of oxen was a

pair (1 Sam. 11:7; Luke 14:19). Using a pair to pull a plow required a yoke to link them together so they could work efficiently. Yokes were usually made of a wooden beam shaped to fit over the necks of the two animals and held in place by wooden or leather fasteners.

The yoke was also used as a symbol of the burden or oppression of heavy responsibility, duty, sin, or punishment (1 Kin. 12:4–14; Jer. 27:8–12; Acts 15:10). In New Testament times, the phrase "take the yoke of" was used by the Jewish rabbis to mean, "become the pupil of" a certain teacher. Jesus gave a gentle invitation to His disciples: "Take My yoke upon you and learn from Me, for I am gentle and lowly in heart, and you will find rest for your souls. For My yoke is easy and My burden is light" (Matt. 11:29–30).

ZACCHAEUS [zack KEY us] (pure)

A chief tax collector of Jericho who had grown rich by overtaxing the people. When Jesus visited Jericho, Zacchaeus climbed a tree in order to see Jesus (Luke 19:3). Jesus asked him to come down and then went to visit Zacchaeus as a guest. As a result of Jesus' visit, Zacchaeus became a follower of the Lord, repented of his sins, and made restitution for his wrongdoing. He gave half of his goods to the poor and restored four-fold those whom he had cheated. In associating with people like Zacchaeus, Jesus showed that He came to call sinners to repentance.

ZACHARIAS [zack ah RYE us] (the Lord has remembered)

The father of John the Baptist. Zacharias was a priest of the division of Abijah. His wife, Elizabeth, was one "of the daughters of Aaron" (Luke 1:5), meaning she also was of priestly descent. Zacharias was promised by an angel in his old age that he would be the father of the forerunner of the Messiah. Because he doubted this promise, he was struck speechless until after his son was born (see Luke 1:13; 3:2).

ZADOK [ZAY dock] (just, righteous)

A high priest in the time of David. Zadok was a son of Ahitub (2 Sam. 8:17) and a descendant of Aaron through Eleazar (1 Chr. 24:3). During David's reign he served jointly as high priest with Abiathar (2 Sam. 8:17).

Both Zadok and Abiathar fled from Jerusalem with David when the King's son Absalom attempted to take over the throne. They brought the ark of the covenant out with them. After Absalom had been killed, David asked Zadok and Abiathar to urge the people to recall David to the throne (2 Sam. 19:11).

When David was dying, another of his sons, Adonijah, tried to take the throne. This time only Zadok remained faithful to the king. When David heard of the plot, he ordered Zadok and the prophet Nathan to anoint Solomon king (1 Kin. 1:7–8, 32–45).

Consequently, Abiathar was deposed and Zadok held the high priesthood alone (1 Kin. 2:26–27). In this way the high priesthood was restored to the line of Eleazar, son of Aaron.

ZEALOT [ZELL uht] (devoted supporter)

A nickname given to Simon, one of Jesus' twelve apostles (Luke 6:15; Acts 1:13), perhaps to distinguish him from Simon Peter. Simon the Zealot is also called Simon the Canaanite (Matt. 10:4; Mark 3:18; Cananaean in NRSV; Simon the Zealot in REB). The Aramaic form of the name means "to be jealous" or "zealous."

Simon was given this name probably because he had been a member of a Jewish political party known as the Zealots. A Zealot was a member of a fanatical Jewish sect that militantly opposed the Roman domination of Palestine during the first century A.D. When the Jews rebelled against the Romans in A.D. 66 and tried to gain their independence, the Zealots were in the forefront of the revolt. They thought of themselves as following in the footsteps of men like Simeon and Levi (Gen. 34:1–31), Phinehas (Num. 25:1–13), and Elijah (1 Kin. 18:40; 19:10–14) who were devoted supporters of the Lord and His laws and who were ready to fight for them.

Like the Pharisees, the Zealots were devoted to the Jewish law and religion. But unlike most Pharisees, they thought it was treason against God to pay tribute to the Roman emperor, since God alone was Israel's king. They were willing to fight to the death for Jewish independence.

The Zealots eventually degenerated into a group of assassins known as Sicarii (Latin, daggermen). Their increasing fanaticism was one factor that provoked the Roman-Jewish war. The Zealots took control of Jerusalem in A.D. 66, a move that led to the siege of Jerusalem and its fall in A.D. 70. The last stronghold of the Zealots, the fortress of Masada, fell to the Romans in A.D. 73.

ZEBOIIM [zeh BOY yim]

One of the five cities of the plain in the Valley of Siddim destroyed along with Sodom and Gomorrah (Gen. 10:19; 14:2). The prophet Hosea used Admah and Zeboiim (Hos. 11:8; Zeboim in KJV) as examples of God's judgment on wicked cities. Many scholars believe Zeboiim was situated near the southern end of the Dead Sea in an area presently covered by water. Others believe it was located near the eastern shore of the Dead Sea.

ZEBULUN [ZEBB you lun]

The tenth of Jacob's 12 sons; the sixth and last son of Leah (Gen. 30:19–20; 35:23; 1 Chr. 2:1). Zebulun had three sons: Sered, Elon, and Jahleel (Gen. 46:14; Num. 26:26–27). These are the only details about Zebulun that appear in the Bible.

ZEBULUN, TRIBE OF

The tribe that sprang from Zebulun, son of Jacob (Num. 1:9; Deut. 27:13; Josh. 19:10, 16; Judg. 1:30). The tribe was divided into three great families headed by Zebulun's three sons (Num. 26:26–27). At the first census taken in the wilderness, the tribe numbered 57,400 fighting men (Num. 1:30–31). The second census included 60,500 members of the tribe of Zebulun (Num. 26:27).

Zebulun played an important role in Israel's history during the period of the judges. Its fighting men were an important part of Barak's force against Sisera (Judg. 4:6–10; 5:14, 18) and of Gideon's army against the Midianites (Judg. 6:35). Elon the Zebulunite judged Israel for ten years (Judg. 12:12). At Hebron, 50,000 Zebulunites joined the other tribes in proclaiming David king (1 Chr. 12:33, 40).

Although Zebulun suffered during the Assyrian wars, when Tiglath-Pileser carried away captives to Assyria (2 Kin. 15:29), Isaiah prophesied that in the future Zebulun would be greatly blessed: "The land of Zebulun and the land of Naphtali . . . in Galilee of the Gentiles. The people who walked in darkness have seen a great light; those who dwelt in the land of the shadow of death, upon them a light has shined" (Is. 9:1–2). According to the Gospel of Matthew, this prophecy was fulfilled when Jesus began His Galilean ministry (Matt. 4:12–17). Nazareth, Jesus' hometown, and Cana, where He performed His first miracle, both lay in the territory of Zebulun.

ZECHARIAH [zeck ah RIE a] *(the Lord remembers)*

1. The fifteenth king of Israel (2 Kin. 14:29; 15:8, 11; Zachariah in KJV), the last of the house of Jehu. The son of Jeroboam II, Zechariah became king when his father died. He reigned only six months (about 753/52 B.C.) before being assassinated by Shallum.

ZECHARIAH [zeck ah RIE a] *(the Lord remembers)*

2. A prophet in the days of Ezra (Ezra 5:1; 6:14; Zech. 1:1, 7; 7:1, 8) and author of the Book of Zechariah. A leader in the restoration of the nation of Israel following the Babylonian captivity, Zechariah was a contemporary of the prophet Haggai, the governor Zerubbabel, and the high priest Joshua. Zechariah himself was an important person during the period of the restoration of the community of Israel in the land of Palestine after the captivity.

Z

The Book of Zechariah begins with a note concerning the prophet. He is named as a grandson of Iddo, one of the heads of the priestly families who returned with Zerubbabel from Babylon (Zech. 1:1, 7; also Ezra 5:1; 6:14). This means that Zechariah himself was probably a priest and that his prophetic activity was in close association with the religious center of the nation. His vision of Joshua the high priest (Zech. 3:1–5) takes on added importance, since he served as a priest in association with Joshua.

Zechariah began his ministry while still a young man (Zech. 2:4) in 520 B.C., two months after Haggai completed the prophecies that are recorded in the Book of Haggai.

ZEDEKIAH [zedd eh KIE ah] *(the Lord my righteousness)*

The last king of Judah (597–586 B.C.). The son of Josiah, Zedekiah was successor to Jehoiachin as king (2 Kin. 24:17–20; 25:1–7; 2 Chr. 36:10–13). After Jehoiachin had reigned only three months, he was deposed and carried off to Babylonia. Nebuchadnezzar installed Zedekiah on the throne as a puppet king and made him swear an oath that he would remain loyal (2 Chr. 36:13; Ezek. 17:13). Zedekiah's original name was Mattaniah, but Nebuchadnezzar renamed him to demonstrate his authority over him (2 Kin. 24:17). Although Zedekiah reigned in Jerusalem for 11 years, he was never fully accepted as their king by the people of Judah.

Because Zedekiah was a weak and indecisive ruler, he faced constant political unrest. Almost from the first he appeared restless about his oath of loyalty to Babylon, although he reaffirmed that commitment in the fourth year of this reign (Jer. 51:59). However, he was under constant pressure from his advisors to revolt and look to Egypt for help. A new coalition composed of Edom, Moab, Ammon, and Phoenicia was forming against Babylonia, and they urged Judah to join (Jer. 27:3). Adding to the general unrest was the message of false prophets who declared that the yoke of Babylon had been broken (Jer. 28).

In his ninth year Zedekiah revolted against Babylonia. King Nebuchadnezzar invaded Judah and besieged Jerusalem. While Jerusalem was under siege, other Judean cities were falling to the Babylonians (Jer. 34:7).

The final months of the siege were desperate times for Zedekiah and the inhabitants of Jerusalem. The king made frequent calls on the prophet Jeremiah, seeking an encouraging word from the Lord. Jeremiah's message consistently offered only one alternative: surrender to Nebuchadnezzar in order to live in peace and save Jerusalem. To his credit, Zedekiah was not arrogant and heartless (Jer. 36:22–23). But he regarded God's prophetic word superstitiously and "did not humble himself before Jeremiah the prophet, who spoke from the mouth of the Lord" (2 Chr. 36:12).

In 586 B.C. the wall of Jerusalem was breached, and Zedekiah fled the city. The army of the Babylonians pursued the king, overtaking him in the plains of Jericho. He was brought before Nebuchadnezzar and forced to watch the killing of his sons. Then his own eyes were put out and he was led away to Babylonia (2 Kin. 25:6–7). Zedekiah died during the years of the captivity of the Jewish people in Babylon. His reign marked the end of the nation of Judah as an independent, self-governing country.

ZEPHANIAH [zeff ah NIE ah] *(the Lord has hidden)*

An Old Testament prophet and the author of the Book of Zephaniah (Zeph. 1:1). As God's spokesman to the southern kingdom of Judah, Zephaniah began his ministry about 627 B.C., the same year as the great prophet Jeremiah. Zephaniah was a member of the royal house of Judah, since he traced his ancestry back to King Hezekiah. He prophesied during the reign of King Josiah (ruled 640–609 B.C.). One theme of his message was that through His judgment God would preserve a remnant, a small group of people who would continue to serve as His faithful servants in the world (Zeph. 3:8–13).

ZERUBBABEL [zeh RUB uh buhl]
(offspring of Babylon)

Head of the tribe of Judah at the time of the return from the Babylonian captivity; prime builder of the second temple. Zerubbabel is a shadowy figure who emerges as the political and spiritual head of the tribe of Judah at the time of the Babylonian captivity. Zerubbabel led the first group of captives back to Jerusalem and set about rebuilding the temple on the old site. For some 20 years he was closely associated with prophets, priests, and kings until the new temple was dedicated and the Jewish sacrificial system was reestablished.

As a child of the captivity, Zerubbabel's name literally means "offspring of Babylon." He was the son of Shealtiel or Salathiel (Ezra 3:2, 8; Hag. 1:1; Matt. 1:12) and the grandson of Jehoiachin, the captive king of Judah (1 Chr. 3:17). Zerubbabel was probably Shealtiel's adopted or levirate son (1 Chr. 3:19). Whatever his blood

ZERUBBABEL

relationship to king Jehoiachin, Zerubbabel was Jehoiachin's legal successor and heir.

A descendant of David, Zerubbabel was in the direct line of the ancestry of Jesus (Luke 3:27; Matt. 1:12). Zerubbabel apparently attained considerable status with his captors while living in Babylon. During the early reign of Darius, he was recognized as a "prince of Judah" (Ezra 1:8). Zerubbabel was probably in the king's service since he had been appointed by the Persians as governor of Judah (Hag. 1:1).

With the blessings of Cyrus (Ezra 1:1–2), Zerubbabel and Jeshua the high priest led the first band of captives back to Jerusalem (Ezra 2:2). They also returned the gold and silver vessels that Nebuchadnezzar had removed from the ill-fated temple (Ezra 1:11). Almost immediately they set up an altar for burnt offerings, kept the Feast of Tabernacles, and took steps to rebuild the temple (Ezra 3:2–3, 8).

After rebuilding the temple foundation the first two years, construction came to a standstill for 17 years. This delay came principally because of opposition from settlers in Samaria who wanted to help with the building (Ezra 4:1–2). When the offer was refused because of the Samaritans' association with heathen worship, the Samaritans disrupted the building project (Ezra 4:4). Counselors were hired who misrepresented the captives in court (Ezra 4:5), causing the Persian king to withdraw his support (Ezra 4:21). The delay in building also was due to the preoccupation of Zerubbabel and other captives with building houses for themselves (Hag. 1:2–4).

Urged by the prophets Haggai and Zechariah (Ezra 5:1–2), Zerubbabel diligently resumed work on the temple in the second year of the reign of Darius Hystaspes of Persia (Hag. 1:14). This renewed effort to build the temple was a model of cooperation involving the captives, the prophets, and Persian kings (Ezra 6:14). Zerubbabel received considerable grants of money and materials from Persia (Ezra 6:5) and continuing encouragement from the prophets Haggai and Zechariah (Ezra 5:2).

The temple was finished in four years (516/515 B.C.) and dedicated with great pomp and rejoicing (Ezra 6:16). The celebration was climaxed with the observance of the Passover (Ezra 6:19). If there was a discordant note, it likely came from older Jews who had earlier wept because the new temple lacked the splendor of Solomon's temple (Ezra 3:12).

For some mysterious reason, Zerubbabel is not mentioned in connection with the temple dedication. Neither is he mentioned after this time. Perhaps he died or retired from public life upon completion of the temple. His influence was so great, however, that historians designate the second temple as "Zerubbabel's Temple."

God was apparently pleased with Zerubbabel's role in bringing the captives home and reestablishing temple worship (Ezra 3:10). On God's instructions, Haggai promised Zerubbabel a special blessing: "I will take you, Zerubbabel My servant, the son of Shealtiel, says the Lord, and will make you as a signet ring; for I have chosen you" (Hag. 2:23).

ZEUS [zoose]

The principal god of the ancient Greeks, considered ruler of the heavens and father of other gods. The Romans equated Zeus with their own supreme god, Jupiter. Barnabas was called Zeus by the people after the apostle Paul performed a miraculous healing at Lystra (Acts 14:12–13; 19:35; Jupiter, KJV). The temple of Zeus at Athens was the largest in Greece. His statue at Olympia was one of the seven wonders of the ancient world.

ZIKLAG [ZIKK lag]

A city in the Negev, or southern Judah (Josh. 15:1, 31), assigned to the tribe of Simeon (Josh. 19:5; 1 Chr. 4:30). When David was pursued by Saul, he and his 600 men fled to the land of the Philistines and found sanctuary with Achish, king of Gath. Achish gave the city of Ziklag to David and his men, and it became David's military base for raids against the nomadic tribes of the Negev (1 Sam. 27:1–12). Many of Saul's followers defected to David and joined David at Ziklag (1 Chr. 12:1–22).

Ziklag is probably Tell esh-Sheriah, about 20 miles (33 kilometers) southwest of Gaza.

ZIMRI [ZIMM rye] ([God is] *my protection*)

The fifth king of Israel (1 Kin. 16:8–20). Before he became king, Zimri was a servant of King Elah and commander of half of his chariots. One day, Zimri killed the drunken Elah and proclaimed himself king. When Omri, the commander of Elah's army, heard about the assassination, he abandoned the siege of Gibbethon and besieged Tirzah, the capital city. When Zimri saw that the city was taken, he "burned the king's house down upon himself" (1 Kin. 16:18). Zimri's reign lasted only seven days (1 Kin. 16:15).

ZION [ZIE un]

The City of David and the city of God. The designation of Zion underwent a distinct progression in its usage throughout the Bible. The first mention of Zion in the Bible is in 2 Samuel 5:7: "David took the stronghold of Zion (that is, the City of David)." Zion, therefore, was the name of the ancient Jebusite fortress situated on the southeast hill of Jerusalem

at the junction of the Kidron Valley and the Tyropoeon Valley.

The name came to stand not only for the fortress but also for the hill on which the fortress stood. After David captured "the stronghold of Zion" by defeating the Jebusites, he called Zion "the City of David" (1 Kin. 8:1; 1 Chr. 11:5; 2 Chr. 5:2).

When Solomon built the temple on Mount Moriah (a hill distinct and separate from Mount Zion), and moved the ark of the covenant there, the word *Zion* expanded in meaning to include also the temple and the temple area (Ps. 2:6; 48:2, 11–12; 132:13). It was only a short step until Zion was used as a name for the city of Jerusalem, the land of Judah, and the people of Israel as a whole (Is. 40:9; Jer. 31:12). The prophet Zechariah spoke of the sons of Zion (Zech. 9:13). By this time the word *Zion* had come to mean the entire nation of Israel.

The most important use of the word *Zion* is in a religious or theological sense. Zion is used figuratively of Israel as the people of God (Is. 60:14). The spiritual meaning of Zion is continued in the New Testament, where it is given the Christian meaning of God's spiritual kingdom, the church of God, the heavenly Jerusalem (Heb. 12:22; Rev. 14:1; Sion in KJV).

See also JERUSALEM.

ZIPPORAH [zip POE rah] *(female bird)*

A daughter of Jethro, priest of Midian, and wife of Moses (Ex. 2:21–22; 4:25; 18:2–4). Their sons were Gershom and Eliezer. When the Lord sought to kill Moses because Eliezer had not been circumcised, Zipporah grabbed a sharp stone and circumcised the child. She and the two sons must have returned to Jethro rather than continuing on to Egypt with Moses, because she is not mentioned again until after the Exodus. Along with Jethro, she and her two sons visited Moses in the wilderness after the Hebrew people left Egypt (Ex. 18:1–5).

Z

ZOBAH [ZOE bah]

An Aramean kingdom situated in Syria, south of Hamath, northeast of Damascus, and east of Byblos in the Bekaa Valley between the Lebanon and Anti-Lebanon Mountains. Generally speaking, Zobah was the land between the Orontes River and the Euphrates River.

Saul fought successfully against the kings of Zobah (1 Sam. 14:47). David clashed with Hadadezer, king of Zobah (2 Sam. 8:3; 1 Chr. 18:3). When the Syrians of Damascus tried to aid Hadadezer, David slaughtered them (2 Sam. 8:5; 1 Chr. 18:5).

David took much bronze as booty from Berothai, Betah (or Tibhath), and Chun, cities of Zobah (2 Sam. 8:8; 1 Chr. 18:8). When Israel battled the Ammonites, the Ammonites hired mercenaries from Zobah (2 Sam. 10:6). Israel was caught between the Ammonites and the Syrians (2 Sam. 10:8). Israel overcame the fighting on two fronts (2 Sam. 10:9–14). The Syrians of Zobah rallied their forces under Hadadezer's commander, Shobach, but were defeated (2 Sam. 10:15–19).

ZOPHAR [ZOE fer]

The third of the "friends" of Job to speak. He is called a Naamathite (Job 2:11; 11:1; 20:1; 42:9), indicating he was from Naamah, in northern Arabia. Zophar's two discourses are found in Job 11:1–20 and 20:1–29. He accused Job of wickedness and hypocrisy, urged Job to turn from his rebellion, and charged that God was punishing Job far less than his sins deserved (Job 11:6).